PHOTOSHOP 4
INTERACTIVE
COURSE

SHERRY LONDON

WAITE GROUP PRESS™
A Division of
Sams Publishing

Corte Madera, CA

PUBLISHER • Mitchell Waite
ASSOCIATE PUBLISHER • Charles Drucker

ACQUISITIONS MANAGER • Susan Walton

EDITORIAL DIRECTOR • John Crudo
PROJECT EDITORS • Tom and Carol Christensen
and Stephanie Wall
DEVELOPMENT EDITOR • Kathy Grider Carlyle
TECHNICAL EDITOR • Rita Amladi
COPY EDITOR • Michelle Goodman/Creative Solutions

PRODUCTION MANAGER • Cecile Kaufman

SENIOR DESIGNER • Sestina Quarequio
DESIGNER • Karen Johnston
PRODUCTION EDITOR • K.D. Sullivan/Creative Solutions
PRODUCTION • Jeanne Clark, Elizabeth Deeter, Ayanna Lacey,
Polly Lavrick
ILLUSTRATIONS • Marvin Van Tiem
COVER ILLUSTRATION • Robert Dougherty
QUIZ AUTHORS • Craig M. Swanson and Nancy Jacobs

© 1997 by The Waite Group, Inc.
Published by Waite Group Press™,
200 Tamal Plaza, Corte Madera, CA 94925

Waite Group Press is a division of Sams Publishing.

Printed in the United States of America
97 98 99 • 10 9 8 7 6 5 4 3 2

Library of Congress Cataloging-in-Publication Data
London, Sherry.
    Photoshop 4 interactive course / Sherry London.
        p.   cm.
    Includes index.
    ISBN 1-57169-036-0
    1. Computer graphics. 2. Adobe Photoshop (Computer file)
I. Title.
T385.L657 1997
006.6'869--dc21

97-10548
CIP

www.waite.com/ezone
eZone Guided Tour

The *Interactive Course* title in your hands provides you with an unprecedented training system. *Photoshop 4 Interactive Course* is everything you're used to from Waite Group Press: thorough, hands-on coverage of this important, cutting-edge programming language. There is far more, however, to the *Interactive Course* than the pages you are now holding. Using your Internet connection, you also get access to the eZone where you'll find dedicated services designed to assist you through the book and make sure you really understand the subject.

FREE TUTORS, TESTING, CERTIFICATION, AND RESOURCES

The eZone provides a host of services and resources designed to help you work through this book. If you get hung up with a particular lesson, all you have to do is ask an online mentor, a live expert in the subject you're studying. A mailing list lets you exchange ideas and hints with others taking the same course. A resource page links you to the hottest related Web sites, and a monthly newsletter keeps you up to date with eZone enhancements and industry developments. Figure 1 shows the page.

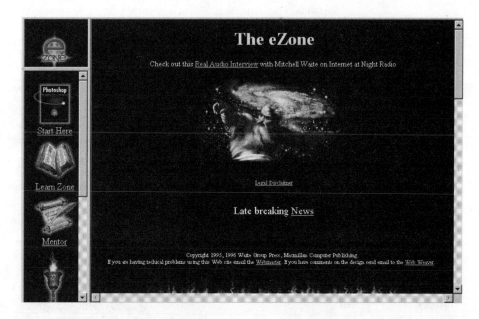

Figure 1
The eZone home page...a whole new way to learn

You'll also be able to work toward a certificate of completion. You can take lesson quizzes online, receive an immediate grade, and track your progress through the course. The chapters are available online, too, so that you can refer to them when you need to. Once you've finished the course with a passing grade, you can print a personalized certificate of completion, suitable for framing.

Best of all, there's no additional cost for all of these services. They are included in the price of the book. Once you journey into the eZone, you'll never want to go back to traditional book learning.

EXPLORING THE EZONE

You'll find the eZone on the World Wide Web. Fire up your Web browser and enter the following site:

`http://www.waite.com/ezone`

From there, click the eZone icon and you're on your way.

NOTE

If your browser does not support frames, or if you prefer frameless pages, click the No Frames link instead of the eZone icon. Your browser must support "cookies," so Microsoft Internet Explorer (version 3.01 or later) or Netscape Navigator (version 3 or later) is required.

Navigating the eZone

As you can see in Figure 2, the screen is divided into three frames. The eZone icon in the top left frame is always visible. This icon is a link back to the eZone home page. No matter where you are, you can always find your way home by clicking this icon.

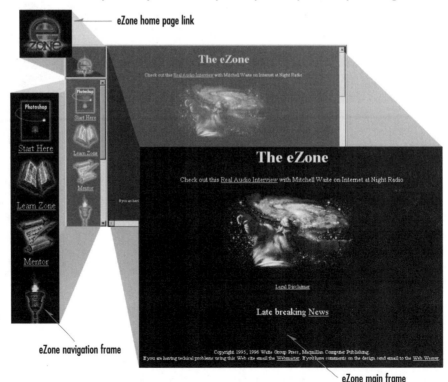

Figure 2
There are three frames in the eZone

Beneath the eZone icon is a navigation frame containing several icons. Each of these icons links to an area of the eZone. You'll learn about each of these areas as you read through this guide.

The largest frame on the page is the main frame. This is where you'll find the information. Scroll down this frame and you'll see text-based links to the eZone areas. Keep going and you'll find the latest eZone news and information, updated regularly. Be sure to check out this information each time you enter the eZone.

Start Here

Click the *Start Here* icon in the navigation frame. This takes you to the Getting Started page where you'll find different sets of instructions. Your options are:

```
I am a GUEST and visiting the EZONE.
I HAVE the EZONE BOOK and I am ready to start the course.
I want to BUY an EZONE COURSE and get my Book.
```

Clicking on these options provides instructions for how to sign on as a Guest, register for a course for which you have a book, or sign up for a course and order the corresponding book.

In the next couple of pages, you'll see how to explore the eZone as a Guest, register yourself, enroll in a course, and take advantage of the many service areas provided at no additional charge.

Signing on as a Guest

On your first visit to the eZone, consider signing on as a Guest, even if you have a book and are anxious to get started. Signing on as a Guest lets you roam the eZone and familiarize yourself with its various areas and features before setting any options. You can view the first chapter of any available course and take the quizzes for that chapter (although Guests' scores aren't saved).

You can ask support questions, view the latest news, and even view the FAQs for a course. Until you register, you can't ask the mentors any questions, sign up for the eZone newsletter, or access the resource links page, but there's still plenty of stuff to check out as a Guest.

To explore the eZone as a Guest, click the *Learn Zone* icon in the navigation frame or on the word "Learn" at the bottom of the main frame. The first time you do this, the Registration Page appears. As a Guest, you can ignore this form.

Just click the *Guest* link, and the Course Matrix appears. From here, you can navigate the eZone in the same manner as registered course members. Remember, however, that access for Guests is limited.

THE INITIATE ZONE

Once you're comfortable navigating the eZone, we know you'll be anxious to start learning and taking advantage of this cutting-edge training system.

The first thing you have to do is create an entry for yourself in the eZone records by registering. Click on the Initiation icon in the navigation frame or on the Initiate link at the bottom of the main frame, and you move into the *Initiate Zone*, shown in Figure 3.

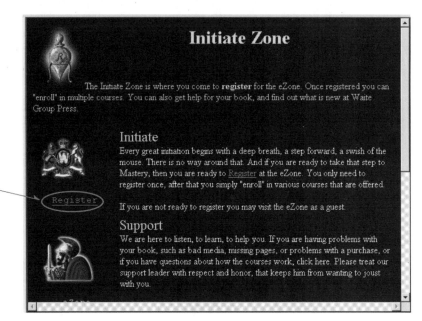

Click here to begin
eZone registration

Figure 3
Go to the Initiate
Zone to start your
training

The Initiate Zone contains three options: *Initiate (Register), Support,* and *Announcements and What's New*. Use the *Support* option to report difficulties you are having with your *Interactive Course* material and services: problems with the book or CD, trouble getting eZone to work, whatever you need. This is not, however, where you'll ask questions related to the course content. Answering those questions is the mentor's job. The *Announcements and What's New* option lets you quickly find out about the latest additions and deletions at the eZone. It also contains information about upcoming courses.

Initiate (Register)

But what you want right now is the *Initiate (Register)* option. Click the *Register* link and a registration form appears.

 NOTE

You don't need a book to register in the eZone; in fact, you can pre-register and order an *Interactive Course* title while you're online. When your copy arrives, you'll already have a recognized password and ID, so that you can enroll immediately in your course of choice.

You need to fill out the registration form completely. Click inside each text box, then type in the appropriate information; pressing the TAB key cycles you through these text fields. In addition to a little information about yourself, you'll need to enter:

`Requested User ID`—Type the name you'd like to use online.
`Password (5-8 Characters)`—Type the password you'd like to use online.
`Password (Verify)`—Retype your selected password, to be sure it's properly recorded.

Once you've supplied all the information, click the *Register* button to submit the form to the eZone's data banks. A confirming message lets you know that you've successfully registered. Registration is important. If you don't register, you can't take advantage of the full power of the eZone.

Entering the eZone as a Registered User

Once you've registered, you'll use your unique ID and password to enter the eZone. Next time you enter the eZone, you need only click the *Learn Zone* icon in the navigation frame or the *Learn* link in the main frame. A simple two-line form pops up, allowing you to type in the user ID and password you created when you registered.

THE LEARN ZONE

Now that you're registered, it's time to get down to business. Much of the course work is done in the *Learn Zone*, shown in Figure 4. To get here, click the *Learn* icon in the navigation frame.

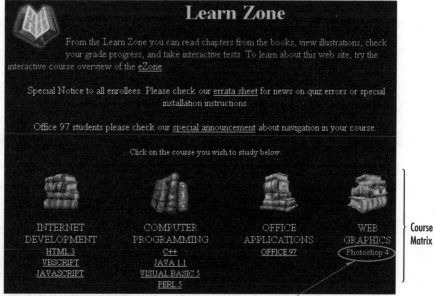

Figure 4
Use the Course Matrix in the Learn Zone to select courses

The Course Matrix

When you enter the Learn Zone, you'll see lists of courses and certification programs. This is called the Course Matrix, and it provides a way to select the various eZone courses. Under each discipline—such as Web Graphics or Internet Development—are a list of core courses. To select the *Photoshop 4 Interactive Course* using this Course Matrix, click on the *Photoshop 4* link in the column labeled "Web Graphics." In a moment, a three-columned table appears.

Verification

The first time you select a specific course, you must enroll. You'll need a copy of the book to do so. You will be asked to provide a specific word from the book. This verifies that you have the proper book for the selected course. The verification process uses the familiar page-line-word formula; in other words, you'll need to look and enter a word from a specified line of text on a specified page of your book. Click your mouse in the text box and type the specified word to verify that you have the course book.

Passing Percentage

You can also set a minimum passing percentage for your course. This determines what percentage of test questions you need to answer correctly in order to pass the course. The percentage is preset at 70%, but you can select 50%, 60%, 70%, 80%, 90%, or 100%.

To set a minimum passing percentage, click the text box for this option to see a list of choices, then click the option you prefer. Once you've typed in the correct word and set the desired passing percentage, click the *Verify* button to enroll in the course. The Chapters Grid appears.

The Chapters Grid

The table shown in Figure 5 displays the chapters of this book, and it shows your completion status and average score for each of them.

Click here to go back to the
Course Matrix

Click on a chapter to view
its quizzes

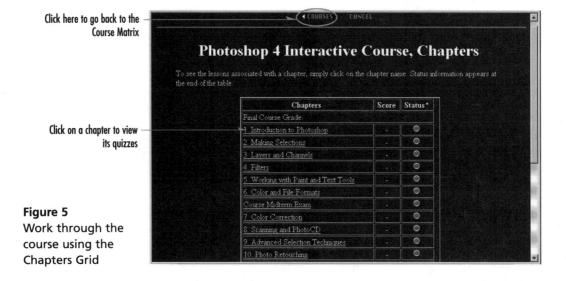

Figure 5
Work through the
course using the
Chapters Grid

The left-hand column lists the chapters of the book; clicking on a chapter lets you view the lessons within it. The middle column, Score, shows your current overall grade for the section (as a percentage). The Status column uses a colored indicator to let you know with a glance whether you've passed (green), failed (red), are still working through (yellow), or have not yet started (gray) a particular chapter.

Click a chapter, and the Lessons Grid appears. (Remember, only the first lesson is enabled for Guests.)

The Lessons Grid

As you take the course, the Lessons Grid (Figure 6) tracks your performance within each section of the book. You can use it to read a chapter lesson or take the related lesson quiz.

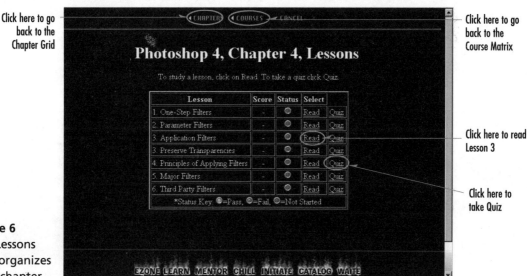

Click here to go back to the Chapter Grid

Click here to go back to the Course Matrix

Click here to read Lesson 3

Click here to take Quiz

Figure 6
The Lessons Grid organizes each chapter

To read a lesson, click the *Read* link in the Select column. To take a quiz, click the *Quiz* link in the Select column. The LEDs in the status column show whether you've passed (green), failed (red), or not yet started (gray) each quiz. A percentage grade appears for each completed quiz in the Score column.

Most likely, you'll achieve the best results if you read through the lessons, then take the quiz. If you prefer, however, you can jump directly to the corresponding quiz, without reading through the lesson.

Testing

Each quiz is a multiple-choice questionnaire. In some quizzes, there is only one answer to each question, but others allow more than one answer. Read the instructions for your course so you know how the quizzes work.

Taking Quizzes

To answer a quiz question, click the check box next to the answer you want to choose. When you've answered all the questions, click the *Grade My Choices* button. Your quiz is corrected and your score shown. To record your score, click either the *Lessons* or *Chapters* link at the top of the main frame.

CAUTION

Do not use your browser's Back button after taking a quiz. If you use the Back button instead of the Lessons or Chapters link, your score will not be recorded.

Midterm and Final Exams

The *Interactive Course* includes midterm and final examinations. The midterm covers the first half of the book, while the final is comprehensive. These exams follow the same multiple-choice format as the quizzes. Because they cover more, however, they're somewhat longer. Once you have successfully passed all the quizzes, as well as the midterm and final exams, you'll be eligible to download a certificate of completion from Waite Group Press.

MENTOR ZONE

In the *Mentor Zone*, shown in Figure 7, you can review FAQs (Frequently Asked Questions) for each chapter. You can also ask a question of a live expert, called a mentor, who is standing by to assist you. The mentor is familiar with the book, an expert in the subject, and can provide you with a specific answer to your content-related question, usually

Click on this pull-down menu to view a list of chapters. Click on the chapter to which your question relates.

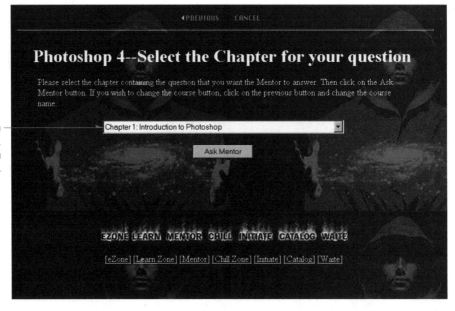

Figure 7
Get personalized help in the Mentor Zone

within one business day. You can get to this area by clicking on the Mentor icon in the navigation frame.

Just the FAQs

Before you ask a mentor a question, you're first shown a set of FAQs. Be sure to read through the list. Since you have a limited number of questions you may ask, you'll want to use your questions carefully. Chances are that an answer to your question has already been posted, in which case you can get an answer without having to ask it yourself. In any event, you may learn about an issue you hadn't even considered.

If the FAQ list does not contain the answer you need, you'll want to submit your own question to the mentor.

Ask Your Mentor

eZone students may ask 10 questions of their course mentor. This limit ensures that mentors will have the opportunity to answer all readers' questions. Questions must be directly related to chapter material. If you ask unrelated or inappropriate questions, you won't get an answer; however, the question will still be deducted from your allotment.

If the FAQ doesn't provide you with an answer to your question, click the button labeled *Ask Mentor*. The first time you contact the mentor, the rules and conditions for the mentor questions are provided. After reading these, click the *Accept* button to continue. In a moment, a form like the one shown in Figure 8 appears.

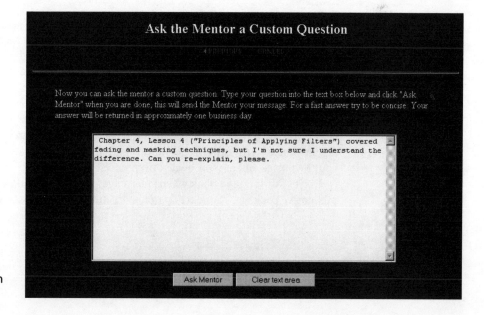

Figure 8
Use this form to send your question to your mentor

This form specifies the course, the chapter, and other information pertinent to your question. The mentor e-mails the answer to your question directly to you, but keep in mind that Mentor Zone questions must be *directly* related to the chapter subject matter.

More Assistance

Keep in mind that there are other sources of assistance in the eZone, too. If you are experiencing technical problems with the book or CD, you'll want to contact the Webmaster; you'll find a link on the eZone's main page. If you want to discuss related issues, such as developments and applications, check out the newsgroups available in the Chill Zone. There are other ways to discuss issues with real people, as you'll discover, when you visit the eZone.

CHILL ZONE

Think of the Chill Zone as your student lounge, a place where students hang out and discuss their classes. But the Chill Zone does a student lounge one better—it's also a library chock full of information. It's a place where you can interact with others reading the same book and find expert resources to assist you as you develop and use your new skills. Perhaps the coolest thing about the Chill Zone is that its options are all included with the cost of your book.

To get into the Chill Zone, click the Chill Zone icon in the navigation frame. Once there, you can click three Chill Zone options:

Discussion List—You can subscribe (or unsubscribe) to a dedicated newsgroup centered on your book.

Newsletter—Select this option to subscribe (or unsubscribe) to the quarterly eZone newsletter.

Resources—These are links to Web sites, tools, and other useful materials related to the course subject.

To select a Chill Zone option, click the link and follow the onscreen instructions.

THE EZONE AWAITS

As you have seen from this tour, this *Interactive Course* book is a lot more than the pages before you. It's a full-blown, personalized training system—including textbook, testing, guidance, certification, and support—that you can pick up and work through at your own pace and at your own convenience.

Don't settle for just a book when you can get a whole education. Thanks to this comprehensive package, you're ready to log on and learn in the eZone.

Dedication

To Willam and Jeanne Mickelson—Uncle Billy and Aunt Jeanne—my favorite aunt and uncle. Thank you both for so many happy memories and pleasant times. Aunt Jeanne even forgave me for putting perfume on my uncle's just-ironed socks when I was a child, and Uncle Billy's art school project, which hung over our mantel, made me think that I would like to be an artist, too.

About the Author

Sherry London has been working with computer graphics applications since the days of "Paint" on the Atari 800. She has used Adobe Photoshop since version 1.0 appeared. Since 1989, Sherry London has been reviewing graphics software and writing how-to articles for a number of publications. She is currently a contributing editor for *Computer Artist* magazine and has contributed articles to *MacWeek* and *MacUser* magazines as well. She is quite active on CompuServe as one of the Mac Photoshop Section Leaders in the Adobe Photoshop forum. She has also been a Section Leader on the CompuServe Crafts forum and a sysop on Ziff's Download and Support forum.

Professionally, Sherry London has used Photoshop both as a graphic artist and as a fiber artist. She has been doing needlework design since 1973, and has used Photoshop as the basis for several needlepoint works that are currently in a travelling exhibit sponsored by the Embroiderer's Guild of America. She also does a large amount of digital photo-retouching. She is a principal of London Computing: PhotoFX, a full service design studio.

Sherry London has a background in education and has worked as an instructional systems designer. She has taught classes in management information systems at Drexel University in Philadelphia, PA, and now teaches Photoshop and Pre-Press at Moore College of Art and Design. She is also the author of *Photoshop Special Effects How-To, Photoshop Texture Magic,* and (with Eric Reinfeld) *Real World Adobe After Effects.*

Sherry is open to questions and comments. She can be reached at her CompuServe account (`76004.1536@compuserve.com`). In addition, you will find her at the Adobe forum. Pop in and say hello.

Table of Contents

Contents

Acknowledgments

There is no way that I could have written a book of this magnitude without the help and support of many others who have given so generously of their time and expertise. I would like to thank these individuals and companies.

The Photoshop vendor community:
The following companies have graciously supplied equipment for this project:
DayStar—nPower 360+ multiprocessing card to help Photoshop reach its speed potential
Light Source—Colortron II which has been so helpful for calibration and color matching
Olympus—a CD-ROM writer which has become an essential part of my studio
Umax—Power Look II scanner which produces superb scans

These companies and their representatives have supplied software, conversation, and inspiration:

Adobe Systems: Rebecca Michals, Patricia Pane, and Sonya Schaefer in PR
Alien Skin Software: Michael Pilmer
Andromeda Software: LouAnn Barbeau
AutoFX: Cliff Weems
Binuscan: Lisa Morris
Box Top Software: Travis Anton
Chroma: Lorena Peer
Cytopia Software
DataStream: Sam Moore
Digital Frontiers: Douglas Frohman
Extensis: Kevin Hurst
Fractal Design: Teri Campbell
Image Express: Herb Paynter
Live Picture: Holly Fisher
MetaTools: Theresa Bridwell
Mclean Public Relations: Eileen Ebner
MultiMedia Marketing GambH: Willi Penner
Second Glance Software: Lance Gilbert
Specular International: Jason Dirks
Total Integration: Patty Skurski
Visu: Michel de Groot
Vivid Details: Kirk Lyford
Xaos Tools

The Online community:
CIS Adobe Forum staff—for friendship and support
CIS Photoshop Forum members—for asking me questions and helping me answer them

Significant others:
Carolyn and Rich Cross—for opening up your photo albums so generously
Barbara Desai—for finding pictures of exotic locales (and daughters), for always being there when needed, and for one of the warmest friendships I have ever known
Rosalie Guzofsky of Moore College of Art and Design—for supporting this effort so ably
Geneen Kashmar, Melaine Reed, Ellen Zucker—for recapturing all of my screen shots for Photoshop 4
Eric Reinfeld—for art and conversation
Ed and Mei Scott—for the incredible gift of those wonderful China photographs and for being such gracious hosts
All of the folks profiled in the book—a sincere thanks for your time and your knowledge

Very significant others:
Carol Christensen, my project editor—for laughter through it all
Rita Amladi—for the tech edit and a glowing introduction
Norm London, my husband—for tolerating rotten dinners and a distracted wife

Foreword

Photoshop can be a real eye opener. It can also be a mindboggling experience fraught with indecision on the "right" approach to take when collaging, color correcting, file prepping, and applying creative techniques. Some of us get it right by spending a small fortune on on-the-job mistake redemption, not to mention far too many hours spent in front of the computer.

While these events can be a real religious experience, most of us would prefer to be led by an expert who has seen, done, and experienced it all. Sherry London, in my experience, is just that person—completely qualified to write a course on Photoshop. Over the couple of years that I have come to know her, I have enjoyed her art, her books, and winced at hearing her many war stories on using Photoshop.

In this book, she presents her profound knowledge of art, production, and Photoshop with a humorous touch. I found myself chuckling over many of her anecdotes while filing away a special technique or workaround. Most of all, she writes as only a woman writer could—unpretentiously and drawing from her background. Her analogies are right on target, related to her experience (in fine arts, weaving, and crafts), and very witty. In my opinion, that's really what it takes to teach Photoshop right. Students usually get it the first time around.

I hope you enjoy this book as much as I did. The book is unique in the structure it offers: a lecture, hands-on exercises, quizzes, and lab assignments to let the topics really sink in. It's well conceived and it really works! If you are an instructor, this book will make it all too easy to lay down the structure of your class. If you are a student tackling this book on your own, you will undoubtedly see the wisdom in this form of presentation within the first two chapters and really benefit from it.

Despite following a structure, Sherry's exercises offer many points of departure, and on several occasions, I found myself happily lost in some new discovery of my own. I wish you many such serendipitous discoveries in reading this book.

Rita Amladi
Orion Arts & Communications
Trainer and Consultant
Former head of Adobe Photoshop Technical Support

INTRODUCTION

Photoshop 4 Interactive Course is a unique book. Much of its uniqueness derives from the format and structure of the Waite Group Press *Interactive* series. You are guided step-by-step through the often confusing ground of learning a new application. You can measure your understanding of the topic through the enclosed quizzes, and you are given real-world projects to complete. At the end of the book, you can earn a Certificate of Completion or even college credit as a reward for a job well-done.

Photoshop has the reputation of being a very difficult program. It's not, really. However, it is very deep in that every action can typically be done in multiple ways. Photoshop is also many different programs in one. For the print professional, it is a pre-press program where images are scanned, color-corrected, and prepared for printing. For the photographer, Photoshop is a master photo lab that contains many more tools than those available in the "real world." For the multimedia artist, Photoshop is one step in a workflow that leads to final production of a CD-ROM, a videotape, or a Web page. What will Photoshop be for you?

About *Photoshop 4 Interactive Course*

Photoshop 4 Interactive Course is designed as a tutorial with multiple methods and exercises for you to understand and practice Photoshop. This book is broken into 15 Chapters with structured Lessons and Hands On Exercises within each Chapter. At the end of each Lesson you will find a multiple-choice quiz that is designed to test your understanding and comprehension of the material you just read.

The Hands On Exercises, found throughout each Chapter, allow you to practice the technique you just read about. Be sure to read each step of the exercise completely before you execute it. Frequently, the first part of a direction will tell you what you are going to do; the rest of the Step expands upon the first sentence and gives specific instructions. If you read an instruction like the one that follows, and do not read the whole instruction before starting, you may attempt to perform the same action twice.

In addition to the quizzes and Hands On Exercises you will find Labs in Appendix C. The Labs are broken down by Chapter and contain Exercises for the various applications you encountered in the reading. They are designed for practice and application of the tools and techniques you read about. Be sure to do these Labs because they will further your ability to work effectively with Photoshop.

Certification Through Moore College of Art and Design

One of the unique qualities of this book is the opportunity for certification plus credits through Moore College of Art and Design. Moore College is an independent, four-year women's college located in Philadelphia. Founded in 1848, Moore College offers Bachelor of Fine Arts degrees in nine majors in the fine and professional arts, and certifcate programs in Desktop Publishing and Computer Graphics open to men and women. Completion of this book will provide you with information similar to Photoshop training at Moore.

After you have completed and submitted the enclosed final exam and received a passing score (as explained in Appendix D), you may submit a request for Level II certification. The exam for this level of certification offers the opportunity for you to apply your knowledge of Photoshop. Once you have achieved Level II certification, you will be awarded three credits in Moore's Continuing Studies Division.

Using This Book—A Word About Conventions

Photoshop allows you to customize your working environment in many ways. Because of this, there were no assumptions made regarding how your system was set up. However, there are some assumptions with regards to the directions for selecting brushes and colors. The instructions are based upon your use of the default brushes and the default palette sizes. In addition, unless otherwise stated in the instructions, the assumption was made that you are using the Photoshop Color Picker on either platform.

There are also some conventions used in this book that you should know about. Remembering this information will make work through the exercises substantially easier.

Filter -> Blur -> Gaussian Blur, 3

Commands shown in this format refer to menu items and options on those items. In this example, you would select the Filter menu, choose the Blur category, and a Gaussian Blur. You would then set the amount of the Gaussian Blur to 3.

File -> New -> Name: Motif, Width: 40 pixels, Height: 40 pixels, Resolution: 72, Mode: RGB Color, Contents: White

A program feature allows you to name an image as you create it or duplicate it. Type the word following the Name into the Name box in the dialog. Enter the dimensions into the appropriate boxes.

File -> New, 200, 200, RGB 72 dpi

This is a shortened form of the command that you will see when it does not matter what you name the image. The numbers after the commas refer to the options in the dialog box. All dimensions, unless otherwise stated, are in pixels throughout the book. You would create a document 200 pixels wide by 200 pixels high. The mode is RGB, with a resolution of 72 dots per inch.

Duplicate the image (Image -> Duplicate -> Working-> OK).

If there is a word other than OK after the Duplicate ->, type it in the As area of the dialog box. If the words "Merged Layers Only" appear anywhere in the instructions, then you are being asked to check the box "Merged Layers Only" in the Duplicate dialog.

Duplicate the image (Image -> Duplicate -> OK)

There is no name needed. The image will be duplicated with the original file name and the word "copy" after it.

eZone

Perhaps the most important way this book differs from other Photoshop books is that it is a Waite Group Press *Interactive Course* book, which gives you access to the revolutionary new Web learning available through the eZone. This is not just a publisher's hype; by connecting you to Waite Group Press via the World Wide Web, the eZone plays a significant role in helping you learn Photoshop.

ABOUT THE CD-ROM

Installing the CD-ROM

The companion CD-ROM contains all the project files developed by the author, plus utility software from third parties. The project files may be opened directly from the CD-ROM by Photoshop, edited, and saved to a location on your own hard drive. Should you want to copy the project files to your hard drive, please follow the steps for your particular operating system.

If you don't have a Web browser installed on your computer, we have provided Microsoft's Internet Explorer 3 on the CD. A full description of Internet Explorer's features may be found in Appendix E, but we have included quick start instructions here for your convenience.

For a detailed listing of what's on the CD-ROM and where you can find it, refer to the following listing.

Windows 95/NT 4 Installation Instructions

Please use the following steps to copy the project files to your hard drive.

1.   Insert the CD-ROM into your CD-ROM drive.

2.   From the Windows 95 desktop, double-click on the My Computer icon.

3.   Double-click on your hard drive and create a new folder, such as Photoshop 4 Interactive Course, by right-clicking on the background and

selecting New and then Folder. A folder called New Folder will be created on your hard drive with the name highlighted. Type in the name you want and press the Enter key.

4. Go back to your drive window and double-click on the icon that represents your CD-ROM. You will see a window with four folders in it: 3RDPARTY, ARCHIVES, CHAPTERS, and EXPLORER.

5. Double-click on the CHAPTERS folder. You will see a window with chapter folders in it. Select the chapter folders you want to copy (control-click on the folders if you're not copying all of them) and drag your selection to the folder you created on your hard drive. You might need to reposition your windows to make the window for your hard drive visible. Depending on how fast your computer is and on the options set for your computer, the copying process may take a few moments to a few minutes.

To install Explorer under Windows 95, select Run from the Start menu. Type

`d:\explorer\ie301m95.exe`

and click OK.

To install Explorer under Windows NT 4.0, select Run from the Start menu and type

`d:\explorer\ie301mnt.exe`

and click OK. Follow the onscreen prompts to finish the installation. If your CD-ROM drive is not D:, substitute the drive letter with one that corresponds to your system.

Windows 3.x and NT 3.5.1 Installation Instructions

Please use the following steps to copy the project files to your hard drive.

1. Insert the CD-ROM into your CD-ROM drive.

2. Run File Manager.

3. Click on the drive icon you want to copy your files to, and double-click on the top-most directory to make it your current directory.

4. Create a new directory by selecting File, Create Directory. Type in a directory name of your choice, such as PSHOP4IC, and click OK.

5. Refresh the directory list by double-clicking on the top-most directory twice. Now click on the directory you just created.

6. Now, double-click on the icon that represents your CD-ROM drive. You will see four directories: 3RDPARTY, ARCHIVES, CHAPTERS, and EXPLORER.

7. Double-click on the CHAPTERS folder. You will see a window with chapter folders in it. Select the chapter folders you want to copy (control-click on the folders if you're not copying all of them) and drag your selection to the folder you created on your hard drive. Depending on how fast your computer is and on the options set for your computer, the copying process may take a few moments to a few minutes.

To install Explorer, select Run from either File Manager or Program Manager and type

```
D:\EXPLORER\WIN31NT3.51\SETUP.EXE
```

and click OK. Follow the onscreen prompts to finish the installation. If your CD-ROM drive is not D:, substitute the drive letter with one that corresponds to your system.

Macintosh Installation Instructions

Please use the following steps to copy the project files to your hard drive.

1. Insert the CD-ROM into your CD-ROM drive.

2. When an icon for the CD appears on your desktop, open the disc by double-clicking on its icon. You will see a window with four folders in it: 3RDPARTY, ARCHIVES, CHAPTERS, and EXPLORER.

3. Double-click on your hard drive and create a new folder, such as Photoshop 4 Interactive Course, by selecting File, New, and then Folder from the Window menu. A folder called New Folder will be created on your hard drive with the name highlighted. Type in the name you want and press the Enter key.

4. Double-click on the CHAPTERS folder. You will see a window with chapter folders in it. Select the folders you want to copy (shift-click on the folders if you're not copying all of them) and drag your selection to the folder you created on your hard drive. You might need to reposition your windows to make the window for your hard drive visible. Depending on how fast your computer is and on the options set for your computer, the copying process may take a few moments to a few minutes.

Please use the following steps to copy the project files to your hard drive.

1. Double-click on your CD-ROM's icon to open its window.

2. Double-click on the EXPLORER folder, and double-click on the file IE Installer. Follow the instructions on the screen to finish the installation.

THIRD-PARTY SOFTWARE

The CD-ROM contains various plug-ins, utilities, and demos for your enjoyment. Each program has either a dedicated installer or is a plug-in which you place directly into your

Photoshop plug-ins folder. Table I-1 outlines what's on the CD-ROM, what folder or directory it's in, and what the installer is named.

Table I-1 Contents of the CD-ROM

Directory	Contents of Directory
3RDPARTY	
ACROBAT	Adobe Acrobat Reader 3.0
AR16E30.EXE	Windows 3.1 installer
AR32E30.EXE	Windows 95/NT installer
Install Acrobat Reader 3.0	Macintosh installer
ALIENSKN	Eye Candy
Install Eye Candy 3.0 Demo	Macintosh installer
SETUP.EXE	Windows installer
AUTOFX	
PGRAPHIC	Photo/Graphic Edges 3.0
Install Demo	Macintosh installer
SETUPEX.EXE	Windows installer
TGRAPHIC	Typo/Graphic Edges 3.0
Install Demo	Macintosh installer
SETUPEX.EXE	Windows installer
EXTENSIS	
IHANCE2	Intellihance
SETUP.EXE	Windows installer
Intellihance™ 2.0	
Demo Installer	Macintosh installer
PhotoTools™ 1.0	
Demo Installer	Macintosh installer
FRONTIERS	
HVSColor Mac	Read HVS Color Demo ReadMe
HVSCOLOR	Read README.TXT
HVSJPEG	Read READDEMO.TXT
METATOOL	Kai's PowerTools demo
MAC	
KPT3 Demo Install.1	Macintosh installer

Directory	Contents of Directory
WINDOWS	
SETUP.EXE	Windows installer
SHOWBIZ	Free Flux
SETUP.EXE	Windows installer
SPECULAR	
Collage 2.0 Demo Installer	Macintosh installer
TextureScape™ Demo Installer	Macintosh installer
ARCHIVES	Distribution files
CHAPTERS	
CHAP01	Chapter 1 projects
EXAMPLES	Example files
FIGURES	Book figures
LABS	
START	Start lab files
END	Finished lab files
CHAP02	Chapter 2 projects
EXAMPLES	
START	Start example files
END	Finished example files
FIGURES	Book figures
LABS	
START	Start lab files
END	Finished lab files
CHAP03	Chapter 3 projects
EXAMPLES	
START	Start example files
END	Finished example files
FIGURES	Book figures
LABS	
START	Start lab files
END	Finished lab files

continued on next page

continued from previous page

Directory	Contents of Directory
CHAP04	Chapter 4 projects
EXAMPLES	
START	Start example files
END	Finished example files
FIGURES	Book figures
LABS	
START	Start lab files
END	Finished lab files
CHAP05	Chapter 5 projects
EXAMPLES	
START	Start example files
END	Finished example files
FIGURES	Book figures
LABS	
START	Start lab files
END	Finished lab files
CHAP06	Chapter 6 projects
EXAMPLES	
START	Start example files
END	Finished example files
FIGURES	Book figures
LABS	
START	Start lab files
END	Finished lab files
CHAP07	Chapter 7 projects
EXAMPLES	
START	Start example files
END	Finished example files
FIGURES	Book figures
LABS	
START	Start lab files
END	Finished lab files

Directory	Contents of Directory
CHAP08	Chapter 8 projects
EXAMPLES	Example files
FIGURES	Book figures
LABS	
START	Start lab files
END	Finished lab files
CHAP09	Chapter 9 projects
EXAMPLES	
START	Start example files
END	Finished example files
FIGURES	Book figures
LABS	
START	Start lab files
END	Finished lab files
CHAP10	Chapter 10 projects
EXAMPLES	Example files
LABS	Lab files
CHAP11	Chapter 11 projects
EXAMPLES	
START	Start example files
END	Finished example files
FIGURES	Book figures
LABS	
START	Start lab files
END	Finished lab files
CHAP12	Chapter 12 projects
EXAMPLES	
START	Start example files
END	Finished example files
FIGURES	Book figures

continued on next page

continued from previous page

Directory	Contents of Directory
LABS	
START	Start lab files
END	Finished lab files
CHAP13	Chapter 13 projects
EXAMPLES	
START	Start example files
END	Finished example files
FIGURES	Book figures
LABS	
START	Start lab files
END	Finished lab files
CHAP14	Chapter 14 projects
EXAMPLES	
START	Start example files
END	Finished example files
FIGURES	Book figures
LABS	
START	Start lab files
END	Finished lab files
CHAP15	Chapter 15 projects
EXAMPLES	Example files
FIGURES	Book figures
EXPLORER	
IE301M95.EXE	Windows 95 installer
IE301MNT.EXE	Windows NT 4 installer
IE Installer	Macintosh installer
WIN31NT3.51	
SETUP.EXE	Windows 3.1/NT 3.51 installer

CHAPTER 1

INTRODUCTION TO PHOTOSHOP

Adobe Photoshop is the standard workhorse application of many graphics professionals using the Macintosh and Windows platforms. It can be used for scanning, original drawing, color correction, digital compositing and manipulation, and image format conversion, as well as for many other graphic arts activities. In this introductory chapter, you will learn how Photoshop differs from drawing programs like Illustrator and Freehand and you will become familiar with the tools and interface items in the program.

Here are some assumptions this book makes.

- You already know how to use your computer's operating system.

- You know how to use the mouse.

● Photoshop is already installed on your computer. If it is not, you need to read the manual that comes with Photoshop to install the program. If you are having a problem with crashes, read the sections in Chapter 14, "Configuring and Optimizing Photoshop," discussing problem solving on the PC and the Mac.

Here are some assumptions this book *doesn't* make.

● That you have any previous knowledge of either Photoshop or any other graphics program.

● That you possess any knowledge of traditional art techniques.

This book will guide you through the world of Photoshop even if you have never touched a paintbrush or a painting program. *Photoshop 4 Interactive Course* won't make you into a world-class artist, but it will teach you how to utilize the resources of this incredibly versatile tool.

At the end of this chapter, you should be able to

● Describe the difference between a raster and a vector image.

● Hide or show any palette.

● Select foreground and background colors.

● Change the preferences settings to work with full-sized brush previews.

● Define and briefly describe the various color modes in which Photoshop operates.

● Create a new file, select or change the color mode, and save a file.

● Use the Tools Options to set the behavior of Photoshop's tools.

● Change the Opacity and Apply modes for various tools.

● Identify the function of each tool on the Tool palette.

A brief word of warning: This chapter is long! It has the largest number of new concepts of any chapter in this book. However, it is not difficult. It is just introduces you to Photoshop and lets you meet all the tools. You will utilize every skill learned in this chapter as you progress through the book.

Think of this chapter as your first anatomy lecture. You need to know the general structure of the body before you understand how all its parts work. That is what will happen here. You will meet the skeleton of Photoshop. It's a lot to learn in one sitting—but since you are working in a virtual rather than a real classroom, you can take your time. Even if it seems overwhelming, remember that each time you use a new skill, it gets easier—and you will use all these new skills many times in the remaining chapters.

WHAT IS PHOTOSHOP AND WHO NEEDS IT?

Photoshop is a graphics program from Adobe Systems, Inc. It is used to design and edit photographic (*continuous tone*) images. It is used by artists, photographers, and businesspeople worldwide. Photoshop allows you to manipulate pictures and create alternate realities. You can put someone's head on another person's body. You can color grass purple. You can place the Eiffel Tower next to the Great Wall of China. You can do all this even if you are not capable of drawing a straight line.

Intended Audience

Many of Photoshop's features are as accessible to the artistically challenged as they are to talented painters. (Of course, if you cannot draw a tiger on a blank piece of paper, you will still not be able to draw one on the screen—but you can scan one and change it as you wish.)

Photoshop has the reputation of being a difficult program. However, it is not really difficult, just very dense—there is quite a lot to learn. Despite this, the program can be used on many levels, and there are very few people who use *every* existing feature. Photoshop can be used to scan images and save them—that's easy. It can also be used at a much more advanced level to build complex images from many scans and to recolor, retouch, or remove images from their current backgrounds.

Raster and Vector Programs

Photoshop is a *raster* image program. This means it works with pixels and enables you to manipulate pixel-based images. *Pixels* are the smallest piece of an image, like atoms in nature. Each Photoshop file is made up of many pixels. If you use the Pencil tool with the smallest brush and create a single dot, this is a *pixel*. Each pixel can have its own color and transparency. You can create, delete, move, copy, and paste individual and groups of pixels. However, once you have moved a pixel from one place in the image to another and deselected it, the computer has no way of knowing which pixel was moved. It cannot tell the difference between a group of pixels that look like a square or a group of pixels that look like a circle. Although Photoshop has ways for you to select parts of an image, it may not be easy to find the pixels again.

In this respect, Photoshop differs completely from a *vector* (drawing/illustration) program such as Adobe Illustrator.

A vector program makes shapes the computer can identify and remember. If you draw a square in a vector program, it remains a square. You can easily select and move it. You can place it in front or in back of another object. If you decide to overlap the square and the circle and later change your mind, both objects are still whole (see Figure 1-1). In a raster program, you lose whatever part of the image is under the overlapping areas (see Figure 1-2).

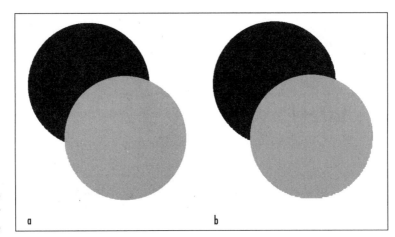

Figure 1-1
Vector image
before (a) and after
(b) moving circle

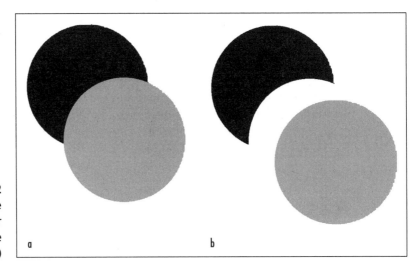

Figure 1-2
Raster image
before (a) and after
(b) moving circle
(note whitespace)

There are other differences between raster and vector graphics programs, but they aren't important right now.

Raster and vector programs are typically used for different purposes. You use Photoshop to composite a group of photographs for the cover of a brochure and Illustrator to set the type in a circle or to create an abstract, hard-edge drawing with only a few colors. There are also many times, as you will discover working through this course, when you want to use Illustrator and Photoshop together.

QUIZ 1

1. Photoshop can be used in the following ways:
   a. Scanning
   b. Digital composition

   c. Image format conversion
   d. Color correction

2. Photoshop is a(n)
   a. Illustrator program.
   b. Vector program.
   c. Raster program.
   d. Editing program.

3. Raster images are different from vector images in that they
   a. Can be grouped together.
   b. Are pixel-based.
   c. Remain intact when moving or overlapping other objects.
   d. Cannot be copied.

4. A photo has many pixels, and every pixel
   a. Can have its own color.
   b. Can be a different shape.
   c. Can be moved, copied, or deleted.
   d. Is the smallest part of an image.

5. What kind of images do vector programs create?
   a. Shapes the computer can identify and remember
   b. Ones that can easily be moved or resized
   c. Bitmapped images
   d. Black-and-white images

PHOTOSHOP'S ANATOMY

Figure 1-3 shows the Macintosh Photoshop environment when you start the program (after you open a new, empty file). The Windows environment is similar, but the Windows window-in-a-window interface gives it a slightly different look. The basic parts of Photoshop are

● **The Menu Bar**

● **The Toolbox**

● **The Floating Palettes**

● **The Document Window**

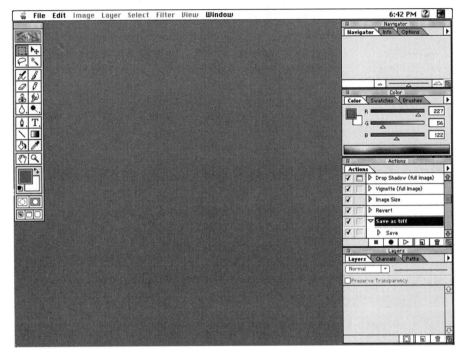

Figure 1-3
The Photoshop
interface

The Menu Bar

The Menu Bar holds all the Photoshop commands. A triangle next to a command indicates there is another menu of commands in it. An ellipsis after a menu item indicates a dialog box with options will be presented if it is selected. Figure 1-4 shows the Image menu. The Rotate Canvas command has another menu under it (it has a triangle indicating that), but the Apply Image command gives you a new dialog box if you select it (it has an ellipsis next to the command).

Figure 1-4
Image menu with
additional menus
or dialog boxes
indicated

CREATING A NEW IMAGE

As a first exercise, let's create a brand new image file.

1. Pull down the File menu and select the New option. The dialog box shown in Figure 1-5 appears. The numbers and units of measure you see differ from the figure shown, based on the last image you created and the settings in the Preferences file.

2. You may type in a title for your image if you wish. Titles for new images are optional. For this example, just type the word Test.

3. The next section in the dialog box asks you to specify the Width, Height, Resolution, and Mode. As you change these settings, a new image size is calculated. You may select any unit of measure you prefer, but it is usually easiest to work in pixels. Make your image 400 pixels wide × 400 pixels high. Set the resolution to 72 pixels per inch.

4. You may not know what the term *resolution* means, but you don't need to right now. You will learn all about resolution and pixels-per-inch in Chapter 6, "Color and File Formats."

5. Select the RGB mode for the image by moving to it in the Mode drop-down menu if the field does not already read RGB. You can see the drop-down menu by clicking on the triangle next to the Mode field. We'll talk about the meaning of RGB a bit later in this chapter.

6. Finally, you need to select the background color for your image. You can choose white, your current background color, or no color at all—just a transparent image. For now, select white as your contents color.

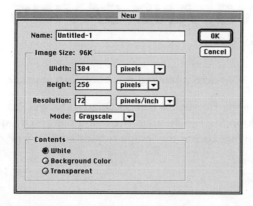

Figure 1-5
Dialog box for creating a new image

7. Click OK. Your new image file appears in a window. Notice the title bar of the file shows you the name and the current color mode.

8. Repeat Steps 1 through 7 and create another new document 300×300 pixels in CMYK mode. Call it CMYK test.

9. Close both windows by clicking on their Close boxes in the standard Macintosh or Windows fashion. Do not save.

 Tip   To select the entire width or height field so you can type in it and replace its former contents, click on the name next to it. This selects the entire field (it turns black). You can do this for almost every dialog box in Photoshop that requires typing (the biggest exception to this rule is in the Color Picker dialog). You can tell if a box needs a value typed in by looking at it. It will have a small triangle next to the box if you are supposed to select from a list. If it doesn't have the triangle, you are supposed to type in it.

Command Watch

You can use the keyboard to create a new image. On the Macintosh, press ⌘+N to open a new document. On the Windows platform, press CTRL+N.

There is also a keyboard command to open an existing document. Use ⌘+O on the Mac and CTRL+O on Windows.

OPENING, DUPLICATING, CLONING, AND SAVING AN IMAGE

1. Put the CD-ROM accompanying this book into your CD-ROM drive.

2. Open the image Flower.Psd (File → Open → Flower.Psd). To open the image, click on the File menu in the menu bar and drag your mouse to the Open command. Locate the image requested (Flower.Psd). Click OK when you find it.

This image comes from the *Grammar of Ornament* CD-ROM by Direct Imagination. The *Grammar of Ornament* is a classic reference of decorative arts from ancient Egypt, Greece, and Rome through a variety of cultures and eras. The CD-ROM is a digital re-creation of this monumental work. Check out the vendor listings at the back of this book for more information on this and any others product mentioned.

In most chapters, you will be asked to copy an image before using it. Here's how: Pull down the Image menu and select the Duplicate command (Image → Duplicate). You see a dialog box. Just press RETURN. A copy of the flower image appears. It is called Flower.Psd copy.

Sometimes you might want to create a new image the same size as one of your opened images. You can do this as part of the Open command you learned in the last Hands On.

3. Create a new file (File → New). When the dialog box appears, instead of typing in the height and width, pull down the Windows menu on the Photoshop menu bar. Figure 1-6 shows the Windows menu open. The flower file appears at the bottom of the menu. Selecting Flower.Psd tells Photoshop you want a *new* image with the same size, resolution, and color mode as the Flower.Psd image. This is a handy thing to know, and it is not well-documented in the manual. Figure 1-7 shows the New dialog box after you have selected the flower image as the model.

4. Click on the Flower.Psd copy image (or select it by highlighting its name in the Windows menu of the menu bar).

5. Save the image by choosing Save from the File menu. Since you did not save this image before, Photoshop gives you a chance to change the file name. Name the image Flower2.Psd and click OK. You may have to select a new directory on your hard drive if the Save location points to the CD-ROM. You cannot save a file to a CD-ROM because it is a read-only device.

Figure 1-6
Windows menu
with list of open
images

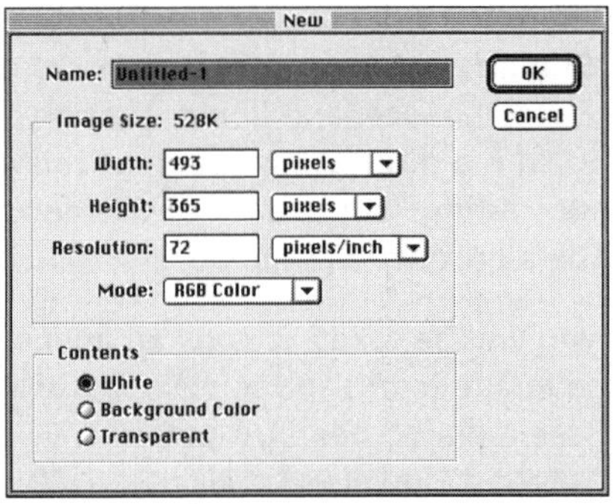

Figure 1-7
New dialog box
showing new size
attributes

Toolbox and Tool Options Palette

The next most important part of the Photoshop interface is the Toolbox. Figure 1-8 shows the Toolbox with all the tools labeled. The next section discusses those tools in detail. Each tool has a dialog box attached, enabling you to select additional options for the tools. You can access this Options dialog box by pressing RETURN when a tool is selected or by double-clicking on the tool itself. The only tools for which double-clicking does not show the Options palette are the Hand and the Zoom tool. Double-clicking on one of these tools causes a different behavior. Double-clicking on the Hand tool makes the view of your image as large as will fit into the window (if the image is small, it increases more than 100%). Double-clicking on the Zoom tool displays your image (or a portion of it) at 1:1 ratio, regardless of how large the image is. The only tool that does not have any options at all is the Type tool.

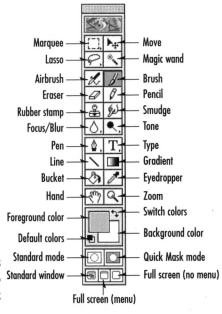

Figure 1-8
The Photoshop
Toolbox

What Is a Viewing Ratio?

Photoshop can display your image in a variety of views, or magnification levels. These enlargements and reductions only affect the way the image is displayed onscreen—the actual image pixels do not change at all.

A 1:1 ratio means every pixel in the image is shown on the screen. If the image is displayed at 1:2 ratio, you see it *half-size,* so only half the pixels are visible. If you view an image at 2:1 ratio, each pixel becomes twice as large.

You can use the Navigator palette to determine the magnification level of the image, or you can type a percentage into either the bottom of the window or the Navigator palette (more on this in a bit!).

Color Pickers

Photoshop keeps two current colors. They are the foreground color and the background color, located in the swatch area of the Toolbox (refer to Figure 1-8 again for the location). The Foreground color is used by the active painting tool (such as the Pencil, Brush, Airbrush, Bucket, or Line tool). The background color is used when erasing or clearing the screen, or when creating a gradient. These colors can be changed by clicking on them. A single click brings up either the Photoshop Color Picker, shown in Figure 1-9, or the standard Color Picker for Macintosh or Windows, shown in Figures 1-10 and 1-11. You can specify which picker you prefer by selecting the one you want in the General Preferences dialog. While you should be familiar with how the standard Color Picker works on your platform, let's spend a bit of time looking at the Photoshop Color Picker.

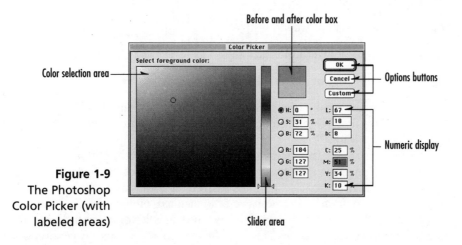

Figure 1-9
The Photoshop
Color Picker (with
labeled areas)

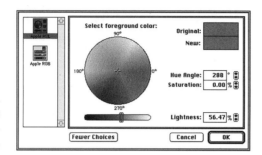

Figure 1-10
The Apple Color
Picker

Figure 1-11
The Windows Color
Picker

The Color Picker dialog is divided into five parts:

● **The Options Buttons**

● **The Slider Area**

● **The Color Selection Area**

● **The Before and After Color Box**

● **The Numeric Display**

The Options area enables you to confirm and leave (OK), cancel and leave (Cancel), or select a Custom color (Custom). The Custom colors are discussed in Chapter 12, "Using Spot Color."

With Photoshop's default settings, you'll notice that the radio button next to the H in the HSB Numerical Display area is selected. This turns the slider into a Hue Selection slider. The Hue Selection slider lets you select the basic color you want (*hue* is the proper term for it). This means you can pick red, pink, green, chartreuse, and so on. Sliding the double arrows up and down the Hue Selector makes the color inside the Color Selection area change. This is the first selection you typically perform when entering the dialog box.

The colors in the Color Selection area are consistent, regardless of the hue selected. The upper-left corner of the Color Selection area always contains pure white (RGB: 255, 255, 255). The lower-left and -right corners always contain pure black (RGB: 0, 0, 0). The upper-right corner always contains whatever hue you selected from the Hue Selection slider. This is the purest, most saturated color in the Color Selection area. If you drag the cursor to the upper-right corner of the Color Picker as far up as it will move diagonally, you will see that in the Numerical Display area, the Saturation and Brightness read 100, 100. If you drag the Hue Slider up and down, the Saturation and Brightness numbers do not change—regardless of the hue—as long as you keep the cursor in the upper-right corner of the Color Selection area. In addition, if you read the K: % in the CMYK part of the Numerical Display, it is usually at 0%, and never more than 1% or 2%.

An easy way to select a shade of gray is to drag your cursor as far left as it goes, then drag it up and down the left edge of the Color Selection area. This always picks a neutral gray (one in which the RGB values are the same).

The rest of the Color Selection area is a mix of white-to-hue, white-to-black, and hue-to-black. You can set your foreground or background color to anything within the Color Selection area simply by dragging the circular cursor over it and clicking. This puts your chosen color in the top area of the Before and After display. The bottom box contains the *before* color. If you select a color fairly close to the upper-right corner (a fairly saturated color), you may see a triangle with an exclamation point pop up. This is the *Gamut Warning*. It tells you the selected color cannot be printed in the standard CMYK process inks. The color appearing inside the triangle (usually a muddy, dull color) is the closest color that can print. If you click on the triangle, that color becomes your *after*—or selected—color, and the warning disappears.

A Short Introduction to Printing

One of the most common reasons people use Photoshop is to prepare images for conventional printing. Most of the mailers you receive and magazines you read are printed conventionally on a printing press using an ink system known as Process Color. In order to print what looks like full color, only four inks are used. These inks are cyan, magenta, yellow, and black. Together they are referred to as CMYK inks or process color. There are many issues and intricacies involved in preparing images to print in process color. Much of the problem revolves around the fact that the four ink colors are not sufficient to produce many of the colors you see on your screen. Chapter 6, "Color and File Formats," and Chapter 15, "Photoshop Output," discuss printing and CMYK issues in more detail.

The Numerical Display area shows the actual numeric values of the color selected in four different color spaces. The color spaces are *HSB* (Hue-Saturation-Brightness), *Lab* (Lightness-color channel a-color channel b), *RGB* (Red-Green-Blue), and *CMYK* (Cyan-Magenta-Yellow-Black). You can type in the values in any one of the numeric displays, if you prefer.

Do not type in a CMYK color definition when you are in an RGB color document. The color you see will not be accurate—even, or especially, when you change the image to CMYK mode.

You may also change the function of the Slider area by clicking on a different radio button. If you select the S button in HSB, the slider changes to whatever Hue your cursor is on, in intensities varying from fully saturated to fully desaturated. If you select B in the HSB area, the slider varies the brightness of the Color Selection area. If you select either R, G, or B in the RGB area, the slider varies the amount of whichever button you choose, and the Color Selection slider shows all the possible choices for that specific amount of the color component.

Command Watch

Here are some convenient commands for working with the color Swatches in the Toolbox:

Ⓓ sets the foreground/background color Swatches back to the black-and-white default.

Ⓧ switches the foreground/background color Swatches so the foreground color becomes the background color, and vice versa.

When you use the Eyedropper tool, clicking on a pixel sets the foreground color to that pixel's color, and (OPTION)+click (Mac) or (ALT)+click (Windows) sets the background color.

CHOOSING A COLOR

1. Pull down the File Menu and click on Preferences → General (or press Mac: ⌘+Ⓚ, Windows: (CTRL)+Ⓚ). This opens the General Preferences dialog. Make sure the Color Picker is set to Photoshop. If it is not, pull down the menu and click on Photoshop to change it. Exit Preferences.

2. Click on the foreground color in the Swatches area of the Toolbox. Make sure the radio button next to the H in the HSB area is selected.

3. Drag the Hue slider all the way to the top. This sets the Color Selection area to Red.

4. Drag the circular cursor to the upper-right corner. The RGB numeric read-out area should say R:255, G:0, and B:0.

5. Drag the cursor down the right side of the Color Selection area until the numeric readout is R:55, G:0, B:0.

6. Drag the cursor back to the upper-right corner. Now drag it diagonally toward the lower-left corner until the Gamut Warning disappears. The RGB values are close to R:217, G:21, B:21.

7. Without moving the cursor in the Color Selection area, drag the Hue Slider down until the Gamut Warning reappears. This should be close to R:217, G:21, B:123. This shows you that the Gamut Warning changes based on the hue and value selected.

8. Type the numbers 91, 177, 71 into the R, G, and B numeric boxes (R:91, G:177, B:71). Notice how the Hue Slider moves to shades of green.

9. Click on the S: (Saturation) radio button. Drag the slider up and down, and notice how the color gets more intense as the slider moves up, then fades to gray as the slider moves down.

10. Click on the B: (Brightness) radio button. Drag the slider to the top and notice that the colors get very bright. Drag the slider to the bottom and notice that the colors in the Color Selection area change to black.

11. Click on the R: (Red) radio button. Type in the RGB values of 91, 177, 71 again. The Color Selection area changes to show all the colors possible with a Red value of 217. To prove this, move the circular cursor anywhere within the Color Selection area. Notice that the R: value in the numeric readout never changes.

12. Type in the RGB values of 91, 177, 71 again. The slider shows all the colors possible with G:177 and B:71 if you only alter the amount of Red. Drag the slider up and down and notice that only the R: amount changes. The colors in the slider vary from a mustard yellow when Red is at 255, to a blue-green when Red is at 0.

13. Drag the Slider until the Red value reads 181.

14. Click on the H: (Hue) radio button and click OK to accept the color.

15. Press ⓧ to exchange the foreground and background colors.

16. Press ⓓ to return the colors back to the black-and-white default.

Floating Palettes

The Floating palettes comprise the final area of the interface. These palettes add functionality to Photoshop and can be hidden or shown through the Window → Palettes menu item. Each palette performs its own function and has an associated menu inside the triangle above the palette scroll bar. The palettes are called floating because they always stay in front of the image you have open. You can never cover a Floating palette with an image—Photoshop does not let you do that. When you open Photoshop for the first time after it is installed, you see the default arrangement of floating boxes across the right side of your screen. The boxes contain the tabbed Floating palettes. Since they are tabbed, the palettes can be made to share boxes so they occupy less space. They can also be minimized by clicking on the box at the upper-right corner of the palette. This expands the palette in stages, then minimizes it to show only the Tab area. Figure 1-12 shows the default arrangement of the Floating palettes. All the palettes are visible.

Command Watch

Press TAB to remove the Floating palettes from the screen temporarily. You can get them back by pressing TAB again.

To remove just the Toolbox, select the Hide Tools option in the Window menu. To remove just the Floating palettes, press SHIFT+TAB.

Figure 1-12
The default
arrangement of
Floating palettes

If you remove the Floating Palettes from the screen this way, make sure they are visible when you exit Photoshop. If you forget to make these palettes visible when you quit, the Mac version of Photoshop has an annoying tendency to cut off the top of the Toolbox the next time it loads. If this happens, you need to go into the Preferences → General dialog and click on the bar that says Reset Palette Locations to Default.

REARRANGING PALETTES

The palettes can be moved into each other and regrouped as you wish. Try this:

1. Move your cursor to the Tab area of the Color palette. Press the mouse button and hold it down. A dotted-line Marquee surrounds the Color palette.

2. Drag the Color palette (still by its tab) to the center of the screen.

3. Select the Swatches palette by clicking on its tab. A solid black line appears around the Swatches palette. Let go of the mouse button. The Swatches palette has now been transferred into the Color palette container.

4. Click on the Color tab to bring it forward, then click on the collapse button in the upper-right of the container. Move the container to the extreme lower-right of your screen. You can move it by dragging the shaded bar on top.

5. Move the Layers/Channels/Paths palette above the Color/Swatches container. Notice that as you get the palette close to the other one, it snaps to align itself. As you move the palette up, it also snaps to the top of the Color/Swatches palette.

6. Drag the Actions palette to the center of your screen. Drag the Brushes palette container down until it snaps to the Layers/Channels/Paths palette.

7. Drag the Options palette by its tab, and place it in the Brushes container.

8. Finally, drag the Actions palette by its tab and place it into the Info/Navigator container at the top of the screen. The container the Actions palette occupied disappears as soon as it is empty.

You will probably find this arrangement of palettes useful. You can leave the palettes arranged like this, or change them to suit your needs.

Let's look at each palette.

Brushes

The Brushes palette shows all the brushes available for a specific tool. There are two versions of the Brushes palette: smooth (*anti-aliased*) and jagged (*aliased*). The anti-aliased brush set (see Figure 1-13) is used with the painting tools producing smooth edges: the Paintbrush, Airbrush, Rubber Stamp tool, Smudge tool, Toning tools, and Focus tools. The jagged set of brushes is used with the Pencil tool (see Figure 1-14).

The Eraser tool uses whichever brush set is needed for the specific Eraser tool selected. To select a brush, simply click on it with the desired tool selected. The tool remembers which brush it used last.

The Brushes menu allows you to create, save, delete, and modify the brushes in the palette (see Figure 1-15). You can create complete sets of these brushes to load or remove as desired. You can create either standard or custom brushes. A *standard brush* is rounded and is based on a circle. A *custom brush* can be any shape you want. You will create a custom brush later in this chapter. Now, however, let's create a standard brush.

Figure 1-13
Smooth (anti-aliased) brush set

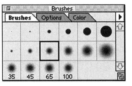

Figure 1-14
Jagged (aliased) brush set

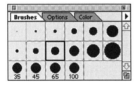

Figure 1-15
Brushes palette menu

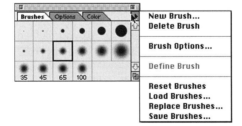

CREATING STANDARD BRUSHES

1. Click on the first brush in the Brushes palette. It is a single-pixel brush.

2. From the Brushes palette menu, select New.... The dialog shown in Figure 1-16 appears.

3. The Diameter setting controls the size of the brush. Drag the slider up and down a few times to see what effect it has in the preview area of the dialog. You can see the brush growing and contracting in shape each time you stop dragging. Drag the slider to 73. This creates a brush 73 pixels large (just over 1 inch in screen pixels on most screens). When you then drag the slider to 74, it looks as if the brush is smaller. Not so! Notice that a tiny 1:2 pops over the preview. It indicates you are now viewing the preview at half size. If you drag the slider to its maximum of 999, the viewing ratio changes to 1:16. A 999-pixel brush would be so slow to use that it is impractical. Set the brush diameter to 25 pixels.

4. The next attribute that needs to be set is *hardness*. The hardness is used by the anti-aliased brush set to determine the amount of transparency at the edges of the brush. An anti-aliased brush always does a little blending between the color of the brush and the color on which it is painted. A brush with 100% hardness takes approximately 3 pixels to change from the brush to the painted-upon color. A brush with 100% softness (which is 0% hardness) contains 1 center pixel in the exact foreground color, and the remaining pixels all blend toward the colors being painted upon. Set the hardness to 50%. This creates a soft brush. You can either drag the slider or click on Hardness and type in the value of 50.

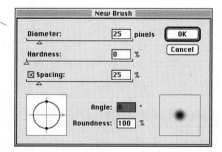

Figure 1-16
The New Brush
creation dialog

5. The third slider is for spacing. This attribute is optional. If you turn off the check mark, the brush repeats itself every pixel. This may make the coverage too heavy. The most common spacing is the default of 25%. If you change the spacing to 100%, the brush does not cover itself at all as it paints. This is an easy way to create dotted lines or spotted areas. The maximum spacing is 999 pixels. If you use this spacing, you can randomly scatter brushstrokes over your image. For now, just set the spacing to 50%.

6. The next set of attributes concern the roundness and the angle of the brush. If you have a circular brush, the angle does not matter—you don't see any changes as the brush rotates. However, if you flatten the brush, the angle makes a big difference. You can set both the angle and the roundness either visually or by the numbers. At the left of the brush edit dialog, you will see the roundness and the angle visual settings. Roundness is represented by the dot on the top and bottom of the brush outline. The angle is set by the arrows. Place your cursor on the top dot and press the mouse button down. Drag the dot until it meets the bottom one in the center of the brush outline. The numeric readout says the roundness is 0%. Grab the point of the arrow and rotate the brush until the numeric readout says 45%.

7. Click OK. You will see that your new brush was added to the palette. We will try it out a little bit later in this chapter. You have created a soft knife-edged brush that is useful in creating ribbons.

You can also save and load complete sets of brushes. In the Goodies folder/directory of your copy of Photoshop, there are additional sets of brushes provided by Adobe. You can delete a brush by clicking on it and selecting Delete from the Brushes palette menu. You can edit any brush by either double-clicking on it or selecting Brush Options in the Brushes palette menu (refer to Figure 1-15). When you load a new brush set (Load Brushes...), Photoshop appends the brushes onto the current brush set. If you select Replace Brushes... from the Brushes palette menu, the new brush set removes all the old brushes and replaces them. If you want to return to the set of brushes installed with Photoshop, the command Reset Brushes... does that for you. You can save a set of brushes for later recall by selecting the Save Brushes... command. This saves all the brushes currently open into one set you can reload as you wish. While brushes are not removed from your palette when you quit Photoshop, brushes you haven't saved will be lost if your system crashes and the Preferences file becomes corrupt. So, if you create brushes you like, save them.

Command Watch

These are the shortcuts for the Brushes palette:

Action	Mac key	Windows key
Delete Brush	⌘+click	CTRL+click
Previous Brush	[[	[[

Action	Mac key	Windows key
Next Brush	[]	[]
First Brush in set	SHIFT+[]	SHIFT+[]
Last Brush in set	SHIFT+[]	SHIFT+[]
Edit Brush settings	double-click	double-click

Options Palette

The Options palette enables you to customize the performance of the tools in the Toolbox. It becomes the active palette when you either select it manually, double-click on a tool in the Toolbox, or press RETURN or ENTER on your keyboard. The specifics in the Options palette will change with every tool. If you click on each tool in the Toolbox with the Options palette open, you can watch the options change. We will look at the options for each tool as we discuss them a little later. The two items in the Options palette menu allow you to reset either just the tool you are using or all the tools back to their default conditions.

Color Palette

The Color palette enables you to quickly select the foreground and background colors without opening the Photoshop Color Picker accessed by clicking on the color Swatches in the Toolbox. Any change you make in the palette is immediately reflected in the foreground or background color and cannot be undone. Figure 1-17 shows the Color palette.

The Color palette menu (see Figure 1-18) allows you to change the *color space* of the sliders, as well as change the color bar displayed. You can mix-and-match as you wish (for example, if you want to choose colors in CMYK color space by moving Hue-Saturation-Brightness or RGB sliders).

Figure 1-17
Color palette

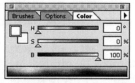

Figure 1-18
Color palette menu

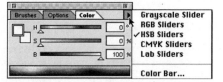

THE COLOR PALETTE

1. Select File → Preferences → General from the main menu bar. Make sure Dynamic Color Sliders is checked. Press OK to exit the Preferences dialog.

2. Press Ⓓ to set the colors back to the black-and-white default.

3. Select HSB Sliders from the Color palette menu.

4. Drag the Hue slider to 227°. The color does not change because the saturation and brightness are still set to 0, and the color looks black.

5. Drag the Brightness slider to 68%. Though the color is now a light gray (since the saturation is still 0), the Saturation slider shows a variety of grays to blues.

6. Drag the Saturation slider to 85%. Notice that the Gamut Warning appears. If you decrease the saturation to about 48%, this warning disappears.

7. Open the Color palette menu and select Color Bar.... You can set the Color Bar so it only shows a Gradient from your foreground to background color by selecting the Current Colors option from the drop-down menu in the dialog. With colors set up this way, the Gradient does not change when you select a new color from the bar (though if you switch to another program, then redisplay the Photoshop screen, the sliders change).

8. Select Color Bar... from the Color palette menu again. Select RGB Spectrum. Select a foreground color. Press the Modifier key (Mac: OPTION, Windows: ALT) and choose a new background color.

   It is often more practical to select colors that exist in the CMYK color space, especially if the image will eventually be printed. Select CMYK Spectrum as the color bar. You may leave the sliders set to HSB or change them to RGB as you prefer.

Swatches Palette

The Swatches palette enables you to keep a variety of your favorite colors already pre-mixed. You may create, save, and recall as many palette sets as you want. Figure 1-19 shows the Swatches palette, and Figure 1-20 shows the Swatches palette menu. You can also add and delete colors from the Swatches palette. As with the Brushes palette, you have the option of replacing the color set with another one (Replace Swatches...) or appending the new color set onto the bottom of the current one (Load Swatches...).

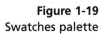

Figure 1-19
Swatches palette

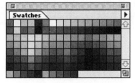

Figure 1-20
Swatches palette
menu

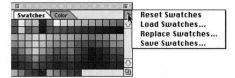

You may also reset the Swatches to their default condition any time you wish (Reset Swatches). You can change the current foreground color by clicking on any color in the Swatches palette.

The Swatches palette is very useful for preparing images with only 256 colors. This type of low-color image is commonly used for ones displayed over the Internet or in multimedia applications. In Chapter 6, "Color and File Formats," and Chapter 13, "Beyond Photoshop," we will look at ways to use 256 colors (Indexed Color mode).

Command Watch

Here are the keystrokes for using the Swatches palette:

Action	Cursor shape	Mac key	Windows key
Change foreground color	Eyedropper	Click on swatch	Click on swatch
Change background color	Eyedropper	OPTION+click swatch	ALT+click swatch
Delete a color	Scissors	⌘+click	CTRL+click
Add a color	Bucket	SHIFT+click	SHIFT+click

Navigator Palette

The Navigator palette lets you control the magnification level of your image. It gives you a very fast way to view any area of your image. The Navigator palette shows you a proxy of your image (a reasonably sized thumbnail) and gives you a slider ranging from about 12% to 1600% magnification of the original. Figure 1-21 shows the Navigator palette.

Figure 1-21
Navigator palette

Values smaller than 100% show you a reduced view of the image, and values above 100% show you enlarged pixels in the image window. The Navigator proxy itself does not change. You have a number of ways to set a value into the Navigator palette:

- Drag the slider in either direction.

- Click on the smaller or larger mountains at either end of the slider to enlarge or reduce the image by a set percentage.

- Type the exact magnification in the numeric box left of the palette.

- Drag a Marquee in the proxy area with the modifier key pressed (Mac: ⌘, Windows: CTRL).

The Navigator palette menu only contains an option for the color used to outline the viewing area in the proxy. Figure 1-22 shows this dialog.

Layers Palette

The Layers palette enables you to control the various elements of your image. Layers act like sheets of acetate and allow you to create images you can change easily, time and time again. The use of Layers is one of the main topics in learning to master Photoshop. Since much of what you will learn in this course concerns Layers, this section does nothing more than introduce you to the palette itself and its associated menu, as shown in Figures 1-23 and 1-24. In order to understand Layers, you need to know much more about Photoshop itself first. You will work with Layers in Chapter 2, "Making Selections," and in Chapter 3, "Layers and Channels." You will then work with them in just about every chapter in this book.

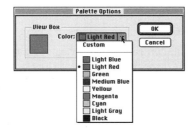

Figure 1-22
Navigator Palette
Options dialog

Figure 1-23
Layers palette

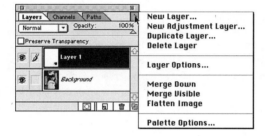

Figure 1-24
Layers palette
menu

Channels Palette

The Channels palette is another very important Floating Palette, but one merely introduced here. Figure 1-25 shows the Channels palette and Figure 1-26 shows the Channels palette menu. Channels are used for two purposes in Photoshop: to store color information and to store selection information. The color information is stored in the channels created by the color space you select. For example, an RGB image has three color channels: a red, a green, and a blue. A CMYK image has four color channels: cyan, magenta, yellow, and black. A grayscale image has only the black channel. These channels are created the moment you open a new document or change from one color mode to another. You can create additional channels, however, as you work. These additional channels, called *Alpha channels*, store information that helps you select portions of your image more easily. Chapters 2 and 3 contain much more information on creating and using channels.

Figure 1-25
Channels palette

Figure 1-26
Channels palette
menu

Paths Palette

Earlier in this lecture, we discussed the topic of raster versus vector graphics. Photoshop is a raster graphics program. However, to make life easier for you, the Adobe software engineers devised a way to use vector-based selections. The Paths palette holds the commands to create those selections and work with vector paths. The options in the Paths palette let you create, save, and delete paths. In addition, you can stroke a path (trace around it with one of the painting tools), edit the curves in it, change it into a standard selection, and use it as a *clipping path* (a way of removing background from a file when it is placed in a page layout or illustration program so only the image inside the path is visible). Figure 1-27 shows the Paths palette, and Figure 1-28 shows the Paths palette menu. You will learn how to create and work with paths in Chapter 9, "Advanced Selection Techniques."

Figure 1-27
Paths palette

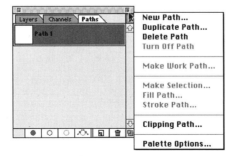

Figure 1-28
Paths palette menu

Info Palette

The Info palette is shown in Figure 1-29 and its menu is in Figure 1-30. This palette is one of the most important and underused of all Photoshop features. It gives you measurements in your image. It can measure the color under your cursor in a variety of color spaces. It can measure the size of selection. It can measure the distance and angle of any area you move in your image. For this reason, it should be easily accessible at all times. The Info palette is not difficult to use. All you need to do is read it. If it is visible, it is operational and automatic. The Info palette will become much more important when color corrections are discussed in Chapter 7, "Color Correction."

Actions Palette

Many programs use the function keys to perform common operations. In some programs, the function keys are always needed to execute the command, and remembering what each function key does is one of the hardest things to learn about the program. Photoshop believes in free choice, however, and includes an Actions palette—a place you can click to execute a series of commands you have chosen as most important to you. In addition, you can associate these commands with a function key—though you do not need to. Even better is the ability of the Actions palette to remember a *sequence* of commands—a simple scripting ability that lets you change a whole folder of files from one file type, for example, to another. Figure 1-31 shows the Actions palette set that comes when you install Photoshop. Figure 1-32 shows the Actions palette menu. You can save multiple sets of actions so you can load whichever one seems most appropriate for the tasks at hand.

Figure 1-29
Info palette

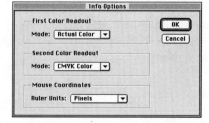

Figure 1-30
Info palette menu

Figure 1-31
Actions palette

Figure 1-32
Actions palette
menu

USING ACTIONS

The CD-ROM contains a set of actions for commands frequently performed in this book. They are all simple actions—just replacements for menu commands. You will learn how to create your own actions in Chapter 14, "Configuring and Optimizing Photoshop," (though you can work through that chapter out-of-turn if you want). Let's load and try out this Action set.

1. Pull down the Actions palette menu in the triangle over the palette scroll bar. Select Load Actions.... You will see a standard file open dialog. Load the set Certified.Atn. This appends the actions to the bottom of your current set. Figure 1-33 shows the new Actions palette (expanded all the way).

   If you have closed the Flower.Psd image, open it again (File → Open → Flower.Psd).

2. Pull down the Actions palette menu and see if there is a check mark next to the Button Mode setting. If there is not, select Button mode. Your palette will look like Figure 1-33.

Figure 1-33
Actions palette
with Certified
Actions set loaded
(Button mode)

3. Click on the Grayscale button. Your image becomes gray.

4. Undo (Mac: ⌘+Z, Windows: CTRL+Z).

5. Select the Button mode again in the Actions palette menu. The check mark disappears and the Actions palette looks like the one in Figure 1-34. To play the Grayscale action again, click on the Grayscale action to highlight it. Now click on the Play button at the bottom of the palette (it is the third icon—the one that looks like a triangle).

6. Undo (Mac: ⌘+Z, Windows: CTRL+Z).

7. You may now close the Flower.Psd image (Mac: ⌘+W, Windows: CTRL+W).

1. What are the basic parts of Photoshop?
   a. Menu bar
   b. Title bar
   c. Floating Palettes
   d. Toolbox

2. The menu bar holds all the Photoshop commands. What does the triangle next to a menu command mean?
   a. The command has a shortcut associated with it.
   b. A dialog box with options will appear.
   c. The command executes immediately.
   d. Another menu of commands appears.

3. Every tool on the Toolbox has a corresponding
   a. Menu command.
   b. Options palette.
   c. Dialog box.
   d. Pop-up menu.

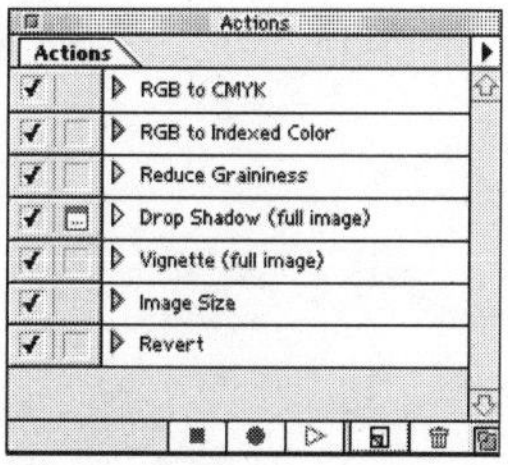

Figure 1-34
Actions palette
with Certified
Actions set loaded
(Normal mode)

4. What do all the Floating palettes have in common?
   a. They always remain on top.
   b. They can be hidden.
   c. They add functionality to Photoshop.
   d. They have an associated menu that can be activated by clicking on the triangle.

5. Which palette allows you to save a pre-mix of your favorite colors?
   a. Colors palette
   b. Swatches palette
   c. Options palette
   d. Channels palette

PHOTOSHOP TOOLS

The next area to consider in the Photoshop environment is the Toolbox. Here you will find the painting implements and selection instruments needed to make Photoshop do your bidding. The tools in the Toolbox are very easy to select. Each one has an associated letter you just press on the keyboard. Since it is usually easier to press a key than to mouse over to the Toolbox, it is worth taking the time to learn the shortcuts listed in the Command Watch section that follows. The tools can also be grouped together by function:

Selection tools	Marquee, Lasso, Magic Wand, Pen, Move
Painting tools	Brush, Airbrush, Pencil, Eraser
Paint utility tools	Gradient, Bucket, Type, Line
Utility tools	Crop, Hand, Zoom, Eyedropper
Image manipulation tools	Rubber Stamp, Smudge, Focus, Tone

In this introduction, you will see the tool icon and its Tool Options palette, learn about its function, and try it out. The more complex tools like the selection tools are covered in much more detail in later chapters.

Command Watch

Here are the keystroke shortcuts for each of the tools and icons in the Toolbox:

Press This	To Get This
A	Airbrush
B	Brush (Paintbrush)
C	Crop tool
D	Default colors
E	Eraser
F	Full Screen (change screen modes)
G	Gradient tool
H	Hand tool
I	Eyedropper tool
K	Bucket tool
L	Lasso tool
M	Marquee tool
N	Line tool
O	Tone tools
P	Pen tool
Q	Quick Mask Mode (toggle between Quick Mask and regular selection modes)
R	Blur tool (Focus tools)
S	Rubber Stamp tool
T	Type tool
U	Smudge tool (toggle between Smudge and Fingerpaint)
V	Move tool
W	Magic Wand tool
X	Exchange foreground and background colors
Y	Pencil tool
Z	Zoom tool

Utility Tools

The Crop, Hand, Zoom, and Eyedropper tools form the utility section of the Toolbox. They let you move easily in a large image, get in close enough to see fine detail, pick up color, and get rid of wasted areas on a canvas.

Zoom Tool (Z)

This tool allows you to get close to an area you need to see in detail or move out until you can see the entire image. You can enlarge or shrink your image on the screen by a factor of 16. The Zoom tool *does not change the pixels in your image*. It merely selects which pixels to show at any given ratio. If you zoom out all the way and shrink your image down to 1:16 ratio, you see very few of the pixels in the image. However, they are still there, waiting for you to look at them again. This is how the Zoom tool differs from the Image Size command. Image Size *does* change the pixels in your image permanently.

There are so many shortcuts to the Zoom tool that it is rarely necessary to select it from the Toolbox. It is always available to you, regardless of the tool you have selected, by holding down spacebar+⌘ on the Mac or spacebar+CTRL on Windows. OPTION+spacebar (Mac) or ALT+spacebar (Windows) reduces the image view on screen. You can also enlarge an area as much as it fits on the screen, using the Zoom tool as if it were a Marquee and dragging it to enclose the area of interest.

If you double-click on the Zoom tool, it shows your image at 1:1 ratio. 1:1 ratio means the screen shows 1 pixel for every pixel in your image (so you can see everything in your image). If you begin to enlarge the screen view (to 2:1 ratio or greater), Photoshop shows you fatter pixels. At 2:1 ratio, you see a grid of 2×2 pixels for every pixel in your image. As you go up to 16:1, each pixel is portrayed onscreen as a grid of 16 pixels square. This allows you precise control over the changes you make to an image since—if you wanted—you could alter every pixel in the image by hand, one by one (of course, that would be very time consuming!).

Figure 1-35 shows the Zoom Tool Options dialog. As you can see, you can click once to zoom to Actual Pixels or Fit on Screen. You can also choose Resize Windows to Fit. When you select this option, Photoshop enlarges the actual window size as you zoom in. This can be very useful. Remember, however, you can also zoom in and out via the Navigator palette.

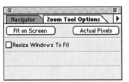

Figure 1-35
Zoom Tool Options
dialog

Here are the keyboard shortcuts for zooming in and out on an image:

Action	Mac key	Windows key
Zoom in	⌘+spacebar	CTRL+spacebar
Zoom out	OPTION+spacebar	ALT+spacebar
Zoom in	⌘+++	CTRL+++
Zoom out	⌘+-	CTRL+-
Zoom to 1:1	double-click on the Zoom tool (both platforms)	
Fit in window	double-click on the Hand tool (both platforms)	

Hand Tool (H)

Figure 1-36 shows the options for the Hand tool. The Hand tool enables you to quickly move from one part of a large image to another. You could use the scroll bars on the right and bottom of the image window, but you will discover that the Hand tool works much faster. Plus, you do not need to mouse over to it. It is always available by pressing the spacebar, regardless of the tool in use. Double-clicking the Hand tool fits the image to the screen so you can see the entire image. It is often faster to use the Hand tool than the Navigator palette as you work.

Eyedropper (I)

The Eyedropper tool lets you select foreground and background colors from the image. Its options, as shown in Figure 1-37, allow you to select the size of the area sampled. A point-by-point sample picks up the actual color of the pixel clicked. A 3×3 or 5×5 sample gives you the average of the colors around the area on which you clicked. Unless you need to pick up a specific pixel, you should select a 3×3 or 5×5 area. That way, a randomly colored pixel will not throw off the color sample.

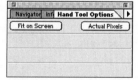

Figure 1-36
Hand Tool Options
dialog

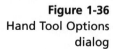

Figure 1-37
Eyedropper
Options dialog

Crop Tool (©)

The Crop tool enables you to select a rectangular area of an image and remove the rest of it. This lets you give an image a new center of interest and remove unneeded background areas. The basic process is simple: All you need to do is select a rectangular area of the image by dragging with the Crop tool. When you then double-click *inside* that rectangular area, the rest of the image is removed. The Crop tool lives inside the Toolbox location also housing the Marquee tools (the upper-left square on in the Toolbox). However, the Crop tool can do much more. Figure 1-38 shows the Crop Tool Options dialog.

If you scan a photograph and the photo is a little bit crooked, you can use the Crop tool to rotate and crop the scan at the same time. If you need an area of the image to be an exact size or resolution, you can use the Crop tool to resize and crop it at the same time. Finally, if you want to resize an image so it is the exact size of another open image, the Crop tool can do that, too. You can move the Crop Marquee (the border defining what to crop) once you place it, if it is not in exactly the right location. Let's work through an exercise so you can see exactly how the Crop tool behaves.

*H*ANDS ON

THE CROP TOOL

1. Open the image Tocrop01.Psd on the enclosed CD-ROM (File → Open → Tocrop01.Psd). Duplicate it (Image → Duplicate → OK).

2. Press © to get the Crop tool. You will see that the image—taken at an elementary school Halloween parade—needs cropping badly. (It also needs a better photograph and better scan, but that's another story!) Of course, it was deliberately scanned crookedly to give you something to straighten.

3. Press [RETURN] to bring up the Crop Tool Options dialog. Make sure the Fixed Target Size box is *not* checked.

4. Place the Crop cursor on the upper-left corner of the *image* (not the *window*—place it where the picture actually starts), and drag it to the lower-right corner. This forms the basic selection. Now you need to rotate it to enclose only the image.

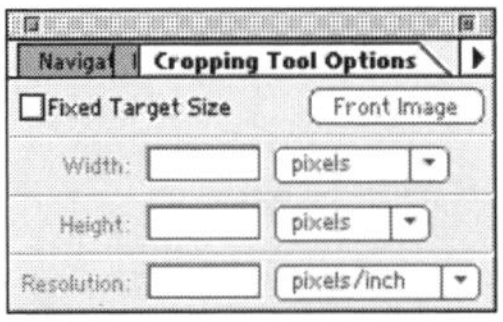

Figure 1-38
Cropping Tool
Options dialog

5. Drag the cursor outside the Marquee (the dotted lines). It changes to a curved, double-pointed arrow as it nears the Marquee. This means you can rotate the Marquee. Press the mouse and rotate the Marquee until it is parallel to the sides of the image. It loses the exact area you want to crop, but that's OK.

6. Now, you can reposition the Crop Marquee so it matches the image exactly. Just press the mouse button down on any corner of the Marquee and drag the corner to the corner of the image itself. Figure 1-39 shows the Crop Marquee correctly placed before the image is cropped.

7. If you place the cursor inside the Crop Marquee, it becomes a tiny arrowhead. Double-clicking with the arrowhead cursor crops the image. To cancel the cropping action and remove the Crop Marquee, you can either press ESC or Mac: ⌘+., Windows: CTRL+.. Move your cursor so you see the arrowhead and double-click to crop. Your image is now straight.

8. While nothing can change this image into a work of art, it can be further cropped and made into a wallet-size photo for a proud parent to carry. A typical wallet-size photo is about 2.35 inches wide × 3 inches high. Click on the Fixed Target Size check box in the Cropping Tool Options dialog. Make sure the dimensions are set to Inches (pull down the small dimensions menus to change this). Click on Width and type **2.25**. Click on Height and type **3.00**. Set the Resolution: to **300**.

9. Position the cursor somewhat to the upper-left of the monster in the red shirt. You need to select his image. Drag the Marquee so it encloses him, but none of the red cone in the image. You can move the entire Marquee just by dragging inside it. The Fixed Size you requested turns any portion of the image you enclose into that exact size. You are actually changing pixels in this image by your actions, which is further explained in Chapter 8, "Scanning and PhotoCD."

Figure 1-39
Crop Marquee placed correctly to crop image

When you have selected the best compromise you can—not too much space above the child's head, none of the red cone, most of the hair on the left side of his arm—double-click inside the selection with the arrowhead cursor to crop the image. The monster gets much bigger as the image is resized to 2.25×3 inches at 300 pixels per inch. Figure 1-40 shows the finished image. Save the image to your hard drive as Monster.Psd (File → Save → Monster.Psd, Photoshop 3.0 format).

10. To continue in proud parent mode, open the image Tocrop02.Psd (File → Open → Tocrop02.Psd). Duplicate the image (Image → Duplicate → OK).

    This image does not need to be straightened, but it needs to be the same size as the brother monster. Click on the monster image. In the Cropping Tool Options dialog, click on the button that says Front Image. This action reads the size of the image into the Fixed Size dialog so you can get an identical match in size with a different image.

11. Click on the Tocrop02.Psd Copy image to activate it. Position the cursor at the upper-left of the clown—on the young lady whose hand is being held by the teacher. Drag it so it encloses the clown almost to her waist but does not select any of the red cone. Try to get the child centered vertically in the image. Move the Crop Marquee as needed, or resize by dragging on the corners. Remember that you can press ESC any time if you are unhappy with your results.

    When you are satisfied with the position of the Crop Marquee, double-click inside it to finish the cropping. Figure 1-41 shows the finished image.

Figure 1-40
Resized and
cropped monster

Figure 1-41
Monster's sister
cropped to match

12. Click on the Fixed Target Size check box in the Cropping Tool Options dialog box to deselect it. It is always a good idea to leave this box unchecked so you do not accidentally crop something to an unintended size. Now is the best time to start developing smart work habits. (Sorry to sound preachy, but many good habits pay off very quickly in Photoshop.)

Selection Tools

The Selection tools enable you to choose an area of the image in which to constrain image changes. When you make a selection, you tell Photoshop that any editing you do only changes pixels within the selection. The process of making selections is crucial to Photoshop. In a vector graphics program such as Adobe Illustrator, it is easy for the program to know what you want to change. You select an object, and the computer knows what an object is. In a raster program such as Photoshop, the computer can't spot the Eiffel Tower in an image any more than it can tell if you scanned the image from a slab of roast beef! Pixels are pixels, and none of them hold any specific meaning to the program. Therefore, you need to tell Photoshop what pixels you want to be considered a unit. Sometimes, this is very easy: You can draw a square shape with the Marquee tool and all is well. Other times, it becomes a major challenge: Your client wants you to change the highlights in a model's hair from blonde to red. Having a large number of different ways to make a selection is essential. The tools in the Toolbox that deal with selections are a start, although there are many more selection commands and techniques you can use. However, the tools below provide the very basics in firepower.

Marquee (M)

The Marquee is the most basic of the selection tools. It is a rectangle or an ellipse, and can be drawn at any size. Many painting programs have shape tools that allow you to draw filled and unfilled circles and rectangles. Photoshop does not. It uses the

Marquee shapes for that. First you select an area, then you fill it or stroke it. Here is a small tryout of the Marquee tool's features.

THE MARQUEE TOOL

1. Create a new document (File → New → Name: Practice, Width: 400 pixels, Height: 400 pixels, Resolution: 72, Mode: RGB Color, Contents: White).

2. Use the Color palette to set your foreground color to Hue: 353, Saturation: 100%, Brightness: 79%.

3. Click on the Marquee tool in the Toolbox. Press RETURN to bring up the Marquee Options dialog. You see the image shown in Figure 1-42.

4. Set the Shape to Rectangular, the Style to Normal, and give it a Feather of 0.

5. Put the cursor near the upper-left corner of your image, and press the mouse button. This sets the upper-left corner of the Marquee. Drag the Marquee diagonally toward the right about 2 inches or so (exact amounts are not critical here). Stop pressing the mouse button. You see a rectangle made up of dotted lines that look like they are in motion. This is the selection outline (also affectionately called the *marching ants*).

   If you click anywhere else in the image, you lose the selection. Try it. This action is called *deselecting*. You can also deselect by selecting None from the Select menu or by pressing Mac: ⌘+D, Windows: CTRL+D.

6. Repeat Step 5 so you have a selection again. This time, fill the rectangle with the foreground color (press OPTION+DELETE on the Mac or ALT+DELETE on Windows). Deselect (Mac: ⌘+D, Windows: CTRL+D).

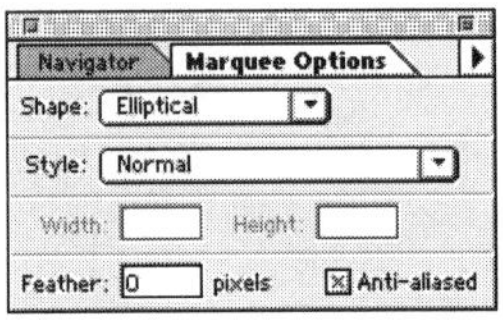

Figure 1-42
The Marquee
Options dialog

7. Repeat Step 5 on a clean portion of your image. This time, instead of filling the rectangle, use the Marquee as a template for a square and draw a line around it—called *Stroking* the selection (Edit → Stroke → 1 pixels, Outside, Blending: Normal, Opacity: 100%). You now have an outline around the rectangle.

8. Press ⓜ on your keyboard. Now the Marquee is elliptical in shape (if you press ⓜ again, it turns back into a rectangle). Find another clean spot on your image and press SHIFT. Drag out the Marquee about an inch or so while keeping SHIFT pressed. You have a perfect circle.

   Rule: To make a perfect circle or square, draw with SHIFT *pressed.* Fill (Mac: OPTION+DELETE, Windows: ALT+DELETE). Deselect (Mac: ⌘+D, Windows: CTRL+D).

9. If you look carefully at the circle, you will see that the edges look a bit jagged. Click on the Anti-aliased box in the Marquee Options dialog. Draw a circle again as you did in Step 8. Fill. This time, it is much smoother. Use the Zoom tool (Mac: ⌘+spacebar, Windows: CTRL+spacebar) to drag a square around the circle. This magnifies the image so you can clearly see the effect anti-aliasing has getting smooth edges on the circle. Press the spacebar to get the Hand tool, and scroll so you can see your original circle. There is a big difference in the edges of the two circles, as you can see in Figure 1-43. Double-click on the Hand tool to make the image fit the screen.

10. Set the Feather to 5. Draw a circle and fill. The Feather radius gives the circle a very soft edge. The larger the Feather number, the softer the selection. You may prefer to work with no Feather on the Marquee and apply it only when you want by using the Select → Feather command. However, you should know that the option exists.

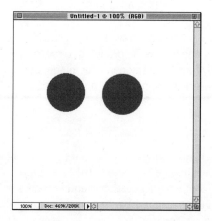

Figure 1-43
Aliased and anti-aliased edges

11. Press Ⓜ to set the Marquee back to a rectangle. Change the Feather back to 0.

12. Another useful feature is the ability to set a fixed size to the Marquee. To use this feature, pull down the Style menu in the Marquee Options dialog. Change the Style to Fixed Size. In the Height and Width fields, type **90**. Remember, you can click on the field's name to select it, so you can easily enter a new number.

   Place your cursor in the middle of your image and click. You immediately see the marching ants. Anywhere you click makes a new selection spring up. Therefore, when you use a fixed-size Marquee, you need to deselect by pressing ⌘+Ⓓ (Mac) or CTRL+Ⓓ (Windows), or by using the Select → None Command from the menu.

   Another reason the Fixed Size Marquee is so useful is because you can easily drag it anywhere in the image and position it exactly where you want. Try it. Drag the Marquee so it sits over the anti-aliased circle.

Command Watch

These keyboard commands select and deselect images:

Action	Mac keystroke	Windows keystroke
Select all	⌘+Ⓐ	CTRL+Ⓐ
Select none	⌘+Ⓓ	CTRL+Ⓓ

These commands help you to change the shape of the Marquee tool:

Action	Mac keystroke	Windows keystroke
Make a square or circle	SHIFT+drag	SHIFT+drag
Draw from center	OPTION+drag	ALT+drag

You may press both keys at once to draw a perfect square or circle from the center. You can press SHIFT at any time while dragging to make a perfect geometric figure. However, if you already have a selection in your image, pressing SHIFT as you start a new one does *not* deselect the original; it simply creates an additional selection.

Lasso (Ⓛ)

The Lasso tool is the freehand sibling of the Marquee tool. Using it, you can draw a selection of any shape you wish. Figure 1-44 shows the Lasso Options dialog box. You cannot fix the size of the Lasso, but you can Feather it and anti-alias it. There are two versions of the Lasso tool. With the Freehand Lasso, you can simply draw as if using a brush, in order to create a selection. You can get straight line segments by pressing OPTION (Mac)

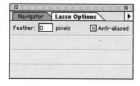

Figure 1-44
The Lasso Options
dialog

or ALT (Windows) while using this tool. This *rubber-bands* (i.e., locks the starting point and lets you stretch and move the end point until it reaches the place that you want it) the lines so you can get straight-sided selections of any size and shape. You can also select the Polygon Lasso mode directly. Pressing OPTION (Mac) or ALT (Windows) lets you toggle between the two modes. In Freehand mode, you can close a selection by releasing the mouse button or reaching the starting point again. If you are in Polygon Lasso mode, you can close a selection by double-clicking (or by finishing the shape).

Magic Wand Tool (W)

The Magic Wand tool enables you to select pixels close to one another in color. You can specify how close by typing in a number from 0 to 255 in the Tolerance field of the Magic Wand Options dialog. Figure 1-45 shows this dialog box. If the Tolerance is set to 0, the Magic Wand only picks up pixels next to the pixel on which you clicked and identical to it in color. If you set the Tolerance to 255, it selects the entire image. The ideal Tolerance is somewhere in between. Chapter 2, "Making Selections," will more thoroughly discuss Tolerance and using the Magic Wand. The Magic Wand is one of the tools used to help separate the Eiffel Tower (or your object of interest) from the rest of an image.

Pen Tool (P)

The Pen tool allows you to create a vector outline around an area of an image so you can select it. It is very useful when there is no other way to separate the pixels you want from the pixels you don't want to manipulate. In the Eiffel Tower example, if the tower has colors so far apart that the Magic Wand cannot build a selection, the Pen tool can be used to trace the edges manually. Chapter 9, "Advanced Selection Techniques," discusses the specifics of using the Pen tool. The Pen tool is actually a series of five tools that fly out of the Toolbox. They are the Pen, Selection, Add Point, Delete Point, and Convert Direction Point tools.

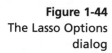

Figure 1-45
Magic Wand
Options dialog box

Move Tool (ⓥ*)*

The Move tool can be placed in either the selection category or utility category of tools. This chapter groups it with the selection tools simply because it is used to *move* a selection (or a Layer). By itself, the Move tool cannot *create* a selection—it can only move it from one place to another. It can be used within a single image, or it can be used to drag-and-drop between images. Chapters 2 and 3 will give you practice using the Move tool. You can access the Move tool at any time by pressing ⌘ on the Mac or CTRL on Windows. The only time this keystroke does not call up the Move tool is when the Hand tool is selected. The one option in the Move tool dialog is Pixel Doubling. With this box selected, Photoshop works more quickly, since it uses a coarser view of the pixels while moving them around (a 200% *fat bit* view). The pixels *resolve* back to their true state when the move is done.

Painting Tools

The four Painting tools discussed here have many features in common. The Pencil, Airbrush, and Brush are the primary means for original drawing in Photoshop. They use the foreground color to place pixels on the image. The Eraser removes the drawing (think of it as painting with the background color), but lets you mimic the activity of any of the other painting tools in order to do so. All the drawing tools enable you to control the Opacity (or Pressure, in the case of the Airbrush), the Apply mode (how the paint is applied), the fadeout (how quickly the paintbrush dries out), and the Stylus Pressure options (if you are using a pressure-sensitive drawing tablet).

Opacity is the degree of coverage you get when working with a painting tool. Opacity works on a scale of 0 to 100. If the Opacity is 100%, the paint will cover over any color underneath it. However, it is possible to only partially paint over other pixels. At 0%, no new paint is seen. You can control the Opacity of the paint tool by the Slider in the Tool Options dialog, or you can press a number from ⓪ to ⑨ on the keyboard. ① gives you 10% Opacity, ② gives you 20% Opacity, and so on. Pressing ⓪ resets the Opacity to 100%. However, typing **33** gives you 33% Opacity, and typing **95** gives you 95% Opacity. This feature works the same way for the Airbrush tool, but instead of Opacity, the characteristic of partial coverage is called Pressure.

The Apply mode is the method used to determine how the paint you put down reacts with the paint (pixels) already in the image. Normal Apply mode works exactly as you would expect paint to react in the real world. The other Apply modes paint on lighter or darker pixels, create overlay effects, or select some other aspect of the foreground color as a basis for applying paint. The Apply modes are discussed a bit later in this chapter.

The Fadeout rate controls the length of the brushstroke. If you have no Fadeout rate, you can paint on the image as if you have a brush that never runs out of paint. As long as the mouse button is pressed, the tool continues to paint. You may also opt to have the paint strokes act as if they are coming from a brush that *does* dry out. By setting the Fadeout rate (check the Fadeout: box and type in a number from **1** to **9999**), you can control how quickly the paint runs out. You can have the paint simply run out (by selecting the Transparent Option). Or, by selecting background, you can change the foreground color into the background color over a specified distance. This option is very useful for painting with a Gradient. The Fadeout rate uses the brush size to determine the distance. A larger brush therefore goes much further on the same settings than a small brush before it either runs out of paint or changes to the background color.

Finally, all the Paint tools can use the Stylus Pressure settings if you have a drawing tablet—such as the Wacom tablet—that lets you change the brushstroke based on how hard you press. The Pencil and Brush tools enable you to control the size, color, and Opacity by the degree of pressure you exert on the drawing tablet. The Airbrush lets you control the size or pressure of the stroke, and the Eraser options change depending on which Eraser tool you select.

You can also use SHIFT to modify the performance of the Paint tools. Pressing SHIFT constrains your brushstroke to the horizontal or vertical, depending on which way you begin dragging the cursor. If you press SHIFT after you paint a stroke then click the mouse button, a straight line appears between the last pixel painted and the place on which you just clicked. This makes it very easy to paint connected straight-line segments.

Pencil (Y)

The Pencil tool leaves aliased pixels in the foreground color wherever it is clicked or dragged in the image. To paint with the Pencil tool, you must keep the mouse button pressed for as long as you want the paint to appear. A large brush size creates a jagged line. Since the Pencil only uses the foreground color, it does not soften the brush edge at all. The Pencil is the only tool that is always aliased (you can also choose to make the Line tool aliased). Because of this, it is really useful when you want to work on images for Internet delivery.

The Pencil Options dialog, as you can see in Figure 1-46, has an option for Auto Erase, which is unique to the Pencil tool. If you click twice on the same pixel with the Pencil when Auto Erase is selected, the pixel changes from the foreground color to the background color. This option cannot really be used to erase an entire stroke just placed on the image, unless you have enough hand control to retrace your stroke exactly. However, once the color changes to the background color, the Pencil paints in the background color until you release the mouse button. The Auto Erase function of the Pencil is an historical link to the first Macintosh painting program, MacPaint. It was especially suited for working in what was then called Fat Bit mode. You can obtain the same effect as Fat Bit mode by working in 8:1 (800%) or 16:1 (1600%) magnification. If you are doing a pixel-level edit on an image, Auto Erase is as useful today as it was a decade or so ago.

Figure 1-46
Pencil Options
dialog

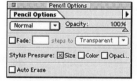

Brush (B)

The Brush tool is a paintbrush—the standard way to place a soft-edged Layer of opaque pixels on the image. Figure 1-47 shows the Paintbrush Options dialog. Notice that it, too, has a unique feature: the Wet Edges option. The Wet Edges option converts the paintbrush into a watercolor brush. Your foreground color shows up only on the edges of the paint stroke, while the center of the stroke contains a more transparent version of the color (which, on a white background, makes it look like a lighter shade). If you brush over the stroke, you can see the second brushstroke over the first. The wet edge looks as if the watercolor had started to dry along the border of the brushstroke. This effect is especially lovely if you are using a Wacom or other pressure-sensitive tablet and can control your stroke size easily. If you stroke over the same area enough times, the color builds up to your foreground color.

Airbrush (A)

The Airbrush tool is the digital equivalent of the artist's airbrush. It lets you apply a gradual buildup of color to an area. The Airbrush, as you can see in Figure 1-48, is unique because it has a Pressure setting rather than an Opacity control. However, they both serve same purpose.

If you keep the mouse button pressed without moving the mouse and you are using the Pencil or the Brush, nothing happens. The color you are placing on the image does not change. However, if you try this with the Airbrush, the color continues to build up. Even if you have the Pressure at 100%, the brushstroke spreads and becomes irregular around the edges as if paint were being absorbed by textured paper. With less Pressure, the color inside the brush builds up first, then it begins to creep outside the brushstroke.

The Airbrush enables you to lay down a very soft wash of color and gradually darken it. Unlike using the Gradient tool, however, you have full control of how the color builds up. If you have ever used a real airbrush, you will feel very comfortable using the virtual one Photoshop provides.

Eraser (E)

The Pencil, Brush, and Airbrush tools have a drop-down menu that starts with Normal. The Eraser's default on that menu is Paintbrush (see Figure 1-49).

Figure 1-47
Paintbrush Options
dialog

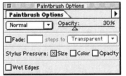

Figure 1-48
Airbrush Options
dialog

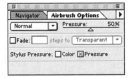

Figure 1-49
Eraser Options
dialog

There is a button that reads Erase Image, and there is a check box that reads Erase to Saved.

Let's look at these features. In Photoshop 2.5 and earlier, the Eraser was a block that simply covered the erased area with opaque background color. It could not transparently erase, change size, or leave anti-aliased edges. This changed with Photoshop 3.0. The old Block Eraser is still available and still useful—but now, you can also select an Eraser that imitates the Pencil, Airbrush, or Paintbrush tool, complete with Wet Edges and all other attributes.

The Eraser can also be used as a fast way to clear the screen. By clicking on the Erase Image button, you get a dialog asking if it is OK to fill the image with an opaque coat of background color. This feature is actually a bit annoying because it takes several additional keystrokes. The Photoshop 2.5 method of double-clicking on the Eraser tool was much faster (although it was too easy to accidentally erase the image).

Command Watch

There are several ways to clear the screen:

- **Double-click on the Eraser tool. Then click on the Erase Image button in the Eraser Options dialog box that appears.**

- **Click on the Eraser tool. Then press** RETURN. **Then click on the Erase Image button in the Eraser Options dialog box that appears.**

- **Select the entire image (Mac:** ⌘+A, **Windows:** CTRL+A, **or Edit →Select All). Press** DELETE. **Deselect.**

- **Press** D **to set your default colors of black and white. Press** X **to exchange the foreground and background colors and make white the foreground color. Press** OPTION+DELETE **(Mac) or** ALT+DELETE **(Windows) to fill the image with white. Press** X **again.**

- **Press** D **to set your default colors of black and white. Press** ⌘+DELETE **(Mac) or** CTRL+DELETE **(Windows). This is the fastest method.**

The Eraser tool has one more unique twist. It enables you to erase to the saved version of your image. This feature is known as the Magic Eraser in many programs. The Erase to Saved feature lets you selectively restore an area of the image if you have made a massive blunder, or lets you brush back in an area with any Eraser tool *at any level of Opacity*. This makes performing some special effects quite easy.

Paint Utility Tools

The Gradient, Paint Bucket, Line, and Type tools get the joint title of Paint Utility tools because, although they are tools using the foreground and background colors, they do not require the same amount of hand control the Painting tools. They are, therefore, special cases of Painting tools.

Gradient Tool (G)

A Gradient is a smooth wash of color moving from one color to another without letting the eye detect where one color stops and the other begins. Rainbows and sunsets are nature's gradients. Gradients are also called fountains, washes, ramps, or blends in other graphics programs.

While you could use the Airbrush tool set to Fade from foreground to background in order to produce a smooth color blend, it is much easier to use the Gradient tool. Photoshop allows you to make Gradients that blend between two or more colors. The blend goes from your foreground color to your background color (or through a range of colors you select). Figure 1-50 shows the Gradient Tool Options dialog, and there are definitely a lot of options. In addition to the Apply Mode and Opacity options, you can pick the Gradient, Type, Dither, and Mask characteristics for the blend. In addition, you can select the Edit button to create or style your own Gradient blends. Let's look at this more closely.

Figure 1-51 shows the list of prebuilt Gradient styles you see when you pull down the Gradient menu. The most generic styles are the foreground to background, foreground to Transparent, and Transparent to foreground, because these react to the colors in the Toolbox. All the other Gradients have the specific colors built into them and produce results regardless of your current color choices. The other Gradient that's most common is the Spectrum, which cycles around the color wheel and is the rainbow Gradient.

Figure 1-50
Gradient Tool
Options dialog

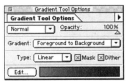

Figure 1-51
Prebuilt Gradients

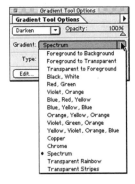

You also have a choice of Gradient types: linear or radial. A Linear Gradient produces a line of color across your image or selection area. In a Radial Gradient, the first color in the Gradient forms the center of a circle, and the last color is at the outside of the circle. This allows you to create a very convincing sphere if you select only two colors and move from light to dark.

You can set the midpoint of the Gradient—the point at which one color becomes more dominant than the other—interactively, by dragging, in the Edit dialog.

Finally, you can select whether to *dither* your Gradient or use the *Mask*. Dithering blends the first color into the second by leaving flecks of colors in the area in which the two meet, rather than changing colors in a straight line. This produces a Gradient less likely to develop *banding* (areas in which you can see the color change) when the image is printed. The Mask flag tells Photoshop to use—or not use—the Transparency in the Gradient. You can set up Gradients in the Editor with areas of varying transparency.

The Gradient tool requires a click-and-drag motion to be applied. Try this Hands On, just so you know how to create Gradients and work the tool. We will take it in a few stages. First, you will see how to apply a simple Gradient to your image. Then you will see how to build a Gradient without, and finally with, Transparency. This is a much longer Hands On than you have seen so far, but the Gradient tool needs more explanation than most of the other tools—although it is easy, and a lot of fun, to use.

USING THE GRADIENT TOOL

1. Create a new document (File → New → Name: Test, Width: 400 pixels, Height: 400 pixels, Resolution: 72, Mode: RGB Color, Contents: White).

   Press D to set the colors back to the black-and-white default.

2. Double-click on the Gradient tool. Set the Apply mode to Normal, the Opacity to 100, the Gradient to Foreground to Background, the Type to Linear, and check the Dither and Mask boxes.

3. Place your cursor in the upper-left corner of the image, and click and hold the mouse button. Drag the rubber-band cursor to the lower-left corner of the image. Let go of the mouse button. You will see a Gradient that moves diagonally across the image.

4. Change your foreground color to red (click on the first box in the Swatches palette).

5. Change your background color to blue (Mac: OPTION+click, Windows: ALT+click on the fifth box in the Swatches palette).

6. This time, place your cursor in the middle of the image at the very top, press SHIFT, and drag the rubber-band cursor to the bottom of the image. You will see a horizontal Gradient covering the previous one.

7. Make a few short drags of the cursor in the image (do not start on one side of the image; start in the center and drag the rubber-band cursor just a short distance in any direction). What happens? You get solid red and solid blue with a much shorter Gradient in between.

Rule 1: Unless a Gradient has transparency or there is a selection, it always covers the entire image.

Rule 2: The blend area is only as wide as the distance between your starting and stopping points.

8. Press the Edit button. Figure 1-52 shows the Edit dialog.

9. Click on the Duplicate button. Name the Gradient Patriot. Click OK. (You could have also clicked on the New button to create a new Gradient.)

The Gradient shows red changing to blue. Click on the pointer under the red. The triangle on top of the black turns black to indicate that this is the point being edited. The pointer has a small F in it to indicate it is using the foreground color. The three possibilities for color are Foreground (F), Background (B), or Selected (and empty pointer). These pointers are placed on the Gradient based on the colors in the *pointer well*. Notice that clicking on the red pointer at the right side of the editor also places red into the Selected color well. The numeric box shows that the color is located at position 0 on the editor.

10. Drag the small diamond on top of the editor bar to the left, then to the right. Notice that the proportion of red to blue changes. This is the interactive midpoint editing we spoke of earlier. You can see the midpoint value in the numeric box, and you can change it there numerically if you prefer. (Leave it at 50%.)

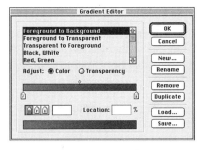

Figure 1-52
Gradient Editor
dialog

11. Click just under the middle of the Gradient editor bar. You create a new point, which shows the Selected color (which is red). Let's change it.

12. Click on the red Color Selector patch. The standard Color Picker window appears. Select white as the color, either by moving the cursor into the upper-left corner or by typing **255** in the Red, Green, and Blue numeric areas. Click OK. The color in the center of the Gradient now changes to white.

13. Drag the White pointer to the left until the numeric area reads 33. Drag the Blue pointer to the left until the numeric area reads 67. This has skewed the Gradient.

14. Press the modifier key (Mac: OPTION, Windows: ALT) and click on the White pointer. Keep the mouse button pressed and drag the *copy* of the white slider all the way to the right. This keystroke should be easy to remember since the OPTION or ALT keys are used to make copies of selections as well. Click on the leftmost point (this is just a safety click—since that point is linked to the foreground color, it cannot be accidentally changed).

    Figure 1-53 shows the finished Gradient in the Editor. Click OK. Apply the Gradient to the image from the upper-left to the lower-right corner.

15. To make part of this Gradient transparent, you need to click on the Adjust: Transparency radio button. The Gradient Editor bar changes to black-to-black. The black signifies 100% Opacity (no transparency at all).

16. Click somewhere under the bar. Drag the new point until the Location is at 80%. Change the Opacity to 0. Click OK.

17. Pick any two other colors as your foreground and background colors. Since you have used foreground and background colors in the Gradient definition, the Gradient colors will change. Drag the rubber-band Gradient cursor from the top of the image to the bottom. The transparency in the Gradient allows the original Gradient to show through.

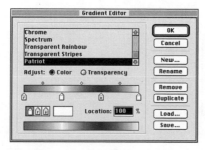

Figure 1-53
Finished Gradient

Paint Bucket Tool (K)

The Paint Bucket tool, whose Options dialog is shown in Figure 1-54, is used for filling an area or selection with the foreground color or a Pattern. This tool, like the Auto Erase feature in the Pencil tool, is an historical link to the first Mac graphics program, MacPaint. You do not need to have an area selected with a Marquee in order to use this tool.

The Paint Bucket tool is one of the lesser-used tools in Photoshop's arsenal. There are other ways to fill an area that are easier and more reliable. The Paint Bucket reacts to the Tolerance setting in the dialog. This is the same Tolerance attribute in the Magic Wand tool. When you click with the Paint Bucket, Photoshop looks at the pixel on which you clicked. It fills with the foreground color or pattern until it hits a pixel outside its Tolerance range. In practical terms, this means the Paint Bucket tool has a nasty habit of leaving halos and glows around areas you want to fill with a solid color. You also need to be very careful where you click—especially if you are trying to fill a narrow area. It is easy to fill the wrong thing and be forced to quickly undo the damage. The Paint Bucket tool is also subject to leaks. If you use it to fill an area inside a line and the line is missing a pixel somewhere, the color will leak into the other areas of the image.

You best strategy for filling most areas is to make a selection (as you will learn in Chapter 2, "Making Selections") and fill it using either the Fill command from the menu or one of the keyboard shortcuts mentioned in the previous Command Watch.

The Sample Merged check box, which is also find on most of the Image manipulation tools, enables you to fill an area based on the colors of the pixels in the layers beneath (if you are using more than one Layer).

Line (N)

The Line tool is very simple. It allows you to draw straight lines and arrows. As with the Gradient tool, when you first click you get a rubber-band line you can pull in any direction. The action to create a line is the same click-hold-drag you used in creating a Gradient. Figure 1-55 shows the Line Tool Options dialog.

In addition to the standard Apply mode and Opacity setting, you can choose whether to anti-alias the line or not. You can select the line width in pixels. You can select an arrow at one or both ends of the line, and you can set the size of the arrowhead in relation to the line width and length. Figure 1-56 shows the Arrowhead Shape dialog.

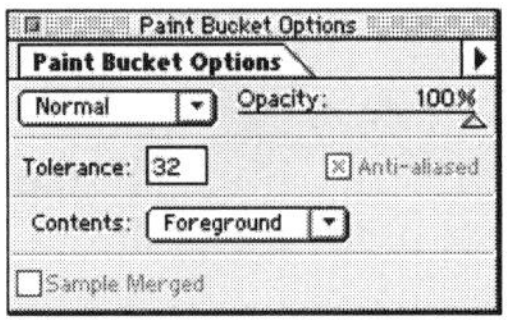

Figure 1-54
Paint Bucket
Options dialog

Figure 1-55
Line Tool Options
dialog

Figure 1-56
Arrowhead Shape
dialog

Type Tool (T)

The Type tool is used to create text in Photoshop. There are no options for the Type tool. Chapter 5, "Working with Paint and Text Tools," discusses the process of creating type in Photoshop. The basic process is very simple: You click anywhere in the image with the Type tool, and a dialog box appears allowing you to select the font you want. You have some limited control over leading and alignment. After you have typed your text into the dialog box and clicked OK, the text is rendered to the screen as a new Layer. If you prefer, you can also select the Outline Type tool (in the same fly-out space in the Toolbox) that leaves a selection Marquee in your image in the shape of the type you created.

Image Manipulation Tools

The Image Manipulation tools differ from the Paint tools because they do not use the foreground or background color. (Caveat: The Smudge tool has a mode that does use the foreground color.) However, like the Paint tools, you use them as if they were brushes.

Toning Tools (O)

The Toning tool is a unique layering of three tools in one. Pressing O more than once cycles through them. The tools are Dodge, Burn, and Sponge. The Dodge and Burn tools are opposites of each other. They can lighten or darken an area of an image. They work best when used with a large, soft brush and an extremely low Exposure setting. As you can see in Figure 1-57, the area normally called the Opacity setting on most Options dialogs is called Exposure in this dialog box. This is because the tool mimics an image editor long used by photographers in the real world to create or remove contrast on an image on film. In addition, where most other tools contain the Apply mode setting, the Dodge and Burn tools let you select Highlights, Midtones, or Shadows as the areas the tool affects.

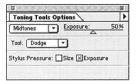

Figure 1-57
Toning Tools
Options dialog for
Dodge and Burn

Figure 1-58 shows the Toning Tools Options dialog with the Sponge tool selected. This tool can either saturate or desaturate any area on which it is used. It has a pressure setting you can control to determine how quickly it builds up. The tool was developed to help prepare RGB images for conversion to CMYK. The problem (to give a short explanation of a very hard concept) when converting images is that the color can change dramatically between color modes, since CMYK cannot produce as many colors as RGB color space. Typically, a color needs to be desaturated in order to fall within the CMYK color space gamut. The Sponge tool is designed to help desaturate areas the Gamut Warning (selected from the View menu) has flagged as problematic. Chapter 6, "Color and File Formats," and Chapter 15, "Photoshop Output," discuss the issue of RGB and CMYK conversions in more detail.

Blur Tool (ⓡ)

The Blur tool is really a part of the Focus tools. It, like the Toning tools, is a toggle (press the keystroke multiple times to change tools). The Blur tool shares the Toolbox location with the Sharpen tool. They are opposites of one another. The Blur tool softens the focus of the area over which it is painted by changing the pixels, so they are closer in color to one another and the borders between neighboring colors become indistinct. The Sharpen tool does just the opposite. It increases the difference between neighboring colors so the image, from a distance, looks as if it is more in focus. Figure 1-59 shows the Focus Tools Options dialog.

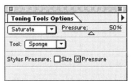

Figure 1-58
Toning Tools
Options for Sponge

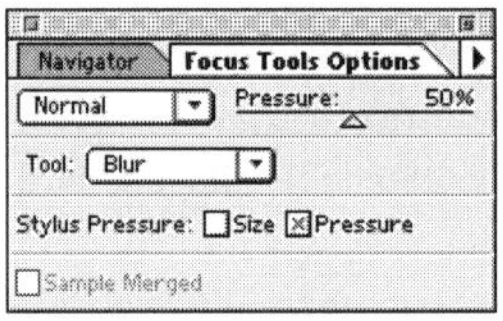

Figure 1-59
Focus Tools Options
dialog

In Chapter 4, "Filters," you will learn about a number of Photoshop *filters*—small image editing functions applied to an entire selection, without requiring brushstrokes. There are a variety of Blur and Sharpen filters. The Blur and Sharpen tools allow you to paint the actions of the filter onto any area you wish, giving you much more control. However, it is very time-consuming to paint over an area with these tools. The larger brush sizes can take a long time to work (especially on slower machines). Therefore, these tools are typically used on small areas only.

Rubber Stamp Tool (Ⓢ)

The Rubber Stamp is probably the most important tool in the Toolbox for photo retouching. It allows you to *clone* (exactly duplicate) areas of an image onto another area. The clone source can be any open image; it does not have to be the same image. It is one of the most flexible of all Photoshop tools. In addition to the Clone Option (which can be aligned or non-aligned), you can paint with a pattern (either aligned to the upper-left corner of the image or not), or you can paint with a portion of your saved or Snapshot image. (A Snapshot takes a picture—in memory—of your image and allows you to return to that point in time later.) Finally, you can use your saved image as a basis for Impressionist art, which uses colors from the saved image to paint with.

The Cloning function is the Rubber Stamp's most frequently used mode. It allows you to repair holes in a garment, remove dirt, or correct blemishes. It can even help you remove a divorced spouse from a wedding picture by covering him or her up with nearby trees!

Figure 1-60 shows the Rubber Stamp Options dialog for this tool, which you will learn much more about in Chapter 10, "Photo Retouching."

Smudge Tool (Ⓤ)

The Smudge tool acts as if you are working on a wet canvas and lets you pull wet paint into neighboring areas of the canvas. Like the Painting tools, it is a click-and-drag tool. When you drag, however, you leave a trail of wet paint. With large brushes, even on a fast machine, this tool can be agonizingly slow.

Figure 1-61 shows the Smudge Tool Options dialog. Note that there is another mode to this tool. It can act just like finger-paint. If you select this feature, it places a dab of the foreground color where you click and blends it into the image.

Figure 1-60
Rubber Stamp
Options dialog

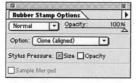

Figure 1-61
Smudge Tool
Options dialog

Non-Tool Icons

The Toolbox also contains icons for several functions that cannot really be considered tools.

Default Colors (D)

The small black-and-white swatch by the foreground and background colors area of the Toolbox allows you to quickly return to the default status of black and white, and foreground and background colors. Typing D is a faster way to do this. You will frequently want to set your colors to black and white, so this is a very valuable timesaving feature.

Exchange Colors (X)

The double-pointing bent arrow between the foreground and background Color Swatches enables you to exchange the foreground and background color by clicking on it. It is usually easier and faster to remember to press X.

Full Screen Modes (F)

There are three viewing or screen modes also available via the Toolbox or by repeatedly pressing F on the keyboard. The *normal screen* mode (the left window control on the Toolbox) allows multiple open images on your desktop. They appear in the standard Macintosh or Windows window with scroll bars and a menu at the top of the screen (Mac) or the application window (Windows).

The *center screen* control icon shows a modified approach, using the entire desktop. The image on both platforms appears against a gray background with a menu at the top of the screen. The only way to scroll through your image is to use the Hand tool, since this mode removes the scroll bars.

The *full screen* mode (the right screen control icon) places the image against a black background with no menus at all. Once again, the Hand tool is needed to scroll through the image. You can get even more screen space by pressing TAB to hide all the palettes and the Toolbox.

Although all the screen controls work with multiple open images, the process may get confused as you change screen modes. Just keep pressing F until the correct image appears in the mode in which you want to see it!

Quick Mask Mode (Q)

When you use the selection tools, typically a marching ant Marquee appears around the selected area. There is another way to view your selection, however: the Quick Mask mode. In Quick Mask mode, the areas not selected appear in red (unless you change the default). All the painting and selection tools work on the selection outline itself, not on the image. If you paint, you paint with shades of gray (or black and white), and you only change the area selected. Painting in white adds to the selection area (as it removes the red rubylith), and painting in black removes areas from the selection. This mode is excellent for fine-tuning selections made by some other method. You can toggle between Quick Mask and Normal modes by pressing Q on the keyboard. You will learn lots more about Quick Mask mode in Chapter 2, "Making Selections," and Chapter 5, "Working with Paint and Text Tools."

Quick Mask mode tends to be confusing at first. You need to forget you are working on a computer and think friskets or rubylith. If you have ever worked with an airbrush, you have masked areas of your image to protect them. That is just what Quick Mask does. It puts a thin film of red digital rubylith over the areas of the image protected from change. Just like the frisket material you might paint onto a wet watercolor for protection, you can remove this film in pieces. Any of Photoshop's tools can then be used to edit this film. When you switch back to the Normal mode, the outer edges of the film define your new selection.

1. Which tools are the Utility tools?
   a. Marquee, Lasso, Magic Wand, Pen, Move
   b. Brush, Airbrush, Pencil, Eraser
   c. Gradient, Bucket, Type, Line
   d. Crop, Hand, Zoom, Eyedropper

2. Which tool allows you to quickly move from one part of an image to another?
   a. Eyedropper
   b. Marquee
   c. Hand
   d. Zoom

3. The Marquee tool is the most basic selection tool. It allows you to
   a. Draw filled and unfilled circles and ellipses.
   b. Draw rectangles and squares.
   c. Select triangular shapes.
   d. Select elliptical and circular shapes.

4. Which of the Painting tools has an Auto Erase option?
   a. Brush
   b. Pencil
   c. Airbrush
   d. Eraser

5. The Gradient tool allows you to create a smooth wash of color that moves from one color to another. What else can the Gradient tool do?
   a. Allows you to create your own Gradient blends
   b. Uses prebuilt Gradient blends
   c. Dithers the blend from one color to the next
   d. Makes colors fade out

COLOR MODES

Photoshop allows you to work in a number of color modes. These color modes are roughly equivalent to the color spaces we discussed earlier. The color mode for an image is selected when you create a new document. It can be changed using the Mode menu. This section gives you a very basic introduction. Chapter 6, "Color and File Formats," will give you more details, as will Chapter 12, "Using Spot Color," and Chapter 15, "Photoshop Output."

Bitmap

A bitmap image contains only black and white pixels. No other color can be used during painting, and neither Layers nor filters are allowed. Images can be rotated 90° or 180° or flipped. No other adjustments are possible. Images can be converted to bitmap mode only if they are already grayscale. Black is the only channel the image can have.

Grayscale

A grayscale image contains up to 256 shades of gray. It, too, has only a black channel, but additional channels can be created (making it a multichannel image). A grayscale image can contain multiple layers. It can be rotated at any angle. Most filters will work on it, though some may not.

Duotone

A duotone image is a grayscale image to be printed in 1 to 4 colors. The same image is printed in each color, but with different values of black (transfer curves). A duotone image only contains one color channel, the Duotone channel, but may have additional alpha channels. The filters that work on a grayscale image work on a duotone one. An image to be printed in three inks is called a tritone, and an image using four inks is a quadtone. An image to be printed in a single ink is called a monotone.

RGB

RGB mode is the standard display mode for monitors. Monitors create color by mixing red, green, and blue phosphors. These three colors, when mixed together, form white. This is *additive* color. It has a wide possible gamut and can contain many colors that are impossible to print. Most scanners (especially desktop models) scan images into RGB color space. This is the mode you are likely to work in most frequently, even if all your work is for print production. In RGB mode, all Photoshop operations are allowed.

CMYK

CMYK mode is a prelude to conventional color printing, which uses four inks—cyan, magenta, yellow, and black—to reproduce all colors. It is a *subtractive* color mode since it is necessary to remove all color in order to produce white. It has a much more limited color gamut than RGB. A CMYK image contains four color channels. This makes it automatically about 25% larger than the same image in RGB mode. It can be layered and rotated at any angle, and can contain additional Alpha channels. Many of the filters, though not all of them, work in CMYK mode.

Lab

Lab color is Photoshop's native color space. It is the mode Photoshop uses to do its color conversion calculations, but you may also choose to work in it as well. It contains three color channels: a Lightness channel that has only grayscale values, and a and b color channels. Most, though not all, filters work in this mode. The color space is based on the work of the CIE standards group as an attempt to create device-independent color—color that can be described without reference to the equipment on which it is displayed, and can be theoretically made to match any device.

Indexed Color

Indexed Color mode is a low-color mode. It can contain a maximum of 256 colors. It stores these colors in a Color Table that can be changed. However, if a color in the Color Table is altered, it changes everywhere it is used in the image. This mode is very useful for images placed in multimedia programs or displayed on the World Wide Web.

An Indexed Color image cannot contain layers and cannot be filtered. Chapter 6, "Color and File Formats," and Chapter 13, "Beyond Photoshop," give more details on using this color mode.

1. How many color modes are there?
   a. 4
   b. 5
   c. 6
   d. 7

2. A image in bitmap mode can
   a. Only contain black or white pixels.
   b. Use Layers and filters.
   c. Be rotated 90° or 180° or flipped.
   d. Have multiple channels.

3. What mode is an image that contains 256 shades of gray, can be rotated any number of degrees, and can contain many layers?
   a. Bitmap
   b. Grayscale
   c. RGB
   d. Duotone

4. What is the standard color mode for most monitors and scanners?
   a. CMYK
   b. Lab
   c. Indexed Color
   d. RGB

5. What are some of the characteristics of CMYK mode?
   a. It's a subtractive mode.
   b. It has a limited gamut.
   c. A CMYK image has four color channels.
   d. It is Photoshop's native color space.

TOOLS AND APPLY MODES

Now is the time to explain that mysterious pull-down in many of the Tool Options dialogs. This menu controls the Apply mode used by the tool. The Apply mode (sometimes called Blending or Transfer mode) determines the interaction of the new brushstroke with the previous image. The Apply modes perform mathematical calculations on the pixels in the image. This math is possible because each color channel of every pixel can be expressed as a number from 0 to 255, where 0 is black and 255 is white.

Earlier in this chapter, you typed the RGB values of 91, 177, 71 into the Numeric Input region of the Color Picker. If you then placed a single pixel of this color in your image, Photoshop actually wrote the value of 91 into that location in the Red channel, 177 into the Green channel, and 71 into the Blue channel. When we discuss channels in more depth in Chapters 2, 3, and 9, you will discover that each channel keeps its image as a grayscale. Therefore, Photoshop recorded your pixel by placing a gray pixel of the correct value at the same location in all the color channels (the RGB channel in this case). Because of this numeric value, arithmetic calculations are possible. In the following descriptions assume the Brush tool is being used. The Brush tool gets its color from the foreground color. In the case of other tools (especially the Image Manipulation tools), the color used in the calculation is coming from a source other than the foreground color. However, the math is the same.

Normal

Normal mode replaces the pixel under the cursor with the foreground color. It uses the full attributes of the color, but respects the Opacity setting (as do all the Apply modes). If the Opacity setting is 100%, Normal mode does a total replace.

Dissolve

At 100% Opacity, Dissolve mode looks just like Normal mode. At lower opacities, Dissolve leaves specks of the new pixels on the image, in response to the degree of transparency requested. At 80% Opacity, most of the new pixels are dotted on top of the previous ones. At 10% Opacity, the new pixels look like a fine, infrequent mist. Dissolve mode resembles the effect you get by filling a toothbrush full of paint and running a finger over it to flick the paint onto a canvas. At high opacities, the paint splatters; at low opacities, the paint is just a light spray.

Behind

This mode only works on a transparent Layer. It only lets the paint stick on areas of the Layer that are totally empty and contain no pixels. It is a good mode to use if you have an object and you wish to paint a shadow behind it (though there are other ways to make a shadow, too). It is also good if you wish to stencil a design onto a Layer. With each new area you add, you protect the work already done.

Clear

Clear mode works only on a Layer, erasing the pixels on that Layer and replacing them with transparency. It is only an option in the Line and Paint Bucket tools, and in the Fill and Stroke commands.

Multiply

Multiply mode is used to darken an image along a curve. That is, not everything in the image darkens to the same degree. This mode takes the value of the pixel in each channel and multiplies it by the value of the foreground color. It divides the result by 255. The color you see on the image is the answer to the math problem. A color multiplied with white always gets the color as its result ($255 \times color \div 255 = color$). In the same manner, if a color is multiplied by black, the result is always black ($0 \times color = 0 \div 255 = 0$). This knowledge can be used to help you predict the results.

Screen

Screen mode is the exact opposite of Multiply mode. It tends to make colors lighter along a curve. Colors screened with white become white, and colors screened with black keep the value of the color.

Overlay

Depending on the color of the original pixel, Overlay mode either multiplies or screens the paint pixel. This mode is similar to placing a transparent, but colored, overlay on an image. The highlights and shadow areas retain their original characteristics, but the midtones accept the overlaid color.

Soft Light

This mode was added in Photoshop 3.0. It favors the original pixels in an image and either lightens the pixel a bit (if the paint color is lighter than 50% gray) or darkens the pixel a bit (if the paint color is darker than 50% gray).

Hard Light

Hard Light mode is very similar in concept to Soft Light mode, though the result is dramatically different. It was also first introduced in Photoshop 3.0. If the paint color is lighter than 50% gray, it is screened onto the original pixel. If the paint color is darker than 50% gray, it is multiplied onto the original pixel. The result is an exaggeration or harshening of the colors in the image. This mode favors the paint color in the result.

Color Dodge

Color Dodge mode is new to Photoshop 4.0. When you use the Dodge tool, you lighten the image. The Color Dodge painting mode does this as well. It looks at each pixel in each color channel and brightens the pixel in the original image, based on the foreground color (or color from the Image Manipulation tool) being used. Painting with black causes no change; painting with white causes the maximum amount of change.

Color Burn

The Color Burn mode is also new to Photoshop 4.0. It is the exact opposite of the Color Dodge mode. Painting with white causes no change, but painting with black causes the maximum amount of change.

Lighten

This mode looks at the original value of the pixel in each channel and compares it to the value in each channel of the color being written to the image. It then selects the *lighter* value in each channel. For example, if a pixel of RGB 91, 177, 71 is placed on top of RGB 100, 40, 24 in Lighten mode, the result is RGB values of 100, 177, 71. This changes the color on the image and makes the image look lighter.

Darken

This mode is the reverse of Lighten, so it selects the *darker* value in each channel. For example, if a pixel of RGB 91, 177, 71 is placed on top of RGB 100, 40, 24 in Lighten mode, the result is RGB values of 91, 40, 24. This changes the color on the image and makes the image look darker.

Difference

Difference mode subtracts the value of the pixel in each color channel from the value of the color being written to the image. The result is the *absolute value*, or the number without any minus signs. It is very hard to predict the colors you will get in Difference mode, but it can create an interesting (though sometimes wild) effect. Painting with shades of gray keep the image in the same color family. Painting with black does not change the image. Painting with white inverts it.

Exclusion

Exclusion mode is another painting mode new to Photoshop 4.0. It is similar to Difference mode regarding the behavior of white and black in the image, but the results look much softer and less wild. This is partly true because the algorithm that is used leaves colors painted with neutral 127 gray at neutral 127 gray, which is not true of the Difference mode. This difference in reaction causes the Exclusion mode to produce softer results.

Hue

Hue mode looks at the Hue of the color being painted and replaces the Hue of the pixel already on the image with the new one. It leaves the saturation and value alone. Black and white do not change, however, and you must be in one of the color modes (not Grayscale or Bitmap) for it to work.

Saturation

Saturation mode looks only at the intensity/purity of the pixel deemed the paint color. It uses this number as the Saturation value for the resulting pixel. This mode is not available in grayscale.

Color

Color mode is used to replace both the Hue and Saturation of a pixel with the Hue and Saturation of the paint pixel. It is an excellent mode for colorizing images. It does not work on images in grayscale mode (though it works well if you change the grayscale image to RGB).

Luminosity

This mode is the inverse of Color mode. The resulting pixel contains the value of the paint pixel, but the Hue and Saturation of the original pixel.

1. What does the Apply mode do?
   a. Stores channel information
   b. Performs mathematical calculations on pixels
   c. Converts an image to grayscale
   d. Determines the interaction of new brushstrokes

2. Which Apply mode resembles splattering or light spray?
   a. Normal mode
   b. Soft Light mode
   c. Dissolve mode
   d. Multiply mode

3. What are the characteristics of the Behind mode?
   a. It is used to darken an image.
   b. It only works on a transparent layer.
   c. It allows paint to stick to areas of a totally empty layer.
   d. It works similarly to a stencil.

4. What mode takes the value of a pixel and multiplies it with the value of the foreground color?
   a. Overlay mode
   b. Soft Light mode
   c. Multiply mode
   d. Screen mode

5. Which color mode lightens an image by brightening each pixel?
   a. Lighten mode
   b. Color Dodge mode
   c. Screen mode
   d. Difference mode

VIP PROFILES

Each chapter contains one or more profiles of people who are important to the study of Photoshop. They are engineers, artists, authors, teachers, or power users of the program. Photoshop users are capable, as a group, of doing phenomenal work because of the work of pioneers in the field. All users of the program build onto whatever innovations and creations came before them. It is important that you learn the history and lore of the program. It is also amazing to see what a life-altering experience Photoshop has been for so many people interviewed for this book.

Mark Hamburg, Adobe Engineer

It is fitting that we start out our series of Profiles of Very Important Photoshopers by meeting Mark Hamburg, Adobe's Lead Photoshop engineer. Mark has been working on the Photoshop project for almost 6 years (since Version 1.0.7 was shipping). The creators of Photoshop are John and Thomas Knoll—but they were not Adobe employees. The brothers developed Photoshop on their own, and Adobe licensed it from them. Mark was the first engineer hired by Adobe specifically for the Photoshop project. While there already was a team at that time looking at porting Photoshop to other platforms, Mark was the first engineer brought in to determine the Photoshop feature set. As the Technical Lead Engineer on the project, he became more and more responsible for guiding the product to its current direction.

Mark has an MS in math from the University of Michigan. While he was interested in graphics for at least 10 years prior to working on Photoshop, his experience prior to Adobe was in word processing on the Mac.

Mark worked originally for Ann Arbor Software on a product called Full Write, which, along with the company itself, was eventually acquired by Ashton-Tate (the company that manufactured the popular database program dBASE). Mark's contribution to Full Write was adding support for Bézier curves to the program as part of a range of built-in drawing features. (Bézier curves are created by vector programs such as Adobe Illustrator, or by the Pen tool in Photoshop.)

What was Mark's first contribution to Photoshop? He added the Pen tool to Version 2.0. Photoshop 2.0 was the work of Tom Knoll and Mark Hamburg with John Knoll's plug-ins. This version added CMYK editing, duotones, the Pen tool, and the first rasterization of the Adobe Illustrator format. Mark has worked on Photoshop—with the exception of six months when he worked on a research project—for the entire length of time he has been at Adobe.

When asked why he thinks the product has been so successful, he replied that it does a broad range of things reliably and with high quality. It is a staple in the studios because it is a stable tool and people can trust its results. It has been amazing to Mark how much the market for the product keeps expanding. Every time he thinks it could be near saturation, the market grows even more. It is a very large market because of the wide range of capabilities in the product. There are long lists of features still under consideration, and the product has come nowhere near to reaching all it can do.

Many of you may have wondered how a product like Photoshop is produced and what it took to get from an idea to the shrink-wrapped box you purchased. Mark described the general process. After a version has been released and is established, the engineering team looks at what is being done by artists and what features are being used—and requested. This gives them a basic target to shoot for. Guided by the Marketing department, they determine a long list of requested changes, enhancements, and new areas to explore. They then evaluate which areas will bring them the greatest reward, then these areas become the areas of highest priority. Once a list of tentative new features for the program is identified, it ultimately comes down to, Mark says, how much Adobe can do and still ship the product in a timely fashion. Obviously, if the engineers insisted on implementing every possible new feature, the product would never get shipped.

Once the feature set is designed, the official cycle begins. First there is the Alpha test stage. At this point, the fears have mostly been determined. The code works—mostly, though it is often still far from stable. While the official definitions of the project life cycle call for the Alpha test to be feature-complete and the Beta test to begin with features already locked down, the reality is somewhat more elastic.

In the Alpha stage, the product is usable but not quite complete. Often, there is a usability study in which long-time users are queried and groups of people are video-taped using the new software in a lab so the engineers can study exactly how they interact with it. The testing provides the much-needed feedback, which can also lead to reworked ideas. The user interface of the program gets tweaked, and the code itself becomes more stable. Finally, the program enters the Beta test stage. At this point, it is given to many more people than during the Alpha test, and the idea is to put the program through the kind of performance testing it will get once it is released. The testers are urged to use the program as much as they can—and to use it for real production work. The object of this phase is to identify and fix all bugs still present in the program. Given the number of different machines and configurations, it seems to be an almost monumental task. During the Beta test, there are fewer changes in the features, but many more bug fixes.

When all the identified bugs are fixed, the engineers produce a release candidate. This *build* of the program is released to a select group of sites who test it for speed and remaining bugs. Mark says that in the tradeoff, if little time remains, they may tolerate a slightly slower speed as long as all of the bugs have been fixed rather than delay the product release to further optimize the code.

Mark's advice for you as you begin working with Photoshop is to start playing with the software and explore all the pieces. Photoshop is a toolbox, and you need to learn how the pieces work together. The easiest way is to just try them—fiddle with all the controls and learn what they do. The manuals—and books like this one—can give you guidance, but you still need to play for yourself.

A Sampling of CompuServe Adobe Forum Sysops

Meet the Sysops on the Adobe Forum. Here's what they have to say about themselves, either in a message or in their CompuServe bios.

Mark Alger, Adobe Forum Sysop

PhD School of Hard Knocks (summa cum loudly with ruffles and flourishes).

I got into Photoshop in a basic case of CPU envy. I was using Photostyler and saw Photoshop running on a Mac at my color separator's shop. I just had to have it. When it came out on the Windows platform, I got it. The rest is a rather sordid history.

My advice to you: Read The Freaking Manual. It is a great one, which is unusual for software products, I know, but true nevertheless.

John Cornicello, Adobe Forum Wizop

I have a BA in Communications.

Got involved through my background in commercial photography, digital imaging, ad agency work, and typesetting. Eventually worked on the Photoshop conferences with Thunder Lizard Productions, and then went on to manage the online services (CIS/AOL) for Adobe.

Advice: Read the manual with Photoshop 4. A LOT has changed (coming from someone who has NOT read the 2.x or 3.x manuals).

Len Hewitt, Adobe Forum Sysop

I think the best advice for learning about Photoshop is to read everything you can about it and then practice, practice, and more practice. Often, just "playing," but with a specific target in view, is a wonderful way of getting comfortable with the program.

Len Hewitt, one of the Adobe Forum's several British sysops, has a background in electronics. He trained as an Electronics Flight Systems Engineer in the Royal Air Force, where he was introduced to computers while working on flight simulators in 1974, but wanted to be a photographer from the age of eight. On leaving the R.A.F. after 12 years' service, he founded Contact Photography and PhotoDesign, which he has run with his business partner since 1980. Contact's first steps into computer graphics were back in 1984, on an Apple IIE with 128K of RAM, for which Len wrote much of his own graphics software in Pascal and Assembler. Len now specializes in industrial and advertising photography, digital retouching, and prepress work using a PC. Married with two grown children, his interests include long distance open (Canadian) canoeing, sea canoeing, real ale, and red wine. He also has a passion for Really Big Dogs!

Robert Phillips, Adobe Forum Sysop

Robert Phillips handles both Windows and Macintosh Illustrator, and the Windows versions of Photoshop. Although not an Adobe employee, he has been regularly involved with the development of these and other Adobe products through Beta testing programs. Robert is proprietor of Classical Typography, a small graphics design organization in northeastern Pennsylvania. In his bread/butter life he is a university-level professor of ancient history. In his spare time he shovels snow. He is coauthor, with Deke McClelland, of the *Photoshop 3.0 Bible—Windows Edition* (IDG Books).

Moe Rubenzahl, Adobe Forum Sysop

BS and MS in Electrical Engineering but now serving in Marketing and Product Development, as well as Marketing Communications capacities.

Began using Photoshop for development of onscreen graphics for Videonics video-editing products. Continued with development of brochures and marketing materials. Today my main use is for graphics for the World Wide Web (see `http://www.videonics.com/`).

Advice for new users: Jump in! Photoshop is such a deep tool; it can be intimidating at first. The most important single piece of advice is to use the Adobe Photoshop Tutorial. It is the single best intro I have found for new—and even somewhat experienced—users. And if I may add one more piece of advice: RAM and disk space. Images inherently need a lot of space and the more RAM you can add, the better.

Carol Steele, Adobe Forum Sysop

Trained as a research chemist with a PhD in Chemistry.

When I made a career change to photography I realised that the future would lie in digital imaging, and so after working with some of the lower-end packages I changed over to Photoshop as it really was (and still is) the industry standard package, which worked far more intuitively to somebody who has darkroom skills.

Unlike a lot of software packages, with Photoshop it really does pay back enormous dividends if you work through the tutorials supplied with the package. They are of enormous benefit. (Author's note: Carol is also from Great Britain.)

Heidi Waldmann, Adobe Forum Sysop

BA, Theology (after near majors in psych and architecture over a span of 15 years—don't ask!).

Got into graphic design accidentally about 11 years ago, and Photoshop is probably the only software I've ever *loved*. I use it to clean up scans, transform clip art, repair torn and faded photos (it's amazing to see details lost for decades appear), and create graphic elements for print and the Web. Even though it's intuitive, Photoshop is one of those "deep" programs—there's always more to explore. Be forewarned: For an addictive personality, it's way more fun to keep exploring than to turn the computer off and get a life…or some sleep…

Advice? Do the tutorials, then go online—-one of Photoshop's great strengths is the enormous breadth and depth of experience its users are willing to share.

JB (Julie) Whitwell, Adobe Forum Wizop

BA French major, English/Spanish co-minors.

Originally started out in the business world doing foreign-language typing, translation, and translation editing. Moved into the computer-based market naturally from there—translation skills are very applicable when it comes to computers and file formats!

Spent some 20 years working for printing/prepress companies, prior to devoting full time to my own business. Primary uses of Photoshop: image capture, image retouching, and other image manipulation required prior to producing the final printed products which include the images.

Secondary use of Photoshop: translation from one graphics file format to another, for specialized purposes!

New user tip: Use Photoshop to prepare your images for printing, rather than relying on similar functions available in the page layout application you use.

CHAPTER SUMMARY

You have learned *what* to do with the basic tools of Photoshop. *Why* you should use each tool will be explained later. You should now be able to open and create images, create Brushes, choose foreground and background colors, and use all the tools in the Toolbox. This is a tremendous amount for you to absorb, and much of it will neither stick with you, nor make much sense, until you start using the program. As you begin to use it, however, the items discussed in this chapter will become second nature.

The next thing you need to do is work through the Lab exercises. This section, which appears in Appendix C, gives you practical experience using the knowledge you just acquired and additional practice in applying your new skills. You are the only one who will know if you actually complete the exercises, but in Photoshop, practice does make perfect. You cannot get comfortable with the program unless you work at it. So, take the time to do these exercises. Many of them even teach additional skills (or tricks) not mentioned in the text. In addition to learning more about Photoshop, you should really *enjoy* the Lab exercises.

CHAPTER 2

MAKING SELECTIONS

earning to make selections is probably the most important Photoshop skill to master. Almost everything you do in Photoshop builds on your ability to select an area of the image on which to work.

Photoshop has a number of selection tools. The Marquee, Lasso, and Magic Wand tools are all used for making selections. In addition, the Select menu has a number of commands that work on the selected areas to expand, contract, feather, or otherwise manipulate them.

At the end of this chapter, you should be able to

⬤ Use any selection tool to create a basic selection.

⬤ Add and subtract areas from a selection.

⬤ Move the selection Marquee without moving the pixels in the selected area.

⬤ Create a selection based on the color values in the image.

● Save a selection for later recall.

● Load a selection from another image.

● Feather a selection.

● Select the border of a selection and describe the specific properties of it.

● Grow a selection or select similar pixels and describe what happens.

● Expand and contract selections.

LESSON 1

WHY USE SELECTIONS?

Photoshop contains many image editing commands. These commands work on either the entire image or on the portion of the image selected. In order to tell Photoshop which pixels to include in the editing command, you need to draw a selection around them. Pixels selected are enclosed with a dotted line called a *Marquee*. The selection Marquee vibrates to call attention to the fact that it's a fluid area. From this motion comes the term *marching ants*, typically used to describe the selection area and used throughout this book.

When a marching ant Marquee is active in your image, your cursor points in the opposite direction as it moves over a selected area. This indicates an active selection—even if the marching ants are hidden at your request.

Command Watch		

Here are some keystrokes for making and dropping selections:

Action	Mac Key	Windows Key
Show/Hide selection Marquee	⌘+H	CTRL+H
Select entire image	⌘+A	CTRL+A
Deselect selection	⌘+D	CTRL+D
Float selection (new layer)	⌘+J	CTRL+J
Cut and float a selection	⌘+OPTION+J	ALT+CTRL+J
Merge down	⌘+E	CTRL+E

1. Besides the Toolbox, where else can you find selection commands?
   a. Tools Option palette
   b. Window menu
   c. Select menu
   d. Marquee Options palette

2. What are some of the things you can do to a selection area?
   a. Feather
   b. Add a border
   c. Expand a selection
   d. Save a selection

3. What are the selection tools in the Toolbox?
   a. Hand tool
   b. Lasso tool
   c. Magic Wand tool
   d. Marquee tool

4. When you create a selection using the Marquee tool, the selection is surrounded by a dotted line, often referred to as
   a. Marching ants
   b. Vibrating line
   c. Marching Marquee
   d. Dotted Marquee

5. There are keystroke shortcuts for making and dropping selections. What is the keystroke shortcut for cutting and floating a selection?
   a. ⌘+H (CTRL+H)
   b. ⌘+J (CTRL+J)
   c. ⌘+A (CTRL+A)
   d. ⌘+OPTION+J (CTRL+ALT+J)

BASIC SELECTION TOOLS

The basic selection tools enable you to create simple selection areas. The Marquee creates selections based on rectangles or ellipses. The Lasso gives you a free-form Marquee shape and allows you to draw your selection.

Marquee

The Marquee tool is used for making rectangular and elliptical selections. As you learned in Chapter 1, "Introduction to Photoshop," you can constrain the Marquee so you get perfect squares and circles, and you can set the Marquee tool to maintain either an exact size or a specific height-to-width ratio.

The strength of the Marquee tool lies in its ability to set the size or ratio of the selection, since it is useless as a selection tool for a complex shape. However, if you need to precisely select rectangular chunks of your image, it is the best choice. It is also very useful for making a fast selection of an object against a solid background to move to another location on the same solid background.

Another use for the Marquee tool is selecting an elliptical area within an image in order to create a *vignette* (a picture that gradually fades into the background). You might see vignettes as a part of old sepia-tone images in which the person in the image fades very softly into the background. Let's use the Marquee tool to create a vignette. The image we will use is called Bhnrgirl.Psd and was taken by photographer Ed Scott of a Montagnard village girl near An Khe, Vietnam, in 1969.

HANDS ON

A MARQUEE SELECTION

1. Open the image Bhnrgirl.Psd. Figure 2-1 shows the original image. Duplicate the image (Image → Duplicate → OK). Do not close the original.

2. Select the Marquee tool and press ⓜ until the Elliptical Marquee appears.

3. Set the fixed size of the Marquee to 500×662 pixels.

4. Drag the Marquee into the image and center it by eye. You can move it as much as you need to. As long as you are using the Rectangular Marquee tool, you can freely move the Marquee without moving any of the pixels *inside* it.

5. To soften the selection, choose Feather... from the Select menu and type **10** as the value. Figure 2-2 shows the Feather dialog.

6. Select Inverse from the Select menu. This reverses the selection. All selected pixels are now deselected, and only the originally unselected pixels are selected.

7. Press ⒟ to set the colors back to the black-and-white default.

Figure 2-1
Montagnard village
girl: original image

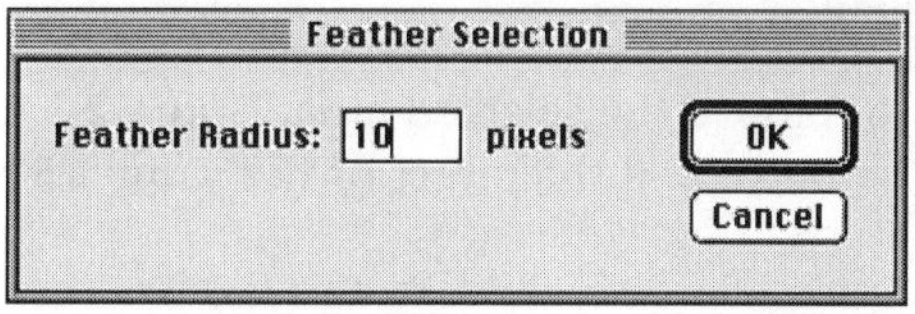

Figure 2-2
Feather dialog

8. Press DELETE to remove the selected area and leave the vignette.

9. Make another duplicate of the original image.

10. This time, let's center the Marquee exactly. There are several ways to do this, but this way is the most accurate. Turn on the Rulers from the View menu (View → Show Rulers; or Mac: ⌘+R, Windows: CTRL+R).

11. Click on the tab for Info Palette to bring it to the front.

12. Check the size of the file in pixels (your Units Preference must be set to Pixels for this to be available) by holding down the mouse on the file size area of the window with OPTION (Mac) or ALT (Windows) pressed. The image is 547×709 pixels. Therefore, the center pixel would be pixel number 274, 355 (half each pixel count and round up to the next number since both dimensions are odd numbers).

13. Make sure that Snap to Guides is selected (View → Snap to Guides should be checked). If not, select the command again in the menu.

14. Drag a Guide from the top ruler (click on the ruler and drag down with the mouse button pressed) until the Info palette says 355. Drag a Guide from the side ruler until the Info palette says 274.

15. Move your cursor until it reaches the intersection of the two Guides. The crosshair cursor for the Marquee turns red when positioned where the two Guides cross.

16. To create an elliptical selection from the center, press the modifier key (Mac: OPTION, Windows: ALT) and press the mouse button. The fixed size elliptical Marquee appears in the image from its center exactly where you want it.

17. Hide the Guides (View → Hide Guides, or Mac: ⌘+;, Windows: CTRL+;).

18. Feather the selection by 25 pixels (Select → Feather, or Mac: SHIFT+⌘+D, Windows: SHIFT+⌘+D).

19. Reverse the selection (Select → Inverse, or Mac: SHIFT+⌘+I, Windows: SHIFT+CTRL+I).

20. Press DELETE to remove the selected area. Figure 2-3 shows the comparison of a 10-pixel vignette and the effect of the softer 25-pixel feathered vignette.

Figure 2-3
Montagnard village
girl with 10-pixel
vignette versus 25-
pixel vignette

Command Watch

You can also use keyboard modifiers to change the way the rectangle and ellipse selections are drawn or behave in the image.

Action	Mac Key	Windows Key
Draw from center	OPTION	ALT
Draw a perfect square or circle	SHIFT	SHIFT
Draw circle or square from center	OPTION+SHIFT	ALT+SHIFT
Inverse the selection	SHIFT+⌘+I	SHIFT+CTRL+I
Feather the selection	SHIFT+⌘+D	SHIFT+CTRL+D

Lasso

The Lasso tool is good for making fast freehand selections. You can use it as you would a pencil (the Freehand Lasso), or you can constrain it to a connect-the-dots tool (Mac: hold down OPTION, Windows: hold down ALT). The connect-the-dots version is called the Polygon Lasso tool. The two versions of the Lasso tool share the same square in the Toolbox. You can select one over the other in one of three ways:

● Press and hold the mouse on the Toolbox square until the other tools appear. Then drag the mouse over the version you want to select it.

● Press the modifier key (Mac: OPTION, Windows: ALT) and click on the tool in the Toolbox to bring up the next one in the same square.

● Repeatedly press the keyboard shortcut until the version you want shows up in the Toolbox.

The Lasso tool can also have an automatic Feather added to it (as can the Marquee tool) if you enter it in the Tool Options dialog box, but it's usually safer to leave the Feather at 0 and manually add any needed amount. This way, the tool always reacts the way you expect.

The Lasso always creates a closed selection. If you do not drag the Freehand Lasso back to its starting point, it draws a straight line between the last point you drew and the starting location of the selection. This is useful because you only need to get the Lasso close enough to let it close up the selection by itself. If you are using the Polygon Lasso, double-click and a straight line will be drawn from that point to the first one.

Although the Lasso is quite good at making fast selections, it is not especially accurate. You will see why in the following exercise combining use of the Marquee and the Lasso. The same example will then be used for the following section of the Magic Wand tool.

THE LASSO TOOL SELECTIONS

1. Open the image Colrwhel.Psd. Duplicate it (Image → Duplicate → OK).

2. Double-click on the Marquee tool. In the Marquee Options palette that appears, set the Shape to Rectangular and the Style to Fixed Size. Enter the values Width: 90 pixels, Height: 90 pixels, and make sure the Feather Radius box is set to 0.

3. Drag the Marquee into the top-left corner so it surrounds the object. Copy it to the clipboard (Mac: ⌘+C, Windows: CTRL+C). Deselect (Mac: ⌘+D, Windows: CTRL+D).

4. Drag the Marquee to the top-right corner of the image and paste from the clipboard (Mac: ⌘+V, Windows: CTRL+V). Deselect (Mac: ⌘+D, Windows: CTRL+D).

5. Drag the Marquee to the bottom-left corner and paste, then place the same image in the bottom-right corner. You have now repeated it four times.

6. Flatten the image (Mac: SHIFT+⌘+E, Windows: SHIFT+CTRL+E).

7. Drag the Marquee back to the second copy (top-right corner). Change the image to grays by choosing the Image → Adjust → Desaturate Option.

8. Drag the Marquee over the bottom-left corner and select the Adjust Hue-Saturation command (Mac: ⌘+U, Windows: CTRL+V). Change the Saturation to -50 by typing in the number or dragging the slider.

9. Drag the Marquee into the bottom-right corner of the image and change the Saturation of the object to -75 as you did in Step 7. Save the file to your hard drive. This prepares it for future use (with the Magic Wand tool).

10. Select the Lasso tool (L). In the Lasso Options dialog, make sure Feather is set to 0 and Anti-aliased is Off.

11. Double-click on the Hand tool to make the image as large as possible on the screen. This lets you see what you are doing.

12. Use the Lasso freehand and draw around the outside of the upper-left object as closely as you can. Look at the image carefully with the marching ants active. Are you very close? (Most of you will not be!)

13. Try it in Polygon Lasso mode and see if you get better results. Was that any better? Probably a little, but most of you will still miss a pixel or two. Look at Figure 2-4 to see the author's attempt at lassoing the object. Even with years of practice, it is not exact. *Do not close this image.* We will get back to it soon.

There has to be a better way to select this flower-like object! This is an easy selection. It was drawn using the Pencil, so it has no anti-aliased edges. Everything is crisp and sharp. It would be much harder if the image was anti-aliased. A better way to do this is by using the Magic Wand tool. However, before we discuss this tool, you need to learn how to add and subtract from your selected areas.

Figure 2-4
a) Lasso in Freehand mode
b) Lasso in Polygon Lasso mode

a

b

1. With the Marquee tool you can
   a. Create a perfect circle selection
   b. Create a freeform selection
   c. Create a rectangular-shaped selection
   d. Create a vignette

2. What is a vignette?
   a. A picture that gradually fades into the background
   b. A selection with the marching ants border
   c. An old sepia-tone image
   d. Another name for an elliptical shape

3. How would you invert a selection using a keyboard shortcut?
   a. ⌘+I (CTRL+I)
   b. ⌘+V (CTRL+V)
   c. SHIFT+⌘+I (SHIFT+CTRL+I)
   d. SHIFT+⌘+V (SHIFT+CTRL+V)

4. Which of the selection tools would you use to create a freeform selection or shape?
   a. Pencil tool
   b. Marquee tool
   c. Magic Wand tool
   d. Lasso tool

5. There are two types of lassos: the Freehand Lasso tool and the _____ Lasso tool.
   a. Circle
   b. Cowboy
   c. Polygon
   d. Square

SELECTION MOVES

It is frequently difficult to select the exact area you want from an image. Therefore, you may need to employ more than one selection method—either in terms of tool use or selection strategy. All the following techniques work with the Marquee, Lasso, and Magic Wand tools using the same set of keystrokes.

Adding to a Selection

After you make a preliminary selection, you may need to add more areas to it. You can do this with any of the three main selection tools by pressing SHIFT as you make another selection with either the same tool or one of the others. Try this simple exercise for practice.

ADDING TO A SELECTION

1. Open the image Redshape.Psd. This image contains several red shapes that are easy to select with either the Lasso or the Marquee tools.

2. Press M to select the Marquee tool. If the shape is elliptical in the Toolbox, press M again. Check the Marquee Options dialog to make sure the style is Normal (if the dialog is not visible, you can simply press RETURN to show it).

3. Start in the upper-left corner of the red shape and drag the Marquee to create a selection that is as large as possible but only contains red pixels. Figure 2-5 shows this first selection.

4. Press the SHIFT key and keep it pressed as you drag the Marquee around the largest selection possible in the highest portion on the right of the shape. Figure 2-6 shows this new selection.

5. Continue to keep SHIFT pressed and make the remaining four selections needed for the entire irregular center shape. It's easier to place the cursor at an unselected corner of a rectangle when starting the selection than to try selecting from the top left—especially if the area is already selected. If you make a mistake, select Undo (Mac: ⌘+Z, Windows: CTRL+Z). This reverses the last command but does not erase your previous selection.

6. You can select noncontiguous areas as easily. Press SHIFT and drag the Marquee around the unconnected shape in the lower-right section of the image.

7. You can use another tool as well. Press L to select the Lasso. Press SHIFT as you start to outline the triangle shape. To make the Lasso rubber-band, either select the Polygon Lasso or press the modifier key as you drag (Mac: OPTION, Windows: ALT). Now click on two points of the triangle, let go, and close up (double-click) the third corner as you add to your selection.

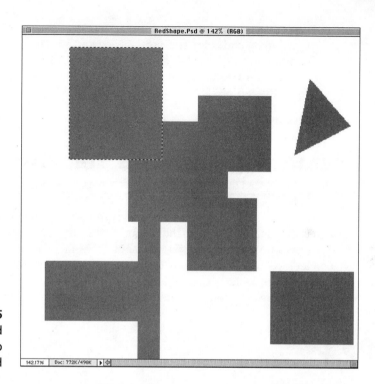

Figure 2-5
The odd-shaped object with the top left corner selected

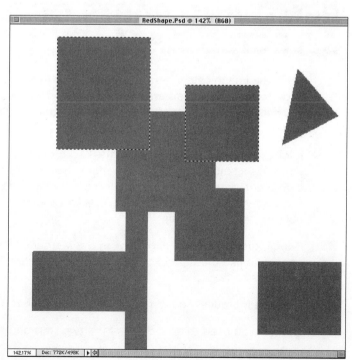

Figure 2-6
The odd-shaped object with a second selection added

8. Now that you have the entire red area selected, select a green area for your foreground color and press OPTION+DELETE (Mac) or ALT+DELETE (Windows) to fill your selection. (After all that work, it would be a shame to waste the selection!) This also shows you how close you came to selecting all the red pixels.

9. Close the image.

Removing Part of a Selection

As you performed the previous selections, you may have selected too much of an area and gotten white pixels along with the red ones. In the example, you were told to undo the selection. This is actually not necessary. You can also reduce the size of a selected area using a modifier key. On the Macintosh, the modifier key for reducing selections is OPTION; on Windows, it is ALT. If you press the modifier key while using the selection tool, you will remove from, rather than add to, your selection. You can see what will happen by looking carefully at the cursor. It contains a small minus sign when you have the correct modifier key pressed. Try this Hands On for practice.

REMOVING PARTS OF A SELECTED AREA

1. Open the image Celebr8.Psd. This file, shown in Figure 2-7, has a gradient background with some stars and an octagon shape in it. For this exercise, you need to select the background of the image—not the border or the objects.

2. It looks like it is not easy to select the background. There is no convenient series of rectangles to select and a number of shapes to remove. You need a different strategy. It is easy to select the background of the image inside the border if you *also* select the objects. Then you can just remove each object from the selection.

3. Double-click on the Marquee tool. In the Marquee Option palette that appears, make the shape Rectangular. Make sure the Feather Radius box is set to 0.

4. Drag the Marquee around the image inside of the red border.

5. Now, all you need to do is deselect the two stars and the octagonal shape.

Figure 2-7
Celebr8.Psd:
a difficult
background
to select

Select the Polygon Lasso tool with no Feather. Press OPTION (Mac) or ALT (Windows) to tell the program you want to subtract from the selection. You may release the modifier key after clicking once with the Polygon Lasso. Now you can rubber-band around the shapes with the Lasso. As you reach the last point before the starting point on each shape, double-click. The shape closes. With each finished shape, your selection becomes smaller.

6. To test your final selection, let's apply a *filter,* a feature of Photoshop that changes the way the image looks without you needing to draw anything. A filter works automatically once chosen. Select Filter → Pixellate → Pointillize from the Filter menu. Select a cell size of 8 and press OK. (This puts fancy confetti-like spots all over your selection.) If your selection is correct, only the Gradient background is filtered. The geometric objects are untouched.

You can use the modifier keys to add and subtract from selections as needed to help build the perfect selection. You can also change tools as needed.

Shrinking a Selection

In the Hands On with the Lasso tool earlier in this chapter, you painstakingly outlined a jagged color wheel to create a selection. You can use the Magic Wand tool (which has not yet been formally introduced) to quickly shrink a Marquee to enclose a specific object. In this example, you simply select some of an object's background and use the Magic Wand tool to subtract it from the selection.

The Magic Wand tool looks at the color you click and builds a selection based on its pixel and the *tolerance* value you set for the tool. Before I explain the function of the

Magic Wand tool any further, try the Hands On. It quickly demonstrates the power of the tool and the technique of *shrinking*.

About Tolerance

No, I'm not trying to tell you to be respectful of others (though that doesn't hurt!). Tolerance, which was first introduced in Chapter 1, determines how close a pixel needs to be in color to another one in order to be included in the action—whichever action is currently being performed. If the pixel is within the tolerance range, it is included; if not, it is not changed.

SHRINKING SELECTIONS

1. Use the Colrwhel.Psd image you were told to modify and leave open. Deselect (Mac: ⌘+ⅅ, Windows: CTRL+ⅅ). Press Ⅼ to select the Freehand Lasso tool.

2. Draw a very loose Marquee around the top left object in the image. Make sure the entire Marquee is drawn on the white background pixels.

3. Double-click on the Magic Wand and set the tolerance to 0. Set Anti-alias to Off. Set Sample Merged to Off.

4. Press and hold the correct modifier key for your platform (Mac: OPTION, Windows, ALT) and click with the Magic Wand on a white pixel *inside* the selection Marquee. The Marquee immediately shrinks to select just the object—you have removed all the background from the selection.

This shows the power of the Magic Wand. After all the fiddling you originally did to outline the color wheel with the Lasso, you can quickly and cleanly select the area with a combination of fast Lasso work and one click of the Magic Wand. Of course, this is a trick example. It works so nicely only because the image is against a solid color background. It would work just as well, however, if the color wheel object had been anti-aliased. This technique is suitable any time you need to extract a complex object surrounded by a single color.

Inverse Selection

Another common strategy for making a difficult selection is to select the areas you *don't* want, then use the Inverse command to select the area *not* previously selected. This works best if the background is solid—or very different in color from the foreground. It is then easy to select the background of an image and inverse the selection.

The Inverse command is located on the Select menu and is used to select the pixels not selected and deselect the pixels that were.

Open the image Colrwhel2.Psd for another short Hands On.

HANDS ON

INVERSE SELECTIONS

1. Double-click on the Hand tool to enlarge the view of the image.

2. Double-click on the Magic Wand and set the tolerance to 0. Set Anti-alias to Off. Set Sample Merged to Off.

3. Click on a white background pixel using the Magic Wand tool. The entire background becomes selected, as shown in Figure 2-8.

4. From the Select menu, choose Inverse. The selection Marquee surrounds every pixel in the image that is not 100% white. (Note: If there are white pixels in the image not connected to the background, these pixels will *not* be selected. The Inverse command does not see color; it simply reverses the selected areas.)

Selecting the Intersection of Two Areas

Although it is not as common an occurrence, there are times you may need to select a portion of an image within the confines of another selection—in other words, the intersection of two selections. Figure 2-9, Jewelbox.Psd, depicts such a need. In this example, you want to select the right half of the jewel box—the section exactly on top of the patterned background. Work through this Hands On to see how it is done.

Figure 2-8
Background selected in Colrwhel2.Psd with one click of the Magic Wand

Figure 2-9
Jewel box
challenge: how to
select the right half
of the box

INTERSECTING SELECTIONS

1. Open the image Jewelbox.Psd.

2. Press w to select the Magic Wand. Set the Tolerance to 30 and Anti-alias Off. Click inside the Jewel box to select it. One click picks up all but the anti-aliased edges of the box. That's fine.

3. Double-click on the Marquee tool. In the Marquee Option palette that appears, set the Shape to Rectangular and the Style to Normal. Make sure the Feather Radius box is set to 0.

4. Press the correct modifier keys for your platform (Mac: SHIFT+OPTION, Windows: SHIFT+ALT). Keep the keys pressed as you drag the Marquee around the entire area of the image backed by the greenish pattern. You do not have to make a rectangular selection that goes to the top and bottom of the image (though doing so has no effect on the results). You must get the left edge of the Marquee correctly placed and at least enclose the full height of the jewel box. The selection Marquee shrinks to enclose only the areas included in *both* selections. Figure 2-10 shows both selections and the final selection. It is a drawing—not a picture of your screen.

Figure 2-10
Jewelbox: two
selections, final
result

5. Once you select the half box, add *noise* to it (Filter → Noise → Add Noise,
   Gaussian, 200). This filter adds random pixels (bits of color) to the image as
   a special effect and is used here just for decoration. The important lesson is
   learning how to select the intersection of two selections.

Moving the Marquee

There may be times when you want to move the selection Marquee but do not want
to move the pixels inside it. A typical reason might be you have drawn a circular Marquee
selection and need to nudge it over a bit. You also might have selected an area with the
Magic Wand and want to duplicate the shape but not the pixels. You easily can move
the Marquee by itself just by dragging it with the mouse. Place the cursor inside the
selected area, press the mouse down, and drag. When you move the cursor into the
selected area, it changes to an arrow with a small, dotted box nearby. As you press
the mouse, you only see the arrowhead. You can move the selection as long as you see
the arrowhead, but keep the mouse button pressed until you are finished dragging.

If you merely click (and release) the mouse, you will lose the selection completely.

Command Watch

Here are some of the keyboard commands to modify the action of the Selection tools.

Action	Mac Key	Windows Key
Add to a selection	SHIFT	SHIFT
Subtract from a selection	OPTION	ALT
Intersect with a selection	SHIFT + OPTION	SHIFT + ALT

Moving a Selection

One of the key things you might want to do with a selection is move it to another location in the current image. You can only move a selection (or the pixels in a selected area) if you have the Move tool active. The Move tool can be selected in one of three ways:

● By clicking on it in the Toolbox

● By pressing V on the keyboard

● By holding down the ⌘ (Mac) or CTRL key (Windows) with any tool except the Hand tool selected

The Move tool does not create a selection but is used to move a selected area either within the image or by dragging it to another one. It is the only tool that allows you to drag-and-drop selections between images.

You can also move selections using the keyboard. The arrow keys function as directional aids. Each key press moves the selection one pixel in the direction of the arrow pressed. You can change this movement to a distance of 10 pixels by holding the SHIFT key as you press the arrow key. This works *only when the Move tool is active.*

Duplicating a Selection

It is easy to move a copy of your selection, rather than the original. Although you can do this with Copy and Paste, it is easier and faster to use the keyboard. On the Mac, press OPTION as you move the selection. In Windows, hold down ALT as you drag. This leaves the original selection alone and creates a floating copy to be positioned wherever you want. Since you also need to use the Move tool, if you have a different tool selected you need to press ⌘ or CTRL to bring up the Move tool, then the OPTION or ALT key to make a copy. Therefore, unless you have the Move tool selected in the Toolbox, to copy a selection you need to press ⌘+OPTION on the Mac or CTRL+ALT on Windows.

1. If you want to add more of an image to your selection, you can use a combination of
   a. ⌘/CTRL+the Lasso tool
   b. SHIFT+the Marquee tool
   c. ⌘/CTRL+the Magic Wand tool
   d. SHIFT+any of the selection tools

2. Pressing ⌘+Z (CTRL+Z) will _____ your last action.
   a. Undo
   b. Copy
   c. Move
   d. Repeat

3. To remove part of a selection, you can press a modifier key as you use one of the selection tools. What is the modifier key in both Mac and Windows?
   a. ⌘ or CTRL
   b. SHIFT
   c. OPTION or ALT
   d. SHIFT+OPTION or SHIFT+ALT

4. In Photoshop, there are many ways of accomplishing the same task. What are a couple ways you can shrink a selection that has a solid background?
   a. Press SHIFT+the Lasso tool.
   b. Use the Magic Wand tool to subtract background from the selection.
   c. Inverse Selection
   d. Reverse Selection

5. What are the three ways you can select the Move tool?
   a. Click on it in the Toolbox.
   b. Press V on the keyboard.
   c. Press ⌘+M (CTRL+M).
   d. Press ⌘/CTRL+any tool except the Hand tool.

MAGIC WAND

The Magic Wand enables you to select areas based on the similarity of their colors. This tool gets its own section because it is probably the most often used of all the selection tools and must be well understood.

The key to the Magic Wand is the correct choice of the Tolerance setting. *Correct* differs for each example, however, and for each area you need to select. Let's start by defining the term *Tolerance*. In this context, Tolerance refers to the similarity between colors. If you set a Tolerance of 0, the Magic Wand picks up contiguous (touching) pixels only if they are identical to the pixel you clicked. The maximum Tolerance setting is 255. At that setting, the Magic Wand selects the entire image. The trick is to find a Tolerance setting that selects most of what you want and nothing (or very little) you don't. Let's explore the Tolerance settings a bit more using the Colrwhel.Psd image you modified (the one with four different versions of the color object).

HANDS ON

MAGIC WAND

This Hands On is an experiment to see how sensitive the Tolerance setting can be and find out what it reacts to in the image. The Colrwhel.Psd image you modified contains four versions of the image. Each object has six petals, with each color touching two to four others.

The original color wheel has petals all set at 100% saturation and brightness. They are as pure as RGB colors get.

The top-right object is solid gray—it is the totally desaturated version of the color wheel. It is there to show you what happens when you convert pure colors into grayscale. These particular colors all convert to the identical value.

The bottom-left color wheel has been desaturated by 50%, and the bottom-right color wheel has been desaturated by 75%. This makes the colors in both objects more similar to each other than the colors in the original.

1. Double-click on the Magic Wand and set the Tolerance to 0. Set Anti-alias to Off. Set Sample Merged to Off. Click on every petal of the three colored objects. Notice that each click only selects one petal.

2. Set the Tolerance to 15 and try again.

3. Now, repeat the clicking on each petal of the three colored objects with the following Tolerance values: 20, 25, 21, 22, 50, 75, 100, 125, 150, 175, 200, 225, 250, 255, 252, 254.

You will notice that groups of similar colors begin to select together as you raise the Tolerance level. The colors on the 75% desaturated image merge first—long before the colors on the other circles begin merging. The colors on the pure object are the last ones to begin being selected together.

What's happening? As you raise the Tolerance, colors sharing similar RGB values begin to look alike to the Magic Wand. The Magic Wand looks at the value in each RGB channel separately and sees how much it differs numerically from the Tolerance setting. It takes all the variances together and evaluates the differences. Based on this, pixels are either in the selection range or out of it.

In this exercise, you saw how changing the Tolerance made a large difference in the areas selected. The exercise was easy because the image lacked any anti-aliased edges. As the edges of an object anti-alias toward the background color, it becomes more difficult to get the Magic Wand tool—or any selection tool—to pick up all the pixels. There are many ways to deal with this problem. In the next section, you will learn how to save your selections—either permanently or temporarily—so you can reload, expand, or contract them as necessary.

1. What is a key option of using the Magic Wand?
   a. Pixels
   b. Tolerance setting
   c. Colors
   d. Transparency

2. The Magic Wand will only select pixels that are
   a. Contiguous (touching).
   b. Similar in color.
   c. Similar in color based on the Tolerance level.
   d. Near each other, but not necessarily touching.

3. Tolerance is defined as
   a. How close one pixel is in color to an adjacent pixel.
   b. The range of variation permitted in a selection area.
   c. How dark one pixel is compared to an adjacent pixel.
   d. How different one pixel is from its surrounding pixels.

4. A high Tolerance number means
   a. More pixels of like color are included in the selection.
   b. Only pixels within a 1-inch×1-inch area are included in the selection.
   c. Only pixels identical in color are included in the selection.
   d. Only contrasting pixels next to each other are included in the selection.

5. What happens as you raise Tolerance levels?
   a. Colors with similar RGB values begin to look alike to the Magic Wand.
   b. Colors with different RGB values begin to look alike to the Magic Wand.
   c. The Magic Wand compares the RGB values of each pixel to the Tolerance level and chooses those in the range.
   d. The Magic Wand compares the RGB values of each pixel to the Tolerance level and chooses those identical in value to the Tolerance level.

SAVING AND LOADING SELECTIONS

If you have never painstakingly created a selection in bits and pieces, then lost it by clicking somewhere accidentally and not pressing Undo fast enough, you're lucky! However, you will probably experience this sometime and become just as frustrated as the rest of us. You can save yourself some of the pain and suffering by learning to use Quick Mask or one of the other selection-saving methods.

Quick Mask

You can convert any selection to a Quick Mask by pressing ⓠ on the keyboard. This creates a *rubylith* (a traditional means for masking images prior to airbrushing) so that only the unmasked area is fully visible. The masked area appears in red (though you can change these settings if you want). Review the section on Quick Mask in Chapter 1 if you do not remember what masking does.

The Quick Mask is a temporary storage area for a selection. It lets you draw and use all the Photoshop tools, but instead of altering the image, the tools work to alter the shape of the mask. For the purpose of this chapter, you need to work in the default colors of black and white when painting on the mask. In Chapter 9, "Advanced Selection Techniques," you will learn about the power of shades of gray in a mask.

The key elements to remember about Quick Mask mode are

● You *remove* areas from the mask by painting with white.

● You *add* areas to the mask by painting them with black.

● Masked areas cannot be changed while the mask is active.

● All tools used while in Quick Mask mode affect *only* the shape of the mask for the image.

After you have fine-tuned your selection in Quick Mask mode, you can either save it to a channel so it is always available, or you can turn it back into a normal selection, and then discard it. Let's see how Quick Mask mode works by creating an image using another of Ed Scott's photographs. This one, Mtnsheep.Psd, is of a *petroglyph*, or rock carving, left by an early Native American group of people. The purpose of the exercise is to create a Quick Mask that smoothes out the basic shape of the petroglyph.

QUICK MASK MODE

1. Open the image Mtnsheep.Psd. Duplicate the image (Image → Duplicate → OK).

2. Double-click on the Magic Wand tool and set the Tolerance to 25. Set Anti-alias to On. Set Sample Merged to Off.

3. Click on a pixel inside the mountain goat. You get more or less of a selection depending on the specific pixel on which you click. If there are entire areas of image missing in the selection, you can add to it by pressing SHIFT and clicking again.

4. When you are happy with the preliminary selection, press Q. You will see an area of red wash over your image, but the area of the goat selected will not change.

5. Make the Channels window visible (Windows → Show Channels) if it is not on your screen. Figure 2-11 shows the Channels palette with the Quick Mask selection.

6. Double-click on the name Quick Mask in the Channels palette. Figure 2-12 shows you the dialog box that appears. You can change both the mask color (red by default) and the opacity of the mask if you want. To pick a different mask color, just click on the color swatch in the dialog box. The color Picker (Photoshop or your platform picker) selected in your Preferences File appears. Red is standard, so unless your image has a lot of red in it when not masked, you might as well leave it alone.

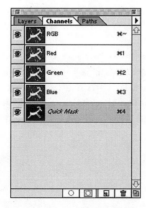

Figure 2-11
Channels palette
showing Quick
Mask

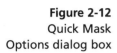

Figure 2-12
Quick Mask
Options dialog box

7. Set the Opacity to 100% so you can see what happens. You need to click OK before you see the change. You can see your mask clearly, but you cannot see through it to make editing changes. Double-click on the Quick Mask name again in the Channels panel to reopen the dialog box, and change the Opacity back to 50%.

8. The settings for Selected-Unselected also can be changed to reverse which portion of the image looks masked.

 Leave this setting alone; do not change it.

The association you want to reinforce with all selections is that drawing in black causes an area to be unchangeable or not selected and white indicates a changeable area. This is really important for consistency. Do not change this on a whim or you will get very confused—and many folks find the issue of channels, selections, and Quick Mask confusing enough without adding more complication.

9. Select the Paintbrush with the 13-pixel hard brush (number 5 from the left on row 1). Press D to set the colors back to the default of black and white. Press X to make white your foreground color.

10. Paint over the area of the goat you wish to select. Make the outlines of the goat smooth and do not leave unselected areas inside him. If you paint too much into the selection, press X to make black the foreground color, and remove the excess. You can switch between black and white as many times as you want.

11. After you make the goat as smooth as you want, select the Type tool bordered with the Elliptical Marquee (this is the Outline Type). Make white your foreground color and click toward the upper-left corner of the image. Type the words Mountain Goat in the dialog box. Select Helvetica for the Font, 40 for the size, Bold, and Anti-aliased. Figure 2-13 shows the setting for the text box.

Figure 2-13
Type Tool Options
dialog box

12. Click OK. Letter outlines are left in the image. Drag the text outlines to where you want them in the image (as you move the Type cursor over the text, the cursor shape changes to the arrow with the Marquee box when positioned directly over the type. This means you can drag the text. If you try to move it when you do not see the arrow cursor, you will lose the selection and have to reopen the Type Tool dialog box).

13. Fill the type with white (Mac: OPTION+DELETE, Windows: ALT+DELETE).

14. Deselect the type either by pressing ⌘+D (Mac) or CTRL+D (Windows).

15. Press Q to exit Quick Mask mode and change the unmasked areas into a selection. Leave the selection active.

16. Darken the selection a little bit. Select Image → Adjust → Hue/Saturation. Change the Lightness setting to -25. Click OK.

17. Select a deep green for your foreground color (RGB 11,47,14). Press SHIFT+DELETE to bring up the Fill dialog. Set the Foreground Color to 100% Opacity in Color mode (pull down the Mode menu to access this list).

18. Reverse the selection (Select → Inverse). With white as your background color, press OPTION. Figure 2-14 shows the finished mountain goat.

19. Do not deselect or close this image. You will need it again shortly.

In this exercise, you see how to create a Quick Mask. Among the uses of Quick Mask is the ability to fine-tune your selection by adding or subtracting to it by *painting on it*. This lets you select areas not color-differentiated enough to be selected via the Magic Wand or requiring more precision than the Lasso affords.

Figure 2-14
Finished Mountain
Goat image

1. What is a Quick Mask?
   a. A hidden selection
   b. A temporary storage area for a selection
   c. A masked selection
   d. A temporary storage area for a mask

2. What is another name for a mask?
   a. Rubycover
   b. Coverlet
   c. Rubylith
   d. Cover mask

3. What kinds of things can you do in Quick Mask mode?
   a. Draw
   b. Alter an image
   c. Use the Photoshop tools
   d. Edit the shape of a mask

4. You can change the color and Opacity of a mask (default is red). Where do you make those changes?
   a. Quick Mask
   b. Channels palette
   c. Quick Mask palette
   d. Channels dialog box

5. What are the key things to remember about the Quick Mask mode (assuming you are working in black and white)?
   a. You can add areas to the mask by painting with black.
   b. Masked areas can be changed while they are active.
   c. Any tools used while in the Quick Mask mode affect an entire image.
   d. You can remove areas from the mask by painting with white.

CHANNELS: AN INTRODUCTION

Photoshop stores your image in channels. It uses two types of channels for storage. The *color channels* (RGB, CMYK, or whatever color space you are using) store the actual image data (what you see on the monitor when look at an image). The *Alpha channels* store selections—areas you want to turn into marching ant Marquees at some point in the future. Let's look at both these types.

In Chapter 1, you learned that an RGB image has three color channels: a Red, a Green, and a Blue. These three channels store all the color information for the image. Think of the color theory you learned in elementary school—red plus yellow makes orange, yellow plus blue makes green, blue plus red makes purple. The color channels of an RGB image work like that too—sort of. There are three primary colors: red, green, and blue. However, these primary colors mix to form white. The color channels can be thought of as a place to store the *primary paint* making up each pixel in the image.

Picture a nice, shiny, ripe tomato at the peak of summer perfection. It is mostly red (189 red on a scale of 0 to 255). It contains a tiny bit of green mixed in with the red (18 on a scale of 0 to 255), and an even smaller amount of blue (2 on a scale of 0 to 255). That is the color formula for the tomato (just like a color formula for paint that needs to be mixed when you pick a sample from a swatch book for your living room). The difference is that the living room paint is placed in one paint can before it shows up on your wall. What if the paint manufacturer decided he could only sell the paint in three separate cans: a red can, a green can, and a blue can? The formula works so that once you put all three coats of paint on the wall, you get the color you want. Let's say you want to paint your wall tomato red. You need one paint can filled with 189 parts of red, a can with 18 parts of green, and a can with 2 parts of blue. After you coat the walls with all three, you see tomato red.

Well, the RGB channels work just like that tomato-colored paint. The portion of each pixel that's red is stored in the red channel, and so on. It all comes together in the Composite channel, which is what you normally view when you look at an image. What is this *portion* stored in the color channel? It is the value of the red, green, or blue component of each pixel. And what is this *value*? It is the gray component of an image—its lightness or darkness. When you look at each color channel, you see a grayscale image representing how much of the color is present in the image.

In an RGB image, the red channel containing a lot of tomato red is mostly white. The value for pure white is 255. The lighter the image, the more of the color it contains. In RGB mode, black (or 0) indicates no color is present; white (or 255) indicates the channel contains pure color. An RGB image that is totally white has a value of 255 in all three channels. This is because the RGB Color System is using the mixture of light as its basis. Physical light becomes white when it adds together red, blue, and green. So, an image containing RGB values of 35, 151, and 40 is heaviest in the green channel and is therefore a shade of green. Note: These values are measured with the Info palette—Photoshop's onscreen densitometer.

This is somewhat easier to understand when you begin to work with CMYK images. They come much closer to following the color mixing theories learned in second grade. At least in CMYK, when a channel is solid white, it is empty rather than filled with color.

So far, this explanation doesn't quite explain why Photoshop uses channels at all. However, the real reason is that printing is done in four inks producing all the colors which are possible to print. By storing the value data for each component of a color in an individual channel, it's much easier for Photoshop to produce color separations—the first step in making printing plates. In order to print something in cyan, magenta, yellow, and black, you have to somehow *get* the image (or the correct percentage of the image) onto a printing plate inked with cyan, magenta, yellow, or black. By storing the image this way from the beginning, it is not much of a stretch.

In the Lab section in Appendix C, you will have a chance to explore this topic a bit more. This knowledge is critical to your understanding of how Photoshop works. You may meet people who have used Photoshop for years and will tell you, "I never mess with channels. They are too hard." Nonsense! These folks are missing one of the most powerful Photoshop features. The only leap of understanding needed for using them is the ability to *see* colors in terms of their grayscale values. In an RGB image, there is a simple correspondence between light and dark pixels, and selected and unselected areas. *Light areas* in an RGB channel show pixels that exist for the channel and can be changed; *dark areas* show pixels that are not in the channel and cannot be changed. Imprint that on your brain! Also remember that this rule holds true *only* for RGB images—which is the other reason that people find this confusing.

The color channels are not the only channels Photoshop can create. Users can create additional channels in any color space but bitmap. These user-created channels—called *Alpha* channels—can be used for a number of different things, but the only one we're interested in right now is its use as a selection channel. You can store your meticulously created selections inside a channel so they can be saved along with the image, and you can reuse them whenever necessary.

What does a selection look like when it is saved? It is a grayscale image in which white indicates areas inside the selection Marquee, and black indicates areas outside the selection Marquee. This should tie all the previous information on color channels into a neat package for you. It all fits—white is present and selected; black is unavailable.

Saving to a Channel

The process of saving a selection to a channel is simple. You can either select the Save Selection option on the Select menu or click on the Save Selection icon at the bottom of the Channels palette. It is the second icon from the left and looks like a marching ants Marquee in a shaded document. Figure 2-15 shows the Save Selection dialog. To accept the defaults in the Save Selection dialog, just click OK. This creates a new channel in the current document. You also have the options of creating a new *document* for the channel (it will be grayscale), or saving the channel so it interacts with an existing alpha channel if there is one.

SAVING A SELECTION

1. Make sure your Channels palette is visible (Window → Palettes → Show Channels).

2. In the Mtnsheep.Psd image, you have the Background selected. Reverse the selection (Select → Inverse).

3. Save the selection to a channel (click on the Shaded Elliptical Marquee icon—the second icon from the left at the bottom of the Channels palette).

4. You will now see a Channel 4. Click on the name Channel 4 to go to that channel.

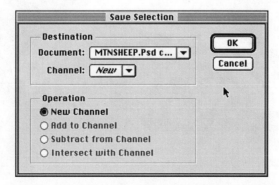

Figure 2-15
Save Selection
dialog

5. Deselect (Mac: ⌘+Ⓓ, Windows: CTRL+Ⓓ). Save the image.

6. Figure 2-16 shows Channel 4. If there are any stray pixels or your edges are not as smooth as you want, use the Paintbrush to clean it up. Remember, white adds to the selection; black subtracts from it.

Command Watch

You can select a channel using the keyboard. In an RGB image, this is how to do it:

Action	Mac Key	Windows Key
Select Composite RGB channel	⌘+Ⓧ	CTRL+Ⓧ
Select Red channel	⌘+Ⓘ	CTRL+Ⓘ
Select Green channel	⌘+Ⓙ	CTRL+Ⓙ
Select Blue channel	⌘+Ⓚ	CTRL+Ⓚ
Select Alpha Channel 4	⌘+Ⓛ	CTRL+Ⓛ
Select Alpha Channel 5-9	⌘+channel#	CTRL+channel#

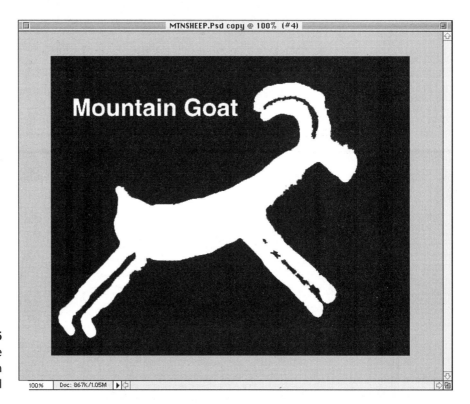

Figure 2-16
Channel 4: The saved selection channel

File Sizes and Channels

Adding alpha channels to images can eat up hard drive storage space quickly. In an RGB image, each color channel takes approximately ⅓ of the file size. If you add another channel to the image, you add up to another ⅓ of the file size. Photoshop compresses images it stores in native Photoshop file format. It is a lossless compression and can significantly reduce the image size. Therefore, it is hard to say exactly how much more room an alpha channel will use. But remember that the amount *does* begin to add up quickly. Therefore, save channels as you work, but think about what you want to actually store with the image long-term.

Only certain file formats enable you to store alpha channels—or more than one alpha channel. Your best strategy is usually to save the channels in a Photoshop image (along with its Layers if there are any), then prepare a final image with a new name for output. Archive the Photoshop formatted image in case any changes are needed later (they always are!).

Loading a Selection from a Channel

The reason you save a selection to a channel is because you may need it again. Let us pretend the client for whom you prepared the Mountain Goat image wants to retrieve the background of the image and change its color—rather than colorizing the image area as you did before. In addition, the client thinks blue is a better color than green. What are your options? (No, screaming is only a temporary relief of stress, and murder is illegal!) You could start over again, or you could load in the channel you already created and saved. That is certainly easier, but you removed the Background. How do you get it back?

That is easy, too. You have the original image, and the channel you saved is inside a file that is *exactly the same size as the original*. This means you can load the channel in your copy and change the original again (making another copy in the process). Try it.

LOADING A SELECTION

1. Click on the Mntsheep.Psd image to activate it. Duplicate the image (Image → Duplicate → OK).

2. Open the Load Selection dialog (Select → Load Selection). Figure 2-17 shows the dialog. Very interesting! The image you are trying to modify is called Mntsheep.Psd Copy 2, but the Load Selection dialog automatically selects the document Mntsheep.Psd Copy. This is the image you want, but how did the program know? Very simple—it is the same size as your current image, and it is the only open image of the same size with a channel that can be loaded! This makes it the only possibility through the dialog box.

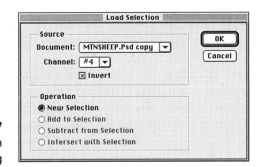

Figure 2-17
The Load Selection
dialog

3. Your selection channel is for the goat and the text. You need to change the Background—the reverse of your selection. Click on the Inverse button in the dialog box to bring in the selection the way you need it. Click OK.

4. Open the Hue/Saturation controls again (Image → Adjust → Hue/Saturation). Change the settings so they match the settings in Figure 2-18. You need to click on the Colorize box, then change the Hue to -117, the Saturation to 63, and the Lightness to 61. You can press ⌘+Ⓗ (Mac) or ⓒⓣⓡⓛ+Ⓗ (Windows) to hide the selection Marquee to see the changes better. This works even while you are inside the Hue/Saturation dialog box.

5. Click OK.

Command Watch

You can also, of course, load channels from the same image in which you are working. You can load them from the Select menu or by using keyboard commands. There are two different sets of keyboard commands—one for when you are looking at the Channels palette; the other, which can be used for Channels 1 through 9, for when you are not viewing the Channels palette.

Action	Mac Key	Windows Key
Load channel—method 1	⌘+click channel name	CTRL+click channel name
Load channel—method 2	⌘+OPTION+Channel#	ALT+CTRL+Channel#

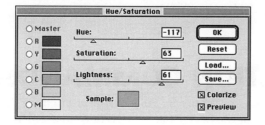

Figure 2-18
The Hue/Saturation
settings

1. What are the types of channels?
   a. CMYK
   b. Alpha
   c. RGB
   d. Color

2. What are Color channels?
   a. They store the CMYK channel information.
   b. They store the image selections.
   c. They store the color information of each pixel in an image.
   d. They store primary paint.

3. What are Alpha channels?
   a. They store selections of images for future use.
   b. They store RGB channel selections.
   c. They are user-created channels.
   d. They store selections of text.

4. Why does Photoshop use channels?
   a. Because printing is done in four inks.
   b. It makes it easier to produce color separations.
   c. That's the way it has always been.
   d. It makes an image easier to edit.

5. What are the ways you can save a channel?
   a. Clicking the Save Selection tool on the Toolbar.
   b. Selecting Save Selection from the Select menu.
   c. Clicking the Save Selection button on the Channels palette.
   d. Choosing Save Selection from the Store Options palette.

SELECTION COMMANDS

Once you create a selection, you can manipulate it in many ways. You can change its color or values, or you can filter it. You can copy, move, or remove it. There are a number of other commands that can also be used on selections—in fact, they can *only* be used on selections. You have already used some of these, but they warrant a more formal introduction.

Hide Edges

You can show or hide selection edges by selecting the Show or Hide command in the View menu, or by pressing ⌘+H (Mac) or CTRL+H (Windows). It is often quite valuable to judge the result of your manipulation of an area by hiding the Marquee. This lets you decide if you like the change *before* it becomes irrevocable. The Hide/Show toggle does not register as a command to the Undo buffer in Photoshop, so you can hide and show the selection Marquee as many times as you want without losing the ability to undo your last real action. You can also use this keyboard toggle when you are inside a dialog box.

The only drawback to hiding the selection Marquee is that it's so easy to forget you have an active selection. In Photoshop, if you have a selection active, the tools and commands only affect that one selection. Therefore, if you try to paint somewhere else in the image, nothing happens—you don't see any painting. You also don't see any warning as to *why* you can't see any paint strokes; however, the strokes are registered into the Undo buffer so it looks like they actually were painted. This might make you wonder why Photoshop has stopped working. Before you think about reinstalling the software, try the Deselect command (Mac: ⌘+D, Windows: CTRL+D). At least 90% of the time, the problem is a forgotten, hidden selection.

Float

There are two types of selections: floating and non-floating. When you first create a selection Marquee, it is *non-floating*. The Marquee simply surrounds the pixels in the image Layer. You can alter a non-floating selection with any filter, or you can change the tonal values or colors in it. However, as soon as you move, rotate, or resize the selection, it becomes a *floating* selection.

In Chapter 1, you learned that one difference between vector and raster programs is raster programs cannot distinguish between background and foreground pixels. Vector programs, however, see foreground areas as separate objects that can be moved, reordered, and manipulated. When a selection in Photoshop is floating, it becomes very similar to a vector-program object. The program knows about its boundary and sees it as something different from the mass of pixels behind it. This means you can move the floating selection, flip it, rotate it, resize it, or perform almost any other manipulation on it without damaging any pixels in your base image, which it passes on top of. If you press (DELETE), however, the selection vanishes, leaving the background color in its place. The original outside the selection Marquee only changes when you deselect the area.

There is also a command called Float (Mac: ⌘+J or Windows: CTRL+J) that *doesn't* create a floating selection. It creates a new Layer (more about this in Chapter 3, "Layers and Channels"). The Float command is used extensively throughout this book, but in Photoshop 4.0, its real name is New Layer via Copy. It is one of the best ways to keep from making accidental changes to your image. When you select the New Layer via Copy command, you preserve the entire underlying image from damage by *raising* the pixels to a new level in the image—where they won't affect anything that isn't on the same Layer. You find this New Layer via Copy command on the Layer menu under the New submenu. Throughout this book, however, the term *float* is used to refer to to the New Layer via Copy command. (It's shorter!)

Try this exercise to see the difference between floating and non-floating selections, and the Layer created using the Float command.

FLOATING SELECTIONS

1. Open the image Mandala.Psd.

2. Double-click on the Marquee tool. In the Marquee Option palette that appears, make the shape Elliptical and the style Normal. Make sure the Feather Radius box is set to 0.

3. Drag a Marquee anywhere in the image.

4. Press (DELETE). The selection vanishes, but so do the pixels inside the Marquee. They are replaced by pixels of the current background color.

5. Undo (Mac: ⌘+Z, Windows: CTRL+Z).

6. Make another elliptical selection. Look at the Layers palette. There is no floating selection.

7. Flip the selection horizontally (Layer → Transform → Flip → Horizontal). Now look at the Layers palette. It shows that you created a floating selection. Leave the image open for a bit.

What happened here? Photoshop automatically creates a floating selection whenever you move a selection area. A selection is moved by dragging it with the Move tool (or key), or by selecting any of the Flip, Rotate, or Effects commands on the Image menu.

Feather

Most of the work you have done so far was with aliased image areas—areas containing hard edges. A *hard edge* has the same color as the object. This is the type of edge created with the Pencil tool and is a throwback to the early days of black-and-white paint programs (such as MacPaint) or early 256-color paint programs such as Studio/8 or Deluxe Paint by Electronic Arts. The problem with a hard edge is it looks jagged if the object contains any curves or lines drawn at angles other than 90, 180, or 45 degrees.

To get around that jagged look (*jaggies* as they are semi-affectionately called), later paint and photo-manipulation programs came up with the concept of *anti-aliasing*. Anti-aliasing means creating edges that are softer because the edge pixels blend the object's color with the background's color so you cannot easily see the edge definition. Typically, anti-aliasing extends about 2 to 3 pixels from the solid color. Figure 2-19 shows the difference between aliased and anti-aliased edges. The first line on the left is drawn with the Line tool set to 3 pixels in width, and the anti-aliased box on the Line Tool Preferences dialog is left unchecked. The second line is drawn with the Line tool set to 3 pixels and Anti-aliased On. You can see how the edge pixels shade toward white. The first S shape is drawn with the Pencil tool and the 1-pixel brush. The second S shape is drawn with the Paintbrush and the 1-pixel brush. The anti-aliasing tricks the eye into thinking it sees a smooth shape even though the anti-aliased line or the S is really just as jagged as the aliased one.

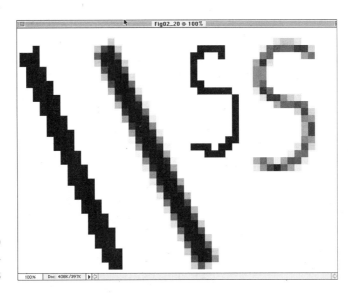

Figure 2-19
Aliased and anti-aliased edges

The Feather command (found on the Select menu) takes this *softening* of a shape a bit further. Anti-aliasing is automatic—when it is used, you cannot control the amount of softening. However, if you have a selection, you can choose to soften it by up to 250 pixels. You have already seen how this feathering can be used to create a soft vignette (in the Montagnard Girl exercise). You will see in Chapter 3 how it is also used to create semi-transparent edge pixels.

The Feather command can only be used on a selection that is not floating. If you try to feather a floating selection, Photoshop feathers it—but it makes it non-floating first! This can be a major problem if you have moved a selection, then decide to feather it thinking that will make it blend into the image better. Wrong move! *Feather first, then move or float.* Try this Hands On to see what happens when you feather a selection.

HANDS ON

FEATHERING A SELECTION

1. Select a nickel-sized area with the Elliptical Marquee from the bottom-left corner of the Mandala image.

2. Select the Move tool ([V]).

3. Copy the selection by pressing the modifier key (Mac: [OPTION], Windows: [ALT]) and dragging it to the center of the Mandala.

4. Apply a 10-pixel feather (Select → Feather, 10 pixels).

5. Whoops! It locked that selection down—not at all what we wanted. Undo (Mac: [⌘]+[Z], Windows: [CTRL]+[Z]).

6. Repeat Steps 1 and 2.

7. This time, feather it before you copy/move it. Give it a 10-pixel feather, then drag-copy it.

8. Drag the selection to the center of the Mandala. Notice how the borders of the selected area softly merge with the area onto which it is dropped. Figure 2-20 shows this clearly. Moving, then feathering a selection results in a hard edge from the original selection and no benefit from the feather—since feathering only shows up when a selection is moved *after* being feathered. When the feathered selection is placed in the center of the Mandala it is very soft, and it looks much smaller than the original selection area. It is—and it isn't.

Figure 2-20
Float then
feathered versus
feathered then
Float

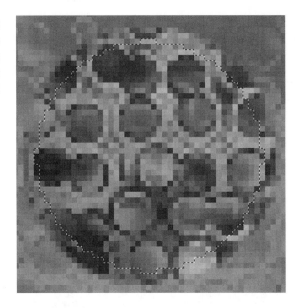

Float then feathered

Feathered then float

9. Select the Fixed Size Style for Elliptical Marquee in the Marquee Options dialog box. Make the height and the width 100 pixels.

10. Drag the Marquee into the center of the Mandala image.

11. Copy it to the clipboard (Mac: ⌘+ⓒ, Windows: CTRL+ⓒ). Create a new document (Mac: ⌘+Ⓝ, Windows: CTRL+Ⓝ). The size defaults to the size of the selection. Notice this is the same 100×100 pixels you specified in the Fixed Size dialog. Click OK. Paste in the selection from the clipboard (Mac: ⌘+Ⓥ, Windows: CTRL+Ⓥ).

12. Return to the Mandala image. Feather the selection by 25 pixels. Drag-copy the selection (Mac: OPTION+drag, Windows: ALT+drag).

13. Repeat Step 10, accepting the default size.

Something very strange has happened. The clipboard copied 100×100 pixels for the non-feathered image, but a whopping 220×220 pixels for the feathered image. The center of the image—the part at *full strength*—is quite a bit smaller than the full selection, however. Feathering has very far-reaching effects. When you feather an image, the selection Marquee shrinks. This is because some the pixels inside the selected area are no longer *fully* selected. The marching ants only surround pixels at least 50% selected. The blending you noticed on the feathered selections occurs because Photoshop only partially selects the pixels inside the feather. The pixels range from fully selected in the center of a selection, to a bit less than 50% selected near the original selection border, to almost totally unselected further out from the original selection border. The degree of selectedness becomes the opacity of the pixel when placed in its new location. The 100% selected pixels are fully opaque. The 50% selected pixels become a 50% blend of the original pixel color and the *receiving* pixel color. The farthest edges of the selection are almost totally transparent on top of the receiving pixels. In Chapter 3, you will learn more about this transparent nature of the pixel.

Stroke

In the primitive paint programs that first appeared with the advent of the personal computer (or in the first MacPaint), there were always tools to draw filled or outlined rectangles and circles. Photoshop has no such tools—at least not on the surface. However, there must be a way to draw the outline of a circle or a square, and of course, there is. It is just not obvious.

The Stroke command (found on the Edit menu) is the mechanism by which you draw outlines around selections. These outlines can be around any selection at all—not just around a square or circle. You can stroke a floating selection, but the command causes the selection to defloat. You can stroke a feathered selection, which creates a very soft edge.

You have a choice of stroking the selection along the inner edge, the outer edge, or the center line. Figure 2-21 shows the Stroke dialog. You will have a chance to experiment with stroking selections in the Labs in Appendix C. As with so many other dialog boxes in Photoshop, you have total control over the Opacity and Apply modes of the stroke. The maximum stroke width is 16 pixels.

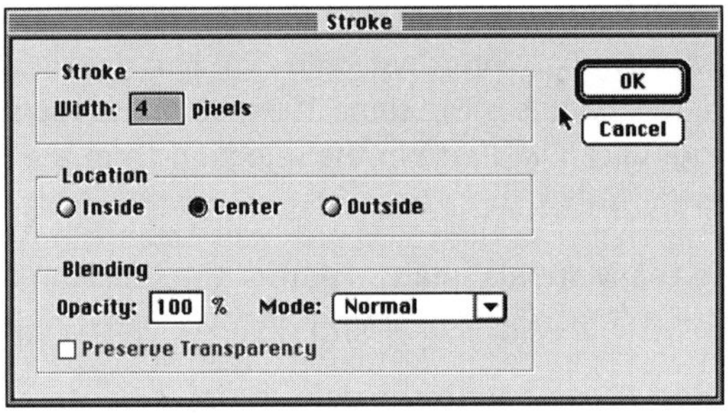

Stroke

Stroke
Width: 4 pixels

OK
Cancel

Location
○ Inside   ● Center   ○ Outside

Blending
Opacity: 100 %   Mode: Normal ▼
☐ Preserve Transparency

Figure 2-21
Stroke dialog box

Border

The Border command is frequently confused with the Stroke command. If an unfeathered selection is stroked, the result is a solid ring of color around the selection Marquee. A Stroked selection is either jagged or anti-aliased, depending on the status of the anti-aliased box in the Marquee Options dialog. A selection made with the Border command is always soft.

The Border command is located in the Modify submenu of the Select menu. Figure 2-22 shows the Border dialog. The maximum border value is 64 pixels.

The Stroke command makes an actual change in the image—it places an area of foreground color around the perimeter of a selection. The Border command has no effect on the base image. However, like the Stroke command and the Feather command, it deselects a floating selection, so be forewarned. It creates a different selection based on the original, but it is not the same. You make a border selection *in order to do something else to the selection.* One common purpose is to apply a blur filter to the border area so it blends better with the surrounding image. You will have a chance to make your own comparisons with the Stroke command in the Lab in Appendix C.

Grow

The Grow command is a way of increasing the active selection area based on the Tolerance setting in the Magic Wand tool. This sensitivity to the Tolerance setting is active even when you use a different selection tool, such as the Lasso or the Marquee. The Grow command is located on the Select menu.

The Grow command works by looking at the pixels in your selection, then reading the Tolerance setting. It selects every pixel contiguous to the original selection falling within the Tolerance setting. A high Tolerance setting allows the selection to expand

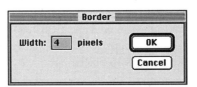

Figure 2-22
Border dialog box

faster, while a low Tolerance setting keeps the growth to a minimum. You can select the Grow command multiple times until you get the selection you want, or the command selects either too much or nothing more. When the selection enlarges to a point at which it reaches pixels of a distinctly different color, it stops growing. There is a Lab in Appendix C that lets you practice and explore this concept.

Similar

If you grow a selection enough times, it has the potential to find every pixel in your image within range. However, there is a faster way. You can use the Similar command (on the Select menu) to find all the pixels in your image that match the range of pixels in your selection.

The Similar command also looks at the Tolerance setting and finds all the pixels that range. Think of the Similar command as being a Grow command on growth hormones. It performs a grow on the entire file—not just on the contiguous pixels. You can also use the Similar command more than once.

Expand

If you find the Grow or Similar commands too unpredictable, you might prefer the Expand command. Grow and Similar expand a selection based on the color of the pixels. The Expand command (Select → Modify → Expand) enlarges the selection based on proximity to the original selection. You enter the number of pixels by which you want to expand the selection, and Photoshop *grows* the selection by that number of pixels in all directions. You can expand a selection by a maximum of 16 pixels at once.

Although this is an easy command to use, it was one of the most valuable new features in the Photoshop 3.0 release. In Chapter 9 you will get a lot more practice making difficult selections. The anti-aliasing edge pixels always prove to be among the peskiest things to try selecting. It is much easier to expand a good selection by a few pixels than to fiddle with the Tolerance setting—which may or may not even help.

Contract

It is also very useful to contract, or shrink, the selection area by a few (or up to 16) pixels. The Select → Modify → Contract command lets you reduce the size of a selection so you can manage the edge pixels by simply cutting them out of the selected area. You will have time in the Lab in Appendix C to work with the Expand and Contract commands.

Smooth

The Smooth command (Select → Modify → Smooth) allows you to smooth the edges of a selection Marquee to even out any bumps and points. This command is not as frequently used as the other Modify commands. However, the command is here if you need it. You can select the number of pixels, up to 16, by which you wish to smooth the selection.

Quiz 7

1. What are the different ways you can hide the edges (Marquee) of a selection?
   a. Choose Hide Edges from the View menu.
   b. Click the Hide Edges tool on the Toolbar.
   c. Press ⌘+H (CTRL+H).
   d. Select Hide Edges from the Select menu.

2. Why would you want to use the Hide Edges command?
   a. To keep the Marquee from printing
   b. To see what an image looks like with the desired changes
   c. So you don't see the marching ants
   d. So you can create another selection

3. How do you create a floating selection?
   a. By moving, rotating, or resizing a selection
   b. By pressing ⌘+J (CTRL+J)
   c. By selecting Float Selection from the Image menu
   d. By clicking the Float button in the Toolbox

4. What command(s) or option(s) would you use to soften the edges of a selection so they blend into the image better?
   a. Click the Feather button in the Toolbox.
   b. Click the Anti-aliased check box on the Marquee Options palette.
   c. Enter a number greater than 0 in the Feather area of the Marquee Options palette.
   d. Choose the Feather command from the Select menu.

5. What are two ways you can draw an outline around a selection?
   a. Click the Line tool button in the Toolbox.
   b. Use the Stroke command (Edit → Stroke).
   c. Use the Show Edges command (View → Show Edges).
   d. Use the Border command (Select → Modify, Border).

VIP PROFILE

Diane Fenster, Artist

Diane Fenster was a frustrated child artist who grew up in New Jersey. Told by her parents that art was not a so-called practical career, she dutifully majored in biology, then moved out to California where she had more freedom do as she wished.

On the loose out west, free and in her early 20s, she gravitated toward graphic design. In those pre-microcomputer days of the mid-70s, she apprenticed and learned about paste-up and layout.

Diane applied for a job at San Francisco State University as a graphic artist for the School of Science and got hired because of her science background. In this position, she grew with the job, taking on more responsibility and trying more challenging techniques, but she finally reached the limits of what a designer could do with a limited budget and no type-creating facilities. Diane also was not fond of "spec-ing" type, so she tried very little beyond the basics since she could not visualize how the type would look when it came back from the typesetters.

But in 1985, what Diane calls her computer guardian angel told her she needed to learn how to use the Mac Plus. She protested, but finally gave in. The murder mystery game *Deja Vu* was her introduction to the computer. Drawn to its 40s ambiance and film noir atmosphere, she became hooked. She learned the Mac by playing that game.

In 1985, the Mac had MacWrite, MacPaint, and MacDraw. New programs appeared slowly in dribs and drabs, and it was easy to keep up with technology and learn one program at a time. Everything was easy to absorb. However, today it has become overwhelming.

As Diane became more comfortable with the computer, she learned how to use it, to enjoy it, and not fear it. It was useful as a graphic design tool. For the first time, Diane could spec type visually rather than by the numbers. From 1985 to 1989, she learned to re-create on the screen what she had previously done by hand.

Then, in 1989, lightning struck. Diane picked up a copy of *Verbum* (an early computer graphics magazine) and read an article about computer artist Joel Sleighton, which described his process of scanning photographs and using a program called Pixel Paint in the background under the photos. That was when Diane first realized it was possible to create artwork—fine art—on the computer. She began the experiment of working digitally and found her life's work.

Diane claims she was like a mad dog back in those days. She stayed up all night and worked all weekend at the computer center at the university. Since all her free time was spent there, her husband, a traditional artist, finally brought his paints to the computer center and started working there—just so he could be near her.

All the programs Diane used had limitations—until she discovered Photoshop. To Diane, Photoshop is the be-all and end-all.

Sonjay Sakhuja, a San Francisco graduate in engineering, started the very first service bureau in Berkeley. He is responsible for performing some of the first color separations on the Mac. He had typed his thesis on a Mac, then went all over the city trying to find place where he could print it. He had an idea in which he interested the Krishna Copy Center: He would manage a DTP organization with laser printers and Macs. A few years later, color appeared, and Sonjay realized the potential for color separations. He consulted with Agfa and Adobe to harness the potential of this new technology and gave a class on the future of color, art, and design. There were five people in this class, including Diane, who became a follower of his and a believer in the potential for the computer to take over the prepress process.

Diane remembers doing an 8-bit image containing fractals for a magazine cover. It took hours to RIP (Raster Image Process) the files, but she ended up with four pieces of film, and, despite the printer's doubts, the image printed fine.

Sonjay introduced Diane to Photoshop. It was then in its first Beta release. Diane ran out and bought a copy as soon as it became available. It was the first piece of software for which she read the manual from cover to cover. She devoured the manual, then sat down and started to play.

Since then, Diane has become one of the best-known Photoshop artists in the country. She designed the cover for the first release of the *MacWorld Photoshop Bible*, by Deke McCelland. She has done covers and editorial images for *MacWorld* magazine, led many seminars, and exhibited in many individual and group shows.

Diane's advice to aspiring Photoshop artists: "Learn one thing at a time and learn it well. You will try many programs. Stay with ones that you find to be intuitive and most creative. Just sit down and play. Take every tool and try it; see what it does. Push every button—don't worry about making mistakes."

Diane thinks books and manuals are good learning tools, but until you see something happen on the screen, you don't really know what it means. You need to see each control, command, and filter and learn what it does to images by moving and trying them.

Photoshop has made Diane the happiest person alive. The anti-aliasing feature is her special delight. She became an artist because of Photoshop, and the increasing complexity and depth of her art is directly attributable to Photoshop 3.0 and the Layers feature. She says she owes her creative career to Apple and Adobe. Even though Diane had dabbled in the arts and photography, it was the computer and Photoshop that made her want to be an artist.

Diane is becoming a better photographer to support the images in her work. She just bought an enlarger and is about to rediscover the printed photograph. She says she wants to be able to take advantage of mistakes and accidents that occur in traditional photography but not on the computer. She wants to capture rough and imperfect textures.

Her additional advice is that Photoshop users "view everything as a potential source of art. Find it in the real world and then, get it into the computer. Try all available means of scanning, drawing, photographing, and videotaping. Always carry a small 35mm camera with slide film everywhere. Create—the world is a source palette.

"Your work is a collaboration between you and the company that engineers the software that you use. We depend on the features, but the creation is our own. Programs should be intuitive, after you have used them for a while, and the software tools need to be as transparent as possible. Practice, practice, practice. Learn what you need to use for your art."

View Diane Fenster's art online:
Fine Art installation online at
`http://www.art.net/Studios/Visual/Fenster/ritofab_Home/fenster.html`
Illustration portfolio at
`http://www.sirius.com/~fenster/`

CHAPTER SUMMARY

This has been a demanding chapter. You learned how to use the Marquee, Lasso, and Magic Wand tools to make selections. In addition, you learned how to use Quick Mask and to save and load selections in channels. You learned to expand and contract your selections and to add and subtract from them manually, too. You learned how to grow a selection and use the Border command, and you have begun to learn how to use the Tolerance setting to control the Magic Wand. These are basic Photoshop skills we will refine in later chapters. *You should not continue on without mastering the techniques discussed in this chapter.* This set of skills is absolutely essential if you are going to perform any serious work with Photoshop.

CHAPTER 3

LAYERS AND CHANNELS

n Chapter 2, "Making Selections," you learned how to make basic selections. Although some of these selections were fairly complex, they are considered basic selections because all the elements in them were either selected or nonselected. The only partial selections were the edges of the selected area. These selections all created mostly black and white channels when saved. Photoshop is capable of much more complex handling of selected areas. This ability stems from the way Photoshop can see values of gray as areas of transparency.

You have also learned that Photoshop can only have one selection Marquee active at a time. Although you can add and subtract from selections, once you deselect, you lose the selection permanently (unless you recover it via a channel mask). However, if you deselect a Floating selection, the pixels under the selection disappear forever. This makes it very difficult if you change your mind. Layers—first introduced in Photoshop 3.0—change this situation and allow you to easily make image revisions.

This chapter introduces you to the full power of Layers and channels. Although you will learn some of the uses for Layers and channels, the emphasis in this chapter is on the commands needed (once again, *how* rather than *why*) to create and manage these Photoshop features. Other chapters give you lots of additional practice in using them. By the end of this chapter, you should be able to

- State the difference between a Layer and a channel and know when to use one or the other

- Save a selected area to a new Layer

- Select, link, export, and reorder Layers

- Set Layer Apply modes and alter Blend If settings

- Create and edit Layer Masks

- Create and use Clipping Groups

- Use the Calculations and Apply Image commands

- Explain how grayscale channels produce transparency

*L*ESSON 1

LAYERS

Picture a transparent sheet of acetate. You can see anything under it. If you place an image on the acetate, it obscures painted areas on the images underneath. However, in places where the acetate is empty, the images underneath still show through. This sheet of acetate is the metaphor Photoshop uses for its Layers feature. If you have any knowledge of traditional animation, you know that a similar process was used. In an old Disney cartoon, for example, each step Mickey Mouse© took was drawn on a new sheet of acetate placed over the background scene—so that the background only needed to be drawn once, not redrawn with every step.

Layers were introduced in Photoshop 3.0 to address the needs of artists who revise images or image composites. Vector programs, you will recall, allow the artist to move objects at any time. The computer always knows what constitutes an object and can find, move, and reorder its position from front to back. This is an advantage that raster programs such as Photoshop do not have—since, once a pixel is in the background plane, the computer cannot differentiate it from any other pixel. Therefore, the computer cannot tell the difference between the Mona Lisa or the Wicked Witch of the West.

Consider this scenario: You just finished working on an advertisement for a client uniting three different groups of people in various locations and a table holding a box of cereal. It took you several days to select the people from the original images, mask them, and composite them with the table and the cereal. Everything is now in the background plane of the image and no selections are active. You send a *comp* (a composite, or a preliminary printout) to the client, who in turn, sends back the message that they want to substitute a different group of people on the left side of the image and want to use a new product shot.

From the work you did in Chapter 2, you should have a good idea how difficult it would be to pull apart this composite once you finish it. If, however, you place each group of people on a different sheet of acetate (layer) as you work and save your image in that format, it is much easier to make these changes. Instead of having to remask the images (and probably start all over again from the originals), you replace the layer containing the unwanted group with the new group, and replace the product layer with the updated product shot. This makes the revisions much less drastic.

This, then, is the major benefit of Layers: the ability to keep an image easily editable. Another major benefit is the ability to make the image in one Layer interact with the images below it in a variety of ways. These ways are the Apply modes you first came across in Chapter 1, "Introduction to Photoshop," when you used the painting tools. Just as you can paint in Multiply or Screen mode, you can set Layers to react to lower Layers using Multiply and Screen modes (and a number of other modes as well). You can also set transparency for Layers.

You can move the image in a Layer by dragging it, just as if you were moving a sheet of acetate of infinite size. You can also change the stacking order of the Layers (to put a different Layer on top, for example). You can link Layers and move two or more of them together.

Layers and RAM

All this flexibility has a price, however. Layers use RAM (Random Access Memory—or just *memory*, in more common terms), and Photoshop is already a very memory-hungry application. Creating a new Layer does not take up much RAM, but *placing* image data on the new Layer requires more memory. Layers add to the stored file size as well. As you work, you will always need to balance your desire for editability against your available memory and hard disk space. Whenever possible, it is better to lean towards editability. In Chapter 14, "Configuring and Optimizing Photoshop," there will be much more information on exactly how Photoshop uses memory and how you can organize your work more efficiently. For now, just be aware that there is a price to pay for keeping images fluid.

Creating a New Layer

Layers are very easy to create. Figure 3-1 shows the Layers palette. There are three icons on the bottom of the palette. The icon on the left is the Layer Mask icon (it helps you mix images with the Layers beneath). The icon at the bottom center of the palette (the one that looks like a square page with a turned corner) is the New Layer icon. The trash can on the right is used to dispose of unwanted Layers.

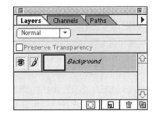

Figure 3-1
Layers palette

You can create a new Layer in several ways:

- By selecting the New Layer command from either the Layers palette menu or the Layer menu (this brings up a Layer Options dialog)

- By clicking on the New Layer icon (there is no dialog—the Layer is created and named by default)

- By floating a selection from another Layer (Mac: ⌘+J, Windows: CTRL+J)

- By clicking on the New Layer icon while there is a Floating selection (this places the Floating selection into a new Layer and deselects it at the same time)

- By dragging down an existing Layer name in the Layers palette until it touches the New Layer icon (this actually duplicates the dragged Layer)

- By dragging or pasting a selection or Layer from another image

The best way to see how to create Layers is to try it. Work through this Hands On.

HANDS ON

CREATING AND NAVIGATING LAYERS

1. Open the image Curtains.Psd.

2. Select the Brush tool (B) using the second brush on the right of the second row (soft, 21-pixel brush).

3. Select the New Layer command on the Layer menu (Layer → New → Layer). Figure 3-2 shows the New Layer dialog box. Although you can name the Layer if you prefer, the default name of Layer 1 is fine for this example. Click OK to exit the dialog box.

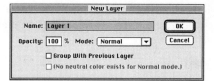

Figure 3-2
New Layer dialog

4. Pick up one of the deeper greens at the left of the image as your fore-ground color (press OPTION [Mac] or ALT [Windows] to make the Paintbrush turn into the Eyedropper tool, and click on the desired color).

5. Paint a nickel-sized circle of color on the new Layer near the center of the image where the lines look as if they are converging. Figure 3-3 shows the image at this point.

6. Create a new Layer, this time by clicking on the New Layer icon at the bottom center of the Layers palette. The Layer is created automatically, without you needing to name it. It is named Layer 2.

7. This time, select the powder blue as your foreground color. Paint a circle of color on this Layer, slightly covering the last circle you painted.

Reordering a Layer

8. Place your cursor on the name Layer 2 in the Layers palette. Press the mouse button and drag the Layer beneath Layer 1. You will see a dark line form between the two Layers when they are in the correct position. When

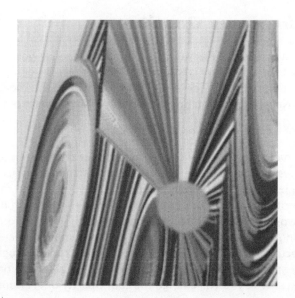

Figure 3-3
Practice image with
one Layer added

you see the dark line, release the mouse button. Layer 2 is now below Layer 1, and the circles you painted overlap in the reverse order.

Moving a Layer

9. Select the Move tool (V̄). Move the powder blue circle somewhere else in the image—it really doesn't matter where. You can place the cursor directly on top of the circle and move it, or you can simply press the mouse button and move the cursor—the circle will follow. This works because of the "sheet of acetate" metaphor. You are not moving the object this way—you are moving *the entire Layer on which the image area resides.*

10. Select one of the stronger yellows in the base image as your foreground color. Create a new Layer and paint a circle of color. If Layer 2 is the active Layer (selected in the Layers palette), when you create a new Layer, Layer 3 is created directly above it.

Changing Layers

11. You do not need to click on a Layer in the Layers palette to select it. You do need to use the Move tool, however. With the Move tool, place the cursor over the object you wish to move or edit. Press CTRL (Mac) or the *right* mouse button (Windows). A small menu appears listing all the Layers that can contain the object. Locate the Layer you want and click. Photoshop then makes active the Layer you selected. Make each of the Layers active to practice this.

Setting Layer Opacity

12. Select one of the flesh-tone pinks in the image as your foreground color. This time, when you create a new Layer, press OPTION (Mac) or ALT (Windows) as you click on the New Layer icon. This modifier key shows you the New Layer dialog just like selecting New Layer from the menu did.

13. Paint a circle of pink on the new Layer.

14. To change the Opacity of the Layer, either drag the Opacity slider on the Layers palette to the left until it reads 50%, or press 5 on the keyboard. As you learned with the painting tools, the number keys can be used to set Opacity in increments of 10 to 100 (number 1 through 0). You can also type a two-digit number into the Opacity field if you type quickly. Photoshop changes the Layer Opacity if you press a number and are using any of the selection tools, or the Move, Hand, Zoom, Crop, or Type tool. If you have any other tool selected (the remaining ones all create or modify pixels on the canvas), you will change the tool Opacity or Pressure instead.

Deleting a Layer

15. Click on Layer 4 in the Layers palette to select it. Drag the Layer name in the palette *to the trash can on the Layers palette*. This deletes the Layer. Do *not* drag it to the desktop trash can. That does not work! Leave this file open because you will continue to use it.

Command Watch: Layer Moves

To change the active Layer, click on the desired object with the Move tool and CTRL (Mac) pressed or right mouse button (Windows) pressed.

Action	Mac Key	Windows Key
Change active Layer—with Move tool selected, click on object with	CTRL	Right mouse button
Bring to front	SHIFT+⌘+]	SHIFT+CTRL+]
Bring forward	⌘+]	CTRL+]
Send to back	SHIFT+⌘+[	SHIFT+CTRL+[
Send backwards	⌘+[	CTRL+[

The exercise above demonstrates most of the basic Layers maneuvers. Here is a summary of the commands you have learned:

1. How to create a new Layer (click on the New Layer icon at the bottom left of the Layers palette)

2. How to create a new Layer and bypass the New Layer dialog box (OPTION+ALT+click on the New Layer icon)

3. How to move the position of an entire image's Layer (use the Move tool and drag the image with the correct Layer selected)

4. How to change the stacking order of a Layer (drag the name of the Layer in the Layers palette to the desired position in the stack)

5. How to set Layer Opacity (drag the Layer Opacity slider, or press the appropriate number key for 10% increments)

6. How to select a Layer without using the Layers palette (using the Move tool, press ⌘ [Mac] or CTRL [Windows], and click on the pixels in the desired Layer)

7. How to delete a Layer (drag its name in the Layers palette to the Trash Can icon on the bottom right of the Layers palette)

Linking Layers

There are times when you want to move the objects in more than one Layer all at once—as if they were linked, or grouped, together. This is easy to do. Let's link Layers 1 and 3 in your practice image.

LINKING LAYERS

1. If you look carefully at the Layers palette shown in Figure 3-1, you will see a column on the left containing an icon of an eye. Next to this column is an empty one (or one containing a paintbrush if it is the active Layer), and just beyond it is the Layer name. That empty middle column is used to link Layers together.

2. Select Layer 1 as your active Layer. A brush appears in the middle column.

3. Click in the link column next to Layer 3. Figure 3-4 shows the Layers palette and the symbol appearing in the link column. The symbol looks like a link in a chain.

4. Select the Move tool (⒱) and move the object in Layer 1. Notice that the circle in Layer 3 now moves with it.

5. To turn off the link, click on it again. Notice that you can break the link by clicking on any link symbol. To create the link, you must click on a layer not selected. To turn it off, if there are only two linked Layers, you can click the link symbol on either one.

6. Link Layers 1 and 3 again.

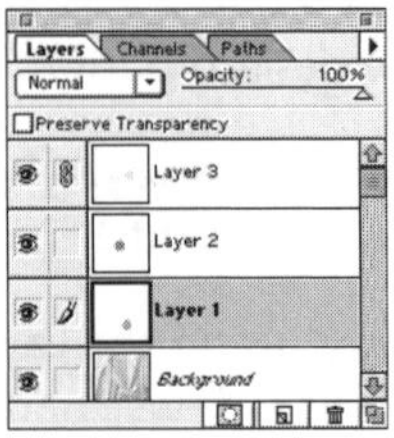

Figure 3-4
Layers palette
showing linked
Layers 1 and 3

7. Link Layer 2 so it moves with the other Layers. It is possible to link the entire image, including the Background Layer if you wish. Try it, but Undo the move immediately (Mac: ⌘+Z, Windows: CTRL+Z). Notice that as you link more Layers, performance suffers and it takes a little while for Photoshop to move everything.

8. Turn off all the links, but leave the image open.

Merging and Flattening Layers

Although you get the maximum in flexibility by leaving all your Layers active, there are times you want to make a single Layer image or make one Layer out of two or more Layers. You can *flatten* the image (using the Flatten command on the Layers palette menu). When you flatten an image, you take the image as it appears on the screen and place it into the background. This leaves a one-Layer image with only the background in it. Any Layers not visible (they do not have the Eye icon showing) when the image is flattened are discarded.

There are also two forms of the Merge command. You can *merge visible* Layers (the Merge Visible command is located on the Layers palette menu). This version of the Merge command takes all the visible Layers and creates either a new background or a Layer from them. If the Background Layer is visible, the remaining Layers are merged into the background. If the background is hidden, then the visible Layers are merged into the lowest Layer in the image. There is also a *Merge Down* command. This command takes the active Layer and merges it into the Layer (or background) beneath. The Merge Down command is excellent when you have just pasted something and want it to immediately join the Layer beneath.

Command Watch		
Here are some keystrokes for merging Layers:		
Action	**Mac Key**	**Windows Key**
Merge Down	⌘+E	CTRL+E
Merge Visible	SHIFT+⌘+E	SHIFT+CTRL+E

There is, unfortunately, no keyboard shortcut for Flatten Image.

What is the difference between a background and a Layer? *Background* is a special case of Layer. It has no transparency. It is always the lowest Layer in the image. It is also *the only Layer that applications other than Photoshop can read*. Page layout programs cannot use the transparency in Photoshop documents (at least, not yet). Therefore, images to be placed in page layout programs (QuarkXPress, Adobe PageMaker) must be flattened before they are exported, saved, or placed. If there is no Background Layer in an image, the Flatten command always creates one and gives it a background color of white.

You can add a background to an image that has none when clicking on the New Layer icon with the modifier key pressed (Mac: OPTION, Windows: ALT), so that a dialog box appears. The very last item on the Mode menu says Background—and the choice is italicized, showing that this is a special class of Layer. If you select Background as the mode for your Layer, you cannot choose an Opacity or a fill color. If your image already has a Background, the choice does not even appear on the Mode menu.

Just as you can create a background if none exists, you can also make a Layer from the background by double-clicking on the Layer name in the Layers palette. This automatically brings up the Make Layer dialog box. Though we will discuss the other options later, for now, all you need to know is that Photoshop automatically renames the background as Layer 0. Figure 3-5 shows this dialog box. Just press RETURN and your background is lifted to become a Layer.

A Layer also differs from the background in that a Layer *has* transparency, and you can set different Apply modes (also called Transfer modes, Layer modes, and Blending modes). These Apply modes control how the Layer interacts with the Layers beneath it (more on this topic in a moment). Let's continue our exploration using the image open from the last Hands On.

FLATTENING AND MERGING LAYERS

1. Move all three circles (on the three Layers) so they just begin overlapping one another.

2. Set the Opacity of Layer 2 to 70%.

3. Click on the Eye icon next to the background in the Layers palette to hide the background.

4. Merge the visible Layers (Mac: SHIFT+⌘+E, Windows: SHIFT+CTRL+E). Figure 3-6 shows the result.

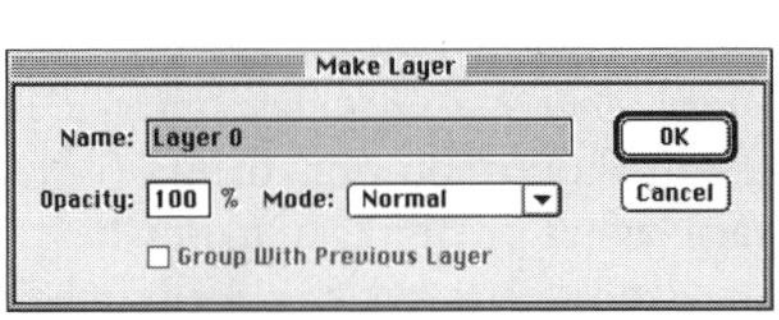

Figure 3-5
Make Layer dialog to create a Layer from the background

> **Make Layer**
>
> Name: `Layer 0`
> Opacity: `100` %   Mode: `Normal` ▾
> ☐ Group With Previous Layer
>
> [OK]
> [Cancel]

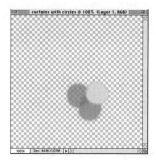

Figure 3-6
Curtains image
merged
(background
hidden)

5. Turn the Eye icon next to the background on again (click on the second column in the Layers palette).

6. Lift the background into a Layer (double-click on the *name* Background in the Layers palette and press RETURN in the dialog box). Figure 3-7 shows the Layers palette after the background is lifted.

7. Set the Opacity of Layer 0 to 80%. Notice that a checkerboard grid begins to show through. This checkerboard is how Photoshop shows transparency. In areas in which there is nothing under a Layer, Photoshop displays this checkerboard. You can change the size or display of this via the Preferences → Transparency&Gamut option in the File menu.

8. You can take a composite view of the image and create a new Layer from it. To do this, first create a new Layer. Then, press OPTION (Mac) or ALT (Windows) before you select the Merge the Visible Layers command from the Layers palette menu (or press Mac: SHIFT+⌘+OPTION+E, Windows: SHIFT+ALT+CTRL+E). Keep the modifier keys pressed until the command is executed. Figure 3-8 shows the Layers palette after the composite is taken.

 The composite view is placed on the active Layer, erasing whatever was there before. So make sure you create a new, empty Layer before doing this. Also, remember that you can drag the composite to the top of the Layer stack, or use it wherever you prefer.

Figure 3-7
Layers palette with
background lifted
into Layer 0

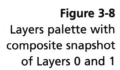

Figure 3-8
Layers palette with
composite snapshot
of Layers 0 and 1

9. Although the new composite Layer looks opaque, it is only 80% opaque even at 100% Opacity on the slider. Press the modifier key (Mac: OPTION, Windows: ALT) and click on the Eye icon next to Layer 2. This turns off all other Layers. You can see that there is transparency in the Layer. The Layer can never become more than 80% opaque because you took a snapshot of the total image with the Opacity of Layer 0 set to 80%. Press the modifier key and click again to show all the layers.

10. Why would you want to take a composite? There are many reasons, but here is one thing you can do now. Flip the Layer vertically (Layer → Transform → Flip Vertical). Set the Opacity to 60%. This adds a new look to the image (not very artistic in this example, but it uses the commands being taught at the moment!).

11. Now it is time to add a new background. Click on the New Layer icon. Scroll down the Mode menu to the very bottom and select Background. Figure 3-9 shows the menu.

12. To make the image a little more interesting, apply the Add Noise filter to the background (Filter → Noise → Add Noise, Gaussian, 600). Figure 3-10 shows the final image.

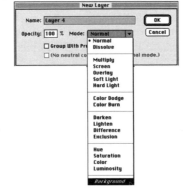

Figure 3-9
Mode menu for
New Layer: notice
the Background
option

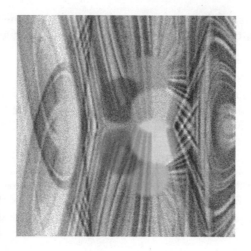

Figure 3-10
Finished Curtains
image

Drag-and-Drop

Photoshop allows you to drag-and-drop Layers and selections between various open images. Anything you drag from one image to another (a selection or a Layer) becomes a new Layer in the receiving image—regardless of the sizes of the two images. You can either drag the object itself from one image into the other or drag the Layer name from the Layers palette into the receiving image. Try this Hands On.

DRAG-AND-DROP

1. Open the images Glitter.Psd and Buttrfly.Psd. The butterfly shape is from the Ultimate Symbol Design Elements collection.

2. Select the Move tool (V) and click on the Butterfly image. Press the mouse button and drag the butterfly as if moving it to a new spot. Keep the mouse button pressed and drag the cursor into the Glitter image. As your cursor moves into the Glitter image, it changes to a hand and you'll see the rectangular outline of the Layer being dragged. When you have positioned the new Layer approximately where you want it, release the mouse button. The Layers palette shows you a new Layer.

3. Undo (Mac: ⌘+Z, Windows: CTRL+Z) so you can try this several different ways.

4. This time, drag the Layer from the Layers palette of the Butterfly image into the center of the Glitter image. The result is exactly the same as before. Undo (Mac: ⌘+Z, Windows: CTRL+Z).

5. Click on the Butterfly image again. Create a selection. You can do this by selecting the nontransparent pixels in the Layer—press the modifier key (Mac: ⌘, Windows: CTRL) and click on the Layer name to load the non-transparent pixels. Drag into the Glitter image. This also results in a new Layer. Undo. Figure 3-11 shows the butterfly selection inside the Glitter image.

6. To more precisely position the butterfly, try this trick with the modifier keys as described in the following Command Watch. Center the butterfly (SHIFT+drag on both platforms). *This is the only way to drag-and-drop between images of the same size so they fall into exact register—one on top of the other.*

7. Move the butterfly towards the upper-left corner of the image (remember, you must use the Move tool or press ⌘ [Mac], or CTRL [Windows]). Leave the image placed there for now. *Do not Undo.*

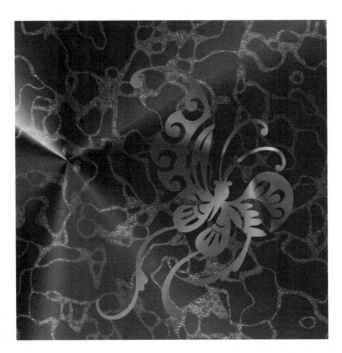

Figure 3-11
Floating butterfly
selection

Command Watch

You can control where a selection or Layer is placed when you drag-and-drop by pressing a modifier key as you drag the object:

Action	Mac Key	Windows Key
Place in center of receiving image	SHIFT+drag	SHIFT+drag

Duplicating a Layer

There are many times you could use two or more copies of a Layer. One major reason is to experiment on the copy without harming the original. Another reason is to set an Apply mode between the two copies to help color- or tone-correct the image. A third reason is to perform a variety of special effects, and a fourth reason is to create a drop shadow.

It is very easy to duplicate a Layer. All you need to do is drag the Layer name onto the New Layer icon. This automatically creates a new Layer with the same name as the original, but with *copy* added after it. Try this, using the Glitter and Butterfly images already open. You will also learn to create a drop shadow (one of several times you are asked to do this in the book).

DUPLICATING A LAYER AND CREATING A DROP SHADOW

1. The Glitter image has a butterfly in it (from the previous exercise). Drag the Butterfly Layer name (Layer 1) in the Layers palette to the New Layer icon at the bottom center of the palette. Layer 1 copy is now the top Layer in the palette.

2. Click the Preserve Transparency box just above the Layer name. This option does not permit any pixels to be created or erased in the Layer. The pixels can be changed, but those present in the image cannot be deleted, nor can new opaque pixels be made. This gives us a very easy way to change the color of an entire Layer object.

3. Select the Eyedropper tool and find a deep brown in the image. Make this your foreground color.

4. Fill the area (Mac: OPTION+DELETE, Windows: ALT+DELETE). Only the butterfly changes color. The background of the butterfly in unaffected.

5. Double-click on the name Layer 1 copy to bring up the Layers Options dialog. Change the Layer name to Shadow.

6. Click the Preserve Transparency box to turn *off* the option. Apply a Gaussian Blur filter (Filter → Blur → Gaussian Blur, Radius: 4).

7. Drag the Shadow Layer in the Layers palette so it is below the original butterfly.

8. With the Move tool (Ⓥ), drag the shadow to the right and a little above the location of the original butterfly so it looks good to you. There is no one correct location. Because the image is dark, the shadow is a bit more difficult to see.

9. This shadow is OK because of the color of the background. However, if you were doing this against a lighter background, you could set the Apply mode for the Shadow Layer to Multiply or Overlay, and you could lower the Opacity of the Layer.

10. The butterfly and shadow are a perfect example of why you might want to link Layers. Link the Butterfly and Shadow Layers and move the butterfly with its shadow to any desired spot in the image.

Exporting Layers

You can copy Layers between images or create new files from them using the Duplicate Layer command in the Layers palette menu. You can also copy them into new Layers in the current image. Figure 3-12 shows the Duplicate Layer dialog. As you can see, you can choose any open image or create a new file.

The only problem with the Duplicate Layer dialog is it only permits you to place one Layer into a new image. If you want to copy the entire image—or just pieces of it—you need to do it a different way. The easiest way to duplicate an entire image (Layers and all) is to use the Image → Duplicate command from the main menu. You have already used this dialog in a Hands On. Now, however, you understand what the Merged Layers Only box means. When checked, it flattens the image while duplicating it.

Figure 3-12
Duplicate Layer
dialog

If you want to copy more than one Layer but not the entire image, you can still use the Image → Duplicate command. This always copies the entire image, but you can then drag the Layers you do *not* want to the Layer Trash Can. You can also drag linked Layers between images, if you drag them from the image rather than from the Layers palette.

If you do not care about retaining all the Layers as they are copied, you can use the trick of getting a snapshot of all the Layers you want to move, then just use the Layers palette menu to duplicate the Layer into a new document. Then, delete the composite Layer from the *original* image.

Dragging more than one Layer

You can also drag-and-drop linked Layers between images. However, you need to have an image already opened to drag them into. If you don't want to copy all the Layers in an image when you only need some of them, you can create a new image and use the Window menu to make it the same size as the image you want to copy. Then, link all the layers you wish to move and drag them to the new image *from the original image* (not from the Layers palette).

DUPLICATING LAYERS

1. Turn off the Eye icon next to the background. Leave the Shadow and Butterfly Layers visible.

2. Make a new Layer (click on the New Layer icon at the bottom of the Layers palette).

3. Press OPTION (Mac) or ALT (Windows) and select Merge Visible from the Layers palette menu. This puts a new combined Layer in the empty, active Layer created in Step 2. This new Layer is selected.

4. Choose Duplicate Layer from the Layers palette menu, and send the Layer to New. Click OK.

5. Open the image RadGrad.Psd.

6. Click on the composite shadow image (Untitled 1). Duplicate the Layer again (Layers palette menu → Duplicate). Send the Layer to the document RadGrad.Psd.

7. Move the Shadow Layer anywhere you want in the image. Figure 3-13 shows the final image.

Figure 3-13
Butterfly and
Shadow
composited over
radial Gradient

Saving a Selection to a Layer

In Chapter 2, you learned how to save a selection to a channel. You can also save a selection to a new Layer. This is one of the most useful of all Layers features. There is a basic, fundamental difference between saving a selection to a Layer and saving one to a channel, however. Saving to a channel saves the *shape and Opacity* of the selection only; saving to a Layer saves the actual *shape data* itself.

Let's examine that last statement. If you select a circular area in an image and save it to a channel, the channel will be all black except for the white circle holding your selection. This is the Opacity data or selection data. The circle is white, meaning the image area inside it is fully selected. The background is black, meaning the image area inside it is not selected at all. The border of the area is likely to contain an anti-aliased region of gray. The pixels in that area are partially selected, and therefore, somewhat transparent. (More on this in a bit.)

When you save a selection to a Layer, however, you are actually saving the image itself—all the color or grayscale pixels comprising that image (remember, in the example above, the saved circular selection contained no indication of what it was in the picture you wanted saved). Channels can only hold grayscale data showing the location of the selection; Layers can hold the actual selected areas.

What Are Floating Selections?

In versions of Photoshop before 4.0, every time you moved a selected area or used the Float command to raise a selection from its background, you got a Floating selection. This was an entry in the Layers palette named *Floating Selection* and was a temporary Layer. Pasting an image or dragging a selection from one image to another also created Floating selections.

In Version 4.0, most operations now create Layers. A Layer is easier to use and cannot be accidentally dropped by clicking on it. You can still create Floating selections, but fewer commands cause them. You will get a Floating selection if

- You create a selection and move it with the Move tool.

- You copy a selected area by dragging with [OPTION] (Mac) or [ALT] (Windows) pressed.

- You make a selection and use one of the Transform commands (Layer → Transform or Layer → Free Transform) on it.

However, all other actions now create a Layer:

- Drag-and-drop with either Layers or selections

- Any use of the Paste or Paste Into commands

- Float command (Layer → New Layer via Copy or Layer → New Layer via Cut)

Do not go out of your way to create Floating selections. One action you should avoid is moving a selection on a Layer. If the Layer only contains the selection (the rest of the Layer is transparent), move the *Layer* to position the object—don't create a selection. *The best reason for loading the nontransparent pixels on a Layer as a selection is to use the selection Marquee in a channel or another layer.*

Saving a selection to a Layer is extremely easy. If you click on the New Layer icon while you have a Floating selection, the selection is placed on the new Layer and the marching ants disappear.

Saving the selection to a Layer is a way of having your cake and eating it too. It allows you to keep multiple selections so they cannot be accidentally deselected or locked in place. It is the reason for having Layers in the first place. Try this Hands On to see the difference between a channel and a Layer selection.

SAVING SELECTIONS

1. Open the image Weaving.Psd.

2. Select the Type tool ([T]) and click in the center of the image. In the dialog box, type the words **Weaving Age**. Press [RETURN] between the two words so Age starts on a new line. Set the Font to Times (boring, but everyone has it)

and the Style to Bold, Italics (also very poor typography but, once again, it is available to everyone reading this book). Set the Font Size to 70 with a Leading of 80. Click on the Alignment: Horizontal Center button. Figure 3-14 shows the Type dialog box correctly completed.

3. The type forms its own Layer. Use the Move tool to position it where you want it to go. Select the nontransparent Layer pixels (Mac: ⌘+click, Windows: CTRL+click on the Layer name in the Layers palette).

4. Drag the Type Layer to the Layers palette Trash Can. The selection outlines remain.

5. Save the selection to a channel (in the Channels palette, click on the Marching Ants icon—the second icon from the lower-left).

6. Deselect (Mac: ⌘+D, Windows: CTRL+D).

7. Look at the channel. You see white text and a black background. This is a map showing the location of your selection, with the white areas selected, the black ones unselected.

8. Drag the icon for Channel 4 to the Load Selection icon at the lower-left corner of the Channels palette (the first icon). You see the white areas in the channel inside the marching ants Marquee.

9. Switch back to the Layers palette. Float the selection (Mac: ⌘+J, Windows: CTRL+J) to make a new Layer.

10. Turn off the Eye icon next to the background in the Layers palette. Although you could not see Layer 1 with everything turned on, you can see it now. You have lifted the area of the image under the words Weaving Age and placed a copy of this text into Layer 1. Turn the Eye icon back on by clicking on it.

11. Since the image data was placed in its own Layer to form text, it can be altered to stand out from the rest of the image. Open the Levels dialog

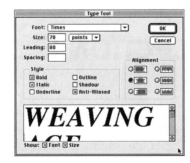

Figure 3-14
Type Tool dialog box for image heading

(Mac: ⌘+Ⓛ, Windows: CTRL+Ⓛ). Drag the Black Output slider to the right until the left Output Levels value reads 133. Click OK. Figure 3-15 shows this dialog. This action makes the image in Layer 1 light enough so it is visible against the background.

12. The image still needs a little more punch. Create a drop shadow for the lettering by duplicating Layer 1, filling the text area with black, and blurring it by 4 pixels with the Gaussian Blur filter. Use the Offset filter (Filter → Other → Offset, 5 pixels right, 5 pixels down) to move the shadow to the right and below the original. Follow the directions earlier in the chapter for making a drop shadow. Figure 3-16 shows the final result.

As you can see from the example, there is a large difference in what is saved between the channel and the Layer. It is very useful to save the selection to a Layer. Remember, you can recover the selection Marquee on any selection pasted or dragged into an image by ⌘+click Layer name (Mac) or CTRL+click Layer name (Windows). Once you have the selection Marquee, it is easy to save the selection to a channel for future use.

Layers, Channels, and Transparency

Channels can hold transparency information by storing values of gray so the selection can be only partially selected. Layers also contain transparency information. This transparency occurs either on the pixel or the Layer level. An entire Layer can be given a transparency level by dragging the Opacity slider on the Layers palette or by pressing

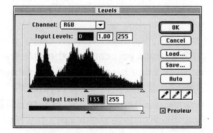

Figure 3-15
Levels dialog

Figure 3-16
Weaving Age
image completed

a number from 1 to 9 on the keyboard while one of the selection tools is active. You can spot a transparent Layer either by being able to see through it to the Layer below, or by seeing the checkerboard pattern through it.

Individual pixels can also be given transparency in a Layer. If you feather a selection, as you did in Chapter 2, then float the selection and turn it into a new Layer, the edges are transparent. If you load a selection from a channel with gray values in it and work with that on a Layer, the pixels that were not solid black or white in the channel have transparency in the Layer. White pixels in a channel produce pixels 100% opaque in a Layer. Black pixels in a channel produce pixels 100% transparent in a Layer. *The darker the pixel in a channel, the more transparent it is when used as a loaded selection in an image.* This may be difficult to visualize, but it is one of the main keys to unlocking the power of Layers and channels. You will have a chance to try several experiments with this in the Lab in Appendix C, "Labs," but for now, try this Hands On to get a practical idea of how channel value affects transparency in a Layer.

LOADING SELECTIONS INTO LAYERS

1. Open the image Blustrata.Psd. This image contains three alpha channels: an aliased circle, an anti-aliased circle, and a heavily feathered circle.

2. Open the Channels palette (Window → Show Channels). Click on Channel 4—Aliased Edge. Zoom in until you can see the pixels along the edge. Figure 3-17(a) shows these edge pixels, which are either solid black or white. Zoom into Channels 5 and 6 as well. Figure 3-17(b) shows the anti-aliased edges of the circle in Channel 5, and Figure 3-17(c) shows the soft, feathered edge in Channel 6. These shades of gray result in different levels of transparency when applied to a Layer.

3. Return to the composite RGB channel (Mac: ⌘ ~, Windows: CTRL ~). Open the Layers palette.

4. Make a new Layer (click on the New Layer icon at the bottom of the Layers palette). Load Channel 4 (Mac: ⌘+OPTION+4, Windows: ALT+CTRL+4).

5. Set your foreground color to a lurid magenta (RGB: 255, 0, 255). This stands out against the background.

6. Fill the area (Mac: OPTION+DELETE, Windows: ALT+DELETE). Deselect (Mac: ⌘+D, Windows: CTRL+D). If you zoom into the edges of the circle, you will see the aliased channel has produced a selection with totally opaque color at the edges and suffers from the same jaggies as that channel.

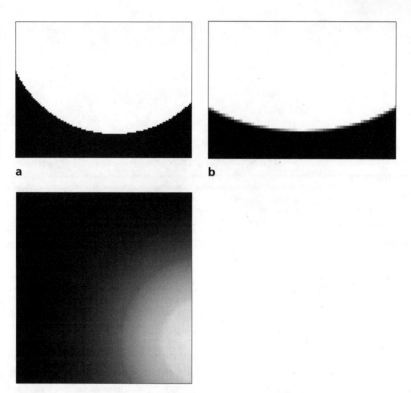

a   b

c

7. Make a new Layer (click on the New Layer icon at the bottom of the Layers palette). Load Channel 5 (Mac: ⌘+OPTION+5, Windows: ALT+CTRL+5). Fill the area (Mac: OPTION+DELETE, Windows: ALT+DELETE). Deselect (Mac: ⌘+D, Windows: CTRL+D). Zoom in on the edges. As you would expect, they are anti-aliased. Select the Move tool (V). The edges are not only anti-aliased; they contain levels of transparency that form the anti-aliasing. Drag the circle several pixels in each direction and notice how the edge pixels adjust to any color they are placed over.

8. Click on the Eye icon next to the background in the Layers palette to turn it off. Notice that the edges of the circle now show up over the checkerboard. The circle itself is opaque—you cannot see through it. However, the edges do allow you to see through in several steps from opaque to fully transparent, and those steps are identical to the lightness of the pixels in the channel producing this object. Turn on the Background again. Figure 3-18 shows a comparison of the two circles with the background turned off.

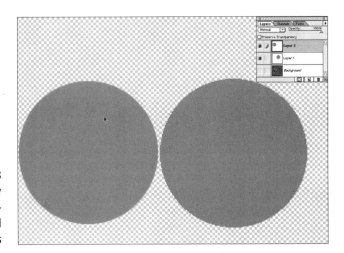

Figure 3-18
Layer transparency
from the anti-
aliased (left) and
aliased circles

9. Double-click on the Magnifier to get back to 1:1 Zoom.

10. Select a bright green for your foreground color (to find a contrasting color so you can see the results better).

11. Make a new Layer (click on the New Layer icon at the bottom of the Layers palette). Load Channel 6 (Mac: ⌘+OPTION+6, Windows: ALT+CTRL+6). Fill the area (Mac: OPTION+DELETE, Windows: ALT+DELETE). Notice how far outside the selection Marquee the new color actually extends. Deselect (Mac: ⌘+D, Windows: CTRL+D). Hide the background (click on the Eye icon to the left in the Layers palette) and notice the much larger area of transparency in the Layer, compared with the other circles. Turn the background back on. Use the Move tool to drag the Layer to see how the edge's color changes as it moves over different colors (including the pink of the other two circles).

If you have had any trouble understanding the relationship between the channel selection and the Layer transparency it creates, redo this exercise and keep at it. You should not move on until you understand the way channel values and Layer transparency relate to one another. You will never be able to use Photoshop to its full potential until you master this concept.

Load Transparency and Preserve Transparency

You have used the Preserve Transparency button to help create a drop shadow. This control enables you to force all pixels to remain at their current level of transparency, regardless of any editing or painting actions you take. When Preserve Transparency is on, you can change the color or value of the pixel, but you cannot alter its degree of seethrough-ness. When you work in the Background Layer and use the Eraser tool or delete an area, it is replaced by whatever color you select as your background color. With Preserve Transparency off (the default condition), if you work in a Layer, Erase or Delete replaces the pixels with totally transparent areas. If, however, Preserve Transparency is on, Erase or Delete uses the background swatch color just as it did when working in the Background Layer.

You can also use the transparency value of a Layer to create a selection. This is the Load Transparency command and is accessible either from the Select → Load Selection menu item or by clicking the Layer name in the Layers palette with ⌘ (Mac) or CTRL (Windows) pressed. Figure 3-19 shows an example of loading the transparency of a Layer as a selection from the menu. There are some interesting differences between the Preserve Transparency and the Load Transparency options, as well as what happens when you combine the two features. These will be practiced during the Lab in Appendix C.

QUIZ 1

1. What are some of the benefits of using Layers?
   a. Background images need only be created once.
   b. It's easier to make edits/changes to an image.
   c. It takes up very little system memory (RAM).
   d. You can make the Layers interact with each other.

2. Layers are very easy to create. What are some of the ways you can create a new Layer?
   a. Click on the Create New Layer tool button in the Toolbox.
   b. Select the New Layer command from Layers menu.
   c. Click the New Layer button on the Layers palette.
   d. Float a selection from another layer (Mac: ⌘+J or Windows: CTRL+J).

3. What are the two ways you can combine Layers into one Layer?
   a. Use the Collapse Layers command.
   b. Use the Merge Layers command.
   c. Use the Combine Layers command.
   d. Use the Flattening Layers command.

Figure 3-19
Load Selection dialog using the transparency of the Layer

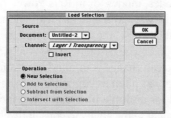

4. What are some of the things you can do with Layers?
    a. Drag-and-drop Layers from one image to another.
    b. Duplicate Layers.
    c. Change the transparency of Layers.
    d. Drag-and-drop images from other graphic applications.

5. How is saving a selection to a Layer different from saving a selection to a channel?
    a. Saving to a channel saves the actual selected area/image. Saving to a Layer saves only the grayscale shape and location.
    b. Saving to a Layer saves the actual selected area/image. Saving to a channel saves only the grayscale shape and location.
    c. Saving to a Layer saves just the background. Saving to a channel saves just the object.
    d. Saving to a channel saves just the background. Saving to a Layer saves just the object and its location.

APPLY MODES

In the old days of Photoshop—Version 2.5 and earlier—the only way to make images interact with one another using anything but Opacity was to use channels or channel commands through a variety of calculations. One of those calculations is *Difference*—the method you will use in the Lab Appendix to check that your answers match the book's answers. Difference is one of the many Apply modes Photoshop permits. These Apply modes use a variety of arithmetic calculations to determine how one image looks when placed on another (or how pixels look after they are altered with a painting tool, as you saw in Chapter 1). The Apply modes used for painting and Layer interaction are mostly the same.

Why Use Apply Modes?

Layer Apply modes are valuable because they let you select how you want one image to blend into another. That is why you also hear them referred to as Blend modes (they can also be called Transfer modes, modes, or in Kai's Power Tools Version 3+–Glue). They can dramatically change the way Layers interact with one another. When you combine the Apply mode with the ability to set the Opacity of the Layer, you get very powerful control over how your image looks. The best part of the Apply modes is also one of the advantages of using Layers: You can change your mind again and again. You can change Apply modes and Layer Opacity as often as you wish, and the activity is nondestructive. Artists have long wished for multiple undos in Photoshop. While this does not exist, you get almost the equivalent in the ability to constantly change the Apply modes.

Selecting Apply Modes

Select the Apply mode you want with the pop-down menu in the Layers palette. It is to the left of the Opacity slider. The default Apply mode is Normal. Normal mode works as if the Layer is the only thing in the image. Anything in the Layer that's 100% opaque covers up the Layers beneath. Figure 3-20 shows the Layers palette with the Apply mode menu open.

Review of Color Arithmetic

The Layers palette contains the same Apply mode choices as the Painting tools options. They are

- Normal
- Dissolve
- Multiply
- Screen
- Overlay
- Soft Light
- Hard Light
- Color Dodge
- Color Burn
- Darken
- Lighten
- Difference
- Exclusion
- Hue
- Saturation
- Color
- Luminosity

Work though the following Hands On to see how much of a difference changing the Apply mode can make.

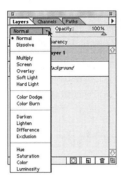

Figure 3-20
Layers palette
Apply mode
options

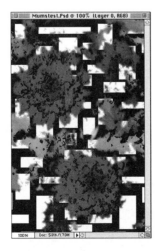

(Hands On logo)

APPLY MODES

1. Open the image Mumstest.Psd. Figure 3-21 shows the original image. Notice there are two hidden Layers (the Eye icon is turned off in the Layers palette). Leave it that way for now.

2. Cycle through the Apply modes for the top Layer and look at each in turn.

   Normal mode is the image as it appears when you first open it.

   In order to see much of the Dissolve mode effect, you need to lessen the Opacity. As you reduce the Opacity, the top image breaks up. Figure 3-22(a) shows this effect at 90% Opacity.

Figure 3-21
Original
Mumstest.Psd
image in Normal
mode

Turn the Opacity back to 100% (press the Ⓞ key). Multiply mode allows only the flower areas over the white squares to show up. This is because anything multiplied with black yields black, and anything multiplied with white keeps its original colors. (All other combinations get darker.) Figure 3-22(b) shows the mums in Multiply mode.

Screen mode is the opposite of Multiply; only the areas over black show up (see Figure 3-22(c)).

Both the Overlay and Hard Light modes look the same in this example. They each show only the bottom black and white Layer. This is why: Overlay mode does not affect either the white or black pixels in the underlying image. Since the underlying image only *has* white or black pixels in it, nothing placed over the image is visible using Overlay. Soft light does not work for the same reason. Soft light typically gives the effect of back-lighting, and also does not change the white or black pixels.

Hard Light shows a difference, however. Hard Light mode makes objects look as if a strong light is shining through them. You can see the underlying Layer, but it is almost as if there is a transparent glow in front of the image. Figure 3-22(d) shows this effect.

Color Dodge and Color Burn show nothing in this example, since they don't work over solid black or white.

Because you are using the Apply mode to place an image over a black and white area, Darken gives results identical to Multiply, and Lighten is the same as Screen. If different colored backgrounds are used, this is not the case.

Difference mode does not make a difference to anything overlaying the black areas in the Background Layer. It inverts the color over the white areas. Numerically, black is 0. Any number subtracted from 0 produces its negative. Difference mode looks at the absolute value of the number (the number itself—without the + or − in it). Therefore, any color that is *differenced* with black will stay the same. White is 255. This is the maximum value a color can have. When you subtract any number from 255, the result leaves a color number as far away from the original as possible—which is its *complement*. Figure 3-22(e) shows this Apply mode. Difference mode can be very attractive. However, this image in Difference mode is not.

Exclusion mode usually gives a less sharp change of colors than Difference mode. However, it treats black and white the same way Difference does, so there is no difference between Difference and Exclusion here.

Hue, Saturation, and Color modes are also unsatisfying with this image. None of these produce any changes. Black and white have no ability to change color because they are completely desaturated. Any hue they possess does not show up because they have no saturation. Plus, they cannot reflect the changes in saturation because they have no hue.

Luminosity mode looks similar in Figure 3-22(f) to Normal mode, but that is because the figure is in grayscale in this book. Normal mode has color; Luminosity mode for this image produces a grayscale as the values of the flower are used to change the values of the areas behind them. Since the underlying Layer is black and white, Luminosity mode changes the values (in black and white) of the underlying Layer to conform to their color equivalents in the Layer above.

3. Turn off the bottom Layer and turn on the Gray Levels Layer. Repeat Step 2 to cycle through the Apply modes. Notice these significant changes once the background is no longer black and white:

Multiply and Screen modes each show results of both Layers: Screen mode does not filter out everything white, and Multiply mode no longer turns anything multiplied with the darkest color to black. This is because the values in the underlying image are not stark black and white.

Overlay and Soft Light modes make a real difference with this new background. Overlay looks like you placed a filter or gel made from the top image over the bottom image. Soft Light looks like you took a flashlight and made it shine through the two Layers from the bottom. The colors produced by Hard Light mode are much more intense than those produced by Overlay mode.

Figure 3-22
Mumstest.Psd
image in
a) Dissolve mode at
90% Opacity
b) Multiply mode
c) Screen mode
d) Hard Light mode
e) Difference mode
f) Luminosity mode

a   b

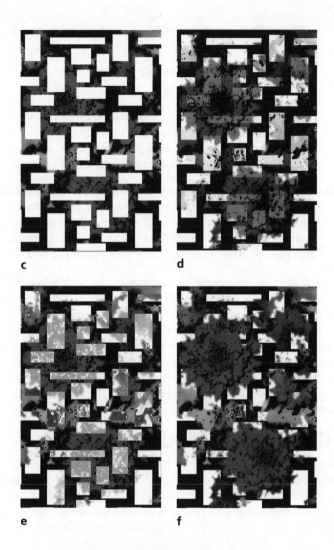

c d

e f

Color Dodge and Color Burn both create changes. Color Dodge *brightens* the bottom image based on the lighter colors. Color Burn *darkens* the base image with the darker values.

Darken and Lighten modes are not the same as Multiply and Screen. Darken does not get as dark as Multiply, and Lighten does not get as light as Screen. This is because the Darken and Lighten modes use the actual values in the calculations (see Chapter 1 to refresh your memory on the math behind the Apply modes if you do not remember).

Difference mode is much more interesting, and the colors vary widely from the originals.

Exclusion mode is very different from Difference, and not nearly as attractive in this instance.

Hue and Saturation modes still make no difference, since you cannot change the hue of a pixel with no saturation, nor can you change the saturation of an already gray pixel. However, Color mode, which changes *both* hue and saturation, works, as does Luminosity mode.

4. As a final test, turn off the bottom two Layers and turn on the Color Levels Layer. Notice the changes that using color brings. There, color interactions become much more complex in almost every mode. Each Apply mode changes the results. The Difference and Hard Light modes are very interesting. The results of Hue and Color modes are subtle and often pleasing.

The color moves possible using Apply modes are practical by no method other than color calculations or color arithmetic. It is almost impossible to paint an image by hand duplicating the results of Difference or Hard Light modes. Artistically, the color changes work (when they do) because they keep images in set numerical relations with one another. Music and mathematics were once taught together as if they were part of the same discipline. There is also a mathematical underpinning in much of what humans find appealing artistically (the Fibonacci progression in math has long been used by fabric designers to design pleasing stripes). The Apply modes work under the same principle.

Filling with Neutral Color

When you create a new Layer, Photoshop adds a totally blank sheet of acetate to your image. It is completely transparent. If you are going to paint on the Layer, this is not a problem. However, if you wish to apply a filter to a Layer, this can be a major problem. There is only one filter that works on a totally transparent Layer: the Clouds filter (Filter → Render → Clouds). Every other filter needs something to work on, in order to produce results. Therefore, Photoshop has provided an easy way to prefill a Layer with something. This something is a color considered neutral by whichever Apply mode you select.

For example, you know that any color, when multiplied with white, yields the original color. Therefore, white is a neutral color for Multiply mode, as well as for Darken mode. As expected, then, black is a neutral color for Screen mode. It is also the neutral color for Lighten and Difference modes. Hard Light, Soft Light, and Overlay modes use 50% black as neutral colors.

To select a neutral color, you simply check the box labeled Fill with Neutral color in the New Layer dialog. If no neutral color is available for the Apply mode, the box is grayed out since Normal mode does not have a neutral color option. You will get a chance to practice with this in the Lab Appendix.

Layer Blend If Options

Layer Blend If options are a bit more esoteric than the features you have met before, but they are very useful when you need them. So far, when you have worked with Layers, you have either set an Apply mode to control how you see the underlying Layer, or you have changed the Opacity of the entire Layer. There is a third way to control how your image reacts to the Layer beneath it: the Blend If dialog.

Blend If was known as Composite Controls in Photoshop versions before 3.0. Its purpose is to selectively enable you to drop out areas of your image based on the values of either the top image or the underlying image. The Blend If sliders are located in the Layer Options dialog you get to if you double-click on a Layer name in the Layers palette. Figure 3-23 shows this dialog. Notice that the Layer Options dialog allows you to change the Layer name, Apply mode, and Opacity as well as the Blending options.

There are three parts to the Blend If dialog. The first part—the small pull-down menu next to the words "Blend If"—selects the Blending channels. The default is gray. The options on this menu change depending on the color space in which you are working. Since we are working with RGB images right now, that is the color space discussed. Gray is your composite RGB channel—what you look at when you view your image in full color. The Blend If dialog allows you to isolate values (or gray levels) within your image. The other menu choices in RGB mode are red, green, or blue. If one of these channels is selected, the image in the specific channel could be added to or removed from the final composite.

The second and third parts of the Blend If controls are the sliders. The top slider is the This Layer slider; the bottom slider is for the Underlying image. The sliders allow you to isolate parts of the image to protect. This is one of those features that is much easier to demonstrate than describe. So work through this Hands On to quickly see how useful these sliders are.

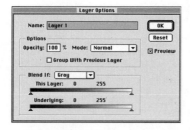

Figure 3-23
Blend If dialog

>

BLEND IF OPTIONS

1. Open the image Maya.Psd. Make sure you have the Layers palette open, too. Notice that there are two Layers, but that the top Layer—the one containing Maya's picture—is set to Normal mode and therefore hides the Layer beneath. Your task is to get the image of Maya to sit on top of the background image and to preserve as much hair detail as possible (this is a preview of material to be covered in Chapter 9, "Advanced Selection Techniques").

2. Let's first experiment with the sliders before doing anything really useful. Drag the left This Layer slider slowly toward the right, pausing for the screen to redraw as you drag. Figure 3-24 shows what the image looks like at a dropout black value of 64. Not pretty! Notice that the image of Maya has started breaking up, and the darkest values in the top Layer are replaced with the background image below.

3. Press the modifier key (Mac: OPTION, Windows: ALT). The Cancel button turns into a Reset button. Keep the modifier key pressed and click Reset. Drag the right This Layer slider slowly to the left. This drops out the background of the top Layer, leaving the figure of Maya sitting on top of the texture beneath. This is the beginning of a very useful effect, and you will return to it.

4. Reset the image again. Drag the left Underlying Layer toward the right slowly. The image begins to break up in a totally different manner. This

Figure 3-24
Maya with only
values lighter than
64 showing

time, as you can see in Figure 3-25, the darkest values from the texture below begin to poke through the image of Maya on top.

5. Reset the image. Drag the right Underlying slider toward the left until the values above the slider read 0 and 59. Look at Figure 3-26. The lightest texture values now show through the top image. Notice that the texture pixels look jaggy as they start to eat away at the top Layer. This is because the slider settings are telling Photoshop to display only the pixels in the top Layer that are located on top of pixels less than or equal to a value of 59 in the underlying Layer. Confusing? Think of it this way. Have you ever drawn a design on paper using glue, then dumped glitter over it? The glitter only sticks to the areas with glue on them, which is how your design shows up. The inverse of this same principle is at work here. The Underlying Layer slider provides the glue. In this case, it says that only pixels between the values of 0 and 59 are sticky. The top Layer's image can only show up where it falls on sticky pixels. Therefore, the darkest values in the background texture are covered by the foreground image—leaving the rest of the image filled with the light stuff from the background texture. Since the selection criteria stops abruptly at value 59, there is a sharp break—and jaggy pixels—in the image.

6. You can soften this jaggy look. Examine Figure 3-27 very carefully. The cursor arrow is positioned just under the right Underlying slider triangle. Notice that this triangle seems to have split apart in the middle slightly (see how the other triangles show a line through their center but are whole). This splitting triangle allows you to feather the edges of the selection so you get a soft blending of the Layers rather than a harsh, jagged blend.

Figure 3-25
Maya appearing over the lightest areas in the underlying image

Figure 3-26
Maya jaggedly
appearing over the
darkest areas in the
underlying image

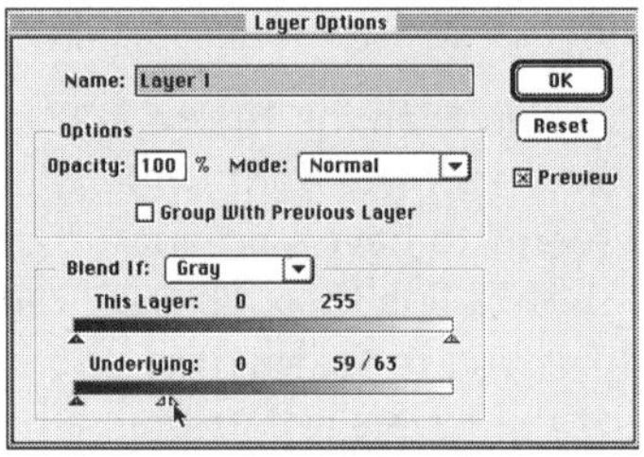

Figure 3-27
Blend If dialog
showing right slider
triangle starting to
separate

Press the modifier key (Mac: OPTION, Windows: ALT) and drag the right side of the right Underlying slider to the right edge. The lightest areas of the underlying image now show up totally feathered into the top image.

This is a good time to stop for a minute and summarize the purpose of each slider.

● The This Layer slider keeps top image data that falls between the light and dark settings on the slider.

● The Underlying slider allows top image data to stick only to the pixels within its range.

● The slider triangles can be split to softly feather the selected range of values.

So far, in this example, you only played with the image. Let's look at it again to see how the Blend If options can perform a useful task.

1. Reset the dialog again (Mac: OPTION, Windows: ALT).

2. Magnify the image so it is at 2:1 ratio (Mac: ⌘+click in the image, Windows: CTRL+click in the image). Notice that your default cursor over the image is the Hand tool (if you have no key pressed). Move the image using this Hand tool so you can clearly see the left side of Maya's hair and the left edge of her shawl.

3. As you drag the right This Layer slider to the left, the light background around Maya begins to fall away. Continue to drag the slider to the left until you can no longer see light pixels around the shawl (approximately value 0 to 64). Notice that you have lost a lot of hair detail at this point (as well as whole chunks in the center of Maya's image). This is the point at which you need to start feathering the selection.

4. Press the modifier key (Mac: OPTION, Windows: ALT) and drag the right portion of the right triangle all the way to the right. The image gets a film over it.

5. Drag the right portion of the right slider to the left (as long as the triangle is split, you do not need to press a modifier key when you drag). The film begins to dissipate. You are looking for the best mix of detail and dropout. You need to find the position of the sliders at which you keep as much hair detail as possible and as little of the light background film as possible. There are many settings that are probably acceptable within this mix. Accept the settings at 0–38÷120. They are a good balance between hair detail and light background. Unfortunately, a good part of Maya is missing as well. That can be remedied, however.

6. Open the image Maya2.Psd. This image is the inside portion of Maya. It has been prepared in advance for you, but you can duplicate it by using the Lasso tool and selecting only the inner areas of the image—the areas you want to remain totally opaque in the final composite.

7. Select the Move tool (V) and drag the trimmed image of Maya on top of the Maya.Psd image. This action restores the areas that should be opaque and leaves the soft edges alone.

You can selectively remove red, green, or blue from the composite image by choosing the areas in the slider associated with those channels. If you remove all pixels from the image containing a value of 255 in the Red channel, the entire pixel is removed—not just the red portion of it (if, for example, the pixel is 255 red and 30 green, the entire pixel disappears, not just the 255 red portion).

The Blend If options allow you very fine control over what appears in the final composite. One of the definite advantages of using the Blend If dialog is that you can change your mind any time. You never destroy the image data itself, and it is always available to you if you need to make modifications.

QUIZ 2

1. What's another name for Apply modes?
   a. Layer modes
   b. Blend modes
   c. Transparency modes
   d. Opacity modes

2. What are some of the Apply modes you can use?
   a. Soft Light
   b. Darken
   c. Opacity
   d. Overlay

3. In order to apply a filter to a new Layer, what must you first do?
   a. Create an object on the Layer.
   b. Prefill the Layer with black.
   c. Nothing, you can apply a filter right away.
   d. Prefill the Layer with a neutral color.

4. What does the Blend If command allow you to do?
   a. Selectively hide parts of your image based on the value of the top image.
   b. Selectively hide parts of your image based on the background color.
   c. Blend all the Layers together based on the value you choose in the Blend If dialog box.
   d. Blend selective Layers together based on the value you choose in the Blend If dialog box.

5. What does the Underlying slider do in the Blend If dialog box?
   a. Keeps the top image data that falls within the slider range.
   b. Allows the top image data to stick only to the pixels within the slider range.
   c. Keeps the background image data that falls within the slider range.
   d. Allows the top image data to stick only to the pixels outside the slider range.

LESSON 3

CHANNELS AND MASKING OPERATIONS

In Chapter 1, you learned about color channels. In Chapter 2, you learned to create selections and save them to *Alpha channels*—special channels added by the user to hold selection information. Earlier in this chapter, you learned how gray values in channels result in levels of transparency in image Layers. Now it is time to do a bit more work with channels. You need to understand how channels and channel math work in order to expand your understanding of Layers. One of the most powerful of the Layer features—Layer Masks—has not yet been introduced. In order to understand Layer Masks, you have to understand channels.

In the old days—before Photoshop 3—almost all image compositing was done in channels. You could cut and paste between images, but you could not set Apply modes. The only way to Multiply two images together was to use Channel Operations (or CHOPs). Photoshop—especially since the addition of Layers—gives you multiple ways to perform almost any task. Many of the things that had to be done in Channel Operations can now be done using Layers. Applying drop shadows is one of the most basic and common activities that used to require Channel Operations. There are still some things that require Channel Operations, but much less than there were. Channel Operations give you most of the Apply modes you already met, plus Add and Subtract, which are not available in Layers. The Hue, Saturation, Color, and Luminosity modes are only accessible as Layer Apply modes.

There are two commands available for Channel Operations. They are the Apply Image command and the Calculations command. After they are introduced, you will learn about their differences and similarities. Both commands, however, work *only on images with exactly the same pixel count in height and width.*

Apply Image

The Apply Image command (found in the Image menu) enables you to place one image on top of the other. In the process, you can set an Apply mode and Opacity, and you can specify a mask. If you have a selection active in the current image, the Apply Image command only affects the selected area. You can think of the command as performing a New Layer and a Merge Layer command in one step. The advantages are

⬤ The Apply Image command works on channels as well as Layers or flat images

⬤ The Apply Image command allows you to confine the command to a selected area

The Apply Image command is very powerful and gives you a great deal of control. It looks more complex than it is. Figure 3-28 shows the dialog. The dialog is organized into two areas: the Source information and the Blending information. Let's look more closely at each section.

The Source information identifies the image being applied to your current image (or Layer, if you are in one). It allows you to specify the source file to use (Source), the Layer within the file (Layer), and the channel within the Layer (Channel). The Source menu picks up all open documents of the same size. An image can be composited with itself as well as with another image. You can even invert your source image if you wish.

The Blending information allows you to specify the Apply mode (Blending), the Opacity (Opacity), and an Alpha channel or image to use as a mask (Mask...). The Target—where you will place the results of the Apply Image command—is *always your current image Layer or channel* (unless you press OPTION [Mac] or ALT [Windows] as you select the command; then you can specify a different target).

Try this Hands On.

APPLY IMAGE

1. Open the images Life.Psd, Beach.Psd, Lifeboss.Psd, and Surf.Psd.

2. Make Life.Psd your current image. It looks like it is blank, but there is a hidden Layer above the background. Leave it hidden for now. The Background Layer is the one that should be selected.

3. Transfer the Surf.Psd image to the Background Layer of Life.Psd by selecting the Apply Image command (Image → Apply Image). In the Source area, select Surf.Psd. Since that image has only one Layer, you have no other options. Leave the channel set to RGB (these are the settings in Figure 3-28). In the Blending area, select the Normal Apply mode at 100% Opacity with no mask. Check the Preview box to turn it on. The Surf image appears inside the blank Background Layer. Click OK.

4. Select the Apply Image command again. This time, apply the Lifeboss.Psd image to the same background using Overlay mode at 100% Opacity. Figure 3-29(a) shows the result. If you look at the Lifeboss.Psd image, you see that it is neutral gray except for what looks like embossed text. If you remember the earlier example with Neutral colors and Apply modes, this gray is neutral and not seen by the Overlay mode. Therefore, it drops out when applied, as if it were not there. Only the embossed edges affect the composite.

5. You can also apply an image to a Layer so it only sticks on the image area of the Layer. This requires using the Preserve Transparency option on the Apply Image dialog. Click on the Eye icon in the Layers palette next to Layer 1 in the Life.Psd image. Black text—matching the embossing— appears in the Layer.

Figure 3-28
Apply Image dialog

6. Select the Apply Image command. Choose Beach.Psd as the Source image (RGB channel). Set the Blending mode to Normal at 100%. Make sure Preserve Transparency is checked. There is no mask. Figure 3-29(b) shows the result. Since the embossing in the image below was done from the same mask, everything fits exactly into place.

You can also use the text as a mask for the image. Since the text is in a Layer, you need to use the Layer transparency itself as your mask. Try this Hands On.

APPLY IMAGE AND MASKING

1. Make the Surf.Psd image your active image.

2. Select the Apply Image command.

3. Choose Beach.Psd as the Source image (RGB channel). Set the Apply mode to Multiply at 100% Opacity. Select Mask.... In the new dialog, select Life.Psd as the mask, Layer 1 as the Layer, and Transparency as the channel. Figure 3-29(c) shows the result, and Figure 3-30 shows the dialog.

The Apply Image command is used throughout this book. It is a very handy command to become accustomed to using.

Command Watch

The Apply Image command always uses the current Layer as the destination for the composite results. However, by pressing the correct modifier key as you select the command from the menu or your Commands palette, you can select the destination of your choice.

Action	Mac key	Windows key
Choose target for result of Apply Image command.	OPTION	ALT
Create smaller dialog box on Calculations command	OPTION	ALT

a

b

Figure 3-29
a) Embossing added to image composite
b) Beach image added to composite
on top Layer
c) Beach image composited onto Surf
image through text mask

c

Figure 3-30
Apply Image dialog
showing mask
information

Calculations Command

The Calculations command is very similar to the Apply Image command. However, it has *no* ability to use the color composite channel of an image in its calculations. Therefore, the Calculations command is best used when you are blending only channels. The sole thing Calculations can do that Apply Image cannot is manipulate the composite color channel image as a grayscale image. Other than that (which you do not need very often), you can use the Apply Image command for everything.

The Calculations dialog looks more complex than Apply Image. This is only because Calculations does not require you to have the active image as one of your sources. Therefore, the Calculations dialog contains a Source 1 and Source 2, a Blending, and a Result section. The dialog is so large, it typically obscures most monitors (but you can press a modifier key [Mac: OPTION, Windows: ALT] to shrink it onscreen).

The example we used for the Apply Image command cannot be used with Calculations because we worked with the RGB channel in color. This time, you will use an image in the CMYK color space as an example. You will use Calculations to make the gold in the image brighter.

CALCULATIONS COMMAND

1. Open the image Dragon.Psd.

2. Select the Calculations command (Image → Calculations).

3. Set both sources to the Yellow channel. Set the Apply mode to Multiply at 100% Opacity, and set the Result to overwrite the Yellow channel. Figure 3-31 shows this dialog box correctly completed.

4. Click on the CMYK composite channel to view the image in color again. You'll see the gold has become much more yellow.

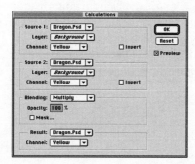

Figure 3-31
Calculations dialog

This is an effect you could not achieve with Layers. The Layers feature does not allow you to work on a specific channel within a Layer simply by dragging and dropping. You must work within either the Apply Image or the Calculations command in order to change the values in a color channel like this. The main disadvantage is that you cannot preview the results of your manipulation of the Yellow channel in color by either the Calculations or the Apply Image command.

The Result section allows you to choose a New or Current channel and a New, Current, or Open image as the place to put the composite. You can also load a composite as a selection.

Both the Apply Image and the Calculations commands can get complex very quickly. They give you a lot of options, such as inverting the image sources or masks. There is no need to make this any more complex than it already is, so it is time to move on. You will use the Apply Image command enough throughout these chapters that you will soon grow comfortable with it.

1. What are the two commands available for channel operations?
   a. Apply Channel
   b. Calculations
   c. Image Calculations
   d. Apply Image

2. What does the Apply Image command allow you to do?
   a. Place one image on top of the other.
   b. Specify a mask.
   c. Work on channels and Layers.
   d. Set the Apply mode and Opacity.

3. In the Apply Image dialog box, the Source information area specifies what?
   a. The Apply mode being applied to your current image.
   b. The image being applied to your stored image.
   c. The channel being applied to your current image.
   d. The image being applied to your current image.

4. In the Apply Image dialog box, the Blending information area specifies what?
   a. The Apply mode and Opacity being applied to your image.
   b. The Apply mode being applied to a stored mask.
   c. The Alpha channel or image to use as a mask.
   d. The image being applied to your current image.

5. How is the Calculations command different from the Apply Image command?
   a. The Calculations command only uses the color channel values of an image in its calculations.
   b. The Calculations command cannot manipulate color channel values, while the Apply Image command can.
   c. The Calculations command cannot use the color composite channel of an image in its calculations.
   d. With the Apply Image command, the image you want to affect must be active. With the Calculations command, it does not have to be active.

LAYER MASKS

One of the main goals when you build an image is to be able to change it as easily as possible. If you keep making changes that lose image detail, however, the image becomes locked in and very hard to change. Layer Masks provide another means of keeping an image fluid. A Layer Mask is an Alpha (or selection) channel associated with a specific Layer in an image. It works like a rubylith or stencil to hide or show areas of the masked Layer. It works exactly like a channel selection does: White areas in the Layer Mask show the image on top. Black areas in a Layer Mask hide the top Layer from view.

You add a Layer Mask to an image via the top Layers menu item, Add Layer Mask. When you create the Layer Mask in this manner, you can either choose Reveal All, which makes the Layer Mask white, or Hide All, which makes the Layer Mask black and hides everything on the Layer. The default is Reveal All. You can also create a Layer Mask by clicking on the Add Layer Mask icon (the circle inside the square), the first icon at the bottom of the Layers palette.

Command Watch: Working with Layer Masks

There are a number of key commands used when working with Layer Masks and Layers to hide and show them:

Action	Key
Show/hide Layer	Click on Eye icon
Show/hide multiple Layers	Drag mouse through row of Eye icons

Action	Mac key	Windows key
Show one Layer/hide rest	OPTION+click on Eye icon	ALT+click on Eye icon
See Layer Mask only	OPTION+click mask	ALT+click mask

Creating Layer Masks

When you create a Layer Mask, you see a second image thumbnail in the Layers palette, next to the image being masked. Figure 3-32 shows the Layers palette with an empty mask attached to Layer 1. The Layer Mask is selected, as you can see by the heavier black line around it. You can also tell the Layer Mask is selected because, instead of the Paintbrush icon in the second column, there appears the same icon as the Add Layer Mask icon at the bottom of the Layers palette.

You can switch between the Layer Mask and the image by clicking on the correct thumbnail in the Layers palette. You need to know which piece is active so you do not accidentally destroy image data.

When the Layer Mask is the selected image, you can only work in grayscale. A Layer Mask is like a channel, and channels can only hold grayscale images. A Layer Mask is created in white by default—all the image data in the Layer is visible. If you invert the default Layer Mask, none of the Layer image will be visible (which is what happens when you select the Hide All option).

What can you put in a Layer Mask? Anything grayscale. Your choices, however, will probably fall within these categories:

⚫ A solid black-and-white mask like the selections you made in Chapter 2

⚫ A Gradient

⚫ A grayscale image

⚫ Hand-painted areas of black and white

Let's look at an example of the first three items on the list (and revisit some work from the last chapter).

In a Layer Mask, you can block out simple shapes, or you can reuse selection masks you created in channels. The easiest way to get the selection channel into the Layer Mask is to use the Apply Image command. This is much better than cut-and-paste because it does not use the clipboard memory. It also places the channel into the Layer Mask in the correct black-and-white relationship. Another easy way is to load the channel and fill the selection in the Layer Mask with black. However, this creates an inverted Layer Mask. You then need to deselect and invert the Layer Mask to get it the right way—or invert the selection before filling it. Unfortunately, you cannot drag-and-drop into a Layer Mask (or a channel). Try this Hands On.

Figure 3-32
Layers palette
showing empty
Layer Mask

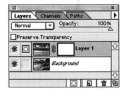

LAYER MASKS: SOLID SELECTION MASKS

1. Open the images Garden.Psd and Family.Psd. The Family image is the same one you used to make a selection channel with Quick Mask in Chapter 2. Now, you are going to move the family from a hotel room in Buffalo, NY to a garden in Singapore.

2. Click on the Family image to make it active. Using the Move tool (V), press SHIFT to keep the image aligned and drag it onto the Garden image. The images were manipulated to be the same size. The Family image appears in the Layers palette of the Garden image as Layer 1.

3. Create a Layer Mask for Layer 1 (click on the Add Layer Mask icon—the left icon at the bottom of the Layers palette). Notice that your color swatches in the Toolbox turn to black and white (which color becomes foreground is not consistent).

4. Select the Marquee tool (M). If the Marquee shape is not elliptical, press M again. Place your cursor in the upper-left corner of the image and drag the Marquee out to the lower-right corner of the image. This creates a circular selection.

5. Reverse the selection (Select → Inverse). Make certain black is your foreground color and fill the area (Mac: OPTION+DELETE, Windows: ALT+DELETE). Like magic, the corners of the Family image are removed and the Garden below is visible.

6. Undo (Mac: ⌘+Z, Windows: CTRL+Z), but leave the selection active. Feather the selection by 50 pixels (Select → Feather, 50). Fill the area (Mac: OPTION+DELETE, Windows: ALT+DELETE) again. Notice how much softer the transition is between the two images. Figure 3-33(a) shows the hard-edge circle and Figure 3-33(b) shows the softer, feathered transition. This action is nondestructive. Unlike the image feathering you have done before, this selection inside the Layer Mask leaves both images totally untouched. Let's prove it.

7. Deselect (Mac: ⌘+D, Windows: CTRL+D). Select the Apply Image command. You will move the Quick Mask channel in the Family image to the Layer Mask in the Garden image. In the Apply Image dialog, select Family.Psd as your source and Channel 4 as the channel. With Preview on, you see the

black and white selection channel. Click OK. Figure 3-33(c) shows the result. Sid and Sandy, with grandchildren Stephanie and David, are now basking in the sun of Singapore.

Did you notice you didn't have to erase the Layer Mask to use the Apply Image command (in Normal mode)? Since all the image data remains intact, there is nothing to

a

b

Figure 3-33
a) Hard-edge transition using a Layer Mask
b) Soft-edge transition using a Layer Mask
c) Finished composite image

c

revert to, and no possibility you will lose any portion of the image. If you were to scribble on the Layer Mask now using black or white paint, you would hide and reveal more of the image. This brings us to the second method of using Layer Masks.

You can also composite two images together softly and seamlessly using a Gradient in the Layer Mask. The Gradient acts exactly the way the vignette Marquee did on the Family image. The top image shows through most strongly where the Layer Mask is white. You will get to try this in the Lab in Appendix C.

A third way you can use the Layer Mask is to apply a true grayscale image. If you place the negative of an image in the Layer Mask, you get a positive image from it. There are many complex effects possible. To get an idea what this technique can do, let's try this Hands On just for fun. The results are wacky, but the technique is simple.

HANDS ON

USING LAYER MASKS WITH GRAYSCALE IMAGES

1. Open the images Swirltex.Psd and Peking.Psd.

2. Click in the Swirltex image. Make a new layer (press the modifier key [Mac: OPTION, Windows: ALT], and click on the New Layer icon at the bottom of the Layers palette).

3. Press D to set the colors back to the default of black and white. Fill the new Layer with black (Mac: OPTION+DELETE, Windows: ALT+DELETE).

4. Create a Layer Mask (click on the Add Layer Mask icon—the left icon at the bottom of the Layers palette).

5. Select the Apply Image command. For Source, choose Peking; for Channel, choose RGB channel and click on the Invert button. Set the Apply mode to Normal at 100% Opacity. Figure 3-34 shows the results.

6. If you need to prove that negatives in the channel yield positive images, invert the Layer Mask (Mac: ⌘+I, Windows: CTRL+I). Now you have a positive of the image in the Layer Mask, but the image itself looks negative. Undo (Mac: ⌘+Z, Windows: CTRL+Z).

7. If you think the color is not lurid enough, you can change the black to another color. Click on the thumbnail of Layer 1 (not the Layer Mask). Select the Image → Adjust → Hue/Saturation command (Mac: ⌘+U, Windows: CTRL+U). Change the setting to conform to the ones in Figure 3-35. Notice the Colorize button is checked—you will not get the same results if it is not.

Figure 3-34
Peking Tombs
image used in
Layer Mask over a
texture

Figure 3-35
Hue/Saturation
settings

8. Leave this example open. You will come back to it in a minute or so.

Painting Layer Masks

You can also paint directly into a Layer Mask. This allows you to control what shows up and what does not in an image. A good example of the use of this technique is shown in the Hands On that follows. In this exercise, you will see how to use the Motion Blur filter and a Layer Mask to control the amount and placement of the filter effect. Thanks go to master Photoshop artist Greg Vander Houwen for sharing this technique.

PAINTED LAYER MASKS

1. Open the image Shuttle.Psd.

2. Drag the icon for the Background Layer to the New Layer icon at the lower-left of the Layers palette. This copies the Background Layer into a new Layer.

3. Select the Background Layer. Apply the Motion Blur filter to the Background (Filter → Blur → Motion Blur, Angle: –30, Distance: 48). You cannot see this in the image as the top Layer hides it.

4. Select the top Layer in the image. Create a Layer Mask (click on the Add Layer Mask icon, the left icon at the bottom of the Layers palette).

5. Press ⒟ to set the colors back to the default of black and white. Choose a soft Paintbrush (65-pixel brush) and the Brush tool (⒝).

6. With black, drag the brush along the lower outside edge of the shuttle. Notice how the motion blur appears. Now, just paint in the blur wherever you want it. If you do not like the results at any point, press ⓧ to exchange the foreground and background colors and paint out the changes. Figure 3-36 shows one solution. You can keep modifying the blur on this image indefinitely, since you never destroy the image data.

Figure 3-36
Motion-blurred
shuttle

Applying Layer Masks

Layers take up a lot of hard drive space if you use many of them. If you create a Layer Mask, the file size of the image grows even larger. Therefore, you may want to permanently set the Layer Mask and not keep the image fluid. To apply the Layer Mask, choose the Remove Layer Mask option on the Layers menu. You are given the opportunity to apply the mask or discard it completely. You can also temporarily disable the Layer Mask if you wish to view the image without it, by selecting the Disable Layer Mask option on the Layers menu.

Let's return to the Peking Tombs image again for some further demonstration.

LINKING, DISABLING, AND APPLYING LAYER MASKS

1. First, let's remove the Layer Mask you previously created. You know you can remove it from the Layers menu at the top of the screen by selecting Remove Layer Mask, then Discard. However, you can also get rid of it like this:

2. Click once on the Preview of the Layer Mask in the Layers palette to select it.

3. Click on the Layers palette trash can. The dialog in Figure 3-37 appears. Select Discard.

4. Open the original Peking.Psd image.

5. Click on the layered image to make it active again. You are going to create a new Layer Mask and fill it with a channel in the original image.

6. Create a Layer Mask (click on the Add Layer Mask icon, the left icon at the bottom of the Layers palette).

7. From the Select menu, choose Load Selection. Select Peking.Psd as the source and Channel 4 as the channel. Do not check the Invert box. Figure 3-38 shows this dialog. Click OK.

Figure 3-37
Discard Layer
Mask dialog

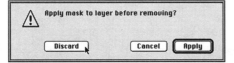

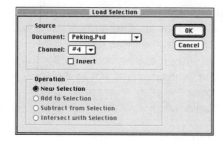

Figure 3-38
Load Selection
dialog

8. Fill the selection with black (Mac: OPTION+DELETE, Windows: ALT+DELETE). Deselect (Mac: ⌘+D, Windows: CTRL+D). You see just the Foo lion this time—without the background.

Explanation

You have created an *inverted* copy of the original channel, which is what you need in order to have a positive show up in the image itself. The Layer Mask was created as Reveal All by default, meaning it is white. When you load the channel, you are selecting the already *white* areas of the *original* channel to be filled. Now, by filling this area with *black*, you create a negative, which is what you wanted.

---

9. Let's look at the Layer Mask itself. Figure 3-39 shows you the actual Layer Mask. Notice that it is a *negative* image. You can draw or paint on this channel as if it were the main image. You can even apply filters to it if you wish.

Figure 3-39
Layer Mask

10. Double-click on the Magic Wand tool and set the Magic Wand options to ⓪ Tolerance and the anti-alias on. Click on the white background of the Layer Mask, then invert the selection (Mac: SHIFT+⌘+I, Windows: SHIFT+CTRL+I). Apply the Bas Relief filter (Filter → Sketch → Bas Relief, Detail: 13, Smoothness: 3, Light Direction: Bottom) as shown in Figure 3-40. Deselect (Mac: ⌘+D, Windows: CTRL+D). If you wish, you may also draw some isolated lines on the Layer Mask in white—just to see how that works.

11. Press the modifier key (Mac: OPTION, Windows: ALT), and click on the Layer Mask preview in the Layers palette again. This restores the view of the image through the Layer Mask.

    At the moment, the Layer and the Layer Mask are *linked* to one another. If you move the image in the Layer or the image in the Layer Mask, both move as one. You can tell because there is a small chain *link* between the Layer and the Layer Mask in the Layers palette. Figure 3-41 shows the Layers palette.

12. Select the Move tool (V). Drag the Layer Mask (or the image) toward the right corner of the document. You have moved both the Layer and the Layer Mask.

13. Click on the link icon between the Layer and the Layer Mask. This turns it off.

14. Click on the Layer Mask so you see the Layer Mask icon in the second column of the Layers palette.

Figure 3-40
Bas Relief
filter dialog

Figure 3-41
Layers palette
showing linked
Layer and Layer
Mask

15. Move the Layer Mask around the image. Notice that the pattern inside the Foo lion changes as you move it. You can drag the Layer Mask around— even almost off the image—and you will not lose any of it, as long as you do not save the image or make any other moves involving the clipboard. You can drag it back and recover it, as long as you do it right away. Also, notice that the background stays black in the image. This is because you are only moving the Layer Mask.

16. Finally, make sure the Layer Mask icon shows up in the second column, and click on the Layers palette trash can. This time, select Apply when the dialog appears.

1. What is a Layer Mask?
   a. A Color channel that works like a rubylith
   b. An Alpha channel that works like a stencil
   c. A Layer that hides all the underlying Layers
   d. An Alpha channel that works with the background

2. When the Layer Mask is selected, you can only work in
   a. RGB Channel
   b. Grayscale
   c. Color
   d. CMYK

3. What can you do with the Layer Mask?
   a. Block out simple shapes
   b. Use the Apply Image command
   c. Reuse selection masks created in channels
   d. Drag-and-drop other images/selections onto the Layer Mask

4. How would you permanently incorporate a Layer Mask into an image?
   a. Choose the Remove Layer Mask option from the Layers menu and choose Apply to Image when prompted.
   b. Activate the Layer Mask, click the Trash button on the Layers palette, and choose Apply to Image when prompted.
   c. Activate the Layer Mask and choose Edit → Delete Layer Mask.
   d. Choose Delete Selection from the Layers palette.

5. How would you apply a grayscale image using the Layer Mask?
   a. Place the negative of an image on the Layer Mask.
   b. Place a black-and-white copy of an image on the Layer Mask.
   c. Place the positive of an image on the Layer Mask and recolor to grayscale.
   d. Select an image and apply a grayscale filter.

LESSON 5

CLIPPING GROUPS

A final feature in using Layers is the Clipping Group. In the section on Channel Operations earlier in this chapter, you saw how to apply an image on top of text in a Layer. There is an easier way. A Clipping Group allows you to use the transparency of a Layer beneath an image as the glue. The top image only shows up where there is glue—image pixels—underneath. You create a Clipping Group by selecting the Group with Previous Layer in the New Layer or Layer Options dialogs. You can also group Layers by placing your cursor on the dividing line between the Layers in the Layer palette, pressing the modifier key (Mac: [OPTION], Windows: [ALT]), and clicking when you see the special cursor appear. This cursor is a tiny black triangle with two overlapping circles nearby. This technique is very easy. Try it, using the Beach, Surf, and text images from before.

HANDS ON

CREATING CLIPPING GROUPS

1. Open the images Surf.Psd, Beach.Psd, Life.Psd, and Pattern.Psd.

2. Click on the Life image and select the Move tool ([V]). Press [SHIFT] and drag the text Layer *from the Layers palette* into the Beach image. This turns the Layer on and makes it visible in the Beach image.

3. Click on the Pattern image, press [SHIFT], and drag it on top of the text in the Beach image. Double-click on the Layer name to open the Layer Options dialog. Click on the box labeled Group with Previous Layer. The pattern now appears only over the text. Figure 3-42(a) shows the image.

4. Press the [SHIFT] and drag the Surf image on top of the Pattern Layer in the Beach image. Use the modifier key (Mac: [OPTION], Windows: [ALT]) and click on the line between the Pattern and Surf Layers to group them. The pattern disappears, and only the Surf Layer is visible. Using the Move tool ([V]), drag the Layer down until the surf appears in the bottom of the word Beach. This shows how you can position the Layer to make the best use of your image while it is still being clipped. Figure 3-42(b) shows the two Grouped Layers.

Figure 3-42
a) Pattern clipped
to text
b) Beach scene with
two
Grouped Layers

a

b

Figure 3-43 shows the Layers palette with the two Grouped Layers. It is important for you to be able to recognize Grouped Layers in the Layers palette just by looking at them. Notice that there is a dotted rather than a solid line between the Grouped Layers. Things do not work the way you expect them to if the Layer is part of a group, so you must be able to spot this immediately.

Figure 3-43
Layers palette
showing Grouped
Layers

Applying the Clipping Group

You can get rid of the Clipping Group and apply it permanently by merging the Layers that are grouped. They must be the only visible Layers, then you can choose Merge Visible Layers from the Layers palette menu. If only two Layers are grouped, you can merge them by using the Merge Down command (Mac: ⌘+E, Windows: CTRL+E) if the top member of the group is the selected Layer and the other group member Layer is directly below it.

1. What does a Clipping Group allow you to do?
   a. Group Layers together.
   b. Use the transparency of a Layer beneath the image as glue, so only the top image shows if there are image pixels underneath.
   c. Group selections from various Layers.
   d. Use the Opacity of a Layer beneath the image as glue so only the bottom image show if there are pixels on top.

2. What are the different ways you can group Layers?
   a. Select Group with Previous Layers from the Layers menu.
   b. Click the Group with Previous Layers box from the New Layer dialog box.
   c. Put your cursor on the dividing line between the Layers on the Layers palette and press the OPTION (or ALT) key.
   d. Select the desired Layers and choose Edit → Group Layers.

3. How can you tell if two or more Layers are linked?
   a. There's a solid line between the Layers on the Layers palette.
   b. There's a chain icon between the Layers on the Layers palette.
   c. There's a interlocking puzzle icon between the Layers on the Layers palette.
   d. There's a dotted line between Layers on the Layers palette.

4. What are the two ways you can get rid of a Clipping Group and permanently apply it to the image?
   a. Choose Merge Visible Layers from the Layers palette menu.
   b. Choose Merge Down from the Layers menu.
   c. Choose Merge All Layers from the Layers palette menu.
   d. Click the Merge All Layers button from the Layers palette.

5. In order to merge Layers using the Merge Down command, what must happen first?
   a. The Layer on the bottom must be selected.
   b. The upper Layer must selected.
   c. Only the Layers you want to merge must be visible.
   d. All the Layers must be hidden.

VIP PROFILE

David Biedny, Author, Digital Guru

David Biedny is one of the authors of the first book ever released on Photoshop, *The Official Guide to Photoshop*, written with artist Bert Monroy. David is also one of the founding editors of *MacUser* and *NewMedia* magazines.

He first got into computers via analog sound synthesizers as a child growing up in South America, where his father was an artist and technologist. David was exposed to both art and technology as his father had drawers full of Letraset press type, and since his father was also a film director, David has access to that technology.

David is completely self-taught. He was an artistic prodigy growing up in Venezuela. He went to college for three years, majoring in Electrical Engineering and Computer Information Studies at Rutgers University and Hunter College in NYC, but he was also working for Ziff-Davis in his third year at college (current publishers of *MacUser*) and had a higher salary than his professors.

David's first computer was an Apple II with some graphics software. He first saw Photoshop—actually before Adobe did—while on retainer for a Silicon Valley graphics firm which shall remain nameless. He was asked to do a technical evaluation of a product for possible acquisition. John Knoll, who with his brother Thomas, had created Photoshop, brought in the program to demo. David was totally blown away by it.

By this time, David had developed considerable experience in multimedia (such as it was back then) and had been working on interactivity assignments in New York since 1985 with his longtime creative collaborator, Bert Monroy. He had the first color MacIIe in New York, and was one of the 12 founders of the recently defunct NYMUG.

David was extremely impressed by Photoshop's ability to take a 24-bit image and reduce it to an 8-bit palette, its file conversion capability, its dithering, and its many Calculations modes. He saw immediately that with the right development, the product would dominate the market. However, after viewing the new software, the director of marketing for the company for which he was consulting asked David how the product differed from MacPaint. In disgust, David walked out on the assignment—and called John Knoll.

This started a long-lasting professional relationship that has lasted to this day. Their phone relationship quickly ripened into a friendship. David tested the fledgling program and provided John and Thomas Knoll with feedback. In the meantime, Bantam Books called him about writing a book on Freehand. David suggested Bantam forget the Freehand book and told Bantam about Photoshop. Bantam was interested, but dubious since this program did not have a manufacturer and had been rejected by just about every major Mac software company.

At this point, John Knoll brought Photoshop to Adobe. It is to Adobe's credit that they immediately realized the potential and brilliance of this product and snatched it up immediately. David called Bantam Books, which was ecstatic over the Adobe purchase, and *The Official Guide to Photoshop* was published six months later.

A while after that, David moved out to California to work at Industrial Light and Magic with John Knoll. Now, even though Photoshop is just one of the tools in his paintbox, the name of David Biedny is inextricably associated with it. Of course, a new book on Channels and Calculations—also written with Bert Monroy and Nathan Moody—helps reinforce that association.

David really likes Photoshop. According to him, it has been the epitome of *form follows function*—the hallmark of good design. For all its power, it is streamlined like an expensive sportscar. The controls are kept to a minimum so as not to detract from performance. It is a unique approach. Photoshop is not really designed for reviewers to look at and "oooh and ahhh." It is designed for people who do hardcore production. The program almost seems to anticipate what you want to do. Even though John Knoll is one of the top five special-effects graphic artists in the world, he realizes instinctively that the gratuitous overuse of graphics in an interface is not a good thing. Even though John Knoll is no longer involved with Photoshop design (Version 4.0 was the first version in which his name does not appear on the About Photoshop credits), David hopes that John's original genius will not be lost as Photoshop continues to evolve.

His advice for you: Many of you just starting out in imaging and media production really only want to know what buttons to push. But that is not a good or productive attitude. Imaging is not a cookbook of recipes. Different problems require different approaches. You need to become a visual problem-solver, and learn to use deductive reasoning. You cannot let yourself become like someone who memorizes a foreign-language dictionary but still cannot put together one coherent sentence. You need to learn how to *use* Photoshop and understand it; learn that it has many ways to do the same thing. You must learn to analyze what you need to do, break it down into steps, understand the ramifications, and then find the correct tools for the task.

In addition, you need to play with the program. The best way to play, though, is to take a specific project and work it through. Take photos and sketch a composite ahead of time, then work it through in Photoshop. Having a goal is critical—in order to arrive anywhere, you must know where your destination is. After you have worked on goal-oriented tasks, your playtime is much more productive.

Finally, don't take anyone's word as gospel. Don't be afraid to ask questions. Read anything you can get your hands on. Learn from as many sources as possible—everyone has something different to teach.

CHAPTER SUMMARY

This chapter covered a large amount of material. Although it only concerned Layers and channels, you learned:

1. How to create, delete, reorder, merge, and flatten Layers

2. How to drag-and-drop

3. How to create transparency in Layers

4. How to use Layer Apply modes

5. How to save a selection to a Layer and a Layer Mask

6. How to use the Apply Image and Calculations commands

7. How to create a variety of Layer Masks

8. How to paint on a Layer Mask, how to hide and show it, and how to apply or discard it

9. How to create and merge Clipping Groups

CHAPTER 4

FILTERS

Filters are the fun part of working with Photoshop. They can be used for either special effects or serious image correction. They are generally very easy to use: Simply select an area of your image, select a filter, and apply. Photoshop's ability to use filters to change the image data gives the program most of its power as an image manipulator.

In this chapter, you will learn techniques to apply to various types of filters. At the end of this chapter, you should be able to

- Apply Photoshop's built-in filters to a selected portion of an image.

- Identify the filters requiring real RAM to work.

- List several ways to work with filters in tight memory situations.

- Define the major classes of filters.

- Apply multiple filters to an image.

● Filter an image so the filters can easily be removed or changed.

● List the principles of suggested filter use.

What are filters? Filters are automated ways to produce specific changes to an image. If you wish to blur an area of an image (or the entire thing), you can apply one of the Blur filters to it rather than hacking away at the whole image with the Blur tool from the Toolbox. Filters also extend Photoshop's capabilities in the same way Extensions add to the capability of the Macintosh Finder. They are *optional* pieces of the program; they can be removed and added to.

We can define a filter in terms of what it *is* and what it *does*. A filter, technically, is a program or piece of code handed a collection of pixels (your selection) to perform some type of manipulation on them (following the rules embedded in the filter code). It then hands the pixels back to Photoshop to redisplay. Filters make use of Photoshop's ability to add functions not built-in or hard-wired to the program. In order to add a filter to Photoshop, you just need to place it within Photoshop's plug-ins folder. Because of this, many companies besides Adobe also write filters for Photoshop. These filters can be purchased (if they are commercial) or downloaded (if they are freeware or shareware), from online services such as CompuServe, America Online, and the Internet. Some of the most popular of these commercial plug-ins (discussed later in this chapter) include

● Eye Candy filters (Alien Skin)

● Kai's Power Tools (MetaTools)

● KPT Convolver (MetaTools)

● Paint Alchemy (Xaos Tools)

● PhotoLab (Cytopia)

● PhotoTools (Extensis)

● Series 1, 2, 3, and 4 Filters (Andromeda)

● Terrazzo (Xaos Tools)

● WildRiverSSK (DataStream)

In addition, these filters can be used in other programs accepting the Adobe plug-in standard, such as Fractal Design Painter, Macromedia Xres, Strata Studio Pro, Specular Collage, Specular Infini-D, Adobe Premiere, Adobe AfterEffects, Adobe Illustrator, Adobe PageMaker, Corel Photo-Paint, and a number of other programs.

Photoshop arrives with 97 *native* filters divided into a number of categories:

- *Artistic filters:* These new filters from the Adobe Gallery Effects set are used to stylize an image and make a photograph look as if it were rendered by hand.

- *Blur filters:* Soften the focus of an image so it looks out of focus in a variety of ways.

- *Brush Strokes filters:* More of the Gallery Effects filters. This set can be applied to a selection to make it look as if a variety of different brushes were used.

- *Distort filters:* Rearrange image data to warp, deform, twist, wrench, and bend it into new shapes.

- *Noise filters:* Add or remove random pixels from images to correct scans or add film grain.

- *Pixelize filters:* Create special effects by grouping pixels in distinct ways, such as Mosaic and Pointillist.

- *Render filters:* Perform image processing tasks, such as cloud creation and lighting.

- *Sharpen filters:* Make the image detail more distinct; improve the focus, and prepare an image for printing.

- *Sketch filters:* Another set of Gallery Effects. These are similar to the Artistic filters in intent and are meant to work on the entire image. They create a variety of novel effects like bas relief, note paper, and chrome.

- *Stylize filters:* Perform a variety of special effects, such as Finding Edges, Embossing, Diffusing, and so on.

- *Texture filters:* This is the final set from the original Adobe Gallery Effects. These filters add areas of texture to your image. The texture can resemble mosaic tiles or an old cracked painting.

- *Video filters:* The two filters in this set help to get noise out of a video capture and enforce NTSC standard (broadcast-safe) colors in your image.

- *Other filters:* Perform functions not covered by the other categories. The most useful of these are High Pass, Minimum, and Maximum.

You can access the filters from the Filters menu in Photoshop. Figure 4-1 shows the Filter menu from my copy of Photoshop and lists both the original filter categories and the third-party filters in my system. Figure 4-2 shows the filters listed under the Distort submenu.

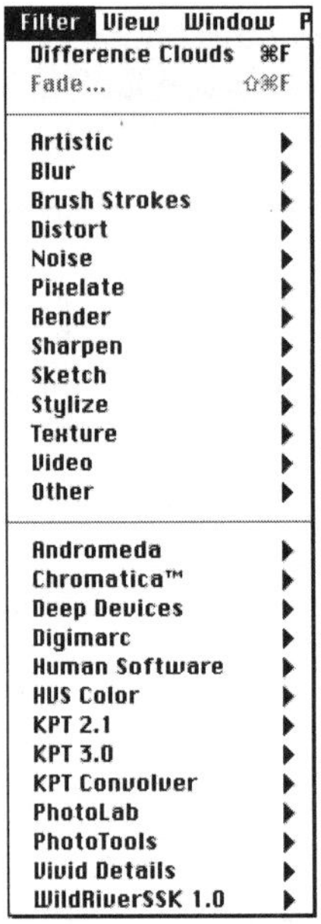

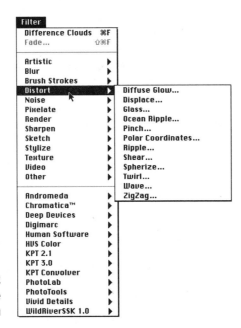

Figure 4-1
Filter menu

Figure 4-2
Filters listed in the
Distort submenu

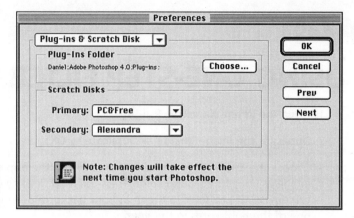

Figure 4-3
Setting the Plug-Ins
Folder location

All the filters are contained in the plug-ins folder when you install Photoshop. However, you can nest folders inside the plug-ins folder as deeply as you wish in order to organize your filters, or you can select a different plug-ins folder by changing the location under Preferences, as shown in Figure 4-3. You can also place an alias to your filters in the selected folder if you wish to keep the filter in another location.

ONE-STEP FILTERS

There are three major types of filter interfaces. They are the One-Step filter, the Parameter filter, and the Application filter. The *one-step* filter has no interface. Once you select it, it is applied immediately because there are no options or controls to select. The Difference Clouds filter is an example of this type of filter. When selected, it applies its own logic to the image. The filter uses the foreground and background colors in the Toolbox and creates clouds. As it adds them to the image, it uses the *difference* (just like the channel arithmetic you first learned in Chapter 1, "Introduction to Photoshop") between the color of the cloud and the original pixel, and places it in the image—hence the name Difference Clouds. You can apply it multiple times, but you cannot select the amount of the effect. All the one-step filters work the same way. Since you cannot control how much they filter an image, all you can do is select them from the menu.

Try this Hands On to add Difference Clouds to your image.

USING ONE-STEP FILTERS

1. Open the image XmasTree.Psd.

2. Duplicate the image (Image → Duplicate → OK).

3. Choose the Eyedropper tool. Select a red from the apple ornament in the image as your foreground color. Press the modifier key (Mac: OPTION, Windows: ALT) to select a green as your background color from the plug of one of the light cords in the image.

4. Apply the Difference Clouds filter (Filter → Render → Difference Clouds) to the copy. Figure 4-4 shows this menu item. The filter is purely for special effects and colors your image somewhat strangely.

5. Visually compare the filtered copy to the original. All the colors were altered dramatically. Figure 4-5(a) shows the original, and Figure 4-5(b) shows the filtered image.

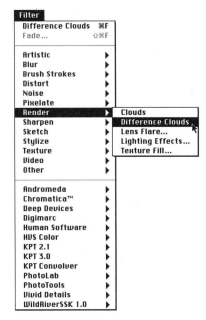

Figure 4-4
Applying the
Difference Clouds
filter

Figure 4-5
a) The original image
b) After the Difference Clouds

a

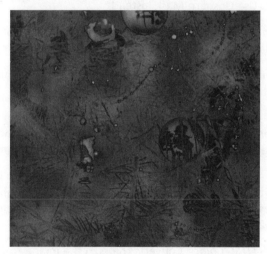

b

Many of the one-step filters are very subtle. A few, like the Difference Clouds filter and the Solarize and Find Edges Filters, make dramatic changes. A few of the one-step filters are not worth using in most cases. Below is the list of one-step filters included in the purchase of Photoshop and a brief description of each:

1. *Blur Menu → Blur:* Produces tiny softening in the image. Use Blur → Gaussian Blur instead.

2. *Blur Menu → Blur More:* Produces a little more softening in the image. Use Blur → Gaussian Blur instead.

3. *Noise Menu → Despeckle:* Very useful Production filter to help remove noise from the image and add values to the Histogram. Use after scanning or importing an image.

4. *Pixelate Menu → Facet:* Creates tiny blobs of color from close-in-tone pixels and is a subtle effect. Helps make images look hand-rendered.

5. *Pixelate Menu → Fragment:* Makes the image look as if it survived a moderate earthquake.

6. *Render Menu → Clouds:* The only filter to work in a totally empty transparent Layer. Replaces any image data with the effect. Uses foreground and background colors to create a cloudlike effect.

7. *Render Menu → Difference Clouds:* Performs a dramatic color change on the image for special effects.

8. *Sharpen Menu → Sharpen:* Increases the focus of an image a very small amount. Use Unsharp Mask instead.

9. *Sharpen Menu → Sharpen More:* Increases the focus of an image a bit more than Sharpen. Use Unsharp Mask instead.

10. *Sharpen Menu → Sharpen Edges:* Increases the focus of the image edges a little bit. Use Unsharp Mask instead.

11. *Stylize → Find Edges*: Removes all parts of the image not considered edges (in other words, areas with a definite color or value change in the image). Leaves a complex line drawing. Invert results for a dramatic effect.

12. *Stylize → Solarize:* Changes the curves in the image so it reverses all the values lighter than 128. White (255) becomes black. A light gray (140) becomes a darker gray (116). The basic formula of the reversal is original value–128=X. 128–X=new pixel color.

13. *Video → NTSC Colors:* Converts colors in the image to colors that are safe on a TV screen and do not bleed or spread.

Command Watch

To reapply the last filter using the previous settings, press ⌘+F (Mac) or CTRL+F (Windows). If you wish to reapply the previous filter but need to change settings, press OPTION+⌘+F (Mac) or ALT+CTRL+F (Windows).

QUIZ 1

1. What are filters?
   a. Cumbersome ways to color an image
   b. Automated ways to produce specific change to an image
   c. Special effects you can apply to an image
   d. Easy and fun to use

2. What are some of the categories of filters that come with Photoshop?
   a. Brush Stroke filters
   b. Texture filters
   c. Bad filters
   d. Artistic filters

3. What is the simplest type of filter interface?
   a. One-step filter
   b. Two-step filter
   c. Difference filter
   d. Single filter

4. What is one of the disadvantages of using the filters mentioned in Question 3?
   a. They're easy to use.
   b. You cannot control how much they filter an image.
   c. They can add dramatic effects to an image.
   d. They can be used multiple times.

5. What are examples of these filters?
   a. Differential Clouds
   b. Gaussian Blur
   c. Despeckle
   d. Electronic

LESSON 2

PARAMETER FILTERS

A *parameter* filter has a control dialog appearing on the screen so you can select various options for it. Most of the parameter filters allow you to see a preview of the filter's effect. There are several types of previews:

● *None:* Very complex filters like Tiles (Filter → Stylize → Tiles) have no preview at all.

● *Small Filter Dialog Preview:* Only a small area of the image is previewed. All the filters on the Artistic, Brush Strokes, Sketch, and Texture menus work this way, as do most of the Pixelate filters.

● *Wire Frame:* This type of preview shows the path the filter will use but may not show the pixel data (sometimes there is a Small Filter Dialog preview along with it).

● *Full Image Preview:* In addition to the small preview in the filter dialog, you can see the effect of the filter in your actual image.

If a preview is available, it works the way the Add Noise filter shown in Figure 4-6 does. The Preview dialog box shows an area of your image with the filter applied. You can click anywhere in your image to place that section of it into the Preview box. In addition, you can see the effect of the filter on the entire image if you have checked the Preview On box (if it's a Full Image preview). You can enlarge or shrink the image in the Preview area by clicking on the + or – under the Preview box, and you can zoom in or zoom out on your actual image while the dialog box is open (using the ⌘+CTRL+spacebar or OPTION+ALT+spacebar method of zooming in or out). You can hide the selection Marquee if there is one (Mac: ⌘+H, Windows: CTRL+H). These controls make it very easy to see how your image will look. Parameter filters also have controls (options) you can set. These options vary by filter. The best way to learn what the options do is simply to try them. As you move the sliders back and forth, you will quickly learn what effect each control has on the specific filter. To see how to use several of the parameter filters, try the Hands On example—it also uses the Difference Clouds filter you already saw and reinforces the Drop Shadow process taught in Chapter 3, "Layers and Channels."

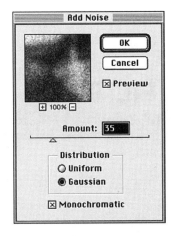

Figure 4-6
A parameter filter
dialog box

Command Watch		
Function	**Mac**	**Windows**
To zoom in from the keyboard:	⌘+spacebar+click	CTRL+spacebar+click
To zoom out from the keyboard:	OPTION+spacebar+click	ALT+spacebar+click
To hide the selection Marquee:	⌘+H	CTRL+H

PARAMETER FILTERS

1. Open the image AfriMask.Psd. Figure 4-7 shows the original image.

2. Duplicate the image (Image → Duplicate → OK).

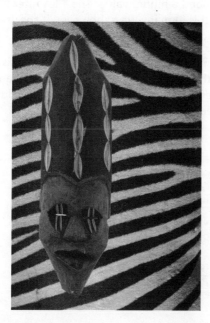

Figure 4-7
Original image

Apply the Difference Clouds Filter

3. The image has a layer and a background. The background contains a zebra-skin section. Layer 1 (the top layer) contains the main image object, a ceremonial mask from Africa. Both images are from the Kai's Power Photos IV collection from MetaTools. Click on the Background Layer name in the Layers palette to make it the active Layer.

4. Select the Eyedropper tool (⬇) and pick a deep ochre (orange-brown) from the face area of the mask as the foreground color. Pick a light gold from the mask's headdress area as the background color.

5. Apply the Difference Clouds filter (Filter → Render → Difference Clouds).

Apply the Mosaic Filter

6. Make Layer 1 the active Layer (click on its name in the Layers palette).

7. Open the Mosaic filter dialog (Filter → Pixelate → Mosaic). Figure 4-8 shows this dialog. Drag the Slider to 11 or type **11**. Try a few other values that way. This filter specifies the exact number of pixels for each square, so a larger image will need a higher value. The Tiles filter (Filter → Stylize → Tiles) is similar to this in many ways; however, it specifies the number of tiles across, so it does not need to change because of the image size.

8. At this point, you might consider this composition finished; however, it could use some other effects such as a drop shadow, and perhaps some definition in the squares left by the Mosaic filter. Let's add a few more filters to it so you can see how they work.

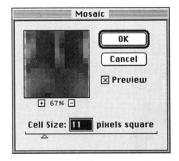

Figure 4-8
Mosaic filter dialog

Emboss the Mask

9. Drag the icon for Layer 1 to the New Layer icon (the center icon at the bottom of the Layers palette). Layer 1 Copy is now the top Layer on the stack. Apply the Find Edges filter (Filter → Stylize → Find Edges). This is a one-step filter, so there are no controls to select. Hmmm... This doesn't look very good. Change the Apply mode for the Layer to Multiply. That looks better.

10. Let's add some definition and 3D to the squares. We can do this by applying the Emboss filter. Open the Emboss filter dialog (Filter → Stylize → Emboss). Figure 4-9 shows this dialog. This parameter filter has three controls. Drag the angle setting to –50 (or +310 depending on how the dial feels like reading). At this setting, the lines look etched into the tiles. At 45°, the lines would be embossed.

11. Set the Height to 3. Set the Amount to 100%. Click OK. You can see the results on your image as you change the settings.

12. The mask image is now too dark. Change the Apply mode to Soft Light. This lets more of the color from the image beneath show through.

Create a Drop Shadow

13. Let's create a drop shadow for this. A *drop shadow* is a very important graphic device that shows depth. This drop shadow recipe needs to become automatic for you, which is why it is repeated from Chapter 3.

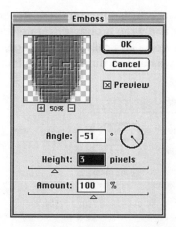

Figure 4-9
Emboss filter dialog

14. Drag the icon for Layer 1 (the original mask) to the New Layer icon (the center icon at the bottom of the Layers palette). The Layer is named Layer 1 Copy 2. Drag it below Layer 1 in the Layer stack (Mac: SHIFT+⌘+2, Windows: SHIFT+CTRL+2).

15. Select a medium blue tone from the image as the foreground color. Fill the image with Preserve Transparency (Mac: SHIFT+OPTION+DELETE, Windows: SHIFT+ALT+DELETE). Change the Apply Mode to Multiply (this enables the shadow color to softly darken the image).

16. You can use the Offset filter to precisely control where the shadow falls. Since this is the filter chapter, let's filter rather than drag the shadow to its desired position. Open the Offset filter dialog (Filter → Other → Offset). Figure 4-10 shows this dialog. Type **18** in the Horizontal field and **12** in the Vertical field. This moves the image 18 pixels to the right and 12 pixels down to offset it from the main object. Click on the Set to Transparent button to make the area to which the image was moved transparent (the Wrap Around setting is most valuable when you create a pattern tile). Click OK.

17. Make sure that you have unchecked the Preserve transparency box. Open the Gaussian Blur filter dialog shown in Figure 4-11. A radius of 8.0 pixels gives a good amount of softening but still shows the shadow. Click OK. The shadow is now complete.

Let's try another filter—this time, on the Background Layer.

Applying the Shear Filter

18. The Shear filter is a special effects filter on the Distort menu that enables you to skew your image and wrap around or create curves and folds. However, the filter only works vertically on the image, and we want to filter it across. Therefore, we need to turn the entire image first.

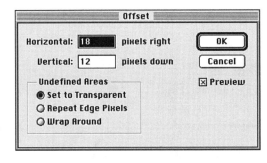

Figure 4-10
Offset filter dialog

Figure 4-11
Gaussian Blur filter
dialog

19. Rotate the entire image 90° clockwise (Image → Rotate Canvas → 90° clockwise).

20. Click on the Background Layer name in the Layers palette to make it the active Layer.

21. Open the Shear filter dialog (Filter → Distort → Shear). Start by clicking on the intersections of the line with the grid square to leave additional points. Click between the top two points and leave a third point in the center. Drag this point to the left as shown in Figure 4-12. Continue to leave points and drag to place the curves until your image looks like the one in Figure 4-12. It does not need to be identical, just close. Click OK to apply the filter. This is the first parameter filter you have used that only has a small filter preview. You cannot see the results on your original image until the filter is applied.

22. You now need to rotate the canvas 90° counterclockwise to put it back as it was (Image → Rotate Canvas → 90° counterclockwise).

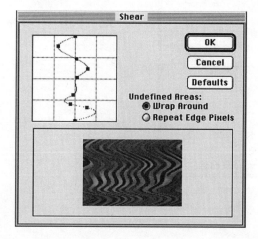

Figure 4-12
Shear filter dialog

You have now used two one-step filters (Difference Clouds and Find Edges), three Full Image Preview parameter filters (Mosaic, Emboss, Gaussian Blur), and one Small Filter Dialog preview filter (Shear).

Add the Twirl Filter

23. Let's add a final effect to the background with the Twirl filter, which has a wire frame preview in addition to a Small Filter Dialog preview.

24. Open the Twirl filter dialog (Filter → Distort → Twirl) as shown in Figure 4-13. This filter swirls your image around a center point at the setting you prefer. Drag the Angle slider to 254° and click OK. Figure 4-14 shows the final result.

Command Watch

Here are some very useful keyboard commands for arranging Layers:

Function	Mac	Windows
Send Layer to top of stack:	⌘+2	CTRL+2
Send Layer forward:	SHIFT+⌘+2	SHIFT+CTRL+2
Send Layer to bottom of stack:	⌘+2	CTRL+2
Send Layer backward:	SHIFT+⌘+2	SHIFT+CTRL+2

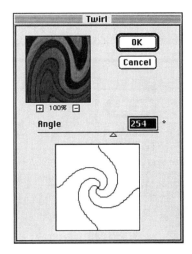

Figure 4-13
Twirl filter dialog

Figure 4-14
Final image with
multiple filters

About Preserve Transparency

You must be very careful when you drag a new layer into an image to read the status of the Preserve Transparency flag. If it is checked in the Layers palette, you can't do anything to the Layer except change the color of pixels already on it. However, when you apply a drop shadow, the easiest way to color it is to make sure Preserve Transparency is on. That way, you can fill the entire shadow Layer and only the object is colored. But you need to make sure the flag is *off* before you try applying a Gaussian Blur, or else nothing will blur.

The easiest way to remember to set or remove the Preserve Transparency flag is by using a version of the Fill command that automatically preserves the Layer's underlying transparency values. From the menus, you can do this using the Edit → Fill command and checking the option for Preserve Transparency. The keyboard equivalent is SHIFT+OPTION+DELETE on the Mac, and SHIFT+ALT+DELETE on Windows.

That was an unusually long Hands On; however, now you should be more comfortable applying a filter to an image.

QUIZ 2

1. In Lesson 1, the simplest type of filter interface was introduced. What is the second simplest type of filter interface?
   a. Circumference filters
   b. Boundary filters
   c. Circumference filters
   d. Parameter filters

2. The filters in Question 1 allow you to preview their effects. There are several types of previews. What are some of them?
   a. Wire Frame preview
   b. Large Filter preview
   c. Full Image preview
   d. Box Filter preview

3. What are some of the things the preview lets you do?
   a. Enlarge or shrink the image in the preview area
   b. Zoom in and out on the actual image while the dialog box is open
   c. Hide the selection Marquee
   d. Click anywhere on your image to place that section in the preview area

4. What are two of the three controls for the Emboss filter?
   a. Angle
   b. Width
   c. Percentage
   d. Amount

5. In order to apply a Gaussian Blur or other blur to a selection, what must be done to the image first?
   a. Save the image.
   b. Create a new Layer.
   c. Preserve transparency.
   d. Add a shadow to the selection.

LESSON 3

APPLICATION FILTERS

The *application* filter uses Photoshop as a shell for another application or program. This class of filter is always a third-party filter. In an application filter, you are really plugging in a totally different program and adding a lot of functionality to Photoshop. For example, Xaos Tools Terrazzo lets you create 17 different types of patterns from your image and looks like a kaleidoscope in constant motion. The Andromeda Series II filter adds a full 3D shape-wrapping function to Photoshop, and Andromeda Series III adds a full screening and Mezzotinting engine. Virtus Alien Skin TextureShop is a full-scale texture generator. The hallmark of this application filter class is that they have multiple screens or preview areas, and they allow you to save and recall sets of options (known as *Presets*). Some of these third-party filters are discussed later in this chapter. The example shown in Figure 4-15, Andromeda Series III Screens, is representative of this genre. Alien Skin Black Box filters are less complex examples of this class. You can work along with the Alien Skin Drop Shadow filter in the Hands On with application filters.

HANDS ON

APPLICATION FILTERS

1. If you have not already done so, install the Black Box Drop Shadow filter in your copy of Photoshop. The filter is in the Filters folder on the CD-ROM. Follow the directions in the Read Me file to install it. Make sure Photoshop is not running when you install the filter.

2. Launch Photoshop.

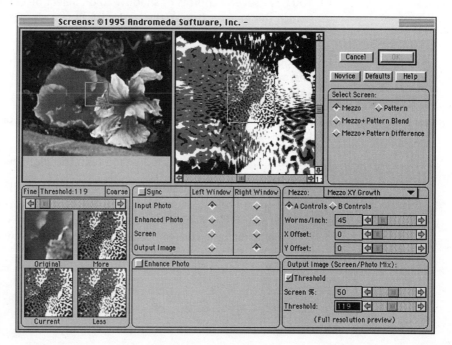

Figure 4-15
Andromeda Series
III Screens

3. Open the image Thai.Psd (File → Open → Thai).

4. Open the Layers palette (Window → Palettes → Show Layers). Notice that this image has several Layers. Layer 0 contains the Thai image, Layer 1 has a background texture, and Layer 2 (which is in the center) is a blank image filled with white in Multiply mode. This is the Layer that will become the drop shadow.

5. Click on Layer 2 in the Layers palette to make it active.

6. This image contains a mask in Channel 4 the shape of the Thai figure. The Alien Skin Drop Shadow filter provides another way to create a drop shadow. It requires a selection, however. Use Channel 4 to make that selection (as you learned in Chapter 3).

7. Load Channel 4 (⌘+OPTION+4 on the Mac or ALT+CTRL+4 on Windows).

8. Open the Drop Shadow filter (Filters → Alien Skin → Drop Shadow). Move the cursor in the Preview box until you can see the area in which you want the shadow to appear.

9. Move all the sliders in the filter dialog from left to right and back again, watching the preview as you go. Set the X Shadow offset to 8 and the Y Shadow offset to 3. Use a Blur of 24 and an Opacity of 55.

10. You have several choices of shadow color. Select black. In Multiply mode (which this Layer is using), the choice of a black shadow subtly darkens the texture beneath it.

11. Click on the Camera icon to save the settings. Name them Thai Shadow. The next time you use this filter, you may simply select these settings in the Settings drop-down menu.

12. Check to make sure your settings are the same as the ones in Figure 4-16. Click OK.

13. Figure 4-17 shows the finished image with the slight shadow applied.

This is a very simple application filter. It has a few more choices than the parameter filters you used before, but it enables you to save settings. The Screens dialog from Andromeda Series III in Figure 4-15 is much more complex. Xaos Paint Alchemy has many different dialog boxes embedded in it and is also a very complex application filter.

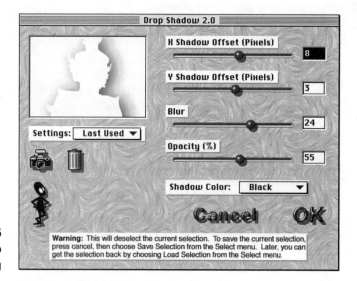

Figure 4-16
Alien Skin Drop
Shadow dialog

Figure 4-17
Image with Drop
Shadow applied

1. What is the third type of filter interface?
   a. Perimeter filters
   b. Two-step filters
   c. Application filters
   d. Program filters

2. The filters in Question 1 are always _____ filters.
   a. Complex
   b. Third-party
   c. Built-in
   d. One-step

3. What are some examples of these filters?
   a. Trekko Tools
   b. Xaos Tools Terrazzo
   c. Andromeda Series II
   d. Virtus Alien Skin TextureShop

4. What are some of the advantages of using this class of filters?
   a. They have multiple preview areas.
   b. They add more dimension and flexibility to Photoshop.
   c. They are difficult to use.
   d. They allow you to save and recall sets of options.

5. What are two of the four options for the Alien Skin/Drop Shadow filter?
   a. Transparency
   b. X Shadow Offset
   c. Blur
   d. Darken

PRINCIPLES OF APPLYING FILTERS

There are no hard and fast rules for applying filters. You need to use the filter you deem most appropriate for the effect you want to achieve. With that said, there are several general principles that can maximize efficiency and make your work more distinctive.

Explore the Filters

The more you know about how each filter reacts, the better you can select one. You can divide filters into two very broad classes: prepress filters, used to correct or enhance an image, and special effects filters, used to change image data by distorting reality. As you experiment with different filters, make note of just what it is a filter changes. Some filters change focus, others change image colors, still others move pixels to create bumps and extrusions. There are other filters that completely obliterate the image data and replace it with a new image, as well as filters that use the image colors to create stylized versions of the original image.

You need to know what each filter does, and, if it has parameters, what they do to control the final effect. Take a copy of an image and just try filter after filter on it. Undo after each try, but note the effects and control settings you like. Such a notebook is a valuable reference. Once you begin using the filters enough, you will come to know what each one does.

Filter in Layers

There may be times you wish to experiment with various combinations of filters but want to keep your options open to change. If you select the area of the image you wish to filter, float it to a new Layer, then apply the filter, you can easily remove the change or lessen its effect by decreasing the transparency or changing the Apply mode. You can then build up a stack of effects you can change as desired. The Hands On with Infinite Changes shows you how to do this.

INFINITE CHANGES

1. Create a new document (File → New → Name: Undoit, Width: 360 pixels, Height: 284 pixels, Resolution: 72, Mode: RGB Color, Contents: White).

2. Create the Gradient layer (Mac: OPTION+click, Windows: ALT+click on the New Layer icon at the bottom of the Layers palette). Accept the default settings, type **Gradient** for the layer name, and click OK.

3. Double-click on the Gradient tool. Set the Apply mode to Normal, the Opacity to 100, the Gradient to Spectrum, the Type to Linear, and check the Dither box. The Mask box does not matter here. Drag the Gradient cursor from the top-left corner of the document to the bottom-right corner. This makes a diagonal rainbow gradient. Since this Layer is floating, you can adjust the Opacity to anything you wish and change it as many times as you want.

4. Create a noise Layer (Mac: OPTION+click, Windows: ALT+click on the New Layer icon at the bottom of the Layers palette). Select Multiply as the mode and check the box that says Fill with Multiply-Neutral color white. Name the Layer Basic Noise.

5. Apply the Add Noise filter (Filter → Noise → Add Noise, Gaussian, 25, Monochrome). Since the Layer is using the Multiply mode, the white pixels show the color of the Gradient Layer. In order to have better use of the noise, you need to get rid of the white pixels.

6. Click the eye icon next to the Gradient Layer so it disappears. The Gradient Layer also disappears from the screen. Now you can see the white pixels.

7. Open the Info palette (Window → Palettes → Show Info). Make sure the top readout on the Info palette says RGB.

8. Double-click on the Magic Wand and set the Tolerance to 0. Set Anti-alias to off. Set Sample Merged to off. Magnify the image until you can clearly see the pixels (use the keyboard shortcut you learned and magnify until the image is 16:1). Move the Magic Wand over the image until you find a pixel that reads R=255, G=255, B=255. This means the pixel is solid white. (If you have trouble finding one, double-click on the Eyedropper tool and make sure the Sample Size Option says Point Sample.) Click on a white pixel. Select all the white pixels in the image (Select → Similar). Press DELETE to remove them. Deselect (Mac: ⌘+D or Windows: CTRL+D).

9. Double-click on the Hand tool to set the image magnification back to 1:1.

10. The final thing to do on this Layer is gently blur it to soften the noise. Apply a Gaussian Blur filter (Filter → Blur → Gaussian Blur, Radius of 0.8). Click in the eye column next to the Gradient layer to turn it back on. Notice that the Gradient now has a very soft texture to it. The Basic Noise Layer should still be in Multiply mode.

11. Drag the icon for the Basic Noise Layer to the New Layer icon at the bottom left of the Layers palette. This copies it into a new Layer. Double-click on the Layer name in the Layers palette and change it to Emboss Layer. Change the Layer Apply mode to Multiply.

12. Apply the Emboss filter to the Layer (Filter → Stylize → Emboss). Set the Angle to 131, the Height to 3, and the Amount to 255. Click OK. You now have a filtered Layer of embossed noise that you can merge with the Gradient Layer, either by changing the Opacity or by changing the Apply mode.

13. Double-click on the Marquee tool and set the options to Shape: Rectangular, Style: Fixed Size, Width: 200, Height: 150, Feather: 0.

14. Click on the Gradient Layer in the Layers palette to make it active. Drag the Marquee into the center of the image. Float the selection (Mac: ⌘+J, Windows: CTRL+J). Select the nontransparent Layer pixels (Mac: ⌘+click, Windows: CTRL+click on the Layer name in the Layers palette).

15. Apply the Polar Coordinates filter to the selection (Filter → Distort → Polar Coordinates, Polar to Rectangular). Deselect (Mac: ⌘+D, Windows: CTRL+D).

16. Double-click on the Layer name in the Layers palette and name it Floater. Change the Apply mode to Difference.

17. Make a new Layer (Mac: OPTION+click, Windows: ALT+click on the New Layer icon at the bottom of the Layers palette). Name the Layer Lens Flare. Set the Apply mode to Overlay and click the box that says Fill with Overlay—Neutral color (50% gray). The Layer should appear just above the Floater Layer.

18. Apply the Lens Flare filter (Filter → Render → Lens Flare, Brightness: 121, Lens Type: 35 MM Prime). Set the center of the flare just a little to the lower right of the center of the image. Click OK.

19. Turn off the eye icons next to the Basic Noise and Emboss layers so you can better see the effect of the Lens Flare filter. Drag the Opacity slider for the Lens Flare layer down to 0, then back up to 100. When you use a neutral fill in Overlay mode, you do not change the underlying values in the Layer beneath. Therefore, only the changes made to the Layer by the Lens Flare filter affect the Gradient beneath. You can drag the Layer around if you wish (but you need to fill the empty portions of it with neutral gray if you move the Lens Flare around). If you want to see more of the Lens Flare, change the Apply mode for that Layer to Hard Light. The gray background still fades from view.

20. You now have almost unlimited settings you can twiddle for this image. Change opacities and Apply modes on the various Layers to experiment with different effects. Finally, set the image as follows, and check your work against Figure 4-18.

Layer	Apply Mode	Opacity
Emboss	Normal	60% Opacity
Basic Noise	Multiply	100% Opacity
Lens Flare	Hard Light	85% Opacity
Floater	Difference	81% Opacity
Gradient	Normal	90% Opacity

You can stack Layers and filter effects as deep as memory allows. This is an excellent way of preserving your ability to change your mind as you work. As you progress through this course, you will also learn ways to change color in Layers and make other modifications enabling you to easily accommodate requests for changes to an image.

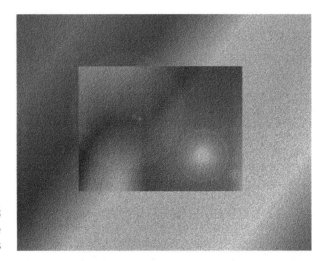

Figure 4-18
Multilayered image
for infinite changes

Command Watch

To float a selection, press ⌘+J (Mac) or CTRL+J (Windows). This creates a new Layer
that does not affect the image data below it. You make whatever changes you wish
to this new Layer without harming anything else in your image. If you decide you do
not want the Layer—you like the filtered result and want to merge it with the Layer
beneath—press ⌘+E (Mac) or CTRL+E (Windows) to Merge Down.

Filter in Channels

You can also filter an individual channel. The two reasons for doing this are

1. To apply a filter when there is not quite enough memory to filter easily.
   This technique works with any filter that can process a grayscale image.
   You apply the filter to each channel individually, but filter all the image
   channels (the RGB or CMYK channels).

2. To apply a filter to only one channel for a special effect.

You can apply a filter to a single channel if it is not grayed out on the Filters menu
when you have the desired channel active. One common reason for applying a filter
to only one channel is to keep a Gradient from banding. You could apply a low, different amount of noise to one or more of the image channels. This light noise (under
6 in value) helps to reduce the banding on output.

Fade Your Filters

A new feature in Photoshop 4.0 enables you to *fade* (selectively undo) a filter after it is applied. The Fade command (located on the Filter menu under the indication of the last filter used) can reduce the filter's intensity so almost none of it—or all of it—is kept. You can set the filter Opacity anywhere from 0% to 100%. At the same time, you can change the filter Apply mode. This means, for example, you can multiply noise into your image. This adds a whole new dimension of flexibility to filters.

Filter with Masks

A very valuable technique for selectively filtering an image is to use an Alpha channel mask. If the mask is black and white, it either filters or does not filter specific areas of the image (see Chapter 2, "Making Selections," and Chapter 3 if you do not remember how to create these masks). You get the most interesting results, however, when you filter through a channel containing shades of gray. You can create a self-mask by duplicating either a grayscale version of the composite color channel or one of the specific color channels, and using it as a mask. If you wish to change mostly the light tones, you create a positive mask; to change mostly the dark tones, you create a negative mask.

Misuse of the Filters

Once you learn what each filter does, you can deliberately use the filter in unexpected ways or at normally undesirable settings to achieve unique special effects. For example, setting the Dust & Scratches filter to a radius of 16 and a threshold of 1 severely removes the image detail. However, by placing it under a copy of the original image that's had the Find Edges filter applied to it, you can get the look of fine ink lines applied over a watercolor wash. Figure 4-19 shows this effect.

Figure 4-19
Dust & Scratches
filter misused

Make the Filters Your Own

Finally, you need to learn to use the filters—especially the special effects ones—in ways showing your creativity and individuality. Some filters have very distinctive looks. The four sets of filters that originally comprised the Adobe Gallery Effects Series of plug-ins (Artistic, Brush Strokes, Sketch, Texture) contain filters which turn your original image into a watercolor, a pen and ink drawing, and so on. They can be useful filters, but you cannot simply apply one to an image and claim to have produced an original work of art. It is too obvious how the effect was obtained.

As you work with the filters, you need to find ways to combine the distinctive filters with the original image so you lessen their right-from-the-box look. One way to do this is to filter in a new Layer and combine the Layers with different Apply modes and Opacity settings. You can even create multiple Layers over the original image.

If you work with generated textures, you can combine several of them together to produce something with your own artistic stamp on it, rather than simply using the algorithm the programmer created. Fractals, too, can be merged with your image data for new and exciting effects.

If you are trying to produce special effects with filters, applying multiple filters to the same selection is often a good technique. However, think very carefully before you apply many different filters to various parts of your image—especially if the filter is a decorative one. Instead of a uniform piece of art, you may instead produce a *filter sampler*. The image in Figure 4-20(a) is another African image from Kai's Power Photos IV collection. The image is so wonderful that even the inappropriate use of too many filters cannot quite destroy it—but it comes close. The image uses the Crosshatch, Add Noise, Crystallize, Conte Crayon, Tiles, Glowing Edges, Bas Relief, and Chrome filters on totally different parts of it. It depicts the effects of too many filters and not enough thought.

Figure 4-20(b) uses as many filters, but much more thought. This image, original-ly designed for an article on filters for *Computer Artist* magazine, uses a collage of images from the MetaTools MetaPhotos Set I. The farmer is composited on top of a seamless repeat pattern created from component images by Real TexureTools AutoTile. The farmer's shadow was done with Auto F/X Power/Pac I. Extensis PhotoEmboss was used to emboss the corn basket and the individual ears of corn. Extensis PhotoBevel was used to create the border on the image. Extensis PhotoText was used to set the type, which was then filtered with the WildRiverSSK MagicMask filter (Metalize). The ram's horn also used the Metalize effect from MagicMask, but the WildRiverSSK MagicCurtain filter was used first to apply shading to both the horn and the ram. The large red pepper was given a weave and smoke treatment in Andromeda Techtures. The farmer's overalls were origi-nally blue with dirt. Chromatica was used to change them to green, but then the WildRiverSSK Chameleon filter was used to change the dirt from bright purple (which is what the Chromatica filter produced) to the reddish mud pictured here. Even though many filters were used here, the image hangs together.

**Figure 4-20
a)** Too many inappropriate filters are used on this image
b) Many filters are used on this image, but it looks fine

a

b

1. Filters can be divided into two very broad classes: _____ filters and
   _____ filters.
   a. Application
   b. Distortion
   c. Prepress
   d. Special Effects

2. Which class of filters is used to correct or enhance an image?
   a. Application
   b. Distortion
   c. Prepress
   d. Special Effects

3. Which class of filters is used to change image data by distorting reality?
   a. Application
   b. Distortion
   c. Prepress
   d. Special Effects

4. Channels can be filtered, too. Why would you want to do this?
   a. Because there is not enough memory to apply a filter easily
   b. To keep a Gradient fill from banding
   c. To add more flexibility to Photoshop
   d. To create a special effect

5. What can you do to reduce the intensity of a filter?
   a. Change the Opacity of the filter.
   b. Change the color of the filter.
   c. Use the Fade command to fade the filter.
   d. Change the filter Apply mode.

MAJOR FILTERS

In this section, we will look at some of the filters in each filter class. Entire books have
been written on the topic of filters and how to use them. It is not possible to cover every
filter in detail here.

Artistic Filters

The 15 filters in the Artistic category were part of the Adobe Gallery Effects series of third-party plug-ins. They are included in Photoshop's native filter list for the first time in Version 4.0. The Artistic filters are used to create a specific art style in your image. Use these filters on an entire image for the best *intended* results. However, you can get more exciting and *personalized* results by combining them with apply modes or other filtering effects. The Artistic filters work in RGB or Grayscale modes only. All the Artistic filters have Small Filter Dialog previews.

The *Colored Pencil* filter takes an image or selection and stylizes it to resemble colored pencils on paper stock. The background color in your Toolbox is the paper color that shows through.

The *Cutout* filter is similar to the Posterize command. It simplifies the colors of your image into the number of levels you request, but it picks colors from the original image—rather than colorspace primitives (RGB or CMYK)—to posterize to.

The *Dry Brush* filter imitates the traditional dry brush technique of dragging a wet paintbrush until it runs out of paint. As the paintbrush dries out, the paint sputters across the area in a very attractive manner.

The *Film Grain* filter is a Noise filter, but it also can lighten and intensify parts of the image. This filter, even at its highest setting, does not overwrite the image the way the Noise filter does at high settings.

The *Fresco* filter is like the Dry Brush filter, but it intensifies the contrast in the image and makes the darks much bolder.

The *Neon Glow* filter makes a strange duo or tritone from your image, depending on your color choices. It uses the settings of the foreground and background colors, as well as a third color chosen in the filter itself. Pick contrasting colors for the most noticeable results. If black and white are your foreground and background colors, you will get a grayscale image with the filter's *Color* color as your glow.

The *Paint Daubs* filter is a mix between the Dust & Scratches filter with a Radius of 16 and a Threshold of 0 (which creates blurry areas of color) and the Unsharp Mask filter. It sort of leaves dabs of color, but the name is not very descriptive of what it actually does.

The *Palette Knife* filter looks as if you are placing flat strokes of color on a canvas underpainted with black. The darkest shadow areas turn solid black, and the image seems to gain in saturation.

The *Plastic Wrap* filter can be used to impart shine to portions of your image, or give the entire image an extremely dimensional look.

The *Poster Edges* filter adds black detail around the edges for a woodcut look. You can get similar results from using the High Pass filter at a setting of 1.6 followed by the Threshold command, and placing this image over the original in Multiply mode.

The *Rough Pastels* filter uses textures in the filter or in another file. The pastels show up on the raised portions of the texture.

The *Smudge Stick* filter looks as if you smudged a chalk or pastel drawing with a towel. This is a good filter to use over the Add Noise filter on a blank image to create texture.

The *Sponge* filter looks like someone is dabbing paint onto the image. You can specify the amount of paint and the size of the sponge.

The *Underpainting* filter yields a skeleton image that uses a texture and is so real, you'd think the paint was still wet. It looks exactly as it should if you had only sketched in the details with thin oils on a canvas.

The *Watercolor* filter is supposed to make an image look as if it were painted with watercolors. It doesn't really. It intensifies the dark areas in the image too much, and the final colors are all extremely strong.

Figure 4-21 shows a sample of all the Artistic filters.

Blur Filters

Blur filters work by lessening the differences between adjacent pixels. If you have an area of white pixels and an area of black pixels, you can make the image look less focused by applying a blur filter, which creates an area of gray. There are six Blur filters: Blur, Blur More, Gaussian Blur, Motion Blur, Radial Blur, and Smart Blur. All work by creating shades of intermediate color in the image. Blur and Blur More are one-step filters. They have very little effect on an image and are rarely used since Gaussian Blur does the same thing with more control.

The *Gaussian Blur* filter is one of the most often used and most useful filters in Photoshop. It is a production filter— it is rarely used by itself. It helps to create drop shadows and is a useful first step in many filter effects recipes.

Motion Blur simulates an object in motion by blurring the ends of it at the angle and amount you specify. It works well when used over the original image, with a Layer mask used to reveal only the specific parts of the image that are moving.

The *Radial Blur* filter can look like a starfield coming at you, or can blur and twist at the same time. It either zooms or spins.

Smart Blur is a new filter in Photoshop 4.0 and blurs the area within similar colors.

Figure 4-22 shows an image with all six Blur filters sequentially applied (Blur, Blur More, Gaussian Blur, Motion Blur, Radial Blur, Smart Blur).

Figure 4-21
Artistic filters (left to right, top to bottom): Colored Pencil, Cutout, Dry Brush, Film Grain, Fresco, Neon Glow, Paint Daubs, Palette Knife, Plastic Wrap, Poster Edges, Rough Pastels, Smudge Stick, Sponge, Underpainting, Watercolor

Figure 4-22
Blur filters (left to right): Blur, Blur More, Gaussian Blur, Motion Blur, Radial Blur, Smart Blur

Brush Strokes Filters

The Brush Strokes filters were once part of the Gallery Effects filter set. They are all new to Photoshop 4.0. They only work in RGB or Grayscale modes, and all of them have Small Filter Dialog previews. They are best used to stylize an image or create texture. The Brush Strokes filters are a great starting point for creating textures. Use them on a blank image that's had Noise added to it.

The *Accented Edges* filter is similar to the Find Edges filter but gives more texture to an image.

The *Angled Strokes* filter looks as if strokes were applied to a canvas in oils with a brush in diagonal lines. You can control which diagonal is used, or you can select both.

The *Crosshatch* filter creates lovely textures—as if a brush were stroked at a criss-cross on the canvas. It can also look like a random weave.

The *Dark Strokes* filter is similar to the Angled Strokes but doesn't show the brush strokes as clearly.

The *Ink Outlines* filter is very similar to the Dark Strokes filter, but you control the Stroke Length rather than the Stroke Direction.

The *Spatter* filter looks as if someone stuffed the image into an airbrush and sprayed it out in little dots of paint.

The *Sprayed Strokes* filter allows you to stroke an image horizontally or vertically. It is similar to the Dark Strokes, Spatter, and Ink Outlines filters.

The *Sumi-e* filter is a calligraphy filter that works very well with text and in Channel Operations (CHOPs). The Stroke Pressure is the one setting that differentiates it from other filters in this category.

Figure 4-23 shows an image with every filter in the Brush Strokes category applied to it.

Figure 4-23
Brush Strokes filters
(left to right, top to
bottom): Accented
Edges, Angled
Strokes, Crosshatch,
Dark Strokes, Ink
Outlines, Spatter,
Sprayed Strokes,
Sumi-e

Try this Hands On, which uses some of the Brush Strokes and Textures filters to create a neutral, yet very textured, background.

BRUSH STROKES FILTERS

1. Create a new image 500×500 pixels.

2. Apply the Grain filter (Filter → Texture → Grain, Intensity: 100, Contrast: 50, Grain Type: Clumped).

3. Apply the Ink Outlines filter (Filter → Brush Strokes → Ink Outlines, Stroke Length: 4, Dark Intensity: 20, Light Intensity: 10).

4. Make a new Layer (Mac: OPTION+click, Windows: ALT+click on the New Layer icon at the bottom of the Layers palette). Set the Apply mode to Multiply and check the box marked Fill with Multiply Neutral Color (white). Click OK.

5. Apply the Texturizer filter to the image (Filter → Texture → Texturizer, Texture: Burlap, Scaling: 200, Relief: 4, Light Direction: Top).

6. The effect is too light to see. Open the Levels command (Mac: ⌘+L, Windows: CTRL+L). Drag the black Input slider until the left Input Levels box reads 215. Click OK.

7. In order to add a filter that works on both Layers at once, you either need to flatten them—limiting what you can do with them afterward—or you need to capture a picture of the two together and filter it. The easiest way to do this is to get the *merged* Layers into a new Layer without losing the original Layers.

8. Make a new Layer (click on the New Layer icon at the bottom of the Layers palette).

9. Press the modifier key (Mac: OPTION, Windows: ALT) and select the Merge Visible command from the Layers menu or Layers palette menu (or press Mac: SHIFT+⌘+OPTION+E, Windows: SHIFT+ALT+CTRL+E).

10. Apply the Angled Strokes filter to this top Layer (Filter → Brush Strokes → Angled Strokes, Direction Balance: 50, Stroke Length: 37, Sharpness: 3). This makes a very attractive texture.

11. Change the Layer Apply mode to Exclusion. You now have a basically gray texture that is very rich but subtle, which almost looks like woven fabric. If you flattened the texture and lightened it, you could use it as a background for a Web page (using the ColorGIF filter, it reduces to 64 colors quite well). Figure 4-24 shows a lightened version of this texture.

Distort Filters

The Distort filters are special effects filters enabling you to apply a variety of changes to your image. They work by moving pixels around in your image. Blur and Sharpen filters change the value of the pixels; the Distort filters actually move the pixels. Let's look at the filters on this submenu.

Figure 4-24
Boucle Woven
texture

The *Diffuse Glow* filter adds a strange glow to your image. It does not really distort it. It is one of the old Gallery Effects filters. Your best friend in this filter will be the Fade Filter... command, which lets you tame this to acceptable levels.

The *Displace* filter is one of the most complex and powerful of all the Distort filters. It enables you to simulate the way an object looks when viewed through glass or water. You can select any Photoshop file as the source for the displacement, and you can select the amount of the displacement. You can also select how the source interacts with the item being displaced: whether it is stretched or tiled. For each pixel being filtered, the Displace filter looks at the matching pixel in the Source image. If the source pixel is a midgray, the filtered pixel does not move. If the source pixel is black, the filtered pixel moves to the right and down. If the source pixel is white, the filtered pixel moves to the left and up. For shades of gray falling on either side of midgray, the filtered pixel is moved less than the maximum displacement.

The *Glass* filter is similar to the Displace filter because it uses Displacement mapping logic. It was designed, however, to simulate the effect of viewing an image through a pane of glass. It was one of the Gallery Effects filters.

The *Ocean Ripples* filter is another Gallery Effects displacement filter. It is supposed to make the image look like it's under water. You cannot select a texture for this effect.

The *Pinch* filter lets you squeeze or expand an image. The squeeze version of the Pinch filter (the positive numbers on the dialog) works as though the pixels are being sucked toward the filter's center. The expand portion of the filter (the negative numbers) looks like a bubble is being blown in the center of the filtered area. The Pinch filter is easy to use but only has a thumbnail preview. It is most useful for production work, such as thinning thick lips or a full nose. In most other situations, it is only a specialty filter.

Polar Coordinates is another specialty filter. It is extremely useful for creating rainbows and text around a circle. It enables you to either change an image into polar coordinates, or assuming the image is already using polar coordinates, change it back to rectangular coordinates. A unique way to use this filter is to apply it to an image, add more drawing to it, then change it back.

The *Ripple* filter does a good job of simulating the movement of water. It allows you to create small, medium, or large ripples. These ripples are straight line, S-shaped waves. You can change the direction of the ripples by dragging the amount slider to the left or right. The Amount slider controls the depth of the ripple.

The *Shear* filter enables you to distort your image horizontally. This is generally an underused filter, but it is very powerful. The 4×4 grid allows you to either slant the image right or left, or perform a Bezier distortion on it. You can click on any point on the distortion line and create a new point. You can then arrange the points to form a distortion curve. You can set the image to wrap around or create a blank canvas as it distorts.

The *Spherize* filter remaps the pixels in the selected area to form a sphere—as if you stretched your image to fit around an overturned bowl. You have control over the amount of the stretching and can even pull the edges toward the center of the image by selecting a negative direction. You can also choose to move the pixels only horizontally or vertically. The sphere created moves pixels only; unlike the Glass Lens filters in the Kai's Power Tools filter pack, no shading is added to the sphere.

The *Twirl* filter enables you to swirl the image from the center of the selected area. You can control the amount and direction of the twirl. This filter is excellent for generating seamless textures when used in conjunction with the Offset filter.

The *Wave* filter allows you to produce distortions based on wave transformations. You can select from Sine, Square, or Triangle forms. You can also select the number of generators, the minimum and maximum amplitude, the minimum and maximum wave length, and the horizontal and vertical scale. This filter creates special effects. It has no preset values, and you need to experiment to discover which settings you like.

The *ZigZag* filter is the filter of choice for creating pond ripples. This is counterintuitive, given the fact there is also a Ripple filter. However, the ZigZag filter does the best job of simulating the motion produced when a stone is thrown into a body of water. There are a number of controls on this filter. You can select the number of ripples and the amount of the ripple. You can also select from three types of ripples: Pond Ripples, Out from Center, or Around Center. The Around Center option looks very much like the Twirl filter except instead of a smooth swirl, it uses the number of ripples setting along each of the four arms of the swirl.

Figure 4-25 shows a combination of all the Distort filters.

Noise Filters

The Noise filters enable you to create and remove *noise* (stray pixels) from your images. All scanned images contain noise. Some of this noise is from dust on the scanner; some is from the film grain. If you are scanning photographs printed on textured paper, the paper texture shows up as noise. If you create flat color in your document and want it to blend in with other areas of a continuous tone image, you have to add noise so it does not look out of place and artificial.

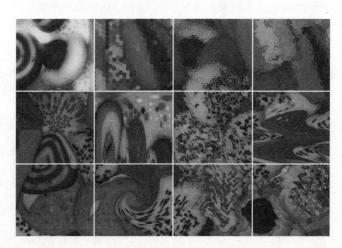

Figure 4-25
Distort filters (left to right, top to bottom): Diffuse Glow, Displace, Glass, Ocean Ripples, Pinch, Polar Coordinates, Ripple, Shear, Spherize, Twirl, Wave, ZigZag

The *Add Noise* filter is probably the most used of all the Noise filters. It adds random pixels of color to your image in the amount you specify. The pixels can be added uniformly, or they can be added using a Gaussian distribution, which looks more random and clumped together. In addition, the noise can be added in color (bits of red, green, or blue), or as monochromatic, in shades of gray. The Add Noise filter provides the perfect basis for creating paper textures in Photoshop, or for creating many special effect textures. In addition, the filter is extremely useful as a prepress filter. It can help to prevent banding when added in small amounts to gradients or graduated areas of an image. It is also useful when retouching and restoring a damaged image to add some noise to the worked-over areas and make them blend better with the original image.

The *Despeckle* filter is used to help remove stray pixels from an image. It is a one-step filter, so you have no control over what it removes and how it works. You can apply the filter multiple times, however, until you get the results you want or the filter looks like it has done as much as it can. The filter works by looking for sharp changes in value in the image. It assumes the value changes are edges needing to be preserved. It leaves these edges alone and slightly blurs the remaining pixels. The final result looks as if noise was removed or lessened in the image. It is often a good idea to use the Despeckle filter before using the Unsharp Mask filter. That way, there is less chance of sharpening the undesirable image noise along with the image detail. In addition, the Despeckle filter can return values of gray to an image that has had Levels applied to it.

The *Dust & Scratches* filter does an excellent job of removing small areas of imperfection in a scanned image. By allowing you to control the threshold and radius of the filter, Dust & Scratches can blend a flawed image area into the surrounding acceptable areas. This is often the better way to handle a long scratch or mote of dust than picking up a nearby area with the Rubber Stamp tool. When you have a tear in an area like an eye, in which there is not much else in the image to use as a source for the Rubber Stamp tool, Dust & Scratches provides an excellent means of blending the damaged area. The filter works by blurring the area towards the median color. This results in an overall softening of image detail inside the selection Marquee. For this reason, Dust & Scratches must be used with great care. Unless the filter is being misused deliberately for special effects, it should not be run against the entire image. To use it properly, you need to very carefully select the imperfection and a bit of its surroundings—as little of the surrounding area as needed to show Photoshop what the good area looks like. You then need to chose the radius and threshold carefully so you only affect the desired area and do not create a general blur there. Luckily, this is a full-preview filter, so you can easily see your results.

The *Median* filter is the final filter in this group—and the least used of the bunch. It helps reduce noise by making the pixels in the selected area more alike. The filter works best when the pixels are fairly close in value to one another. In an image of sharp red and white checkerboard squares, this filter makes no difference at all. You can select the radius of the effect and see a full preview before committing to the change. The filter almost creates a watercolor effect.

Figure 4-26 shows a combination of the four Noise filters.

Figure 4-26
Noise filters (left to right, top to bottom): Add Noise, Despeckle, Dust & Scratches, Median

Pixelate Filters

None of the filters on this menu are especially useful, except for special effects. The common link between these filters is that they all break up an image into flat areas of color and create abstraction rather than reality. All these filters leave the image, for the most part, unrecognizable.

The *Color Halftone* filter enables you to set the screen angles for each color channel. The final effect resembles the color reproduction in old newspapers, in which every portion of the halftone rosette is visible. This filter is useful only for special effects. The smallest dot size is 4. This is not useful for previewing your color separations, though it would be nice if it were. Unless you want a comic book look for color halftones, you are better off creating the effect by splitting all your channels and changing each to a bitmap using the correct screen angle for that plate. Then recombine the images into one.

The *Mezzotint* filter is another poor simulation of the real thing. A mezzotint is a dithered rendition of the image that looks like it was formed by drops of paint. A good mezzotint is delicate and very fine. This filter creates a variety of screens so coarse they are almost unusable—especially for something you really wanted to mezzotint. This is a good filter for you to avoid using. There are other ways to create mezzotints; Waite Group Press' *Photoshop Special Effects How-To* describes a number of them. There is also a wonderful third-party filter set from Andromeda, called Screens, that creates an enormous variety of mezzotints—and does it beautifully.

The *Facet* and *Fragment* filters are one-step filters that are also of marginal use. The Facet filter flattens the detail in the image, attempting to make it look hand-painted. As a mechanical substitute it's not bad, but the computer-induced regularity in the final image makes the output less than artistically successful. The images do look abstracted and impressionistic to an extent (if you can see the effect of the filter at all), but they lack the charm of handmade paintings. The Fragment filter has no charm whatsoever.

According to the Photoshop manual, the Fragment filter creates four copies of the image, offsets them from one another, and averages the results. The results actually look like you tried to take a photograph during an earthquake. If that's that look you want, go for it. However, this filter offers little for me to recommend it.

The *Mosaic* filter divides the image into squares of 2 to 64 pixels. Within each square, the color is averaged. This produces an image that's always less saturated than the original. The filter is very good for helping to produce cubist effects or for simplifying images. It is excellent as a first step in producing Counted Cross Stitch designs or designs for any craft using a grid as a basis.

The *Crystallize* filter also divides your image into solid-colored areas. However, these areas are more organic—crystalline in shape. The filter allows you to set a crystal size from 3 to 300 pixels. This is a very good special effects filter and can produce very attractive results. It is a wonderful filter when applied to an Alpha channel that is then used as a mask to apply other effects.

The *Pointillize* filter replaces the image area with dots—sort of a tribute to Georges Seurat, but the dots do not touch one another. This can be a very lovely special effect and actually does have a number of uses in images intended to be designy rather than realistic. The Pointillize filter works on a totally white image and is sensitive to the foreground and Background colors in the Toolbox.

Figure 4-27 shows a combination of the Pixelate filters.

Render Filters

The Render filters are a group of RAM-hungry filters that create Clouds, Lighting Effects, and Lens Flares. They owe their origins to 3D technology, Ray Tracing, and the study of Fractals.

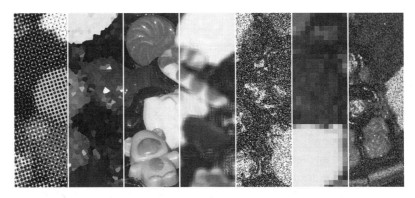

Figure 4-27
Pixelate filters (left to right): Color Halftone, Mezzotint, Facet, Fragment, Mosaic, Crystallize, Pointillize

The *Clouds* filter is the only filter in Photoshop that works on an empty Layer. It uses the foreground and background colors to create wispy formations simulating clouds, smoke, or fog. Since the filter totally replaces anything on the active Layer and is not sensitive to anything on the Layer, it is usually best to run this filter in its own blank Layer. That way, you can easily set the Opacity and Apply mode after the filter has run. The cloud formations produced by this filter resemble clouds as seen from an airplane, rather than clouds seen from the ground moving towards the horizon line. You can build up soft watercolor-washed backgrounds by layering Clouds Layers in different colors and Apply modes on top of each other.

The *Difference Clouds* filter does not work in an empty Layer. It uses the foreground and background colors to create cloud formations, but matches these clouds with the underlying pixels and shows the Difference as the result. If you use black and white as your colors, you invert part of your image. Picking a dark and a light key color in your image seems to work nicely in most cases; however, this is really only a filter for special effects.

You have already used the *Lens Flare* filter. This filter creates the look of the sun bouncing off the lens. It works well in an Overlay or Hard Light Layer filled with neutral color. This is a very RAM-intensive filter, so if you are low on RAM it will not work. It works in RGB mode only. If you are using a 680' Mac, the filter requires an FPU.

The *Lighting* filter is another RAM-intensive filter. This filter simulates the effect of lights shining on the image. Although the interface looks complex, it is actually fairly straightforward. You can add as many lights as you want (and have RAM for), and you can change their color. You can also set the lights up so the final effect imitates the shine you get off a reflective, plastic, or metallic surface. You can add bump maps to your artwork and create 3D effects. The Lighting filter can see bump maps in either the grayscale values of one of the color channels or in any of the Alpha channels. This provides a very easy way to add 3D text to an image with full control over the lighting. You will use this filter in Chapter 5, "Working with Paint and Text Tools."

Glossary

Bump Map: A bump map is an image used as a source to generate 3D textures. When a 3D rendering program reads the source file, it sees the gray values as guides to height. Most often, white areas in the source image are *high* and black is *low*. Neutral gray creates a flat plane. The user normally has control over the actual amount of depth or height.

Sharpen Filters

There are four Sharpen filters: Sharpen, Sharpen More, Sharpen Edges, and Unsharp Mask. Of these, only the last one, Unsharp Mask, gives you control over the results. The other three are one-step filters. The Sharpen filters are the opposite of the Blur filters. While the Blur filters make the image soft and fuzzy, the Sharpen filters help make the image look crisper and more in focus. Almost any scanned image needs some sharpening to correct the softness caused by the scanning process itself. Unless you are working with a drum-scanned image—which should have been sharpened during the scan—you probably need to sharpen your images. The amount of sharpening needed depends on the size of the image, its resolution, its content, and the method of output.

The *Sharpen* and *Sharpen More* filters both give a jolt to your image—usually they're either too gentle or they sharpen the wrong things. There is never any real reason you need to use these filters, although you can strengthen the effect by applying the filter multiple times.

The *Sharpen Edges* filter looks at areas in the image in which there is a distinct change in color. At the break in color, the program finds an edge and sharpens it. The only problem with this is that you still cannot define the amount of sharpening, and your idea of an edge and the image's may be completely different.

The most useful and important filter of this group is the *Unsharp Mask* filter. The term Unsharp refers to the photographic process of sandwiching the original negative and a slightly blurred negative together to make an unsharp negative. The filter works by looking for areas of value change. It then lightens the lighter pixels and darkens the darker ones along the edge to make an apparent improvement in detail. It is a very interesting filter: Although it is easy to use, there is quite a lot of theory about *how* to use it and which settings to use.

Much of the collective wisdom of experienced Photoshop users regarding the topic of unsharp masking comes from two books: *Real World Scanning and Halftones*, by Steve Roth and David Blatner (Peachpit Press, 1993) and *Real World Photoshop*, by Bruce Fraser and David Blatner (Peachpit Press, 1996). Extensive experimentation was done to arrive at the conclusions of these authors. The information included here is derived from their work.

Figure 4-28 shows the Unsharp Mask filter dialog. Notice it contains three components: the Amount, Radius, and Threshold. Let's look at each of these components.

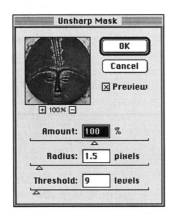

Figure 4-28
Unsharp Mask filter
dialog

The Radius setting is the first setting you should adjust. Radius defines the distance the filter affects. If the Radius is 1, 4 pixels are changed—2 on either side of the edge. For every addition to the Radius, another 4 pixels further from the edge are affected. If the Radius is too small, the unsharp masking is not very effective. If it is too large, a very unpleasant halo results. Oversharpened images look worse than slightly blurry ones. You should start the Radius setting at ½ the dpi of your image. If your image is scanned at 300 dpi, the Radius value should be 1.5 (dpi÷200).

The Amount setting determines just how dark the dark side of the edge gets and how light the edge's light side gets; it controls the change in contrast along the edges. A large Amount setting causes high contrast along the edges. There are many settings yielding almost the same results, but as you increase the Amount setting you need to decrease the Radius to keep the degree of sharpening constant. Typically, a good Amount is around the 200 percent mark. You can start testing the filter at anywhere between 200 percent to 400 percent. If the image is being printed as a halftone, it can stand more sharpening than if it was being printed to film. If you are going to print the image, it can be oversharpened on your screen and still print fine, since the halftoning process removes some of the sharpening from the image.

The Threshold setting determines the values included in the edge-finding process. If the Threshold is set to 0 all values in the image are included, and an edge is found anywhere a pixel differs from another. This has the effect of creating edges in skin tones, clouds, and other areas that should remain smooth. It also creates edges accentuating the noise, dust, and scratches in an image. As a general rule, the Threshold setting should not drop below 4. If you set it too high nothing happens, and you see no change from the filter. Again, as a general rule, the Threshold setting should not exceed 10.

Large images need more sharpening than small ones. Small images need to be sharpened at a lower Radius since their details take up fewer pixels. Images should be sharpened as one of the last steps in the process. Generally, you should sharpen only after all image editing and color correction is done and you are ready to convert the image to CMYK for printing.

Sketch Filters

The Sketch filters are from the Adobe Gallery Effects set of filters. Most of these filters translate the image into some type of two-toned image, usually using the foreground and background colors as the effect colors. They imitate a number of hand-drawn artistic styles. The Sketch filters tend to simplify the shapes in the image using the logic of either the Find Edges or the Threshold commands in order to work. They only work on RGB or grayscale images.

The *Bas Relief* creates an embossing of the image, almost as if drawing it on plaster on a wall. This is an effective filter in black and white but can be confusing—or even awful—in color.

The *Charcoal* filter simulates the look of charcoal sketched on paper. Black and white are your best color choices. The Charcoal filter uses the Threshold command logic for finding the areas of greatest contrast in the image.

The *Chalk & Charcoal* filter allows you to control a drawing with two different media. The Chalk uses the background color, and the Charcoal uses the foreground color. You can set the chalk and the charcoal intensities separately. This filter really looks good in black and white.

The *Chrome* filter changes the image into a usually unrecognizable mess of gray values supposed to look as if they are reflecting light, like chrome does. Tame this filter by placing the original image *above* it in Color mode.

The *Conte Crayon* filter looks best in black and white or with tones of gray. It always uses a midgray for the mixture of foreground and background colors, regardless of what they actually are. The filter is good for reducing colors in images destined for the Web, since an image easily reduces to about six colors. This filter works best on images with areas of contrast—definite lights and darks. On a muddy image, this filter generally produces unrecognizable results.

The *Graphic Pen* filter renders a photograph like an ink-drawn sketch. It uses long strokes (or short dots, depending on the setting) and looks best on a large, contrasty image. The filter uses only two colors with no intermediate shades.

The *Halftone Pattern* filter offers some significant differences from standard bitmap conversion halftoning. It lets you apply a halftone pattern *over* an image—without converting it to bitmap—so you retain areas of gray, but still get a well-defined pattern. The Circle Pattern type of this filter draws a concentric circle over the image and uses it as the halftoning algorithm. It is a very interesting variation.

The *Notepaper* filter is a Threshold filter. In order to make it perform properly (get a result that in any way saves your image detail), you need to figure out the correct Threshold setting first. Try the Threshold command (don't actually process the image), then take the setting you like best and divide it by 255. Multiply the result by 100. Use that number in the dialog box. The filter looks like an embossed version of the Threshold command.

The *Photocopy* filter also is a Threshold filter. Your foreground color is the toner color, and your background color is the paper color. It is suitable for Web output because it reduces the colors in the image to about six. It retains enough detail on a small image to see the original subject, which is very useful.

The *Plaster* filter renders your image into a plaster wall. It depends on the values of your foreground and background colors, however, to determine if the image details indent or emboss.

The *Reticulation* filter is essentially a graytone Mezzotinting filter. It uses a different simplifying logic than the Plaster filter, even though it also creates two main color areas.

The *Stamp* filter is a good choice for Web images since it can retain a lot of detail with few colors. It is very similar to the Photocopy filter, but it can produce a 2-color image, while Photocopy reduces to 6 or more. Because of this, it can be sharper than the Photocopy filter.

The *Torn Edges* filter is a close relative of the Plaster filter except instead of embossing or indenting the Threshold area, the filter produces fuzzy edges along it.

The *Water Paper* filter is an odd duck in this category, because it does not simplify the colors of the image into two tones. It makes the image look as if it was placed in a pail of water and the ink ran off the paper in streaks. The controls in this filter seesaw. When Contrast and Brightness are either high or low, the Fiber Length selection is critical to your liking the results. It must be low or else the image will be all water. If the Brightness and Contrast settings are set towards the middle, the Fiber Length can increase with quite good results.

Figure 4-29 shows a combination of all of the Sketch filters.

Stylize Filters

The Stylize filters are among the most commonly used of the special effects filters. They abstract the image being filtered by changing colors, finding edges, or moving pixels around. Most of them work in the RGB, Grayscale, CMYK, and Lab modes.

The *Diffuse* filter takes all the pixels within the selected area and randomizes them a bit. The effect looks like you took the image and shook it so pixels fell out of place. This is a very handy filter for a number of special effects; however, it may need to be applied many times before successfully blending the pixels in an area together. The interesting thing about this filter is it preserves the original pixel colors—it just rearranges their location in the image. If you only have three colors in a Diffused area, there will remain just three discrete colors after the filter is applied.

The *Emboss* filter is one of the most frequently used filters of the group native to Photoshop. It provides a fast way of adding depth to an image. The Emboss filter enables you to set the angle, height (in pixels), and amount of the emboss. The best results come from a fairly low (2 to 4 pixels) height and a relatively low emboss amount (100 percent to 200 percent). Beyond those limits, the Emboss filter creates a large number of artifacts and odd color flashes. Within those limits the Emboss filter is fairly successful, but it embosses everything in the selected area: noise, film grain, and so on. The final result is mostly neutral gray with color flashes. There are a variety of third-party filters—most notably Alien Skin Black Box—permitting you to emboss an object outline rather than the pixels in it.

Figure 4-29
Sketch filters (top to bottom, left to right): Bas Relief, Chalk & Charcoal, Charcoal, Chrome, Conte Crayon, Graphic Pen, Halftone Pattern, Reticulation, Notepaper, Photocopy, Plaster, Stamp, Torn Edges, Water Paper

The *Extrude* filter enables you to convert your image into a bunch of blocks or pyramids of a varied depth and user-controlled size. This can create some interesting background effects—or very strange foreground effects. It is purely used for fun.

The *Find Edges* filter is another Photoshop workhorse. Although it is useful for special effects, it can add artistically to an image and sometimes be useful in creating masks or image outlines. This filter is effective either exactly as it appears (it is a one-step filter, so you have no control over it), or by inverting it so bright color shows up on black. It also works well when desaturated to grayscale and multiplied with the original image, or used over a random background to add image detail. You can change the edges the image finds by first processing it with the High Pass filter at a fairly low setting.

The *Glowing Edges* filter is an enhancement of the Find Edges filter (and comes from the Gallery Effects set). It automatically performs a find-edges-and-invert, but also lets you select the edge size and the number of edges found.

The *Solarize* filter reverses values greater than 127 in an image. It takes the amount by which a pixel exceeds the value of 127 and subtracts it from 128. If a pixel has a grayscale value of 130 (127+3) before the filter, it has a value of 125 (128–3) after the filter is applied. This remaps the entire light half of an image so no value in it exceeds 127. You can create this same effect using the Curves command. In addition, you can create many more Solarize curves with the Curves command. This is a good graphic technique in an abstract image. You should also experiment with a variety of different curves that reverse themselves.

Trace Contours is similar to the Find Edges filter, but it draws a line around the area requested and allows you to specify the level you wish to trace. This results in a generally less complex image than using the Find Edges filter. Since you have a full preview on this filter, you can fine-tune the effect before applying it. You can also use this filter to help create outlines from images.

The *Tiles* filter breaks up your image into a series of squares separated by the foreground or background color, the inverted image, or the original unchanged image. You can select the maximum number of tiles along the shortest dimension of your image. You can also select a maximum offset distance between tiles. This filter has great potential in creating interesting backgrounds or very abstract renderings on an image.

The *Wind* filter can blow the pixels in your image to the right or left. It can also blast them, blow them strongly, or pull them in both directions at once. This filter can create major havoc with your image detail—which is why you would use it. It is very handy in producing distressed wood textures and other special effects.

Figure 4-30 shows all the Stylize filters. The image has been so distorted by the filters, it is hard to discern the original candy.

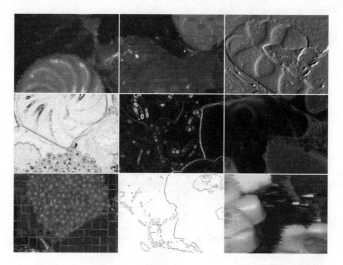

Figure 4-30
Stylize filters (left to right, top to bottom): Diffuse, Extrude, Emboss, Find Edges, Glowing Edges, Solarize, Tiles, Trace Contours, Wind

Texture Filters

The Texture filters are from the Adobe Gallery Effects filter set. They all add some type of texture to your image—either a grain or an embossing—and all of them show texture when added to a blank document. They are wonderful starts for custom textures when combined with other filters. They only work in RGB or grayscale.

The *Craquelure* filter makes an image look like a very old watercolor cracked with age. It makes wonderful textures in blank images.

The *Grain* filter is a superset of the Add Noise filter. It adds a variety of different noises to your repertoire. Many of the settings that work with one type of Grain do not work well with others. Also, some of the Grain types use the foreground and/or background color to create the grain. This filter can be used in texture recipes just as you would use the Add Noise filter.

The *Mosaic Tiles* filter is a close relative of the Craquelure filter. However, it makes irregularly contoured squares at regularly spaced intervals.

The *Patchwork* filter is somewhat misnamed. It looks more like mosaic tiles than patchwork quilts. It takes the tiles and elevates them.

The *Stained Glass* filter is another mosaic tile wanna-be. It really looks like mosaic tiles. Unfortunately, it looks nothing at all like stained glass. It is a crystallize filter with grout and stronger color. You can also add a light source, but it sits smack in the center of the image and cannot be moved.

The *Texturizer* filter just adds texture to an image. Until the Lighting Filter made its debut in Photoshop 3.0, this was the only way to easily add embossed textures and bump maps to images (besides bringing them into Painter). It gives you less control than the Lighting Effects filter, but it is easier to use.

Figure 4-31 shows the various Texture filters.

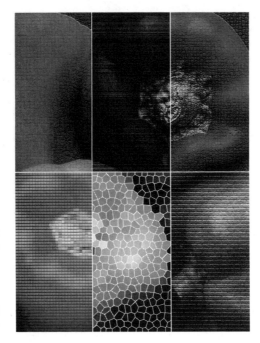

Figure 4-31
Texture filters (left to right, top to bottom): Craquelure, Grain, Mosaic Tiles, Patchwork, Stained Glass, Texturizer

Video Filters

The two Video filters are utility filters. The *NTSC Colors* filters change the colors in your image so they do not bleed or bloom when placed on a regular TV set. The bright reds are the most prominent colors changed. The *DeInterlace* filter improves the quality of a video capture by either removing every other row of pixels and duplicating a row in its place, or by interpolating between two odd or even rows.

Other Filters

The Other category of filters is a collection of filters that do not fit comfortably anywhere else. They are basically utility filters.

The *High Pass* filter removes areas of low intensity from the image. A high setting looks like it's accomplishing little in the way of filtering the image; a low setting (.5 to 1.5) makes the image almost totally gray except at areas of marked color/value changes. One of the best uses for this filter is as a first step before applying either the Find Edges filter or the Threshold command. When you set a low value to the High Pass, then turn the image into a bitmap using the Threshold command, you can get much more image detail than is otherwise possible.

The *Minimum* and *Maximum* filters are inverses of one another. The Minimum filter finds the darkest pixels within a use-specified range, and the Maximum filter pushes the image towards the lightest pixels in the range. The best use for these filters is as a way of thinning or thickening the values in a channel mask. This is especially useful when applying text effects in which you might want to process the text with a fat and thin mask.

The *Offset* filter changes the location of an image within the document borders. You can specify the side-to-side and up-and-down offset amount in pixels and whether the area moved is replaced with the background color, transparency (in a layer), or wrapped-around image. This is one of the most useful of all Photoshop filters, especially in creating patterns. It also allows you to precisely move image areas—either by calculating from the top left of the image, or by figuring in relative numbers.

QUIZ 5

1. What are Artistic filters used for?
   a. To create a specific art style in your image
   b. To create a more beautiful image
   c. To enhance individual parts of an image
   d. To darken your image

2. What are some examples of Brush Strokes Filters?
   a. Angled Strokes
   b. Crosshatch
   c. Semi filter
   d. Spiked

3. What is the most complex and powerful of the Distort filters?
   a. Spherize
   b. Polar Coordinates
   c. Shear
   d. Displace

4. What does the Dust & Scratches filter do?
   a. Cleans and polishes your image
   b. Removes small imperfections of a scanned image
   c. Blends away damaged areas of an image
   d. Creates scratches

5. Graphic Pen, Bas Relief, Notepaper, Torn Edges, Water Paper, and Reticulation all belong to what group of filters?
   a. Render filters
   b. Pixelate filters
   c. Sketch filters
   d. Stylize filters

THIRD-PARTY FILTERS

Adobe has created a standard way for companies to write filters that *plug into* Photoshop. Filters that do not come with Photoshop are called *third-party plug-ins*, and there are many of them on the market. One of the main reasons there are so many is that they can also be used by a large number of programs besides Photoshop. There is a growing list of applications supporting the Adobe Photoshop plug-in architecture. Adobe Premiere, Adobe PageMaker, Adobe Illustrator 6.0+, and Adobe AfterEffects can all use the Photoshop plug-ins—or at least use the third-party ones. So can Fractal Design Painter, Equilibrium deBabelizer, Strata and Specular's 3D programs, and Corel Photo-Paint.

Third-party filters are available commercially through mail order houses or the Adobe Plug-in Connection, or as shareware online (CompuServe, America Online, and the World Wide Web). The ones discussed below are all commercial software and available for purchase. They are listed by company. On the CD-ROM, you will find several articles originally published in *Computer Artist* magazine that go into a little more depth about some of these filter sets.

Imaging Filters

Alien Skin produces the Eye Candy filters (formerly known as the Black Box filters). This set is a special effects filter enabling you to create drop shadows, inner and outer bevels, glows, glass, carves, cutouts, and more. It does an excellent job on text.

The company *a lowly apprentice production* markets PlateMaker, absolutely the best and easiest solution for producing spot color within Photoshop. It allows you to take the Alpha channels you created for your spot colors and save them—along with a composite color preview—as a DCS2 file to place into QuarkXPress and carry enough information to properly separate the file.

Andromeda has four major filter series. Series I performs traditional photographic filter effects. Series II is a full-blown 3D filter enabling you to wrap images around simple shapes inside Photoshop. Series III creates screens and mezzotints for images. Series IV is a texture applicator that allows you to use the textures as is—as color maps, bump maps, or environment maps. There is another small filter, called Velociraptor, that creates unique motion trails.

Auto F/X Corporation produces filters that fuse textures into images and add unusually shaped edges to the borders of images, relieving the boredom of square frames (called Photo/Graphic Edges). They also have a filter that adds irregularly shaped edges to text (called Typo/Graphic Edges). In addition, their Power/Pac I filter automates many of Photoshop's more time-consuming channel operations, such as making drop shadows, glows, embossing, and screen tints of images.

CGSI has a filter set called RealTexture Tools. This Windows-only filter set comes from the world of virtual reality. Autotile creates repeating patterns using an algorithm that analyzes the selection and uses an irregular path through it to make a seamless tile—without the type of fogging created by KPT Seamless Welder from the MetaTools KPT filter set. You can also remove the effects of atmosphere and perspective from an image so it is more easily tiled. The aim of this filer set is to enable a designer to produce seamless tiles usable for terrain maps or walkthroughs in the virtual reality environment.

Chroma has a filter called Chromatica, a color-change filter. This filter allows you to select a portion of an image (for example, a sweater) and replace its color with a new one. As it replaces the color, it keeps the complexity and tonal values of the underlying image. A second filter in the set lets you replace the colors in the image (or in a selected area) with colors extracted from another image. While the Chromassage filter from Second Glance Software swaps a 256-color color table from one image to another, this filter extracts thousands of colors as the color table.

Cytopia offers the PhotoLab collection of filters creating a variety of color changes in the image. The set allows you to create gradients replacing the image values, apply photographic color filters to add or subtract a specific color range, or create sepia-tone images.

Data Stream markets a filter set called WildRiverSSK. It is a wild, marvelous, special effects filter set. There are a number of filters included: DekeBoko (a bevel filter), Chameleon (a color replacement filter), MagicCurtain and MagicFrame (filters that create gradients based on waveforms manipulating the color spectrum). The major filter in this collection is MagicMask, which applies 24 different effects to text or selections, making them look metalized, shadowed, beveled, embossed, woodgrained, wispy, and many more.

Extensis, which has a line of page layout program filters, has also released PhotoTools, a very practical filter set that adds a button bar to Photoshop so you have one-click access to your favorite commands. It also has an Embossing filter, a Drop Shadow filter, and a Bevel filter. In addition, it provides the most workable solution to editing text in Photoshop: PhotoText, which allows you to set blocks of type; kern, track, and change the styles and fonts of individual letters; and lay out a number of blocks of text at one time. It was named one of Computer Artist's Products of the Year in 1996. Extensis also produces Intellihance, a filter that corrects scanned images for tone and sharpness.

Flamingo Bay/Image XPress offers ScanPrep Pro. This Import module enables you to correct your scans in a totally automated fashion. Once you tell the module about the condition of your original (it is light, too dark, previously screened, and so on) and the final output format you want (4-color, the Web, or film recorder), the plug-in takes control of your scanner, scanning and correcting the image for you. It lets you intervene to correct for color cast (since this is difficult for any program to determine). If you do a lot of production scanning, this application quickly pays for itself.

Human Software has a number of filters. Squizz allows you to stretch and deform your image—and paint in or out this warping. The company also has several filters to help you convert Kodak PhotoCDs into CMYK color.

Digital Frontier has two color utilities for Web publishing. HVS ColorGIF 2.0 lets you create GIF files both smaller and better than Photoshop's. The reduction algorithm used allows you to change an image to Indexed Color mode and preserve the tiny amounts of trace colors that give the image its personality. All too often, these traces of color are washed away in Photoshop's native conversions. In addition, HVS ColorGIF 2.0 can convert the images so they look good without needing to dither them (dithering adds to the file size when the image is saved as a GIF). HVS JPEG creates small JPEG images interlaced for fast viewing on the Web and shows you what the JPEG compression does to your image in advance—so you can intelligently trade off size versus quality before you write the file. The two products are marketed as a bundle called Web Focus.

Boxtop Software markets PhotoGIF 2.0 and ProJPEG 2.0. These programs also prepare images for the Web. The products are sold as shareware through the Boxtop Web site. You can see demos of the products at their Web site as well: `http://www.boxtopsoft.com.`

Knoll Brothers—John and Thomas Knoll, the original creators of Photoshop—have also released a product called CyberMesh. CyberMesh is a 3D plug-in enabling you to create a grayscale image to show depth. The filter then builds a 3D model that can be exported into a 3D program for rendering. It uses the grayscale values as the basis for calculating the forms and extrusions needed.

MetaTools markets two filter sets and a number of other products. Kai's Power Tools is the granddaddy of all special effects filters. While it was not the first on the market (Gallery Effects was), it is possibly the best-known and most often used. The filters in KPT 3.0 include the Gradient Designer, Texture Designer (for generating textures), Spheroid Designer, and a variety of noise enhancement filters. The included KPT 2.1 set adds a Fractal Explorer and additional noise filters. KPT Convolver is a tool that makes the Custom filter (Filter → Other → Custom) much more useful. It works with the convolution tables in an interactive method that allows you to fine-tune your effect without having to blindly guess at numbers to plug into the grid. You can freely create blurred, raised, and oddly colored images—or use it for serious color tweaks and color corrections.

M.M.M. Software produces two filter sets, both of which are different and interesting. SISNIKK (Single Image Stereogram Development) enables you to create *stereograms*, those patterned images that reveal a hidden 3D image embedded in them if you stare at them the right way. It does an incredibly good job of it, too. The other filter set is HoloDozo, a 3D plug-in that allows you to wrap an image around one of 28 different 3D shapes. You can create flying saucers, bagels, boxes, cones, domes, and even curly pasta shells.

Second Glance Software markets a number of filters. Chromassage manipulates the image's color table and lets you substitute it with another, which creates some wild color effects. PaintThinner and PhotoSpot are a set allowing you to intelligently reduce the number of colors in your image, then create one plate per color. It is very useful for silk screening. However, it does not halftone the plates, so it is not as useful for spot coloring conventional print applications if the spot color is used in various tints. LaserSeps creates printing plates that also do not halftone; they employ a technique called

Stochastic screening (similar in look to a mezzotint on each plate). The advantage is the image printed this way will not moiré (accidentally misregister in a way causing a weird, unintended pattern to appear). Second Glance also markets Scantastic, an excellent scanner driver for Hewlett-Packard, Apple One, and Epson scanners.

Total Integration markets a large number of utility applications as plug-ins. Epilogue is a full Adobe PostScript rasterizer importing any flavor of EPS file, regardless of the application that created it. Fast/Edit Deluxe enables you to edit small portions of a large file at once and merge the edit back into the original. Unlike Photoshop's built-in Quick Edit, this module allows you to edit files saved in formats other than TIFF. You can even edit Layers from a layered Photoshop file.

Valis, a manufacturer of a number of 3D extensions and shaders for Pixar's Renderman, has a filter that lets you use Flo, a warping application, from within Photoshop. Flo is one in a progression of three products moving from warps to animation: Flo, MetaFlo, and MovieFlo.

Virtus has released Alien Skin TextureShop. This is a remarkable texture generator that can be used through Photoshop or as a stand-alone. The textures it creates are superb, and you can use either the texture, color, or bump map. Unfortunately, the product is very buggy and not well-supported.

Vivid Details has a wonderful filter called TestStrip that is a superset of the Variations command. It enables you to tweak your color corrections and view many different combinations or levels of change at once. You can also print the test strip and send it through production if you wish to find precisely the best correction for your needs.

Xaos Tools offers a number of exceptional filters. Paint Alchemy is a not-to-be-missed brushing engine. It allows you to create textures and backgrounds using brush shapes. For each brush shape, you can specify the coverage, stacking order, angle, Opacity, and color. You can change these attributes to add randomness, or make them vary by original image hue, saturation, or value. Terrazzo is a pattern generator. It takes your image and allows you to create 17 different varieties of repeat patterns from a section of the original. You can save the original tiles for reuse, or you can apply the pattern to the original image. It is like having a kaleidoscope at your fingertips. TypeCaster lets you create 3D type from within Photoshop. TubeTime is a tiny filter that creates TV noise and snow.

1. What third-party package is the best and easiest solution for producing spot color within Photoshop?
   a. Eye Candy
   b. PlateMaker
   c. RealTexture Tools
   d. Chromatica

2. DataStream writes a filter set called _____, which includes filters such as DekoBoko, Chameleon, and MagicCurtain.
   a. PhotoLab
   b. RealTextures
   c. CyberMesh
   d. WildRiverSSK

3. Which of the following packages are color-change filters?
   a. PhotoLab
   b. PlateMaker
   c. Chromassage
   d. Epilogue

4. Which of the following companies make plug-in packages that work well with texture filters?
   a. CGSI
   b. Vivid Details
   c. MetaTools
   d. Valis

5. Paint Alchemy, TubeTime, and Terrazzo are filter packages offered by
   a. Virtus
   b. Cytopia
   c. Xaos Tools
   d. Total Integration

VIP PROFILE

Eric Reinfeld, Photoshop Guru

Eric Reinfeld, a New York artist and principal of Digital Design, is a master of special effects. He has a degree in photography, with a minor in graphic design. Eric has had a somewhat eclectic career. After getting his degree, he became the owner of a dry cleaning establishment! However, he could not shake his creative background and with one look at Photoshop, he was hooked again. He saw such interesting stuff being done with the then-new program that he got a Color Mac II—and never looked back.

Eric had worked a bit with Studio/8 and Studio/32 and PixelPaint (a 24-bit paint program arriving on the scene earlier than Photoshop) and found them decent. But Photoshop—which was still Barney Scan when he saw it for the first time—was really cool.

He played and created weird stuff. He started his new artistic career doing mostly desktop publishing using Quark and PageMaker, and he worked for a belt manufacturer as a designer. He scanned buckles and leather or fabric, and put together belt simulations to show buyers so they could pick out what styles they liked. This meant the sample makers did not need to create actual samples until an interest in the style was generated.

He then went to the American Kennel Club to help them convert from traditional to desktop technologies. They had a Linotronic 300 there, so Eric started doing color separations, creating many pages for magazines and doing more Photoshop. It was there that he started developing type effects with Photoshop. It is the type effects, a consuming passion, for which Eric has become so well-known and sought out (not to mention his design and teaching skills).

On July 2 of 1992 or 1993 (Eric remembers the date but not the year), he got a Quadra 950 and downloaded Kai Krause's Photoshop tips. He began doing CHOPs—for a solid 3 days and nights. That was a major turning point for him.

After his job at the AKC, he got a job at Sterling-Bianca as a senior color desktop technician. He worked there for a year, did a lot of Photoshop work, then left to become a freelancer for his own company, Digital Design.

Eric has since worked with *Business Week*, *Time*, and a number of advertising agencies. He has taught at the Center for Creative Imaging, Pratt Institute, School of Visual Arts, United Digital Artists, and the Thunder Lizard Photoshop conferences.

His advice to beginners: "Eat it up, make it yours, immerse yourself totally. Jump in with a full body and play."

CHAPTER SUMMARY

In this chapter, you learned how to apply Photoshop filters to entire images, selections, layers, and channels within images. You also learned how to filter within memory constraints. You should now be able to use any of Photoshop's built-in filters and personalize filter results. Remember to work the Lab exercises in Appendix C. Also, check the CD-ROM for demos of many of the third-party filters discussed.

CHAPTER 5

WORKING WITH PAINT AND TEXT TOOLS

Photoshop is typically used for manipulating, rather than creating, images. However, it is a very capable paint program besides being an exceptional image editor. This chapter shows you how to use the painting tools in Photoshop to create images and work with text.

At the end of this chapter, you should be able to

- Create custom brushes
- Use an image as a brush source
- Create seamless textures
- Use textures as paper surfaces
- Add color to line art and grayscale images
- Use the Airbrush tool
- Complete an airbrush project
- Use the Type tool

⬤ Describe when to set text in Photoshop, and more importantly, when not to

⬤ Create softly embossed effects with text

IMITATING PAINT ON PAPER

Digital paint programs work by putting pixels on a screen. They can either place *flat* pixels or pretend the pixels are actually ink, chalk, and paint. Most programs can do one or the other. Photoshop falls into the first category (flat pixels on the screen), but you can also make it react to paper texture with a little care, planning, and understanding of the principles involved.

Fractal Design Painter is perhaps the premiere example of a natural media paint program. In fact, Fractal Design has trademarked the term *natural media*. Painter is the perfect companion to Photoshop if you do a lot of original drawing. You can save your images in Photoshop format and move them back and forth between the two programs. Most Photoshop artists regularly use both programs.

The hallmark of Fractal Design Painter's paintbrushes is the way they interact with the canvas. They can be made to simulate chalk, watercolors, crayons, oils, and so on, by using adjustable parameters on the brushstroke to specify whether or not it covers the previous strokes, how much it is absorbed by the drawing surface, and how much paper texture shows through. While you can get some of the same effects using Photoshop, Photoshop was not designed for this purpose and cannot do it all—nor can it do it as elegantly. In this chapter, we'll look first at building brushes, then at creating paper textures, and finally, at using brushes that react to paper textures. You will also learn how to use the Rubber Stamp tool to repair areas of an image.

Brushes

In Chapter 1, "Introduction to Photoshop," you learned how to modify Photoshop's built-in brushes and how to create a custom brush from a grayscale selection. To review: Photoshop allows you to create a circular brush of up to 999 pixels across. You can set the hardness of the brush (how feathered and transparent it is at its edge), the spacing between strokes (up to 999 pixels between brushstrokes), the shape of the ellipse creating the stroke, and the angle of the stroke. These modified brushes allow you to create, for example, a pen nib suitable for calligraphy.

How would you go about creating such a brush? The first step is to analyze what the tool is like in the real world. A calligraphic brush is one that can paint thick or thin lines as the letters are drawn. It is typically a hard edge—though not a jagged edge. So, what brush settings would this translate into? The thick and thin stroke could be accomplished by a sharply angled, fairly thin brush. When the brush is dragged in one direction, the stroke is thin; when it is dragged in the other, the stroke is much thicker. You could even design a pair of matching brushes that angle in opposite directions. If you place them next to one another on the Brushes palette, you can select between them using one key press of the [or] key. To get the hard edge, you create a brush that is almost completely hard—but still anti-aliased. Let's try it.

Command Watch

Remember, you can change your brush size without visiting the Brush palette by pressing the bracket keys on the keyboard.

The left bracket key ([) selects the brush to the left of your current brush in the Brushes palette.

The right bracket key (]) selects the brush to the right of your current brush in the Brushes palette.

You can also think of this as *previous* and *next*.

SHIFT+[selects the *first* brush in the Brushes palette.

SHIFT+] selects the *last* brush in the Brushes palette.

Hands On

CALLIGRAPHIC BRUSH CREATION

1. In the Brush palette menu, select the New Brush... option.

2. Create a small nib brush with the settings Diameter: 11, Hardness: 80%, Spacing: 15, Angle: 43°, and Roundness: 24%. Figure 5-1 shows the dialog with these settings.

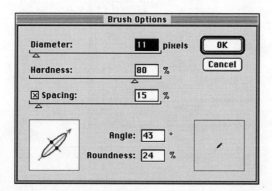

Figure 5-1
Small nib brush creation dialog

3. Try out the brush on your image. See if you like the size, angle, and spacing. Is it hard enough? Too hard? The action of the brush should be smooth but not too soft. If you do not like the settings, adjust them. Try a few variations.

4. Create another new brush that has the same settings but is larger in diameter. To essentially copy the settings from another brush, select the brush, then choose New Brush... from the Brush Palette menu. The dialog contains the settings for the selected brush. Change the diameter to 30 pixels. Figure 5-2 shows this brush.

5. Try it out as well.

6. Clear the image (Select All+DELETE).

7. Create a new image, 800-pixel square.

8. Unless you have exceptional penmanship, you need guidelines to keep your writing from wandering up and down in a given line. Turn on the Rulers (Mac: ⌘+R, Windows: CTRL+R). Pull down a guideline from the top ruler (just place your cursor on the Ruler Bar, press the mouse button, and drag downward). Leave one guide every 50 pixels (according to the side ruler). Your side ruler should show pixels as the unit of measure (if not, set this in the Preferences). If you view your image at 60% to 100% magnification, then you should see ruler marks along the left side every 50 pixels. Figure 5-3 shows the text for you to practice on. Notice the use of both pen sizes.

You can view the invitation without the guidelines by pressing ⌘+; (Mac) or CTRL+; (Windows). Does your example have the same difference in tone (lights and darks) as the example shown in Figure 5-3? It won't—unless you are using a pressure-sensitive tablet and pen rather than a mouse.

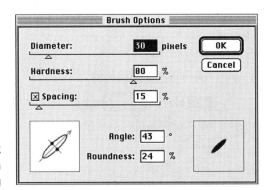

Figure 5-2
Larger nib brush
creation dialog

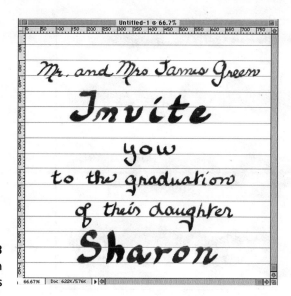

Figure 5-3
Invitation written
with new pen nibs

Pressure

If you create a lot of original art or calligraphy, a drawing tablet is a good investment. Wacom makes cordless drawing tablets that change the characteristics of the stroke based on how hard you press the stylus down (other manufacturers do, too, but Wacom was the original and is the standard against which other tablets are measured). This gives a very natural feel to the artwork, since drawing with a mouse has been compared—semi-affectionately—to drawing with a bar of soap.

Photoshop (and Fractal Design Painter) use the drawing tablet to change the size, color, and Opacity of the brushstroke as you vary the pressure of your stroke. In the Brush Options dialog, there are choices for interpreting pressure input. Figure 5-4 shows the Brush Options dialog. At the bottom, notice the Stylus Pressure setting. The options are not mutually exclusive—you can change brush size, color, and Opacity *at the same time*. If you have selected brush size, the brush varies between the actual size (with maximum pressure) and a very thin stroke. The color option causes a variation between the background color if you make soft strokes and the foreground color if you press hard. The Opacity setting changes the transparency of the stroke from very transparent at low pressure to fully opaque at full pressure. Figure 5-5 shows samples of scribbles with size, color, Opacity, and both size and Opacity selected as the pressure settings.

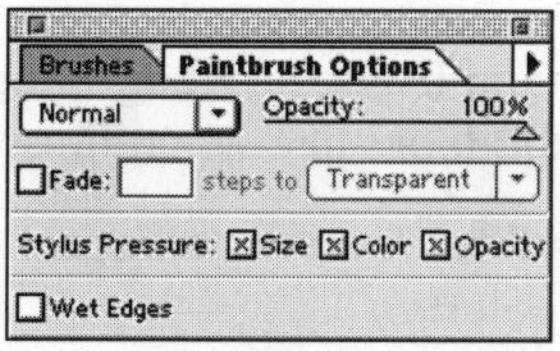

Figure 5-4
Brush Options
dialog showing
pressure settings

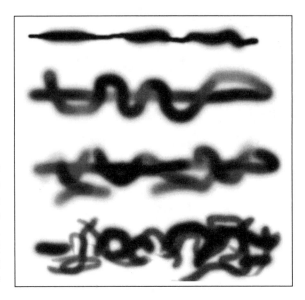

Figure 5-5
Image showing
(from top to
bottom) variations
in brush stroke size,
color, Opacity, and
both size and
Opacity

Creating Custom Brushes

In Chapter 1, you also learned how to capture a small image and use it as a custom brush. The image used was a squiggle—not very exciting, but sufficient to show the basic principle. In this section, you will see how to obtain two completely different effects from custom brushes.

A custom brush created from a piece of a photograph provides an easy way to create a colorized graphic—easier than copying and colorizing the image and laying it out by hand. While you do lose the flexibility of layering a pasteable image gives you, you can make up for it in ease, speed, and a certain serendipity and rhythm.

In this Hands On, you will take an image and create a brush to use as a graphic design. As you do, you will have an opportunity to practice your newfound selection skills.

CUSTOM BRUSHES #1

1. Open the image Manisha.Psd.

2. Using the Color Range command (Select → Color Range...), select Manisha's hair. Figure 5-6 shows what this looks like when finished.

3. Save the selection to a channel (click on the elliptical Marquee icon in the bottom left of the Channels palette).

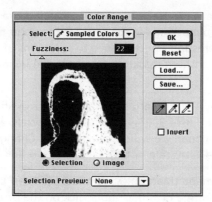

Figure 5-6
Color Range
selection for start
of custom brush

4. Click on the name of a new channel (Channel 4) in the Channels palette to make it active. Manisha's hair offers a convenient way to select her from the background. Using white as the foreground color, paint the mask so all Manisha—except her left shoulder—is selected, and none of the background is. Figure 5-7 shows the finished mask. Notice the hair is deliberately left a bit ragged.

5. Load the selection (Mac: OPTION+click, Windows: ALT+click on Channel 4 in the Channels palette). Copy it to the clipboard (Mac: ⌘+C, Windows: CTRL+C) and paste it into a new file (Mac: ⌘+N, Windows: CTRL+N). Click OK, paste the copy (Mac: ⌘+V, Windows: CTRL+V), and Merge Down (Mac: ⌘+E, Windows: CTRL+E).

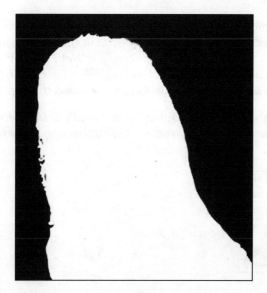

Figure 5-7
Finished mask for
custom brush

6. The original image is very soft. The brush, since it is grayscale, can benefit from some unsharp masking—actually, more than you normally use. It can also create an interesting effect to save two versions of the brush—with differing levels of unsharp masking. Duplicate the image (Image → Duplicate → OK).

7. For this copy, apply the Unsharp Mask filter (Filter → Sharpen → Unsharp Mask) with an amount of 300%, a radius of 3.5 pixels, and a threshold of 4. This is much higher than we would use normally. Change the image to grayscale (Mode → Grayscale → OK).

8. Select the entire image (Mac: ⌘+Ⓐ, Windows: CTRL+Ⓐ). Define it as a brush (Brush palette → Define Brush). Double-click on the brush and set the spacing to 200%.

9. Click on the unsharpened image and duplicate it again (Image → Duplicate → OK).

10. For this copy, apply the Unsharp Mask filter with an amount of 92%, a radius of 2.5 pixels, and a threshold of 0. Change the image to grayscale (Mode → Grayscale → OK). Select the entire image (Mac: ⌘+Ⓐ, Windows: CTRL+Ⓐ). Define it as a brush (Brush palette → Define Brush). Double-click on the brush and set the spacing to 200%.

11. Clear the clutter of open images since you no longer need them. Create a new image at 500×500 pixels.

12. Select a color for your foreground (we used RGB 123, 107, 200 for this example).

13. Double-click on the Brush tool. Set the Brush Options to Normal as the Apply mode (in the Brush palette—not in the Layers palette!), Opacity to 100%, no fade, no pressure options, and Wet Edges off. Select the sharper Manisha brush (the first one you created). Click once in the center of the image towards the left edge. Figure 5-8 shows the approximate location.

14. Now, change the Brush Options Apply mode to Difference. Difference mode is an easy way to create some intersecting imagery with the brush.

Figure 5-8
First brushstroke

15. Add another two brush strokes (Figure 5-9 shows the general locations).

16. Press the modifier key (Mac: OPTION, Windows: ALT) to change the cursor into the Eyedropper, and pick up the solid shade of olive in Manisha's hair on the left side of the lowest image on the screen. This is the inverse of the blue with which you started. When you paint with it in Difference mode, you get your original color. This is a good way to cycle between the original and complementary colors to control the effect you get while painting in Difference mode.

17. Place two more brushstrokes. Figure 5-10 shows the placement.

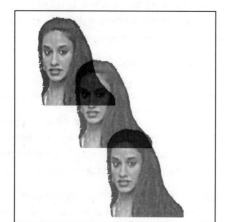

Figure 5-9
Next two
brushstrokes

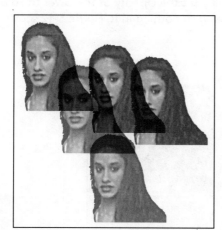

Figure 5-10
Two more
brushstrokes

18. Select the less sharp brush. Click two more times—once with the olive foreground color (near the lower-left corner of the image), and once with the original blue (pick it up as you did in Step 16) between the bottom of the image and the first brushstroke. This completes the foreground of the image. Figure 5-11 shows the result.

19. In order to create a new background, raise the current background into a Layer and remove the white around the brushstrokes. Double-click on the Background in the Layers palette to open the Layer Options dialog. The Layer name changes to Layer 0 automatically. Click OK.

20. Double-click on the Magic Wand and set the Tolerance to 10. Set Anti-alias to On. Click on the white area behind the brushstrokes. Press ⌘ to remove the pixels from the Layer (if they do not disappear, make sure you do not accidentally have Preserve Transparency checked).

21. Make a new Layer (Mac: OPTION+click, Windows: ALT+click on the New Layer icon at the bottom of the Layers palette). Select Background as the new Layer type (you need to scroll to the very bottom of the list).

22. Leave Difference as the painting mode and blue as your foreground color. Drag the brush all over the background image *without* letting up the mouse button. Cover the background with Manisha images, but leave a few clear impressions near the top of the image.

23. Since the background is a little dark and overpowers the image, lift the Background Layer. (Double-click on the Background in the Layers palette to open the Layer Options dialog. The Layer name changes to Layer 0 automatically. Click OK.) Set the Opacity of the Layer to 50%. Create a new Background Layer with nothing in it. Figure 5-12 shows the finished result.

Figure 5-11
Final foreground
brushstrokes

Figure 5-12
Finished image

Whew! That was long! However, it should begin to set your creativity in motion as you see how else you can employ a photograph as a custom brush and graphic element.

The second example in this section shows how to use a painted element as a custom brush. You can build shapes and use them as brushes and assemble them using Layers. In this Hands On, since you already know how to define a custom brush, and even the drawing-impaired can draw a daisy and leaf shape, we will begin with the shapes already created. All you need to do with them is define them as brushes, then paint with them. This Hands On also shows you how to vary the color of the brush as you paint—even if you are not using a tablet.

HANDS ON

BRUSH ELEMENTS

1. Create a new document (File → New → Name: Practice, Width: 400 pixels, Height: 700 pixels, Resolution: 72, Mode: RGB Color, Contents: White).

2. Open the image Flower.Psd. Select the entire image (Mac: ⌘+Ⓐ, Windows: CTRL+Ⓐ) and define the image as a brush. Set the spacing to 150%.

3. Select a clear red for the foreground color and a bright yellow for the background color. These will be the two end colors of the daisies.

4. Double-click on the Brush icon and set the Brush Options to Normal Apply mode and 100% Opacity. Click on the Fade box to select it, and set the

Fade to five steps from Foreground to Background. The brush changes through five colors from red to yellow. Do not select Wet Edges or any pressure settings.

5. Drag the brush inside your new image. As you paint, the colors change. Once the brush has reached the background color, it will not change again unless you begin a new brush stroke. To add red to an area, release the mouse button, then press it again.

6. This creates a small field of daisies. However, it makes it difficult to add leaves to the daisies since the leaves will cover the already-drawn daisies. Here is a better technique: Create a new image the same size as the last one (400×800 pixels).

7. Make a new Layer (click on the New Layer icon at the bottom of the Layers palette). Paint the daisies in this Layer.

8. Open the image Leaf.Psd, select the entire image, and define it as a custom brush. Set the spacing to 300%.

9. Select a leafy shade of green for the foreground color.

10. Click on the Background Layer in the Layers palette to make it active. Click under many of the daisies to add stems. If this becomes boring, define another custom brush that is a horizontally flipped version of the Leaf.Psd image. Figure 5-13 shows this image.

Figure 5-13
Scattering
of daisies

11. Duplicate the image (Image → Duplicate → OK).

12. Select your daisy colors again and make the top Layer active. Paint with the daisy brush until much of the image is covered and you have a field of daisies with only a few green leaves peeking through. Figure 5-14 shows this image.

Wet Edges

The Wet Edges setting on the Brush Options dialog converts your brushes into Watercolor brushes. Repeat the previous Hands On with the Wet Edges setting turned on. Figure 5-15 shows an enlargement of a section of this image so you can see the darker edges and the inner transparency of this brush method.

Basic Patterns for Paper Textures

In order to simulate the effect of paint on a surface, it is necessary to create the textured surface on which to paint. It is also necessary to make that surface permeable to the electronic paint. You already know how to create channels. If a texture is placed in a channel and the channel is loaded as a selection, then you can paint on it and reveal the texture with your brushstrokes.

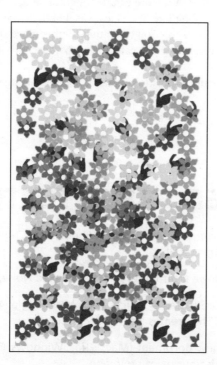

Figure 5-14
Field of daisies

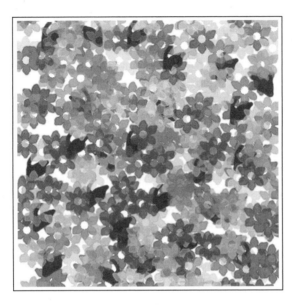

Figure 5-15
Watercolor daisies:
detail

What is a texture? A texture gives visual *feel*. When you look at a texture, you can see what it should feel like. A texture can be rough or smooth, fine or coarse, grainy, bumpy, or stringy. It can look like bricks, canvas, linen, or watercolor paper.

How do you create a texture? You can either fill the image space with one stretching the full size of the canvas, or you can create a pattern and tile it. Let's look at both techniques.

The very easiest texture to create consists of pixels generated by the Add Noise filter, and then embossed. Try this Hands On.

HANDS ON

EMBOSSED PAPER TEXTURE

1. Create a new document (Mac: ⌘+N, Windows: CTRL+N) 400×400 pixels. Make the image grayscale.

2. Apply the Add Noise filter (Filter → Noise → Add Noise, 10, Gaussian).

3. Emboss the texture (Filter → Stylize → Emboss, Angle: 42%, Height: 2, Amount: 300%). This creates a soft, low texture.

4. Create another new document (Mac: ⌘+N, Windows: CTRL+N), 400×400 pixels, RGB. This is your painting image.

5. To prepare the texture for painting, you need to load it into the painting image. Since the painting image is the same size as the texture image and the texture image is grayscale, you can use the Load Selection command to transfer it from one file to the other. Load the selection (Select → Load Selection, Untitled-1, Black Channel). The correct selection appears as the default.

6. Turn off the marching ants so you can paint (Mac: ⌘+Ⓗ, Windows: CTRL+Ⓗ).

7. Try out both the brush and the airbrush. Erase the image (Mac: ⌘+DELETE, Windows: CTRL+DELETE).

8. Return to the grayscale texture image and create a new channel (click on the New Channel icon in the center of the Channels palette).

9. Apply noise again—this time, change the amount to 180.

10. Emboss the noise, using an amount of 100%. Because there is more noise, you need to do less to it.

11. Select the painting image. Load this texture as you did the previous one. Check the Load Selection dialog to make sure that it says Channel #2. Figure 5-16 shows this dialog.

12. Hide the marching ants and paint. Notice the texture made from this noise setting is much coarser and more pronounced. Figure 5-17 shows the effect of both textures.

The foreground color used in Figure 5-17 is black—notice how much lighter it becomes. This is because of the gray values in the texture channel. You can control the effect of the paper texture—how much "paint" is absorbed—by controlling the grayscale levels. A texture map that is medium gray absorbs about half of the "ink." It varies from

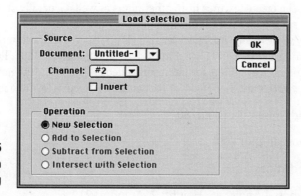

Figure 5-16
Load Selection
dialog

Figure 5-17
Both textures
in use

there by the amount of lighter or darker flecks in the texture. This is a good balance for a paper texture, but you can use the Levels or Curves command to change the texture so it is lighter or darker. You can change the contrast of the texture to make it more or less obvious. You will get a chance to practice this in the Lab exercises in Appendix C, "Labs."

You can store the texture in an Apha channel within your document—which is convenient for keeping the pieces of the project together—or you can use a grayscale or multichannel image. The advantage of using one image to hold a number of textures is that it creates a self-contained library of textures you can easily use. The disadvantage of this method is that you must create a painting the same size as your texture file in order to load the textures as selections. One compromise is to create a small texture file and store the filters and settings for creating the texture in the Caption field of the File Info for the document (File → File Info). That way, you can have a cookbook of texture effects with the recipes stored with them. The textures are fast and easy to create, so you can whip one up to whatever size document you need.

You can create textures from other filters as well. Generally, starting with Add Noise is easy, since it and the Clouds filter are the only Photoshop-native filters that work on a totally white document. However, there is no reason your next step has to be the Emboss filter. You can use Add Noise, Find Edges, and Gaussian Blur a little. You can also use the Wind or Wave filters for interesting effects. If you blur the noise before using Find Edges, you get another effect. A particularly attractive formula is

● Add Noise—Gaussian, 80

● Gaussian Blur—1.8

● Find Edges

● Emboss—Angle: 45, Height: 2, Amount: 210%

Figure 5-18 shows this texture.

You can also create patterns and use them to make interesting tiled paper textures. The only real trick is that a texture generally works best when you do not see any seam line. When you repeat a section of an image, you normally see a line where the original edge is. This does not happen as often with noisy, embossed textures, but it can—and it is very distracting when it does. The next Hands On shows you how to create an easy, seamless texture resembling a stucco wall.

HANDS ON

CREATING A SEAMLESS STUCCO TEXTURE

1. Create a new image 100 pixels square, in grayscale.

2. Fill it with noise (Filter → Noise → Add Noise, 165, Gaussian).

3. Apply the Emboss filter (Filter → Stylize → Emboss, Angle: 45, Height: 2, Amount: 100%).

4. Apply the Offset filter (Filter → Other → Offset, 50 pixels right, 50 pixels down, Wrap around). This amount is one half the image's width and height.

5. Apply the Twirl filter (Filter → Distort → Twirl, -121).

Figure 5-18
Texture created
from Blurred Noise
with Find Edges
and Embossing

6. Apply the Offset filter again with the same settings. The image reverts to its original location.

7. Apply the Twirl filter again using the last settings.

8. Select the entire image (Mac: ⌘+Ⓐ, Windows: CTRL+Ⓐ). Define this as a pattern (Edit → Define Pattern).

9. Create a new RGB image 600×600 pixels. Click on the New Channel icon in the center of the Channels palette to create a new channel. This will be Channel 4.

10. Fill the channel with the pattern (SHIFT+DELETE → Pattern, 100% opacity, Normal). Figure 5-19 shows the texture in repeat.

Before we continue, let's take a minute to define the terms pattern and texture. *Pattern* refers to an image area repeated for effect, in which the repeating elements are obvious. *Texture* consists of repeat units containing random elements, so it does not cause the eye to see regular areas of repetition when it's tiled. Part of the confusion is that the term pattern also refers to any image element that repeats—whether or not your eye is supposed to tell where one tile starts and ends. Figure 5-20(a) shows a seamless texture, and Figure 5-20(b) shows a seamless pattern. Although both are seamless, the texture does not show any repeats, while the pattern features obvious repetition.

What is the purpose of the Offset filter used in this Hands On? The Offset filter is used to show how the pattern will tile. By wrapping the texture and offsetting it by half its length and width, you can see if there will be a seam down the middle. An obvious seam in a pattern is ugly—unless it is intentional. If the pattern is supposed to be a

Figure 5-19
Stucco texture used
as pattern fill

Figure 5-20
a) A seamless texture
b) A seamless pattern

a

b

texture, the seam is very distracting. In order to remove a seam that shows up in the center of an image, you need to change the pixels to eliminate the center line *without disturbing any of the pixels at the edges of the image*. Since those are the edges that will tile, they must be left alone. There are several ways to handle a seam, if one appears when the Offset filter is applied.

One way to remove a seam is to use the Twirl filter. This is what we did in the previous Hands On. The Twirl filter covers that center seam and leaves the tile edges alone. It always yields a seamless pattern, but it is suitable if you want to keep the detail. It is a fairly obvious cover-up that creates a strong pattern to replace the seam. In this Hands On, we used the Twirl filter twice to create a double twirl texture. Another native Photoshop filter useful for removing seams is the Distort → Polar Coordinates filter.

You can also attempt to cover a seam line using the Rubber Stamp tool. By transferring image areas from inside the tile to cover the seam line, you can increase the randomness of the texture and make it seamless. This is a very good method on really random patterns. The Smudge tool is also useful for covering seams. You will get some practice with the Rubber Stamp and Smudge tools in the Lab exercises in Appendix C.

There are also some excellent third-party filters that can help. In Kai's Power Tools (KPT), there is a filter called Seamless Welder. It takes a section of an image and creates a seamless tile from it. It works on any image, but since it works by taking the left edge of the image just outside the tile area and compositing it with the right edge inside the tile area (and repeats this for all the sides), the edges, while seamless, can get very blurry—which causes an obvious pattern when the image is tiled. Also in the KPT filter set is the KPT Twirl filter. This version of twirl also creates kaleidoscopic effects. Figure 5-21(a) shows a farm in China, photographed by Ed Scott, used as a seamless pattern created with the KPT Seamless Welder.

Xaos Tools makes a filter called Terrazzo that creates incredible patterns. It can do kaleidoscopic repeats, plus it can create all 17 possible ways an image can be repeated on a plane. Figure 5-21(b) shows a seamless pattern created by Terrazzo from a portion of the daisy flowers you created earlier in this chapter.

If you want to create high-quality, seamless textures and patterns, RealTexture Tools, Professional Edition, by Computer Graphics System Design Corporation, does an excellent job of making seamless tiles without the blurring that the KPT Seamless Welder produces.

Using the Lighting Filter

The Lighting filter can also be used to create paper textures. The Lighting filter has the ability to use textures, patterns, or gray values as *bump maps*. A bump map is a surface texture that can be applied to another object or image. It works by assuming that gray values can be translated into height. The most common translation assumes white pixels are high and black pixels are low.

Photoshop comes with a large number of Lighting Filter textures that can be copied from the distribution CD-ROM to your hard drive, or used directly from the CD-ROM. They are in a folder titled Textures for Lighting Effects. These textures can be used by themselves and are combined with the Lighting filter for an additional effect. You can apply these textures to an image or Alpha channel by using another Photoshop filter called Texture Fill. The Texture Fill filter is one of the Render filters. It can tile any grayscale image in Photoshop 2.5 or 3.0 format without the added steps of defining a pattern.

Figure 5-21
a) Pattern created using KPT's Seamless Welder
b) Pattern created using Xaos Tools' Terrazzo filter

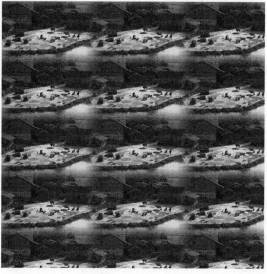

a

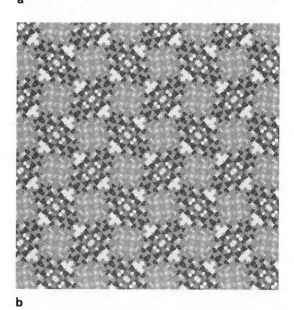

b

If you use one of the Lighting filter textures as a paper texture (and the set of 75 textures does contain some already labeled *paper*), you can quickly create a seamless surface on which to draw. Since the texture is a repeat, the paper will be consistent throughout the image. You can also use the Lighting filter on these textures (or use the textures as height channels) to create paper textures that are not consistent throughout the image. Where the light is more pronounced, the paper absorbs the paint better.

Conversely, you could invert the paper texture to make the overall surface less absorbent. There is a Lab exercise in Appendix C showing you how to use the Lighting filter and these textures.

Simulating Brushstrokes

In Fractal Design Painter, your brush determines whether the brush stroke reacts to the paper texture. Photoshop was not designed to use paper textures, so the process here is not that easy. If you load a paper texture selection, your brush *will* react to it. In Photoshop, there is no choice. Therefore, if you want to specifically imitate the way chalk or charcoal behaves, you need to perform an in-depth analysis of the pressure, amount of absorbency, stroke width, and so on. (Or purchase Painter, which makes the whole process much easier.)

With limited options, you can control the absorbency only by varying the gray values in the paper texture. If you want the surface to repel most of the ink, either change the levels of the Alpha channel or invert the texture in the channel so it is more dark than light. Keep a copy of the original texture so there is a fallback if you are not happy with your results.

1. What is the name of the natural media painter that compliments Photoshop?
   a. Natural Design Painter
   b. Fractal Design Painter
   c. Fraction Paint Painter
   d. Natural Fractal Painter

2. What keys enable you to change brush size without opening the Brushes palette?
   a. ⟮[⟯ and ⟮]⟯
   b. ⟮←⟯ and ⟮→⟯
   c. ⟮>⟯ and ⟮<⟯
   d. ⟮]⟯ and ⟮[⟯

3. Where can you change the size, color, and opacity of a brushstroke reflecting the pressure you put on your strokes?
   a. Drawing Tablet
   b. Drawing palette
   c. Brush Options palette
   d. Pressure Options palette

4. What option on the Brush Option palette converts regular brushes to watercolor ones?
   a. Watercolors
   b. Wet Edges

   c. Water Edges
   d. Wet Colors

5. Which filters or tools can be used to make a seam in a pattern or texture go away?
   a. Offset filter
   b. Twirl filter
   c. Smudge tool
   d. Polar Coordinates filter

LESSON 2

OTHER PAINT PROCESSES

The Paintbrush only provides some of the painting effects Photoshop is capable of. There are many more tools available. You can use Photoshop to color black-and-white images, colorize grayscale images, and act as a digital airbrush. Let's explore some more.

Painting Line Art

You can use Photoshop to color line art—as if you were putting color into a coloring book. You can do this quite easily by painting on the black line art in Darken mode. Darken mode only leaves paint where the foreground color is darker than the pixel already in the image (that is, it only changes lighter colors). If the outline is done in black on a white background, you cannot accidentally paint over the outlines of your image.

Try this short Hands On, using the image of a globe from the Ultimate Symbol Collection's trial disk.

PAINTING LINE ART

1. Open the image Globe.Psd. Duplicate it (Image → Duplicate → OK).

2. Flatten the image (Mac: ⌘+E, Windows: CTRL+E).

3. Select the Paintbrush tool (B) and press ENTER. In the Brush Options dialog, set the Apply mode to Darken and the opacity to 100%.

4. Open the Swatches palette so you can easily choose colors.

5. Use the last brush on the first row (the 19-pixel hard brush). Select red—the first color in the Default Swatches palette.

6. Color in the top six areas of the globe. Figure 5-22 shows the image with the top part colored.

7. Fill in the next section with primary yellow, the third section with green, and the bottom with deep blue.

8. Open the image Dancer.Psd. Select the Move tool (⟨V⟩) and drag the top Layer on top of the colored Globe image. Position the woman toward the right side of the globe so her face is over the yellow area and not on a black line. Change the Apply mode to Multiply. Figure 5-23 shows this image.

The addition of the Mexican dancer to this image in Multiply mode is another example of how you can keep black lines from being overwritten by other images or brushstrokes. When you work in Multiply mode, all black pixels are automatically protected. This also gives you a convenient way to hand-color photos.

Figure 5-22
Ultimate Symbol
Collection Globe
partially colored

Figure 5-23
Dancer added to
globe image

Colorizing an Image

It is possible to hand-color a grayscale image. This is similar to the photographic process people have been doing for years. Tintypes have been a popular art form for almost as long as the camera has been in existence, and they were once the only way to get a color photograph. The only caveat is that you cannot get realistic color in a hand-tinted image. There are too many shades in nature—especially in human skin tones—for an artist, no matter how skilled, to color an image as lifelike as a photograph. You can get close, but there is a sparkle and vibrancy missing. Actually, that's the charm of the tintype. It looks a bit old-fashioned, and it is—the new electronic version of an old craft.

There is a series of postcards and greeting cards designed around partially colorized images. The grayscale image is left in place with only the key elements containing color. The technique is very soft—and very effective. However, if you really need photographic color, do not do use the hand-coloring method.

There are three main ways to paint color onto a grayscale image: using the Multiply mode, using the Color mode, or using a *trick*—a clever technique that can give you photographic color.

Both Multiply and Color modes are simple painting methods. You just paint over your grayscale image with the colors you selected—either from the original or from a color source you prefer. There are some subtle differences in the two modes.

Color mode:

● Gives brighter, clearer, colors

● Does not affect either the lightest or the darkest values in the image

● Allows you to brush over previously colored areas on an image with the same color, without any change

● Can replace the color of a previously painted area by applying brushstrokes over it with a new color

Multiply mode:

● Darkens Fcolors a lot when used over darker grayscale areas

● Changes highlights to your paint color, and may turn the darkest areas to solid black

● Darkens the color by applying repeated strokes over a painted area

● Can also darken the color of a previously painted area by applying brushstrokes of a new color

These differences are attributable to the differences in the math between the Multiply and Color modes. The Multiply mode darkens an image faster in the already darkened areas than it does in the lighter areas. White multiplied with a color yields the color; black multiplied with the color yields black.

Color mode, however, only replaces the Hue and Saturation components of a color. It uses the hue and saturation of the foreground color and the value of the original area. For that reason, neither black nor white can be colorized. Value 255 (white) is always white, regardless of the hue. Black (value 0), always remains black even with the saturation cranked up as far as it will go.

You need to be careful, however, when you paint in Multiply mode. If you keep the mouse button pressed, you can paint over the same areas as many times as you want without changing the color you first put down. However, as soon as you release the mouse button, a new stroke over an already-painted area darkens the image considerably. You will have a chance during the Lab in Appendix C to practice and compare Multiply and Colorize hand-coloring.

One of the most interesting colorizing techniques is the trick method. This requires having an already-colored original, however, and assumes you only want to color *part* of the image or vary the amount of color in the image. The following Hands On teaches you this technique. It really has a lot of possibilities.

TRICK COLORIZING

1. Open the image GCover.Psd. Duplicate it (Image → Duplicate → OK).

2. Drag the icon for the Background Layer to the New Layer icon at the bottom left of the Layers palette. This copies the Background Layer into a new Layer.

3. Desaturate the top Layer (Mac: SHIFT+⌘+U, Windows: SHIFT+CTRL+U). This changes the top image into grayscale, but leaves it as an RGB image so it can be colored.

4. Create a Layer Mask (click on the Add Layer Mask icon—the leftmost icon at the bottom of the Layers palette or choose it from the Layers menu). Your foreground and background colors should change to black and white. If they do not, press D to set them to the default.

5. If you paint on the Layer Mask with solid black, you completely reveal the color image under the grayscale Layer. A much softer technique is setting the brush opacity to 5 and controlling the amount of color you reveal. Set the opacity in the Brush Options dialog to 5 (press the 5 key on your keyboard). You can change your opacity as you wish by pressing the number keys 0 through 9. Remember, 0 is full opacity (not zero opacity).

6. Use black and a brush of suitable size, and color over the flowers in the image (there are four full flowers and three soft partial flowers at the back of the image).

7. Color over some of the leaves as well. Figure 5-24(a) shows the original image, and Figure 5-24(b) shows the areas that need to be revealed.

8. Add some punch to the image by making the right yellow and red flowers almost at full intensity and brightening the centers of the other two whole flowers. You can do this by changing the opacity on the brush or by painting over the area several more times. Figure 5-24(c) shows the final Layer Mask. From this, you can see the areas of varying values on the mask. The darkest values are where the color from the Layer below is most intense.

Using the Airbrush

The Airbrush is one of Photoshop's most interesting paint tools. While most of the painting facilities in Photoshop do not really resemble their counterparts in the analog world, the Airbrush does. It works the same, minus the mess. However, it is the one tool in which you need hand control.

The Airbrush is substantially different from the Paintbrush. The Paintbrush simply flows pixels onto the image at a fixed rate. While you can vary the opacity if you use a pressure sensitive pen, generally, the Paintbrush is very simple. You need hand-eye coordination to make it go where you want, but once you place it in the right location, there are no more choices to make.

The Airbrush, however, reacts to the speed at which you move your hand—even if you are using the mouse. If your finger is heavy on the mouse button and you leave the brush in an area, the paint builds up. This makes the tool both challenging and delightful to use. The most important trick is to keep the pressure setting low. A low pressure setting does two things: It gives you a wide range of build-up values, and it allows you much finer control of the tool. The other trick is to use the widest, softest brush you reasonably can. The final trick is to mask, mask, mask!

If you have ever used an airbrush, you know that it is not just a Paintbrush with a long hose and wide spray. It is a tool that demands a different technique to apply. An analog Airbrush excels at creating lovely gradations and/or soft applications of a single color. The digital version in Photoshop does too. Just as you must create masks to control where the airbrush can and cannot paint in the real world, so must you in Photoshop. You will probably spend much more time masking than actually painting. However, if you are going to use the airbrush, you need to carefully mask your image first.

You will discover your optimum working patterns as you begin using the airbrush. However, until then, use these suggestions for organizing your image:

● *Work in Layers.* The more Layers you use as you airbrush, the easier it is to change something if you do not like the result. If you only mask one area and apply one color spray to it, you can always fix a mistake by deleting the area. However, if you have oversprayed several colors, a mistake can be more costly in terms of time.

● *Keep a thumbnail of your reference image embedded in the drawing.* You can shrink it in size so it fits into your document. Keep it on its own Layer.

a

b

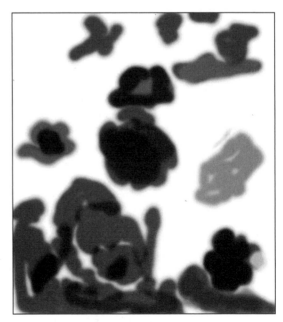

Figure 5-24
a) Original Ground Cover image
b) Areas to be colored
c) Finished Layer Mask

c

● *Create a Layer for your palette.* This keeps the colors used in an image handy—and you don't have to wonder which Swatches document you tucked it away into. If you pick a palette in advance, place dabs of the colors on a blank Layer. If you prefer to select them as you work, dab them on as you use them.

● *Create a template for your image and keep it in an Alpha channel.* You can turn the template on as you paint and see the instructions you will follow. You can also create a template and store it on the Layer above the Background. This works if you have a lot of separate selections in your image.

● *Create each object in a separate file and composite later.* If the final drawing will include a number of airbrushed objects, create each one in its own file first. This makes the project more manageable and easier on RAM.

● *Always fill an area with a solid color before you begin airbrushing.* Even a preliminary light coat will ensure you get a smooth fill.

● *Separate your palettes so you can see the Layers, Channels, Paths, Brush, and Options palettes at the same time.* This is tough onscreen real estate but a blessing as you work. If you are lucky enough to have more than one monitor, use one to store all of the open palettes.

Before you begin the Hands On, here are some painting tips for using the Airbrush:

● *Paint gently.* The Airbrush is sensitive to the time it takes you to move across an area. Work as quickly as possible to keep a light touch.

● *Use as large a brush as you can.* The largest brushes are the most anti-aliased. This helps one stroke blend into the other.

● *Use the brush-outside-the-mask technique to get darker colors around edges.* The mask gives you a sharp, crisp shape. To build up color just at the edge of an object, position your brush mostly outside the mask and let the very edge of the brush build color. This is a much better technique than using a smaller brush for the shadows.

● *Create more masks than you actually need.* Take the time to build as many masks as you think you might possibly need. Build Highlight and Shadow masks. Even if you do not use them, it is better to have more than you need than to have to create more as you paint. Stopping breaks your concentration.

● *Finish an area in one brushstroke.* Try to cultivate a smooth fill of an area. Do not release the mouse button until an entire area is finished. That way, if you are unhappy with your stroke, you can undo it.

With these thoughts in mind, try this airbrushing Hands On. The file is already organized for you, the Alpha channel template is there, a palette is selected, and paths are created. All you need to do is the airbrushing. However, you will also learn how the system works.

AIRBRUSHING

1. Copy the *Lemon lights* lighting style from the CD-ROM.

2. Open the image LemonS.Psd. Duplicate the image (Image → Duplicate → OK) and close the original.

3. Make a new Layer (click on the New Layer icon at the bottom of the Layers palette). This Layer holds the base coat for the airbrushing. Double-click on the Layer name to open the Layer Options dialog and change the name of the Layer to Base Coat.

4. Load the whole lemon path by pressing the modifier key (Mac: ⌘, Windows: CTRL) and clicking on the path name in the Paths palette. Make sure none of the paths in the palette are shaded, and hide the marching ants (Mac: ⌘+H, Windows: CTRL+H).

5. Select the Airbrush tool (A). Set the Pressure to 18% and the Apply mode to Normal.

6. Select the lightest yellow on the color palette embedded in the LemonS.Psd image (press OPTION on the Mac or ALT in Windows to change the cursor into the eyedropper tool). Fill the selection (Mac: OPTION+DELETE, Windows: ALT+DELETE).

7. Press OPTION (Mac) or ALT (Windows) and click the New Layer icon at the bottom of the Layers palette to create a new Layer. Name it Lemon Layer.

8. Since the base coat now obscures the template Layer, click the Eye icon next to the template Layer in the Layers palette to turn it off. Turn the Alpha channel on by clicking the eye column in the Channels palette. Make sure that although the Eye icon is visible, the channel is not selected. You may have to turn on this channel for viewing every time you create a new Layer. Figure 5-25 shows the Template channel.

Figure 5-25
Template channel
for lemon
airbrushing

9. Pick up the medium yellow in your palette. Show the marching ants to make sure your selection is still active, then hide them again. Following the guidelines in the template, spray the yellow over the lemon using a very large brush. The color should be heaviest underneath the lemon in the areas marked *shadow*. Do not try to protect the highlights, but do not spray them as heavily.

10. Load the two highlights paths by dragging the first one to the elliptical Marquee on the Paths palette. Press the SHIFT key and drag the other one onto the elliptical Marquee icon. Both paths should now be selections. Feather the selection by 15 pixels (Mac: SHIFT+⌘+D, Windows: SHIFT+CTRL+D, 15). Hide the marching ants (Mac: ⌘+H, Windows: CTRL+H).

11. Use the 100-pixel brush and select the Eraser tool (E). Choose the Airbrush version of the Eraser. Set the opacity to 10% and the Apply mode to Normal. Very gently remove some color from the highlights areas with the Eraser. Your stroke should be very light, fast, and mostly across the center of the highlights.

12. Make a new Layer by clicking on the New Layer icon at the bottom of the Layers palette. Name it Shadows. Load the whole lemon path (Mac: ⌘+click, Windows: CTRL+click on path name in the Paths palette). Hide the marching ants (Mac: ⌘+H, Windows: CTRL+H).

13. Select the darker yellow. Use a smaller airbrush to darken the shadows area. Note that there is a triangular area toward the left of the lemon that is also fairly dark. You can see this both on the template and the thumbnail.

14. Using the smallest tip on the second row of brushes, paint in the very fine lines toward the left tip of the lemon. Use the Blur tool to blend them in slightly.

15. Make a new Layer by clicking on the New Layer icon at the bottom of the Layers palette. Name it Greens.

16. The whole lemon path should still mask your image.

17. Pick up the green color in the palette. Spray it very gently just over the right tip of the lemon. A little goes a long way! Using the 45-pixel brush, position the cursor so most of the brush is outside the right tip of the lemon. Press the mouse button to release more green on the very tip. The technique of building up color at the very edge by painting mostly outside the masked area is extremely useful. Using the anti-aliased edge of a large brush gives you an enormous amount of control.

18. Pick up the darker neutral brown color in the palette. Spray just a bit of it over the green tip. Very quickly and lightly, spray some across the bottom edge of the lemon to darken it (mostly outside the mask).

19. Make a new Layer (click on the New Layer icon at the bottom of the Layers palette). Name it Tip.

20. Load the Tip path and hide the marching ants. Pick up the lighter neutral brown and spray the entire tip for medium coverage. Use a smaller brush (35 pixels) and spray the edge of the tip joining the lemon with the darker neutral brown. Use the brush-outside-the-mask technique. Spray the entire tip very lightly with a 1000-pixel brush using the green from the palette. Deselect (Mac: ⌘+D, Windows: CTRL+D).

21. Drag the Tip Layer below the base coat Layer in the Layers palette. This hides the pointed edge of the tip.

22. Click on the lemon coat Layer in the Layers palette and drag it to the New Layer icon at the bottom to duplicate it. Name the duplicate Lemon Coat bumps and drag the Layer name to the top of the Layer stack. Load the whole lemon path.

23. To add some texture and dimension to the image, apply the Lighting filter (Filter → Render → Lighting). In the Lighting Filter dialog, shown in Figure 5-26, select the Lemon Lights preset you copied from the CD-ROM for this book. The box "White is high" should be checked. Also, make sure the name of the Texture channel used is Noise.

24. Drag the Layer to the top of the stack and set the opacity on the Layer to 19%. If you still feel the texture is too strong, you can apply a 1.0 Gaussian Blur to it.

25. Finally, let's give the image a bit more noise. Create a new Layer. This time, set the Apply mode to Multiply and check the Fill with Neutral color—White box. Name the Layer Noise 1.

26. Load the whole lemon path. Add noise (Filter → Noise → Add Noise, 10, Gaussian, not monochromatic). The noise adds a bit more texture to the entire image—even in the highlights area in which the Lighting filter did not do much because the area is mostly transparent.

27. To get more texture, drag the icon for the Noise 1 Layer to the New Layer icon at the bottom left of the Layers palette. This also copies the Apply mode (which is Multiply). It gives a subtle darkening of the image.

28. One more enhancement: Make a new Layer. Use the darkest brown to define the right edge of the lemon in front of the tip. Figure 5-27 shows the area to darken. Use the Blur tool with Sample Merged checked to blend it in, and turn down the opacity of the Layer until it looks darkened but not obvious. Figure 5-28 shows the final list of Layers, and Figure 5-29 shows the finished lemon.

You should be very proud of yourself. Oh, all right! If you want one more Layer, create a new one and, using the darkest neutral brown, with the whole lemon path loaded and inverted, spray a cast shadow under the lemon. Use the brush-outside-the-mask technique to keep the shadow localized to just beneath the lemon. You can match your work against the image Lemonlay.Psd if you want. To use the lemon in a composition, click the Eye icons to turn them off next to the Background, Color Palette, and Template Layers. Duplicate the image, Merged Layers only. Trash the two extra Alpha channels in the copy. The lemon is now in its own document and can be dragged in one piece into any other composition.

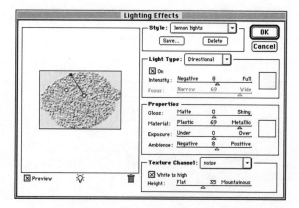

Figure 5-26
Lighting filter
dialog

Figure 5-27
Darkening the
rounded end of
the lemon

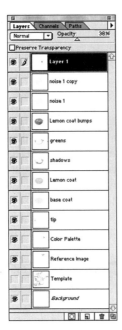

Figure 5-28
Layer list for lemon

Figure 5-29
Finished lemon

QUIZ 2

1. What mode allows you to keep black lines from being overwritten when filling in a picture with color?
   a. Add mode
   b. Multiply mode
   c. Multiplicity mode
   d. Colorize mode

2. What are the three main ways you can paint color onto a grayscale image?
   a. Multiply mode
   b. Fill mode
   c. Color mode
   d. Trick mode

3. Color Mode is different from Multiply Mode. What are some characteristics of Color Mode?
   a. It gives brighter, clearer colors.
   b. You cannot brush over previously colored areas on an image with the same color.
   c. It only replaces the Hue and Saturation components of a color.
   d. It does not affect the lightest or darkest values in the image.

4. When using the Airbrush tool, what is recommended first?
   a. A high pressure setting
   b. A low pressure setting
   c. A calm, relaxed attitude
   d. A small brush

5. Until you are comfortable working with the Airbrush tool, what are some things you can do to organize your image to get the results you want?
   a. Work in Layers.
   b. Create a template for your image and keep it in an Alpha channel.
   c. Create all your objects on one Layer.
   d. Separate all your palettes so you can see them at once.

LESSON 3

TEXT

It took us a long time, but we are finally ready to look at how Photoshop uses text. The short, easy answer is *badly*. As with all generalizations (and short, snappy answers), this is only partially true. Photoshop is a bitmapped (raster) program. To get clear, crisp text, you need to set the text in a vector program or a page layout program such as PageMaker or QuarkXPress. This leads to a number of problems when you combine text with Photoshop.

Text can be set in Photoshop by either typing it into the Text tool dialog or importing it as an EPS file from Illustrator. In either case, as soon as it is deselected and locked into the image, the text is no longer editable. The program cannot tell the difference between pixels that are used in text and pixels that are used to draw the lemon that you worked on previously.

Text Dos and Don'ts

This leads us to formulate several rules when working with text in Photoshop.

● If you do not need to set text in Photoshop, don't.

● Do not type small text (less than 24 point) or large blocks of text in Photoshop. If you need to do this, bring the Photoshop file into your page layout program and place the text over it there. The quality will be much better.

● Large point sizes are acceptable. Use single words or short phrases.

● The best reason for using text in Photoshop is to add images or texture to it, or to mix it in with the base image.

● If you import text from Illustrator, wherever possible, make outlines of the text rather than import text objects.

● If you want to use large type in Photoshop, set it first in Illustrator. You have much more control over your type in Illustrator, and Photoshop sometimes cuts off text descenders when you try to create more than one line (though you can fix this in ATM by selecting Preserve Character Shapes).

● Use Adobe Type Manager (ATM) and Adobe Type Reunion (ATR). They come free of charge with Photoshop. ATM is needed if you want to set anti-aliased text and have it look good. It takes the PostScript code from the font outlines and uses it to make the onscreen display of the fonts acceptable. It is also used to rasterize the fonts into Photoshop. ATR places all the fonts from the same family—book, italic, black, and so on—into one menu item on the Fonts menu and creates a drop-down menu next to each family so you choose the specific member. Without it, each font is listed by itself, causing even a modest font collection to get out of hand.

● Use a Font Manager such as Suitcase, Master Juggler, or ATM 3.0 to cut down the number of fonts open at once. You can create sets of fonts with either program and only load them when you need them.

● Create text in channels or on empty Layers to give yourself the maximum flexibility. If you need to place text onto a nontransparent area, make sure you also create a matching Alpha channel for it so that you can easily re-select the text.

Using the Text Tool

To create type, select the Type tool (T) and click in the area in which you want the text to appear. A dialog box, shown in Figure 5-30, appears. The dialog box is where you actually type what you want to appear on the screen. You can select the font, size, leading, alignment, spacing, and style. Once you have placed the words you want, exiting the Type dialog places the text (in the current color) on the screen as a new Layer. The Preserve Transparency button is automatically enabled for text Layers, and each text object is placed in its own Layer.

If you want to *kern* the text (change the spacing between individual letters), select the part of the word you want to move and use the arrow keys to nudge it closer together or farther apart. If you have ever used a version of Photoshop earlier than 4.0, this is a change in the tool's behavior—and not a particularly welcome one. However, the Text tool only allows you to *create* text objects; you must manipulate them with the Selection and Move tools.

If you get annoyed trying to work with type in Photoshop, there is help. Extensis Corporation has released a set of Photoshop plug-ins called PhotoTools. This filter collection includes PhotoText, a plug-in allowing you to set blocks of text within Photoshop. It gives you much more control over the type than native Photoshop does. Figure 5-31 shows the PhotoText dialog box. Notice that you can change the tracking and font widths. You can move the baseline on part of the text. You can change the color of selected letters or words. Photoshop is still not a good environment for typesetting because it is a raster program (remember that term from Chapter 1?). However, PhotoText makes it much easier if you need to place text into Photoshop.

Anti-Aliasing

The Type tool gives you the choice of bringing in the text as aliased or anti-aliased. Anti-aliased text looks much better, in general, since it softens the jagged edges of the type.

Figure 5-30
Type dialog box:
native Photoshop

However, it looks awful when you print black text against a white background. There, especially at small point sizes, the text looks fuzzy and slightly out of focus. To print black text on a white background, use a different program, one that prints the text smoothly at any size (such as Illustrator, Freehand, PageMaker, or QuarkXPress). Or, create an image that is already at printer resolution so you can place the text without anti-aliasing it and still have it print without being jagged. Placing aliased text is as easy as clicking the anti-aliased box off in the Type dialog box.

Rasterizing from Illustrator

If you have access to Adobe Illustrator, you can greatly simplify your life by using it to create the outlines for any text you want to use in Photoshop. There are several benefits:

- The type can be sized to fit exactly into the area in Photoshop without guessing at the needed point size and making multiple attempts.

- You can apply filters or distortions to the type and create type following a path or surrounding a circle. You cannot do this with any degree of precision within Photoshop.

- You have better control over kerning.

To create type in Illustrator, simply select the text tool and type your word. When finished, change the type to outlines and save as an EPS or Illustrator file. Open Photoshop. You can either use the Place... command to move the text into your Photoshop file, or you can drag the outlines from Illustrator directly into Photoshop.

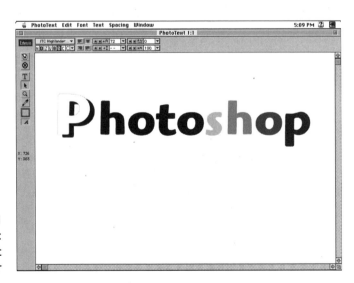

Figure 5-31
Type dialog box:
Extensis PhotoText
filter

Creating Drop Shadows

In Chapter 3, "Layers and Channels," you learned how to create a drop shadow for an image. Creating drop shadows for text is exactly the same thing. Though there are many different ways to create a drop shadow, the easiest one uses the following steps:

1. Create your text in a blank Layer or import the text from Illustrator (which automatically places it into its own Layer using the Place... command).

2. Drag the icon for the text Layer to the New Layer icon at the bottom left of the Layers palette. This copies the text Layer into a new Layer. Name this Layer Shadow and drag it below the text Layer in the Layers palette.

3. Click on the Preserve Transparency box in the Layers palette and fill the image with the foreground color (the one you want to use for your shadow). Then turn off Preserve Transparency so you can perform the next step.

4. Apply a Gaussian Blur to the Shadow Layer. This blur can be anywhere from 4 to 15 pixels, depending on the image size (large images require more blurring than small ones).

5. Drag the Shadow Layer (using the Move tool) to where you want the shadow (typically to the right and down). You can also use the Offset filter (Filter → Other → Offset) to move the shadow a specific number of pixels).

6. Now, set the opacity on the Shadow Layer so the shadow looks right to you.

Creating Natural-Looking Drop Shadows

There are a few things to remember about drop shadows that can help you get better results.

Shadows in nature are never black. Use a dark neutral for your shadow or set the opacity fairly low. If you change your shadow's Apply mode to Multiply, you achieve a much more realistic darkening of your background than you get from a transparent black in Normal mode.

Try Overlay or Hard Light mode for your shadows. Depending on the image, these Apply modes can work very well.

If you want your image to look like it is floating high above the page, use a large offset for the shadow. Soften the shadow as well. To get just a hint of a shadow (as if your object is very close to the page), use a smaller offset and a much less blurred shadow.

You can change a shadow into a glow by changing the color and not offsetting the shadow at all. The Gaussian Blur should be large enough to spread the image outside the original outlines and make it visible behind your text or object.

You can create hard-edge embossing by cutting your text from your Background Layer, making a blurred copy of it in both white and black, and offsetting them under the text Layer in opposite directions. To create soft embossing, blur all three text Layers. Figure 5-32 shows the soft embossing example in the Lab Appendix.

There are several third-party filter sets that help create drop shadows. Alien Skin Black Box, Extensis PhotoTools, and DataStream Wild River SSK have filters that create drop shadows. All the filter sets give you basic control over the shadow color, the shadow offset, and the softness of the shadow. None of these filters creates a moveable drop shadow (a shadow on its own Layer), so the method shown in the Hands On is still the most flexible for simple drop shadows. However, each of the three filter sets has additional filters for use with text (Emboss, Cutout, Carve), making some very complex techniques very easy. The Wild River MagicMask filter performs 24 different text effects and is definitely a showpiece. The text effects are worth the entire price of the filter set.

Screening Text

Another thing commonly done with text in Photoshop is to use it so its color is either stronger than the rest of the image or much more subdued. The process of making the color of part of an image less intense or much lighter is called *screening*. When using text, frequently the image under it is screened back so the text is more visible. You can also fill the text itself with the background image, then screen back the rest of the image. Another common trick is to make a box around the text and screen it back, then cut out the text from the screened box to reveal the original image at full strength.

In order to screen an area of an image, it should be placed on its own Layer. This gives you the maximum amount of flexibility for combining the use of the Levels command with Apply modes and opacity changes. Try this Hands On to see how to screen a text box over an image. The image we will use is another one of photographer Ed Scott's excellent China images. The type is set in ITC Snap.

Figure 5-32
Soft-embossed text

Command Watch: Layer Positioning Keystrokes

Action	Mac Key	Windows Key
Select lower layer	OPTION+[[]	ALT+[[]
Select higher layer	OPTION+[]]	ALT+[]]
Send to back	⌘+[[]	CTRL+[[]
Bring to front	⌘+[]]	CTRL+[]]
Send backward	SHIFT+⌘+[[]	SHIFT+CTRL+[[]
Bring forward	SHIFT+⌘+[]]	SHIFT+CTRL+[]]

HANDS ON

SCREENED BACK TEXT BOX

1. Open the image Visit.Psd. Duplicate it (Image → Duplicate → OK).

2. Drag the icon for the Background Layer to the New Layer icon at the bottom of the Layers palette. This copies the Background Layer into a new Layer. Name the Layer Text Box.

3. The text you will use is in Channel 4. Load Channel 4 (Mac: OPTION+⌘+4, Windows: ALT+⌘+4).

4. Press DELETE to remove the area occupied by the text from the top Layer. Deselect (Mac: ⌘+D, Windows: CTRL+D).

5. Click the Eye icon next to the Background Layer to turn it off temporarily.

6. Change your units to inches (Mac: ⌘+K, ⌘+5; Windows: CTRL+K, CTRL+5). Turn on the Rulers (Mac: ⌘+R, Windows: CTRL+R).

7. Drag Guidelines from the Ruler so the top and bottom guides are each 1 inch from the edges of the image, and the side guidelines are ½ inch from each side edge. Turn on Snap to Guides (View → Snap to Guides, or Mac: SHIFT+⌘+;, Windows: SHIFT+CTRL+;).

8. Double-click on the Marquee tool. In the Marquee Option palette that appears, set Shape to Rectangular and Style Normal. Make sure the Feather Radius box is set to 0.

9. Drag the Rectangular Marquee so it snaps to the guidelines you created.

10. Reverse the selection (Mac: SHIFT+⌘+I, Windows: SHIFT+⌘+I). Press DELETE. This leaves only a box with the text cut out of it on the Layer.

11. Hide the Guides (Mac: ⌘+;, Windows: CTRL+;).

12. Press the modifier key (Mac: ⌘, Windows: CTRL) and click on the Layer name to select the non-transparent pixels on the top Layer.

13. Turn the Eye icon back on next to the Background Layer. The top Layer is still the active one.

14. Create an Adjustment Layer (Mac: ⌘+click, Windows: CTRL+click the New Layer icon on the Layers palette). Select Levels as the Adjustment Layer type.

15. Move the Gamma control (the middle triangle on the Input Slider) to the left until the numeric readout says 1.51. Move the left Output slider towards the right until the numeric readout says 43. Click OK. You have changed the gamma point of the top Layer (the midpoint value in the image), which brightens the image. You have also changed the darkest value in the image from 0 to 90, which lightens the entire image considerably. Click OK.

16. To further emphasize the text, we need to put a stroke around it and the box. Press the modifier key (Mac: OPTION, Windows: ALT) and the left bracket key ([) to make the Text Box Layer active. Using the Eyedropper tool (I), select one of the darker colors in the boys' hair on the full strength image. Press the modifier key (Mac: ⌘, Windows: CTRL) and click on the Layer name to select the non-transparent pixels on the Text Box Layer. Stroke (Edit → Stroke, 3, Outside). Figure 5-33 shows the finished image.

Figure 5-33
Image with text
box screened out

Another way to make the screened box stand out is to set the Apply mode of the Text Box Layer to screen at 65% Opacity. Setting the Apply mode of the Text Box Layer to screen makes the screened image area brighter than in Normal mode. However, you cannot stroke the box while it is in Screen mode, because your outline will also be screened out. You need to load the transparency of the Text Box Layer by pressing the modifier key (Mac: ⌘, Windows: CTRL) and clicking on the Layer name. Then create a new Layer. Stroke the selected area on the new Layer instead of the Text Box Layer. This way, the strong green stroke does not bleach out.

Command Watch: Guides and Grids		
Action	**Mac key**	**Windows key**
Show/Hide Guides	⌘+;	CTRL+;
Snap to Guides	SHIFT+⌘+;	SHIFT+CTRL+;
Lock Guides	⌘+OPTION+;	ALT+CTRL+;
Show/Hide Grid	⌘+"	CTRL+"
Snap to Grid	SHIFT+⌘+"	SHIFT+CTRL+"

1. What are two ways you can set text into an image?
   a. Typing it in using the Text tool
   b. Inserting a text box
   c. Drawing it on using the pencil tool
   d. Importing it as an EPS file from another program

2. What are the two programs that come with Photoshop to help you insert text in an image?
   a. Adobe Illustrator
   b. Adobe Type Manager
   c. Adobe Type Reunion
   d. Adobe Text Manager

3. What is one of the reasons you would add text to an image in Photoshop?
   a. To add pizzazz to your image
   b. To be able to add images or texture to it
   c. It's the best way to add text to your image
   d. To add a caption to your image

4. What is the name of the package of plug-ins for Photoshop created by Extensis Corporation?
   a. TextTools
   b. PhotoPlugIns
   c. PhotoTools
   d. PhotoText

5. What is the name of the process that makes part of an image less intense or lighter?
   a. Lightening
   b. Screening
   c. Highlighting
   d. Clouding

VIP PROFILE

Roberts Howard, Illustrator

Roberts Howard, author of *The Ilustrator's Bible* and *Gouache for Illustrators*, was dragged into the computer age kicking and screaming. Traditionally trained, he was very skeptical of computers. Rob is also the host of the Artists Forum on Compuserve—an excellent source of knowledge and discussions for both digital and traditional artists.

His first computer was an Atari, purchased for its ability to word process, since his manual typewriter had died. He was intrigued with the possibilities of the Atari paint program, though more as a toy than as a production adjunct. He soon discovered his Atari files were not acceptable to publishers and eventually purchased a PC 386 SX with a $99 Adobe software bundle of Illustrator and Streamline.

As Rob became more comfortable with his new purchases, he realized computer technology was going to have a major impact on the art world. He became one of the beta testers for the Windows version of Photoshop 2.5, the first PC release of the software.

He found Photoshop very difficult to learn. Part of the problem was that as an illustrator, he thought of the art process in one way, but the software worked differently. Another problem was the terminology. There was great overlap in the terms used in both the computer and traditional art worlds, but the meanings were different. However, he finally made peace with the program and now uses it constantly.

Today, Rob measures all other pixel-based packages against Adobe Photoshop. He finds that many things are easier to do with Photoshop. Currently, he is performing a great deal of photo-retouching. As an illustrator, he can add emotion to a photograph that a traditional photo-retoucher cannot. On one recent assignment, he transformed a static picture of a helicopter following a car into an emotional chase scene.

He heightened the rise on road, modified the background, and added motion to the road. He then added a foggy feeling to the entire scene. On the hood of the car, he added a Lens Flare and duplicated the grille and headlights, which he placed on top of the original but a bit off register and at 40% Opacity to give it vibration. He also softened and added speed to the rotor of the helicopter, plus he added a lens flare. Photoshop made the process much easier than working conventionally.

His advice to beginners: "The best advice I have seen came from Michael Sullivan at a How Convention. The easier a program is to learn, the harder it is to use in day-to-day work; the harder a program is to learn the more depth it has and the more useful it will be. So, persevere. Photoshop is hard to learn, but the rewards are worth it."

CHAPTER SUMMARY

This chapter covered a lot of ground. You learned

- How to create custom brushes and how to use images as brush sources.

- How to create textures and make them seamless.

- How to use these textures as if they were paper surfaces. You also learned to use these for both original drawing and applying texture to an image that already exists.

- How to use the Airbrush tool and structure a project.

- How to use the Type tool and tips for using it more efficiently. You learned when to set text in Photoshop, and more importantly, when not to.

- How to create softly embossed effects with text.

CHAPTER 6

COLOR AND FILE FORMATS

hotoshop gives the user an almost unlimited—and certainly confusing—number of choices of image mode and file formats. This chapter attempts to put them into perspective for you and help you select the best file format and image mode for your needs. Those needs will vary, depending on the final use of your image. An image that is traditionally printed on a four-color printing press needs to be changed at some point in the process to CMYK mode, and needs to be saved as either a TIFF file or an EPS file. An image destined for use on the World Wide Web must become either an Indexed Color GIF file or an RGB JPEG file (or a file in the new PNG format). If the same image will be used in a multimedia production (placed into Macromedia Director or embedded into a QuickTime movie), it might need to be saved as a PICT file—still in Indexed Color mode. If you work on Windows, you may need to save files in PCX or BMP format for certain applications.

You also have a choice of saving a file with a digital *watermark*—an indicator that helps to identify you as the image's creator and lets anyone who sees it contact you for usage permission.

What are these modes and which file formats do you use for what? These are the questions this chapter addresses. By the end of the chapter, you should be able to

● State the advantages, disadvantages, and active features of using the following image modes:

  RGB

  CMYK

  Lab

  Indexed Color

  Duotone

  Bitmap

● Convert an image from one mode to another

● Create a duotone, tritone, or quadtone using the preset curves

● Change a duotone to a CMYK image and adjust the Printing Inks Setup to see an accurate preview

● Identify the most common file formats for prepress

● State when (and when not) to use TIFF, EPS, PICT, PCX, GIF, and JPEG formats

● Specify which Photoshop features (such as channels, Layers, and color depth) are available in which formats

● Create a GIF89a file with interlacing and transparency

● Create a watermarked version of your image

COLOR SPACE

How do you define or specify a color? A rose may be a rose may be a rose, but what color rose is it? This is a topic that generates much confusion. How do you know which color space to choose?

You select a *color space* (a system for defining a color) when you create a new image. As we discussed in Chapter 1, "Introduction to Photoshop," there are four major systems for defining color. They are

1. RGB: The language of the monitor

2. CMYK: The language of the printing industry

3. HSL: The language of most artists

4. Lab: A universal, device-independent language—sort of an Esperanto based on the physics of color

Photoshop works with all four systems, but only enables you to create documents in three of them. HSL (Hue-Saturation-Light) is not a supported document mode, and unfortunately, this is the color system most artists understand. HSL color is the only color system that works the way you learned to mix colors in elementary school: Colors are located on a color wheel, and adding black makes them darker, while adding gray makes them less saturated.

Each color space has its own range of achievable colors, plus its advantages and disadvantages. Photoshop also works with two colorless color spaces: bitmap and grayscale. Grayscale images contain 256 shades of gray, and bitmapped images have only black or white pixels.

The achievable colors in a color space are called the *gamut* of the color space. They are the colors it's possible to create within that color space. Some colors are totally outside the gamut of colors you can create on a computer. For instance, metallic gold can be simulated, but you cannot create a true metallic gold on the computer regardless of which color space you use. That said, let's take a look first at the true color spaces in Photoshop's Image → Mode menu, then at the other possible document modes.

Lab

L*a*b* (Lightness, plus a and b color channels) is a *tristimulus* color model, meaning it has three values. This color model, which was developed by the Centre Internationale d'Eclairage (CIE), has three channels (Lightness, a, and b). It is a *device-independent* color space. This means, in theory at least, that the colors are defined so they can be unambiguously output on any device supporting this standard, and the color will not vary. Lab color is a mathematically defined color model taking into account the way the human eye perceives color.

Lab color is the color model Photoshop uses internally. When you convert from RGB to CMYK, for example, Photoshop references the Lab color tables to determine how to display the changed pixels. The gamut of Lab colors includes both the RGB and CMYK color ranges. The Adobe Photoshop manual recommends working in Lab mode when you print from Photoshop to a PostScript Level II printer, though most people do not bother. It is also useful when you wish to adjust the image's luminance or color values apart from one another.

You can often create a better grayscale version of a color image simply by using its Lightness channel. If you convert your image to Lab mode and sharpen just the Lightness channel, you can produce a sharper image with much less haloing and distortion than if you worked only in RGB or CMYK mode.

RGB

RGB color space is also a tristimulus model. An RGB image contains three components—a Red, Green, and Blue channel. These channels correspond to the individual phosphors on the computer monitor, which emit red, green, or blue light.

RGB color space is an *additive* color system, meaning all three colors combine to create white. This is why the color in an RGB channel tends to look reversed—as if it were a negative. If you are viewing the channel in grayscale, the white areas in it carry its color information. For example, if you place a red circle in an empty (white) document, you will see no change in the red channel. In the green and blue channels, you will see a black circle. An RGB image starts out *full* (100% red, 100% green, 100% blue), and the process of placing image data into the channels *empties* it.

RGB color space gives you 8 bits of data per channel, or 256 shades of gray. The combination of possibilities yields about 16.7 million colors that can be displayed. However, the specific 16.7 million colors vary based on the monitor used, its age, and its condition. If you display the same file on 15 monitors in a room, the image will look different on all 15 of them!

CMYK

CMYK (Cyan, Magenta, Yellow, Black) is a color mode that would be a tristimulus model in a perfect world. It is a nice theory that the mixture of cyan, magenta, and yellow in varying proportions generates all possible colors, with 100% of each yielding black. In reality, 100% of all three colors gives you a dark mud. Hence the K in CMYK—black ink added for that extra punch, since dark mud is usually not good enough.

CMYK is the color mode of the traditional print world. Four-color process printing is based on this color system. Magazines, newspapers, and almost all printed literature use CMYK inks for their color.

CMYK is a subtractive color space. In RGB mode the colors combine to form white; in CMYK they combine to form black. In the channels, the black areas indicate the amount of the specific color for that plate. The darker the plate or channel, the more of the color it possesses.

There are a huge number of colors that cannot be generated at all in CMYK color space. It has a very small gamut of possible colors. In general, the colors that can be produced in CMYK color space are the less saturated colors in any given range. An exclamation point inside a triangle appears in the color picker, warning you when you attempt to select a color that cannot be printed.

There are a number of different opinions about working in CMYK versus working in RGB for images that will be printed. If your scans are acquired in CMYK mode, the general consensus is for you to stay in CMYK mode (unless you need a filter that does not work in that mode). However, if your scans are done in RGB, you should work in RGB to color correct and manipulate the image, then convert to CMYK as your last step. Doing this gives you the ability to easily *repurpose* your images.

Repurposing is a new buzzword in the industry. It means being able to use the same image for a number of different output methods. If you retain a fully corrected copy of your image in RGB, you can convert it to Indexed Color mode for Web or screen use, and you can send it to an RGB film recorder. You can also use the same image with a composite printer or a coated stock print job, plus you can send it to the newspaper. If you convert to CMYK mode too early, you limit your options somewhat, because you change (degrade) the colors every time you change from one CMYK profile to another or to RGB mode and back. (More on this topic later in the chapter when we discuss RGB to CMYK conversion.)

Indexed Color

Indexed Color space is one of the oldest forms of color available on the computer. This is not a *real* color space, in terms of existing as a theoretical system of color. RGB colors come from the physics of light; CMYK colors come from the realities of the print world; Lab color comes from the musings of scientists about the way in which people perceive color. Indexed Color mode comes from the limitations of computer hardware and of computer memory.

The first microcomputers had two colors: black and white. This is easy for a computer since *binary* (meaning something is either on or off) is its native tongue. Then there were four colors—still easy for the computer. These four colors were dithered (mixed up) to create the illusion of more colors. Computers gradually came to display 8 (the EGA cards), then 16 (standard VGA), then 256 (extended VGA) colors. Eventually, 24-bit color cards became available (16.7 million colors). However, the 256-color format did not disappear.

People discovered that 256 colors are enough for many purposes, especially when the colors are mixed together optically to seem like more. After all, the artist Georges Seurat accomplished this a century ago, resulting in several classic paintings and a new art movement called *pointillism*—a technique of applying small dots of color to a surface so that from a distance they blend together. 256-color images are also good for animation because they display faster and take less room in RAM and hard disk storage space. As more people use the World Wide Web, they too appreciate the 256-color space for its faster download and display times.

How does Indexed Color work? And what does its name mean? Just what is indexing? Let's take a look.

When you create an Indexed Color image, a Color Lookup Table (CLUT) is also generated. This CLUT is the actual index. Think of an index at the back of a book. Its purpose is to keep track of every important idea in a book and help you find it quickly. The Color Lookup Table stores a sample of every color in the image (like the ideas in a book) and the color number associated with it (somewhat like the page number references). This makes it easy to locate every pixel in the image using that color.

If you decide to change a color, you just need to change its sample in the Color Lookup Table and it immediately changes the color everywhere it's used in the image. The Color Lookup Table has 256 entries. This gives you 256 possible colors—one for each paint bucket in the CLUT. The actual gamut of colors you can place in the bucket depends on your hardware. Different color cards may be limited in the total pool of colors from which the final 256 can be selected.

We will discuss Indexed Color space in greater detail in Chapter 13, "Beyond Photoshop," when we talk about Photoshop and Web graphics. There are definite issues such as System palettes and cross-platform considerations that require explanations.

Indexed Color space can actually be a lot of fun. If you like to create wild colors and weird effects, you can manipulate an image's color tables to create some really striking examples. The Lab in Appendix C has a "Just for Fun" exercise you can try that lets you borrow the Color Table of one image and apply it to another.

There are some programs that depend on Indexed Color space to perform Color Table animation. In the earlier days of Microcomputers, CLUT animation was more prevalent than it is now. However, Imaja has a program for the Macintosh called Bliss Paint that turns CLUT animation into performance art. The program lets you paint on a canvas with certain prewritten forms and patterns, plus it enables the colors in the image cycle to change either randomly or based on user input. For example, you can press Ⓑ to place more blue into the image. The program can also respond to musical input and changes colors in time to music. Bliss Paint also creates QuickTime movies of its creations so you can place them into any program that works with animation and video (such as Adobe Premiere, Adobe After Effects, MacroMedia Director, Quark Immedia). You can also bring Bliss Paint images back into Photoshop and composite or rework them.

In Chapter 10, "Photo Retouching," you will learn how to change colors in an Indexed Color grayscale image to create a sepia-toned image (like an old photograph).

When you change an image into Indexed Color mode, you have some choices as to how set the colors. Figure 6-1 shows the Indexed Color conversion dialog. There are three areas on the Indexed Color dialog. They are Resolution, Palette, and Dither. The resolution section enables you to specify the number of colors you want in the finished image (the maximum is 256).

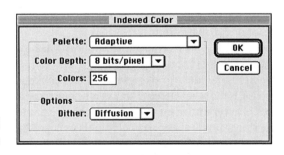

Figure 6-1
Convert to Indexed
Color mode

The Palette section allows you to choose between an Exact palette (if you have less than 256 colors in the image currently, you can opt to keep them all), Macintosh or Windows System palette (the set of colors standard to the Macintosh or Windows operating systems), Adaptive palette (the 256 colors that best describe, in Photoshop's opinion, the image being converted), Web (the 216-color Netscape palette), Custom (using an already-created Color Table), and Previous (using the last Color Lookup Table loaded).

The Dither section lets you choose whether to try to get the look of more colors in the image by dithering (mixing up the pixels), not dithering, or creating a pattern (the way colors are shown on a monitor that only displays 256 colors). There is almost no reason to willingly choose to use a pattern dither. However, there are excellent reasons to select either of the other two. It really depends on *why* you are converting to Indexed Color mode. Non-dithered graphics are much smaller when saved to a GIF file for display on the Web, and they can display much faster. Dithered images may look better and as if they have more colors.

It may be a little bit difficult to picture the next three figures in color (though you can see them on the CD-ROM). However, you can easily see the change occurring when you move from the continuous color of the original to the choppy color changes in the other figures. This is apparent even in grayscale. Figure 6-2(a) shows an image in 24-bit color mode. Figure 6-2(b) shows the same image reduced to 256 colors with no dither, and Figure 6-2(c) shows the image dithered.

All three images were captured at 8:1 resolution on the screen, so you can almost see the individual pixels.

There are some definite disadvantages to working with an Indexed Color image: You cannot use any of the filters; you cannot use Layers; and the Gradient, Focus, Tone, and Smudge tools do not work.

Duotones

The Duotone mode is not a color space either. Rather, it allows you to select from one to four colors that react to the same grayscale image. The common duotone uses two Pantone or other spot color inks and prints the same grayscale image in two passes—one with each ink—using different *transfer* curves with each pass.

About Transfer Curves

A *transfer curve* is the same as a curve you apply using the Curves dialog, but it is used to determine the output densities (gray values) of an image when the image is sent to a PostScript output device like an imagesetter. You can view the transfer curve as a curve or a chart. In chart form, it shows the output value for each input value. Let's see what this means.

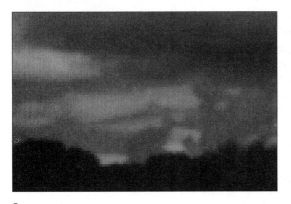

a

b

Figure 6-2
a) Convert to Indexed Color mode
b) Indexed Color, no dither
c) Indexed Color, dithered

c

Figure 6-3 shows a calibration strip produced with the Calibration Strip acquire module from David Pfeiffer & Associates (available on many online services). You can make one for yourself from a posterized Gradient. This strip has 13 gray values in it. Starting at 0% black at the top, it shows the 5%, 10%, 20%, 30%, 40%, 50%, 60%, 70%, 80%, 90%, 95%, and 100% gray values. It is an excellent way of determining if your printer is capable of printing these values so they can be distinguished from one another. In any case, this shows the gray values printing at a 1:1 correspondence—50% gray in the file *should* (barring complications in the printing process itself) print at 50%.

Figure 6-4 shows the Page Setup dialog appearing when you select Transfer. This is a totally demented curve that serves no purpose besides demonstrations and wild special effects.

You can either read the curve points on the graph or read the exact values from the chart. For example, the chart states all gray values of 20% black in the original image are output at 84.4% black. All input values of 80% are output at 27.5%. Using the transfer curve, you can see the changes in Figure 6-5. Figure 6-6 shows an image with the demented curve applied to half of it diagonally across the center using the Curves dialog (a real *transfer* curve must effect the entire image rather than just a section of it).

Figure 6-3
Calibration Strip of
grays from 0% to
100% with extra
5% and 95% values
added

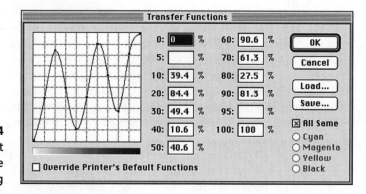

Figure 6-4
Transfer curves set
up in the Page
Setup dialog

Figure 6-5
Calibration strip
with transfer curve
applied

Figure 6-6
Image with same
curve as above
transfer curve
applied

Why Use a Duotone?

Back to the topic of duotones (now that you know what a transfer curve is).

A duotone uses a transfer curve on each printing plate to control the amount of ink in the highlights, midtones, and shadows of the image. The beauty of the duotone is in the subtlety with which the inks interact and in how it produces a stunning piece of work at a lower printing cost (lower cost for two colors; a four-custom-color printing job would be as expensive if not more than CMYK printing).

Many of the works of photographer Ansel Adams were printed as duotones or quadtones with several different transfer curves of black ink. You do not need to use different ink colors to produce a very rich effect. Black built up in different densities over selected values in the image conveys its own visual message.

Duotones (and tritones and quadtones) can also be used to tie together the graphic elements in an ad or brochure. You can use the full colors for the strong elements in the image, then soften them by creating a photographic duotone. Quadtones (four colors) are quite effective in conveying mood. If the curves are properly controlled, the colors can mix so softly you wouldn't believe four strong hues could produce so gentle an output.

Starting a Duotone

The best way to learn to apply a duotone to an image is to start with Photoshop's built-in curves. These curves (and the Pantone or process colors used in them) are guaranteed to work. They have been tested to ensure you get excellent results. Let's change an image to a duotone and try several of the built-in curves to see what they do. We will use a head shot of Maya for this and the other duotone work. This is the same young lady whose picture you used in Chapter 3, "Layers and Channels"; however, in this image, she has grown into a very beautiful young adult.

CREATING A DUOTONE

1. Open the image Mayahead.Psd.

2. Change the Mode to Duotone (Image → Mode → Duotone).

    The image must already be in grayscale mode, as seen in Figure 6-7, before changing to Duotone. If it is not, the Duotone option is dimmed and not selectable.

3. When you select Duotone..., you see a dialog that lets you select the type of duotone and its colors and curve.

4. Click on the Load... button. Photoshop stores a number of preset duotones curves inside the Goodies folder in the Photoshop directory. Go into the Goodies → Duotone Presets → Duotones → Pantone → Duotones, and select the fifth curve on the list. Figure 6-8 shows the file list using the Macintosh O/S. This preset uses black and Pantone 144, an orange color that builds up to 80% in the shadows.

5. After you select the preset, your Duotone dialog will look like Figure 6-9. It shows both the black and the Pantone 144, and a thumbnail of the curves set up for that color. It also shows a Gradient across the bottom, representing the way the colors will overprint. If you change the curves, that Overprint Gradient will change as well.

Figure 6-7
Maya, in grayscale

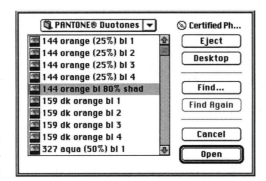

Figure 6-8
Pantone Duotone
curve list

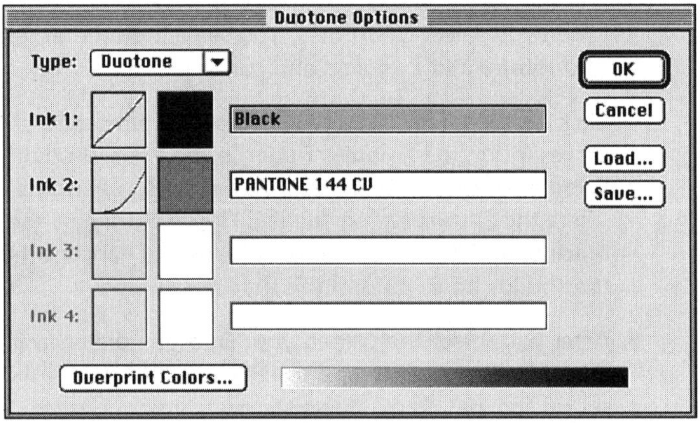

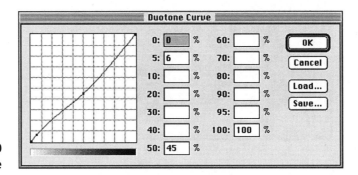

Figure 6-9
Duotone dialog

6. Click on the *curve* next to the black color swatch (clicking on the color swatch brings up the Color Picker). You see the curves shown in Figure 6-10. If you click on the Pantone 144 curve thumbnail, you see the graph in Figure 6-11.

Figure 6-10
Black curve

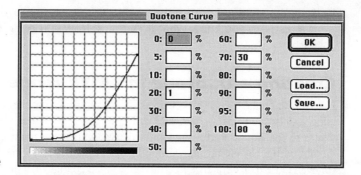

Figure 6-11
Pantone 144 curve

7. Click OK to exit the dialog. The grayscale image has changed to a warm brown image. That warm hue is the result of the overprint at different densities of the black and Pantone 144 inks.

8. You can change the colors making up the Duotone without changing its curves. Select Duotone... from the Mode menu again, and click on the Pantone 144 color swatch. The Photoshop (or system) Color Picker appears. Select Pantone 171 from the Custom color menu. Click OK. The color changes to a medium pink. When you exit the Duotone dialog, notice there is now a soft pink color cast to the image.

 Selecting a color of a substantially different value than the one in the preset curve causes very unexpected changes in the image.

When you choose a new color, if you wish to reuse the old curve, you need to pick one that's close to the original color in value.

9. You can also alter the Curve. Reopen the Duotone dialog (Image → Mode → Duotone...). Click on the curve next to Pantone 171. Change the curve so the 100% input value is also 100% output and 70% input becomes 40% output. Figure 6-12 shows these changes to the graph.

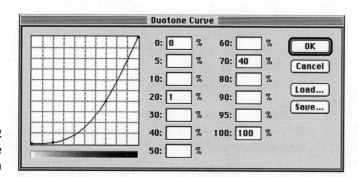

Figure 6-12
Changed curve
graph

10. Save this changed Duotone curve by clicking on the Save... button, and give it a name so you know what it contains. Now you can recall it anytime you wish.

Creating a Duotone in CMYK Mode

It is easy to create a duotone—especially if you use one of the presets. However, creating your own curves is a bit riskier. Rob Day, author of *Designer Photoshop* and frequent visitor to the Adobe Forum on CompuServe, warns that many of the Pantone colors are not within the gamut of a computer monitor and cannot be previewed accurately (or even close to accurately). In addition, a small change on a press—such as the printer not mixing the Pantone ink so that it matches the Pantone selector exactly—can ruin a duotone or at least seriously change the way it looks.

Experimenting with Duotones (courtesy of Rob Day)

One way you can learn how a duotone prints is to use the trim area on a job with two or more Pantone colors, or a Pantone color and black. If there is room along the margin of the job in the area to be cut away, you can try out some duotones and a variety of curves. You might want to create a small Gradient and a small design you use consistently for play. That way, you can keep some of the scraps as reference and compare results on a variety of paper stocks, with as many colors as you get the chance to print. This is an inexpensive way to gain experience with duotones without experimenting on a client's actual job.

> **Warning:** Discuss this with your printer before you decide there is enough room for such experiments. There may be other factors you are unaware of that could make your margin art a problem.

There are a few other facets of duotones that make them trickier than they should be. You have noticed that you cannot preview changes to the Duotone Curves until you have left the dialog box. This makes experimentation very time-consuming. Many Photoshop users have found a way around this. In a recent discussion on the Adobe Forum between New Jersey–based photographer Steve Pollock, Rob Day, and several other users, the following technique was presented. It enables you to work in CMYK color space but print with Pantone inks and preview the results as well as—if not better than—in Duotone mode. The other advantage is you can use Photoshop's Dot Gain settings and prepare your images exactly as you would for CMYK printing (which you will learn in Chapter 15, "Photoshop Output").

The Printing Inks setup (File → Preferences → Printing Inks) controls, among other things, the way Photoshop displays the CMYK colors *on the monitor*. This means you can change the way colors look onscreen without changing the way they will print. This lets you tweak your monitor to make your screen more closely resemble your output. It also enables you to tell the monitor to display cyan in pink, or in any other color you specify. We will use this trick to make the one grayscale image in a duotone occupy two channels in a CMYK image but display in their Pantone preview colors.

In order to understand how this technique works, you need to understand what makes a duotone work. A *duotone* is a grayscale image with only one channel (open the Channels palette and look). However, it has *two* transfer curves—one for each color. This makes it impossible to look at the curve for each channel since there is only one. In the following exercise, you change from the Duotone mode to the Multichannel mode, which gives you two channels and applies the correct transfer curve to each. Follow along.

CREATING DUOTONES IN THE CMYK CHANNELS

1. Open the image Mayahead.Psd.

2. Change the image to Duotone (Mode → Duotone).

3. Load the 506 Burgundy (75%) bl 1 curve.

4. Click on the Overprint Colors... button at the bottom of the dialog. The dialog shown in Figure 6-13 appears. Click in the 1+2 patch (the Color Picker appears) and make note of the color's Lab values. In this case, the overprint color is pure black with a value of 0, 0, 0. Cancel the dialog.

5. Change the Mode to Multichannel (Mode → Multichannel). Open the Channels palette. You should see two channels.

6. Create two new empty channels in the Multichannel image (click twice on

Figure 6-13
Overprint Colors adjustment area

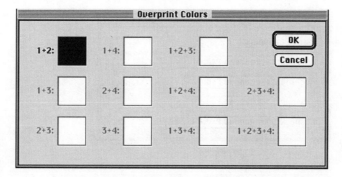

the New Channels icon at the lower center of the Channels palette). If the channels appear in black (as they probably will), invert them (Mac: ⌘+⏉, Windows: CTRL+⏉). The channels must be white.

7. Split the channels apart (Channels Palette menu → Split channels). This puts each channel into its own image. However, you can merge the channels again to form a CMYK image, which you could not do if you hadn't split them apart.

8. Merge the channels together again (Channels Palette menu → Merge Channels), but select CMYK as the mode. Figure 6-14 shows this selection dialog.

9. When you select the mode and click OK, a new dialog, shown in Figure 6-15, appears. This allows you to place any open images of the same size in any channels you wish. Place image #1 in Channel 1 and image #2 in Channel 2, and so on, as shown in the Figure 6-15.

10. The image becomes a CMYK image with data in only two channels. The colors, however, are strange. We need to fix this next. Actually, we don't need to change how the channel prints, only how it looks to *us*.

11. Open the Printing Inks Setup preference (File → Preferences → Printing Inks Setup). Figure 6-16 shows the dialog. Click on the Ink Colors drop-down menu and select Custom... at the top of it.

12. The Ink Colors dialog appears. It is shown in Figure 6-17. Click on the cyan

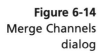

Figure 6-14
Merge Channels
dialog

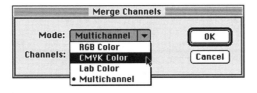

Figure 6-15
Select channels to
merge

Printing Inks Setup

Ink Colors: [SWOP (Coated) ▼]   [OK]

Dot Gain: [20] %   [Cancel]

Gray Balance
C: [1.00]   M: [1.00]   [Load...]
Y: [1.00]   K: [1.00]   [Save...]

☐ Use Dot Gain for Grayscale Images

Figure 6-16
Printing Inks Setup
main screen

color swatch to bring up the Color Picker. Change the color to black (RGB 0, 0, 0). Click OK as many times as needed to exit the dialog. This is a two-step process (unless you know the Lab definition of Pantone 506).

13. Click on the foreground color swatch in the toolbox, and change it to the first Pantone color your duotone uses (this example uses only one, Pantone 506).

14. Repeat Step 11. This time, click in the Magenta swatch to bring up the Color Picker, and click in the Foreground Color swatch in the Toolbox (where you just stored the correct color). This places the RGB equivalent of Pantone 506 into the color preview box of the Magenta channel.

15. Now you need to set the combination of cyan plus magenta to the over-print color from the duotone dialog. Click on the CM: swatch. Change the color to black (Lab 0, 0, 0). Save this print ink setup using a name telling you what it is, such as P506&Bl. This enables you to reuse it when needed.

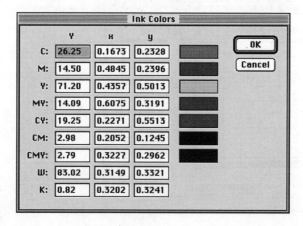

Figure 6-17
Ink Colors dialog

Ink Colors

	Y	x	y	
C:	26.25	0.1673	0.2328	
M:	14.50	0.4845	0.2396	
Y:	71.20	0.4357	0.5013	
MY:	14.09	0.6075	0.3191	
CY:	19.25	0.2271	0.5513	
CM:	2.98	0.2052	0.1245	
CMY:	2.79	0.3227	0.2962	
W:	83.02	0.3149	0.3321	
K:	0.82	0.3202	0.3241	

[OK]   [Cancel]

16. Click OK. Your image now looks just like it did when it was an official duotone.

17. You can use all Photoshop's facilities now. You can easily preview changes to the tone curve too. Open the Curves dialog (Mac: ⌘+Ⓜ, Windows: CTRL+Ⓜ). Select the Magenta Channel in the Curves dialog and drag the curve down from the center until the numeric readout shows Input: 128, Output: 94. This intensifies the Magenta (which is the Pantone 506 when you print). Figure 6-18 shows this curve. As you drag, you see a real-time preview of the color change. This makes it much easier to select curves. Click OK. Save your image.

18. Change your Printing Inks Setup back to the original setting (probably *SWOP Coated* if you never changed it).

 You cannot leave the setup in place for the duotone or you will throw all your other images' displays off kilter and wonder why the printing is so messed up.

So, put everything back in order while you are still thinking about it!

How do you make this image print in the correct colors? That part is easy. Either output the image to an imagesetter from Photoshop, or place it into QuarkXPress or PageMaker. After the cyan and magenta films are produced, tell the printer to use black and Pantone 506 (and identify the correct plate for each).

You can also use CMYK colors to simulate a duotone. This technique, courtesy of New York artist Eric Reinfeld, is used in the Lab in Appendix C. It is one Eric has taught with great success to his publishing clients (such as *Business Week* and *Time* magazines).

Figure 6-18
New Magenta
curve

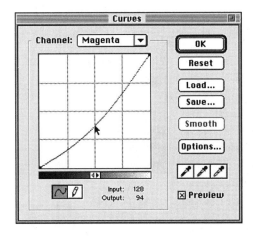

Bitmaps

Bitmaps are also a color space of sorts. They are bi-level images in which any given pixel can be either black or white. In order to convert to Bitmap mode, your image must be a grayscale. Once you have a grayscale image, there are several ways you can convert your image to a bitmap. The most common ways are using the Diffusion Dither or the halftone. Let's try several methods.

CONVERTING TO BITMAP

Steps (Creating a Threshold Bitmap)

1. Open the image Ellen.Psd.

2. This image is already a grayscale so it can simply be converted to bitmap. Select the Mode menu and choose Bitmap. The dialog shown in Figure 6-19 appears.

3. Make a copy of the image (Image → Duplicate → OK).

4. Convert the image to a bitmap (Image → Mode → Bitmap, 50% Threshold, 300 dpi).

   When you convert a grayscale to a bitmap, you need to increase the resolution of the image to maintain the same amount of detail. Usually, you go from 72 dpi (if that is your starting resolution) to 300 dpi. This gives the halftoning room to work.

5. Print the image. Figure 6-20 shows the 50% Threshold conversion.

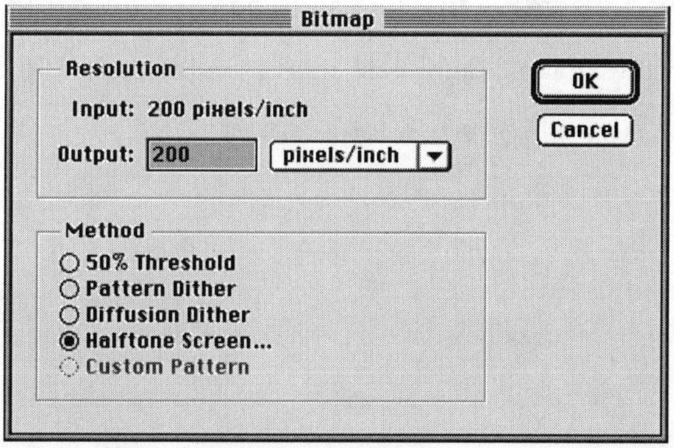

Figure 6-19
Bitmap dialog

Figure 6-20
50% Threshold
bitmap conversion

6. Undo (Mac: ⌘+Z, Windows: CTRL+Z).

Steps (Creating a Pattern Dither Bitmap)

1. Use the Ellen.Psd Copy image.

2. Convert the image to a bitmap (Mode → Bitmap, Pattern Dither, 300 dpi).

3. Print the image. This method is not pictured here. It is not particularly attractive, nor is it useful unless you need to display your image on a screen with a limited number of gray values.

4. Undo (Mac: ⌘+Z, Windows: CTRL+Z).

Steps (Creating a Diffusion Dither Bitmap)

1. Use the Ellen.Psd Copy image.

2. Convert the image to a bitmap (Mode → Bitmap, Diffusion Dither, 300 dpi).

3. Print the image. Figure 6-21 shows the Diffusion Dither conversion.

4. Undo (Mac: ⌘+Z, Windows: CTRL+Z).

Figure 6-21
Diffusion Dither
bitmap conversion

Steps (Creating a Halftone Screen Bitmap)

1. Use the Ellen.Psd Copy image.

2. Convert the image to a bitmap (Mode → Bitmap, Halftone Screen, 300 dpi).

3. In the dialog that appears, leave the angle and frequency information unchanged and select Line as the method.

4. Print the image. Figure 6-22 shows the Halftone Screen conversion.

Figure 6-22
Halftone Screen
bitmap conversion

5. Undo (Mac: ⌘+Z, Windows: CTRL+Z).

6. Repeat this exercise again using the Round spot as the halftone.

7. Undo (Mac: ⌘+Z, Windows: CTRL+Z).

1. Of the four major systems used for defining colors, which one is the universal device-independent system (language)?
   a. RGB
   b. CMYK
   c. HSL
   d. Lab

2. What are gamut colors?
   a. Colors simulated on the computer
   b. Colors that can be created on the computer within its color space
   c. Colors outside the color space
   d. Colors that can't be printed

3. Which statements are true about Lab color space?
   a. It is a device-independent color space.
   b. Color doesn't print well on most printers.
   c. It is a mathematically defined color model.
   d. It is the color model Photoshop uses internally.

4. Which of the following color systems is the oldest form of color?
   a. RGB
   b. CMYK
   c. Indexed Color
   d. Duotones

5. What are some of the reasons one would use duotones, instead of a traditional color system?
   a. The way the gray inks interact can produce a stunning piece of work at a lower printing cost.
   b. They can be used to tie graphic elements in an ad or brochure.
   c. They create a stunning color image.
   d. They produce poor quality images and are difficult to print.

FILE FORMATS

Photoshop can open and write a very large number of file formats. Some people use Photoshop for its file format conversion capabilities alone! Question are always asked, however, about which is the best file format or which formats should be used for what. Let's try to clear up the confusion.

For starters, when Photoshop has an image it is editing, you can save it in any file format you want (given color space considerations and a few other factors). The image data itself should not change, regardless of the format (unless the format is JPEG), though the extras that can be saved along with it (such as Layers and Channels) will change.

Opening Files

Photoshop can open a large number of file formats. The list of files it can read is not always the same list as the files it can *write*. You can tell what file type you are opening through the File Open dialog, though the specifics differ by platform.

On the Macintosh, you can see the file format of an image at the bottom of the File Open dialog. Figure 6-23 shows the area specifying the file type. If you have saved the file without a custom preview icon, you can also tell the file type from the image icon (if the image was originally saved with Photoshop).

If you are working on the Windows platform, you can see the file type in the File Open dialog if you select the Details button to the right of the dialog. Figure 6-24 shows this for Windows 95. In Windows 3.1, you will only know the file type from the extension.

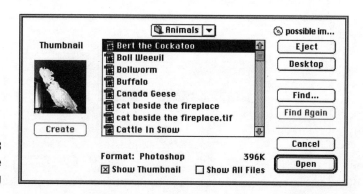

Figure 6-23
Macintosh File
Open dialog

Figure 6-24
Windows 95 File
Open dialog

You can open files that are saved on Windows in the Macintosh version of Photoshop and vice versa. They move cross-platform very well. However, depending on how you have *named* them, you may not originally see them listed in the File Open dialog.

On the Macintosh, you cannot open a PC file into Photoshop by dragging it to the program icon or by double-clicking. Because the file is from the PC, the Macintosh operating system does not properly see the file as a Photoshop document. However, you *can* open it from Photoshop. If you have given the file an *extension* (three letters preceded by a period identifying the file format, such as .PSD for a Photoshop file) Photoshop understands, the file will appear—as does the .PCX file in Figure 6-25, in the Photoshop File Open dialog.

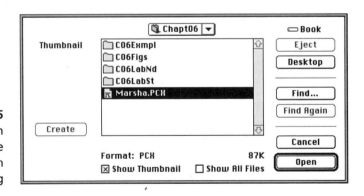

Figure 6-25
PC Image with
extension in the
Mac File Open
dialog

If you did not name it with a valid extension, it will not appear in the list unless you check the Show All Files box, as shown in Figure 6-26. Notice that Photoshop has selected the Raw file format for the copy of Figure 6-26. You need to change it to PCX if you want the file to open properly. To change the file type, click and drag the menu down where it says Raw. You will see the entire list of available file types.

The situation of the PC is very similar. If you named the file so the PC understands the file type extension, Win/Photoshop shows it in the File Open list and opens it without a problem, as you can see in Figure 6-27. However, if you failed to give it a proper name, your only chance of opening it is via the Open As command in the File menu. Figure 6-28 shows the File Open dialog for the randomly named images created at the time this chapter was written. When the File → Open As command is invoked, Windows does its best to read the unfamiliar Macintosh file name. The configuration used here is a bit of a hybrid—Windows 95 running on the Macintosh via a DOS Compatibility card. While Windows 95 should allow you to see long Macintosh file names, the Mac version of it does not. Therefore, the file names look the way they would under Windows 3.1—truncated and creatively rearranged so Windows gets the typical 8.3 file name it expects. The last three characters have no relation to the actual file name whatsoever. You need to tell Windows what the file format is so it can open the strange file.

Now, let's look at how you can save a file in the various file formats, and when and why you would want to.

Photoshop (.PSD)

Images can be saved in Photoshop 3.0 or Photoshop 2.0 formats. If you wish to save images with Layers, Photoshop 3.0 format is the only one that allows you to do so. Photoshop format also enables you to have up to 16 alpha channels. You can save files in any color mode. Photoshop format compresses images when it saves them so they take up no more disk space than absolutely necessary. The compression, however, is *lossless*—not one pixel in the image is removed or changed when the image is reloaded.

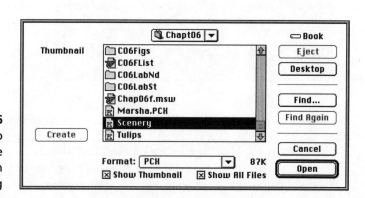

Figure 6-26
PC Image with no extension in the Mac File Open dialog

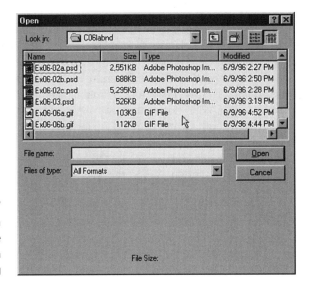

Figure 6-27
Mac Image with extension in the Windows File Open dialog

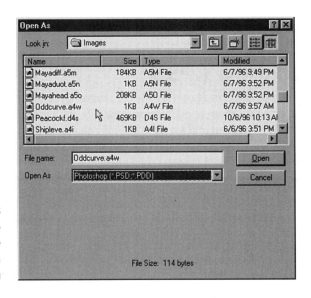

Figure 6-28
Mac Image with no extension in the Windows File Open As dialog

Images saved in Photoshop format can be easily exchanged between the PC and the Mac. If you give them the PC extension of .PSD, they can be opened by drag-and-drop on the Mac or found in the File Open dialog of Windows—regardless of their original platform. Without the correct extension, they can be opened from the File → Open dialog of either program by clicking on the Show All Files control. With few exceptions, they cannot be placed in any page layout program, nor can they export their transparency to a page layout program. In order to use the transparency of an image, you need to create a clipping Path (see Chapters 9 and 15 for more information on that).

TIFF (.TIF)

A TIFF file (Tagged Image File Format) is one of the two most common file formats for placing an image into a page layout program. Although you cannot save Layers with this format, you can save channels. However, most other programs have no idea what to do with these extra channels, so there is really little reason to save them with the image. There is a good reason not to save them, however, as QuarkXPress is known to scramble both the preview and the printing of TIFF images with embedded channels.

There is a lot of misconception about the TIFF format. Most of it stems from ancient programming history (about two years ago or so!). In the beginning, there were Mac TIFFs and PC TIFFs (and there still are). The Mac TIFF files used the Motorola method of writing the file, and the PC TIFFs used the Intel method of writing the file (which they both still do). These two methods reversed the order in which the individual bits of data were written. The problem occurred when you tried to move the files cross-platform. The PC applications could not read Mac files and vice versa. This is no longer the case. All the major cross-platform applications can easily read TIFFs written in both Motorola and Intel order. You may still have problems with some smaller, older, or non-standard applications. In addition, the TIFF file format is a moving target. There are several different versions of it, and it is not unknown for a program (including Photoshop) to balk at opening one that is quite outdated or rare.

TIFFs are very useful for prepress work. They can be reduced in size or cropped within a page layout program, and the computer will not need to send the entire file to the imagesetter to print a portion of it. This makes the image RIP faster. You can also modify a TIFF file in the page layout program by changing its color (if it is grayscale) or varying its opacity, and you can also set Trapping. TIFF files can be saved in either Mac or PC order. They can be saved as uncompressed or as LZW compressed images (though LZW compressed TIFFs have a nasty tendency to get corrupt or to not open).

You can save TIFF files in RGB, CMYK, Grayscale, or Bitmap mode. When you place a bitmap TIFF file into a page layout program, the white pixels become transparent. If you are working in PageMaker 6.0, you can even create a Clipping Path for the TIFF file.

EPS (.EPS)

EPS is the other popular format for placing images into a page layout program. EPS (Encapsulated PostScript File) images must be printed on a PostScript printer or imagesetter. They are larger than TIFF files, but they load much faster into a page layout program because they have previews already embedded in them.

The EPS file Photoshop creates is a bitmapped EPS file. You cannot open and edit it in Adobe Illustrator, although you can place it in an Illustrator image. The idea of an EPS file is that the program in which it is placed does not have to do anything with the file but output it. This means when you place an EPS file in a page layout program, the program cannot touch it. The file will *knockout* (remove the colors under it) by default, and you cannot set *trapping* (the way the colors overlap to prevent white areas from showing if the printing press does not align the color plates exactly). You cannot change the colors in the image. You cannot change the opacity. If you place the image in a picture box smaller than the image or you try to crop the image, it must send the entire image to the imagesetter anyway, before the excess areas are tossed away.

However, you can embed a Clipping Path in an EPS file (so you can remove background and whitespace from around an image and give it an irregular boundary). You can send a Transfer curve with an image so it will print differently than it displays. You might want to include a custom Transfer curve to compensate for dot gain or for a miscalibrated imagesetter.

PC and Mac EPS files are different. The Mac uses a PICT preview, while the PC uses a TIFF preview. Photoshop can read either flavor on either platform, but many other programs cannot. Save the EPS file for whichever platform will send it to the imagesetter. Unless you are going to use a system that doesn't accept it (such as UNIX), save the image with binary rather than ASCII encoding. This makes a much smaller file. You also have the option of creating an EPS file with a JPEG (a severely compressed) preview. Tread carefully if you select this option. There have been many reports on the Adobe Forum of trouble and incompatibilities with the JPEG preview format.

EPS files can also be saved in a DCS (Desktop Color Separation) flavor. This is a five-file set that is pre-separated. Your image must be in CMYK mode, then you can create a file that has a master image plus four additional files—one for each of the CMYK channels. This is a robust format, though it can be broken if you move or rename one of the pieces.

PCX (.PCX)

PCX format is a PC format. It was originally created by Zsoft for PC Paintbrush. It became a de facto standard on the PC platform and is used by many graphics programs. It is basically a 256-color format, though it has been extended to hold 24-bit data. Since PCX was one of the original graphics file formats, there are many versions of it. Therefore, there is a good chance Photoshop won't be able to open one of them from an older or less popular program. Use it with care, and don't save in this format if you have an alternative. The Windows version of Photoshop warns you that it cannot save printing preferences or configurations with this file format.

PICT (.PCT or .PIC)

The PICT format is the Mac equivalent of the PCX format, except there aren't a huge number of different PICT formats. There are vector PICT files and bitmapped PICT files. There is only one reason to use this format: if you need to place it into a Mac multimedia program. This format is very bad news when placed in a page layout program. Do not use it in PageMaker or QuarkXPress, as it rarely images the way it should.

PICT files can be saved as 2-bit, 4-bit, or 8-bit files in grayscale mode, and as 16-bit or 24-bit files in color. You can save an Indexed Color file as a PICT. You can also add JPEG compression to a PICT file.

TARGA (.TGA)

TARGA files were among the earliest of the 24-bit–capable graphics formats. At one time, they were excellent vehicles for cross-platform transfer. The format has almost died out, however, and there is very little reason to use it now. There are several flavors of TARGA files, and it is quite possible to meet one that is not compatible with Photoshop.

JPEG

The JPEG format is a product of the Joint Photographic Experts Group. It is a *lossy* method of compression, meaning it changes the actual pixels in the image when it saves the file. It throws away color differences in the file so it can make the file smaller when saving it.

The file format was developed as a way to deal with the huge hard disk space requirements of graphics files. JPEG compression works by tossing away pixels that probably won't matter in an image. There are different levels of JPEG compression. Using them, you trade off file size for quality. A high compression setting creates a very small image size with a large loss in image quality. A small compression ratio makes a larger file but does not degrade the image.

The loss in image quality using a high JPEG setting should not be noticeable when the image is printed. However, if you edit a file that has been JPEG'd, then save it as a JPEG file again, it will suffer a second round of image loss. If you zoom into a JPEG'd image, you can see the damage or loss that has occurred. There is a characteristic 8×8 grid appearing in an image saved as a JPEG file. Figure 6-29 shows this in an enlarged form of a file saved as a JPEG at low quality. The best procedure is to always save a copy of your image in a format other than JPEG in case you need to make changes.

Figure 6-29
JPEG loss to the image: a characteristic 8×8 grid

JPEG files are becoming more common for use on the Web, where they can produce 24-bit color with a small file size and a reasonable download time. Files saved as JPEGs from Photoshop move easily across platforms. The Adobe Forum on CompuServe has seen a number of complaints about incompatibilities between Mac and PC JPEG files not created from Photoshop.

Figure 6-30 shows the File Save dialog for JPEG images. It enables you to select from three options: Baseline Standard (the normal compression to get the best quality with the least amount of loss), Baseline Optimized (this setting optimizes quality over file size), and Progressive (the format for the World Wide Web allowing a file to be downloaded in 3 to 5 passes, so image data is visible even before the file is completely transmitted). In addition, you can select from 10 quality settings that determine the trade-off between image size and image quality.

GIF and GIF89a

The GIF89a format is the current darling of the format world and the star format on the World Wide Web. The GIF format was developed and popularized through use on CompuServe, where it was promoted as perhaps the first cross-platform graphics file format. In fact, the name GIF means Graphic Interchange Format.

In order to save a GIF file, your image must be in Indexed Color mode. This limits the GIF format to 256 colors. You can save a regular GIF file from the File → Save As menu. The format is listed as CompuServe GIF.

The GIF89a file format is a variant of the GIF format, allowing you to make selected colors in the image transparent and interlace the file. These features make this format ideally suited for the Web. To save a file as a GIF89a, you must *export* it (File → Export) as a GIF89a file rather than *saving* it. Let's look at how this file format works.

Interlacing is a method of displaying a file quickly. The file displays first at a very low resolution—it is blocky and highly pixellated. With each successive pass, the file comes more into focus as the blocky pixels are refined and finally displayed at their full resolution. This method lets you see a file being downloaded so you can decide whether to wait for the entire file to display or move on. Figure 6-31 shows the GIF89a Export dialog. To interlace the file so it displays quickly, you only need to check the Interlace box.

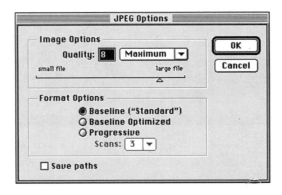

Figure 6-30
JPEG File Save
dialog

Figure 6-31
GIF89a Export
dialog

You can create transparent backgrounds in the GIF89a format in several ways.

The best results (the most visually pleasing in Photoshop) are obtained by exporting an image while it is in RGB mode. You can place your image on a Layer with the transparency you desire. If you wish to feather the edge of your image first to soften it, you may do so. Hide the Eye (Visibility icon) of any Layer that should not appear in the finished image, and select File → Export → GIF89a. When you export an image already containing transparency, the settings are automatically transferred to the Export dialog so you don't need select the areas you wish to be transparent. The Export command converts the image to Index Color and automatically creates an Alpha channel for the transparency.

Select the desired palette (Exact, Adaptive, or System). Select Interlace (or not) as you prefer. You may load another Color Lookup Table if you wish. You may also select the Transparency Index Color, which defaults to a Netscape Gray. This is the color replacing all pixels that will be transparent in your finished image. You may click Preview to see how the image will look in a browser. When you are satisfied, click OK.

You may also choose to convert your image to Indexed Color before you export it. This enables you to tweak the colors in the image if you wish. You can select the transparent areas yourself using the Eyedropper to select colors to "drop out." If you want to make a color transparent, make sure it does not appear anywhere else in the image. Pick a foreign color (one not in your image) as your transparency index color, so you make sure you don't drop out anything you do not intend to. You may drop out as many colors as you wish.

You may find that it is easier to create a channel that maps your transparency. When using a channel, you cannot inadvertently drop out colors in the middle of your image, which you easily can if you select dropout colors with the Eyedropper.

PNG (.PNG)

The PNG format is a fairly new format for Web graphics. It is designed to replace the GIF format, which has raised some concerns about legal usage rights lately. The PNG format is available directly from the File Save menu. It can save RGB images with no prior conversion and can interlace the image for a progressive download.

1. Photoshop can read and write many file formats. In fact, many people use Photoshop for
   a. Its storing abilities.
   b. Its file format conversion abilities.
   c. Its cross-platform abilities.
   d. Its file reading abilities.

2. If you save an image as a Photoshop file, it will have which of the following characteristics?
   a. The file will have a .Psd file name extension.
   b. The file will retain its layers.
   c. It can easily be exchanged between the Mac and PC worlds.
   d. The image will lose its color channels.

3. A TIFF file is one of the two most common file formats. TIFF files are very useful for which of the following reasons?
   a. They can be saved in RGB, CMYK, Grayscale, or Bitmap modes.
   b. They can be saved and used on both PCs and Macs.
   c. All major cross-platform applications can read TIFF files.
   d. They are easy to resize, crop, and recolor.

4. Besides TIFF files, what are some other file formats for images?
   a. EPS
   b. PCS
   c. GIF
   d. PCX

5. The most popular graphic image for the World Wide Web is the GIF file. In order to save a GIF file, your image must be
   a. In CMYK Color mode.
   b. In Indexed Color mode.
   c. Under 4095K in size.
   d. Exported to another application to save.

WATERMARKING YOUR IMAGE

As image distribution moves into new channels, it has become increasingly difficult for artists to control the copyrights on or track the use of their images. Photoshop 4.0 ships with a system by Digimarc designed to help artists control their rights to images.

Digimarc is a company maintaining a database of artists and their works. It enables people to locate an artist whose work they wish to use if the image has been *stamped* with contact information when saved. In order to put artists and clients together, Digimarc has created the Embed Watermark and Read Watermark filters (Filter → Digimarc →).

If the Read Watermark filter is present in the Plug-Ins folder, Photoshop automatically scans any file it opens to see if the file is branded with an artist's *watermark*. What is a watermark? In traditional printing, a watermark is a stamp or logo applied to paper to identify the maker. It acts as both a certificate of authenticity and a means of identification. It is subtle enough not to detract from the printed page, but visible if you know to look for it.

A digital watermark serves the same purpose. It is a pattern of noise applied to an image in a way the computer can read, although most viewers of the image should not be able to see it (though you, as the creator of the image, will probably notice the slight image changes). If you use the Digimarc system (and there are other systems available which are not included with Photoshop), you can select the strength of the watermark. The higher the strength, the more visible the watermark is in the finished image. However, the stronger the watermark, the more likely it is to survive a variety of image manipulations—such as resizing, blurring, sharpening, and printing.

Yes, the watermark is designed to be present in a printed image. That way, if it is scanned back into a computer, the branding and contact information is still readable. The watermark is also designed to withstand JPEG compression and changing images from one file format to another or into different color spaces.

Bundling the Digimarc filters with Photoshop was a very clever move for the company. However, they are doing this to make a profit. The maintenance of a database of artists is expensive. Therefore, the service is not free. If you wish to register your images and obtain a unique ID to identify yourself as the creator, there is a $150 per year charge. For this fee, you receive a unique ID and are listed in the Web database of artists. You may choose to place your images into the public domain or into a restricted usage class when branding them. If you restrict the use of your images, you can then instruct Digimarc as to how you wish to be contacted—directly or through a representative. You can select whether or not to make your address and phone number public. Figure 6-32 shows the Embed Watermark dialog. You can find Digimarc on the Web at `http://www.digimarc.com`.

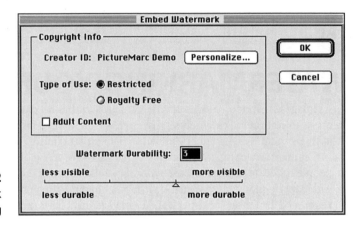

Figure 6-32
Embed Watermark
dialog

Interested parties can search the Digimarc database on the Web or can phone in a fax-back request for information. You will also receive reports of the number of requests for information your images have produced. The database is available 24 hours a day.

1. Channels have made it more difficult for artists to do what?
   a. Create images for the World Wide Web
   b. Track use of their images
   c. Control the copyrights on their images
   d. Create black and white images

2. What is a watermark?
   a. An almost invisible marking that serves as a certificate of authenticity and identification
   b. A line signifying the highest level of water
   c. A mark on paper created by an object with condensation
   d. A stamp or logo branded onto paper to identify the maker

3. Digimarc has created two types of filters to create and read watermarks. What are they?
   a. Embed Watermark filter
   b. Write Watermark filter
   c. Read Watermark filter
   d. Scan Watermark filter

4. What is a digital watermark?
   a. A pattern or image embedded within an image
   b. A pattern of noise applied to an image only readable by a computer.
   c. A microscopic graphic with a code or signature added to an image or graphic
   d. An electronic signature attached to an image

5. What are the advantages of applying a stronger digital watermark to an image?
   a. It is more likely to survive resizing, blurring, and printing of the image.
   b. The watermark will be more visible.
   c. It doesn't brand the image like a traditional watermark.
   d. It is more likely to withstand JPEG compression.

VIP PROFILE

Andrew Rodney

Andrew Rodney received a degree in photography from the Art Center College of Design in Pasadena, CA, in the pre-Photoshop year of 1988.

Once out of school, he bought a Macintosh computer from which to run his business. The computer was supposed to be a serious business machine, not a graphics workstation. However, in 1990, when Photoshop appeared on the scene, Andrew went into a computer store for software, saw a Mac IIcx running in color, and fell in love.

He purchased the color Mac and Photoshop, telling his wife he could probably use Photoshop to help his photography business. It wasn't Photoshop, though, that had caught his eye—it was the color! Photoshop was an excuse to convince his wife he *needed* that computer.

However, he soon became addicted to it and figured it could be a good way to promote his business. The advertising and commercial photography industries were very competitive, and not many photographers were using Photoshop back then. His business took off as he began to apply the new technology.

In 1994, Andrew and his wife moved to Santa Fe, New Mexico. He now does imaging and training in Photoshop for Camera and Darkroom Digital. He runs the digital facility, which consists mainly of sales and training. He works with Kodak, DayStar, Agfa, and Nikon equipment (among others), and provides high-end imaging and scanning services.

Recently, he began working with digital cameras and writing for *PhotoElectronic Imaging*. Basically, Andrew says, everything that has happened in his professional life since 1990 was because of Photoshop.

His advice to new users: "A lot of folks can do good Photoshop work, but you need to understand imaging fundamentals as well. GIGO (Garbage In, Garbage Out). Photoshop is a link in the chain—make sure you get good training from books or classes on input, color management systems, and output methods."

Andrew has made a number of contributions to this book. Most of his tips appear in Chapter 8, "Scanning and PhotoCD." Andrew is also active online in the AOL and CompuServe Photoshop forums.

CHAPTER SUMMARY

In this chapter you learned about color modes and file formats. You learned how to create duotones and change them to CMYK images for ease of manipulation. You learned how to create GIF89a files from Indexed Color images. You also learned about TIFF and EPS files and when they should be used for prepress.

CHAPTER 7

COLOR CORRECTION

One of the most important skills you need to learn in Photoshop is the art of color correction. The colors you see in real life, the colors you scan, the colors on your monitor, and the colors that print are all different. Your goal is to learn how to make them as similar as possible. An introductory course in Photoshop is *not* a good place for you to learn about all the intricacies of color management and advanced tonal correction theories. So we'll try to keep this as simple as possible—even though it is not a simple subject.

You can think of color correction as four separate issues:

- Getting accurate colors into Photoshop from a scanner or PhotoCD (Chapter 8, "Scanning and PhotoCD")

- Getting good color output from Photoshop (Chapter 15, "Photoshop Output")

● Using Photoshop's color manipulation commands to adjust colors in an image (this chapter)

● Calibrating your system to work with *known* color characteristics (Chapter 15)

This course, as a whole, really only covers Photoshop's own manipulation commands in detail. Other chapters in this book introduce you to the topics of color for printing so you know the scope of the problem—if not its solution. Once you have finished this course, you are ready for three excellent books that take you much deeper into the issues. *Real World Photoshop* by Bruce Fraser and David Blatner (Peachpit Press) is the best technical book written on the topic of Photoshop prepress and color management (getting images ready for printing and using color management systems). The other two recommended books are by Dan Margulis, who is also a contributing editor of *Computer Artist* magazine. Dan's books are *Professional Photoshop* and *MakeReady*. Both deal with color correction strategies and issues involved in CMYK editing. The approach is much different from *Real World Photoshop*, but it is important for you to understand both ways of looking at the topic.

That's down the road, however. First, you need to learn what Photoshop can do for images that are already scanned or acquired. What do you do if you don't like the color, or if the image is faded or dull? This chapter teaches you how to use the color correction features of Photoshop to make the color and tonal values look better.

By the end of this chapter, you should be able to

● Define and explain the White, Black, and Gamma points.

● Set the White, Black, and Gamma points in the Levels dialog.

● Explain the concept of a Histogram and use the Levels histogram to see where an image needs correction.

● Explain the concept of *key:* low key, high key, and key.

● Remove color cast from an image using Levels, Curves, Hue/Saturation, Color Balance, or Variations.

● Change the tonal values in an image using the Curves command.

● Use the Info palette to sample specific areas of the image.

● Create and use Adjustment Layers.

Much of the information in this chapter (and some of the writing as well) was contributed by Jim Rich and Eric Reinfeld. Eric's explanations of using levels and curves are very helpful. Jim contributes his extensive experience in color correcting images for print. All the theoretical explanations are Jim's. In addition, my discussions online over the years with Dan Margulis and Bruce Fraser—as well as my reading their books—help to make this information as complete and accurate as possible. (I, of course, take full responsibility in the event of an error, but it is important for you to know that this chapter was not written in a vacuum, but rather has evolved from much contact with many experts.)

Photoshop has such a rich set of color correction and color manipulation commands that a beginner can quickly become overwhelmed. Figure 7-1 shows the Image →Adjust menu options. There are *14* menu items. Good grief, 14 different commands to help adjust color! Never fear. You really don't have to use them all. In fact, there are only three of these commands (Levels, Curves, Hue/Saturation) you really need to master, and some (such as Contrast and Brightness) you shouldn't even use at all. Other commands (Posterize, Threshold, Inverse) are typically used for special effects rather than color correction.

Adjusting color is part science and a lot of experimentation. The major challenge is determining what needs correction before you begin doing anything. Do you try to make your onscreen image look just like the photograph did before you scanned it? That's fine, but the colors in the photograph may not have been accurate. If you adjust the colors of the image to look good on your monitor, they might look totally different on a different monitor. Finally, the way the image looks on your screen and the way it prints out are usually two very different things.

To simplify your learning process, let's discuss color corrections based, for now, on how things look on your monitor (or, on my monitor as I write this chapter). You must realize that this is an oversimplification and *we are not going to discuss accurate color just yet*. Concentrate on learning the *techniques* of correcting color—even if the color itself isn't quite correct.

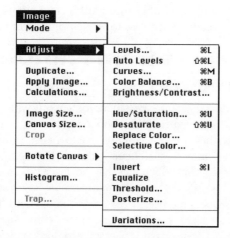

Figure 7-1
Image → Adjust
menu options

When you color correct an image, you should follow this basic workflow:

1. *Determine what needs fixing.* If you don't know where you're going, how will you know when you've arrived?

2. *Clean up the obvious flaws.* Get rid of dust and scratches before you perform your color moves.

3. *Do your global color corrections.* Remove any color cast and major image problems.

4. *Fix any remaining areas of trouble.* Use paths to select the trouble spots and fix them in their own layers.

BASIC CONCEPTS

Color adjustments cause data loss *because the image data is remapped.* When you open an image that was never adjusted, it contains as much information as it will ever have. Any adjustments toss away bits of the original pixel data. This is not always bad, since you want to improve the levels of color and tone in your image. However, each time you make an adjustment you destroy more information. Therefore, you want to keep unrecoverable *color moves* to a minimum.

Photoshop 4.0 has a new way to make recoverable adjustments. It enables you to create a different type of layer than the ones we have discussed before. *Adjustment Layers* let you make nondestructive and infinitely undoable color moves. After you learn about the color correction, you will learn how to create Adjustment Layers.

What to Expect from Photoshop's Color Correction

Each Photoshop user has different expectations for working with color images and making color separations. Some expect Photoshop to produce great results with little effort. Others are concerned they do not have enough experience and skill. What makes the color image reproduction process difficult is that each imaging situation is different. Each image is unique to itself and requires that the image processing controls be adjusted specifically for each situation, in order to obtain the best results. Therefore, if you expect the color reproduction process to be one group of Photoshop settings you never change, be prepared for a letdown. To learn about and consequently become proficient with color reproduction methods, it is necessary to think on your feet.

At first color reproduction might seem impossible to figure out, but it is not. Color reproduction fundamentals can be learned and, with some experience, transformed into refined skills. The fundamentals enable you to grasp the key concepts of

● Knowing the color terminology

● Learning to look at and evaluate images

● Understanding how the Photoshop image processing controls affect the final reproduction

● How to apply the fundamental knowledge and achieve good results for each particular imaging situation

If you are new to imaging, this chapter provides a basis for *beginning* to understand important concepts and apply imaging techniques. There is a lot that can go wrong when trying to adjust an image. You need to really understand the number of variables within the color imaging process so it becomes more manageable.

Learning the Critical Image Variables

Jim Rich—author of *Photoshop in Black and White*, contributor to such books as *Imaging Essentials* and *Production Essentials,* and noted color correction specialist—recommends you understand what to look for in an image before you start adjusting its controls. He identifies three *critical variables:*

1. Neutral grays

2. Image Contrast (Tone Reproduction)

3. Color Areas (red, green, blue, cyan, magenta, yellow)

Each of these variables has a specific function in the image.

Neutrality refers to neutral gray image areas seen as gray tones. Gray tones within images vary from light to dark and do not (in other words, should not) appear as colorful hues of red, green, blue, cyan, magenta, or yellow. Neutral highlights appear white, shadows appear black, and midtones appear in various shades of gray. Photoshop has specific features controlling neutral areas. An alternative term for neutral gray is *gray balance.* Figure 7-2 shows an image with many neutral gray tones (in the bird and the roof).

Tone reproduction is a term used to describe the contrast of an image. This is one of the most important image-processing adjustments. Figure 7-3(a) shows an image with a high contrast; Figure 7-3(b) shows the Histogram for that image.

If the image's contrast is correct, then other color correction problems don't seem as tough to deal with. Altering gray balance and performing selective color usually become less necessary, and if needed, easier to adjust. Figure 7-4(a) shows an image with average contrast; Figure 7-4(b) shows the Histogram for that image.

Figure 7-2
Image with neutral
gray tones

Figure 7-3
a) High contrast
image
b) Histogram for
high contrast
image

a

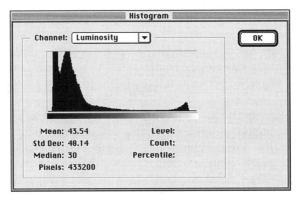

b

Figure 7-4
a) Average contrast image
b) Levels Histogram for average contrast image

a

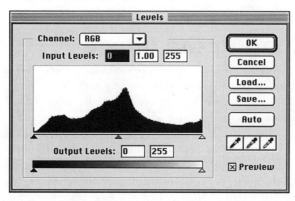

b

The tone reproduction characteristics are identified by image areas such as highlights, shadows, and midtones. Other technical terms are interchangeable to describe image contrast. These terms include but are not limited to gamma, tone shape, gradation, and luminosity. Levels and Curves are the Photoshop tools to adjust image contrast. Figure 7-5(a) shows an image with a low contrast; Figure 7-5(b) shows the Histogram for that image.

Color areas of an image are the hues areas, such as red, green, blue, cyan, magenta, and yellow (RGBCMY). Each color area has tones within the hues ranging from light to dark. Though generally not characterized by highlights, shadows, and midtones, color areas are directly affected by highlight, shadow, and midtone adjustments.

The terms most commonly associated with color image areas are *color correction* or *selective color correction*. Photoshop has specific features controlling selective color areas. These include Hue & Saturation and Selective Color.

Figure 7-5
a) Low contrast
image
b) Histogram for
low contrast image

a

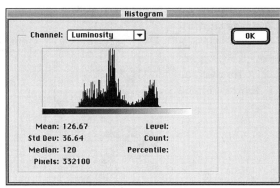

b

Evaluating the Image

As we mentioned before, the first step in color correction is to determine what needs correction. If you can't state what is wrong with the image, how will you know when you get it right? Is there enough contrast in the image, or is it very flat? Are the hues (the major colors) in the image what and where you want them? You need to begin by looking at the image, then analyzing it. In this process, you can identify the important image areas such as the neutral highlight, midtone, and shadow areas along with the important color areas.

The Info palette is one of the major tools to use. Measuring images is important to get good color results. Neutral gray is a good place to start measuring an image. It is easiest to define and use as a reference point for reproducing all types of images. Neutral gray image areas of color originals, digital files, or the final reproduction are referred to as highlight, shadow, and midtone areas. Neutral highlights appear white, shadows appear black, and midtones appear in various shades of gray. Exact neutral areas do not appear colorful, such as hues of red, green, blue, cyan, magenta, or yellow. If a neutral area of the original or reproduction looks colored, it is considered to have a color cast.

Let's evaluate the Rooftop.Psd image mentioned above.

EVALUATING AN IMAGE

1. Open the image Rooftop.Psd.

2. Can you find the neutral areas? The neutral shadows are the blackest parts of the image (the pitch/tar lines in the roof). The neutral highlights are the lightest (the pigeon's feathers). The neutral midtones in this image are the roof areas and the shaded feathers on the pigeon. You can locate these areas using the Levels command, the Info palette, and the Histogram, as you will see in a little while.

3. How about the image contrast? Is it high, average, or low? The image has an average-to-high contrast. Once again, the Levels command can confirm this for you.

4. Finally, can you identify the color areas? The pigeon and the roof are neutral and really have no color, but the sky and the trees hold definite color.

5. Is there a color cast? In this image, it is difficult to know without actually measuring the image with the Levels Histogram and/or the Info palette. We will come back to this question in a bit.

Where do we go from here? You still must learn how to measure the image. Especially in this image, where on the surface, it looks like neutral areas are neutral, you do not know if you need to perform any image corrections until you actually see the numbers. They will tell us if neutrals are actually in balance, the image needs more contrast, or there is a color cast.

Measuring Neutral in RGB

Measuring neutral gray in original transparencies, digital images, or on a color monitor is straightforward. Equal amounts of RGB digital values from light to dark achieve neutral gray. The whitest digital value measures 255. This is the brightness image area. The blackest digital value measures 0. This is the darkest image area.

Measuring Neutral in CMYK

In the CMYK printing process, creating neutral gray with halftone dot values is not easily achieved at first. You might think that equal amounts of cyan, magenta, and yellow are needed to make neutral gray. However, mixing equal amounts of them up yields a pinkish gray.

To make a neutral gray with cyan, magenta, and yellow, a special relationship is needed. This relationship or balance (or proportion) is necessary because of the impurities in the CMY printing inks. When this relationship is achieved, you get neutral gray tones in the reproduction from light to dark. This is referred to as *gray balance*. Think of it as a cookie recipe: If the ingredients are used in correct balance, the cookies bake right. If you use too much sugar, the cookies come out too sweet; too much flour, they come out too hard and tasteless; too much butter, they run in the pan; or too little butter, they stick to the pan.

To determine the correct gray balance for an image reproduction, compare it with the color original. If neutral areas in the reproduction look like the original image, the correct gray balance was achieved. Measuring a gray original establishes the input-to-output relationships of neutrality of RGB to CMY. Table 7-1 represents Photoshop default values that create neutral gray using CMYK halftone values.

Table 7-1 Typical Photoshop Neutral Balanced Values for RGB and CMY (Photoshop Default Preferences)

	Cyan	Magenta	Yellow	Red	Green	Blue
	Percent Values			Digital Values		
Paper White	0%	0%	0%	255	255	255
Highlight	5%	3%	3%	244	244	244
1/4 tone	29%	19%	20%	190	190	190
Midtone	49%	36%	36%	128	128	128
3/4 tone	62%	49%	47%	68	68	68
Shadow	65%	53%	51%	5	5	5
Extreme	65%	53%	51%	0	0	0
Black point						

Determining Neutral Gray

Originally neutral gray is determined by trial and error and is usually unique to the scanning and image reproduction system. The gray values shown above and below are typical for print and nonprint applications, and provide a good starting point to establish gray. As each color system is fine-tuned, these values are slightly altered to compensate for the intricacies of a color reproduction system. In Photoshop, gray balance values are built into the color separation portion of the program (Color Settings/Printing Ink Tables). Gray balance results can be viewed in the Preferences Separation Setup dialog box. As the Printing Ink tables are altered, the gray balance also changes. Chapter 15 gets into some of the complexities of CMYK printing and setting up the Color Reproduction Preferences (Color Settings).

Quiz 1

1. How many Photoshop commands are there on the Adjust menu to help you adjust the color of an image?
   a. 10
   b. 14
   c. 20
   d. 5

2. What is the basic workflow you should follow to correct image color?
   a. 1) See what needs to be fixed, 2) Clean up obvious flaws, 3) Perform global color corrections, and 4) Fix remaining troubles.
   b. 1) Clean up obvious flaws, 2) See what else needs to be fixed, 3) Perform global color corrections, and 4) Fix remaining troubles.
   c. 1) Clean up obvious flaws, 2) Perform global color corrections, and 3) Determine what remains to be corrected.
   d. 1) Perform global color corrections, and 2) Clean up obvious flaws and troubles.

3. What are some of the skills required to understand color reproduction?
   a. Looking at and evaluating images
   b. Understanding how Photoshop image-processing controls affect the image
   c. Knowing how to use the Photoshop tools
   d. Knowing color terminology

4. It is recommended you understand what to look at in an image before you adjust it. What are the three critical variables you can use to evaluate an image?
   a. Color areas (RGB, CMYK)
   b. Image contrast
   c. Neutral grays
   d. Image depth

5. What are the two Photoshop tools used for adjusting image contrast?
   a. Variations
   b. Curves
   c. Levels
   d. Equalize

APPLYING NEUTRALITY, TONE CORRECTIONS, AND COLOR CORRECTION

The next section takes a closer look at using the concepts of neutrality, tone reproduction, and color areas.

Color Casts: A Fact of Life

Most color images have some type of color cast. It is sometimes difficult to decide how to adjust color casts in highlights, shadows, and midtones of each original. Some color casts are slight, some are dramatic. Color casts can be overcome by adjusting the color image either during the scanning, the desktop color separation process, or a combination of both.

Once neutral gray values are determined, the operator uses neutral gray to adjust the neutral areas of the reproduction. These critical decisions are made by looking at and measuring the image, and determining what halftone output values are needed to achieve neutral gray for highlights, shadows, and midtones for the reproduction. If a color cast is in the image, the operator decides how much of a color cast to maintain, practically reduce, or completely eliminate. This skill is learned by looking at the final results and remembering the RGB and CMYK halftone values that produce certain visual results.

Tone Reproduction: Image Contrast

Tone reproduction is a term used to describe the contrast of an image. When highlight and shadows are set correctly, the lightest and darkest image areas make the reproduction look like the original. This gives the final reproduction highlights and shadows the correct amount of white and black detail. If highlight and shadow areas are not adjusted correctly, each reproduction will be visually inaccurate.

The midtone areas are between the highlights and the shadows. Adjusting midtones achieves the correct contrast in the reproduction. Midtones affect the amount of lightness and darkness of both the neutral and color areas.

Guidelines for Highlights, Shadows, and Midtones

Neutrality is a good guide for determining where and how to adjust highlight, shadow, and midtone areas from the start of the image reproduction process. To start the adjustment process, work with highlight areas first. Find a neutral white area that carries the whitest image details. This is called the *diffuse highlight*. Use target values of cyan=5%, magenta=3%, and yellow=3%.

Next, work with the shadow areas. Find the darkest neutral black of the image area. If using the Photoshop default settings, use target values of cyan=65%, magenta=53%, and yellow=51%. Do not set a black value.

Midtone adjustments are based on two factors:

● **Image content, which measures if the image is average, light, or dark**

● **Neutral gray adjustments**

Color Areas

Color areas are seen as hues in original images and reproductions by a variety of objects and scenes. These areas are made up of colorful ranges of tones and hues in red, green, blue, cyan, magenta, and yellow areas. Though generally not characterized by highlights, shadows, and midtones, color areas are directly affected by highlight, shadow, and midtone adjustments. Color areas are usually thought of and controlled in terms of selective areas such as red, green, blue, cyan, magenta, and yellow (RGBCMY).

The purpose of selective color correction is to control specific hues and/or the amount of saturation in each color area, individually in a selected color (RGBCMY).

While there are other methods of selective color correction—such as using masks—the system of using six color areas and four different color inks (making 24 possible interactions) is the best-known method for scanners and desktop color software applications.

Other selective color adjustments include neutral gradation controls permitting only neutral or near-neutral gray areas of the reproduction to be adjusted without affecting color areas like neutral shadows.

When discussing color areas, two terms are often used: saturated and desaturated. A saturated color appears bright. Conversely, the desaturated colors appear less bright and closer to neutral gray.

1. What is used to adjust neutral areas of reproduction?
   a. Halftones
   b. Neutral gray
   c. Layers
   d. Tints

2. What is tone reproduction?
   a. Shadow reproduction
   b. Depth of an image
   c. Contrast of an image
   d. Highlighting of an image

3. What are midtones?
   a. The areas between the highlights and shadows of an image.
   b. The area between the RGB and CMYK color channels.
   c. They affect the amount of lightness and darkness of the neutral and color areas.
   d. The tones between the neutral gray areas and color areas.

4. Midtone adjustments are based on what two factors?
   a. Color area adjustments
   b. Image content
   c. Neutral gray adjustments
   d. Image contrast

5. What is the purpose of selective color correction?
   a. To selectively adjust color shadows and highlights
   b. To adjust the Hues and Saturation of the neutral gray areas
   c. To control specific Hues in each color area
   d. To control the amount of Saturation in each color area

GETTING GOOD NEUTRAL AND COLOR AREAS

The Info palette is Photoshop's Densitometer—it samples the values of pixels in the image and reports the result in a variety of color spaces. It is the major tool you need to evaluate your image. Regardless of the accuracy of your monitor or whatever settings you choose, the RGB values for an image in RGB mode (or CMYK values for an image in CMYK mode) are the same—for the same file—on any system, monitor, or platform. Dan Margulis claims he can edit a color image on a black-and-white monitor, and that as long as he has the Photoshop Info palette, he can make the image print correctly.

This is an important point. This claim might seem like a major feat if you're new to Photoshop, but if you are experienced, it is just a day-to-day function of a skilled color operator. To do this, the Info palette reports pixel values. The experienced color expert knows when the values make sense in an image and when they do not. Here are some general rules:

● The lightest areas in the image (Highlights) should not have values higher than 245 in an RGB file, or values less than 5% in a CMYK file.

● The darkest areas in the image (Shadows) should not have values lower than 15 in an RGB file, or values greater than 90 to 95% in a CMYK file.

● Areas supposed to look neutral gray in an RGB image (areas with no color in them) should have the same values in the Red, Green, and Blue channels.

Using the Info Palette

Let's look at the Rooftop.Psd image again and see if we can use the Info palette to find highlight, shadow, and midtone areas, and see if our neutrals really are such.

Info Palette Options

Before you use the Info palette, you must make certain it is set up for your needs. The Palette Options selection is the only choice on the Info Palette menu. Figure 7-6 shows these options. The two sections concerning us now are the First and Second Readout sections.

Since the image is in RGB mode, you can set the First Readout to either RGB or Actual Color. Set the Second Readout to CMYK (if the image were grayscale, that setting would be better). The settings enable you to see the color as it appears in the various color spaces. The CMYK numbers you see on the palette are not etched in stone, as long as the image is in RGB mode. These values depend on the state—or status—of the Color Settings you have selected (or have not yet learned how to use—in which case, you will get default numbers). If you change the Color Settings, the CMYK values also change. However, if you do not change the settings, you can safely expect to see the CMYK values show up in the final film—as long as your monitor is calibrated and the service bureau makes no drastic mistakes. For right now, select CMYK as the Second Readout and don't worry about Color Settings until Chapter 15.

Taking Measurements

Now that you have the Info palette set up in a useful way, you are ready to explore the Rooftop.Psd to see if it needs work. The Info palette performs its function as a Densitometer by reading and reporting on the values under the cursor. As long as you keep the cursor in the active image, the Info palette gives you the color of every pixel it passes over. Hmmm...

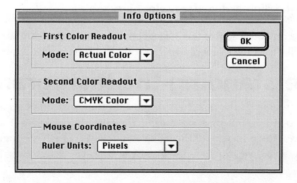

Figure 7-6
Info palette options

Every pixel it passes over... But what if the pixel represents noise—a random, stray dot of color appearing where it isn't expected? If the pixel is out of sync with its surrounding colors, the Info palette reports it anyway. Unless... You need to set the behavior for the Eyedropper tool so it samples a 3×3 or 5×5 grid of pixels and averages their color. That way, a single, stray pixel cannot throw your calculations out of whack. To do this, double-click on the Eyedropper tool to bring up the Eyedropper options. Set the Sample size to 5×5.

Finally, you are ready.

THE INFO PALETTE

1. Drag the cursor over the image and notice how the numbers in the Info palette change.

2. Place your cursor on the pigeon's eye. You should get an RGB readout of approximately 32, 27, 27.

3. Drag your cursor around the light spot on the pigeon's body just under his wing. Look at the Readout. Which RGB color seems to always read the highest? It should be red, but not by a huge amount.

4. Drag the cursor around the sky area to the right of the image. Your readings should be close to RGB 95, 135, 170. This means blue is the dominant color, which is what you would expect from the sky.

5. Drag your cursor over the roof. On the darkest blotch on the roof, is the color true black? No. The values are much greater than RGB 0, 0, 0 (in the 20s).

6. Finally, is the roof really neutral gray in the scan? Not quite; red seems to be the slightly dominant color here, too.

Read on and discover the next steps you need to perform to correct this image and others like it—now that we have discovered it seems to have a minor neutrality problem.

Understanding the Histogram

The Histogram is the next most important tool. Instead of seeing each pixel or pixel group to give a spot-by-spot reading, the Histogram looks at the entire image at once and gives you a picture of the values it contains. The Histogram is a bar chart showing how an image is broken down into digital values called *levels*. By changing the levels, you alter the tonal range, contrast, color areas, and neutrality of the image. You can alter an image's Histogram in a number of ways. The Histogram shows shadow and darker areas of the image towards the left side of the scale. The midtone areas are found in the middle, and the highlight areas are to the right.

Along with the Info palette, the Histogram is your best source of information about what needs correcting. The image Histogram appears in the Levels command dialog and in its own Image → Histogram command. Let's look first at the stand-alone Histogram (which cannot be changed).

Figure 7-7 shows a grayscale image of two cats. Figure 7-8 shows the Histogram for the image. The Histogram (found under the Image → Histogram command) graphically plots the values of the image. You can see by looking at Figure 7-8 that the image does not contain many light values. It leans toward the darker tones. The numeric pixel values in an image range from 0 to 255 in each channel. A grayscale image only contains one channel—the black channel. This makes it very easy to read this Histogram. A value of 255 is pure white, and a value of 0 is black.

By reading the Histogram, you can see that at value level 231, there is 1 pixel (Count=1), and that 100% of the image values are at this value or darker (Percentile=100). This image has no pixels lighter than 231. That makes this a *low key* image. And you thought low key meant shy and laid back! *Key* is a photographer's term referring to the tonal value of an image. A *high key* image has values leaning toward the highlights, and a *key* image is evenly balanced.

While this Histogram cannot be changed (you can only use it to determine how many pixels fall within a specific range of values), you can change the one found in the Levels command. Figure 7-9 shows the Levels Command Histogram for the two cats image. Notice that the graph is identical. It is only the items around the graph that differ.

Figure 7-7
Two cats: an image
in grayscale

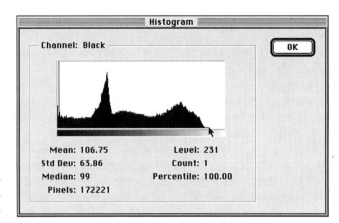

Figure 7-8
Histogram for two
cats image

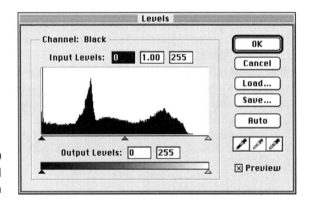

Figure 7-9
Levels Command
Histogram

The top region is the Input region. This is where you adjust for color and tone. It has three sliders: the Black point (black triangle on the left controlling the shadows in the image), White point (white triangle on the right controlling the highlights), and Gamma (the gray triangle in the middle controlling the midtones). You can change the graph by moving any of the sliders. This reapportions the curve. If you drag the White point toward the left to Level 231 (where the lightest pixel in the image is located) and click OK, the curve changes to the one in Figure 7-10. You won't see it unless you reopen the Levels dialog. Notice the *gaps*. These gaps in the Histogram show how the values in the image were stretched so they could fit over the entire length of the graph (from 0 to 255). By setting the White point to 231, you actually moved it to 255 when you clicked OK. This leaves holes in the Histogram in which there are no pixels at a given level. That is the data loss you were warned about earlier.

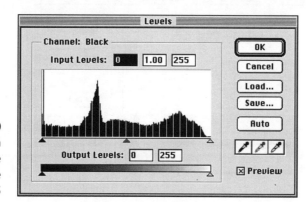

Figure 7-10
Histogram with gaps when image highlights move from 231 to 255

If you move the White and Black points too close together, you risk posterizing the image. *Posterizing* an image means compressing the values so you see an obvious jump from one value to the next. Figure 7-11 shows the two cats image posterized (using the Posterize command) into four levels of gray. You can see each value distinctly. That's fine when you do it deliberately, but not when it happens as a result of poor color correction. Figure 7-12 shows the posterized Histogram. You can clearly see the gaps where values are missing.

Figure 7-11
Two cats posterized to four levels

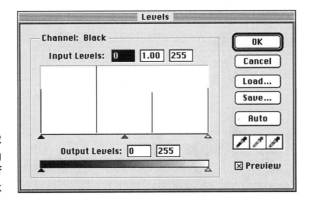

Figure 7-12
Histogram showing only four values of black

Levels Command

The Levels command is usually the first adjustment command to use. Even if you do not want to adjust the image with this command, it is wise to check it for an initial reading of the value ranges in your image.

Here are the things you can do with the Levels command:

● Set White, Black, and Gamma points

● Set a maximum Black output value for the image

● Set a minimum White output value for the image

● Change the color definitions for the White and Black points

● Adjust the White, Black, and Gamma points for each individual channel in the image—either to remove a color cast or to improve tonal quality

Experience shows that dividing the Levels command into three adjustment classifications—manual, semi-automatic, and automatic—makes it easier to understand.

Manual Modes

The Manual mode is used in conjunction with the Eyedropper tool in the Tool palette, reading the values in the Color palette or Info palette, then dragging the endpoints of the input Levels slider manually to make a change meeting your target tone reproduction requirements. This method works predictably in RGB, LAB, and CMYK modes. It requires a lot of expertise and can be very time-consuming. The gamma (midtone) slider adjustment in the Levels dialog box is always performed manually.

The Levels command has a midtone adjustment slider ranging in value from 0.10 to 9.99, with the 1.0 value being equidistant from the light and dark sliders. The default gamma is always 1.0, but in the master channel (the composite channel), changing the gamma slider in one direction or another alters the tone curve and makes the image lighter or darker (by changing the place at which the values in the image become middle gray).

Semi-Automatic Modes

The Semi-automatic mode involves using the Set White (highlight), Set Black (shadow), and Set Gray (midtone) Eyedropper controls. These features define and let you manually apply target values to an image area. The *target values* are the actual values you want the White, Black, and Gray points to be. You need to set these before you use the Eyedropper. To set them, double-click on the Eyedropper in the Levels command dialog, and use the Color Picker to select the desired value. You can also refer to the chart above for the most common settings.

Setting White and Black points with the Levels Eyedropper works predictably only in RGB mode. Typical highlight values are 5% cyan, 3% magenta, 3% yellow, and 0% black. The Shadow values in the Levels and Curves Color Picker vary due to the Preference setting for Printing Inks and Separation Setup. Don't change the Color Picker shadow values for CMY in this dialog box, but you can adjust the Color Picker black (K) values. Technically, it is possible to keyboard CMY shadow values into the Color Picker, but the color separation output is not affected accurately.

If you accidentally keyboard CMY shadow values into the Color Picker and can't remember what was there before, just type all **0**s into the RGB value area. This makes the CMYK values reflect the actual halftone shadow point values you are requesting in the digital CMYK file and the halftone film. The CMYK values are based on the Printing Ink and Separation Setup Preference settings. Since the black printer halftone dot value is adjustable, it may be altered based on the previously found target values.

When the Black Ink Limit is applied, the black halftone dot value is limited by that Preference setting. This creates a slight prediction error, so the black halftone dot values do not agree exactly with the values that come out on film.

The midtone Eyedropper affects neutral and color image areas but does not change the image contrast. In Photoshop terms, it does not affect the image's luminosity. This is an expert tool only available in the RGB mode. It works by applying the Color Picker values to an image area. There are many possibilities with this feature. The most straightforward approach with this tool is to consider adjusting *slightly* color-casted midtone areas. Using it on extreme color casts can be a disaster. For example, if a neutral area is dramatically magenta or yellow and you apply the midtone Eyedropper to it in an attempt to make it neutral, it introduces a color cast into other image areas. For color reproduction, this is a very tricky tool that must be used carefully.

Auto Modes

The Automatic method requires that the target White and Black points are set in the appropriate Color Pickers. Clicking on the Auto button allows the program to automatically pick the White and Black points. Photoshop makes calculations based on the brightest and darkest pixels, and applies the target values in the Color Picker. This might seem like the best method for setting white and black, but if the whitest or blackest pixels are outside the image areas of interest, or if they are not neutral, you get poor results.

You can apply an autolevels correction either from within the Levels command by clicking on the Auto Levels button, or by simply applying the Auto Levels command from the Image → Adjust menu. In either case, it is a quick-and-dirty approach suitable for fast corrections before trying a special effect, but not acceptable for quality color correction.

Let's try a Hands On exercise so you can see how the Levels command works. The image, another one from Ed Scott's China series, has a very bad yellow color cast. You will learn how to quickly remove the color cast. It is important to remember that when we adjust the input Histogram using the three triangles on the input slider, we redistribute the curve.

THE LEVELS COMMAND

Setup

1. Open the image Dadson.Psd. Duplicate the image (Image → Duplicate → OK). Figure 7-13 shows the original image (you can also see it on the color pages).

Figure 7-13
Color-casted
Dadson.Psd image

2. Drag the icon for the Background Layer to the New Layer icon (the center icon at the bottom of the Layers palette). This enables you to work on the duplicate in the image so you can easily see the before and after by clicking the Eye icon, and you can mix the corrected copy with the original if needed. Eric Reinfeld strongly recommends setting up your image this way (and doing your local corrections in yet another copied Layer). Unless you are using Adjustment Layers (discussed later in this chapter), this is the best way of structuring your image for correction.

3. Open the Info palette (Window → Palettes → Show Info). If you do not have the palette set to RGB and CMYK color readouts, change them using the Palette options under the triangle menu on the right side.

4. Double click on the Eyedropper tool and set the Eyedropper options to use a 3×3 sample. This setting is very helpful since it averages the pixels, compensating for any pixels that differ substantially from the rest of the area.

5. Take a variety of readings using the Info palette—especially along the highlight areas of the child's face. Notice in the CMYK readout how high the Yellow value is. Normal skin tones have a lot of yellow, but this image has too much.

Setting Initial White and Black Values

6. The next step is to set the target White and Black points. Photoshop defaults to RGB 0, 0, 0 for the Black point and RGB 255, 255, 255 for the White point. These values are usually too sharp—especially if you want to set the White and Black points with the White and Black point Eyedropper tools.

7. Double-click on the Black Eyedropper at the bottom right of the Levels command. The Photoshop (or system) Color Picker appears. Select RGB 5, 5, 5 as the value for solid black.

8. Double-click on the White Eyedropper at the bottom right of the Levels command. The Photoshop (or system) Color Picker appears. Select RGB 244, 244, 244 as the value for solid white. This white is far off enough from true white that it prints with a tiny halftone dot. Solid white (the color of paper) should only be found in *specular* highlights (the glint of sun on jewelry, for example).

Identifying Highlight and Shadow Image Areas

9. Levels has a feature permitting the user to visually locate specific highlight and shadow areas on the image. This feature is called Thresholding or Clipping. This is available on the Macintosh platform only. To use the Thresholding feature, hold down OPTION as you slide the right or left triangle of the input levels below the Histogram back and forth. (The Preview option must be turned off and LUT Animation must be selected in the General Preferences for this effect to work.) The advantage of Thresholding, if your system supports it, is that you can quickly identify the brightest and darkest portions of the image. When you use this feature, the brightest or darkest parts of the image are the ones that turn white or black first.

Selecting White and Black Points from the Image

10. In Chapter 15, you will learn more about making highlight and shadow selections based on the output method for the image. The main point to understand right now is this: When you set the highlight for an image, you want to select the image's lightest point that still contains some detail. When you set the shadow, you also want to pick a point just removed from being solid black. For both the highlight (White point) and the shadow (Black point), you want to select areas of the image to be neutral. This has made an incredible difference in the image already.

Selecting the Neutral Gamma Point

11. Look at the child's pants at the extreme left of the image. The dominant color is a bit greenish. Click on the gamma Eyedropper (its default is set to middle, neutral gray: RGB 127, 127, 127). Drag the Eyedropper into the image and find a value in the pants close to a middle gray (at least in the Green channel). Click there with the Eyedropper. This removes the remaining color cast. Click OK to save your changes and exit the dialog. You can see this image in the color pages at the center of the book.

Levels: The Workflow

Why did the corrections above help the image? We removed the yellow color cast by three clicks because the White and Black point neutralized the highlights and shadows in the image, and the Gamma point changed midtones (which had a green cast by then) to neutral gray. This does not always work with every image, but it is the first thing to try when you need to remove a color cast. Your normal routine in Levels should be to

- Set the White and Black points by dragging them or by using the Eyedroppers.

- Set the Gamma point with the Eyedropper if needed.

- If there is still a color cast, adjust the Gamma points on the individual channels.

- If the image is too dark or too light, readjust the White or Black points, or drag the Gamma slider in the composite channel.

- Finally, if you need to control the output tones, drag the Output sliders to remove the solid whites and blacks from the image.

Removing Color Cast in the Individual Channels

You can also remove color cast in an image globally by adjusting the Gamma slider in the individual channels. If you are editing in RGB, dragging the Gamma slider in either direction moves the image toward one color or another. Here is the list:

Table 7-2 Complementary Colors when Adjusting Gamma in Levels Channels

Channel	Color on the Left	Color on the Right
Red	Red	Cyan
Green	Green	Magenta
Blue	Blue	Yellow

The following Hands On shows you how to adjust the gamma in the individual channels. You will adjust a dining room that is much too blue. The room is actually neutral, with a brown table and white carpeting. The walls are also a shade of off-white. The cake icing is a hot pink; however, the scan is an accurate representation of the photograph, which was of abysmal quality.

GAMMA ADJUSTMENT IN CHANNELS

1. Open the image Blueroom.Psd.

2. Check the image with the Info palette. Notice that on the RGB scale, the blue is much higher than the other two colors in all the image's neutral areas. In the CMYK scale, there is almost no yellow. If you look at the opposite colors in Table 7-2, you can easily see why too much blue also equals too little yellow. The colors are complementary colors—opposites on the color wheel.

3. We need to adjust the Blue channel first to see if bringing more yellow into the image can help it. Open the Levels dialog (Mac: ⌘+Ⓛ, Windows: CTRL+Ⓛ).

4. While the Levels dialog is open, look at the Info palette. There is an extra column of numbers. The column on the left is the value before the levels change. The column on the right is the color value after the levels move. This is invaluable when you need to know exactly how much you are moving each color. Another little Levels trick is to keep the preview turned off. Click on the title bar and you get a before and after when you release the mouse. This won't work if the preview is turned on.

5. Figure 7-14 shows the Blue channel in the Levels dialog. Notice that the Histogram does not stretch toward the left. First, move the Black point slider to the right until it touches the area in which the image data begins.

6. Check the image with the Info palette by moving the cursor over the neutral areas. This helps, but not enough.

7. Move the Gamma (midpoint) slider towards the right until the Info palette readings show you have approximately equal RGB readings in each channel. The numbers in Figure 7-14 are a reasonable compromise.

8. Some of the red readings look like they should be higher. Select the Red channel in the Levels dialog and change the Gamma point by moving it a small distance to the left. This brings in a bit more red. You may use the settings in Figure 7-15.

9. Click OK. We have made a massive difference in the image with very little effort.

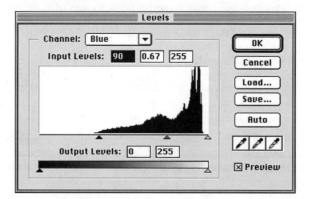

Figure 7-14
Blue Channel Levels
Histogram

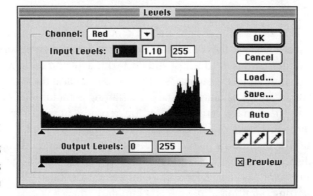

Figure 7-15
Red Channel Levels
Histogram

Changing Brightness with the Gamma Slider

You can change the brightness of an image using the Gamma (midpoint) slider in the Composite channel of the image. If you slide the Gamma point left, you make the image lighter; slide it to the right, and you make it darker. When you do this, you adjust the image's midtone curve. This can be used to bring an image into *key*.

More About Midtones

Before you adjust the midtones, you need to properly adjust the highlights and shadows. Color images have a variety of light and dark tones reflecting the original scene. One of the main factors for achieving a good color reproduction is to identify the distribution of tones within an image. One method of characterizing the distribution of light and dark tones is to classify images into categories. Since many variations exist among types of image categories, a simpler approach to reproducing different types of images is establishing three basic classes:

1. *Average images:* These have equal amounts of light and dark tones.

2. *Light images:* These have predominantly light tones.

3. *Dark images:* These have a majority of dark tones.

A popular term often used to describe image class is *keyness*. The context for keyness is high key for light images, low key for dark images.

An *average* image is not too light or too dark. It contains an even distribution of all levels of tones and colors. High key images are light-looking images. A light image means the color original consists mostly of light tones and colors. Low key images are dark-looking images. A dark image means the color original consists of mostly dark tones and colors.

Adjusting Light- and Dark-Looking Color Images

Since there are varieties of light and dark image categories, only experience will tell you how much to change the color controls to optimize various types of light and dark images.

To understand how to adjust and deal with light and dark images, you need to first establish how an average image is reproduced (establish the average image parameters). The average image parameters establish a starting point for reproducing all types of color images. The average setup is based on reproducing most average original images with little modification. To use this strategy, highlights and shadows are defined and adjusted with little change and are applied with standard midtones settings, pre-established neutral values, and Hue & Saturation (color correction) values.

Once color parameters for average images are identified, the approach is to use them as a starting point for adjusting light and dark images.

Guidelines for Highlight and Shadow Setting of Light and Dark Images

When your image differs significantly from the average, here are some tactics you can use to adjust it:

● Find and adjust your highlights based on the neutral white carrying the whitest image details.

● Find and adjust your shadow areas based on the darkest neutral black image area.

After highlights and shadows are adjusted:

● *For a high key image:* Increase midtone areas to bring out or better separate the highlight to midtone details.

● *For a low key image:* Decrease midtone areas to bring out or better separate the shadow details.

Since each image has its own unique distribution of tones, only experience can tell you exactly how much to adjust a midtone. However, the principles of adjusting midtones for average, light, and dark images are the basis for achieving good contrast in a color reproduction.

Reducing Contrast with the Output Sliders

We have said very little about use of the Output sliders. They have two main uses. One you have already seen in Chapter 3, "Layers and Channels." It is possible to screen back an image (make it look lighter on top of the original) by adjusting the Output sliders. That makes it easy to create lighter areas in an image, so you can place text or make it stand out from the background.

A second use for Output sliders is decreasing the contrast in an image to produce a smaller range of tonal values. You can cut an image with a full range of values (0 to 255) down to 15 to 240 if you wish, so it prints better without having areas be too black or glaringly paper-white because their halftone dot was too small for the press to reproduce (all presses have a minimum and maximum halftone dot they can hold). You can adjust your image for the conditions of the printing press by changing the Output sliders in the Levels command.

Curves Command

In the first Hands On using the Levels command, you were told that changing the Histogram altered the *curve* of the image. There is another command—Curves—that does this as well, and offers you more control in certain instances.

The Curves command works very much like the Levels command. With Curves, you get to be more precise in targeting areas of our image and altering them. With Levels, you use a Histogram to alter where data falls on it. With Curves, you see data plotted across a curve at a 45° angle. With Levels, you used a three-position slider to move data. With Curves, you can add up to 14 points to control data. Figure 7-16 shows the Curves dialog. Notice that, unlike Levels, it gives you no information about the image you adjust—the original curve is the same for every image.

When you open Curves, you find there are two points laid down for you—at White and Black points—just like in Levels. If you click in the center of the line, you add a point at the 50% value. As you move the point up, you lighten the image or change its gamma. As you drag the 50% dot towards the bottom, you darken the image or make it less bright. You can add a point between the black and the 50% mark to give you a point that controls the shadows. A point between white and 50% enables you to control the 1/4s or highlights.

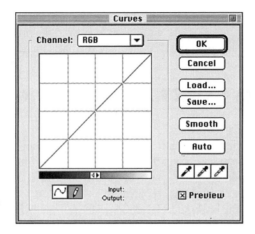

Figure 7-16
Curves dialog

As you add points, you can target specific areas of each image. Whenever you take the cursor out over the image, it turns into the Eyedropper tool. As you hold down the mouse, you can see where that particular pixel value lies against the curve. This lets you target any specific value and change it to another one—something you cannot do with Levels. At the bottom of the Curves palette, you see input and output values. When you move a point on the curve, you can clearly see the new value to which you are moving it.

When adjusting color, it is important to remember you can adjust an RGB image in the Composite channel. This means you can adjust it globally, using the Eyedropper to target values. You see your points against the curve. In CMYK, you do not see your points against the curve. You can only see your points against the curve if you work in the individual channels. CMYK must be handled separately, but together: They must be handled separately in the sense that they need to be adjusted individually, but under the same interface, one at a time. Hold down the CMYK radio button on top of the grid, scroll down to the channel you want to edit, and adjust the curve. Unfortunately, you can only see one curve at a time.

To change the size of the visual grid, click on it while holding down (OPTION) (Mac) or (ALT) (Windows). This gives you a 10×10 grid instead of the default 4×4 grid.

Try this Hands On.

CURVES

1. Open the image Weaving.Psd. This is Ed Scott's image from Chapter 3.

2. Explore some of the neutral areas with the Info palette. Yes, it is too blue. Hair can be blue-black, but not *that* blue-black. Let's adjust this a bit.

3. Open the Curves dialog (Image → Adjust → Curves or Mac: ⌘+Ⓜ, Windows: CTRL+Ⓜ). How do you remember Ⓜ as the Curves command? A lowercase m is curvy.

4. Since the image is too blue, let's look at the Blue curve first. It is behind the Channel drop-down menu (or press Mac: ⌘+③, Windows: CTRL+③).

5. Place your cursor over the top of the girl's dress, and look at the Info palette as you drag. Click in the center of the girl's back. Figure 7-17(a) shows the image with the Eyedropper cursor marking the spot clicked. Figure 7-17(b) shows the Curves dialog. The circle at level 127 in the Blue channel shows the spot on the curve in which the clicked-upon point falls. Notice that the Input and Output values for the point are both 127. This is because you have not adjusted anything yet. Figure 7-17(c) shows the Info palette at that point—and it shows them for all the channels, not just the Blue channel. From the values, you can see the Blue value is much too high (though the 128 reading is just slightly different from the reading you get in the Curves dialog).

6. There are two methods of adjusting the curve: the Pencil and the Curve tool. The Pencil is very good for making tiny spot corrections, and the Curves tool is better for keeping a smooth curve. Select the Curves tool. Drag the cursor back to the point *on the curve* at which the input and output read 127 (this time, keep the cursor on the line—not in the image). Click to place a point along the line at the 127 input and output mark (or as close as you can get to it). When you read the Info palette in Step 5, at the target point, the Green channel was 67 and the Red channel was 46. In order to make the dress neutral, we need to make the RGB values approximately the same. Therefore, drag the 127 input point down to the place at which the output says 67. Figure 7-17(d) shows this curve.

7. Since we adjusted the Blue channel to meet the value of the Green channel, we do not need to make any adjustments there (at least, not right now). Switch to the Red channel (Mac: ⌘+①, Windows: CTRL+①). According to the Info palette in Figure 7-17(c), we need to move the Red curve at input point 46 up to output point 67 to neutralize that portion of the image. Do this now—locate input point 46 along the red curve, click, and drag the point up until the output point says 67.

8. Look at the image. You have unfortunately fixed one problem by creating another. The image is now too red in the highlights. Therefore, you need to "lock down" a portion of the curve. If you Reset the dialog now (by pressing Mac: OPTION or Windows: ALT), you lose the changes to the Blue channel as well. So, don't do that. Instead, place your cursor over the point which you created on the curve, press the mouse button, and drag the point from the image. It gets thrown away. You can drag a curve back to its original condition by removing all the points this way.

a

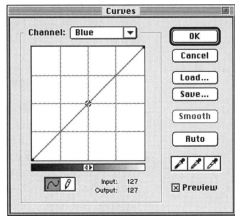

b

Figure 7-17
a) Image with
Eyedropper at
target point
b) Curves dialog
showing location of
target point
c) Info palette at
target point
d) Blue Channel
Correction curve

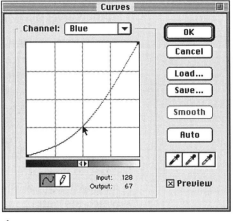

c

d

9. It is often necessary to anchor or lock-down specific points along the curve to keep them from moving when other points are adjusted. We need to do this with the Red channel now. Click on the intersection of each of the grid squares to lock down the quartertone, midpoint, and three-quartertone points. Figure 7-18(a) shows this curve.

10. Toss away the point at 64, 64 in the curve. Locate input point 46 and drag it to output point 67. Figure 7-18(b) shows the curve.

Figure 7-18
a) Five-point Lockdown curve in Red channel
b) Corrected Red curve

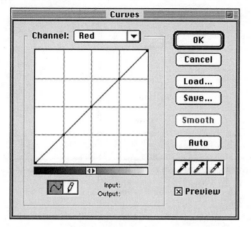

a

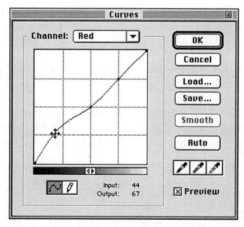

b

11. Even though the dress seems more neutral now where we corrected both channels, if you sweep your cursor off the image itself and read the values, the Blue channel still is too low in some places and too high in others. Let's make a few more adjustments there. Switch to the Blue Channel curve.

12. Drag the points in the Blue curve so your curve looks like the curve in Figure 7-19. The precise settings are Input 100/Output 32, Input 128/Output 68 (your original), Input 152/Output 108, and Input 191/Output 191. How were these points selected? The original adjustment was added from the original Lockdown curve. Readings were then taken from highlight and shadow points, and this curve appeared the best compromise.

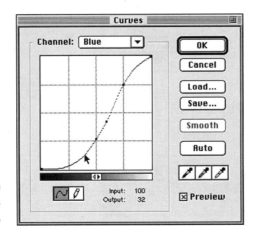

Figure 7-19
Readjusted Blue
curve

13. The image could be somewhat lighter, however. For this, we need to make a midpoint adjustment in the master curve. Switch to the Composite channel (Mac: ⌘ ~, Windows: CTRL ~).

14. Drag the 128 input point (the midpoint) up to the 140 output point as shown in Figure 7-20. This lightens the entire image.

15. Before you click OK, save this curve. In the Curves dialog, click on the Save button. Name the curve Girl.ACV. You will use this again at the end of this chapter.

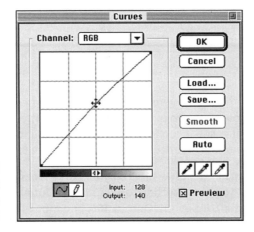

Figure 7-20
Midpoint
adjustment on the
master channel

Making a Lockdown Curve

Anchoring or locking down points on a Photoshop curve is a necessary and common practice. One method of creating pre-established points on a curve is to make a Lockdown curve. This is done by anchoring key points, then saving the curve (using the Load & Save feature). Typically, five-point Lockdown curves are used for manual highlight, 1/4 tone, midtone, 3/4 tone, and shadow adjustments, and ten-point Lockdown curves are used for very specific tone adjustments. The Lab in Appendix C guides you through the process of creating these.

Making Precise Points on the Curve Using the Transfer Function

When in the Transfer Function dialog (from the Page Setup dialog), key in the points, such as highlight, 1/4 tone, midtone, 3/4 tone, and shadow. Use the values exactly corresponding to the curve points you want locked down. The Lab in Appendix C shows you how.

Curves and Photoshop Modes

Depending on the color mode used, the Curves dialog offers three, four, or five sets of curves. Lab has three possible channels to adjust: one for L, A, and B. Typically the L channel (luminance) adjusts image contrast. RGB has four possible options to adjust the image channels. The master channel controls all colors together. There are three individual color curves, one for each channel, R, G, and B. CMYK has five possible options to adjust the image channels. The master channel controls all colors. There are four individual color curves, one for each C, M, Y, and K channels.

Curves Controls

The Curves tool influences the tone reproduction (contrast) and neutrality of an image. The Curves dialog box, as its name suggests, allows adjustments of the image's tonal reproduction characteristics by adjusting a curve. The Curves tool is the most precise tone reproduction image processing tool in Photoshop. It is possible to adjust specific areas of an image's tones such as highlight, 1/4 tone, midtone, 3/4 tone, and shadow values, or multiple points along the curve (up to 16 points). This is the traditional terminology used in the prepress and imaging field and makes Curves the easiest tool to use when communicating specific Dot or % values for different types of paper and printing presses.

Highlight (white) and shadow (black) adjustments are done with Curves through their respective Color Pickers, just as you set them in the Levels command. The highlight and shadow adjustment with this tool can be divided into three classifications: manual, semi-automatic, and automatic.

Manual Mode

The Manual mode is used in conjunction with the Eyedropper tool, reading the values in the Color palette or Info palette, then dragging the points of the curve manually to make a change meeting your target tone reproduction requirements. This method works predictably in RGB, LAB, and CMYK modes.

Semi-Automatic Mode

The Semi-automatic mode involves using the Set White (highlight), Set Black (shadow), and Set Gray (midtone) Eyedropper controls. These features define and let you manually apply target values to an image area. The highlight and shadow target values are previously set up (from within the Curves Color Picker), as is the midtone adjustment for neutrality.

Setting White and Black points with the Eyedropper works predictably only in RGB mode. Typical highlight values are 5% cyan, 3% magenta, 3% yellow, and 0% black.

Using Curves Visually

Curves has a feature permitting the user to visually locate specific highlight and shadow areas on the curve. These areas are indicated by an open circle appearing on the curve. To get the circle, hold the mouse button down while the pointer is over the selected areas on the image. (This method was demonstrated in the Hands On above.) Be careful not to have any of the curve's Eyedroppers active when probing the image (this can apply the target values at the wrong point in the image).

Shadow Target Values in Curves

Shadow values in the Levels and Curves Color Picker vary due to the Preference setting for Printing Inks and Separation Setup. The Color Picker shadow values for CMY should be altered manually in this dialog box, but the Color Picker black values can be adjusted. Technically, it is possible to enter CMY shadow values into the Color Picker, but the color separation output is not affected.

If you accidentally placed CMY shadow values into the Color Picker and can't remember what was previously used, you can recover them to ensure you specify accurate shadow point values in the Color Picker by having it place 0s in the RGB dialog box. This makes the CMYK values reflect the actual halftone shadow point values you're requesting in the digital CMYK file and the halftone film. The CMYK values are based on the Printing Ink and Separation Setup Preference settings.

Since the black printer halftone dot value is adjustable, it should be altered based on the previously found target values.

When the Black Ink Limit is applied, the black halftone dot value is limited by that Preference setting. This creates a slight prediction error, so the black halftone dot values do not exactly match the values that come out on film.

Midtone Eyedropper

The midtone Eyedropper affects neutral and color image areas, but does not change the image contrast. In Photoshop terms, it does not affect luminosity. It is an expert tool only available in the RGB mode.

It works by applying the Color Picker values to an image area. There are many possibilities with this feature. The most straightforward approach with this tool is to consider adjusting slightly casted midtone areas. Using it on extreme color casts can be a disaster. For example, if a neutral area is dramatically magenta or yellow and you apply the midtone Eyedropper to it in an attempt to neutralize the area, it introduces a color cast into other image areas. This is a very tricky tool for color reproduction. Use it carefully.

Auto Modes

The Automatic method requires the target White and Black points set in the appropriate Color Pickers. Clicking on the Auto button allows the program to automatically pick the White and Black points. Photoshop makes calculations based on the brightest and darkest pixels, and applies the target values in the Color Picker. This might seem like the best method to set white and black, but if the whitest or blackest pixels are outside the image areas of interest, or if they are not neutral, you get poor results.

The Curves Tool Display

When working with Curves, you can select either the Levels or % mode. You do this by clicking on the double arrow in the gradation bar. In the % mode, dragging down a point lightens an image. When working in Levels mode in the Curves dialog, dragging down a point darkens an image. You must drag the mouse in the image or have the cursor over an area in the curve to get the input and output values to display. Figure 7-21 shows the same master channel adjustment as Figure 7-20, but in % mode. Notice that the same point is now lower, the input/output display is in %, and the white portion of the gradient bar is to the left.

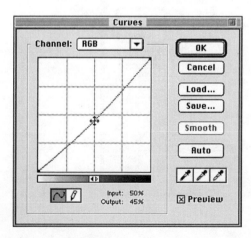

Figure 7-21
% Mode in the
Curves dialog

Levels Versus % Mode

To learn more about this feature, select the % mode and make a dramatic minus mid-tone change, then click on the double arrow in the gradation bar to see the effect in the Levels mode. Visually, it is in the opposite position in the Levels mode.

Creating a Refined Grid

When Photoshop starts up, the Curves dialog offers a display grid in increments of 25%. Hold down (OPTION) (Mac) or (ALT) (Windows) and click inside the Curves dialog to display a refined grid in 10% increments. Figure 7-22 shows this 10-point grid. This grid creates a Zone system very familiar to photographers, in which image values are distributed over 11 *zones*—from 0 to 10.

Why Curves and Not Levels?

As you gain experience, you will find yourself using Curves for color correction much more often than Levels. Curves is a sophisticated tool for adjusting image contrast and altering color casts. Levels does not offer as much flexibility and is not capable of specific image-processing refinements. However, Levels does offer its own advantages.

For example, Levels offers the Thresholding feature useful for finding highlights and shadow points of RGB images (not available with CMYK or LAB modes). For Thresholding to work, make sure the Preview button is unchecked.

Using Curves and Levels: A Summary

The Levels and Curves dialogs are your first weapon for attacking an image needing correction. You've now tried both methods. Let's look at the process again in a bit more detail, from a theoretical perspective.

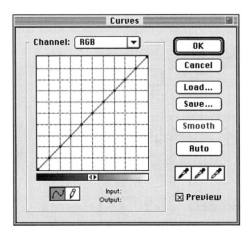

Figure 7-22
10 point grid

Adjusting Highlights and Shadows of RGB and CMYK Images

Adjusting the image to reflect the proper highlight and shadow range is a critical step in achieving a good quality color reproduction. This process frames the images so the tonal range can be adjusted to give the best results in the reproduction. For example, when reproducing an image, if the highlights are too light they may not print. If they're too dark, the images may lack contrast. Follow the steps illustrating how the highlights and shadow points of an image can be properly identified and adjusted.

1. Identify target values.

2. Use highlight dot values from the gray balance chart. Typical printing target values for highlights are 5% cyan, 3% magenta, 3% yellow. Nonprint applications use 245 red, 245 green, 245 blue.

3. Use Curves or Levels to find and set highlight and shadow areas on the RGB image.

4. Highlight set up (pre-adjustments for RGB images only).

5. Open the Curves or Levels dialog box by selecting Image/Adjust from the menu bar. Double-click on the Set White point (highlight) button. This brings up the Color Picker for the Select White Target Color controls. Set the C to 5%, M to 3%, Y to 3%, and K to 0%.

6. Shadow set up (pre-adjustments for RGB images only).

7. Double-click on the Set Black point (shadow) button in the Curves dialog box. This brings up the Color Picker for the Select the Black Target Color controls.

> To identify the predetermined shadow point values, it is sometimes necessary to place 0s in the RGB dialog box. This makes CMYK values reflect the actual halftone shadow point values that will potentially come out on halftone film. Other CMY values can be dialed into this dialog box, but they are not the values on the final color separation. The Cyan, Magenta, and Yellow are preset based on the earlier Preference settings (Printing Ink Colors and Separation Setup). The black printer halftone dot values in the Color Picker are adjustable and should be altered based on the previously determined target values. A typical adjustment to the black printer halftone dot value is from 95% to 80%.

8. Locate the highlight areas.

9. Determine where to place the White point or the highlight in the image. Use the visual approach of examining the white and black areas of the image in conjunction with the Info palette. The Levels Threshold feature can help.

10. Click-and-drag the right hand (White point) Input Levels triangle. Hold down OPTION. Slide the triangle to the left, then back to the right (make sure you have Video LUT Animation checked in the Preferences dialog box, and make sure Preview is not checked). The areas that turn white first are the highlight areas. Return the slider to the full right position. This is an easy method for quickly identifying the lightest or darkest image areas. This method works on a Macintosh system only.

11. Locate the shadow areas. Determine where the Black point or shadow will be placed.

12. The Levels tool can help click-and-drag the left (black) Input Levels triangle. Hold down OPTION. Slide the triangle to the right, then back to the left. The areas that turn black first are the shadow areas. Return the slider to the full right position.

13. Set the White and Black points. To set the White point on an RGB image, click once on the Set White Eyedropper button, then click on the image area chosen as the neutral white with detail. (This is the area described in Step 4.)

14. If the image is in the CMYK mode, manually drag the end points of the curve until the Info palette has what you believe are the correct target values in the highlight image area.

15. In either case—using RGB or CMYK images—examine the Info palette setting before applying the halftone values to the image. After the halftone values are applied, confirm the selection using the Eyedropper, and measure the before and after CMYK values in the Info palette Densitometer in the image area you chose as the lightest neutral area with detail. When in the RGB mode, this tool lets you easily correct a color-casted neutral highlight area.

16. To set the Black point of an RGB image, select the Set Black Eyedropper button, then choose the darkest near-neutral image area (use the RGB values in the Info palette to identify this point). This sets CMYK values in the shadow. Make sure the halftone values are applied using the Eyedropper, and measure the before and after CMYK values in the Info palette Densitometer in the image area you chose as the darkest neutral shadow area. If the adjustments are significant, they make a dramatic change to the screen image. If they are minor, the change is not too apparent.

17. Note that this tool only neutralizes the shadow point. It does not allow color casts to be easily changed in neutral shadow areas; this is done later on.

18. If the image is in the CMYK mode, manually dragging the endpoints does not usually work well unless the image's neutral shadow point was set close to the correct values. This method usually ruins the image's saturation if the shadow point is dramatically off.

19. If using supplied CMYK images, a method of correcting neutral or near-neutral shadow areas with color casts is using the black color of the Selective Color feature. This permits changing just the neutral black point without affecting the saturated colors. This is a good way to correct for color casts in neutral shadows. Adjustments are accomplished by adjusting the slider of CMYK until the desired values are achieved in the Info palette.

Adjusting Midtones

Determine the correction for the midtone areas using the master channel in Curves or Levels for an overall midtone change. This alters all colors simultaneously in RGB or CMYK. If the image requires specific midtone adjustments for color casts, they can be done with individual channels.

More About Midtones

After the highlight and shadow areas are established, midtones must be adjusted. You can make a single point midtone adjustment with either the Levels or Curves tool. The Curves tool, however, allows multiple points of control over the adjustment of tones between the highlight and shadows. This is usually necessary to create good color results. Typically, a total of five points are used on the whole curve. Two points are for the highlight and shadow, and three are used for the midtone, the 1/4 midtone, and 3/4 midtone. Up to 16 points are available with Curves.

Guidelines to adjust midtones ensure that neutral image areas are gray balanced, light images require an increase in midtones, dark images require a decrease in the midtone, and average images require little or no change at all.

Since each image has its own unique distribution of tones, only experience can tell you exactly how much to adjust a midtone. But the principles of adjusting midtones for average, light, and dark images are the basis for achieving good contrast in a color reproduction.

To adjust a midtone area manually on the curve, move the cursor up to intersect a part of the line forming the curve, and click to place a point at that spot. You can then drag the point up or down to increase or decrease values in the image along the curve. When making adjustments with one control point, the Curves tool works much like the Levels Gamma adjustment. The unique adjustment feature of the Curves tool is that it allows more than a single midtone control point. In fact, it offers up to 16 additional points that can be placed or locked down along the curve. This allows very specific areas of tones to change without strongly affecting other image areas. To prevent other areas from changing values, anchor those points on the curve.

Guidelines to adjust midtones ensure that neutral image areas are gray balanced, light images require an increase in midtones, dark images require a decrease in midtones, and average images require little or no change at all. Using the Info palette is a must.

Since each image has its own unique distribution of tones, only experience can tell you exactly how much to adjust a midtone. But the principles of adjusting midtones for average, light, and dark images are the basis for achieving good contrast in a color reproduction.

Images Without Clearly Defined Highlight Areas

If there are not any near-neutral white areas in the image, there are a few things you can do. In some instances, it is necessary to take an educated guess at placing the highlight. Here are some tips on what to look for.

1. Set up a standard curve you have learned from experience that places the highlight well. Tests can illustrate if the standard curve will work on most images. If it does, it is a good basis for images without highlight.

2. If your monitor is calibrated, use Curves or Levels to make manual adjustments until the image looks OK on the screen. Then make a proof. After some experience, you will get an idea of how to make color correction adjustments based on the relationship of the image on the monitor to the proof.

3. Instead of using neutral gray for the highlight, use a color. This is a very expert technique. What makes it difficult is that the color balances are different than gray balance. For example, in a Portrait image there may not be any defined near-neutral highlight area. We took an educated guess and examined a blonde hair with the Info palette. We found 8% cyan, 9% magenta, and 13% yellow. The guess was to make sure the blonde hair was nice and yellow golden. We used the Curves White point Eyedropper tool and keyboarded in 5% cyan, 6% magenta, and 10% yellow. This ensured the hair was golden blonde and made sure the image had good highlight contrast. This technique is easier in the RGB mode, but can be done in the CMYK mode by manually moving each channel with the curve.

Images Without a Shadow Point

These techniques are similar to the highlight adjustment methods.

1. Set up a standard curve you have learned from experience that places the shadow well. Tests can show if the standard curve will work on most images. If it does, it is a good basis for images without shadow.

2. If your monitor is calibrated, use Curves or Levels to make manual shadow adjustments until the image looks OK on the screen. Then make a proof. After some experience, you will get an idea of how to make color correction adjustments based on the relationship of the image on the monitor to the proof. Be careful when dragging the shadow endpoints because this can ruin the saturation of the image. It can make the image colors either oversaturated or desaturated. If that happens, use Hue & Saturation or Selective Color to fix the saturation problems.

Grayscale Images

Grayscale images are much easier to correct than color images since they are so much less complex. You can use Levels or Curves with them, too. In general, you need to make sure there is fairly sharp contrast in a grayscale image since it has no color to distract the viewer.

Making Snappy Grayscale Images

The Curves command helps produce the snappiest grayscale images. One typical technique for getting good contrast in a grayscale image is creating an S-curve that anchors the midpoint of the image, but which makes the quarter point a bit lighter and the three-quarter point a bit darker. This enhances the contrast quite a bit and can improve many images. Use it gently, however, as you risk posterizing the image if you are heavy-handed. Figure 7-23(a) shows an image with very little contrast. Figure 7-23(b) shows the correction curve for the image—notice the S-shape. Figure 7-23(c) shows the corrected image.

Getting Good Black and White from a Color Print

In general, you get the best reproduction of graytones by starting with a black-and-white image. Often that is not possible. Perhaps the most frequent reproduction need you will come across is processing color originals as grayscale.

There are three major ways to convert a color image to black and white:

● Image → Mode → Grayscale

● Convert the image to Lab mode and keep only the Luminance channel

● Mix two of the channels (usually Red and Green) together using the Apply Image command

Of these three methods, converting to grayscale mode generally yields the worst results. Try this Hands On to see all three methods in action.

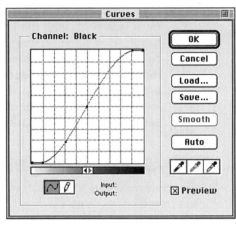

a

b

Figure 7-23
a) Low contrast image: Grayscale
b) Correction curve
c) Corrected image

c

CONVERTING TO GRAYSCALE

1. Open the image Hakone.Psd.

2. Duplicate the image (Image → Duplicate) three times. Give these images names as you duplicate them. Name one copy Gray, another copy Lab, and the third copy ApplyImg.

3. Click on the Gray image to make it active. Change the image to grayscale (Image → Mode → Grayscale, OK).

4. Click on the Lab image to make it active. Change the image to Lab (Image → Mode → Lab, OK). In the Channels palette, drag the A and B channels to the Channels palette trash can. This leaves you with a multi-channel image. Now, change the image mode to grayscale (Image → Mode → Grayscale, OK).

5. Click on the ApplyImg image to make it active.

6. Click on each channel to view it. Typically, the Red channel carries the image detail, the Green channel carries the luminance, and the Blue channel carries the most noise. In this image, the Red and Green channels are the best of the three, and the Green channel is better than the Red.

7. Drag the icon for the Green channel to the New Channel icon in the bottom center of the Channels palette. This duplicates the channel.

8. Open the Apply Image command. You will see the dialog as it appears in Figure 7-24. Select the Red channel as your Source channel. Apply 40% of the Red channel to the current area (Channel 4) in Normal mode. Click OK.

9. Now, you can either throw away all the other channels and convert the remaining one to grayscale instead of multi-channel, or you can duplicate the channel into its own image—which still needs to be converted from multi-channel mode to grayscale.

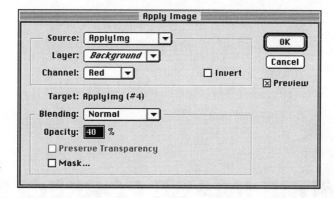

Figure 7-24
Apply Image dialog

QUIZ 3

1. What does the Info palette do?
   a. It monitors the RGB and CMYK channels and tells you when to make adjustments to the color.
   b. It evaluates your image.
   c. It samples the values of the pixels and reports the results in a variety of color spaces.
   d. It translates color values and stores the information in channels.

2. Before sampling pixels, you need to set the behavior of which tool?
   a. Selection tool
   b. Eyedropper tool
   c. Magic Wand tool
   d. Hand tool

3. What is the Histogram?
   a. A bar chart showing which colors are in an image.
   b. A bar chart showing how an image is broken down into digital values, or levels.
   c. A chart depicting the history of the pixels in the image.
   d. It shows the shadow and darker areas of an image.

4. What are some things you can do with the Levels command?
   a. Set a minimum black output for the image.
   b. Set Black, White, and Gamma points.
   c. Change the color definitions for black and white.
   d. You can evaluate the RGB and CMYK color channels using the Histogram.

5. You can remove the color cast from an image globally by
   a. Clicking on the Remove button in the Info palette.
   b. Adjusting the Gamma slider in individual channels.
   c. Changing the color of the pixels.
   d. Adding a new Layer and modifying the channels.

MORE IMAGE CORRECTION TOOLS

Once you have made the global corrections to your image, you may find you still need to tweak it for better color. These tweaks can be in terms of saturation or selective color (needing to make the magentas more green, for example). Or, you may need to physically change a color in a specific location in the image without affecting anything else in the image. There are several more commands for you to learn. They are the Hue/Saturation command, Color Balance command, Selective Color command, and the Variations command.

Applying Selective Color Corrections

The Hue/Saturation and the Selective Color commands are the two main tools to make selective color changes to images. These are changes affecting only part of the image, rather than the entire image, as do the Levels and Curves commands. With selective color correction, you can usually make changes to only part of the image *without making a specific Marquee selection*. You can isolate just the magentas or the blues in the image.

Hue/Saturation Command

The Hue/Saturation command is not as refined a tool as Selective Color, but it does have some good points. The most effective use of the Hue/Saturation tool is to just use the Saturation feature to selectively saturate colors, or to make dramatic color changes with the Hue feature. Then, use the Selective Color tool to fine-tune the selective color image areas.

The Hue & Saturation control is difficult to work with because it does not let you adjust one color component at a time, as is usually necessary in high-quality color work. Trying to adjust one color area by moving one of the three features (HSL) changes two or three of the color components of the hue. This makes it almost impossible to use this tool to adjust and control particular color hues independently. It is possible to use all the features of this tool, but it takes experience and skill.

For example, trying to adjust one color like magenta to create a particular CMYK hue in a deep red area of an image is very difficult. It is usually necessary to work with all three features—Hue, Saturation, and Lightness—to some extent. The more experience you gain with this tool, however, the more you will learn about how all three features interact.

The Hue/Saturation command has two main features for adjusting the color of images:

● **To color correct images used for print and nonprint applications**

● **To Colorize images to create special effects**

Hue/Saturation has options for adjusting color image areas globally (on all color image areas) or selectively (on specific color image areas). The Hue/Saturation dialog box is divided into six specific color areas: RGBCMY. It offers three adjustments for Hue, Saturation, and Lightness, which can work globally or on the specific colors.

Global Mode

In the global mode the *Hue* feature changes the hues as if they were on a circle. This feature is useful for making dramatic changes to hues of an image or within a selection. The range is +180 to −180.

Saturation works globally on all hues. Less Saturation moves all colors toward gray, more Saturation makes all the colors brighter.

Lightness makes the overall image whiter or blacker.

Hue and Saturation of Specific Colors

This mode allows changing the Hue, Saturation, or Lightness of individual colors: red, green, blue, cyan, magenta, or yellow (RGBCMY).

The Hue control changes the color chosen. It permits the adjustment of two components making up a particular hue. This alters the hue between the two colors to either side of the color being adjusted. The following table describes the adjustments.

Table 7-3 Hue Adjustments in Various Colors

Color Adjusted	Between	And
Red	Magenta	Yellow
Yellow	Red	Green
Green	Yellow	Cyan
Cyan	Green	Blue
Blue	Cyan	Magenta
Magenta	Blue	Red

Saturation adjusts the amount of grayness of the chosen color. More saturation adjusts components of the color to brighten the hue. Less saturation adjusts the components of the color to make the hue gray.

Lightness makes the specific color image area whiter or blacker.

Let's try an example with Hue/Saturation.

Here are the keystroke shortcuts for some of the color correction commands.

Command Watch

Action	Mac Key	Windows Key
Levels	⌘+L	CTRL+L
Levels at last setting	OPTION+⌘+L	ALT+CTRL+L
AutoLevels	SHIFT+⌘+L	SHIFT+CTRL+L
Curves	⌘+M	CTRL+M
Curves at last settings	OPTION+⌘+M	ALT+CTRL+M
Hue/Saturation	⌘+U	CTRL+U
Hue/Saturation last setting	OPTION+⌘+U	ALT+CTRL+U
Color Balance	⌘+B	CTRL+B
Color Balance last setting	OPTION+⌘+B	ALT+CTRL+B

HUE/SATURATION

1. Open the saved copy of the Weaving.Psd you corrected earlier in this chapter (if you don't have it, open Weaving2.Psd).

2. Although the color in this image is much better than the color in the original, the yellow looks unnaturally sharp (of course, Ed Scott—the photographer—is probably the only one who knows how accurate the original image actually was—maybe the yellow is supposed to be that bright!). However, we will attempt to remove some of the yellow from the image.

3. Open the Hue/Saturation dialog, shown in Figure 7-25.

4. Just to get an idea of what this command can do, make sure that the master channel radio button is selected, and slowly drag the Hue slider to the left, then to the right. Pause to let the screen display catch up so you can see how the Hues rotate around the color wheel. In the master channel, when you move the Hue slider, the entire image changes color. The color relationships are maintained from one color to another, but everything rotates around the color wheel.

5. Return the Hue slider to the center (0 in the Numeric readout).

6. Drag the Saturation slider slowly in both directions. To the left, it changes the image to gray, and to the right, it adds more color. Return it to the 0 position.

7. Drag the Lightness slider to the left and right. Notice that the entire image becomes darker (left) or lighter (right). This is very useful when you want to screen back an image to place text over it (of course you can also do this with Levels or Curves, but Hue/Saturation may be even easier). Return it to the original position.

Figure 7-25
Hue/Saturation
dialog

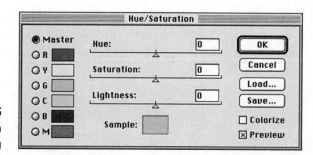

8. Click on the Colorize button to place a check mark in it. Now, slowly drag the Hue slider and the Saturation slider to try different combinations. The Colorize button is really a special effect rather than a color correction device. Uncheck the Colorize box, and the image returns to its original state.

9. Now, click on the R radio button to select only the reds in the image. Move the Hue slider in both directions and notice how you influence the image from magenta to yellow. Return the slider to the 0 position. Now, try the Saturation slider in both directions. You can tell how much red is in the image by the amount of change occurring. Once again, leave the slider in the 0 position.

10. Click on each of the YGCBM radio buttons and drag the saturation slider to see how much of each color is in the image. Leave all sliders back at their starting points. Notice there is relatively little green, blue, cyan, or magenta in the image.

11. Now, let's make some changes. Since the yellow seems a bit too harsh, we need to correct it. Moving the Yellow Hue slider though only makes the image too magenta or too green. A better way is to desaturate the yellow a bit. If you drag the cursor over the girl's yellow shuttle (the stick wrapped with yellow yarn on top of the loom), you notice that as you read the CMYK values on the Info palette, you see areas that have ! instead of % marks. That's the way Photoshop tells you an area is not within the CMYK gamut. Check out the area at location 318, 237 on the Info palette. You see the ! displayed.

12. We need to desaturate this area a bit to bring the yellow within the CMYK gamut. Click in the Y radio button. Drag the Saturation slider down to around –19. Check the shuttle area with the cursor and read the Info palette. While you still see ! on the left side of the double-number display (the original color), the right side (the new colors) should not show you any of the gamut colors.

13. While you are in the yellow area anyway, drag the Hue slider toward the left to –2. This gentle change makes the yellow a bit less glaring, too.

14. Click OK. Undo (Mac: ⌘+Z, Windows: CTRL+Z) and Redo (Mac: ⌘+Z, Windows: CTRL+Z) a few times to see if you like the changes. They are an improvement, so leave them changed. You may save and close the image.

Selective Color

When selective color correction is applied it can influence all the color areas of the complete image, but its main effect is on the most saturated color image areas. The midtones are not affected as dramatically as the more saturated areas. For example, measure a deep red color in CMYK. The red measures C=20%, M=90%, Y=90%, K=10%. If the magenta was increased in the saturated area from 90% to 100%, there is a 10% change of magenta in reds. Then measure a face or lighter red area. The magenta in those areas does not increase by 10%, but is influenced by the increase of magenta in reds by 4% or 5%. This illustrates the way sophisticated selective color correction tools work and provides a basis to discuss the Photoshop Selective color features.

The Selective color tool in Photoshop (Image → Adjust → Selective Color) is the main color tool to apply selective color corrections. It works best when your image is already in CMYK mode, but can be used—though not with as much success—when you are in RGB mode. It not only offers features to adjust specific hues such as RGBCMY, it provides the White, Neutral, and Black features. The White feature controls the highlight areas of an image. The Neutral feature controls the midtone image areas. They both affect neutral and color image areas.

The Black feature of Selective Color primarily controls the extreme neutral shadow point of an image. It does not affect pure hues or saturated color areas. This means the Black feature does not have a major effect on color areas; it is capable of easily adjusting the total ink density of CMYK files. This is the tool to effectively re-adjust neutral shadows of supplied CMYK images. Theoretically, the Black feature should work the same way on RGB files, but the Preference settings influence and override its functionality.

Crossover Colors

Color correction crossover is phenomena that happens when visually different color areas are affected by a particular selective color correction adjustment.

For example, the color orange is seen by selective color features as partially yellow and red. The orange color is affected by both red and yellow selective color correction controls to some degree (it crosses over between both colors).

Identify and Compensate for Any Color Interactions

Highlights, shadows, midtones, and neutrals affect color areas. Color areas need to be adjusted last to ensure the correct color/hue and saturation is achieved. The amount of adjustment depends on how much hue and saturation change is desired and the amount of midtone adjustment to create good contrast, based on the expectations of the customer.

The key interactions to beware of are midtone adjustments. Any type of midtone adjustment affects neutral and color image areas. When midtones are adjusted, it is necessary to check and/or read just the color correction. It is critical that this is done by measuring the color areas before the midtone adjustment, to know how the hue and saturation were affected.

Selective Color Masking

Another way to apply selective color corrections is generating selections in Photoshop. There are many tools to create selections that isolate an image area. It is necessary to use the ones you are comfortable with. Once the selection is created, any of the image processing tools can be used to alter the color. Each color imaging situation lends itself to certain image processing tools. There is no hard and fast rule here, but working within a selection, there are two basic imaging situations guiding the user:

● If the color area requires a slight change—but no more than about 20% per color

● If it needs dramatic color adjustments

While there are exceptions to these guidelines, their purpose is to ensure the image contrast is not degraded when making selective color corrections with the selections. Both Curves and Selective color are very effective for making slight changes to a color area.

If a large color change is necessary, it is best to use the Hue feature of the Hue & Saturation tool. This method causes a dramatic hue shift. Then, use Curves or Selective color to fine-tune the color.

Dodge and Burn

Photoshop offers other features for specific image areas, such as the Dodge and Burn tools. These are good for fixing small areas with color problems. A good way to use these tools is with single color channels, the Info palette, and two windows open. Open one window and work on one Black and White channel with the Dodge or Burn tool, being careful to watch the output values and the new window as it updates the color image.

Using the Color Balance Command

The Color Balance command is a commonly used tool whose function is not incredibly unique. Figure 7-26 shows the Color Balance dialog. Notice that the three sliders let you move between colors just as you would using the Gamma slider in the Levels dialog. The only advantage of using the Color Balance dialog is you can localize the changes to the highlights, midtones, or shadows only, and you can preserve the luminosity of changed areas. This is an easy command to use, but there is very little reason you would need it.

Using Variations

Variations (Image → Adjust → Variations) is an interactive method of color correction. Figure 7-27 shows the Variations dialog using the Blueroom.Psd image from earlier in this chapter. In the upper-left corner, you'll see the original image. There is also a current pick reflecting the changes. The current pick is also the center square in the color correction area. The radio buttons on the right are for selecting the areas to adjust. These

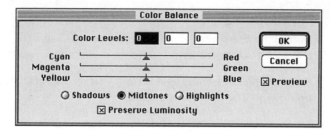

Figure 7-26
Color Balance
dialog

areas are shadows, midtones, highlights, and saturation. The Fine and Coarse slider adjusts the harshness of correction. The main area with all the squares is for color correction. The three squares on the right are for adjusting lightness and darkness.

Many people consider Variations no more than a toy, and not a serious color correction tool. However, it can perform serious color correction and is much easier for a beginner to learn than some of the other adjustment methods. It is always useful for special effects, too. One of the main problems with Variations is the small size of the image previews from which you must select. However, this is remedied by the third-party plug-in TestStrip, by Vivid Details, which is a superset of Variations.

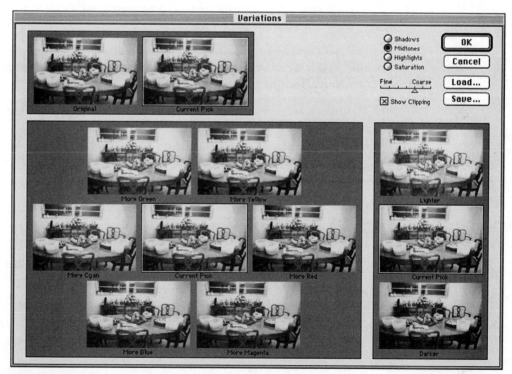

Figure 7-27
Variations dialog

The process:

1. Determine the problem with the image. Is it too light, too dark, too blue, and so on? Once the evaluation has been made, you can correct it.

2. First, set the coarseness to a setting you're comfortable with. This depends on how great a change you need.

3. Try to set the lightness and darkness first. Click on whichever one you feel is necessary. Each time you click, all the squares except the original update to reflect the change.

4. Remember to always work in opposites.

5. Let's say the image is too red. Find the box that says More Red, look to see which color is opposite, and add more of the opposite color. This starts neutralizing the color cast. Make necessary color moves that may involve the other colors as you see the image update.

6. These settings can be saved for other images. Click on the Save button, name the color correction, and choose a destination.

7. Saved settings can also be applied to other images. Open Variations, click on the Load button to find the settings, and open.

8. Always undo and compare the before and after images. Eric Reinfeld (who wrote this set of instructions) always does this a number of times before making a decision.

Now that you know the general rules, let's try correcting the BlueRoom.Psd using Variations and see if the process is any easier.

VARIATIONS

1. Open the image BlueRoom.Psd. We already know this image is too blue.

2. Drag the Coarseness slider to the right as far as it goes. Yuk! All the changes are too sharp. While we should set lightness and darkness first, the tone of this image seems fine right now. The blueness of it is overwhelming, however.

3. We know yellow is the opposite of blue. Therefore, drag the Coarseness slider to the left until the yellow image looks more acceptable than the current image (one click to the right of center). Click to make it the current image.

4. The image is still a bit too blue, but the yellow image is too yellow. Drag the Coarseness slider back one notch to the left (it is now in the center). That's better. Click on the yellow image to make it the current image.

5. Now that the color is better, the image is too light. Click on the Darker image to make it current. Hmmm...

6. The Darker sample looks better than the Current image, but is too dark. Move the Coarseness slider back to the left one notch to make a smaller change, and click on the new Darker sample to select it.

7. The image looks much better now. Click on the Shadows radio button. Make sure you have Clipping selected. Several of the image previews show that shadow areas are clipped to black if these previews are chosen. Since the entire image was too blue, it is likely the shadows are also too blue. Click on the Yellow preview to select it. Click OK to exit the dialog and save the changes.

8. Undo and redo a few times. It's definitely an improvement!

Applying USM (Unsharp Masking)

USM is typically the final image processing adjustment. USM is applied to add sharpness lost during the original scanning process. High-end scanners and some desktop scanners allow the user to add sharpness as the image is being processed. This is usually a good feature to have during the scanning process, although you must be careful not to oversharpen an image as you acquire it.

Some folks argue that USM is best performed in the RGB or LAB mode. All these methods work, but Jim Rich believes you have more control over each of the final channels by applying USM at the CMYK stage of the process just before the image is output. Refer to Chapter 4, "Filters," for the details of the Unsharp Mask (USM) adjustment range.

Determining the correct amount of sharpness is a subjective decision. If the effect is taken so far that it creates distinct white or black lines in the contrast or transition areas of an image, you have oversharpened it. Note that the amount of sharpness shown onscreen is often softened by the actual printing process, so experiment with different settings.

Most images only require USM applied overall. Some images need USM applied to individual channels.

1. What are the two main tools to make selective color changes to images?
   a. Hue/Saturation command
   b. Color Balance command
   c. Variations command
   d. Selective Color command

2. What is the most effective use for the Hue/Saturation tool?
   a. To fine-tune the selective color area
   b. To selectively saturate colors or make dramatic color changes with the Hue feature
   c. To colorize an image to create special effects
   d. To color-correct images used for printing

3. The Selective Color tool is the main color tool for color corrections, it works best when your image is in
   a. RGB mode.
   b. CMYK mode.
   c. RGBCMY mode.
   d. black and white mode.

4. Which of the Adjust tools are good for fixing small areas?
   a. Color Balance
   b. Dodge and Burn
   c. Variations
   d. Selective Color

5. Variations is an interactive color correction tool. What kind of things can you do with this tool?
   a. Adjust the shadows and highlights
   b. Adjust the Hue/Saturation
   c. Adjust the midtones
   d. Adjust the lightness and darkness

ADJUSTMENT LAYERS

Photoshop 4.0 has added an entirely new way of performing color corrections—one with massive benefits and almost no tradeoffs required. So why wait until the *end* of this chapter to present it? The new feature—Adjustment Layers—builds on the color correction tools you just learned. Nothing covered in this chapter is really rendered obsolete by the new feature.

Adjustment Layers are Layers containing *color correction information only*. They allow you to make nondestructive color correction moves that can be changed at any time. So far, the advice you received is to make as many of the corrections at once as you can, using as few of the different commands as possible, so you do not destroy any more image data than you absolutely must to get decent color. With Adjustment Layers, you no longer need to worry about destroying data if you need to make multiple color moves—or if you realize you have over- or undercorrected an image in progress.

Creating an Adjustment Layer

You can create an Adjustment Layer in several ways:

● Layer menu → New → Adjustment Layer

● Layer palette menu → New → Adjustment Layer

● Click on the New Layer icon with the modifier key (Mac: ⌘, Windows: CTRL) pressed

You can create a number of different types of Adjustment Layers, but each type of adjustment can only be made in its own Layer. There is an Adjustment Layer for the following commands:

● Levels

● Curves

● Brightness/Contrast

● Color Balance

● Hue/Saturation

● Selective Color

● Posterize

● Invert

● Threshold

Let's try an example using the Weaving.Psd image again (now you will see why we saved the Curves settings).

ADJUSTMENT LAYERS

1. Open the Weaving.Psd image (the *uncorrected* one).

2. Create a new Adjustment Layer (Mac: ⌘+click on New Layer icon, Windows: CTRL+click on New Layer icon). Figure 7-28 shows the dialog that appears.

3. Pull down the Type menu and select Curves as the Adjustment type. Figure 7-29 shows this dialog.

4. As soon as you click OK, you see the standard Curves dialog (if you chose a different type of adjustment, that command would appear).

5. Load the Girl.ACV curve you created (it is on the CD-ROM if you did not save it). This brings in all the corrections you previously created. If you did not have a precreated set of curves, you would proceed exactly as you did to create the curves the first time.

6. Click OK. The image looks just as it did when you used the Curves command without an Adjustment Layer. The difference is you can go back at any time and re-adjust the Curves by double-clicking on the Adjustment Layer—or you can toss it away completely and start over if you do not like your changes. Figure 7-30 shows the Layers palette after the Curve Adjustment Layer is added. Notice that the second column in the Layers palette shows a circle inside a rectangle—exactly the same icon as appears on a Layer when the Layer Mask is being edited. This is because an Adjustment Layer and a Layer Mask are very similar.

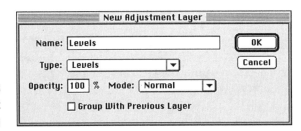

Figure 7-28
New Adjustment
Layer dialog

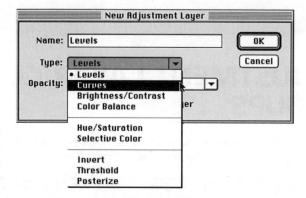

Figure 7-29
Specifying the
Adjustment Layer
Type

Figure 7-30
Layers palette
showing Curves
Adjustment Layer

Performing Local Corrections

An Adjustment Layer normally applies the correction to all visible portions of an image. If you have areas on several Layers beneath the Adjustment Layer, all the parts you can see are changed. You can make the correction affect only one of the objects below by placing it directly above the object and creating a Clipping Group. Since this is hard to visualize, let's try a fast example.

ADJUSTMENT LAYER CLIPPING GROUPS

1. Open the image Layers.Psd. It contains three Layers, but only two look visible—as you can see in Figure 7-31(a).

2. Click on the Sun Layer to make it the active Layer. Create an Adjustment Layer (Mac: ⌘+click, Windows: CTRL+click on the New Layer icon at the bottom of the Layers palette).

3. Select the Hue/Saturation Adjustment Layer as the Type.

4. Drag the Hue to +41—which changes the Layers under the Adjustment Layer (the Star and the Sun) to green.

5. Place your cursor over the *preview* of the Adjustment Layer in the Layers palette and double-click to bring up the Layer Options dialog (if you are not over the preview, you bring up the Hue/Saturation dialog instead). Click on the box that says Group with Previous Layer. This isolates the hue change to only the Sun layer—which you can now see clearly, as shown in Figure 7-31(b).

Figure 7-31
a) Layers.Psd
b) Layers.Psd with Sun Layer adjusted

a

b

6. Click on the Moon Layer to make it active and create an Adjustment Layer (Mac: ⌘+click, Windows: CTRL+click on the New Layer icon at the bottom of the Layers palette). Select a Hue/Saturation Layer.

7. Set the Hue to –58, the Saturation to –62, and the Lightness to –24 as shown in Figure 7-32.

8. Repeat Step 5 with the new Adjustment Layer to group it with the moon image only.

9. Open the image Sunpat.Psd. Select the entire image (Mac: ⌘+A, Windows: CTRL+A). Define this as a pattern (Edit → Define Pattern).

Figure 7-32
Hue/Saturation settings for the moon

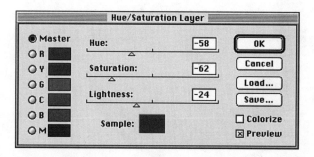

10. The Adjustment Layer is really a Layer Mask, and can be painted on just as you paint into and out of a Layer Mask with black, white, and shades of gray. Therefore, we can fill it with a pattern that reveals the original colors of the image before the Adjustment Layer was applied. Fill the image with the pattern (SHIFT+DELETE → Pattern, 100% Opacity, Normal).

11. Hmmm.... You can barely see this. Let's edit the Hue/Saturation for the moon and change the colors. Double-click on the Adjustment Layer *name* (remember, double-clicking on Preview brings up the Options dialog—not what we want right now). Change the Hue to −137, the Saturation to 67, and the Lightness to 40, as shown in Figure 7-33. Now you can see the pattern clearly, as shown in Figure 7-34.

12. Click OK to save the changes.

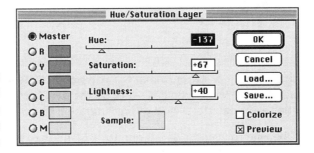

Figure 7-33
Changed Hue/Saturation settings for the moon

Figure 7-34
Finished Layers image

In addition to allowing for nondestructive color changes, the Adjustment Layer allows you to correct isolated portions of an image. If you have an area selected (surrounded by a Marquee) when you create the Adjustment Layer, it is automatically masked.

Adjustment Layers and Apply Modes

Another wonderful feature of Adjustment Layers is that you can change the Opacity and Apply mode. One excellent way to color correct an image before introducing the Adjustment Layers is to duplicate an image that is too light into a new Layer, then place the Layer into Multiply mode. This allows you to correct the image using its own tones—sometimes a far better method than Levels or Curves, as the image itself applies its own curve.

The drawback to this correction approach is its cost in RAM and disk space—it doubles the size of the image. Now, however, there is no need to duplicate the original Layer at all. All you need to do is select a Levels or Curves Adjustment Layer and *without making any adjustment to the levels or curves*, change the Adjustment Layer Apply mode to Multiply. You will use this technique in Chapter 10, "Photo Retouching."

Quiz 5

1. What are Adjustment Layers, and what do they enable you to do?
   a. They allow you to make nondestructive color correction.
   b. They allow you to stack one Layer on top of the other for a variety of effects.
   c. They contain color correction information only.
   d. They are used to keep track of Hue/Saturation changes.

2. What are the different types of Adjustment Layers you can create?
   a. Invert Adjustment Layer
   b. Levels Adjustment Layer
   c. Threshold Adjustment Layer
   d. Variation Adjustment Layer

3. How can you create an Adjustment Layer?
   a. From the menu bar, choose Image → Adjust → Add New Layer.
   b. From the menu bar, choose Layer → Adjustment Layer.
   c. From the Image palette menu, choose Layer → Add Adjustment Layer.
   d. From the Layer palette menu, choose New Adjustment Layer from the drop-down list.

4. When you apply an Adjustment Layer to an image, what does it normally affect?
   a. All visible portions of the background image only
   b. All visible portions of all Layers
   c. All visible portions of an image
   d. All visible portions of the top Layer only

5. Besides allowing for nondestructive color changes, what else does the Adjustment Layer allow you to do?
    a. Make global color corrections to an image
    b. Make corrections to isolated portions of a particular Layer
    c. Make corrections to isolated portions of an image
    d. Reduce the size of image

VIP PROFILES

The Profiles in this chapter feature the co-authors of *Real World Photoshop*.

Bruce Fraser, Graphics Expert/Writer

Bruce Fraser is co-author of *Real World Photoshop*, one of the most highly regarded Photoshop books ever written. It took 1½ years to write book—the authors had to learn many things they thought they knew. It proved to be the most difficult book any of them (Bruce, co-author David Blatner, and editor Steve Roth) had ever worked on.

Bruce is also a contributing editor of *MacWeek* and *MacUser* magazines, as well as a frequent visitor and helper on the Adobe CompuServe forum.

Bruce began as an amateur photographer. In 1984, his roommate purchased a 128KB Mac. Bruce was hooked, and by early 1985, he was working at TechArt—one of the first service bureaus in the country—using PageMaker 1. He started working for *MacWeek* in 1986 or 1987. He also worked for one of the first digital prepress shops. Plus, he freelanced for Peat-Marwick, where he went from doing simple bullet charts to creating presentation graphics.

Bruce first "met" Photoshop while writing a review of scanners for *MacWeek*. Photoshop was still Barneyscan, and Bruce was awed by the possibilities. As easy as it was, though, getting images into Photoshop, getting them out was a real challenge. There were very few printers or slide recorders on the market. Because of this, the original technology seemed mostly suited for hobbyists, but there was always the intriguing possibility that it might be much more. And by the time Photoshop reached version 2.5, it was. It had become a serious prepress tool.

Bruce's advice to you: Be prepared for lifelong learning; don't try to solve all the problems at once. Many folks start out using Photoshop by scanning in images, but scanning is an art in itself. If you start with prescanned images instead, you will learn the program more easily (use Photoshop's images on the CD-ROM or stock photos). When you have succeeded in getting the images to output predictably, then it is time to learn to scan.

Concentrate on the stuff you are good at. If you are an airbrush artist, learn to use the airbrush in Photoshop first.

Bruce is upset with the number of traditional photographers who are afraid Photoshop will make them redundant. Images come from a conscious act on the part of the imagemaker—that can never be replaced. Photographers are needed more than ever. Photoshop is a hugely enabling technology.

David Blatner, Graphics Expert/Consultant/Author

David Blatner, co-author of *Real World Photoshop* and noted expert on QuarkXPress, started working with computers at age 9 and was teaching the BASIC programming language by age 12. He taught adults and became an intern at Xerox Parc at the age of 14. He started working on the Alto machine with the first GUI (Graphical User Interface)—a precursor to the Mac. After having gotten so early a start, David then lost interest in computers and went into theater. He has a degree in theater administration. However, he did maintain enough interest in computers to continue with them at summer jobs. It was at one of these summer jobs that he first started to use QuarkXPress in 1987.

David also worked in a service bureau doing color separations on a Linotronic 100—in which he had to register film by eye. He began to take an interest in PostScript programming.

When David graduated from college, he needed an income, so he started consulting, training, and doing PostScript programming. People liked his work because he was both technical and artistic—a combination that is not easy to find. It gave balance to his advice and consultations.

In 1990, he wrote his first book on QuarkXPress. Since then, he has written or co-authored seven books. His most recent is *Real World QuarkImmedia*.

David became involved with Photoshop through his interest in QuarkXPress. He needed to do digital imaging—hence his introduction to Photoshop.

Digital imaging is a richer subject than page layout; there is so much more to it. However, because of his work with XPress, David approached Photoshop not for the cool effects, but rather to learn how to use the tools efficiently. David says that he has the eye of a designer, but not the hands. Since he does not feel totally at ease as an artist, he has become an expert on imaging.

David feels that Photoshop is such an incredible tool, he is almost embarrassed wishing Adobe would focus more on solving higher-end production issues, rather than developing more cool effects. He would like to be able to lock down a point or multiple points on the Info palette, make corrections, and see what happens to those specific points. However, one of the things David finds most exciting about Photoshop is how many different people in so many different industries use it. Medical imaging, scientific, engineering, design—all these diverse fields can all use the same program.

David's advice to you: Take time to play. It is only in playing that you ever really learn the program. The biggest problem for artists and designers working in the industry is needing to get proficient so fast that they don't learn anything beyond what is required to get the immediate job done. So, find an idea and try to do it in Photoshop. Take the time to learn the features of the program and the ways to use it most efficiently.

CHAPTER SUMMARY

This has really been a long haul. The color correction chapter is one of the longest and most complex in the book. In this chapter, you learned the process for correcting images and saw a number of the tools needed to do this. You learned to set white and black points, highlights, shadows, and midtones. You learned to read a Histogram and the Info palette, and to use the two tools together. You learned how to use levels and how to create curves for correcting images and removing color casts. You also learned a variety of ways to convert an image to grayscale. You met the Hue/Saturation, Color Balance, and Variations commands. Finally, you learned how to create Adjustment Layers for global, local, and selected corrections.

CHAPTER 8

SCANNING AND PHOTOCD

One of the most important steps in producing good output from Photoshop is acquiring good images. Although you can create images in Photoshop from scratch, much of the work most people do contains some prepared imagery. You can obtain images from a number of sources:

- Video cameras
- Kodak PhotoCD
- Other graphics applications, such as 3D programs or vector drawing programs

If you scan images, you can scan photographs or original drawings. You can also place objects on your scanner. One interesting texture was created for a Boston design firm from a slab of raw roast beef placed on the scanner (although how they cleaned the scanner afterwards remains a mystery!). Many artists prefer to paint with traditional media, then scan their originals into the computer. So you see, you have many options.

Chapter 13 adds to your input options by showing you how to work with Photoshop, vector, 3D, and video programs together. However, the many types of hardware, such as digital and video cameras, are somewhat beyond the scope of this book. This chapter introduces you to the basics of scanning and using PhotoCD images.

At the end of this chapter, you should be able to

● Scan images into Photoshop at the correct dimensions for the output device you selected.

● Select the best settings on your scanner driver to enhance the image before acquisition.

● State the difference between resampling and resizing an image and how resolution affects each of these.

● Define and differentiate the concepts of ppi, dpi, and lpi.

● State the benefits and drawbacks of scanning into RGB, CMYK, or Lab color space.

● Discuss ways to scan and clean up line art.

● Use the Kodak CMS to read images from a Kodak PhotoCD.

IMAGE SIZE AND RESOLUTION

There is no concept that Photoshop newcomers find as consistently difficult to understand as the issue of image size and image resolution. This is because these are terms that almost function as moving targets. Let's take a few moments to define each.

Image size sounds like it should be easy. Obviously, it tells you how large an image is. But *large* in relation to what? In feet? In centimeters? Every instance of largeness must have a unit of measure attached. Photoshop gives you a wide variety of units of measure from which to choose. You can measure the dimensions of a Photoshop file in

● Pixels

● Points

● Picas

● Inches

● Centimeters

This abundance of measurement units, however, can cause you to try to compare apples and oranges (or points and pixels), which works no better in the digital world than it does in the physical world. The other problem is that—with the exception of the pixels measurement—all the other dimensions are relative measurements and are linked to the resolution of the image.

Image resolution is the number of pixels per inch (ppi) or per centimeter that your image contains. This resolution amount is used to help determine the physical size of an image when you are ready to print it or export it to another application.

Image Resolution and Physical Image Size

In the previous section, we said that all dimensions except for pixels are relative—only the measurement in pixels is absolute. This is perhaps the key concept in understanding resolution and image size. Except for pixels, all measurements use the qualifier *x pixels per inch (or centimeter)*. Therefore, if you have an image you created at 3 inches×3 inches, you need to state that your image is 3 inches square at 300 pixels per inch (or whatever your resolution is set to).

Resolution is fluid. If you change it to 100 pixels per inch, you change the physical (output) size of the image but you may not change the number of pixels in it.

It may help to mentally perform this experiment. Fill a measuring cup with water up to the ¾ cup line. Get two differently shaped containers. One should be a common water drinking glass, the other, a wide, flat-bottomed bowl. Pour the water from the measuring cup into the glass. How high is the water? (About 2 to 3 inches is typical.) Pour the water from the glass into the bowl. How high is it now? (It should be much lower.)

Has the amount of water changed? No—not unless you spilled some. The only thing that changed was the shape of the container. In a narrow container, the water is higher; in a wide container, the same amount of water is much lower. You can directly compare this to image resolution and image size. The container is the analog equivalent to the image resolution. If the resolution is very high, it makes the physical image size (the depth of the water) smaller since it forces the pixels into a smaller area (think of the narrow glass forcing the pixels to stack up on top of each other). A smaller resolution gives these pixels more room to spread out. They are not as deep, but they are wider and cover a larger physical area.

You can also prove this mathematically. If you have an image 3 inches square at 300 pixels per inch, it contains 900 pixels in each dimension (3 inches×300 pixels per inch=300×3=900). If you change the resolution to 100 pixels per inch, your image becomes 9 inches square (900 pixels÷100 pixels per inch=900÷100=9). If you resize the resolution to 600 pixels per inch, the image will shrink to 1.5 inches square. The image, however, still contains only 900 pixels in each dimension. Like the water, the atomic structure of the image remains the same. It is only the viewing lens that changes.

In this course, you have created almost all the new images by specifying pixels in the Unit of Measure box. You also set the Units Preference to pixels. As you can see from this discussion, only the pixel count gives you an absolute number that does not vary when the image resolution changes. If you get used to thinking in pixels, then much of the calculating you need to do becomes very easy.

Another Perspective

Since the information on resolution is so tough to understand, it might be helpful to discuss it in more than one way. Andrew Rodney of Camera and Darkroom Digital in Santa Fe, NM, wrote the following sidebar and uses it in his classes as a training piece on resolution:

We like to think about digital files in terms of pixels. A pixel (short for *Picture Element*—use that at your next party to impress your friends) is the smallest unit of measurement when discussing a digital file. This is where we will begin. All digital files should be thought of as nothing more than a series of pixels running the length and width of the image. Forget for now all that stuff about dots per inch, pixels per inch, and so on. We'll get to that in a second. For now, just realize that once you scan an image, it's composed of pixels!

OK, let's now try and discuss how all those pixels come into our unit of measurement. We will work with inches. If you have an original that's 4 inches×5 inches, and you need to scan it, it seems reasonable that the final image will be composed of a series of pixels running from one end to the other. Let's say you have a digital file that started its life as a 4×5-inch transparency. We want to scan it and we need to set the resolution. This is when we need to determine what we intend to do with this image after the scan. How will it be output?

Output devices, be they printers or even monitors, have to lay out the pixels in a row. Before we scan our image, we have to figure out how it will be output. How many pixels in, say, an inch will our output device lay out? Let's say we have a printer that is 300 dots per inch. 300 dots per inch and 300 pixels per inch are interchangeable. It's like calling 12 inches a foot. In reality, output devices lay down *dots*. So when we talk about output devices, we should say dots per inch (dpi) rather than pixels per inch (ppi). However, if we have a file that's 300 pixels per inch, and we feed it to a device that can lay down 300 dots per inch, we will get output that's *1* inch!

This is the concept of resolution in its simplest terms. You have a file. It is composed of pixels. You send those pixels to a device. That device lays down a set number of pixels (remember, dots) in a row. That's not so hard to understand, is it? This is one reason we like to deal with pixels when describing a file. At some point, those pixels get laid down on a device. Let's talk about another output device: your monitor. Yes, a monitor is an output device much like a printer. Most monitors output 72 dpi. What if we have a file 216 pixels wide? If our monitor is displaying 72 pixels per inch, that file will show up (at 1:1) in Photoshop at 3 inches (216÷72=3).

We will do an exercise in Photoshop soon that will introduce you to the Image Size dialog. This handy dialog is also useful as a resolution calculator. For now, just be concerned with the total length and width of a file in pixels and how those pixels are fed to an output device. Here's another quick example. Suppose we have a file that's 4000×5000 pixels. Our original was a 4×5 negative. We know our output device is a film recorder and its output resolution is 1000 dpi. How large will the film be after we feed a 4000×5000 pixel file to a device that lays down 1000 dots in an inch? The correct answer is 4×5 inches.

Let's look at the same example in a different light. We still have a 4000×5000 pixel file. You now have an output device like a Kodak dye subprinter. Its output resolution is 203 dpi (but for the sake of easy math, let's say it's 200 dpi). How large would the files output? 4000÷200=20 inches and 5000÷200=25 inches. The only problem is our printer can't output a print this large. OK, let's do this one more time. Now we are going out to an Iris Ink Jet printer. Its output resolution is 300 dpi. The Iris can produce a very large print. Taking the same 4000×5000 pixel file, the output is 13.3×16.6 inches (4000÷300=13.3 and 5000×300=16.6).

Here's the deal. In *all* cases the same digital file, the 4000×5000 pixel file, produced different-sized output! In other words, if you work with pixels and you know the output resolution of your device, you can always figure out how large the output will be.

Image Size Command

The Image Size command is used to both resize and resample images. When you *resize* an image, you change the physical dimensions of its *output* (as we did above—the same amount of water, new container). When you *resample* an image, you actually change the *amount* of "water"—the number of pixels in the image.

The Image Size dialog box is divided into two parts: one displays the image in pixel count, the other in physical size. There is an option box that lets you decide if you wish to resample. When you allow resampling, you can change either the pixel count (by pixels or percent) or the height, width, or resolution. If you only want to resize the image, uncheck the Resample Image box, which locks the pixel count of the image and lets you only change the height, width, or resolution. Furthermore, the dialog recalculates all the other dimensions for you by just changing *one* dimension. The behavior of the dialog does not change based on your Units preference (as the dialog did in Version 3.0.5 and earlier). However, keeping your units in pixels is still the safest way to work. Let's look at an example.

HANDS ON

RESIZING AND RESAMPLING IMAGES

1. Check the setting in the File → Preferences → Units to make sure it is set to pixels. If not, change it.

2. Open the image CharlesR.Psd. This is an image of the Charles River in Boston.

3. Figure 8-1 shows the image with its Print Preview size window. You can see this by clicking and holding down the mouse button on the numeric information box at the bottom left of the image window (on the Mac) or the bottom of the application window (on Windows). The print size shows relative to an 8.5×11 inch page (or the page size and orientation selected in your Page Setup dialog).

Figure 8-1
Print Preview window shows the image's relative size on a printed page

4. Next, press the modifier key (Mac: OPTION, Windows: ALT) and click and hold the mouse button on the same area that showed you the Print Preview window. This time, you see the Image Size information box. It tells you the image is 641×453 pixels at 132 pixels per inch. It also uses 851KB in memory.

5. Open the Image Size dialog (Image → Image Size). Figure 8-2 shows the dialog box. It is divided into two main sections: the Pixel Dimensions and the Print Size. A third section at the bottom lets you determine whether to constrain the image proportions or resample the image, and the dialog also lets you specify the Interpolation Method for resampling. Always leave the Interpolation Method at Bicubic unless you have a very good reason not to (the Interpolation Methods are explained in more detail in Chapter 14, "Configuring and Optimizing Photoshop"). For now, uncheck the Resample Image box.

6. Change the resolution to 600 pixels per inch. Look at the Pixel Dimensions. They have not changed at all. This shows that you can easily change the resolution of an image without changing the number of pixels it contains—our definition of *resizing*—as long as the Resample Image box is not checked. You can see that the physical size has changed, however, in the Print Size section (if your Units are set to Inches in the dialog). The width has gone from 4.856 to 1.068 inches. Click OK.

7. Look at the Print Preview box again. This time, it is very small. Notice that the image has not moved on your screen. Not a single pixel in the image has been changed.

8. Undo (Mac: ⌘+Z, Windows: CTRL+Z).

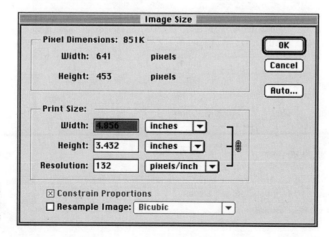

Figure 8-2
Image Size dialog:
Resample Image off

9. Select the Image Size command again. This time, make sure the Resample Image box *is* checked. Then change the resolution to 600 pixels per inch. Figure 8-3 shows this dialog. What happened? Look at the File Size. It is now 17.2MB! The dimensions in inches did not change at all. However, look at the Pixel Size area. The number of pixels has increased to 2914 (from 641). This meets our definition of image *resampling*. In order to change the number of pixels from 641 to 2914, the computer has to *invent* an additional 2271 pixels.

10. Press the modifier key (Mac: OPTION, Windows: ALT) and click the Reset button. There is one anomaly to explore. The Print Size dialog gives you the option of setting the new size by percent as well as by inches, centimeters, picas, points, or columns. Leave the Resample Image box checked. Change the Units for Width to Percent, but leave the Width set to 100%. Change the resolution to 600 ppi. The number of pixels in the image does not change, but the printing size does. Press the Cancel button to leave the dialog but leave the CharlesR.Psd image open.

What have you learned?

● You can *resize* an image by changing its resolution if you do *not* check the Resample Image box. This changes the physical size of the output image without changing the number of pixels.

● You can *resample* an image by changing the resolution if you *do* check the Resample Image box. This alters the number of pixels in the image, creating or removing enough of them to keep the image at its current physical output size.

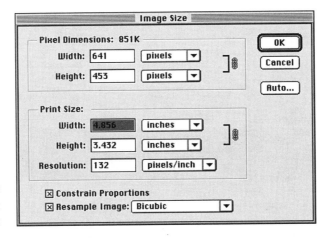

Figure 8-3
Image Size dialog:
Resample Image on

The other thing you should know is that *down-sampling* is OK (reducing the number of pixels in the image), but *up-sampling* (making more pixels) is not OK and can cause a serious amount of image degradation. Don't up-sample if you can avoid it.

HANDS ON

UP-SAMPLING (WHY YOU SHOULDN'T DO IT!)

1. Double-click on the Marquee tool. In the Marquee Option palette that appears, set Shape to Rectangular and Style to Fixed Size. Enter these values: Width, 200 pixels; Height, 200 pixels. Make sure the Feather Radius box is set to 0.

2. Drag the Marquee into the Charles River image so it surrounds the autos at the bottom of the image and fits against the image's bottom edge. Crop the image (Image → Crop) to the size of the Marquee.

3. Duplicate the image (Image → Duplicate → OK).

4. Apply the Image Size command (Image → Image Size) and leave the Resample Image box *on*. Set the resolution to 800 pixels per inch and click OK.

5. Double-click on the Magnifier tool to view the image at 1:1 ratio.

Look carefully at the resampled image. If you look at the highway divider, you can clearly see the pixels in the image. This should not be the case! Seeing pixels at 1:1 is *always* bad. This occurred because there was not enough information in the original image for the computer to use as a basis for color decisions. Therefore, the computer duplicated nearby pixels and interpolated their colors. This eventually caused the pixels to group themselves in block-like formations of similar colors so that it looks like you are seeing individual large pixels. Not a pretty sight! The image is much too soft and noisy to be used. The moral is, don't up-sample an image if you need to use it photographically when you are done. Instead, scan it at a higher resolution so that you capture it at the size that you need.

PPI, DPI, and LPI

Now that you know the difference between resolution and image size, and between resampling and resizing, you need to nail down the illusive terms ppi, dpi, and lpi. We are slowly working our way toward trying to determine scan sizes.

dpi means dots per inch. This is, for our purposes, identical to the pixels per inch (ppi) you used in the Image Size dialog. However, technically, it refers to the individual spots of ink a printer or imagesetter can produce. Digital images are stored in pixels per inch; output devices create dots per inch. In both cases, all the dots, spots, or pixels in a given device are the same size. *lpi*, or lines per inch, refers to the halftoning that occurs when an image is printed conventionally or on most desktop printers. These dots *do* vary in size, though they are printed at a fixed interval. This interval is called the *screen ruling*—or lines per inch (lpi).

The key thing to know about a line screen is that your image resolution should be larger than the line screen you select. How much larger is up for debate, but the general consensus is that if your resolution is 1.5 times your line screen, you have sufficient detail in the image. More traditional rules recommend 2 to 2.5 times the line screen as a good amount of detail. There is no profit in having more image resolution than you need since that just slows down the processor without adding any quality to the finished image.

What line screen do you need? That depends on the printing press, the paper you use, and the quality you want. Generally, newsprint requires a line screen of about 85 lpi, a decent quality coated stock (glossy paper) needs a line screen of 133, and high quality magazine printing demands 150 to 200 lpi. A 300 to 600 dpi laser printer uses a halftone of 53 to 63 lpi.

What Is Halftoning?

Look at a photograph in a newspaper. The dots comprising it are large enough to see without the use of a magnifier. These dots you see are the line screening (or halftoning). They are spots of black ink and empty paper that produce the visual illusion of gray tones. The name *halftone* for a printed grayscale image comes from the fact that there are only two colors used (ink and paper).

A printing press or most desktop printers can only lay down one color at a time. In addition, they can only print a single value of that color. The action is very basic: A printer can place a spot of ink or not place a spot of ink. The color of the ink as it is placed does not vary. However, the location of the ink and its size and shape vary. This variation is what makes the optical illusion of graduated color appear.

When you send a grayscale image (or a single channel of a CMYK document) to an imagesetter, it converts the image into black and white by a process known as *halftoning*. It uses a screen with dots of a user-specified shape and size to break up the image into areas of black or white. Where the image is darkest you see dots closer together, making the image look dark. In the lighter areas, the dots are far apart. You can try this for yourself by converting a grayscale image to a bitmap image using the halftone option you learned in Chapter 6, "Color and File Formats." Figure 8-4 shows an image being broken up into digital halftones by an elliptical line screen.

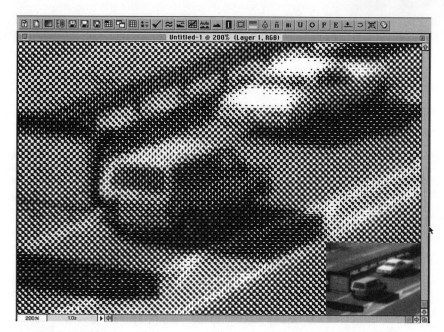

Figure 8-4
Halftones

Determining Scanning Resolution

You now have all the information you need to make an intelligent choice of scan size. You need to know two things:

● Your finished output size

● The line screen you need in order to print

Printing to a Continuous Tone Device

Andrew Rodney offers the following advice if you are not going to halftone your output: Dye sublimation printers and film recorders do not halftone their output. Therefore, for continuous tone output to a device like a dye sub, you don't need more than a 200-ppi scan. The human eye can't see any difference. This is one reason that the original dye subs from Kodak (XL-7700) were mere 203-dpi devices.

However, when you combine type *and* images, you really need 300 dpi or the type looks soft. Therefore, if you are just printing photos, 200 dpi is fine. Combine photos and type, and you need 300 dpi. Some manufacturers try and trick folks into believing that higher output resolutions mean better quality, but on this type of device, it just isn't needed.

The rest should be easy—but it isn't always. Many folks get confused when they need to scan an image that won't be printed the same size as the original. Often, you need to change the size of an image you are scanning. Depending on the options your scanner gives you for setting the scan size, you may need to calculate the new dimensions in a variety of ways:

- As the raw number of pixels to be scanned (easiest if your scanner driver permits it)

- As an enlargement/reduction percentage (unfortunately, the most common calculation)

- Scanning resolution (probably the second most common method, and the most confusing)

- In inches, picas, points, or centimeters

Let's look at each situation using the following example:

Original image dimensions: 5 inches wide, 3 inches high

Printing specs: 150 lpi (resolution of 300 ppi)

It is easy to output your image at the same size as the original. To print at 150 lpi, a safe amount is 2 times the lpi=300 dpi. Scan at 300 ppi. You will get a scan of

- 1500 pixels (5 inch width×300 ppi) × 900 pixels (3 inch height×300 ppi)

- 100% enlargement (in other words, the same input and output size)

- Scan resolution of 300 ppi

- 5×3 inches

That is simple! However, what happens if you need to change the size of the original?

Needed size: 4 inches wide, keep same proportions

Here is the math behind each calculation (for those of you who, like me, are a bit mathematically challenged).

● *In pixels:* 4 inches×300 ppi=1200 pixels wide. Typically, if your scanner driver allows you to enter the exact number of pixels to scan, it simply calculates the other dimension based on the area you selected during the pre-scan operation (discussed in the following text). This means you should not have to calculate more than one dimension.

● *In percentage:* If the original was 5 inches and the scan must be 4 inches, then there is a ratio of 4:5—the scan must be $^4/_5$ of the original. $^4/_5$=.8 or 80%. You need to scan your original at 80% with a resolution of 300 ppi.

● *Resolution:* Printer drivers that only allow you to specify scan resolution rather than dimensions are a major pain. Although the *scan* resolution and the *print* resolution do not have to be the same, this is the part most beginners find so confusing. Your scanner knows the actual physical dimensions of an area you select on it. When you drag a Marquee around the area you wish to scan, the scanner can calculate its real world dimensions. So, if you select an area that's really 5×3 inches, the scanner knows those dimensions. However, you must trick the scanner into grabbing the needed number of pixels. If you set your scan resolution at 300 ppi (the resolution you need for printing), the scanner grabs 1500×900 pixels, which is too big. Therefore, the calculation must figure out how many dpi you need to grab in 5 inches to end up with 1200 pixels. Where did the 1200 pixels come from? Your output is 300 ppi and the desired width is 4 inches. 300×4=1200 (pixels). Therefore, the final calculation is 1200 (needed pixels)÷5 (original inches)=240 (ppi). Set the resolution to 240 and scan the image. To get the correct dimensions after scanning the image, use the Image Size command to change the resolution to 300 ppi—without resampling the number of pixels in the image.

● *In units of measure, such as inches:* Leave your resolution set at 300 ppi and change the size of the scan to 4 inches wide. Let the scanner calculate the width. Sometimes it is not possible to obtain the exact dimensions you want. This is due to rounding problems as the scanner calculates dimensions. It moves the numbers you type to the nearest possible numbers. You can make the image adhere more closely to the exact dimensions you need once it is scanned. If the size you need changes to something a bit smaller, you can make the dimensions a bit larger so you have room to reduce the image size later.

After we look at the process of scanning, we will return to this example using a real image and see how each of these adjustments produces the same result.

QUIZ 1

1. Where are some of the places you can find images?
   a. Video cameras
   b. Other graphics applications
   c. Photo album
   d. The Internet

2. What units of measure can you use in Photoshop?
   a. Pixels
   b. Centimeters
   c. Millimeters
   d. Points

3. All measurement units are relative and linked to image resolution, with the exception of _____.
   a. Picas
   b. Pixels
   c. Inches
   d. Centimeters

4. What is *pixel* short for?
   a. Picture Image Boxes
   b. Picture Boxes
   c. Picture Image Excel
   d. Picture Element

5. What command is used to resize and resample an image?
   a. Resize command
   b. Resize and Resample command
   c. Image Size command
   d. Pixel Size command

LESSON 2

USING A SCANNER

There are a number of basic types of scanners: drum scanners, flatbed scanners, film scanners, and hand-held. Drum scanners are very expensive and are used mainly by service bureaus for prepress. These scanners have exceptional quality. However, since they are so expensive and not commonly found in most studios, we will not discuss them in great detail here.

On the very low end are the hand-held scanners. Since the price of desktop scanners has dropped, this lower-end category is fading somewhat. The hand-held scanners enable you to acquire an image by moving the scanner over the image. This typically results in slanted images that are not good quality. Since the quality of hand-held scanners is so low, we will not focus on them either.

The flatbed scanners are the most common scanners for image acquisition on the desktop. They range in price from about $300 to more than $7000. Many of the higher-priced models also come with film scanners to acquire image negatives or to scan slides. The difference in price is a reflection of quality, software, dynamic range, bit-depth, and sometimes, options (such as film scanners or batch imaging capabilities).

Scanner Color Space, Bit-Depth, and Dynamic Range

You already know about the four major color spaces—grayscale, RGB, CMYK, and Lab. Most scanners can acquire images in grayscale or RGB. Drum scanners and some high-end desktop scanners can also scan images and transform them into CMYK or Lab color space. In addition, most scanners can acquire images in bitmap (black-and-white) mode. This is called line art.

Scanners are sold with specific bit-depths. This number, generally between 24 and 48, indicates how many colors a scanner can capture and see as different. A 24-bit scanner can see over 16 million colors. Photoshop normally works in a 24-bit color gamut. Why would you need a scanner that has a higher bit-depth?

Photoshop also supports some 48-bit and 36-bit scanners. The scanner hands over the higher bit-depth data for Photoshop to use only with Levels and Curves. The Image → Mode dialog lets you specify whether you want an 8-bit or 16-bit channel depth. The higher bit-depth scanners allow you to capture more of the colors in a specific image. A scanner, such as the Umax PowerLook II, which has a 36-bit-depth, can see more colors than Photoshop can use. It can, therefore, scan the image and keep the best range of colors that fits into 24-bit color space.

Even more important than the bit-depth is the *dynamic range* of a scanner. The dynamic range is an indication of how capable the scanner is at obtaining the highlights and shadows in an image. A scanner with a high dynamic range can capture more shades in the shadows before they turn black and more highlight areas before they turn solid white. If these additional levels are present in your image, they enable you to make adjustments you otherwise could not. For example, if you scan a forest scene with deep shadows, you can use curves to lighten some of the range. However, if your scanner sees all the shadow area as solid black, you will only be creating gray shadows by changing the curves. As long as there are different shades in the shadows, however, you can selectively lighten some of them.

Resolution, Dynamic Range, and Scanner Bit-Depth

Andrew Rodney again contributes his expanded view: There are three important hardware specs that prospective scanner buyers should keep in mind: resolution, dynamic range, and bit-depth. Unfortunately, most buyers concentrate on resolution first and pay least attention to the most important spec: dynamic range. Obviously, you want a scanner that has a high enough resolution for your needs.

What is the smallest original you'll scan and how big will it need to be enlarged? If you primarily scan large format originals like 4×5s and the scans are used for conventional 4-color reproduction, super-high resolution shouldn't be much of a factor. Even scanning with a quality factor of 2× and printing on a 200-line screen, it's unlikely you'll need any more then 400 ppi to 1200 ppi (the latter giving you 3× enlargement or output of 12×15). For small originals such as 35mms, you would need to blow them up 11× to fill a two-page spread, but of course, 35mms don't generally make the best spreads due to their small size.

Dynamic range (also known as density range) is one of the most important specs in determining the quality of the final scan. The dynamic range is a measure of the difference between the lightest highlight and the blackest black (D-max) that a unit can scan. Film has a far wider dynamic range than printed material. If you measure the density range of a print, it is in the neighborhood of 2.7. The density of a transparency could be from 3.3 to as high as 3.7 or in an extreme case of litho film or an E-6 control strip, 4.0! Since this unit of measure is log-E, the difference between a dynamic range of 3.6 and 3.7 can be significant. Therefore, if you attempt to scan an original with a density range of 3.5 on a scanner with a dynamic range of 3.3, shadow and/or highlight detail will not be captured. Subtle shadow detail is recorded as black rather than a very dark shade of dark gray. This means a loss of detail in what could be important areas of your original. The ScanMate has a stated dynamic range of 4.0, while the Agfa has a dynamic range of 3.7. Either one is more than suitable for scanning film! Keep in mind what your final output will be too. Ink on paper does not show the subtle details in shadows and highlights like a high-end film recorder does.

Bit-depth is a spec that most scanner manufacturers are proud to state (unlike dynamic range). Nearly all imaging applications work with 24-bit color files (8 bits per color). But having a higher bit-depth prior to converting a file to 24 bits means the data is broken up into finer steps or shades of tonality. The idea is if a scanner can operate in more than 8 bits per color, it has more data to work with to produce the *best* 8 bits of data for use in your imaging software. This, in fact, is quite true. If, however you have a scanner that only has a dynamic range of 3.3 and your original has a range of 3.6, the extra bits only divide more steps of pure black into black! If the scanner can't see into areas of tonality, having extra bit-depth does nothing. Therefore, an ideal scanner is one that captures the entire range of density found in your original and also deals with more than 8 bits of data at the scan stage. A 48-bit scanner with a dynamic range of 3.3 is no match for a scanner that has 36 bits and a dynamic range of 3.6 (assuming your original has a density range of 3.6)!

Scanner Controls

Each scanner comes with its own driver. This driver is the software controlling the behavior of the scanner. It is usually a plug-in Import module for Photoshop (it appears on the File → Import menu). In order to use the scanner, you need to connect it according to the manufacturer's instructions, then install the driver as instructed in the scanner manual. Once everything is set up, you start to scan by placing your image on the scanner bed, closing the top of the scanner, and then selecting the scanner driver under the File → Import menu.

Figure 8-5 shows the Umax PowerLook II scanner driver control screen. This is a good example of a scanner driver because it contains a wide range of features you'd want in a scanner. The scanner driver contains most of the same color correction tools discussed in Chapter 7, "Color Correction." However, they are now part of the scanner software so that the image you bring into Photoshop is captured correctly and needs less adjustment after being acquired. This is desirable because each time you adjust an image, you lose data. If you adjust it in the scanner, however, you still capture a full range of values. Even better, when you make adjustments at the scanner level, you get a smooth—rather than a *gappy*—histogram.

Figure 8-6 shows the Levels histogram for the image you see on the scanner bed in Figure 8-5. The scan uses the settings shown in Figure 8-5 as well. Notice the Levels histogram shows that the scan does not come close to containing any white. If you use the Levels command to change the White Point in Photoshop, you will see a result that looks like Figure 8-7. This is a broken (or gappy) histogram. It contains obvious gaps in the tonal range of the image. Figure 8-8 shows the histogram for the same White Point correction performed in the scanner driver using the Levels command. Notice that a full range of values is captured.

The PowerLook II scanner driver also contains settings that allow you to set White, Black, and Gamma points, change curves, and correct color cast and color balance. You can change the units you use for scanning (in Figure 8-5, they are set to inches, and the measurement is the physical one read from the area marqueed on the scanner bed). You can also set the Preferences to specify the minimum and maximum RGB values you wish to include in the scan. This is the equivalent of setting values on the Output sliders in the Levels command in Photoshop—so you can keep true black and true white out of your images. The PowerLook software also contains such goodies as the ability to flip or rotate an image during scanning, or scan an image's negative (especially useful if you are scanning a photographic film negative). It even contains a Magnifier so you can enlarge the preview for a closer look.

When you purchase a scanner, you need to use the software that comes with it to acquire your image. The PowerLook II scanner software is excellent, and the Power Look 2000 comes with high-end binuscan software. Agfa also makes models with excellent software. The new line of Sapphire scanners from Linotype-Hell is very expensive but has perhaps the most impressive software ever shipped with a desktop scanner.

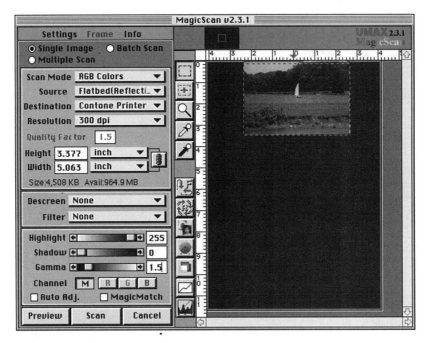

Figure 8-5
Scanner driver
control screen for
Umax PowerLook II

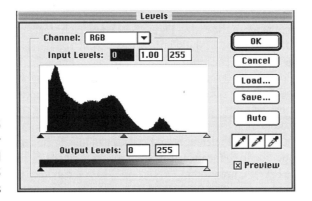

Figure 8-6
Histogram for
image scanned
with Figure 8-5
settings

There are, however, a few multi-scanner software drivers available. Second Glance Software manufactures the Scantastic scanner driver. This driver supports Epson, Hewlett-Packard, and Apple scanners. It provides most of the tools the PowerLook driver contains and is better than many of the manufacturers' drivers because of the scanners it supports. If you own one of the supported scanners, it is a good driver to purchase (Epson scanners ship with it anyway).

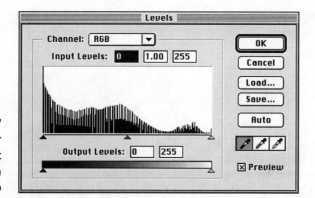

Figure 8-7
Histogram for
White Point
corrected in
Photoshop

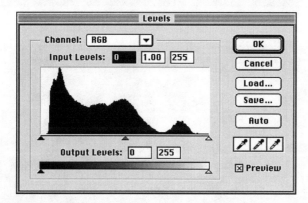

Figure 8-8
Histogram for
White Point set in
the scanner driver

What Can You Scan?

A flatbed scanner lets you scan photographs—that's obvious. But it does not limit you to photographs. You can scan any printed material. However, images that have already been printed pick up the halftone pattern when scanned. When you print them out again, they will *moiré*.

A moiré is a pattern that is both distracting and unintended. It occurs when an image is badly or improperly halftoned—usually at the wrong angles. With previously printed material, it occurs when you try to halftone a halftone. You should not scan any copyrighted material—which most printed items are. However, clients are prone to handing you printed logos and asking you to revise and reprint them. When you are stuck, you have no choice—you have to scan material that includes halftone.

Some of the newer scanner drivers contain descreening features. These features let you acquire images that were previously screened or halftoned and help remove those patterns. Figure 8-9 shows the cover from the Photoshop 3.0 CD-ROM scanned without descreening. Figure 8-10 shows the same image scanned using the Umax PowerLook II descreening feature. There is a very big difference—and even more were you to see it in color. (Hint: The color versions of these figures are on the CD-ROM.)

Figure 8-9
CD-ROM cover
scanned without
descreening

Figure 8-10
CD-ROM cover
scanned and
descreened

You are not limited to scanning printed paper. Several art supply mail order houses (Flax and Sax) sell textured, marbled, and lace papers. There are wonderful things to scan and use as backgrounds. Handmade papers make marvelous backgrounds as well. If you are creating images that will not be resold, you can also scan origami paper. With any of the art papers, however, you should check into copyrights if you use them for commercial purposes.

If you have access to *old* or non-patterned fabrics, they should be scannable and in the public domain. Modern printed fabrics are generally copyrighted and contain such a notice along their selvage. However, if you are doing quilt design, you can certainly scan your fabrics as an aid to designing.

The scanner can be used for 3D objects as well. You can scan fruit, coins, almost anything that fits the scanner screen and holds still! Tinsel makes a very interesting image, as do bunches of various yarns placed on the scanner. The mylar from old balloons or the holograms on some paper dinnerware catch the lights of the scanner in a very intriguing fashion. Use your imagination (just don't use roadkill—which, believe it or not, has also been done!).

Setting Units on the Scanner

You were promised a demo of setting the scan size from the example above. Here it is.

- *In pixels:* 4 inches×300 dpi=1200 pixels wide. In the Umax driver, adjust the Marquee around the area to scan. For our example, the real units are be 5 inches×3 inches when you enclose the area to scan. You only need to change the units of the width to pixels and enter the number 1200. The scanner immediately calculates the height as 720 pixels. When you press the scan button, the image is acquired at the exact size of 1200×720 pixels. Figure 8-11 shows the scanner dialog with the units set to pixels.

- *In percentage:* If the original was 5 inches and the scan must be 4 inches, then there is a ratio of 4:5 (the scan must be 4/5 of the original). 4/5=.8 or 80%. In the Umax scanner driver, one of the available units is percent. If you select this as your unit and set it to 80%, you capture an image that is 1200×720 pixels—identical to the method above. Figure 8-12 shows this dialog.

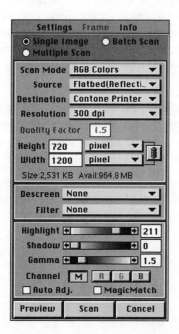

Figure 8-11
Units set to pixels

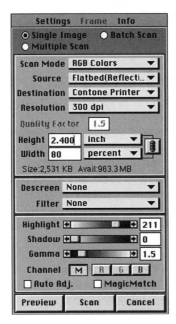

Figure 8-12
Width unit set to
percent

🔵 *Resolution:* Select an area that is really 5×3 inches. The final calculation is 1200 (pixels)÷5 (inches)=240 (dpi). Set the resolution to 240 and scan the image. Figure 8-13 shows this setting in the scanner dialog. To get the correct dimensions after you scan the image, use the Image Size command to change the resolution to 300 dpi—without resampling the number of pixels in the image.

Figure 8-14 shows the Image Size dialog. Notice the image is exactly the same 1200×720 pixels as in the other methods. Also notice that when you change the resolution to 300 from 240 in the Image Size command, the file size and number of pixels do not change (the units are set to pixels).

🔵 *In units of measure, such as inches:* Leave your resolution set at 300 dpi and change the size of the scan to 4 inches wide. Let the scanner calculate the height. This is a very easy way to change the size of the image. Figure 8-15 shows this dialog.

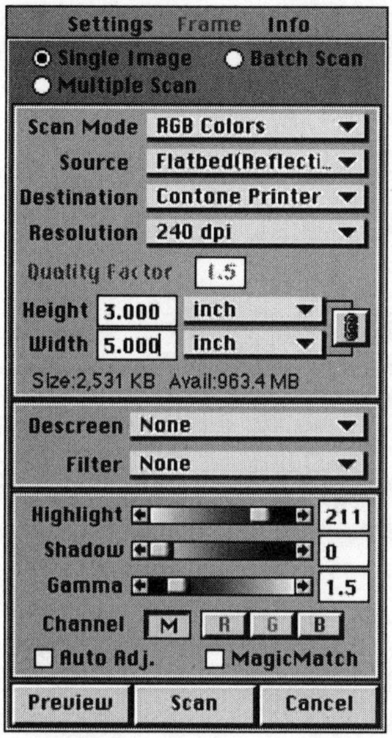

Figure 8-13
Resolution changed
for scan

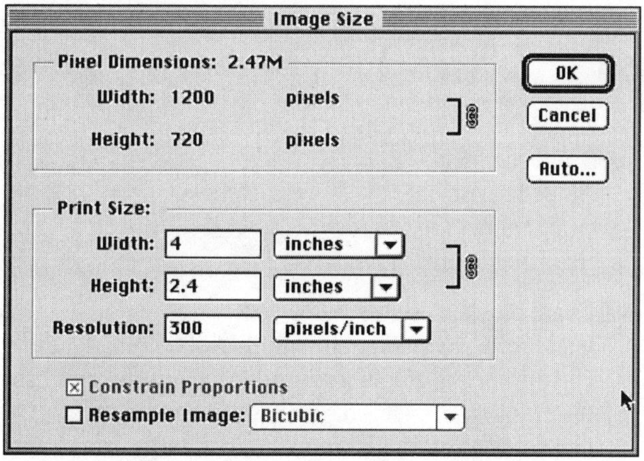

Figure 8-14
Image Size dialog

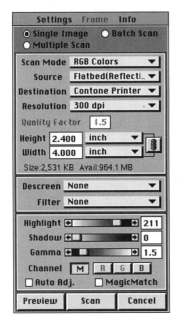

Figure 8-15
Units set to inches

1. What are the basic scanners available today?
   a. Drum scanners
   b. Flatbed scanners
   c. Film scanners
   d. Hand-held scanners

2. What are bit-depths?
   a. The number of pixels×the number of colors in an image
   b. The number of colors a scanner can capture and distinguish
   c. The number of pixels a scanner can capture
   d. The number of dots a scanner can identify at one time

3. What is dynamic range?
   a. A group of continuously scanned pixels
   b. A 24-bit range of colors identifiable by a scanner
   c. The capability of a scanner to capture an image's highlights and shadows
   d. A black-and-white scan of continuous pixels in an image

4. Before using a scanner, what else must you have installed?
   a. Scanner software
   b. Scanner drivers
   c. Photoshop
   d. A controller card

5. What is a moiré?
   a. A badly scanned image
   b. A pattern that is both distracting and unintended
   c. A collage of distracting patterns
   d. A mosaic image

SCANNING LINE ART

A scanner is also used to acquire *line art*, black-and-white images that may need to be traced or executed in Adobe Illustrator or another vector drawing program. Line art needs to be captured at a higher resolution than grayscale or color images. Typically, you need to scan it at 600 to 1200 dpi.

Cleaning Scans

If you scan a pencil sketch or any other line art, any stray mark becomes a smudge on the image. Figure 8-16 shows a frog relief taken from the book *African Designs from Traditional Sources*, one of the Dover copyright-free design series books. This is a fairly clean scan, but notice how jagged the edges are and how many spots of white exist inside the black areas. Also notice there are spots of black in the background.

You need to give this image a preliminary clean-up, regardless of whether you want to work with it in Photoshop or Illustrator. The easiest way to do this is by erasing the obvious flaws from the background, then selecting the background. Since you cannot use the Magic Wand tool on a bitmap image, you need to change the mode to grayscale but leave the ratio at 1:1. Set the Tolerance on the Magic Wand tool to 0 and uncheck the anti-alias box. The white spots in the frog (that you want to remove) are not selected when you select the background. Inverse the selection, then remove any white lines included by mistake. Fill the selection with black. Inverse the selection again and fill with white. You can then reconvert the image to bitmap using the 50% Threshold option and the same input and output resolutions.

This is enough cleaning to preserve the hand drawn look of the image (if it is hand drawn). However, if you need to place the image into a vector program, it will be very jagged and will contain a large number of control points—which is bad because it can cause a PostScript Limitcheck error in the imagesetter.

Figure 8-16
Frog scan in need
of clean-up

Try this trick described by Kai Krause in his famous Photoshop Tips postings on America Online. Once the image is in grayscale, add a Gaussian Blur to it. It may require a blur of 4 to 6 pixels to get enough gray shades. Open the Levels dialog and move the White and Black Input sliders towards the center. Do not adjust the Gamma point. You can slide the three triangles to the right or left, but keep the Gamma untouched. Find the point where the edges look the smoothest. Then click OK. Figure 8-17 shows the Levels set this way for a blurred version of the frog. Figure 8-18 shows the smoother frog.

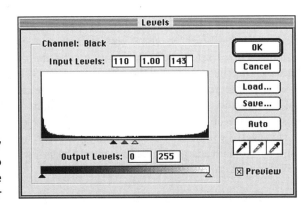

Figure 8-17
Frog Levels to
make the image
smoother

Figure 8-18
Smoothed frog

Autotracing

You can place your cleaned line art into Adobe Illustrator, or you can move it into a dedicated *autotrace* program such as Adobe Streamline. This enables you to prepare the image automatically to change it into vector format. You could also create Paths in Photoshop and export them to Adobe Illustrator, or you could create a Bézier point over each element of the scan in your vector drawing program.

1. What is line art?
   a. Images that need to be traced
   b. Images that are black and white
   c. Black-and-white images that have no fills
   d. Images created with the Pencil tool

2. Line art should be scanned in at higher resolutions than grayscale or color. What is the recommended resolution?
   a. 300 to 600 dpi
   b. 600 ppi
   c. 600 to 1000 ppi
   d. 600 to 1200 dpi

3. What can you do to minimize the jagged edges of an image you will be importing into Adobe Illustrator (and other vector programs)?
   a. Erase the obvious edges.
   b. Add the Gaussian Blur filter to the image.
   c. Use the Magic Wand tool to smooth out the edges.
   d. Put the image into Anti-aliased mode.

4. In order to use the Magic Wand on a bitmap image, what do you have to do with the image?
   a. Change the mode of the image to grayscale with a 1:1 ratio.
   b. Change the mode of the image to CMYK with a 2:1 ratio.
   c. Set the Tolerance level on the Magic Wand to 0.
   d. Set the Tolerance level on the Magic Wand between 3 and 10.

5. Adobe Streamline is what kind of application?
   a. Line duplication application
   b. Line art applet
   c. Autotrace program
   d. Sketching program

PHOTOCD

Another method of obtaining images that is becoming increasingly popular is the Kodak PhotoCD.

The PhotoCD is a technology developed by Kodak to store a large number of digital images, each in five or six different resolutions. It is a compact image storage format that allows you to place approximately 100 images on a single CD-ROM.

PhotoCD Technology

You can purchase a wide variety of stock images in PhotoCD format from many vendors. Image Club, a division of Adobe Corporation, carries many of these PhotoCDs. You can also take a roll of exposed film to a local camera store (or service bureau) and have the film returned on PhotoCD. The price is much less expensive *per image* if you have the film developed when the PhotoCD is created (but you end up paying for an entire CD-ROM when there may only be a few usable images on the roll). It is more expensive to get negatives copied to PhotoCD. Some establishments, however, charge the same amount for uncut negatives as they do for undeveloped film. The lowest price recently seen was $.24 per uncut negative. The price can easily reach over $3.00. There is a difference in quality in the various places that create PhotoCDs and to a certain extent, you do get what you pay for.

PhotoCDs are created by scanning images using a CCD scanner with a dynamic range of 2.7 (soon to be 3.3). The images are then written to a PhotoCD. Each image is stored so that, on the consumer level PhotoCD, you can acquire one of five different resolutions (in pixels):

- 192×128

- 384×256

- 768×512

- 1536×1024

- 3072×2048 (about 18MB)

There is also a professional level Kodak PhotoCD which has one higher resolution image (72MB).

About PhotoCDs

We have to thank Andrew Rodney for contributing this section to the chapter:

A PhotoCD scan is known as an *image pack*. This is because the actual file on the CD is really a package of possible final files and resolutions. The image pack must be *acquired,* which is accomplished by various software packages. The acquire process is one in which the user specifies the size or resolution desired, along with other possible parameters. The image pack can be acquired in one of five or six (for the Pro) possible resolutions, depending on the intended needs of the file. In other words, a PCD~Image pack can be acquired as a thumbnail-sized image or a high-resolution image as large as 18MB for the Master scan and 72MB for the Pro scan. Typically, when creating scans, the image resolution must be specified at the time of actual scanning. This limitation is not present with PhotoCD. Once an image pack is created and stored on the CD, the user can acquire it for various needs repeatedly simply by specifying the size required. This gives PhotoCD a great deal of flexibility. Since the image pack is a compressed proprietary file format that Kodak created, it's possible to store at least 100 to as many as 130 scans (image packs) on one Master PhotoCD disk. Due to the larger files possible with the Pro scans, the number of images that can be stored is less, perhaps 30. The sixth, larger image pack is optional (and a separate file), so it is possible to store more images from larger format originals on the Pro disks if needed.

Another limitation of conventional scans is that they should be optimized for a specific output. For example, nearly all color photos that have been reproduced in print during the last 20 years were actually scanned in order for the printer to create the plates necessary to print on a 4-color press. The original images are placed on a very expensive unit called a drum scanner. The image is digitized into what we commonly call a color separation. This term is accurate because in addition to digitizing the image, a file is created separating all the colors into cyan, magenta, yellow, and black. A color separation is nothing more than a scanned image digitized into these four separate colors after which four pieces of film are created to represent each color for the press. A scanned image for 4-color reproduction is usually a file in what's called a CYMK colorspace and is optimized for a specific press condition. This optimization is done at the time the original is scanned, and the size or resolution is set at this stage. If the original needs to be printed months later at say, twice the size, the camera original must be rescanned to that specific size. PhotoCD does not have this limitation because once it's scanned, it becomes an image pack that can be acquired in various sizes. Additionally, PhotoCD image packs are not stored as CYMK or RGB files because PhotoCD makes *no* assumptions about how the scans will be used. Therefore, the image pack is stored in a special format developed by Kodak called PhotoYCC. PhotoYCC is a device-independent colorspace much like CIE/LAB. Think of PhotoYCC and this image pack as a piece of digital clay. It can be shaped and molded via the acquire process to fit various needs now and in the future. Conventional scans are optimized for specific output needs. Therefore, while such a scan produces superb results to a 4-color press, the same file produces inferior output to a film recorder or digital printer. PhotoCD scans are optimized for no single output. During the acquire stage, the tools are presented to the user so this digital lump of clay can be optimized for the intended output needs. The image pack can be acquired any number of ways, any number of times, so that one scan can be used for virtually any output.

This flexibility is a great asset and advantage to PhotoCD scans. However, the quality of the output greatly depends on the skill and knowledge of the user acquiring the image pack! Many early users of PhotoCD saw poor results when they ultimately output the files. The reason was the method by which they acquired the files. Again, this process of acquiring the PhotoYCC data is critical! Think of a PhotoCD image pack as a roll of unlabeled film. Suppose you had to take a photograph and had no idea what kind of film was in your camera. Obviously, if you had different brands of film of different speeds, your results could vary. Imagine if the film could be black-and-white, or color, or even infrared. The image pack operates in the same way before acquiring. You could acquire an image pack from a color slide as a CYMK file, RGB file, or even a grayscale file, as well as many other choices. Therefore, it's important to understand that the image pack truly is a lump of digital clay waiting for you to properly acquire the file.

It's not in the scope of this section to discuss all the possible tools available to the user for performing the critical acquiring process. It is possible to acquire PhotoCD images so the final results are nothing short of superb. Kodak has several products enabling the user to acquire PhotoCD files. Most of these tools operate inside image editing programs such as Photoshop. Those of you already involved in digital imaging might wish to examine Kodak's Color Management System (KCMS) for acquiring files. This method produces excellent results using what's known as *Device Color Profiles*. A profile is used for each intended output and optimizes the PhotoYCC conversion to just the right file for a specified output device. This KCMS software is included in the Macintosh version of Photoshop. Kodak and DayStar Digital have jointly created a package called ColorMatch, which takes the KCMS several steps further by allowing the user to work with a calibrated monitor and use the KCMS on files other than PhotoCD. Know that the quality of a PhotoCD scan is excellent and the quality of your final output greatly depends on how the conversion of PhotoYCC to a specific file is accomplished.

One other factor to consider is the degree of sharpening you must apply to a PhotoCD scan before output. *All* scans require some degree of sharpening, and this is another item that should be optimized for a specific output device. Remember that PCD files are created with *no* intended output, so *no* sharpening is applied at the scan stage. Therefore, the user must apply some degree of sharpening to the file (and more on some types of files—such as those intended for newspapers—than others). Since most sharpening filters used in image processing applications are resolution dependent, the size and kind of output device dictates the different degrees of sharpening required. Again, Kodak has wisely avoided sharpening the image pack, giving you the flexibility to use the scan any number of ways.

Importing a PhotoCD Using Kodak's Acquire Module

There are three basic ways to open a PhotoCD image in Photoshop. You can use the Open command as you normally would. When you do this, you need to select the Photos folder, rather than the PhotoCD folder (these are the two folder/directories at the top level of the PhotoCD). This changes your PhotoCD image into a PICT file. However, it is not the recommended way to open a PhotoCD image. Figure 8-19 shows the Open dialog using the standard Photoshop Open command.

When you install Photoshop, there is a KCMS (Kodak Color Management System) application also installed onto your system. On the Mac, a number of Extensions are placed into the System folder with the intention that they run every time you use the computer. These load the routines needed to read data off the PhotoCD. You can use

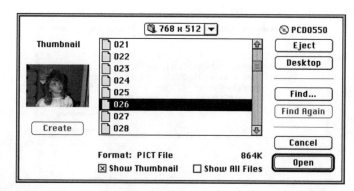

Figure 8-19
Standard
Photoshop Open
command

the Open command to access the *Precision Transforms* stored within the Acquire software. These Source and Destination transforms enable you to specify the type of film from which the PhotoCD was created and how you will use it.

Figure 8-20 shows the dialog appearing when you select the Open command and the PhotoCD folder with the KCMS enabled. You can select the Source of your image; Figure 8-21 shows this dialog. You can also select the destination of the image, as shown in Figure 8-22. This list of printers or targets allows the KCMS to translate the PhotoCD image into the color space and gamut of the desired destination. Finally, you can click on the Info button to see information about the specific image you wish to acquire. Figure 8-23 shows this feature.

The difference in quality between using the standard Open command and the KCMS-enhanced Open command is nothing short of astounding. The CD-ROM for this book contains two images, AlexOpen.Psd and AlexKCMS.Psd. Take a look at them to see the difference in quality. After you see the changes possible with the KCMS, you may never use any other method again unless it is to purchase the upgrade to the Kodak KCMS directly available from Kodak. That is the third method for acquiring a PhotoCD. It allows for more targets for the image, but it is an extra expense.

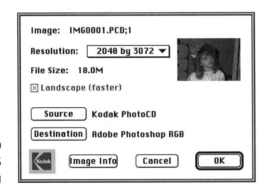

Figure 8-20
Photoshop KCMS
Open dialog

Figure 8-21
Selecting the Image
Source

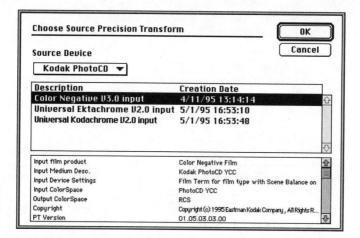

Figure 8-22
Selecting the Image
Destination

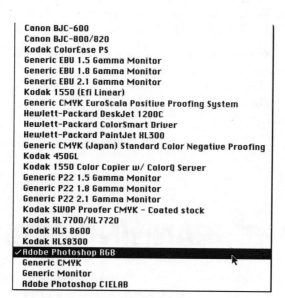

Figure 8-23
Image Info

1. What is a PhotoCD?
   a. A technology created by Kodak to store a large number of digital images
   b. A CD with photo images, similar to clip art CDs
   c. A compact image storage format
   d. A picture of a compact disc

2. What kind of scanner is used to scan photos?
   a. Flat-bed scanner
   b. CCD scanner
   c. Film scanner
   d. Hand-held scanner

3. Images are stored five times on a PhotoCD, each at a different resolution. What are these resolutions?
   a. 1536×1024
   b. 768×512
   c. 3072×2048
   d. 384×256

4. What is a color separation?
   a. CMYK color channel
   b. A scanned image digitized into four separate colors
   c. The boundary between two or more different color pixels
   d. A scanned image digitized into 4-color film layers

5. A PhotoCD scan is known as an image pack and is stored in a special format. What is the name of this special format?
   a. PhotoLab
   b. ColorLab
   c. PhotoCMYK
   d. PhotoYCC

SMART SCANNING SCRIPTS

One of the things many Photoshop users have requested is a batch image acquisition mode—the ability to scan and process a number of images at once. The other desired feature is a *smart* program that decides how to make the best use of each scan—to make it clean, crisp, and focused.

Some scanners have the ability to feed successive scans into an unattended scanner, especially if you are scanning slides. Transparency scanners can store up a group of slides for scanning all at once. The problem occurs when the conditions of the slides vary, making the scanner operator adjust white and black points and other corrective settings. Wouldn't it be nice if the scanner or a program could see the adjustments needed? There are several programs on the market which attempt to do just that. Each has its strengths and its weaknesses.

Intellihance: Add Image Captures

Intellihance, by Extensis Corporation, is a Photoshop plug-in that accepts a scanned image as input. You can use the automatic settings or fine-tune them in terms of desired contrast, brightness, saturation, sharpness, and despeckling. The plug-in appears on the Filters menu.

binuscan

An intelligent batch processing program external to Photoshop is binuscan. To make the best use of binuscan, you need to capture totally raw scans from the scanner with no corrections whatsoever. You then drag these images into a waiting folder where they are picked up and processed by binuscan. This is very useful across a network, since many people can place images into the folder and they are processed consistently.

binuscan is a very high-end correction program and requires you to calibrate both your scanner and the printer to the targets it provides. It is also quite expensive. However, in a large organization where speed and consistency are important, it quickly pays for itself. The only real problem with binuscan is it gets no improvement from the intelligence and features of the scanner itself as you are instructed to capture only totally raw scans.

Scan Prep Pro

Scan Prep Pro has a lot of interesting features. It is a Photoshop Acquire module that controls your scanner for you. If your scanner is among the list of supported scanners—and most medium- to high-range scanners are—Scan Prep Pro invokes your scanner driver so you get the best use from whatever capability and dynamic range your scanner possesses. You tell Scan Prep Pro about the condition of your image: Is it too light? Too dark? Too fuzzy? Previously screened? Figure 8-24 shows this dialog. As you can see, there are many options to set.

You can prepare your images for CMYK separations, for a film recorder, for the Internet, or for a specific printer. Once the image has been scanned, the program takes over. Based on the settings you give it, it invokes a series of Photoshop commands such as Levels, Color Balance, and more—too fast for you to watch what it is doing. It makes all these changes on a copy of the image so you do not lose your original.

Several features are especially worth noting: You can select the color correction tool of choice, and you have control over the color cast. Plus, it has a feature called *copy dot* that does a phenomenal job of preparing line art for output. In addition, it enables you to process an image that is already in your system—whether you created it previously or scanned it. This allows you to set up consistent processing steps, even for images you need to build first before you can separate them. It also contains a series of Separation Tables that may give you better results than the ones inside Photoshop.

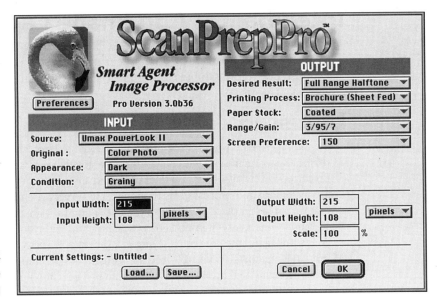

Figure 8-24
Scan Prep Pro
Acquire dialog

1. What are some of the programs that make image adjustments while scanning?
   a. Intelliscan
   b. Intellihance
   c. binuscan
   d. Scan Prep Pro

2. Which scanner program is a high-level program requiring you to recalibrate your scanner?
   a. Intelliscan
   b. Intellihance
   c. binuscan
   d. Scan Prep Pro

3. The Scan Prep Pro is a Photoshop Acquire module that can be used to scan images for
   a. CMYK separations.
   b. Internet.
   c. Film Recorder.
   d. Screen savers.

4. Which feature of Scan Prep Pro enables you to prepare line art?
   a. Draw.dot
   b. CopyLine
   c. Copy.dot
   d. ArtLine

5. Which scanner programs are Photoshop plug-ins that appear on the filters menu?
   a. Intelliscan
   b. Intellihance
   c. binuscan
   d. Scan Prep Pro

VIP PROFILE

Steve Roth, Author and Seminar Leader

Steve Roth is one of the co-founders of Thunder Lizard Productions—the company that puts on the Photoshop, QuarkXPress, PageMaker, and Illustrator conferences. He is co-author of *Real World Scanning and Halftones* and *Real World PostScript*, a contributing editor for *MacWorld*, and editor of *Real World Photoshop* published by Peachpit Press.

In the late '80s, Steve was the editor of *Personal Publishing* magazine and became involved with the then very new PostScript language. He helped write the seminal information on how halftoning works and how PostScript actually images things.

As part of his work for both *Personal Publishing* and the books he was writing, Steve got to evaluate a large number of scanners. With almost all of them, the only tonal correction possible was Brightness and Contrast. That was extremely frustrating as Brightness and Contrast corrections are simply not sufficient for producing decently corrected output.

DataCopy was a company that sold scanners, and their scanner came with a program called MacImage, which let you apply tonal *curves* to images. It was amazing how well images were improved by applying these curves.

Finally, Steve got in a Barneyscan with the Barneyscan XP software (the software, written by John and Thomas Knoll, that became Photoshop). He found the Levels command, played with it for five minutes, and saw Nirvana. It had the best interface he'd ever seen. Suddenly, mere mortals could make drastic improvements to almost unusable scans (there was almost no shadow detail from the early desktop scanners).

Steve became an evangelist for *non-linear correction* (Levels and Curves). Finally, there was a tool that produced usable images! After the advent of Photoshop, the changes became more evolutionary, rather than revolutionary. Since then, Photoshop has become much easier and more comprehensive. Steve has gone on to explore many more techniques for scanning and correcting images.

Steve is not a digital artist. He characterizes himself as a "workman-like publisher" who wants an easy way to take images and get them into publications in good-looking form without a lot of time and hassle.

He has several suggestions for new users of Photoshop:

● Don't use Brightness and Contrast to correct images (use Levels and Curves)

● WYGIWYG (What You Get Is What You Get)—you can't get more from the technology than it can offer

● Consider the incredible value to a customer to have a consultant or employee who knows the technical stuff cold. It is important that you can solve people's problems with graphics output for them, and clients are willing to pay a premium for people who can do this.

CHAPTER SUMMARY

We have covered a lot of ground in this chapter. You learned how to use the same features of Levels, Curves, Color Balance, and White, Black, and Gamma points that you met in Chapter 7 within a scanner dialog to acquire images. You learned how to use your scanner and how to calculate the scanning size, percentage, and resolution. You learned the basics of using Kodak's PhotoCD format. You also learned about some additional programs that can help improve the quality of your scans.

CHAPTER 9

ADVANCED SELECTION TECHNIQUES

I n Chapter 3, "Layers and Channels," you learned to make basic selections. These were mostly hard-edged selections—something was either selected or not selected. Photoshop is also capable of making partial selections. These are selections based on grayscale masks, so that if a filter were applied to the selection, its effect would be less in some places than others.

In this chapter you will learn how to

- Use the Path tool to make smooth selections.
- Create a selection based on colors in the image.
- Minimize color spill.
- Create a mask based on the image detail itself.
- Create selections that preserve hair and fuzz detail.

ADDITIONAL SELECTION METHODS

In Chapter 3 you learned how to use the three selection tools that are located in Photoshop's Toolbox—the Marquee, the Lasso, and the Magic Wand. You also learned how to save these selections to a layer or to a channel, and how to reload the Channel selection. You learned, as well, how to use the Quick Mask feature to paint selections. Two selection methods were not discussed—using the Path tool, and using the Color Range command (in the Select menu).

Path Tool

The Path tool lets you draw vector-like shapes inside of Photoshop. It uses the same Pen tool that is in Adobe Illustrator, and should be familiar to you if you have used an illustration program like Adobe Illustrator, Macromedia Freehand, or CorelDRAW!. The Path tool can draw both straight and curved shapes. These shapes (or paths) can be saved with the image and reused, and can also be dragged from image to image. They can be exchanged with Illustrator (either dragged-and-dropped, or copied and pasted). A saved path takes up much less room in a file than does an extra channel. However, a path makes a sharp-edged selection—it does not hold grayscale information as a channel can.

The advantage to drawing a path, in addition to the savings in file size, is that it lets you select something that may be otherwise unselectable. Even though the Lasso tool can draw a freehand selection, your hand may not be steady enough to make a smooth selection, and an errant click can lose a large amount of work. A path is infinitely modifiable, and can be very smooth.

Once you have created a path, you can change it into a selection, or stroke it to give color to the outline. One interesting difference between stroking a path and stroking a selection (using the Edit → Stroke command) is that you can stroke a path using any painting tool in the Toolbox. Let's take a closer look at the Paths palette and its functions.

Paths Palette and Paths Palette Menu

The tools to create paths are located on the Toolbar and they all pop out from the Pen tool (P). They include the Pen, Direct Selection, Add Anchor Point, Delete Anchor Point, and Convert Anchor Point tools. Figure 9-1 shows the Paths palette. There are two main sections to the Paths palette—the Paths list, and the Icon bar across the bottom.

Figure 9-1
Paths palette

The Icon bar is used to perform a variety of actions on the paths once they have been created. All of the commands on the Icon bar are also available on the Paths palette menu, shown in Figure 9-2. The Paths palette menu contains additional commands as well.

Toolbar

All of the tools that you need to use to manipulate paths are accessible from the Toolbox. If you click on the Pen tool, the other tools are revealed.

1. *Pen tool:* The Pen tool is used to create new points on the path.

2. *Direct Selection tool:* The Direct Selection (arrow) tool is used to move points on the path, edit the shape of the curve, or move the entire path. When you are using any of the path tools, you can press ⌘ (Mac) or CTRL (Windows) to get the Direct Selection tool. How do you remember this? Easy! The ⌘ (Mac) or CTRL (Windows) key helps you move objects. When one of the path tools is active, the Direct Selection tool is used to move things—and the same "helper" key works.

3. *Add Anchor Point tool:* This tool adds a new point along the path at the place where you click. On the Macintosh, you can access this tool while the Pen tool is in use by pressing CTRL (sorry, Windows users...there is no short-cut here) and clicking where you want a new point to be inserted. If you are editing a curve with the Direct Selection tool, you can add a new point by pressing ⌘+OPTION (Mac) or ALT+CTRL (Windows) and clicking some-where on the path.

4. *Delete Anchor Point tool:* This tool removes a point along the path when you click on an existing anchor point. You can access this tool while the Pen tool is in use by pressing CTRL on the Mac (no Windows shortcut here, either) and clicking on the anchor point that you want to remove. If you

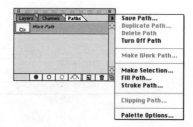

Figure 9-2
Paths palette menu

are editing a curve with the Direct Selection tool, you can remove an anchor point by pressing ⌘+OPTION (Mac) or ALT+CTRL (Windows) and clicking on the anchor point to be removed.

5. *Convert Anchor Point tool:* This tool lets you change the nature of the curve that you are creating. If you have drawn a smooth curve, you can make it a corner or line segment by clicking on the anchor point with the Convert Direction tool. If you click on the direction point rather than the anchor point, you can move the individual direction point by itself to create a sharp point. If you click on a line segment point with this tool and drag the mouse, you can make direction handles appear. The handles will show a smooth point. There is no key shortcut on Windows when you are using the Pen tool (the Mac shortcut is ⌘+CTRL). While you are using the Direct Selection tool, you can access this tool by pressing CTRL on *either* platform.

Command Watch

Here are some keystrokes for working with paths.

When the Pen tool is in use, you can do the following:

Action	Mac Key	Windows Key	By Clicking On
Add another anchor point	CTRL	N/A	Path
Remove anchor point	CTRL	N/A	Anchor point
Make corner point	CTRL+⌘	N/A	Anchor point
Make smooth point	CTRL+⌘	N/A	Anchor point
Move single-direction point	CTRL+⌘	N/A	Direction point
Smooth direction points	CTRL+⌘	N/A	Direction point
Move a point	⌘	CTRL	Anchor point
Move a direction point	⌘	CTRL	Direction point
Select additional points	⌘+SHIFT	CTRL+SHIFT	Anchor point
Select *all* points	⌘+OPTION	ALT+CTRL	Anywhere on path
Copy path	⌘+OPTION+drag	ALT+CTRL+drag	Anywhere on path

When the Arrow tool is in use, you can:

Action	Mac Key	Windows Key	By Clicking On
Add another anchor point	⌘+OPTION	ALT+CTRL	Path
Remove anchor point	⌘+OPTION	ALT+CTRL	Anchor point
Make corner point	CTRL	CTRL	Anchor point
Make smooth point	CTRL	CTRL	Anchor point
Move single-direction point	CTRL	CTRL	Direction point
Smooth direction points	CTRL	CTRL	Direction point
Select additional points	SHIFT	SHIFT	Anchor point
Select *all* points	OPTION	ALT	Anywhere on path
Copy path	OPTION+drag	ALT+drag	Anywhere on path

The Path List

The Path list area is used for selecting the path on which to work. Clicking on a path name makes the path active. When it is active, it can be modified, moved, selected, stroked, or filled. To hide all your paths, click on the area under all the path names. If you have a lot of paths, make sure there is always some blank space under them so you can easily hide them. The paths stay visible, regardless of which other palette (such as channels or Layers) is selected. You can also hide the paths by selecting the Turn Off Path option in the Paths palette menu.

The Icon Bar

You can use the Icon bar as a shortcut once you have drawn a path. The Icon bar actions vary, based on whether you click on the icon or drag a path onto the icon.

1. *Fill Path:* This fills the active path with the current foreground color if you click on it. If you drag a path onto it, it fills that path with the current foreground color, regardless of whether the path was selected when you began to drag. If you click on the icon with the modifier key pressed (Mac: OPTION, Windows: ALT), you will see a pop-up Options dialog (the same one that is available under the Fill Path option in the Paths palette menu).

2. *Stroke Path:* If you click on the Stroke Path icon with a painting tool selected, you will trace around the edge of the path with that painting tool (and whichever brush and painting characteristics are currently selected). If you click on the Stroke Path icon with no painting tool selected, you will stroke the path using whichever tool was last selected in the dialog of the Stroke Path command that is accessed via the Paths palette menu. Dragging a path onto the Stroke Path icon performs the same actions on that path even if it was not previously selected. If you click on the icon with the modifier key pressed (Mac: OPTION, Windows: ALT), you will see a pop-up

Options dialog (the same one that is available under the Stroke Path option in the Paths Palette menu).

3. *Path into Selection:* Clicking on the Path-to-Selection icon places the marching ants marquee around the currently active path. Dragging a single path onto the icon selects that path. Once you have a path selected, you can modify that selection by dragging additional paths onto the icon and pressing the modifier keystrokes listed in the Command Watch. These are the same keystrokes used to load a selection from the Channels palette. If you click on the icon with the modifier key pressed (Mac: OPTION, Windows: ALT), you will see a pop-up Options dialog (the same one that is available under the Make Selection option in the Paths Palette menu).

4. *Selection into Path:* Clicking on the Selection-to-Path icon creates a new path from the selected area. It uses the Tolerance last set up in the dialog in the Paths Palette menu. (*Tolerance* refers to how closely the Path "hugs" the actual pixels in the selection. A low number follows the pixels exactly—which can result in a jagged rendering and output problems. A high number conforms much more loosely to the selection and outputs better, but is much less accurate. The "correct" number is a compromise. It will also get larger as the number of pixels in your selection increases.) If you click on the icon with the modifier key pressed (Mac: OPTION, Windows: ALT), you will see a pop-up Options dialog (the same one that is available under the Make Path option in the Paths Palette menu).

5. *New Path:* If you have an active path labeled *Work Path*, clicking on this icon saves the path using the default name. If no path is active when you click on this icon, or your active path has already been saved, you start a new path with the default name. If you drag a saved path to the icon, you will duplicate it. If you drag a *Work Path* to the icon, you will save it under the default name. If you click on the icon with the modifier key pressed (Mac: OPTION, Windows: ALT), you will be able to give it a new name.

6. *Remove Path:* If you drag a path onto this icon, it removes it from the image. If you click on the icon, you are asked if you *really* want to delete it. If you click on the icon with the modifier key pressed (Mac: OPTION, Windows: ALT), the path is deleted without asking for confirmation.

Command Watch

To make selections from paths, press the following keys and drag the path in the Paths palette onto the Path-to-Selection icon at the bottom of the Paths palette.

Action	Mac Key	Windows Key
Select single path	Drag path	Drag path
Add path		`SHIFT`+drag path

The next two keystrokes bring up a Make Selection dialog set with the correct options:

Action	Mac Key	Windows Key
Subtract path	`OPTION`+drag path	`ALT`+drag path
Intersect path	`OPTION`+`SHIFT`+drag path	`ALT`+`SHIFT`+drag path

You can perform the same actions more easily by using the keys and clicking on the path names themselves in the Paths palette. The little cursors will guide you.

Action	Mac Key	Windows Key	You See
Select single path	`⌘`	`CTRL`	
Add path	`SHIFT`	`SHIFT`	
Subtract path	`OPTION`	`CTRL`	
Intersect path	`OPTION`+`SHIFT`	`ALT`+`SHIFT`	

Paths Palette Menu

Using the Icon bar is a quick way to perform most of the commands you need. However, choosing the commands from the Paths palette menu or the Icon bar by pressing `ALT` (Windows) or `OPTION` (Mac) usually gives you more control. Let's take a look at the specific commands.

1. *New Path:* This is the same as dragging a Work Path to the New Path icon, but you are given the opportunity to select the name of your choice.

2. *Duplicate Path:* This is the same as dragging a Saved Path to the New Path icon, but you can select a name for the path.

3. *Delete Path:* This removes the path from the document.

4. *Turn Off Path:* This is the same as clicking on whitespace below the paths in the Path list.

5. *Make Work Path:* This menu command is available only when you have a marching ants selection active. It lets you change a selection into a path. This is a good way to save a simple selection without the overhead of a channel. When you select this command, you see a dialog that asks for a Tolerance setting. The setting controls how tightly the path hugs the original selection. It also controls how many points are added to the path.

Although you might think that a tight Tolerance is better (small numbers=tighter Tolerance), that is not always the case. Figure 9-3(a) shows a shape with a path created at Tolerance of 1.0. The path is very awkward and looks jagged. Figure 9-3(b) shows that it *is* jagged when it is filled— probably not at all what you had in mind.

Figure 9-3(c) shows the same shape with a path created at 5.0 Tolerance setting. This makes a very nice, smooth shape. It does not, however, conform precisely to the original shape boundaries. If the path is in turn selected and filled, the darker areas are left over from the original shape and help show the degree to which the new selection fails to match the original. However, it is much better than the shape that was filled from a 1.0 Tolerance.

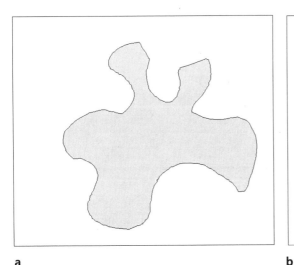

a

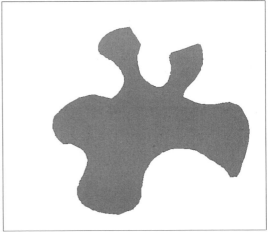

b

Figure 9-3
a) Path created at 1.0 Tolerance from selection
b) Filled selection made from path created at 1.0 Tolerance from selection
c) Path created at 5.0 Tolerance from selection

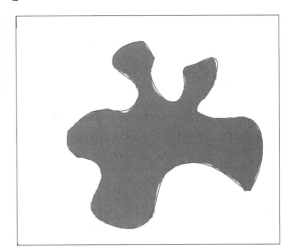

c

6. *Make Selection:* This command turns a path into a selection. It enables you to add, subtract from, or intersect with the current selection (in case you do not remember the key commands). In addition, you can specify a Feather for the selection and decide if the selection is to be anti-aliased. Figure 9-4 shows this dialog.

7. *Fill Subpath:* This is the same as selecting the Fill Path icon, but you have all of the choices shown in Figure 9-5.

8. *Stroke Subpath:* This command is the same as the Stroke Path icon, but it lets you specify the tool that you want to use rather than using whichever tool was last selected.

9. *Clipping Path:* You can specify that a path become a clipping path. If you then save the file as an EPS and list the same path as a clipping path, you can drop out everything outside of the clipping path when you place the image into a page layout program such as Adobe PageMaker or QuarkXPress. You will learn more about clipping paths in Chapter 15, "Photoshop Output."

10. *Palette Options:* This lets you choose the size of the thumbnail on the Paths palette.

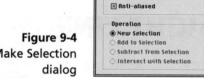

Figure 9-4
Make Selection
dialog

Figure 9-5
Fill Path dialog

Drawing Paths

If you have used an illustration program, the process of drawing paths will be easy for you. If you have not, it may take a bit of time for you to become comfortable with the Pen tool. The Pen tool draws either straight lines or Bézier curves. A *Bézier curve* is a mathematical construct. In practical terms, it is a way of drawing a curve so that you can control the shape of the curve very precisely. You do this by placing an anchor point and then shaping the curve with the two direction points that seesaw out from the anchor point. Figure 9-6 shows the anatomy of a Bézier curve.

An *anchor point* is the actual point that is placed by the Pen tool.

Direction points are the control points at the opposite ends of the direction line that goes through the center of the anchor point. The direction points can be altered individually on each side of the curve to change the distances traveled by the curve; however, they will always remain smooth (like a seesaw, when one direction point moves up, the other angles down). The only way to make the line between the direction points bend is to change the point from a smooth point to a corner point.

A *segment* is the area of the path between two anchor points. It can be straight or curved.

So, how do you draw a path? You need to lay down a series of clicks and drags. Let's start with a very easy example—a rectangular object. In order to draw a path around this object, all you need to do is click.

DRAWING STRAIGHT LINE SEGMENTS

1. Open the image Rectangl.Psd.

2. Select the Pen tool (P).

3. Click once on the top-left corner of the shape. Figure 9-7 shows a paint-by-numbers (or click-by-numbers) view of the object.

Figure 9-6
Anatomy of a
Bézier curve

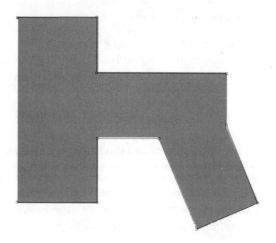

Figure 9-7
A straight line path

4. Simply continue to click at the numbers in order until you finish number 11. Point 12 is the same as Point 1. When you place your cursor directly over Point 1, you will see a tiny loop appear on the pen cursor. This signifies that you are over the starting point and are about to make a closed shape. When you see the loop, click to close the shape.

5. Magnify the shape so that you are looking at it in 2:1 view. Click on the Arrow tool. Move any points that were not placed precisely right by clicking on them and dragging them to a better location.

6. When you are happy with the path, drag the path entry in the Paths palette down to the New Path icon on the Paths palette.

This is fairly easy. If you had pressed [SHIFT] as you clicked on horizontal and vertical lines, you could have constrained the lines to be straight (45, 90, or 180 degrees).

It is a bit trickier to draw curved lines. When you draw a curve, you need to click to set an anchor point, continue to hold the mouse button down, and then drag in the direction in which you are going. That sets the direction points (and that is how they got their name). In the next Hands On, you will be guided in every stroke that you make.

HANDS ON

BÉZIER CURVES

1. Open the image Eight.Psd. You will see a figure 8 that is created from anchor points with all of their direction points showing. You will never see a path look like this. This image was specially built for you.

2. Select the Pen tool (P).

3. Click on the first point (the one where the straight arrow is pointing). Figure 9-8 shows you this image. Hold down the mouse button as you click, and drag the direction point that appears until it lays on top of the direction point in the example file.

4. Move in the direction of the curved arrow by letting go of the mouse button, and clicking/holding/dragging on the next point. Drag until the direction points lie on top of the ones in the image. When the direction points are in the same place, the curve that occurs is the same.

5. Finish the image by clicking/holding/dragging on each anchor point in turn. Close the shape at the top and drag until the lower direction point on this last point lies on top of the one in the image.

6. If needed, select the Direct Selection tool (Mac: ⌘, Windows: CTRL) and reshape the curve. If you were close as you drew, you should not need to do much editing.

This is the process of creating a curved Bézier path. You can draw your paths "fast and sloppy" and edit them after the points have been placed, or you can set each point precisely and shape it using the key commands shown in the Command Watch above. Either way gives you the same results.

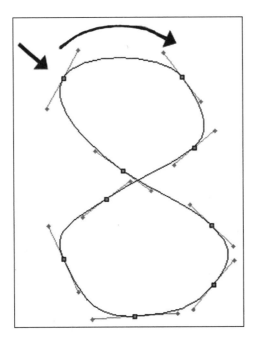

Figure 9-8
Figure 8 shape
for trying out
Bézier curves

Select → Color Range

Using the Color Range command is very similar to using the Magic Wand to choose a color range and then selecting the Similar command from the Select menu. However, pixels selected with the Magic Wand are always fully selected (except at the anti-aliased edges). Pixels selected using the Color Range command need not be fully selected. You can tell this if you save a selection to a channel. The Magic Wand selection is white on a black background with sharply defined edges (assuming no feathering or anti-aliasing). The Color Range selection, depending upon the fuzziness setting, forms a grayscale image. Fuzziness is somewhat like Tolerance, but it smoothes the selection and partially selects additional pixels, based on how near the pixel is in color/value to the ones in the "non-fuzzy" selection.

Fully versus Partially Selected Selections

When you drag a Marquee around an object, select it with the Magic Wand tool, or select it using the Color Range command, each pixel in the object can be fully or partially selected. A fully selected pixel participates in whatever is done to it 100%. If it is moved, every speck of color in the pixel goes along. If it is filtered, the pixel receives the full effect of the filter.

The Marquee, the Lasso, and the Magic Wand tools always fully select the pixels, unless the pixel is part of a feathered edge (softened for blending with the Feather command, a feather on the tool, or anti-aliasing). The Color Range command only partially selects the pixels that are near to the color clicked upon.

A fully selected pixel shows up as white in a saved Alpha channel. A partially selected pixel is a shade of gray.

Figure 9-9(a) shows the original image. This is an image of trees shot against a blue California sky. In Figure 9-9(b), the Color Range dialog is open and shows a selection made by dragging the Eyedropper+ tool across the top part of the sky. The Fuzziness is 0, and you can see exactly which pixels were selected. Figure 9-9(c) shows the same selection with a Fuzziness of 126. At this point, all of the sky is at least partially selected. Figure 9-9(d) shows the selection at a Fuzziness of 200. This selection is enough that if you were to use the Color Balance command on this image, you would slightly shift the color balance of the trees as well as the sky and introduce a completely new color cast to the image. (The Color Balance command lets you alter the relationship between complementary colors in an image.) Try this Hands On.

Figure 9-9
a) Original image of the tree and flower shot against blue sky
b) Color Range command, Fuzziness = 0
c) Color Range command, Fuzziness = 126
d) Channel created from the Color Range command, Fuzziness = 200

a

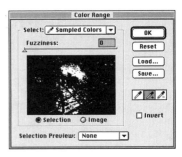

b

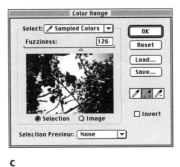

c

d

HANDS ON

COLOR BALANCE

1. Open the image TreeSky.Psd. Duplicate the image (Image → Duplicate → OK).

2. Three channels have been created and labeled for you. Load Channel 4 (Mac: OPTION+⌘+4, Windows: ALT+CTRL+4). This channel contains the selection created with the Fuzziness of 0.

3. Hide the marching ants (Mac: ⌘+H, Windows: CTRL+H).

4. Open the Adjust Color Balance dialog (Image → Adjust → Color Balance). Press the Midtones radio button at the bottom of the screen, and drag the Yellow/Blue slider all the way to the right (toward blue) so that it reads +100. This makes the blue in the image much more pronounced. Click OK. The image now has pixels of deeper blue in it where the selection existed. This is not a satisfactory look. The pixels are too scattered and hard-edged.

5. Click on the original image and duplicate it (Image → Duplicate → OK).

6. Load Channel 5 (Mac: OPTION+⌘+5, Windows: ALT+CTRL+5). This selection is the same as the previous one but has the Fuzziness raised to 126. Repeat Steps 3 and 4 to add more blue to this image. This time, the color changes softly throughout the affected area. This is a good use of the soft-selection capability of the Color Range command.

7. Repeat Steps 5 and 6, using Channel 6 as the channel to load. This selection, made with the Fuzziness at 200, really allows a blue cast to develop in the image. Although you cannot see much difference using blue, try this again and add magenta (-100 on the slider) to the image instead. It makes the image look as if it were shot at twilight, and the trees and leaves take on the same subtle coloring.

Now that you have seen how an image can be altered from a Color Range selection, let's discuss how you go about creating one.

The Color Range command is accessed via the Select menu. If you look at Figure 9-10, which shows the image of the ram that Photoshop needs so much (sorry about that one!), you see that there are three Eyedropper tools. The plain Eyedropper selects all pixels that are the same color as the one on which you click. You can use the Eyedropper+ tool (or press SHIFT) to add more colors to the selection range. The Eyedropper– tool removes colors from the selection. You can also press OPTION (Mac) or ALT (Windows) to access this if you are using the plain Eyedropper.

You have a wide selection of options for viewing your selection-in-process as well. You can look at the selection in the dialog (Selection radio button) or at the image itself

Figure 9-10
The Color Range
dialog

(Image radio button). The Selection Preview menu controls how the original image looks while you are in the Color Range dialog. You can see the image unaltered (None), which lets you select colors on the image and see the mask in the dialog (if you combine this with the Selection button). You may also see the original image as a grayscale (white selected and black not), against a white or black matte (the color of the unselected areas), or as a Quick Mask (with whichever color you selected as a rubylith). Actually, these are too many options—viewing your original image with no preview and the Selection in the dialog usually works just fine!

Of much more value is the ability to use a variety of *automatic* selections. Figure 9-11 shows you the What to Select menu in the dialog. While the most common option is to select whichever colors you sample from your image, you can also automatically select each of the color components individually: the Highlights, Midtones, or Shadow areas, or the Out-of-Gamut colors (the colors that are not printable in the normal 4-color printing process).

In order to make a selection, you drag the Eyedropper (usually the plain one with (SHIFT) pressed) across the range of colors you want to select. Add color areas slowly and watch the mask build up on the screen. When you are satisfied that you have selected the area that you want, click OK. This converts the mask that you created into a selection—it can then be used and discarded, changed into a Quick Mask, or saved into a channel. If you want to save file space, you could also use the Save... button in the Color Range dialog to save the selection as a special Selection image and then load it into the dialog when you want to use it. This is also handy if you have several versions of the same image and need to select the same portion of the image multiple times.

1. What does the Direct Selection tool enable you to do?
   a. Create new points on the path
   b. Move points on the path, edit shape of a curve, or move entire path
   c. Add a new point along the path
   d. Change the nature of a curve

Figure 9-11
Selection menu in
the Color Range
dialog

2. What do Palette Options allow for?
   a. Specify the tool to be used
   b. Turn a path into a selection
   c. Specify that a path become a clipping path
   d. Choose the size of the thumbnail of the Paths palette

3. What is a Bézier curve?
   a. A curve based on two outside anchor points and one mobile inner point
   b. A single anchor point with two direction points that seesaw out
   c. An immobile curve—the shape cannot be changed
   d. A four-point curve with two stationary and two mobile points

4. What is true of a fully selected pixel?
   a. Shows up as white in a saved Alpha channel
   b. Shows up as black in a saved Alpha channel
   c. Is controlled by the Color Range command
   d. Participates at % effectiveness of the command applied to it

5. The Color command allows for what feature?
   a. Switch between color extremes in an image
   b. Balance red, blue, and green channels
   c. Switch between black and white in an image
   d. Alter complementary colors in an image

LESSON 2

DIFFICULT SELECTION PROBLEMS

One of the most common—and most difficult—image editing tasks is to create an image silhouette (or *silo* for short). This involves extracting a person, animal, or object from its background and placing it onto a new background. There are a few potential problem areas:

● Making the outline selection to separate image from background

● Getting a smooth edge

● Making the silo blend seamlessly into its new background

● Repairing color spill on the detail edges

● Preserving fine edge details like hair, fur, and fuzz

In Chapter 3 and in the earlier portions of this chapter, you learned ways to create selections to separate an image from its background. You can build a selection using any combination of the Marquee, Lasso, and Magic Wand tools. You can use the Color Range command or build paths around an object. Once you have the selection, you can save it as a channel or a Quick Mask. You can also use the Layer Options "Blend If" sliders to composite one image onto another. This is really a quite impressive array of options, but it is not yet enough. You need to know how to use an image to create its own mask. The rest of this chapter will be devoted to learning how to

- Determine the characteristics of the mask edge that you want

- Remove any color spill

- Create a self-mask

- Restore fine edge detail to the image composite

Anti-Aliasing and Edges

In several of the previous chapters, you were introduced to the concept of anti-aliasing. This is the creation of pixels along the edge of an object that changes the color at the edge from the object color to the background color over a distance of about 3–5 pixels. This is done to soften the edge—the place where the colors meet and mix then fools the eye into thinking that the object belonged there originally. When the anti-aliasing is stretched out over a distance longer than 3–5 pixels, it is called *feathering*—and must be specifically set/requested by the user via the Select → Feather command (or, if you like to live dangerously, in the Marquee or Lasso tools—but don't live *this* dangerously!).

Both anti-aliasing and feathering are techniques to make the edges look smooth and not jagged. However, both techniques break down when there is a major difference in the color of an original background and the color of a background onto which you want to place a new object. When you move an object from its original background, you tend to pick up edges that are diluted with the color of the background. This is called *color spill*. When you take these diluted edges with you to a new background, it quickly becomes obvious that the object does not belong. These edges, if permitted to remain, are the sign of either a too-hasty composite, or a person who is not experienced enough with Photoshop. In either case, the edges generally also cause a very unhappy client. The edges are not always easy to remove—even for an experienced Photoshop user—but you must do something to get rid of them.

Your basic options are to

- Defringe

- Choke (contract) the selection to eliminate the edge area

- Neutralize the color spill

Defringing

The Defringe command is located on the Layer menu under the Matting submenu. It is listed with two other commands—Remove White Matte and Remove Black Matte. Of the three commands, only Defringe has a chance of doing something useful (the other two commands generally cause a major mess). Defringe lets you replace edge pixels of a range of your choice (1–64 pixels) with color from the inside portion of the image. This can be quite useful—but not always.

If the object you are moving is fairly solid and has low edge detail, but contains a decided color spill, Defringe does a wonderful job of removing the color spill. However, if the image has a lot of edge detail, Defringe does a very good job of removing that as well. Defringe works on either a floating selection or on an entire layer (not the Background layer). The selection can be feathered or not. Sometimes the results will be less drastic on a feathered edge. Figure 9-12 shows the Defringe command dialog. You will have an opportunity in the Lab section in Appendix C, "Labs," to make your own decisions regarding the usefulness of this command.

Choking the Selection

Choking is a term borrowed from the prepress process called *trapping*. Images are trapped to keep white paper from showing through if the image's printing plates misregister or misalign a little bit. To choke an object means to contract (or make smaller) the edges of that object. This can help to remove the color spill by selecting less of the edge area of the image. Predictably, since this is Photoshop, there are many ways to do this. Here are three of these ways.

Modify the Selection Boundary

Once you have a selection Marquee around your desired object (created from any of the various ways you have learned), you can contract that selection by a pixel or more. This lets you shrink the selection Marquee so it moves away from the original borders and closer to the center of the selection by however many pixels you select. Figure 9-13 shows an object (the light blob) whose original boundary was first selected and the Marquee contracted by 8 pixels.

Figure 9-12
Defringe dialog

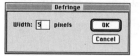

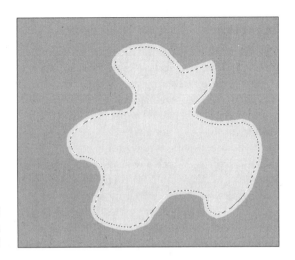

Figure 9-13
Selection
contracted

You can see the new set of marching ants inside the original shape. You can modify the selection borders using the Select → Modify submenu. Figure 9-14 shows this submenu, which enables you to expand, smooth, or border the selection as well. If the selection had a feathered edge originally, it will retain that feathered edge after the selection has been contracted.

Minimize the Selection Border

Photoshop also contains a filter that enables you to choke in a channel (the filter works anywhere, but using for the purpose of choking a selection works best within an Alpha channel). If you have saved your selection as a new channel, you may use this method of making the selection smaller. The filter is the Minimize filter (Filter → Other → Minimum). It looks at the pixels in the channel and asks you to type in the number of pixels to minimize. The Minimum filter selects the darker of the pixels for the distance that you specify. Figure 9-15 shows the same blob as Figure 9-13. The middle gray "border" area shows the area cut off in the channel by the Minimum filter (the light area is what is left). This method tends to leave a jagged edge area if the channel was not feathered. If the selection in the channel had a soft edge, it will keep the soft edge, but there may be some artificial corner/points created in the selection when the filter has finished.

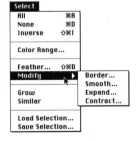

Figure 9-14
Select → Modify
submenu

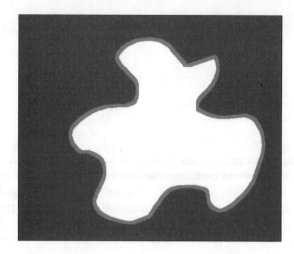

Figure 9-15
Selection
Minimized (Filter →
Other → Minimum)

Levels Choked Selection

The final method of choking the selection is to use the Levels command on a channel. This gives you very fine control over the amount by which you can shrink the selection. The principle behind this method is to get some edge blurring into the channel and then selectively move the blurred edges toward white or black. Since this method is much less "automated" than the others, a Hands On demonstration is in order.

CHOKING USING LEVELS

1. Open the image Blob.Psd. This is the same blob image that has been used in previous examples.

2. Apply a Gaussian Blur to the image (Filter → Blur → Gaussian Blur, 2). The amount of the blur should be fairly small—just enough to add a bit of gray levels to the image.

3. Open the Levels dialog (Mac: ⌘+L, Windows: CTRL+L). Figure 9-16 shows the levels for the blurred blob. Notice the typical pattern in the Histogram—high white and black with a sharp drop-off of numbers of pixels as you reach the midtones.

Figure 9-16
Levels for
blurred blob

4. If you drag the Black Input slider toward the right, you will decrease the size of the white blob. You can control the amount of the choke by the amount that you drag the Black slider. Figure 9-17 shows the Levels sliders with the three Input sliders positioned at the right of the image. Drag the Black Input slider so that your screen matches this example. Figure 9-18 shows in middle gray the area that was removed from the selection.

The Levels method of choking almost always retains the soft edge (the only way to remove it is to drag the three sliders on top of one another at the right side of the image). This is the preferred way of choking a selection, though the other methods are fine in fairly simple situations.

Figure 9-17
Levels for
choked blob

Figure 9-18
Choked blob
superimposed over
original (medium
gray area is
removed)

The sky in this image by Ed Scott is a bit too cloudy.

You can take a synthetic sky...

...and replace the original. (Chapter 2 Lab—Making Selections)

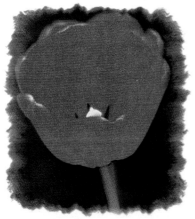

You can remove an image from its background...

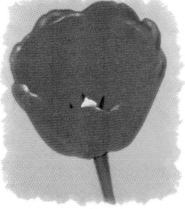

...and salvage the edge detail in a simple image. (Chapter 9—Advanced Selection Techniques)

You can also replace a plain background...

...with a fancier one. (Chapter 3—Layers and Channels)

You can take a much harder-to-select image by Ed Scott...

...and still preserve fine details like wisps of hair. (Chapter 9—Advanced Techniques)

You can create your own brushes from photographs. (Chapter 5—Working with Paint and Text Tools)

You can create images with wonderful variations in texture. (Chapter 4—Filters)

You can airbrush simple forms... (Chapter 5—Working with Paint and Text Tools)

...or much more complex ones. (Chapter 5 Lab—Working with Paint and Text Tools)

This original photograph by Ed Scott is too yellow.

It can be neutralized. (Chapter 7—Color Correction)

This room is much too blue...

...but it can be corrected... (Chapter 7—Color Correction)

...or made much more wild. (Chapter 7 Lab—Color Correction)

The atmosphere in this image by Ed Scott is a bit too blue.

It can be made warmer and more yellow. (Chapter 7—Color Correction)

COLOR EFFECTS

This fairly dull marina can be made exciting when combined in Difference Mode. (Chapter 3 Lab—Layers and Channels)

This photo of artist Eric Reinfeld's niece and nephew...

...can very easily become a 4-color CMYK quadtone. (Chapter 12— Spot Color)

This photo by Ed Scott of a tomb in Beijing ...

This detail photograph of a Foo lion (taken by Ed Scott)...

...can be prepared as a three-color spot printing job. (Chapter 12—Spot Color)

...can be given a wild new color look. (Chapter 3—Layers and Channels)

Through the magic of Photoshop, a Buffalo hotel...

...and a garden in Singapore (photo by Kiran Desai)...

...can be combined. (Chapter 3—Layers and Channels)

This damaged photo from the author's attic can be repaired and sepiatoned. (Chapter 10—Photo Retouching)

This petroglyph, photographed by Ed Scott,...

Ed Scott's photo of a girl in northern Thailand...

...is given a soft oval vignette. (Chapter 2—Making Selections)

...can be stylized and re-colored. (Chapter 3—Layers and Channels)

COLLAGE

A koala...

a bear...

and a parrot...

under an umbrella...

near a bamboo grove...

into a real zoo! (Chapter 11—Photo Montage)

can turn a lovely patio...

Line art can also be filtered through a Quick Mask. (Chapter 2 Lab—Making Selections)

This crab from the Ultimate Symbol Collection becomes a watercolor. (Chapter 4 Lab—Filters)

You can take an ordinary photograph and make it into a stylized woodcut. (Chapter 4 Lab—Filters)

Halloween can be scary even without using the Find Edges filter. (Chapter 4 Lab—Filters)

Line art can be stamped like a cookie cutter to pick up filtered fabric. (Chapter 2 Lab—Making Selections)

A flower arrangement is embossed and enhanced with multiple filters. (Chapter 4 Lab—Filters)

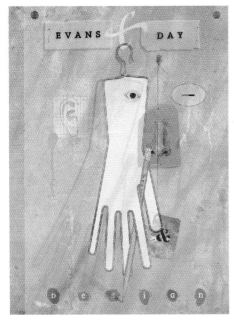

Artwork by graphic designer Rob Day
for Evans Day Design

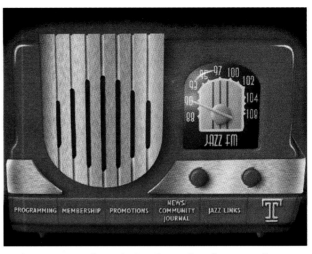

Web page interface design by artist/photographer
Steve Pollock

Self-promo piece by artist Eric Reinfeld

Web page by illustrator Rob Howard

Neutralize the Color Spill

If defringing your selection does more harm than good, and choking the selection still does not get rid of enough edge detail to help, then you must take the next step of trying to neutralize the color spill. Once again, there are several techniques that you can use. The example is an image of a tulip which is to be placed onto a new background. The four techniques that you will learn all start with an already created mask. You will learn how to build this self-mask in the last section of this chapter.

Fill with Background Image

One way to eliminate color spill is to fill the edges of an object with the background on which you will place the object. This pre-compositing step replaces the semi-transparent edge area with pixels of the correct color. The only disadvantage to this technique is that you really need to know where you are going to place the image before you can get rid of the color spill. Since the replacement color is as fixed as the original color, you cannot easily change your mind.

Let's try this method.

REPLACING COLOR SPILL WITH THE BACKGROUND IMAGE

1. Open the image Tulip.Psd.

2. Load Channel 4 (Mac: OPTION+⌘+4, Windows: ALT+CTRL+4). This is the channel called "Image Mask." Float the selection (Mac: ⌘+J, Windows: CTRL+J).

3. Create a new document (Mac: ⌘+N, Windows: CTRL+N). To make it the correct size, select the Tulip document in the Windows menu.

4. Set your foreground color to RGB 255,201,48. This is an egg yolk yellow. Fill the new document with the foreground color (Mac: OPTION+DELETE, Windows: ALT+DELETE).

5. Click on the original Tulip image. Press SHIFT and drag the Floating Selection from the Layers palette into the new image. Figure 9-19 shows this image. Notice the dark line around the tulip. That is where the original selection picked up the color spill.

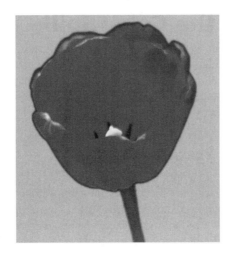

Figure 9-19
Color spill around
the edge of the
tulip

6. Select the Layer pixels (Select → All → press an arrow key once, then back, and then press ⌘+E for the Mac or CTRL+E for Windows). This selects every pixel on the layer that is not 100% transparent.

7. Create a border selection of 15 pixels (Select → Modify → Border, 15). This border area is wide enough to include all of the color spill area. You may need to experiment a few times with this number when you use your own examples. Always Undo the border command before reselecting a border amount or the program becomes very confused.

8. Feather this border area by 2 or 3 pixels (Select → Feather, 2).

9. Press Q to turn on the Quick Mask and look at the selection. If you cannot see the Quick Mask because both it and the tulip are red, double-click on the Quick Mask entry in the Channels palette and change the mask color to blue.

10. The one area that needs to be cleaned up is at the bottom of the tulip stem. The Quick Mask has the inner edge of the stem included in the border. It needs to remain as it was originally. Use a bit of black paint to remove it from the selection. When you are satisfied, press Q again to return to the normal selection mode.

11. Fill the selection (Mac: OPTION+DELETE, Windows: ALT+DELETE) with the foreground color (which is the background color of the image). Figure 9-20 shows the image after this step. The image that has been filled with the background color is slightly smaller than the original tulip. This is because the spill area has been made the same color as the background. If the background is not solid, you can fill it with the image in one of several ways.

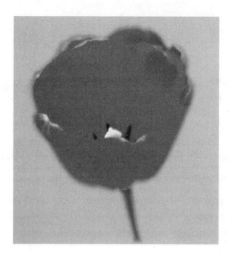

Figure 9-20
Color spill removed

● You can take a snapshot of the background with the Object Layer turned off. You can then use the Edit → Fill command and fill from Snapshot.

● You can duplicate the Background Layer as Layer 1 and save the image before you drag the new object (the tulip) into it. You can then select the top Layer and delete the image from it. When you drag the new object, Merge Down (Mac: ⌘+E, Windows, CTRL+E) so that it occupies the empty Layer. Prepare the border selection as you did in the Hands On and fill the border from Saved (Edit → Fill, from Saved).

Either of these two fill techniques works well. The Fill from Saved requires less RAM, however. You can also experiment with a variety of Fill modes (Normal, Lighten, Darken, Color, Overlay) to see which one works best.

Paint on Preserve Transparency

If you feel that object has gotten too small when you remove the color spill, you may prefer to paint back the edge area of the image. This technique, and the one that follows, can do just that.

When the Preserve Transparency button is enabled for a Layer, the pixels can be altered in color, but they cannot be removed or added to. The practical value of this is that it always lets you "paint within the lines." Areas that should not be filled *cannot* be filled. Therefore, if you create a border selection as you did previously, and place the selection into its own Layer, you can turn on Preserve Transparency and simply paint over the nontransparent pixels, using the Rubber Stamp tool. This puts the colors that *you* want at the edges of the object. The disadvantage of this technique is that if these edge pixels are semi-transparent (as they should be), they may not cover the edges of the object. You might need to delete the object border area first.

PAINTING ON TRANSPARENCY

1. Open the Tulip.Psd image if it is not already open. Repeat Steps 1–8 in the Replacing Color Spill example. Duplicate the image (Image → Duplicate → OK). The final exercise also picks up from this point, so it is easier to make a spare copy than it is to redo all of the steps.

2. Now that you have your border selection, float and cut the selection to a new Layer (Mac: ⌘+OPTION+J, Windows: ALT+CTRL+J). This removes the selection from the object and makes it a new Layer.

3. Turn on the Preserve Transparency button above the Layer names area of the Layers palette.

4. In this image, use the Paintbrush and pick up colors from the edge of the tulip. Paint the edges of the tulip border selection the same color as the inner, uncontaminated areas of the tulip. (In other images, you might prefer to use the Rubber Stamp tool to replace the color at the edges of the object.)

5. Drag the Layer that contains the painted edges below the original object and see if you prefer the way it looks there.

6. You may also want to uncheck the Preserve Transparency button and add a small Gaussian Blur (1 or 2 pixels—or more if the image is a larger size) to the Edges Layer. This can help to soften the transition. You can constrain the blur to the inner part of the tulip edges in this example by clicking on the transparent background outside of the tulip with the Magic Wand. Inverse the selection. When you apply the blur, it will blur more on the inner edge than the outer one.

Paint Through an Edge Mask

The technique of painting through a mask that only lets you recreate the edges is very similar to the Paint-On-Transparency technique. However, it can also be used to recreate extremely fine edge detail. Peter Fink teaches this technique in his courses, and also describes it in his excellent 1995 book, *Photoshop Knocks Their Socks Off*.

This technique lets you isolate the contaminated edges in the image. The portion of the image that is not contaminated is moved to a new location. You can then paint back in the detail around the edges by creating a mask/selection that only contains the edges. Since this is easier to show than to explain, try this Hands On.

SIMPLE EDGE MASK

Open the image Tulip.Psd.

1. Drag the Image Mask channel (Channel 4) to the New Channel icon at the bottom center of the Channels palette. This duplicates the channel. (The Image Mask is the channel that created your original selection.)

2. Apply a Gaussian Blur of 3.0 to the duplicated channel to give it enough gray pixels to create a Choke Mask (Filter → Blur → Gaussian Blur, 3).

3. Click on the Eye icon next to the RGB channel and turn it on so that you can see the channel as you create the Choke Mask. (The Image Mask copy channel is still the active channel.)

4. Open the Levels dialog (Mac: ⌘+L, Windows: CTRL+L). Drag the Black Input slider to the right so that the mask shrinks smaller than the tulip and you can see edges of the tulip from behind the mask. Click OK.

5. Double-click on the name of the Image Mask copy in the Channels palette and change the name to Choke Mask.

6. This is the mask that you use to move the tulip into its new file. Load the Choke Mask channel (Mac: OPTION+⌘+5, Windows: ALT+CTRL+5). Float the selection (Mac: ⌘+J, Windows: CTRL+J).

7. Create a new document (Mac: ⌘+N, Windows: CTRL+N). Set your foreground color to RGB 255,201,48. Fill the new document with the foreground color (Mac: OPTION+DELETE, Windows: ALT+DELETE).

8. Click on the original tulip image. SHIFT+drag the new layer from the Layers palette into the new image. This time, there is no color spill.

9. It is now time to build the Edge Mask. Click on the tulip image—which is where your other two channels are located. Open the Calculations dialog (Image → Calculations). Figure 9-21 shows this dialog and the correct responses. You are going to Multiply the Choke Mask and the Image Mask to create an Edge Mask. Just as in *real* multiplication, it does not matter which one comes first. However, the smaller channel (the Choke Mask) needs to be inverted (the check box) so that it knocks out all of the inside of the tulip (leaves an area of black). This leaves the edge of the tulip the only selected area in the channel. This selection is placed in a new channel. Click OK and change the new channel name to Edge Mask.

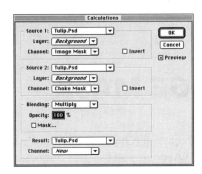

Figure 9-21
Calculations dialog
to create Edge
Mask

10. Apply a 1-pixel Gaussian Blur to the channel. This helps to blend the edges a little bit better as your selection goes over the original.

11. Click on the new image that contains the moved tulip. Load the Edge Mask selection into the tulip Layer. Figure 9-22 shows the Load Selection dialog for this (since the selection is coming from another file). You need to load the Edge Mask from the Tulip.Psd image.

12. Once you have the mask loaded, you can paint the colors from the edge of the tulip back into the mask, or you can use the Rubber Stamp tool.

What is especially good about this technique is that you are adding edge detail to the Layer so that the object itself is complete and uncontaminated by any background color. Since the object is on a Layer, you can move it and recomposite it with any other background—thus avoiding the "locked-in-place" syndrome that the first color spill removal method produced. Also, since the Edge Mask was not totally white, there is some transparency that will help blend the object with any eventual background.

Use a Layer Mask

The final method of removing color spill is not automated at all. It has the advantage of always working, though it is more time-consuming than the more automated methods that can be used. However, sometimes the image will just not cooperate, and nothing seems to produce a satisfactory mask for it. Other times, you may have a mask that does 99% of the job and you just hate one corner of the image because it retains a tiny bit of color spill. In these situations, it is just as easy to add a Layer Mask to the image and gently remove the color spill pixels with delicate brushwork.

Figure 9-22
Load Selection
dialog

In this Hands On, you use the Defringe command and a delete "trick" to get close to the needed edge effect. A Layer Mask will bring you the rest of the way.

HANDS ON

PAINTING INTO A LAYER MASK

1. Open the Tulip.Psd image (again). Duplicate the image (Image → Duplicate → OK).

2. Drag the icon for the Background Layer to the New Layer icon at the bottom left of the Layers palette. This will copy the Background Layer into a new Layer.

3. Using the Eyedropper tool, select the deeper yellow at the center of the tulip as your foreground color.

4. Click on the Background Layer to make it active. Fill the background (Mac: OPTION+DELETE, Windows: ALT+DELETE) with the foreground color.

5. Click on Layer 1 (the tulip) to make it the active Layer. Load Channel 4 (Mac: OPTION+⌘+4, Windows: ALT+CTRL+4). This is the Image Mask that you have used before.

6. Reverse the selection (Select → Inverse). Press DELETE. This gives you the color spill edge that you have seen in all of the methods so far. *Do not deselect.* Press DELETE two more times. The edge spill gets a little bit lighter.

7. This technique works because there are partially selected pixels at the edge of the selection. Each time you press DELETE, you remove a bit more of these edge pixels. This sometimes gets you the effect that you want all by itself!

8. There is still some edge contamination, so you can use the Defringe command on it. Reverse the selection (Select → Inverse). Press → once to float the selection, and then ← to move it back where it was. Apply the Defringe command (Select → Modify → Defringe, Radius=3).

9. Make a new Layer (click on the New Layer icon at the bottom of the Layers palette). Drag Layer 1 into the trash can on the Layers palette. You no longer need it.

10. Figure 9-23 shows the tulip after Step 8 with arrows indicating areas of remaining color spill (areas that do not look like shadows on the edge of the flower).

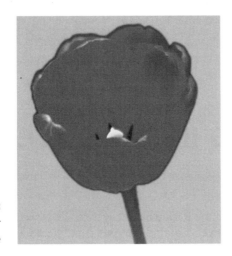

Figure 9-23
Tulip with color
spill still in image

11. Create a Layer Mask (Layers menu → Add Layer Mask). Select the Paintbrush and make black your foreground color. Use a soft-edged brush and very gently paint outside of the tulip area with black paint so that the edge of the brush just begins to eat away at the color spill edges. Figure 9-24(a) shows the completed mask, and Figure 9-24(b) shows the finished tulip.

Figure 9-24
a) Layer Mask to
remove color spill
b) Finished tulip

a   b

1. What is the concept of anti-aliasing?
   a. Create pixels along the edge of an object to change the color of the edge to the background color.
   b. Create a sharp, crisp line between the image of the object and the background.
   c. Remove an image from the background.
   d. Create jagged edges.

2. What is color spill?
   a. Edges that are defringed with the color of the background.
   b. Edges that are choked with the color of the background.
   c. Edges that are neutralized with the color of the background.
   d. Edges that are diluted with the color of the background.

3. Which technique is best for re-creating fine edge detail?
   a. Choke an image
   b. Paint through a mask
   c. Paint-On-Transparency
   d. Fill the edges

4. Of the methods to remove color spill, which is not an automated process?
   a. Paint-On-Transparency
   b. Paint through an Edge Mask
   c. Fill with background image
   d. Use a Layer Mask

5. What is one advantage to fixing a color spill by painting through an Edge Mask?
   a. Adds edge detail to the Layer so the object is uncontaminated by the background.
   b. Creates a smaller file so it uses less room when the image is saved.
   c. The Edge Mask will be totally black and allow for some transparency.
   d. It is not an automated system and thus produces a more clear picture.

MAKING IMAGE MASKS

The previous section described the process of removing color spill. However, giving you a precreated mask for the tulip was a bit like those cartoons that explain a math concept by replacing the essential steps with the notation "and here a miracle happens."

The "miracle" was the creation of that original mask. Until you can produce that, the other techniques cannot be as effective.

You have learned a great number of ways to produce a mask for an image and save it into a channel. One of the best ways is to have the Image Mask itself. This process starts with the search for a suitable channel.

Finding the Channel with the Most Contrast

The idea of self-masking images is to find an image channel that shows the most contrast between what you want to keep and what you want to remove, and to use that channel to help build a mask. Once you find the channel, you can *make a copy of it* and use curves or levels to bring the channel down to mostly black or white. This is much easier to show than to explain. Follow along...

LOCATING A SUITABLE CHANNEL

1. Open the image Girl.Psd. This is another one of Ed Scott's China series of photos. Duplicate the image (Image → Duplicate → OK).

2. Examine the Red, Green, and Blue channels carefully.

3. Pick the channel that has the best contrast. The Blue channel does not—all of the values are similar there. Either the Red or Green channel would work. The Green channel seems to have the most overall contrast, so it is the best. Drag the Green channel to the New Channel icon to make it into a new channel (one that will not affect the colors in the image).

4. You can also convert the image to CMYK or Lab mode and look at those channels as well. Sometimes one of those will provide better contrast.

In this instance, there is not too much reason to hunt further. The Green channel provides as much contrast as needed to develop a good black-and-white mask. A "textbook" example of a perfect channel for a mask occurs in the Tulip image that you used in Lesson 2. In that image, the Red channel shows excellent contrast and needs little work in order to be used as a mask. Figure 9-25 shows the Red channel for the Tulip image.

Figure 9-25
Tulip.Psd: Red
channel

Using Curves

Now that you have located the candidate channel, the next step is to change the channel so that the parts of the channel you want to see are white and the parts of the channel you want to remove from your image are black. The Curves command generally does the best job. You use the Pencil tool in the Curves dialog to draw the white area out so that it embraces all of the area you want, and draw the dark area of the Curves dialog so that it "eats up" the areas that you don't want. This is easy to do when the image cooperates!

Look at Figure 9-25 again. The Red channel for the tulip is mostly there. The tulip is very light, and the background is dark. The tulip stem, though somewhat dark, is lighter than the background. Figure 9-26 shows the Curve dialog with the light areas forced to white and the dark areas forced to black.

Figure 9-27 shows a copy of the Red tulip channel after that curve is applied. The mask is almost perfect. It requires only a light touch-up with black paint and a small blur to make it an accurate mask.

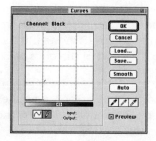

Figure 9-26
Curves dialog
for tulip showing
tone forcing

Figure 9-27
Almost finished
mask for tulip
(after applying
curves)

Most images are not that perfect. The Girl.Psd image is not as easy to mask since the young lady's hair is dark and her shirt light against a midtone background. For this image, you need to bring the lights and darks to white and the midtones to black in the Curves dialog box. Work along in this Hands On.

DEVELOPING AN IMAGE MASK

1. Drag the icon for the Green channel to the New Channel icon in the bottom center of the Channels palette to duplicate the channel. It will be called Green copy.

2. By looking at the Green channel of the Girl, you can tell that there is a shadow in the background that is darker than most of the area and close in tone to the girl's hair. If you make a very crude selection of that area with the Lasso, you can pick up one of the midtone grays from the nearby background and fill the selection. Figure 9-28 shows this selection. This helps to keep the shadow from becoming part of the girl's hair.

3. Open the Curves dialog (Mac: ⌘+Ⓜ, Windows: CTRL+Ⓜ). Make sure that the Curves dialog is set up so the dark areas are on the left and bottom—white is top and right (click on the double arrow on the Gradient bar to switch directions if you need to).

Figure 9-28
Shadow selection

4. The curve you create here differs from the Tulip curve because you need to turn the darkest and lightest tones in the image to white (selected) and the midtones to black (not selected). Use the Pencil tool in the Curves dialog. Drag the Pencil along the top edge of the Curves grid from the left edge about 2/3 of the distance of the first quarter of the grid. This turns the girl's hair to white. Figure 9-29 shows the actual curve that needs to be drawn.

5. Draw the right-top area of the curve to change the girl's clothing to white. Then draw a line at the bottom of the grid between the two top lines. This forces the midtones in the image to black.

6. Click on the Smooth button to get some gray tones in the edges, and click OK. Figure 9-30 shows the mask after curves have been applied. What have you accomplished? You have just made the beginnings of a mask for the young girl without drawing paths or clicking on the Magic Wand tool, and you have the start of a very accurate mask.

Figure 9-29
Curve for
masking girl

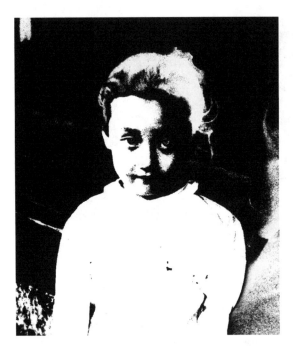

Figure 9-30
Mask after the
Curves command
has been applied

7. Use the Lasso tool to quickly select the areas inside of the girl that should be white, and fill them with white. Then select the outside areas, and fill them with black.

8. Double-click on the Green Channel Copy name in the Channels palette to open the Channel options dialog. Change the Opacity to 100%.

9. Click on the Eye icon next to the RGB channel to turn it on. Now you can see a solid color background around the figure. This tells you how close your mask is to being finished. Figure 9-31 shows the girl surrounded by a solid background. There is still work to be done.

10. Change the Opacity of the channel back to 50%. Paint in the rest of the details using white to add to the selected areas and black to remove areas from the selection (and cover them with the frisket color). Get as much of the obvious hair as you can, but do not worry about the fine wisps for now. Figure 9-32 shows the almost finished mask.

11. Change the Opacity on the channel back to 100% and look at the channel. Make sure that you have no background selected. Double-click on the Green Channel Copy name in the Channels palette and change the Color Indicates radio button to Selected Areas. This lets you see if the selection fits inside the borders of the girl (the Eye icon for the RGB channel must still be turned *on*).

Figure 9-31
Mask in progress

Figure 9-32
Almost finished
mask

12. With the 100% opaque mask still covering the girl, apply a Gaussian Blur to the channel (Filter → Blur → Gaussian Blur, 2). Open the Levels dialog (Mac: ⌘+L, Windows: CTRL+L).

13. Drag the White Input slider toward the left as shown in Figure 9-33 until the white numeric readout says about 92, or the opaque Image Mask shrinks inside of the outline of the girl.

    You should be able to see the hint of a glow from behind the mask. Now you are done (well, with this mask at least!). Figure 9-34 shows the girl with the opaque mask. Double-click on the channel and change the Color Indicates button back to Masked Areas.

14. Click on the RGB channel to make it active. Load Channel 4 (Mac: OPTION+⌘+4, Windows: ALT+CTRL+4). Float the selection (Mac: ⌘+J,

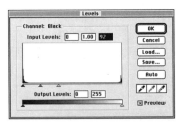

Figure 9-33
Levels dialog to
Choke Mask

Figure 9-34
Girl with opaque
choke mask

Windows: CTRL+J). Make a new Layer—press the modifier key (Mac: OPTION, Windows: ALT) and click on the New Layer icon at the bottom of the Layers palette. Turn the Eye icon for the Background Layer off so that you can see the results of your effort. Figure 9-35 shows the girl against a solid background. The mask keeps very little fine detail but should have no color spill.

You will need to make more modifications to this image. If you are not going to continue on with this chapter right now, save your work to your hard drive.

Salvaging Image Details: Hair and Fuzz

The previous exercise created a silhouetted figure that is quite satisfactory for many purposes. The process, once you master it, is very fast, and most masks of the complexity that you just did can be produced in 5–10 minutes. However, for high-end work, you will want to keep as much of the image detail as possible. That is the mark of the true Photoshop master. However, the hair or image detail is, as discussed earlier, contaminated with the background color. Therefore, you will get much better results by painting the fine details back into the image through a more complex Edge Mask than you used for the tulip example.

The procedure for creating this Edge Mask is very similar to that of the tulip Edge Mask. However, the tulip was the "perfect candidate" for the Edge Mask, and this image

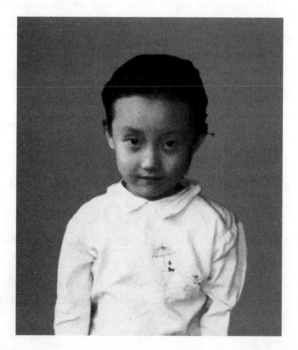

Figure 9-35
Girl silhouetted
against solid
background

will take much more work. If you try to move an object from a background, and there is a very sharp contrast between the object and the background, the editing is fairly easy. With this image of the young girl, the hair detail you are trying to preserve is dark but the background is in the midtones. In order for this technique to work, you need to be able to force the background to solid black or white.

Let's talk strategy before jumping into the Hands On. The process of creating the Edge Mask is to

- Find a suitable channel (or channels)

- Force the background area to black (or white) using levels, curves, or a combination of both

- Keep as much original tone in the edges as possible

- Piece the Edge Mask together, if needed

- Build the final Edge Mask by multiplying an inverted, choked copy of the original Image Mask with the Edge Mask

- Load the Edge Mask into a new Layer of the image

- Paint in the details through the mask

Because the detail you want to keep in this image is dark, you need to force the background to white and then invert the entire channel. Furthermore, you cannot allow the hair detail to become completely black, or the resulting mask will not have the subtlety that is needed. Basically, the hair detail should not change in value at all (until it is inverted to form the channel).

Because of the values in the image (and the ones you want to keep), neither a global levels or curves change is possible. You need to select the background area and "level" the *selection* to white as the only means of making a decent Edge Mask. Follow along.

CREATING A "DETAIL-PRESERVING" EDGE MASK

Open the saved Girl.Psd image with the Image Mask channel in it.

1. Click on the RGB channel to make it active if it is not already. Make the Background Layer the current Layer (this is the original image). Duplicate the Layer (Layers palette menu → Duplicate Layer → New) into a new document.

2. This is the point at which you would begin the search for the "best" channel for your Edge Mask. To shorten that search, the best channel is the Lightness channel of the image in Lab mode. Therefore, change the image to Lab mode (Image → Mode → Lab).

3. In the Channels palette, click on the name Lightness to make that the active channel. Duplicate the channel by dragging it to the New Channel icon at the bottom center of the Channels palette.

4. After you have duplicated the Lightness channel, change the image back to RGB mode (Image → Mode → RGB).

5. "Pre-fill" the shadow behind the girl's head (in the new channel) as you did in the last exercise by enclosing the area with the Lasso tool and filling it with a nearby shade of gray.

6. The only way to make the hair detail white and the background dark is to first select all or most of the background. Therefore, open the Color Range dialog (Select → Color Range).

7. Select the Eyedropper tool. Press [SHIFT] to make it work in "add" mode and drag the cursor across the two surfaces of the riser (the step-like thing) to the left of the girl. Figure 9-36 shows the Color Range dialog. Set the Fuzziness to about 15 or so. The "trick" is to set the values so that the hair detail is not changed but the best amount of the background changes to white in the Color Range dialog box. You might want to set the Image Preview to Black Matte to see exactly what is happening on the image.

8. Select the Lasso tool ([L]) and add the side of the image and the girl's shirt to the selection (press [SHIFT] as you drag the Lasso around groups of unselected pixels). Figure 9-37 shows the marching ants when you have finished your selection.

9. Open the Levels dialog (Mac: ⌘+[L], Windows: [CTRL]+[L]). Drag the Gamma slider (the middle one) toward the left almost all of the way. Now drag the White Point slider almost to the left edge. Figure 9-38 shows this dialog

Figure 9-36
Color Range dialog

Figure 9-37
Selection to
change background
tone

with the correct settings (your histogram will vary depending upon how much of the girl's shirt you selected, but the numeric setting can still stay the same). This step will result in a very light image with the girl's hair as the only dark area.

10. Deselect (Mac: ⌘+D, Windows: CTRL+D). Invert the channel (Mac: ⌘+I, Windows: CTRL+I). Use the Lasso tool to remove everything but the hair.

11. Apply a very tiny Gaussian Blur (from 0.4 to 0.8 pixels). Use the Paintbrush to touch up any needed areas and to further define the black areas (do not touch the tones in the white areas—you need these values to keep the edge detail realistic). Name this channel Almost Edge Mask.

12. Drag the icon for the Image Mask channel to the New Channel icon in the bottom center of the Channels palette to duplicate the channel. Name the channel Choke Mask. You need to re-choke this channel to make it smaller. Do this by applying the Threshold command (Image → Adjust → Threshold) to the image. Drag the Threshold slider to the right all the way. Click OK.

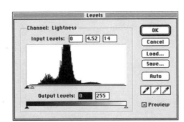

Figure 9-38
Levels dialog

13. You need to blur the edge of this choked mask to make it blend with the inside of the Edge Mask. Apply a 1.5 to 2.0 Gaussian Blur.

14. Open the Calculations dialog. Select the Choke Mask as Source 1, and click on the Invert box. Select the Almost Edge Mask as Source 2. Set the Blending to Multiply. Make the Target a New Channel in the current image. Click OK. Name the channel Edge Mask. Figure 9-39 shows this finished Edge Mask.

15. Select the RGB channel. Switch to the Layers palette and make a new Layer (click on the New Layer icon at the bottom of the Layers palette).

16. If this new Layer is not at the top of the list in the Layers palette, drag it there. Load the Edge Mask channel.

17. Double-click on the Rubber Stamp tool and make sure that the Sample Merged box is checked. You might want to hide the marching ants and turn on the Eye icon next to the Edge Mask channel so that you can see where to paint. Use the Rubber Stamp tool to add the rest of the girl's hair and wisps around her face. You might want to cut down the Opacity of the Rubber Stamp tool as well so that you can build the hair to the darkness that you prefer. When you are finished, deselect (Mac: ⌘+D, Windows: CTRL+D).

Figure 9-39
Finished Edge
Mask

Turn off the Eye icons next to all of the Layers except for the girl and her hair. If you do not, you will pick up the background color as you add back the image detail, and you will now have a new color contamination with which to contend. If only those two Layers are visible, you will get no color spill, and you will be able to freely change backgrounds. The transparency in the Edge Mask means that the image will merge seamlessly with any new background.

18. Let's finish this so that the background is worth the effort. Create a new Layer that hides the original image. Using the Eyedropper, pick up the green-blue color in the upper-left corner of the original image. Fill the image (Mac: OPTION+DELETE, Windows: ALT+DELETE) with this color.

19. Open the image Lattice.Psd. Select the entire image (Mac: ⌘+A, Windows: CTRL+A). Define this as a pattern (Edit → Define Pattern).

20. Click on the girl image again to select it. Create another new Layer above the green-blue one. Fill the image with the pattern (SHIFT+DELETE → Pattern, 100% Opacity, Normal). Turn the Opacity down to 12%.

21. Make the Hair Layer the active one. Merge Down (Mac: ⌘+E, Windows: CTRL+E). This creates one Layer from the Hair and the Girl below it. If there are any "join faults" where the hair wisps were added, repair those now. Press the modifier key (Mac: OPTION, Windows: ALT).

22. Drag the icon for the silhouetted girl Layer to the New Layer icon at the bottom left of the Layers palette. You are now going to make a drop shadow. Move the copy one Layer down in the Layer stack. Turn on the Preserve Transparency button. Fill the image (Mac: OPTION+DELETE, Windows: ALT+DELETE) with the green-blue foreground color (black is too harsh for the shadow here). Click the Preserve Transparency button off and set the Layer Apply mode to Multiply.

23. Select the Move tool (V) and move the Shadow Layer to the right and down a bit to mimic the image lighting. Apply a 5–8 pixel Gaussian Blur. Set the Layer Opacity to about 42%. Breathe a huge sigh of relief as you have now finished this! Figure 9-40 shows this image as a vignette with an embossed version of the background pattern under the vignette (the instructions for the embossing are on the CD-ROM).

How do you apply what you have learned here to another image? The example that you did was very hard. Few images can be more difficult unless there is no contrast at all between the edge detail and the background. The one thing that you may have to do in other images, however, is to build the Edge Mask from several different channels if no single channel is best for all of the detail that you need to re-create. If that is the case, then build non-overlapping "temp" channels and add them all together one at a time either with the Calculations command or by dragging the Marching Ants Marquee up to each channel with SHIFT pressed.

Figure 9-40
Finished image
(vignetted)

1. In making an Image Mask, what are the qualities you should look for in a candidate channel?
   a. Very little contrast
   b. Similar channel values
   c. Always choose the Green channel
   d. A high amount of contrast

2. When making Image Masks, the second step involves changing the channel parts so the parts of the channel you want to see are white and the parts you need to remove are black. What is the best tool for completing this task?
   a. Lasso tool
   b. Marquee tool
   c. Pencil tool
   d. Paintbrush tool

3. When the detail and the background blend too closely in an image, which of the following is the best means for making a decent Edge Mask?
   a. Global level change
   b. Curves change
   c. Level the background to white
   d. Level the image to white

4. If you need to build the Edge Mask from several different channels because a single channel is not sufficient for the detail, which is the best means for doing so?
   a. Build non-overlapping temp channels
   b. Build overlapping temp channels
   c. Build non-overlapping perm channels
   d. Build overlapping perm channels

5. In the above question, what is step two?
   a. Add them all together simultaneously with the Calculations command
   b. Add them all together one at a time with the Calculations command
   c. Leave them as is
   d. Apply them together one at a time with the Threshold command

VIP PROFILES

Cliff Weems, President of Auto F/X Corporation

Cliff Weems is the president, owner, and guiding light of Auto F/X Corporation of Exeter, NH. His original product was the Photo/Graphic Edges series of CDs that enabled a designer to add a deckled or otherwise textured edging around the border of an image. The company has lately started to convert these edges into a filter that can automatically size the edge to the image and let the designer select the edge and heavily customize it.

Cliff started his Macintosh career as an art director. He had worked in the Navy in satellite communications, and became comfortable there with the use of computers. When he left the Navy, he realized he wanted to work as a "creative." He purchased one of the early Macintosh computers and trained himself as a designer/desktop publisher. He started by using PageMaker 1.0 and Digital Darkroom.

His was the first ad agency in Exeter to use a Macintosh, and many clients came to the agency simply for that reason. Cliff saw early on that this was the direction for the future of commercial graphics.

Early in the 1990s, Cliff became interested in the design of software aimed at designers. He saw many gaps in the available software, and wanted different things for designers than what was out there. Photo/Graphic Edges was released in 1994 and was an instant hit. It is possible to make unusual edges around an image, but this product—which was not a filter set when first released—made it *practical* for a designer to take the time to add a deckled edge to an image.

Having been a designer gives Cliff a unique perspective on creating software for designers—and allows him to give advice that comes from the heart of his experience in the industry. Cliff sees the typical designer as someone who needs to turn around jobs very quickly in order to make a reasonable living. Yet the pull of creativity is very strong—if you were not creative, then this wouldn't attract you as a way to make a living.

Therefore, most designers are torn between the desire to create a unique piece of work, and the need to do it in a short enough time span that the job is still profitable. Designers no longer have the time they were once given. In today's competitive climate, it is no longer enough to make a quick marker comp. You need to make it almost polished enough for production—which often means locating a stock photo, setting and kerning the type, in addition to creating a killer idea.

As powerful as Photoshop is, it still limits an artist's creativity. Some effects are simply not possible at all; others take too long. While an artist has always been somewhat limited by the confines of what can be done within the realm of practicality, the computer artist is definitely a captive to the capabilities of the computer. It is certainly possible to design a project that cannot be executed on the computer. What is needed is a set of tools that enables the artist to quickly and easily perform multi-step complex sequences of events somewhat on "autopilot." The paradox, though, is you still need to understand what is being done to your image and remain able to guide the steps that happen automatically. More powerful software will always equal more creativity. It is this type of software that Cliff and his company are trying to create. Cliff sees Auto F/X as the bridge between art and technology—making it easier for the designer to design cool things.

Cliff has some advice for you, which he knows sounds somewhat strange coming from a special effects filter developer. He says that you need first and foremost to remember that the computer is much like a pen. A pen is a tool, but the mind of the designer is the real key. Too many young digital designers expect the software to "do" the creativity for them, and software needs to have the flexibility to enable the designer to do custom—not prepackaged stuff—that is new and different. Filters are a frequently misused tool and can become cliched very quickly. You need to take control of the filter, and not let it control you.

Since a designer needs to be able to make a living, quick results are needed to maintain profitability. You also need to learn the best techniques for performing common tasks—such as silhouetting images or making drop shadows. You can sit in front of a computer all day and still not be profitable. Photoshop is so powerful that many users do things in an inefficient way. You need knowledge of the efficient use of features in order to use more complex effects and enhance your creativity. The more you know about working "smart," the easier it is to dream up an idea and say, "Yes, I know how I will do that," and then finish the job within budget.

David Xanakis, President of XRX, Inc.

David Xanakis is president of XRX, Inc., the parent company of *Knitter's* and *Weaver's* magazines and Xanakis Design Services. He also conducts "traveling" seminars called Navigating Photoshop, Navigate Illustrator, and Preparing Graphics for the World Wide Web.

David was trained as a pianist and composer. He then developed an interest in weaving and, along with Elaine Rowley and Alexis Xenakis, started *Weaver's* magazine. He did a lot of editing and writing for the magazine and also spent a lot of time figuring out extremely complex weaves.

David first met the name Adobe when his company switched over to digital magazine production in 1987 with the purchase of QuarkXPress and Adobe Illustrator. Later, he received a mailing from Adobe of a poster with light bulbs advertising the brand-new program Photoshop. He was knocked out by the poster. He had wanted to be able to work with photos and had been frustrated with Digital Darkroom and Image Studio as being needlessly complicated and limiting. He immediately purchased Photoshop because he liked Adobe's reputation and felt that the company generally knew what it was doing.

When he first purchased the program, David says that he was bowled over. It was so easy to use. He played with it endlessly and couldn't leave it alone. He worked to determine strategies such as how to use it with low RAM. He ran distortions on individual channels changing the variables for each channel. He scanned popcorn, ball bearings, and anything else that fit on the scanner bed and didn't run away.

At first, Photoshop was just a hobby, albeit an obsessive one. But when Version 2 shipped, his company's printer, St. Croix Press of New Richmond, Wisconsin, told him about a color separator in Minneapolis—Tom Forsite of GV Graphics—who was experimenting with calibrating his digital scans to St. Croix' presses. Paulette Bertrand, St. Croix' Service Bureau Director, used Tom's scans placed in QuarkXpress, ran the film, and oversaw the press test. The results were excellent and she began encouraging some of St. Croix' more advanced clients to attempt to use the new technology. David was among those clients and he thought he understood that many clients were already working with digital photo files.

Encouraged—and by this time modestly proficient at Photoshop—his company printed their magazine's cover and center spread. David and his partners were pleased with the results and next produced a 110-page magazine. Only after they had finished printing the magazine did they discover that St. Croix's only other client to make use of digital images had done so only on a single page of their book. To the best of their knowledge, *Knitter's* magazine was the first nationally distributed magazine to be produced entirely by digital methods, just as, a few years earlier, *Knitter's* magazine was the first magazine to be entirely produced in the then-new program QuarkXpress.

The change to new technology is never easy. In the very first days of David company's use of the computer, floppy disks were sent to a service bureau in Denver (at that time one of only three in the United States). Film was output from one of the very first Linotronics which imaged type and graphics at 600 dpi. Even so, the job took days. When David began to use Photoshop in his production, he found that he needed to buy several Syquest drives and about 50 Syquest cartridges. He also found that the original color separations, however high their quality, were also fairly expensive. While experimenting with different vendors, he discovered that not all separators were equally skillful.

David said that at first, he really didn't know anything about color management or calibration and there was very little information available. He was forced to solve each problem as it occurred. He learned about color shifts and how to avoid them, monitor calibration, how to make squeaky-clean PostScript files ("clean" meaning files that were so efficient that they imaged in five minutes or less per film). He learned that you do not resize or rotate files in QuarkXpress or apply bolding to roman fonts. He learned to rasterize Adobe Illustrator files and to do his own trapping and imposition. He managed, over a period of about a year, to reduce imposition costs from $8,000 to about $900 per issue by designing his magazine's pages so that they could easily be taken apart and imposed. Eventually, most of the problems were solved. *Knitter's* magazine, a quarterly publication, began to make use of full digital methods with Issue 27. The current Issue is 44.

David says he used to be intimidated by professional scans but will now modify a commercial scan without hesitation. He has learned to solve the perplexing problems of color shifts on certain colors of yarns. He read Kodak's white papers, which described a problem with certain dyes which reflect UV list during outdoor photo shoots and cause major color shifts on film. These colors are usually the bright fashion reds and greens. The problem is not apparent until the photos are developed in the lab: reds move toward burgundy or orange, greens toward brown. The magazine has learned to spot this as a potential problem, to check for it, and to correct it so that the pictures of the sweaters always match the actual yarn colors.

Photoshop is a big aid in making print look good, and David takes great pleasure in teaching people how to use the program (plus the bells and whistles). He teaches ways to get a scan from an inexpensive scanner and to get it to look good on press, using Unsharp Masking, color management in practical terms, calibration, dot gain, printing ink settings, and minimum and maximum dots (putting dots back into images and cutting down on shadows). He also teaches ways to make local color corrections in a hurry and what to do about soft edges.

David feels that Photoshop is probably the best piece of microcomputer software ever written and is still in awe of the people who wrote it. He says he still cannot believe that the original program contained as much as it did and that the programmers could have produced a program that was so far in advance of any real need at the time of its introduction. For the first several years, he suspects, 98% of Photoshop users made use of about 2% of the program's capability. The program was not just a little ahead of its time, but miles ahead. It was so much better than anyone had expected. He thinks that users back then would have been thrilled to get a program that would do 20% of what it could do. The program is still enormous and many users do not use it to full capability. It is still maintaining its place and even today has no real competition.

Version 3.0 of Photoshop had an incredible simplicity of use with its only failing, David thinks, its color-separation procedure and methods. He uses the program on a regular basis and says he learns something new about it nearly every day.

David's advice to you: Photoshop may seem intimidating, but it is really easy once you get used to it. Buy a few books and start doing some straightforward things. Don't fear the program. It has so many ways to do the same thing. And with the ability to Revert, Erase to Save, take a Snapshot, and use Layers and Duplicate images, you never need to be afraid of destroying your image as you experiment. Just jump into it, have fun, and see what Photoshop can do.

CHAPTER SUMMARY

This is a very important chapter. This chapter contains much of the knowledge needed to make images behave when you attempt to composite them with other images or with different backgrounds. In this chapter, you learned how to create paths and use the Color Range command. You also learned about color spill and how to remove it, and how to create masks from the image data itself. Finally, you learned how to build an Edge Mask to help restore detail to an image.

CHAPTER 10

PHOTO RETOUCHING

Chapters 7, 8, and 9 introduced you to scanning, color correction, and the various color spaces within Photoshop. This chapter helps you use this newly acquired knowledge to help heal ill photographs. There are many reasons why images may need to be *healed*. The photographic materials themselves decay over time, and images fade—or their color was not satisfactory to begin with. People put images into plastic albums, and over a period of a few years, the photos are damaged almost beyond repair. Photos get old and crack, get left in the rain, get caught in a flood, or eaten by the dog.

The topic of photo retouching can be divided into two somewhat separate categories: the need to restore an image, and the need to manipulate an image to add or remove things (like color casts, dust, small or large objects, phone wires, and people). My first commercial photo-retouching assignment was

471

to "fix" a wedding picture to remove the groom! I've since made quite a habit of "boyfriend-ectomies." Strangely enough, I've rarely been asked to remove the *girl*.

In this chapter, you will learn

⬤ The typical sequence of steps in an image-retouching process.

⬤ How to use the Rubber Stamp tool to repair image imperfections.

⬤ How and when to use (or not use) the Dust&Scratches filter.

⬤ How to repair skin tones and remove blemishes.

⬤ How to use the Toning tools to emphasize shadows and highlights.

⬤ How to add and remove objects and people from an image.

⬤ How to create sepia-toned images.

⬤ How to colorize flesh tones in an image.

Photo retouching and restoration projects usually involve one of two possible output processes—output to a film recorder so that a new photograph can be made, or traditional prepress output to an imagesetter for conventional printing. A third alternative—output to a photographic quality dye-sublimation printer—is also increasingly common. It is critical that you know in advance what your output method will be. You need to prepare an image very differently depending upon its final form. The output method impacts the scan resolution and the color space decisions.

WORKFLOW

There are a fairly predictable number of steps in a photo-retouching or restoration project:

⬤ Acquire the image or images

⬤ Crop the image if needed

⬤ Perform global color correction

⬤ Fix the problem areas of the image

⬤ Apply the Unsharp Mask filter

⬤ Output

Acquiring Images

The two major ways in which a photograph can be acquired are by scanning or via PhotoCD. If you are being asked to restore an old photograph, you will almost always have to scan rather than acquire from a PhotoCD. You can scan either the original or a slide/ negative (if you have access to a transparency scanner—and you have the negative). Scanning for photo retouching is no different than scanning for any other reason. However, some older photographs may be very delicate and need to be handled with extreme care.

Sepia-toned photographs may present a problem, however, if they are badly torn or damaged. Many CCD scanners (typical desktop scanners) which scan in one pass produce sharp blue and orange lines around the damaged area. These lines identify the damage, but they are somewhat hard to eradicate. One solution is to scan in three passes if your scanner has the capability. Another solution, that usually works better, is to scan the image first in color in a very small scan so you can capture the color of the sepia-tone. Then scan at the needed resolution in grayscale and reapply the sepia-tone to the image when it is fully restored. The grayscale correction process is much easier as well.

Resolution

If you are going to send your output to a film recorder, you need to be prepared to create a huge input file. Film recorders typically need a 2KB, 4KB, or 8KB file as output. K stands for *thousands,* and, in this case, it means "thousands of *pixels.*" A 2KB file requires 2,048 pixels across its longest dimension. A 4KB file needs 4,096 pixels and an 8KB file needs 8,192 pixels. Physical dimensions do not have much meaning to a film recorder. They do not understand *inches* or *points* or any measurement except for pixels.

This is frequently the most difficult thing for new users to understand. On the Adobe Forum on CompuServe, at least once a week someone asks, "What is the resolution of a film recorder?" or "What is the resolution of slide film?" The answer is "It doesn't matter." All the film recorder requires is an image with enough pixels to keep it happy. It does not bother with pixels-per-inch.

A 2KB file will weigh in at almost 9MB, a 4KB file at about 45+MB, and an 8KB file at a whopping 137+MB. Which one should you choose? If depends on the final output size of the image. If the image is destined to be enlarged to 8×10 or more, you really need to produce an 8KB file. Unless your film recorder does an incredibly good job of up-sizing the image, a smaller file is going to be too "soft" (fuzzy, pixellated) when the image is enlarged. A 2KB file is barely sufficient for anything except slide presentations. For most normal uses, a 4KB file should be fine.

The other thing you need to consider is the aspect ratio of a slide and the aspect ratio of the image to be output. Typical photograph sizes are 4×6, 5×7, 8×10, 11×17. The aspect ratio of a film recorder is 1:1.5. While the 4×6 image exactly fits that, the rest do not. This is not a problem if the ratio is less than that. It enters into the calculations if the ratio is greater. You also need to leave a bit of space around the edges of the image for the slide housing if you are producing a slide, or for the film printing equipment, if the photo is to be printed by machine rather than manually, a 7% border area is common. So, since you will probably sacrifice some of the edge area, you do not need to capture 8,192 pixels for an 8KB file—though it never hurts anything except your computer's performance and hard drive capacity to scan in more than you need.

If the "long side" of the image needs to be 8,192 pixels, how do you determine the "short" side? Part of this depends on your scanner driver. Figure 10-1 shows the dialog box of the ScanTastic scanner driver, by Second Glance Software. This driver can be used by scanners from Epson, Hewlett-Packard, and Apple. When you choose pixels as your units and enter the precise number of pixels for either the length or the width, the scanner driver calculates the other dimension based on your rectangular selection. Should you need to put an exact number into both fields, a little bit of arithmetic would be needed. If your original is 4″ × 6″ and the 6″ side translates into 8,192 pixels, then you divide that number by 6 inches which gives you the number of pixels per inch that that number represents (1,365.3 pixels per inch). That number multiplied by 4 gives you the needed pixel count for the other dimension (5,461 pixels).

If you are scanning your image for output to an image setter or to a photo-realistic printer, then you need many fewer pixels. The general rule is that 1.5 to 2 times the final line screen is sufficient resolution. Chapter 15, "Photoshop Output," has much more of an explanation of line screens and the printing process. For now, just remember these as *baseline* suggestions of resolutions:

- If you are printing on high-quality coated stock, scan at 266ppi for a line screen of 130 or 300ppi for a line screen of 150.

- If you are printing on uncoated stock, scan at a ppi of 200 for output at a line screen of 100 to 125.

- If you are printing on newsprint, scan at a ppi of 170 for a line screen of 85.

- Photo-realistic printers do not use a line screen, so you can scan at a resolution of 300ppi for best quality.

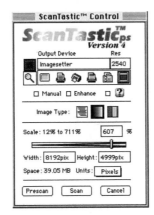

Figure 10-1
ScanTastic scanner
plug-in dialog

Color Space

The choice of output device also affects your color space. A film recorder is an RGB device. It can only handle files that are in RGB color space. This actually makes it easier as there is no need to convert the image into CMYK color space. You will keep the dynamic range of the image when you output to film. The uncertainty that is introduced in this process, however, is at the photo lab itself. If you are not doing the printing of the final film, then you have little control over the color corrections used by the operator to print the image. Slide film has no need to color correct when printed, so what appears on slide is what went out of the computer. However, you cannot print a positive from a slide, and slide film used to shoot negatives is a chancy process. One of the better techniques of communicating the colors needed on the final photograph is to image the pictures twice—once on slide film and once on regular film. The slides can then be used by the lab to see how the color is supposed to look.

If you are using a conventional paper-printing process, you will need to convert your image to CMYK so that it can be printed. Some scanners give you the option of scanning directly into CMYK color space (the scanner does the conversion for you). There is great debate in the digital imaging/prepress community as to whether it is better to edit in RGB and change to CMYK as a final step or to work in the output color mode. More Photoshop professionals who visit the Adobe Forum on CompuServe, including Bruce Fraser, coauthor of *Real World Photoshop*, from Peachpit Press, seem to feel that working in RGB is best. Dan Margulis, author of *Professional Photoshop*, from Wiley, makes a case for the other argument. Dan also writes for *Computer Artist* magazine, and his article on the merits of RGB versus CMYK editing is part of his newest book, *MakeReady*.

1. Why do sepia-toned photographs present problems?
    a. The scanner will not scan this type of photo.
    b. They are too delicate to place in a scanner.
    c. When torn they may be scanned and create blue and orange lines.
    d. You cannot mend these photos by any means.

2. File recorders typically need what size file as an output?
    a. 2KB, 4KB, 8KB
    b. 2", 4", 8"
    c. 2MB, 4MB, 8MB
    d. 2:4:8 ratio

3. What is the resolution of a film recorder?
    a. 8 pixels-per-inch
    b. 137+MB
    c. 4 pixels-per-inch
    d. It does not matter

4. In comparing an image to output with a ScanTastic scanner driver, and in an attempt for best resolution for an image where the long side needs to be 9,500 pixels, what is the value of the short side in pixels for an original 8×10 photo?
   a. 4,750 pixels
   b. 3,800 pixels
   c. 9,600 pixels
   d. 1,900 pixels

5. A film recorder is a(n) _____ device and can only handle files that are in _____ color space.
   a. CMYX, RGB
   b. CMYX, CMYX
   c. RGB, RGB
   d. RGB, CMYX

LESSON 2

IMAGE SIZE, RESTORATION, AND RAM

If you are asked to restore a photo taken from an old locket so that it can be enlarged to an 8×10 image, refuse! People frequently have very unrealistic ideas as to what a computer can do. A 4×6 original enlarges very nicely to 8×10. An image the size of your fingernail does not. If a photographer cannot enlarge an image photographically to a given size (with reasonable detail), then you will not be able to do so either. You will have better luck on a scanner that works at a higher resolution, but you need to be able to capture enough pixels to get all of the details. If there is not enough detail in the original, all you are capturing is 8,000+ pixels of mush.

Beware, as well, of missing body parts that you are asked to re-create. If you can grab an eye from another image that is taken at the same angle, you might be able to replace a missing one. If a dog has eaten half the picture of Uncle John's face, you might even be a good enough artist to put it back together again, but, if you do, will it still look like Uncle John? Steven Johnson, noted photographer, cautions about restoring an old photograph if the changes alter the appearance of the person in the image. It is perhaps more ethical to let half of Uncle John look the way he actually did than to create a fiction loosely based on fact.

Another consideration in whether you actually want to restore a badly damaged image is whether it needs to be restored or redrawn! An artist can draw or paint a portrait; no one can really draw or paint a photograph. If you look at an image of a human face (view the image, Manisha.Psd, that is used in Chapter 7), you can see at 16:1 magnification, by moving the cursor over it with the Info palette open, no two adjacent pixels are the identical color. An artist can paint something that looks like a person, but it is unlikely that he or she can paint it with such realism that it will look like a photo (nor should it). If you are asked to restore something that is so badly damaged that it cannot be fixed without substantial redrawing, you might want to consider doing a less-than-realistic artistic rendering of the photograph rather than trying to restore it. The caveat here, is, of course, that better artists do a better job than those less skilled in hand rendering.

Finally, consider some of the more spectacular controversies that have appeared about retouched images and truth versus photographic lies. The furor over the *National Geographic* cover (where the pyramids were moved slightly to make the cover look better) and over the prison picture of O. J. Simpson on the cover of *Time* magazine (where his skin tone was darkened) are two examples that spring readily to mind.

Image and RAM

A 137MB file needs a computer with a lot of RAM (or a person with large hard drive and a huge amount of patience). Since Photoshop slows down if an image is too large to fit into RAM, a professional retoucher needs a high-powered machine. A machine with 80MB of RAM (70MB of which can be used to open a Photoshop file) is not enough. Photoshop needs 3–5 times the image size to keep an image in RAM. For a 150MB image, that means 450–750MB of RAM—an almost impossible, and certainly unaffordable, amount. However, the more RAM you have, the faster you will be able to work. You can certainly use the QuickEdit facility of Photoshop or the third-party program from Total Integration, FastEdit/Deluxe, to help cut down on RAM requirements, but you need to be careful that you do not make tonal changes or image corrections that will become obvious when the image is put back together again (Chapter 14, "Configuring and Optimizing Photoshop," discusses these two programs in more detail).

For this chapter, you will correct an image that should be much larger than it is. For the sake of your sanity, the file size has been kept low. The image is from my attic—a family Thanksgiving some time in the early 1950s (I am the young girl in the lower left of the image). The image is cracked in a number of places—that is what happens when a photo is rolled up! It is approximately 10×6 inches long and is a black and white print that almost looks home-developed—except that nobody in the family ever had photography as a hobby. Although there is substantial damage to the image, it is fixable. It is the type of damage that looks worse than it is. None of the damage is on critical locations in the faces, there is sufficient detail in most areas, and the photograph is printed on smooth paper so that the scan does not pick up paper texture in addition to the cracks.

1. For a very small photo, what is the best guideline for deciding how much it can be enlarged?
   a. No matter the original size, an image can be enlarged to any size.
   b. If a photographer can enlarge the image nicely, so can Photoshop.
   c. Three times its original size
   d. Five times its original size

2. To keep a Photoshop image open in RAM, what does it need?
   a. 1–3 times the image size
   b. 3–5 times the image size
   c. 5–7 times the image size
   d. 7–9 times the image size

3. Identify the best method for deciding if a photo needs restoration or to be redrawn.
   a. Refer to the Info palette and check for two adjacent pixels identical in color.
   b. Need a 16:1 magnification
   c. Ask a painter.
   d. Need a 5:1 magnification

4. How much RAM is necessary to keep a 300MB image open?
   a. 900–1500MB of RAM
   b. 950–1550MB of RAM
   c. 1000–2000MB of RAM
   d. 2000–2500MB of RAM

5. Which Photoshop utility can be used to cheat the RAM requirements?
   a. FastEdit/Deluxe
   b. Total Integration
   c. Lasso tool
   d. QuickEdit

SCANNING AND CROPPING THE IMAGE

The first step in a computer photo-retouching project is to scan the image. It should be scanned at either the size you need or slightly larger. For this exercise, a 2KB file has been included on the CD-ROM. The original scan is for an 8KB file but a 40+MB file is a bit taxing as a learning device. A good practice (if you have the RAM and hard disk space) is to also scan the most damaged of the faces a second time at a larger size. This size should be an even multiple (usually twice the size) so that it is easy to reduce and place back into position. The blending that occurs when an image is resized can be helpful in covering up some of the most difficult of the retouching marks on faces.

For this exercise, three areas have been saved for you at two times the final size if you wish to use them. This is so that there is more detail to edit. The files are MacBilly.Psd, Grandpop.Psd, and Rutharry.Psd.

Once the image is scanned, it needs to be cropped to the final output proportions. Figure 10-2 shows the scan of the Thanksgiving dinner. The final output size should be 8×10, but the original is 6×10—the proportions simply will not work. You need to either remove some of the people from the image—something that the picture's owner would probably not like, or invent part of the image at the top or bottom. The other solution—and the one you'll use here, is not to bother getting the correct proportions. The image can be printed on lager paper with blank space on it and framed to fit.

The bottom of this image is a bad place to *create* detail. You would have to draw the bottom of the tablecloth and probably the actual table as well. You would also have to add legs and clothing details to the figures on the left and right of the image (the author, and cousin Larry). This seems hardly worth the effort. At the top of the image, you would need to continue the Venetian blinds, the wallpaper, and the chain for the chandelier. This is also messy, but more realistic than re-creating body parts. However, if you remove the chandelier from the image (it is ugly and adds nothing anyway!), the task becomes easier. You can also, possibly, remove the half of a window above the diners and just continue the wallpaper up to the image borders. If it becomes impossible to match the blinds on the left side, you could carefully replace that wall with wallpaper as well (though having to mask everything is also time-consuming).

Let's start the retouching process by cropping the image and making it the correct size.

Figure 10-2
Original
Thanksgiving photo

CROPPING

1. Open the image Thanksgv.Psd.

2. Notice that there is a border on the left side of the image (your left), and there is a lot of damage at the very top of the image. Use the Crop tool to cut away those areas. Figure 10-3 shows the Crop tool Marquee around the image.

3. How does this image compare to the 8×10 proportion that is needed? Double-click on the Marquee tool. In the Marquee Options palette that appears, make the shape Rectangular and the style Constrained Aspect Ratio. Enter the values Width: **10**, Height: **8** and make sure that the Feather Radius box is set to 0. Drag the Marquee out from the bottom-right corner of the image. If you keep to these proportions, unfortunately, you will remove too much of the width of the image. So, concede defeat and work with what you have.

QUIZ 3

1. What is the first step in computer photo retouching?
   a. Crop the image.
   b. Recolor the image.
   c. Fold the image in half.
   d. Scan the image.

Figure 10-3
Area to be cropped

2. When the output size is not proportional to the original image, which technique is typically most desirable to the photo owner?
   a. Print the image to larger paper that will include blank space.
   b. Cut the edges of the image off.
   c. Split the image in half.
   d. This project is impossible to do.

3. Which tool should be used in the retouching process of cropping the image to get rid of damaged areas?
   a. Lasso tool
   b. Cut tool
   c. Crop tool
   d. Pen tool

4. When checking the proportions of creating an image into a 4×6 photo, which style would you set the Options palette at?
   a. Constrained Ratio
   b. Constrained Aspect Ratio
   c. Rectangular
   d. Square

5. In the above question, what numbers would you enter for the Width, Height, and Feather Radius box?
   a. 4,6,0
   b. 6,4,1
   c. 4,6,1
   d. 6,4,0

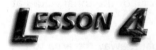

TONE AND GLOBAL CORRECTING

There is one glaring, major problem on this image that needs to be fixed. The left side of the image, left of the last major crack, is much lighter than the rest of the image. There is no global correction that will fix this. There is a sneaky local correction, however. It is so simple, but it could take hours done any other way.

TONE CORRECTION

1. Using the Lasso tool, outline the left side of the image up to the crack. Figure 10-4 shows the area to be outlined. If you drag the Lasso over the crack first and then draw a half circle outside of the image until you get close to your starting point, you can let go and get a perfect selection.

2. It is possible (indeed, likely) that you may not have selected quite up to the crack in all locations. It is easier to make the selection too large than it is to try to cover up problem areas later. Expand (Select → Modify → Expand) the selection by 4 pixels.

3. In most projects, you would also feather the selection at this point. However, since the selection boundary is an area that has to be fixed, there is no point to softening the selection.

4. Create an Adjustment Layer (Mac: ⌘+click, Windows: CTRL+click on the New Layer icon at the bottom of the Layers palette). Since there is an active selection, the Adjustment Layer is already masked to that selection. Choose Levels as the Adjustment Layer type. Figure 10-5 shows this dialog. Set the Layer apply mode to Multiply in the Dialog, and click OK. When the Levels Dialog appears, *do not change anything*. Just click OK. This action allows you to set up a local correction for the section so that it matches the rest of the image. To correct this would throw off all of the tonal values at this stage.

5. Use the black paint on the Adjustment Layer to paint away the area to the right of the crack that you might have picked up in the masked area. Correct, if needed, with white to paint the mask back in.

6. It is easy to tell where the mask should be. Not only is the crack there, but the color changes. Make sure that you zoom out to 1:1 so you can accurately see what you are doing. Remember: You can press the spacebar to access the Hand tool so you can scroll around the image, or you can scroll via the Navigator palette—which is usually faster.

7. The area you multiplied is now much darker than the rest of the image. The cure? Reduce the Opacity of the Layer. Somewhere at about 37–42% Opacity, the top Layer contains the tonal range at the main image.

Figure 10-4
Area to be lassoed
for correction in an
Adjustment Layer

8. Under normal circumstances, you might wish to keep the Adjustment Layer around for later adjustments if necessary, but it is less complex to remove it. Merge Down (Mac: ⌘+E, Windows: CTRL+E).

The tone is now nice and even throughout. Well, it *is* even—but it is way too light. Figure 10-6 shows the Histogram in the Levels dialog. You can see the effect of the local correction in the Histogram. It is in the jagged lines at the top of the right portion of the graph. This is where gaps were left in the left side of the image. It is best to do the global, grossly needed color or tone corrections before starting the clean-up campaign on the image because there is less chance of the edits becoming obvious that way. So, the next step is to globally correct the image tone. As you can see in the Histogram, there is a very low dynamic range to this image. It has no punch at all and needs more lights and darks.

Figure 10-5
New Adjustment
Layer dialog

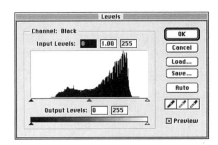

Figure 10-6
Histogram after
local correction

Global Correction

Chapter 9, "Advanced Selection Techniques," discussed color corrections. The best way to color correct this image is to use the Multiply trick again—this time with the entire image. Here are the steps so you can follow along.

MULTIPLY CORRECTION

1. Create an Adjustment Layer (Mac: ⌘+click, Windows: CTRL+click on the New Layer icon at the bottom of the Layers palette). Set the Apply mode to Multiply. Click OK. *Do not adjust the Histogram at this time.*

2. This gives a very dark image, but it has much more life to it. If you check the darkest areas in the image with the Info palette, you see that the dark areas are still not black. They are about 94% black at their darkest. This is good. You do not want to lose the shadow areas of the image.

3. Drag the Opacity on the Multiply Layer back to about 80%. This gives you even more assurance that you will not lose your shadows.

The image still needs more punch in the highlights. Because you are using an Adjustment Layer, the Histogram can be tweaked indefinitely without destroying image data. Open the Levels dialog. The Histogram, shown in Figure 10-7, shows that the image is still lacking in light values (though it is also not reaching near black). It needs lighter values near the right of the Histogram. Drag the White Point Input slider to the left until the numeric area reads 0, 100, 206. Drag the Black Input Slider until it reads 30. Figure 10-8 shows the new settings in the Levels dialog. Notice that the Histogram itself does not change. Figure 10-9 shows the image corrected globally using the steps above. You can go back and adjust the shadows again later if they look too light when you are finished.

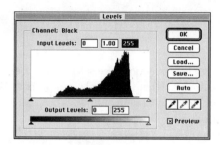

Figure 10-7
Histogram after
Multiply correction

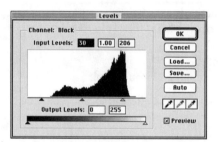

Figure 10-8
Histogram after
Levels correction

Figure 10-9
Photograph fully
tone corrected

Why did you choose 206 for the white point? Usually, you would try to leave the white point somewhere where it does not cut off any of the white values already in the image. However, the whitest areas in *this* image are the torn paper areas that you need to repair. Therefore, you can cut into the whites in the histogram since the specular highlights on the people's glasses (which would normally be the strongest whites in the image) are not yet showing up as white, either.

1. In the situation where you may not have selected close enough to an image when making adjustments, what is a simple tool to fix this?
   a. Use the Lasso tool to create a new outline.
   b. You cannot fix this.
   c. Expand the selection by four pixels.
   d. Select the selection by four pixels.

2. Identify the two methods for scrolling around an image.
   a. Press the spacebar to obtain the Hand tool.
   b. Lasso tool
   c. Navigator palette
   d. Press (CTRL) to obtain the Marquee tool.

3. Where do you look to see the effect of local corrections?
   a. Desktop
   b. File saved
   c. New file
   d. Histogram

4. Which is the correct order to color correct an image using the Multiplicity trick?
   a. Create an Adjustment Layer, set Apply mode to Multiply, and adjust the Histogram.
   b. Create an Adjustment Layer, set Apply mode to Multiply, and drag the Opacity on the multiple Layer to a percentage where shadowing is not lost.
   c. At the Histogram, set the Apply mode to Multiply, and change the Opacity.
   d. Create an Adjustment Layer and set the Opacity to 80%.

5. Typically, which is the best method for deciding where to set the white point?
   a. It should always be set at 206.
   b. The lowest point possible, usually around 60
   c. It should be somewhere where it does not cut off any of the white values already in the image.
   d. The point in which all torn portions are well hidden

MINOR IMPERFECTIONS

After you have corrected for tone, you can start on either major repair work or minor repair work. It is often easier to do the small things first. There are two filters that are used for minor surgery on the image. They are Despeckle and Dust&Scratches.

Despeckle

After you have corrected for tone, you can despeckle the image. This filter (Filter →
Noise → Despeckle) removes tiny stray pixels that are a different color than the pixels they are near. This has the effect of softening and somewhat blurring the image, but
it also can put back a full range of image tones into the Histogram. It is a single-step
filter, so there is nothing to choose other than the filter itself. Apply it once, now—you
may wish to use it again after you have flattened the image to help re-create a full tonal
range if necessary.

DESPECKLE FILTER

1. Select the Despeckle filter (Filter → Noise → Despeckle).

2. Open the Levels dialog just to see what it has done to the Histogram (Mac:
   ⌘+L, Windows: CTRL+L). Figure 10-10 shows the Levels dialog after the
   Despeckle filter has been used. Do not change anything in the Levels dia-
   log. Cancel it. Notice that since you are still using an Adjustment Layer, the
   Histogram does not re-adjust to reflect changed values.

That wasn't much of a Hands On, but there isn't much to say except that the Despeckle
helps to remove excess noise from the image so that it becomes a little smoother and
easier to retouch.

Meet the Family

Since it is now time to start correcting pieces of this image rather than the entire image,
it is time to be introduced to "the family." It is much easier to refer to the diners by name
than to say "the woman on the left sitting between two men." Saying "Let's fix Aunt Ida's
hair" is much more easily understood. Figure 10-11 shows the Thanksgiving partici-
pants and their names. Missing (mostly) from this image are the author's parents. There

Figure 10-10
Histogram after the
Despeckle filter has
been applied

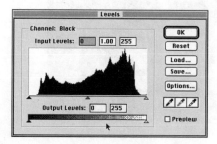

is another version of this photograph that shows half of Mother, holding a towel, and standing next to me. Father was taking the picture. Actually, the photos behind the diners were retouched so that my parents could join the group. You see their wedding picture in one image and Father as a soldier in the other. Sister is also missing from this picture as she was not yet born. Why is a family picture being used for this exercise? One certainly cannot *buy* a picture in this bad of a condition in order to show you how to repair damage!

Dust&Scratches

The Dust&Scratches filter is very powerful at repairing tiny damaged areas of the image. The purpose of this filter is to look at an area of damage and its surrounding pixels and change the color of the damage to that of the pixels near it. It does this by selectively blurring the area using your input values for Radius and Tolerance. In a way, this is almost a mini-unsharp mask (USM), but it never sharpens—it only blurs. However, the concepts of Tolerance (the amount of change needed in a pixel color) and Radius (how many pixels away from the current pixel) are the same as in USM.

Dust&Scratches can do too good of a job fixing the damages sometimes. It has a tendency to over-blur and soften the surrounding area so, as it "fixes" the damage, it creates a similar-toned blob that stands out like a stoplight on a dark night. This is a fix?

In order to use Dust&Scratches, you need to tame it and make it do something useful. It can sometimes be of more help than the Rubber Stamp tool. There are two basic strategies that you can use with the Dust&Scratches filter. You can filter as tiny a selection as possible that still gets some of the area surrounding the damage, or you can select a wider area, float the selection, and then filter the resulting Layer. Let's try this Hands On with a few different Dust&Scratches techniques. You will get to see the filter when it helps—and when it does not. *Remember to work in the Background Layer rather than in the Adjustment Layer.*

Figure 10-11
Family introduced

DUST&SCRATCHES: FLOATING METHOD

1. Magnify Grandpop's left shoulder (your left) until you can clearly see the spot of white on it. This is a minor flaked-off area in the print. Figure 10-12 shows this area encircled.

2. Double-click on the Lasso tool and set the Feather on the Lasso to 2. While it is usually best to use the Lasso without a feather, for this filtering process, it is much easier to set a feather in advance. Just remember to set the Feather back to 0 when you are through with these corrections, or your tool will not behave as expected the next time you use it.

3. Draw a Marquee around the damaged area using the Lasso. Draw the Marquee a few pixels larger than the damage. Figure 10-13 shows the lassoed area.

4. Float the selection (Mac: ⌘+J, Windows: CTRL+J).

Area of damage —————

Figure 10-12
Small area of
damage

Figure 10-13
Lasso around
damaged area

5. Apply the Dust&Scratches filter (Filter → Noise → Dust&Scratches). Start with the Radius set to 1 and the Threshold set to 0. This is as little of the filter as you can apply. Look at the Preview. If the damage disappears, then you can click OK. It doesn't in this case. Carefully drag the Radius slider to the right, one number at a time (or press the up and down arrows to advance the slider by one). When you no longer see the damage, stop. The white area disappears completely at a radius of 4.

6. Drag the Threshold slider to the right until most of the damage appears again. Now drag it back toward the left one number at a time (or use the down arrow) until the damage again disappears. This happens at a Threshold of 1. These become your filter settings—for this area at least. Click OK.

7. The marqueed area is now very smooth. Luckily, so is most of the coat that you are fixing. However, you can check to make sure that you change the minimum number of pixels. Set the Apply mode to Darken. This makes sure that only lighter pixels are changed (the damage is much lighter than the surrounding area).

8. You can also make sure that you do not change the darkest pixels from the original image. Double-click on the Layer name in the Layers palette to open the Layer Options. Figure 10-14 shows the Blend If dialog with the settings needed to ensure that only the damaged area is changed.

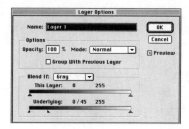

Figure 10-14
Float controls

9. You can also drag the Opacity slider to see if you can get by with a more transparent patch. In this example, you cannot. The patch becomes very visible as soon as you lower the Opacity.

10. **Merge Down** (Mac: ⌘+E, Windows: CTRL+E).

That fixes one tiny hole—though the Rubber Stamp tool would have done a much faster job. It works almost as well on the crack in the turkey. Try that on your own using the same technique.

When you float the damage, you need to make a new *Layer* with the Floating selection. You need to apply the filter twice to the area (and it cannot include both damaged areas on the turkey—you have to handle them one at a time). The larger area cannot adequately be patched with this technique because it is too large.

Apply the filter once at a low radius to fix whatever damage it can. Then, apply it again to the part of the turkey damage that did not get filtered well enough the first time. You need to set the Underlying Layer value much lower than you did on the jacket, however. The patch will never become invisible; *you* will know it is there. Because the damage is so stark, it is much harder to hide. However, if you fix it using the Dust&Scratches filter and decide it needs more work, it is easier to hide using the Rubber Stamp tool after it has gotten a first "coat" with Dust&Scratches. Figure 10-15(a) and 10-15(b) show the turkey before and after the partial fix.

The ideal way to apply the Dust&Scratches filter is to find a setting that applies equally well to all of the bits and pieces of damage in an image. If you can locate such a magic setting, then you can quickly lasso an area, and use the keyboard command to reapply the last filter (Mac: ⌘+F, Windows: CTRL+F). In this image, one area that will accept a magic setting is the wallpaper. Try this Hands on.

Figure 10-15
a) Turkey before patch
b) Turkey after patch

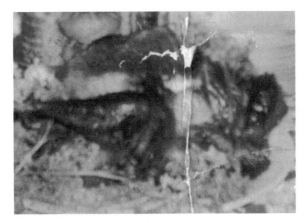

a

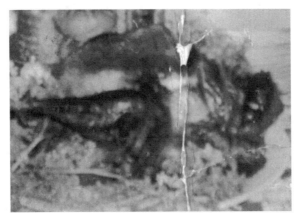

b

HANDS ON

DUST&SCRATCHES: LASSO VERSION

1. Magnify the image to a ratio of 1:1. Press the spacebar and scroll around the wallpaper in the upper portion of the image. You will notice a number of lighter splotches.

2. Draw a Marquee around one of the small areas that is lighter than it should be. The Marquee should enclose just enough of the background for the filter to know what color the area should be.

3. Hide the marching ants (Mac: ⌘+H, Windows: CTRL+H).

4. Apply the Dust&Scratches filter. The setting that seems to work best here is a Radius of 3 and a Tolerance of 2.

5. Deselect (Mac: ⌘+D, Windows: CTRL+D).

6. Continue to repeat Steps 2–5.

It is a good practice to hide the Marquee before you filter, just in case the filter makes a mess. You cannot judge this with the marching ants visible. Therefore, if you hide them first, you can quickly undo the filter if its setting is not helping.

The Dust&Scratches filter can also be useful in covering up long scratches in light-colored areas of low contrast. Uncle Billy's shirt is a good candidate for this use of the filter. Figure 10-16(a) shows the scratch on Uncle Billy's shirt before it is fixed along with the area to be filtered enclosed in a Marquee. Figure 10-16(b) shows the mended shirt.

1. Name the two filters used for minor corrections on an image.
   a. Despeckle and Defreckle
   b. Dust&Scratches
   c. Despeckle and Dust
   d. Despeckle and Dust&Scratches

Figure 10-16
a) Shirt in need of repair
b) Shirt mended

a

b

2. What is the primary purpose of the despeckling function?
   a. To remove tiny stray pixels that are different in color than the others that are near
   b. To correct the tone of an image
   c. To add pixels that are similar in color to others that are near
   d. To correct the stray spots or blemishes found on an image

3. How does the Dust&Scratches filter accomplish the task of repairing tiny damaged areas?
   a. By blurring the area through the usage of the USM input value
   b. By removing stray pixels that are different in color than the ones in the surrounding area
   c. By blurring the area using input values such as Radius and Tolerance
   d. By sharpening the edges of the surrounding areas to the damaged portion

4. Which is the ideal setting for applying the Dust&Scratches filter?
   a. The damaged areas need to be greater than a pinhead in size.
   b. One that fits all the damaged areas equally
   c. One where each damaged area has an individual setting
   d. The color is mostly black.

5. Which filter is best for covering up long scratches in light-colored areas of low contrast?
   a. Despeckle
   b. Histogram
   c. Layers
   d. Dust&Scratches

MAJOR PROBLEMS

The very serious cracks in the Thanksgiving image need more help than the Dust&Scratches filter can provide. The Rubber Stamp tool is the most useful tool in the photo retoucher's arsenal. Although it is easy to use, it is a little trickier to use *correctly*.

Using the Rubber Stamp

In a tutorial for a very early grayscale editing program, there was a forerunner of the Rubber Stamp tool, and the instructions said it could be used to clone parts of image to other locations in the same image. The tutorial showed the tool being used to copy a palm tree to another part of the image. This made no sense at all, since a Lasso could supposedly cut out the area, which could then be copied and pasted wherever. When using the clone tool in this program, it was almost impossible to separate the palm tree from the sky behind it—which really looked rotten in its new location. The tones didn't fit at all.

The anecdote above addresses one of the most common misconceptions about the Rubber Stamp tool. It should *not* be used to clone objects from one place to another. You have much better tools for doing just that. Instead, the Rubber Stamp tool, in Clone mode, excels at covering up blemishes and problems in an image with tiny nearby areas of detail. In other words, if you want another tree in an image, cut and paste the first one. Put it on a *Layer*, and blend it in. However, if Sister Susie has a smudge on her cheek, remove it using bits of "skin pixels" from close to the problem spot. If she has braces on her teeth, that, too, can be removed with the Rubber Stamp tool.

There is a major catch-22 about using the Rubber Stamp tool. If you clone from areas too close to the damage, you risk leaving very ugly tire tracks. This is because the tool begins to copy the copied area and ends up making repeating areas that are obvious and unacceptable as in Figure 10-17(a). If you clone from too far away from the damage, the color and tonal values will be wrong—and the result will be ugly, obvious, and unacceptable as in Figure 10-17(b). The basic technique for using the Rubber Stamp tool is simple. Set the Rubber Stamp tool options to Clone Aligned. Select a brush. Press the modifier key (Mac: OPTION, Windows: ALT) and click the spot on the image from which you want to copy. Release the mouse button. Move the cursor to the spot where you wish to place the copied texture, and press and hold the mouse button to draw. Your Source (the first click) and Target (the place where the drawing occurs) are now linked. You will continue to copy the image from the same distance away for as long as you do not select another Clone Source.

Figure 10-17
a) Clone source too close to object
b) Clone source too far away

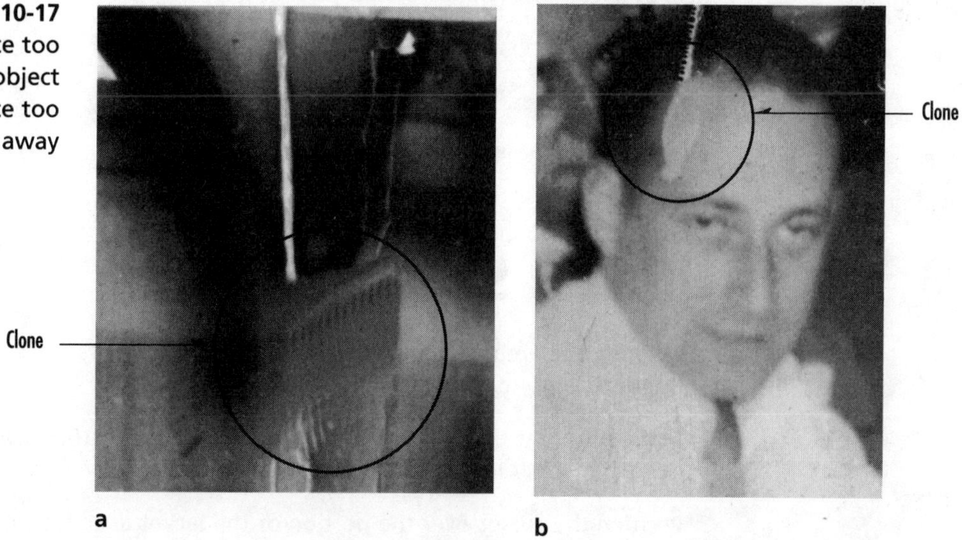

Clone

Clone

a

b

To use the Rubber Stamp tool well, there are some tricks that you must use:

● Clone as close as possible if you are working on skin tones.

● Do not use any single clone source for long. Keep moving the clone source.

● If you are fixing up skin tones, clone from both the shadow and the light side of the damage area.

● Use the Rubber Stamp tool with less than full Opacity if none of the nearby tones seems right, or you need to blend a dark and light clone version. Be careful using the tool with less than 100% Opacity, however, because you can remove too much of the underlying grain and make the image area fuzzy.

● Consider using the Rubber Stamp tool in Darken or Lighten mode if the damage is very different from surrounding areas.

● To keep your options open, select an area to be fixed, float it, and make it into a Layer. Do your editing on the *Layered* version and blend it into the original. Set the Rubber Stamp tool to Sample Merged Layers.

● Watch Russel Brown's retouching tricks on the Photoshop 4.0 CD-ROM. They are excellent and show how to remove wine stains (or discolorations) from a color image and how to handle "rainbow" pixels that show up on a video capture or low-end scanner. The tips are not repeated here since you have access to them on the CD-ROM.

With these tips in mind, let's start fixing some of the major damage on the practice image.

RUBBER STAMP TOOL

1. Magnify the area of the image around Cousin Robert's jacket. Select the Rubber Stamp tool.

2. Make sure that the Rubber Stamp Options are set to 100% Opacity and Normal mode, Clone Aligned.

3. Position the cursor over the portion of the jacket as shown in Figure 10-18. Press the modifier key (Mac: OPTION, Windows: ALT) and click where Figure 10-18 shows the Rubber Stamp icon.

Figure 10-18
Jacket detail and
Clone Source

4. Carefully cover over the major blob of damage on the jacket. Change the Clone Source often.

5. To fix the long crack at the right of the jacket, use the *powder-puff* method. Select a Clone Source nearby and stamp once on the crack. Select another and stamp again. Keep patting fixes over the crack until it is all covered. Then, use the Rubber Stamp tool with longer strokes to even out the coverage. You will end up cloning over areas that were not originally damaged, as you need to make a fairly uniform surface.

6. Set the Rubber Stamp tool Opacity to 40% and the Apply mode to Dissolve. Add back a little noise in the areas that have gotten too smooth. Use the Blur tool at a mid-range pressure to smooth some of the Dissolve mode pixels if they are too sharp. Figure 10-19 shows the mostly fixed jacket.

Let's look at another area of damage—the damaged skin tones on Uncle Billy's face. This is a more difficult area to correct. Not only are skin tones hard to correct normally, since they vary so much that you must use close-by pixels in order to do the repair, but this area contains a dark black streak that also destroys the near-by pixels that you want to use.

Figure 10-19
Jacket detail mostly
fixed

FIXING GRAYSCALE FLESHTONES

1. Open the image MacBilly.Psd. It has already been corrected so that it matches the color corrections you applied to the entire image. However, it is twice the size of the same area in the large image. If you were doing this on your own, you would need to remember to apply the same corrections to the image "pieces" as you did to the image so that they would blend together. Figure 10-20 shows this area.

2. Uncle Billy's hair is the easiest thing to fix first. Use the powder-puff stamping technique again and pick up various areas of from the hair detail nearby.

3. Look closely at the skin tones on Uncle Billy's face—both near the damaged area and then over the rest of the face. The area of shadow around his left ear and jaw provides the best match to the damaged tones. Use that area of the face as the clone source for the damage. Figure 10-21 shows the first area in which to click. The Rubber Stamp icon is the Clone Source, and the Plus sign (+) shows the target.

Figure 10-20
Uncle Billy and
Uncle Mac, detail
to be fixed

Figure 10-21
Clone Source and
Clone Target

4. Carefully repair the damaged skin. You will need to powder-puff more hair over the top of the repair. If there is a line between the shadow and the lighter areas at the right edge of the repair when you are done, you can modify it by selecting the forehead as the Clone Source and placing the Rubber Stamp tool in Lighten mode at 40-50% Opacity. Carefully even out the tones. Figure 10-22 shows Uncle Billy fully retouched.

Figure 10-22
Uncle Billy,
retouched

5. The damage to Uncle Mac's face is equally tricky to repair. You need to use a small, hard brush to fix the collar detail, and the powder-puff technique with a soft brush to fix his clothes. Once that is done, you can use the powder-puff technique on his hair, as well. Bring the skin tone up into his hair area and then powder-puff over them with pixels from the hair.

6. Using the Lasso, draw a Marquee around all of Uncle Mac's face and hair. Make sure that all of the damage is included in the selected area. Float the selection (Mac: ⌘+J, Windows: CTRL+J) to a new Layer. This lets you experiment and start over if you don't like the results. It also gives you better flexibility in applying changes to the image. Make sure that the Rubber Stamp Options is set to Sample Merged.

7. Start fixing the image at the shadows area above the shirt collar. Use mostly the powder-puff technique. Try to keep the shadows consistent with the original image as you repair it. You may need to sample a bit farther away from the damage as the damage has also introduced false shadows—which you need to remove.

8. When you reach the eye area, carefully try to reconstruct the outer shape of the eye. Do the best you can—it is not clear what shape that outer edge had before the image was damaged.

9. When you are done, evaluate your results. If the shadow detail is not quite right and you are unhappy with your results, add a Layer Mask to the Layer. This lets you replace the original shadows (paint on the mask with black) and use a very fine brush (with white) to replace just the area that was cracked. You can continue to modify the mask to keep what you like about your corrections and remove what you don't like. You can then either flatten the image (if you are happy with the results) or simply apply the mask to the Layer and try again. Figure 10-23 shows Uncle Mac repaired. The file, MacBillD.Psd on your CD-ROM, shows this image with Layer mask in place if you want to examine this process.

10. You now need to replace the small section that you retouched into the main image. Duplicate the image (Image → Duplicate → OK). Reduce the copy by 50% (Image → Image Size → 50%).

11. Use the Move tool ((V)) and drag the small image into the original. If you altered the copies to the same tonal specifications, the two images should merge easily.

Figure 10-23
Uncle Mac,
repaired

12. If you have trouble aligning the images, click on the Background Layer to make it active. Turn off the Eye icon on the top Layer (the new image section that you dragged in). Click on the New Channel icon in the center of the Channels palette to create a new channel. Leave the new channel as your "write-able" channel, and click on the Eye icon for the Black channel. This lets you see your main image. Magnify Uncle Mac's face so that you can clearly see his eye. Using a small, hard Paintbrush, paint the *channel* so that his eye is the only thing selected (WARNING: Make sure that you are changing only the channel!). Now, click on the Black channel to make it active, but leave the Eye icon turned on by the new channel. Back in your main image, make Layer 1 active. Use the Move tool ([V]) and drag Uncle Mac's eye on the top Layer so that it shows through the mask. The two images should be aligned.

13. If there is a difference in tone between the two image Layers and you can see the square section that you just put into the image, use the Eraser in Airbrush mode with a soft brush to erase the edges of the top *Layer* so that the two Layers blend. You can use the Paintbrush and a harder brush to remove detail up to the area where the tones look correct. If you want to be able to change your mind, use a Layer Mask rather than the Eraser tool, and paint areas in or out using soft brushes to merge them.

14. Once you are happy with the results, flatten the image and save it.

Replacing Detail

There are four basic ways to replace missing detail in the image:

⚫ You can draw it.

⚫ You can steal it from another part of the image or from another image.

⚫ You can remove the object in question and replace it with something else.

⚫ If the detail is in the image but is too light or too dark, you can bring out the details and only replace the critical ones in the image.

In the next section, you will learn how to use all of these techniques on the Thanksgiving image.

Drawing Detail

When there are small areas of damage that cannot be cloned, you may be able to add them back with a Paintbrush. The better an artist you are, of course, the easier this is to do. However, even the seriously "drawing impaired" can work with the Paintbrush a *little*. A fork on the Thanksgiving table is cracked. It is too blurred to be able to clone. Figure 10-24(a) shows this area of the image. You could remove the fork completely from the image, or repaint it. It is good practice for you to try to repaint it. You can repaint it by cloning to repair the damage using the background of the tablecloth and then painting in the fork over the tablecloth, or you can use Layers and a Layer Mask to make sure that you do not inadvertently damage anything when you paint. That is the tactic you shall use.

PAINTING DETAIL

1. Use the Rubber Stamp tool to repair the damaged area of the tablecloth until you get near the fork. Use mostly long strokes with a little of the powder-puff technique.

2. Drag a Marquee around the tines and base of the fork and float the selection (Mac: ⌘+J, Windows: CTRL+J) to a new Layer.

3. Immediately duplicate the Layer by dragging its icon to the New Layer icon at the bottom left of the Layers palette.

4. Turn the Eye icon off for the top Layer and make the middle Layer the current one (click on the Layer name for the middle Layer in the Layers palette).

5. Clone over the damage on the fork using the color of the tablecloth in the background. This will be the surface on which the fork rests.

6. Select the top Layer to make it active and turn on its Eye icon.

7. Turn off the Eye icon for the middle Layer.

8. Use the Paintbrush tool and sample the color of the fork (Mac: OPTION key, Windows: ALT key to get Eyedropper). Set the brush Opacity to 100% and paint over the entire area of the fork tines and fork base with the sampled color. Make sure that no area of damage is left.

9. Create a Layer Mask (click on the Add Layer Mask icon—the leftmost icon at the bottom of the Layers palette). Fill it with black (make black the foreground color and press SHIFT+DELETE). You will see only the bottom Layer.

10. Use white paint to make the fork tines appear. Paint over the area of the fork tines and the gray that was used in the top Layer's image will return. The best result is obtained by setting a Fade distance on the Brush tool the length of the fork tines. The file Fork.Psd on the CD-ROM for this book shows this part of the image as a Layered document so you can see the three Layers and the Layer Mask. Figure 10-24(b) shows the finished fork.

**Figure 10-24
a)** The fork before
being repaired
repair **b)** Finished
fork

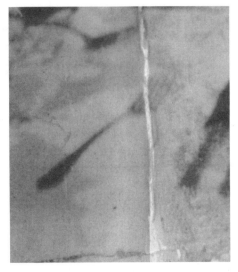

a

b

Stealing a "Patch"

In one of the earlier sections of this chapter, you left the turkey only partially corrected. In this section, you will steal, borrow—or whatever term you wish to use—a portion
of the turkey that is okay to patch up the remaining hole in the turkey breast. The strategy is simple—find another area of the image that you want to use, make a selection
the size of the hole, and move the good image over it.

Hands On

STEALING A PATCH

1. Use the Lasso tool to draw a Marquee around the hole on the turkey breast. Figure 10-25 shows both the turkey and the marquee'd area.

2. With the Lasso tool still active, drag the Marquee to the area of the turkey leg that seems to contain skin. (You are only dragging the Marquee—not the image data.) Feather the selection (Select → Feather, 2 pixels).

3. Drag a copy (Mac: ⌘+OPTION+drag, Windows: CTRL+ALT+drag) of the selected area back to the area of damage.

4. Make a new Layer (click on the New Layer icon at the bottom of the Layers palette). Create a Layer Mask (click on the Add Layer Mask icon—the leftmost icon at the bottom of the Layers palette).

5. Paint the Layer Mask to blend in the damaged area. You should be good at this by now!

6. Apply the Layer Mask (Layer menu → Remove Layer Mask → Apply).

7. Now you can use the Rubber Stamp tool to pick up areas around the borders of the former hole to blend in all of the patch. Figure 10-26 shows the finished patch with the rest of the turkey repaired as well.

Figure 10-25
Unpatched turkey breast

Figure 10-26
Patched turkey
breast

8. Use mostly the powder-puff technique to fix the remaining scratches and imperfections on the turkey.

Replacing Objects

Sometimes objects are so damaged that the best thing to do is either remove them by covering them over with the background or surrounding areas, or replace them with other objects from a different image. In the Thanksgiving image, there are two photos in the background behind Uncle Mac. These photos were so damaged that it was hard to repair them (see Figure 10-27(a). Instead, two other photos—Figures 10-27(b) and 10-27(c) were placed in the frames.

Here's how it was done:

The replacement images were dragged into the image window as a new Layer and then scaled and placed in perspective using the Free Transform command (Layer → Free Transform). You will learn how to do this in Chapter 11, "Photo-Montage."

The image Photos.Psd has the Layers for this process. Open the file and look at both the Layer and the Layer Masks that were created. Figure 10-27(d) shows the finished area of the image.

Recapturing Detail

Sometimes an area of the image is under- or over-exposed, but the contrast detail is still in the image. As long as the image has not blown out to solid white, solid black, or solid-anything else, you can get some of this detail back.

The very young Sherry is over-exposed in the Thanksgiving image. By using the Multiply technique that you used earlier to set the tonal balance, you can bring out the details of the face. The procedure follows.

a

b

c

d

Figure 10-27
a) Original damaged small photos
b) Soldier photo
c) Wedding image
d) Soldier and Wedding images placed into main image

RECAPTURING IMAGE DETAIL

1. Draw a Marquee around the area of Sherry's head. Figure 10-28(a) shows this step.

2. Float the selection (Mac: ⌘+J, Windows: CTRL+J) to a new Layer.

3. Set the Apply mode to Multiply.

4. Drag the icon for Layer 1 to the New Layer icon at the bottom left of the Layers palette. This will copy the Layer into a new Layer. Its Apply mode will automatically be Multiply.

5. Repeat Step 5. Turn the Opacity down to 27%. What you are doing in Steps 3–6 is to darken the feature detail. Even though the skin is also getting dark, that can be removed. You want to multiply until the dark areas are as dark as you want.

6. Click the Eye icon on the Background Layer off, so the image can no longer be seen.

7. Merge the visible Layers (Layers palette menu → Merge Layers).

8. Create a Layer Mask (click on the Add Layer Mask icon—the leftmost icon at the bottom of the Layers palette).

9. Paint out all of the area around Sherry's face on the mask with black so that it is no longer visible.

10. Double-click on the Layer name to open the Layer Options dialog. Press the Modifier key (Mac: OPTION, Windows: ALT) and drag the left half of the This Layer slider to the left until the image reaches the desired tones. Figure 10-28(b) shows this dialog with suggested settings for this image.

11. Use a light gray and a soft brush to tone down the shadow under Sherry's jaw line. Flatten the image (Layers palette menu → Flatten image). Figure 10-28(c) shows the finished retouching.

Figure 10-28
a) Sherry,
unretouched
b) Layer Options
dialog **c)** Sherry,
retouched

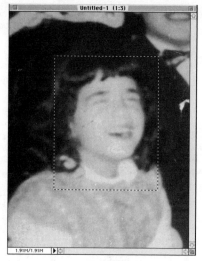

b

a

c

Finishing Up

At this point, you should be able to remove all of the scratches and damage from the Thanksgiving image. This is the point at which you add the Unsharp Masking to the image. The USM amount will differ depending upon whether you wish to print this image or send it to a film recorder. Any image that will be halftoned can stand a greater amount of USM. You are generally safe applying an amount that leaves the beginning of a halo on the screen. If you are sending the image to a film recorder, however, all of the sharpening will be seen. Therefore, do not over-sharpen the image. If it does not look good on the screen, it will not look good when it is printed. Chapter 4, "Filters," went into detail about Unsharp Masking. Review that chapter again if you are unsure. Figure 10-29 shows the fully retouched image.

1. The Rubber Stamp tool, in Clone mode, is best for which feature?
   a. Cloning objects from one place to another
   b. Removing a smudge from a cheek
   c. Removing braces from teeth
   d. Covering blemishes in areas with tiny nearby areas of detail

2. The Rubber Stamp tool has one tricky catch to its use, what is it?
   a. The risk of copying already copied areas and making errors when you clone from areas too close to the damage.
   b. Tonal and color values will be wrong if you clone from too far away from the damage.
   c. Tonal and color values will be wrong if you clone from too close to the damage.
   d. The risk of copying already copied areas and making errors when you clone from areas too close to the damage.

3. Which tool is best for drawing in detail when cloning cannot be utilized?
   a. Marquee
   b. Lasso
   c. Paintbrush
   d. Rubber Stamp

Figure 10-29
Thanksgiving
retouched

4. Stealing from part of a undamaged image to replace damage on another image is called *stealing a patch*. This technique involves which process?
   a. Feather the damaged section of the image in need of fixing, drag a copy to the good image, make a new Layer, create a Layer Mask, apply the Layer Mask, and use the Rubber Stamp tool.
   b. There is no such thing as *stealing a patch*.
   c. Feather the good section of the image to be stolen from, drag a copy to the area of damage, make a new Layer, create a Layer Mask, paint the Layer Mask to blend in the damaged area, apply the Layer Mask, and use the Rubber Stamp tool.
   d. Lasso and copy from the good image, drag to the damaged image, and use the Rubber Stamp tool.

5. For an over-exposed image, which technique is used to the bring out the detail?
   a. Drawing
   b. Multiply
   c. Replacing
   d. Stealing a patch

RETOUCHING TECHNIQUES

Two very common retouching requests are to use a sepia-tone on a grayscale image or to colorize a grayscale image.

Sepia-tones

Sepia-tones can be added to an image in a number of ways. The easiest way is to use a filter called GradTone from the Cytopia Software PhotoLab filter set. This method gives the best sepia range for the least effort. Figure 10-30 shows the filter dialog. You can create your own range of Sepia colors or use the built-in sepia gradation. One way of developing your own sepia ranges is to scan a sepia-toned image and "borrow" the color range that it generates. You can use that range in the CSI GradTone filter or in the Indexed Color method shown here. Unfortunately, this filter is only available on the Macintosh.

Another easy way to apply a sepia-tone is to change the image temporarily to Indexed Color mode. By itself, this yields a very posterized (sharp color changes) image. However, you can fix this by a slightly sneaky trick. Here are the steps (you will get a chance to practice in the Lab section in Appendix C).

Steps to create an Indexed Color sepia-tone:

1. **Create a Gradient that contains the color range that you want in your sepia-tone (or use or adjust the sample on the CD-ROM, Gradtone.Psd).**

2. Change this Gradient to Indexed Color mode (Mode → Indexed Color, Exact). Save the Color Table (Mode → Color Table → Save). This has already been done in Sepia.CLUT.

3. Change a copy of your intended image to Indexed Color mode (Mode → Indexed Color, Custom and select the Color Table that you previously created). The image must be in RGB mode first for this to work properly. Figure 10-31 shows the Indexed Color dialog. Click OK.

4. The image will probably be posterized (very splotchy) and unusable in this state—though occasionally, it will be fine just as it is.

5. Change the Mode back to RGB (Mode → RGB).

6. Apply a Gaussian Blur to this image until the colors in the image blend. Do not worry about losing image sharpness.

7. Open another copy of the image that you wish to sepia-tone. Make sure that you have changed the grayscale to RGB. Using the Move tool (⟨V⟩), drag the blurred copy over the original. Set the Layer Apply mode to Color. It looks much better now.

Here is another technique that gets results that are surprisingly close to those achieved by the CSI GradTone filter. A successful sepia-tone places saturated color in the dark areas of the image but, generally, keeps the light tones in an image fairly neutral. This Color Mode technique can do this for a sepia color of your choice. Once again, general directions are given here, and the specifics for working with the Thanksgiving image are in the Lab exercises in Appendix C.

1. Open the image that you wish to sepia-tone.

2. Change the mode to RGB (Mode → RGB).

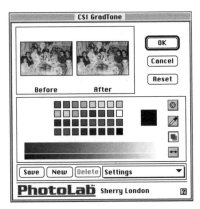

Figure 10-30
CSI GradTone filter
dialog

Figure 10-31
Indexed Color
dialog

3. Make a new Layer (press the modifier key (Mac: OPTION, Windows: ALT) and click on the New Layer icon at the bottom of the Layers palette).

4. Fill this Layer (SHIFT+DELETE) with the sepia color of your choice. No clue? Try RGB 51, 19, 9 or RGB 30, 0, 0.

5. Set the Apply mode to Color.

6. In the Channels palette, click on the New Channel icon in the center of the Channels palette to create a new channel.

7. Use the Apply Image command to place a copy of the original grayscale image into this channel.

8. Use the Levels command to make this channel copy of the image a bit darker than you would want it to print (if you were printing it). You are going to use this channel as a mask, and anything black in it will not be changed in your image. Since you want to keep the darks in your image fully saturated, you want to emphasize these dark tones. Set the Black slider further into the image where data occurs. You might even want to use the Gamma slider to darken the midpoint a *little* bit. Figure 10-32 shows the Levels dialog for this change.

9. Load Channel 4 (Mac: OPTION+⌘+4, Windows: ALT-CTRL+4).

10. Desaturate the image through this mask (Image → Adjust → Desaturate). The loaded channel that was value-pushed toward black keeps the color in the dark areas of the image and gradually removes it from the lighter areas.

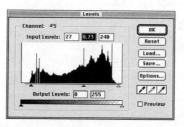

Figure 10-32
Levels dialog to
correct for
sepia-tone

A final way to create a sepia-tone is to use the Duotone feature of Photoshop. This feature is discussed in Chapter 12, "Using Spot Color." Indexed Color mode is also discussed in Chapters 6 and 13.

Colorizing Images

If you wish to colorize photographs, the process is the same as discussed in Chapter 6, "Color and File Formats." The only tricky part is getting convincing flesh tones. One photo-retouching project was brought in by a new grandmother. She discovered that a grayscale photo of her daughter looked amazingly similar to a color photo just taken of her new granddaughter. She wanted the baby's mother's photo colored to match. In this instance, the flesh tones could be "borrowed" from the matching image. Sample selected areas of the flesh and hair tones in the reference image and use those tones to paint the black and white image in Color mode. The key to as realistic a fleshtone as you will get is to sample a number of the tones in various portions of the face and hair. This image will still lack some of the sparkle of the true color image, but it will be much closer than if you had simply chosen one flesh color and painted.

One of the major problems in restoring old photographs is that many of them were printed on textured paper. Sometimes this paper has almost halftone-like dots. Other times it is flecked paper—almost like the paper texture of a dollar bill. Photographs printed on cloth are also in existence. These all present a challenge. While you can blur the texture somewhat, you may also blur the image beyond the point where sharpening it is able to help.

One technique that can be useful is to try to even out the texture with the Paintbrush. This is not as unreasonable as it sounds. If the paper texture shows up as areas that are too light in an image, you can set the Apply mode on the Paintbrush to Darken and sample a color that is just a bit darker than the exposed grain but lighter than most of the areas near the grain. Using the Paintbrush at a very low Opacity, you can carefully darken the texture. The Darken mode will make sure that only lighter pixels are affected. If the texture is too dark, you can do the reverse.

This technique can also be used to cover very fine scratches in an area. The trick here is to sample a color that is not as far away in value from the damaged area as the areas that surround the damage. For example, if you tried to paint with a dark brown to cover white damage in a medium brown area, you would also cover the pixels that were not part of the damage. That is why you need to find a middle color—so you can confine the painting to the area you want to change.

If you are working in a color image, you could try Russel Brown's trick to see if you can neutralize the texture if it is confined to only some of the channels.

Covering Spots in "Batch"

If there are a lot of scratched or scraped areas inside of an area of flat color, you may be able to patch just about every one at once, rather than needing to hack away at it with the Rubber Stamp tool or Dust&Scratches. This time-saving advice comes from noted photographer Steven Johnson.

Duplicate the area that needs to be patched by selecting it and floating the selection to a new Layer. Set the Layer Apply mode to Darken (or Lighten if the damage is dark) and move the Layer a few pixels up, down, or sideways until the damage disappears. Make sure that you do not cause the image to look double-exposed. Flatten the image when you are satisfied with the results.

Removing People and Pets

There are a number of ways to approach the subject of removing pets, people, or other unwanted objects in an image. An unwanted groom can be removed by covering him completely with nearby trees (at an outdoor wedding). A prom night can be rewritten—or rephotographed in the computer. A "boyfriend-ectomy" can extract a girl from the embrace of her boyfriend in her mother's living room near an open deck, and place her in an outdoor setting totally unrelated to anything that actually happened.

In Chapters 3 and 9, you learned how to create selections based on masks. The process of extracting a person is no different. The areas of difficulty are creating the selection to begin with and making sure that merging with a new image leaves no telltale seams behind. You can use the Select → Modify → Contract Command to help keep a line from showing around a person you are moving to a new background.

There is a skill to be learned, however, if you are using the Rubber Stamp to cover over an object or person when you need to continue a pattern or need to extend a specific area.

The pull for the Venetian blinds in the Thanksgiving image adds nothing to the picture and needs to be removed. However, it appears in areas of wallpaper. The wallpaper pattern needs to be continued to the window ledge, and the blinds need to be redrawn correctly. In order to remove the pull, you need to pick a known spot on the wallpaper directly under the area to be removed. You then need to drag the Rubber Stamp tool upward in a straight line so that it covers the pull and redraws the wallpaper pattern directly under it. In this instance, it is OK to let the texture duplicate itself. Figure 10-33(a) shows the original area of the image with the start points and direction marked on it. Notice that the direction arrow is parallel to the wallpaper rather than to the pull. Figure 10-33(b) shows the retouched area. After the window sill was re-created, a batch repair was done on it as shown previously.

Figure 10-33
a) Venetian blind pull that needs to be removed **b)** Image area retouched

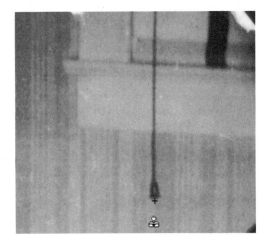

a

b

QUIZ 7

1. Sepia-tones can be added in a number of ways. Identify them.
   a. Indexed Color mode and Color mode technique
   b. GradTone filter from Cytopia Software PhotoLab filter set, Indexed Color mode, and the Duotone feature of Photoshop
   c. Texture helper, Indexed Color mode, and Color mode technique
   d. GradTone filter from Cytopia Software PhotoLab filter set, Indexed Color mode, Color mode technique, and the Duotone feature of Photoshop

2. What are the two most common retouching requests on photographs?
   a. Cut people out.
   b. Sepia-tone on a grayscale image.
   c. Colorize a grayscale image.
   d. Tonal changes on a grayscale image.

3. In the situation where a photo is printed on textured paper, which tool is used to smooth out the texture?
   a. Paintbrush
   b. Lasso
   c. Marquee
   d. Histogram

4. What is a tricky way to remove scratches inside an area of flat color?
   a. Dust&Scratches
   b. Rubber Stamp Tool
   c. Cover spots in Batch
   d. Lasso and copy

5. Which command can be used to help eliminate a line from showing around a person when moving him or her to another background?
   a. Modify → Select → Contract command
   b. Select → Modify → Contract command
   c. Contract command → Select Modify
   d. None of the above

VIP PROFILE

Dan Margulis, Author of *Professional Photoshop*

Dan Margulis is a professional pre-press manager with over 20 years experience heading electronics departments at high-end trade shops. He is the author of *Professional Photoshop* (John Wiley & Sons, 1995), the leading guide to color correction and image enhancement. His column, "Makeready," which focuses on practical production issues, appears in *Computer Artist* magazine. Topics covered in the column form the basis of his newest book, *Makeready: A Prepress Resource* (MIS: Press, 1996).

Dan first encountered color pictures being manipulated on a desktop computer in the mid-80s. This was in a secret room located deep in the bowels of leading software company, where inveterate developers were working with a prototype of what became the Macintosh II. "It was not, of course, a very impressive demonstration by today's standards," Dan says, but as soon as he saw it, he went out and bought Apple stock, because he knew that he had just seen the end of the half-million-dollar color retouching stations he was familiar with.

Dan continues: "Photoshop was five years away at that point, but something like Photoshop was clearly inevitable. Naturally, early versions of Photoshop could not create professional color any more than early versions of QuarkXPress or PageMaker could create professional typography. But I've been using the program for high-end work since Photoshop 2.0 came out in 1991. After that, it was just a matter of time before Photoshop replaced the 'high-end' systems I was more familiar with—and the time has recently come."

When Photoshop 4 was announced and Dan reviewed it, he led with the following:

"Quick. What do art directors, photographers, webmeisters, printers, service bureaus, ad agencies, retouchers, game developers, motion picture special effects teams, and multimedia mavens all have in common?

Yes, they are mostly crazy. Yes, they mostly work with Macintoshes. Yes, they mostly have some dealings with PostScript. But, transcending this, they all use a single program, the only one in the history of the industry ever to have such a monopoly, both the beefiest cash cow in the field of and the brightest star in the brilliant constellation of products of its distinguished parent, the driving force behind color's move to the desktop, the ubiquitous, two-million user, preeminent graphic software of our time, Adobe Photoshop."

Dan's advice to you: "Photoshop at first impresses you with brute force, but the program is a fox, not a lion. The really dramatic effects are easily learned. *Nobody* ever masters all the ins and outs of the program. There is always a new complexity, always a new technique. Don't be buffaloed either by things you don't understand or by experts spouting jargon—if they're using terminology you don't understand, chances are they don't understand it either."

CHAPTER SUMMARY

This chapter showed you the basics of retouching images. The chapter builds on many techniques that you learned in other chapters. You need the color correction skills from Chapter 8, the scanning skills from Chapter 7, the selection, masking, Layers and channels skills from Chapters 2, 3, and 9. These chapters all need to work together to give you the background to manipulate a photograph.

You have learned the workflow steps needed in a typical project. You have also learned how to change tonal values, how to use the Rubber Stamp tool and the critical photoretouching filters of Gaussian Blur, Unsharp Mask, and Dust&Scratches. In addition, you have practiced covering holes, scrapes, and other image wounds. You have learned how to apply a sepia-tone to an image and how to minimize paper grain.

CHAPTER 11

PHOTO-MONTAGE

ayers make it easy to create composite images. Using Layers, you can combine and merge separate images in ways that would be very difficult in a single-Layered program. This chapter looks at ways to combine images. At this point in your study of Photoshop, you have acquired most of the basic skills for using this program. You know how to scan, color-correct, make selections, and make masks. All of these skills come together when you create photo-montages.

This chapter looks at the thought process that goes into making a photo-montage. It also describes techniques used by many artists to create these very popular types of images.

At the end of this chapter, you should be able to

⬤ Remove images from their backgrounds.

⬤ Create a Roadmap channel as a thumbnail for the composite.

519

- Use the Roadmap to place images into your composite.

- Use the Transform and Free Transform commands.

- Use the Image Size and Canvas Size commands.

- Create an Adjustment Layer.

- Create a "coloring" Layer.

- Link Layers so that they move as one.

- Create a Clipping Group.

The process of creating a photo-montage is similar to the process that you used to do photo-retouching. The main difference is that in a photo-montage you need to perform the same set of actions on more than one image, and then fit the images together into a new and coherent whole.

There is an old saying that "if you don't know where you want to go, any road will take you there." This is very true of photo-montage. It is always helpful to have a plan. Even if you have to adjust the plan as you go along, at least you'll know whether you're supposed to be traveling toward California or New York!

The plan comes first, then you acquire photos or illustrations to form the montage. You need to color-correct, retouch, mask the images, and extract what you want from their backgrounds. You then need to crop the images and resize them to fit. Next, you need to place them in a single file and arrange the pieces. Finally, you can perform the finishing touches of adding transparency and Apply modes to make everything fit together, or you can recolor the separate pieces to make them look as if they belong in the original photograph.

In this chapter, the basic compositing sections use one continuing example—one that is dedicated to all of you who have ever said, "Gee, my house is a zoo!"

MAKE-READY

Make-ready is a convenient name to use to describe the procedures needed to prepare the pieces of a photo-montage so that you can put them all together. The activities in this category include creating a map of the final composite, physically acquiring the images to use, and masking them to extract the details that you want.

Developing an Idea

First comes the idea. If you have no idea for your composite, you don't know whether to gather photos of France or photos of your community swimming pool! A photomontage should have a purpose, a theme. There should be some reason why you are putting together bits and pieces of different images. It doesn't have to be great art—it just has to have some type of internal consistency. It is physically possible to place a baseball cap, a soda bottle, and a duck in the same image, but why? However, if you put the baseball cap on the duck's head and the soda can in its wing, and add the text, "Come quack for the home team!" it begins to make sense.

So—you need an idea.

Creating a Map

Once you have an idea or direction, the next thing you need is a plan. The plan consists of two parts—a list of images that you need, and a rough idea of what you want to do with them. Figure 11-1 shows the base image that you will use in this chapter. It is a picture taken through an open patio door. The dark interior makes a very nice

Figure 11-1
View to the outside—the original "base" image

contrast to the brightness of the outside, and it offers the possibility of making the "outside" into something somewhat less than realistic—or possible. It is a good image for some creative and lighthearted "play."

For this photo-montage, you are going to add a koala, a parrot, and a bear casually sitting on the patio. You do not always need to have a base image, as the patio scene will be for us. However, it can help to give structure to the final composite. The humor in this montage will come from the incongruity of these animals just resting on the patio as if they belonged there.

You will also switch the shrubbery in the background to make the koala feel more at home—a bamboo backdrop (well, the koala would probably be happier if he were a panda, but so be it!). The umbrella is also very washed out, so you will replace that, too.

At this point in the process, it can be very helpful to draw a map, or thumbnail, of the desired montage. You don't have to go into great detail, but you basically want to block out the areas where you plan to use each image. This helps to organize the drawing and to get an idea of the relative size of each of the image pieces. There are a few possible scenarios for drawing this thumbnail:

- You have a really good idea of where everything can go, so you are able to draw the thumbnail immediately.

- You don't even know which images you are going to use at this point. You can acquire the images first and then create a thumbnail.

- You have the images, but you cannot quite picture them working together. Quickly cut out each of the image elements with the Lasso tool and reduce each in size (in a copy) to 72 ppi so that the image actually resamples (see Chapter 8, "Scanning and PhotoCD" if you do not remember the difference between resampling and resizing). Drag all of the elements into one image and scale, rotate, and move them in relationship to one another until you get the arrangement that you want. At this point, you can draw the thumbnail.

The third option is probably the most realistic one. It has the advantage of being fast—since you are resampling your images down to 72 dpi (which is screen resolution). It also allows you to distort the images as many times as you need to arrive at a decent composite without having to worry about the image degrading in quality. Since you will be redoing this at high resolution, it does not matter if the image is unusable—you are only interested in relative placement and sizing.

Once you have the images arranged as you think you want them in the "test" composite, how do you draw a thumbnail and what do you do with it? So far in these chapters, you have been using the Alpha channels to create selections. While that is their main purpose, they can also be used as non-printable notes areas. You did something similar to this in Chapter 5, "Working with Paint and Text Tools," when you worked with the Airbrush, but you used a Layer for notes then. You could do your thumbnail in a

Layer if you were careful, but Layers print. If you forget to remove the Notes Layer, this can lead to printing disasters. An Alpha channel cannot print by accident. Therefore, you can place your tracing into an Alpha channel in your photo-montage and turn on the Eye icon to see it. Let's work through this example.

DRAWING THUMBNAILS

1. Open the images Room.Psd, Bear.Psd, Parrot.Psd, Umbrella.Psd, and Koala.Psd. These are the major elements in the montage.

2. Duplicate each image and reduce the duplicate to 72 ppi. In the Image Size dialog, make sure that the Resample Image box is checked. Change the Resolution to 72 ppi.

3. The Room.Psd image is your base image. Therefore, no image can be wider or taller than this. Activate each image and double-click on the Magnifier tool to see each image at 1:1 ratio. The umbrella is much too big. Resize that one so it is smaller than the room image before you do anything else. Remember, you can see the image size on the Mac by pressing OPTION and dragging down the area where the RAM usage is displayed at the bottom of the image window. On Windows, you can get this size by pressing ALT and clicking on the RAM usage area at the bottom of the application window. Change the size of the umbrella to 2.5 inches wide (at 72 ppi).

4. Use the Lasso to quickly outline the umbrella. Use the Move tool (V) or press ⌘ to drag the umbrella on top of the Room image (with the umbrella selected, just drag and drop it). Drag the new umbrella on top of the washed-out one.

5. The umbrella is at the wrong angle and the wrong size. It needs to be rotated and scaled. Since these are commands that have not yet been discussed, open the image TestComp.Psd. This image is already prepared for you so that you can draw a thumbnail. (You can close without saving the other images now as you will not be needing them again right away.)

6. Click on the New Channel icon toward the bottom right of the Channels palette to create a new channel. If the channel is created in solid black (as it probably will be), invert it (Mac: ⌘+I, Windows: CTRL+I).

7. Select the Paintbrush tool with a hard brush. The second or third brush in the Brushes palette on the top row is a good choice.

8. Click the Eye icon on the RGB channel to make the image data visible. However, Channel 4 needs to be only channel that is selected for writing. Figure 11-2 shows the Channels palette set up properly for this.

9. Trace the outline of the room to make the first part of the thumbnail. Then trace around the umbrella, the koala, the parrot, and the bear. Trace enough of the details so you can get an idea what is happening in the image. Figure 11-3 shows the finished thumbnail—crude but good enough to use.

10. Your next step is to get the thumbnail channel into the base image.

11. Open the full-size Room.Psd image and duplicate it.

12. Change your Units Preference back to Pixels.

13. Determine the pixel count for the Room.Psd image (it is 806×1188).

14. Resize (resample) the thumbnail image (Image → Image Size → Width: 806 pixels, Height: 1188 pixels, uncheck Constrain Proportions, check Resample Image). Although setting the width *should* give you exactly the correct height, the rounding errors when you reduced the image to get the thumbnail may make the up-sampling of the channel off by a few pixels. By unchecking Constrain Proportions, you can set both height and width measurements exactly.

15. Check to make sure that the Channels palette is the active palette view. Drag the channel containing the thumbnail into the Room.Psd Copy image. Double-click on the channel and change the Opacity of the channel to 100%.

16. Name this channel Road Map. That way it will be easy to identify.

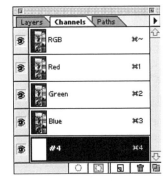

Figure 11-2
Channels palette set up for tracing the RGB image

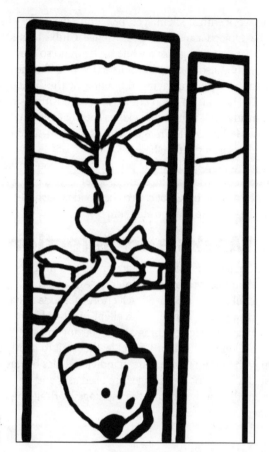

Figure 11-3
Thumbnail

17. Click on the RGB channel to make the RGB channel active, and then turn on the Eye icon next to Channel 4. You can clearly see your outlines from the thumbnail.

18. Save this image as Composit.Psd.

Acquiring Pieces

The image acquisition process, for most folks, actually takes place concurrently with the *get an idea* phase of the project. Once you have an idea of what you want to do, you need to get or create the images that you need. If you are working on a tight budget or a tight deadline, your idea may be dictated by what you already have.

There are several ways for you to acquire images. You can scan them from photographs or from objects placed directly on the scanner. You can bring them into Photoshop from a PhotoCD of your own or stock images. You can create the image in any application that allows you to open the file in Photoshop.

If you like to work with stock images, one group that is very useful for doing photo-montages is the ObjectGear series from Image Club. This series of photo-objects features images that are shot against a white background so they are easy to remove from the background. They also contain both drop (looking like the object is above the canvas) and cast (accurately portraying the angle of the light) shadows. Kai's Power Photos (Series 1–4) are also a good choice for compositing since many of the images contain paths already built to help you extract the images from their backgrounds. They also contain what MetaTools calls *Transflectance* channels—Alpha channels to help remove the white space but preserve the shadows.

If you scan photographs, the same principles that you learned in Chapter 8 apply here. Do as much correction at the scanner level as you can. Scan the images at least as large as you need them to be. Color correct them and retouch them as needed in Photoshop before you cut them out to composite them.

Making Masks and Selections

After all of your images are scanned or acquired, you need to remove the objects that you want from their backgrounds. Chapter 9, "Advanced Selection Techniques" went into copious detail about advanced selection methods. That material will not be repeated here. However, it would be excellent practice for you to stop now and take the time to cut away the backgrounds on the starting images. When you remove each image from its background, add a 1-pixel feather to it to gently soften the edges. You should end up with four images that are in individual files but are on transparent Layers (the Room.Psd and Bamboo.Psd images are used *as is* and do not need to be removed from a background). You will create the montage by dragging these Layers into your composite image.

CREATING SILHOUETTES FROM THE STARTING IMAGES

1. Open the saved Composit.Psd image.

2. Drag the icon for the Background Layer to the New Layer icon (the center icon at the bottom of the Layers palette). This will copy the Background Layer into a new Layer. Remove the contents of both windows from the room image on the new Layer. This is easy to do. Use the Polygon Lasso tool. Feather the selection by 1 pixel before you delete. Change the Layer name to Door Frame. Figure 11-4 shows the Door Frame Layer.

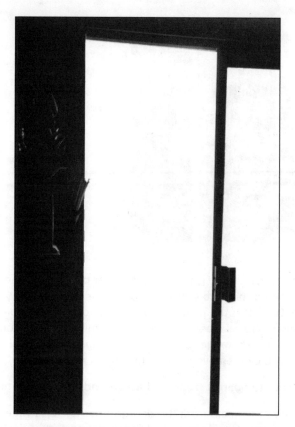

Figure 11-4
Door Frame Layer

3. Drag the icon for the Background Layer to the New Layer icon (the center icon at the bottom of the Layers palette) again. Name this Layer Patio.

4. Drag a Rectangular Marquee around the plant on the floor of the patio on the left side of the image. This plant will be covered over by the bear, so you need to move it to a "safer" spot. Copy it to the clipboard (Mac: ⌘+C, Windows: CTRL+C). Create a new document (Mac: ⌘+N, Windows: CTRL+N). Paste in the selection from the clipboard (Mac: ⌘+V, Windows: CTRL+V). It will appear as Layer 1. Remove the background of the flower. Save this image as FleurPot.Psd.

5. Return to the Composit.Psd image. Remove the umbrella, the door frame, and the background trees from the Patio Layer. Cut out the trees inside of the patio fence in the left half of the window. You do not need to remove the insides of the fence on the right half (the blue side). Figure 11-5 shows this image. You have left only the bottom halves of the images that appear inside the patio glass doors.

Figure 11-5
Patio Layer

6. In the bear image, just extract the bear on the left (the one lying down). You do not need to salvage all of his fur detail unless you want the practice. Duplicate the bear image (and the other image pieces) before you begin to create masks or to select them. Double-click on the Background Layer in each image to create Layer 0 (make the image a Floating Layer) so that you can remove the background.

7. Remove the parrot from the background. You do not need the branch.

8. Remove the koala from the background. Try to salvage the hair around the koala's ears. You do not need the tree branch that the animal is holding.

9. Remove the umbrella from the Umbrella.Psd image.

This gives you the images that you need to composite. Your next task is to correctly size them to fit in the image. You will try a variety of commands on the Layer menu to do this (probably more than you really need to, but it is good practice).

Transform Commands

Once you have finished the make-ready portion of your montage, you need to physically move the images into the place you have planned for them to go. The Road Map channel that you created is your guide. The image manipulation commands on the Layer menu are the main tools that you need to nudge the montage pieces into their new home. This section looks at these Layer commands: Free Transform, Numeric Transform, and the *component commands*—Flip, Scale, Rotate, Skew, Distort, and Perspective. The Image Size and Canvas Size commands (from the Image menu) are also shown.

This is a very interesting group of commands. The thing that makes them unique is that you can perform any of the Transform commands from the Layer menu while you are executing any other of them. You can twist and mold your image into any shape before you say "OK." If you decide to skew your image and then think that maybe you'd like to rotate it, the Layer → Transform and Layer → Free Transform menu items remain active throughout so you can mix and match them. (The only other function in Photoshop that allows other menu items to be selected in the middle of a dialog or activity is the New File command—which allows you to select any open image as the template.)

"Okay, so what's the big deal," you may ask. The big deal is that every time you scale, rotate, skew, distort, or otherwise mangle an image, you degrade the quality of the image (its sharpness and definition). It is possible to change a beautiful image into a blurry mess of pixels and once the image is deformed, it cannot be healed. So—you only want to do this once to any given image. Photoshop's capability to let you do all of your mangling in the course of one operation makes it less likely for you to cause a major mess (or at least one that cannot be undone).

What Is a Bounding Box?

When you select a Transform command, a rectangular box with solid lines appears around the area to be transformed. If you have an active selection, the bounding box is the smallest rectangle that can enclose the selection. If there is no selection, the bounding box is the smallest rectangle that can enclose all of the non-transparent pixels on the Layer.

The bounding box contains hollow squares in each corner and in the center of each side. These are the *handles* that you use to grab the image so you can skew, scale, or distort it. You rotate the image by dragging the cursor outside of the bounding box.

Think about the ability to do multiple transforms in one step as if you were making 10 copies in a copier. If you copy the same image 10 times, each copy is at least as crisp as all of the other copies. Contrast this with making a copy, then copying the copy, then copying the copy of the copy, and so on. By copy number 10, it is a wonder if anything shows up at all. By letting you do everything you want to an image at one time, you can preserve as much of the original as possible.

In the sections that follow, the Transform commands are presented as needed to make the montage—rather than in any specific order. However, let's define briefly what each type of transformation does.

● *Flip* (horizontal or vertical) creates horizontal or vertical mirror images.

● *Scale* changes the size of an object proportionally or non-proportionally.

● *Rotate* changes the orientation of an object, revolving it around its center point.

● *Skew* changes a rectangle (the bounding box of the object) into a parallelogram.

● *Perspective* makes a trapezoid from the rectangle so that the sides, if extended, would converge at a vanishing point.

● *Distort* allows you to move each corner of a rectangle independently of the others.

Flip

In order to get the flower pot to sit against the right wall of the image, you need to flip the image over so that the flat side of the pot is toward the right. Figure 11-6 shows the flower pot *before* it is flipped. In which direction should it be flipped? You have a choice of Horizontal or Vertical.

The answer is that the flower pot needs to be flipped horizontally. Why? A horizontal flip, somewhat non-intuitively, flips the image from left to right maintaining the same horizontal axis (the horizon would cross your screen from left to right as well). A vertical flip flips the image along its vertical axis (up and down).

Add the flower pot to the composite image by flipping it horizontally (Layer → Transform → Flip Horizontal) and dragging it to the composite image (with the Move tool or ⌘). Place it against the far right wall along the bottom of the image. Remember to change the Layer name to Flower Pot so that you can easily see what is on the Layer, and drag it below the Door Frame Layer.

Figure 11-6
Flower pot

Image Size

The koala bear is really too big to fit in the area where he is supposed to go in the Composit.Psd image. You need to make him the right size to fit in the image. Here is one technique that helps to make him fit—and it uses the image map that you created earlier in the chapter.

SCALING AN IMAGE USING THE IMAGE SIZE COMMAND

1. Turn on the Eye icon next to the Road Map channel in the Channels palette of the Composit.Psd image.

2. Drag the Rectangular Marquee around the outline of the koala that appears.

3. Open the Info palette (Window → Palettes → Show Info). The size of the selection is shown in the W: and H: rows of the Info palette. The koala is approximately 211×271 pixels in the example.

4. Now measure the koala that you need to place in the composite image. You really only need to get the height measurement—if that is correct, the width will be automatically scaled to match. The koala is approximately 411 pixels high. It will need to be resized.

5. Duplicate the koala image that you prepared for the composite (the one without the background). Crop it so that the image contains just the koala with no extra space around it. This makes it easy to do the math—there is no need to!

6. Use the Image Size command to reduce the koala to 271 pixels high (Image → Image Size → Height: 271 pixels).

7. Use the Move tool ([V]) and drag the koala into the composite image. The Road Map channel will turn itself off. Turn the Eye icon next to the Road Map channel back on, and move the koala into place.

8. Drag the Koala Layer in the Layers palette below that of the door frame. Figure 11-7 shows the Layers palette at this point.

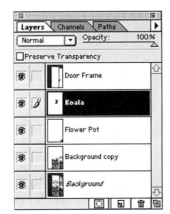

Figure 11-7
Layers palette after
placement of koala

When you calculate image dimensions in pixels, the image resolution does not matter. Therefore, using pixels is the most exact way to determine by how much you need to reduce an image. You can use exact amounts and do not need to worry about percentages—or about different image resolutions.

Scale

The Scale command (Layer → Transform → Scale) is used to reduce or enlarge the size of a selection. It can be used on any Layer that has a selection, or it can be used on a non-Background Layer with no selection. If there is no selection Marquee, the Scale command will affect all non-transparent pixels on the Layer.

You can scale a selection proportionally or non-proportionally. To scale a selection without regard to its proportions, you just need to drag one of the *box points* at a corner or sides of the image. That will *anchor* the scaling to the corner diagonally opposite the one that you move. If you want the transformation to take place from the center out, press (OPTION) as you drag on any point. If you want to maintain the image proportions, you need to press (SHIFT) as you drag a *corner* point (and yes, you may press (SHIFT) and (OPTION) at the same time).

The cursor changes when you select the Scale command. It will become an double-pointed arrow only when it is over a *draggable* corner point. After you have sized the selection to the desired amount, the cursor becomes an arrowhead when it is inside of the selected area and a regular cursor arrow outside of the selected area. To execute the command, double-click inside of the Marquee where you see the arrowhead or press (ENTER) or (RETURN). Press (⌘)+(.) (Mac) or (CTRL)+(.) (Windows) or the (ESC) key on either platform to change your mind and cancel the command. Let's try this with the parrot—which is small enough to fit in the composite image so that it can be scaled "in place" there.

SCALING AN IMAGE

1. Open the parrot image that has been prepared for compositing and is already free from its background.

2. Drag the parrot into the composite image.

3. Turn on the Eye icon next to the Road Map channel in the Channels palette.

4. Use the Move tool (V) to position the parrot so that its head is in the correct position according to the Road Map.

5. Select the Layer → Transform → Scale command. A rectangle with hollow boxes at the sides and corners appears around the image. Figure 11-8 shows this position.

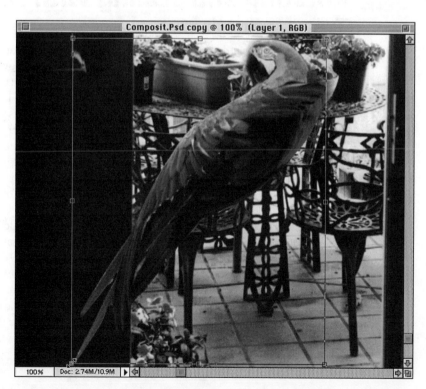

Figure 11-8
Parrot ready to be
scaled

6. Press [SHIFT] and drag the bottom-left corner up until it makes the parrot the same height as the parrot in the Road Map. Note: The parrot will not "fit" into the Road Map as it is scaled. You need to make sure that the height is the same, however.

7. Move the cursor inside of the parrot selection. The cursor will become an arrowhead. Double-click the mouse to execute the Scale command.

8. Use the Move tool ([V]) to place the parrot so that it fits into its space in the Road Map.

9. Turn off the Eye icon next to the Road Map channel so that you can see what you have done. If you need to move the parrot so that it holds onto the table, do so now.

10. Double-click on the Parrot Layer and change the name of the Layer to Parrot for easy identification.

11. Drag the Parrot Layer below the Door Frame Layer in the Layers palette.

Rotating and Scaling with Free Transform

The Rotate command is used to revolve the selection to a new angle. It works on either a selection or Layer *or on the entire image.* So that you can know which it plans to do (rotate a Layer or the whole image), there are actually *two* rotate commands. The Rotate Canvas command is located in the Image menu, where it indicates that you can .change the orientation of the entire image. This command lets you rotate or flip your whole image. You can specify 90, 180, or an arbitrary number of degrees to rotate.

The Rotate command located in the Layer → Transform menu allows you to turn a Layer or selection at either fixed intervals of 90 and 180 degrees, or you can rotate the image "by eye" until it looks right. The Layer → Transform → Numeric Transform command has a section where you can specify the exact angle of rotation if you do not want 90 or 180 degrees.

The Rotate command (whichever one you select) is a destructive command, so you need to use it with care. You can rotate an image by 180 degrees as many times as you need without causing a problem. It is also fairly safe to rotate at 90 degree angles. However, rotating the image, selection, or Layer at other intervals causes image distortion and image loss, so you do not want to rotate anything this way more than once. If you need to "try out" a number of different possibilities, make a copy of the image first, and experiment on the copy. When you are sure of the correct angle, use the original image and rotate to the angle that you prefer.

Rotating Images Around a Center Point

If you ever need to rotate multiple copies of the same image (to "fan" them around a center, for example), create new copies for each rotation and specifically move them to the new location. Example: You have a leaf that you want to use to make a rosette by rotating it in increments of 40 degrees around the center. Since a circle has 360 degrees, you need nine copies of the image. The easy way to do it would be to copy the first leaf and rotate it by 40 degrees, then copy the rotated leaf and rotate *it* by 40 degrees, and so on. This is a bad move. By the time you have completed the circle, your leaf is so distorted and soft it is almost unrecognizable. Instead, copy the first leaf and rotate by 40 degrees. Make another copy of the original and rotate it by 80 degrees. Continue to make copies of the original and rotate them to precise places around the circle. You can try this in the Lab exercise section in Appendix C.

In the photo-montage that you are building, the one element that needs to be rotated is the umbrella. It also needs to be sized correctly. In addition, it is too big to fit "whole" into the base image.

If it's too big, how should you resize it? Well, you could use the Image Size command on it *before* you move it to the composite. If you were to reduce the image size so that it is smaller than the pixel width of the composite image, that would work. But there is another way...

Photoshop 4.0 contains a feature known as *big data*. This feature, new to Photoshop in Version 4.0, allows you to drop larger images into smaller ones. When you do, the *extra* data that you cannot see will remain inside the edges of the image. If you move the larger Layer, the extra stuff shows up. (In earlier versions of Photoshop, Layers were clipped to the size of the image.)

Using Big Data

When you bring a larger image (in pixels) into a smaller one, the image area that does not fit into the window remains attached to the image. The overflow is available for use if you move the image, but it will not print, and you cannot view it on the screen. You can remove the overflow image by using the Select All command and then choosing Image → Crop.

If you have this extra data in a Photoshop image, you can change your mind about the exact area of the Layer that is to "show up" in your project. However, you pay a price for this. Your file size increases and so does the amount of RAM needed to edit the image.

Here are the statistics for the Room.Psd image with the Umbrella.Psd image dragged into it.

Description	RAM requirements	File size
Umbrella reduced before placing	4.74MB	3.7MB
Umbrella left whole	4.81MB	3.9MB
Umbrella with *extra* data clipped off	5.57MB	4.5MB

To clip the hidden data, select the visible area of the Layer and create a new Layer via Cut (Mac: SHIFT+⌘+J, Windows: SHIFT+CTRL+J). Then, drag the original Layer to the Layer palette trash can.

This Hands On guides you through the process of scaling an image that is too big to fit in the document and shows you how you can combine the operations of scaling, moving, and rotating the umbrella into one sequence using the Free Transform command (Layer → Free Transform).

Command Watch

You can use these keyboard shortcuts for the Transform commands:

Command	Mac	Windows
Free Transform	⌘+T	CTRL+T
Numeric Transform	SHIFT+⌘+T	SHIFT+CTRL+T

ROTATING IMAGES

Drag the *original* umbrella into the composite image.

1. Turn on the Eye icon for the Road Map channel in the Channels palette. Press ⌘ (Mac) or CTRL (Windows) and drag the umbrella so that the point where the spokes meet the pole is directly underneath the same spot on the Road Map. This will allow you to scale the umbrella "in place" from the center of the image.

2. Change the Layer name to Umbrella and drag the Layer in the Layers palette below the Koala Layer (the koala needs to look as if it is in front of the umbrella). Turn off the Eye icons for the Koala, Parrot, and Door Frame Layers so that it is easier to work (you will turn them on again when the transform is done).

3. Make the Info palette visible (Window → Palettes → Show Info).

4. Select the Free Transform command (Mac: ⌘+T, Windows: CTRL+T). A box with hollow corners appears around the umbrella.

5. Place your cursor on the top-right corner and press [SHIFT] (this keeps the image proportions as you scale the umbrella) and [OPTION] (Mac) or [ALT] (Windows) (this causes the scaling to occur from the center of the image). Drag the corner toward the bottom left until the bounding box touches the top of the umbrella in the Road Map. If you look at the Info palette, it shows that you are scaling the umbrella approximately 69%. Repeat this step, if needed, until the umbrella is the correct size for the image.

6. Place your cursor outside of the bounding box. As you move it near the right side, it will change to a double-pointed curved arrow. This is the Rotate cursor. Drag the cursor in the direction that you wish the image to rotate (up and left). The needed rotation is about 8 degrees if you watch the Info palette as you rotate. Figure 11-9 shows the umbrella being rotated, and Figure 11-10 shows the Info palette, which registers the angle of rotation.

Figure 11-9
Umbrella being
rotated

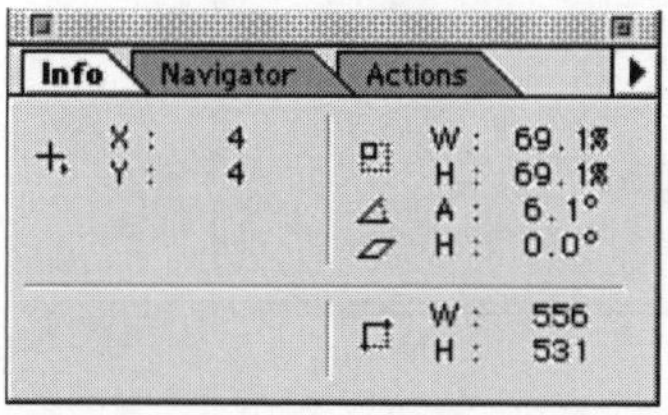

Figure 11-10
Info palette
showing angle of
rotation

7. Because the right edge of the umbrella is cut off in the original image, the umbrella needs to be placed against the right edge of the composite. This does not give you much maneuvering room for placement (other than moving it up or down). If the koala looks like it is hanging in thin air, you need to move the koala, not the umbrella. Do not worry for now that the umbrella may not reach the table or that parts of the koala are missing from the image. You will fix that up in a bit.

8. Continue to rotate and/or scale the umbrella until it occupies its correct spot in the thumbnail. To "set" the transformation, double-click inside of the bounding rectangle.

Before you continue the chapter, place the bear into the composite image. The bear is already at the correct size and just needs to be dragged into place. The Layer needs to be placed below that of the parrot, so the parrot's tail looks like it is over the bear's back. Use the Road Map channel to properly place the bear once you have dragged the image into the montage.

Canvas Size

The Canvas Size command is very useful when you need to give yourself more white space in an image but do not want to change the size of any of the elements in the image. Figure 11-11 shows the Canvas Size dialog set up for the Bamboo.Psd image. It contains the desired number of pixels in the New Size fields.

The Anchor: boxes on the dialog are very interesting. The image is set up so that it will appear in the exact center of the new margins (Anchor: center box selected). If you click on any of the other boxes, the placement on the new canvas will change. Clicking on the Anchor: upper-left box puts the current image into the upper-left corner of the new canvas size. The boxes are visual; click on the one that describes the location where you want the current image to appear.

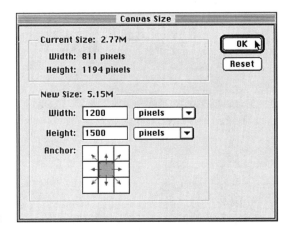

Figure 11-11
Canvas Size dialog

Your choice of background color also affects the Canvas Size command—your background color is what is used for the new margins that you add to the image (if you make the canvas size larger). You can also use Canvas Size to trim away areas of the image. A warning dialog will alert you to confirm that you wish to remove image data.

Let's try changing the canvas size of the Bamboo.Psd image.

HANDS ON

IMAGE SIZE COMMAND

1. Open the Bamboo.Psd image and duplicate it (Image → Duplicate → OK).

2. Double-click on the Background Layer in the Layers palette to open the Layer Options dialog. Press RETURN to change the Layer into Layer 0. Freeing the Layer from its background when you change the Canvas Size makes the Transformation commands easier to use.

3. Open the Canvas Size dialog (Image → Canvas Size). Set the width to 1,200 pixels and the height to 1,500 pixels. Leave the Anchor: in the center.

4. Click OK.

Now, you can use this enlarged image as a basis for some "silly putty" experiments. Usually, there has been some artistic justification for the image manipulations in addition to the pedagogical reasons. However, right now the need to learn the commands is driving the artistic design—the only reason to use *these* commands in *this* composite is so that you can learn them.

Skew

The Skew command allows you to angle the image without changing its orientation. You can move the image diagonally either along the length or the width. If you are trying to skew something on the Background Layer, you must have a selection or the Transform menu will be grayed out. If you are working in a Layer and have no selection, you will skew the Layer contents (the non-transparent pixels).

The method that you use to skew an object depends upon whether you have selected the Free Transform or the Transform → Skew command (you can perform this operation using either command, and change your mind in the middle). To slant the image, you need to grab the center handle along the side that you wish to move.

Command Watch

The Skew command is accessible via the Layer → Transform → Skew menu item or the Layer → Free Transform menu item (Mac: ⌘+T, Windows: CTRL+T).

Action	Mac Key	Windows Key
To skew using the Skew command		
Skew single side:	Drag one of the center box handles on the bounding box	
Skew both sides from center:	OPTION	ALT
To skew using the Free Transform command		
Skew single side—one point only:	⌘	CTRL
Skew 1 point on top and bottom:	⌘+OPTION	CTRL+ALT

HANDS ON

USING THE SKEW COMMAND

Important: In order to complete the next three Hands On exercises as part of the same Transform command, you need to set up your image so that it is in a window that is larger than the image size. Here are the steps to follow to make sure that your transformations will look like the book's regardless of your monitor size:

1. Create a new image that is 460×460 pixels.

2. Place this image behind the "enlarge canvas size" copy of the Bamboo.Psd image.

3. Drag the window of the bamboo image so that it is the same size as the new, empty document. This step simply sizes the *window*—not the image.

4. On the Navigator palette (Window → Show Navigator), drag your cursor over the percentage box to highlight it and type the number 20. Press RETURN. The image will zoom out to 20%. Work with this view as you skew, distort, and apply perspective to the image.

5. Use the "enlarged canvas size" version of the Bamboo.Psd image. Select the Image → Effects → Skew command.

6. Drag the right center box up until a corner touches the top of the image.

7. Wait for the image to redraw. Drag the left center box down until a corner touches the bottom of the image. Note: You could also press the modifier key (Mac: OPTION, Windows: ALT) to do Steps 1 and 2 at one time.

8. Do not "set" this transformation. You are going to distort it further.

Distort

The Distort command allows you to move any one corner of the image at a time in any direction without regard to image shape. Where the Skew command constrains either the length or the width of the image and takes the basic shape of a parallelogram, the Distort command knows no such restrictions. You can seriously pull your image out of line with this command.

It works the same way that the Skew command does with respect to image selections: You need a selection in the Background Layer but do not need a selection in one of the transparent Layers.

Select the Distort command from the Layer → Transform menu. Pull the bottom right-hand corner of the image over to the right side of the canvas, while keeping the bottom edge of the image parallel to the top edge. Figure 11-12 shows this action.

Figure 11-12
Using the Distort
command

Perspective

The Perspective command is used to (*surprise*) show perspective. It can make an image look like it is towering overhead or fading off into the sunset. When you use the Perspective command, two corners of the image always move in opposite directions at one time. For example, if you move the left corner toward the left of the image, the parallel right corner moves toward the right of the image by the same amount.

The direction in which you first drag a corner determines the corner that will move in synch with it. If your dragging motion is down or up, both points on the same side will move together. If you drag toward the right or left, then either the top or the bottom points (depending upon which corner you selected) will move in synch. You can also drag any center from side-to-side. This anchors the opposite side.

THE PERSPECTIVE COMMAND

1. Continue to use the "enlarged canvas size" version of the bamboo image. You need to rescale the image before applying perspective.

2. Select the Free Transform command (Mac: ⌘+T, Windows: CTRL+T) and wait until the screen redraw is complete. Drag the upper-left corner bounding box so that it is over the upper-left corner of the actual image.

3. Press and hold SHIFT to constrain proportions and drag the lower-right corner of the bounding box toward the lower right until part of the right side of the bounding box just touches the upper-right corner of the image. Figure 11-13(a) shows the position of the bounding box at this point.

4. Select the Image → Effects → Perspective command. Drag the upper-right corner of the bounding box until it touches the upper-right corner of the image window.

5. Drag the lower-left corner of the bounding box down until part of the left side bounding box outline touches the bottom-left corner of the image. Figure 11-13(b) shows the position of the bounding box at this point.

6. Double-click inside of the bounding box to "set" the transformation or press ENTER or RETURN.

7. Drag the image into the composite and move the Layer below all of the other Layers except the Background. If you can tolerate the distorted bamboo, leave it alone. If you really hate the way it looks, trash the Layer and drag the original bamboo image in its place. Figure 11-14 shows the composite image with all of the elements in place.

Figure 11-13
a) Bamboo grove perspective, part 1
b) Bamboo grove perspective, part 2

a

b

Figure 11-14
Composite image
with all elements in
position

Here is a summary of the modifier keys when used with the Free Transform command:

Action	Mac Key	Windows Key
Constrain proportions/direction	SHIFT	SHIFT
Mirror	OPTION	ALT
Move single corner point	⌘	CTRL
Skew (drag side-center handle)	⌘	CTRL
Perspective	SHIFT + ⌘ + OPTION	SHIFT + ALT + CTRL

QUIZ 1

1. What is the process of Photo-Montage?
   a. Taking more than one photo and adding them together as one image
   b. Eliminating portions of a photo to create an image
   c. Taking only two photos and creating one by blending them together
   d. Retouching damaged areas of a photo

2. In a group of two or more photos, the base image is a good reference point to what?
   a. The color scheme
   b. The height and width of the other images
   c. The tonal changes
   d. Which tools are used

3. Name the two functions in Photoshop that allow other menu items to be selected in the middle of a dialog or activity
   a. Free command and Open command
   b. Transform commands and Open command
   c. Transform commands and New File command
   d. Free command and New File command

4. What is the most exact way to determine the size to which an image needs to be reduced?
   a. Inches
   b. Percentages
   c. RAM
   d. Pixels

5. The Photoshop 4.0 feature "big data" allows for which of the following?
   a. Store larger files
   b. Drop larger images into smaller ones
   c. Layers to be clipped to an image size
   d. Complete removal of extraneous data

LESSON 2

IMAGE LIQUIDITY

One of the best reasons to use Layers, and to leave the image Layered after the montage is complete, is to allow for unexpected changes. So long as the image is kept in Layers, it can easily be changed if a client decides that an element is in the wrong place, a color is not exactly right, or a logo needs to be replaced.

For this reason, you should make as few permanent changes to image data as possible. This naturally causes a trade-off between the size of the image (which, in our example, has gotten huge) and keeping open your image options. It is best to try to keep the Layers and Layer Masks active as long as possible.

Memory Management

Layers use RAM. Each Layer that you add uses more RAM. The additional amount of RAM and disk space needed is incremental. A full Layer uses much more RAM and disk space than a Layer that only contains something small (the Parrot Layer occupies much less RAM and disk space than the Bamboo Layer).

You can tell how much RAM an image is using by looking at the numbers in the Window information area at the base of the image (on the Mac) or at the bottom of the screen (Windows). For example, the numbers on the Composit.Psd image after all image elements have been place read 2.74M/18.1M. The first number is the amount of RAM needed to edit the image if it were a single Layer with no additional channels. The second number indicates the amount of RAM that the image currently needs. RAM, in this case, also means scratch disk space if there is not enough free RAM in your Photoshop partition.

You can continue to work on an image until it slows down unbearably. At that point, you might want to consider merging some Layers or building intermediate files to make image editing faster. You could also use a plug-in called FastEdit Deluxe, from Total Integration, to edit only a portion of your image at a time. FastEdit Deluxe, unlike the built-in QuickEdit feature (in the File menu), allows you to edit portions of images in Photoshop 3.0 format that contain Layers.

Layer Controls

In the "My house is a zoo" montage that you have been creating, all of the major elements are on separate Layers for maximum flexibility. You can easily move and reposition each Layer, but you are still only taking advantage of part of the power of the Layers architecture. The other Layer-related features that give added flexibility are Layer Masks, Clipping Groups, and Apply modes.

Layer Masks

You have already used Layer Masks in earlier chapters and should know how valuable they are. In this collage, you can use a Layer Mask to make it look as if the umbrella is going behind a flower bowl rather than ending in thin air.

*H*ANDS *O*N

ADDING A LAYER MASK

1. Click on the Umbrella Layer in the composite image and then create a Layer Mask (click on the Add Layer Mask icon—the leftmost icon at the bottom of the Layers palette).

2. Using black as your foreground color, pick a medium brush and paint over the edge of the umbrella until it looks as if the bottom of the pole is behind the flowers. Remember: Painting with *black* in the Layer Mask *hides* what is in the current Layer, painting with *white* in the Layer Mask *reveals* it.

3. If it looks as if the umbrella should be continued still further so that it ends in the table, you might want to drag the umbrella, and the koala that is clinging onto it, a bit farther toward the right to put it firmly behind the flowers. To move both Layers at one time, click in the Link column next to the Eye column on the Koala Layer. A symbol that looks like a Link in a chain appears. This icon is the Linking icon and indicates that the two Layers will move together. Figure 11-15 shows the Layers palette with the Umbrella and Koala Layers linked.

How else might you use a Layer Mask in the composite? If you did not feather your images as much as they need, you can repair the feather by using a Layer Mask and painting outside the image area in the Layer with a very large, *soft* brush and black paint. Let the edge of the brush just touch the edge of the image area. As the brush starts to

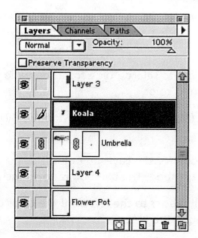

Figure 11-15
Layers palette
showing two Layers
linked for moving

leave black "paint" in the mask, the edges of the object in the Layer will soften and feather. You can control this very precisely with the Layer Mask—if the edge gets too soft, just paint over it with white and try again. It makes an infinite undo.

You can also use Layer Masks to blend two or more images together seamlessly. This is a special effect that you can practice in the Lab section in Appendix C.

Apply Modes

You can use the Layer Apply modes to keep an image fluid. Any Apply mode can be added and removed from a Layer at any time without damaging the image data. You can use the Apply modes for special effects, but you can also use them for things like color correction. Here's how.

HANDS ON

APPLY MODES FOR COLOR CORRECTION

The bamboo background and the umbrella that are behind the right-hand portion of the sliding glass door need to be made much more blue to look as if the door is in front of them. You can add this blue color cast using a solid Layer of blue and the Color Apply mode.

1. Open the Composit.Psd image.

2. Click on the Koala Layer to make it active and then click on the New Layer icon at the bottom left of the Layers palette to add a new Layer (this puts the new Layer directly above the koala).

3. Using the Rectangular Marquee, select the area of the bamboo that is behind the right side of the patio door. Draw the rectangle only down to the fence.

4. Use the Eyedropper tool to select a blue from the patio tiles behind the door as your foreground color.

5. Fill the selected area (Mac: [OPTION]+[DELETE], Windows: [ALT]+[DELETE]) with the solid blue.

6. Change the Apply mode for the Layer to Color. This makes the Layer a *colorized* blue over the bamboo. The bamboo is now much too blue.

7. Drag the Layer Opacity slider to the left until the color cast matches the area that shows through the fence (about 74%).

8. If you wish to give added intensity to the area, you can increase the saturation by about 35-40% using the Image→ Adjust→ Hue/Saturation command.

You can color correct any Layer that needs it using a solid color Layer above it and Color mode. You can change the solid Layer at any time by using the Adjust→ Hue/Saturation command, and the changes are completely non-destructive.

You could also use an Adjustment Layer to do the same thing. Let's try it that way as well—now that you have tried the "manual" approach.

1. Drag the blue Layer that you created to the Layer trash can.

2. Click on the Koala Layer to make it active. Using the Rectangular Marquee, select the area of the bamboo that is behind the right side of the patio door. Draw the rectangle only down to the fence.

3. Create a new Adjustment Layer (Mac: ⌘+click on New Layer icon, Windows: CTRL+click on the New Layer icon). Make it a Hue/Saturation Layer in Normal Apply mode.

4. In the dialog box, click on Colorize. Drag the Hue slider to –142, the Saturation slider to 42%, and the Lightness slider to –17. These settings best approximate the blue that you selected before. Click OK.

5. The image is much too blue. Drag the Opacity slider in the Layers palette (for the Hue/Saturation Layer) to about 62%.

Which method should you use—a Layer in Color mode or a colorized Hue/Saturation Layer? It is close to being a toss-up. If the area were very large, the Color mode Layer would probably take up more room. This is just another example of multiple ways to do almost anything in Photoshop.

Clipping Groups

A final Layers feature is the Clipping Group. This feature allows you to trim one Layer so that it conforms to the shape of the Layer beneath it. It is a wonderful, fast way to make type from a picture. It is also an easy way to make the flower pot at the bottom left of our composite image take on the same blue color as the rest of the items behind the plate glass window.

You can change a Layer into a clipping group by placing an X in the box marked *Group with previous Layer* in the Layer Options dialog. Figure 11-16 shows this dialog. You can also accomplish the same thing by pressing OPTION (Mac) or ALT (Windows) and placing the cursor directly over the dividing line between the two Layers in the Layers palette. When you are in the correct spot, the hand cursor will change to the *grouping* cursor, two overlapping circles and a tiny left-pointing wedge. When you see this cursor appear, click once. The solid line between the two Layers changes to a dotted line and the lower Layer name is underlined. They are also slightly indented in the Layers palette. This is visual confirmation that a clipping group has indeed been established. Let's try it with the flower pot.

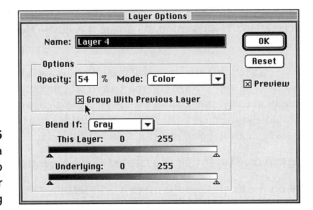

Figure 11-16
Establishing a clipping group using the Layer Options dialog

CLIPPING GROUPS

1. Open the Composit.Psd image.

2. Click on the Flower Pot Layer name in the Layers palette to make the Layer active.

3. Make a new Layer (click on the New Layer icon at the bottom of the Layers palette). The new Layer will appear directly above the Flower Pot Layer.

4. Drag a Rectangular Marquee around the entire area of the flower pot. Fill the area with the same blue that you used for the Color Layer above or sample a different blue from the darkest area of the patio floor behind the plate glass window.

5. Set the Apply mode to Color as you did earlier.

6. Double-click on the Layer name to open the Layer Options dialog and click on the box marked *Group with Previous Layer*. This looks like it cuts out the areas of the solid blue rectangle that are on top of the flower pot. In reality, not a single pixel is removed, but only the pixels that are over the flower pot are visible. Drag the Opacity slider lower until you have an acceptable color cast (about 54%).

You could achieve the same results by filling the entire Layer with blue and then clipping, but that would increase the disk and RAM usage very much for no good reason. If you fill an area just a bit larger than the object that is used for clipping, that is good enough. You could also use an Adjustment Layer and clip the Adjustment Layer to the Flower Pot Layer (or select the Flower Pot Layer and add the flower pot to the Adjustment Layer that you created previously by clicking the Adjustment Layer to make it active and filling the selection with white—which removes the mask from the area and allows the color correction to affect the flower pot).

Intermediate Files

You can reduce the storage requirements on a photo-montage by using intermediate files to build groups of effects and then flattening a copy of the finished version. You can then use this flattened copy in your final composite. For example, you could have built the koala hanging onto the umbrella in one image and brought them both into the composite as a single entity. You could create objects and their shadows in the same manner. As long as you keep the images with the original Layers, you can always go back and make changes.

Finishing the Photo-Montage

The practice photo-montage looks fairly good, but it needs some finishing touches for more realism.

1. You need to go back and create part of the koala's leg and arm where the tree was removed. You can use the Rubber Stamp tool for that.

2. The parrot's tail feathers should leave a shadow over the bear. Remember how to create a drop shadow? Duplicate the image and drag the copy below the original Layer. Turn on the Preserve Transparency option and fill the non-transparent pixels with black (or your shadow color). Turn the Preserve Transparency option back off and apply a Gaussian Blur to the Layer. Drag the Layer into the correct position for a shadow. You might want to use a Layer Mask on the Shadow Layer to remove the shadow of the parrot where it would not realistically occur (between the table and the bear).

3. The koala's head should cast a shadow on the umbrella.

4. The bear should have a cast shadow (not a drop shadow) along the patio floor (elongate a drop shadow using the Skew, Distort, or Perspective command).

5. These shadows add enough to an already too-large file that you might want to create intermediate files for them.

1. What is the advantage to using Layers when working on a photo-montage?
   a. They are fun.
   b. They allow you to make changes even after the image is complete.
   c. They create more RAM.
   d. None of the above.

2. If you see the numbers 2.74M/18.1M at the bottom of your PC screen while working on an image, what does the second number indicate?
   a. The dimensions of the image
   b. The amount of RAM remaining on your hard drive
   c. The amount of RAM the image currently needs
   d. The amount of RAM needed to edit an image in a single Layer with no additional channels

3. What is the Layers feature Clipping Group used for?
   a. To trim one Layer so that it conforms to the shape of the Layer beneath it
   b. To cut and paste pieces of one figure to another
   c. To clip multiple Layers at one time
   d. All of the above

4. Intermediate files are handy for what?
   a. Saving time
   b. Saving storage
   c. Saving amount of work
   d. Saving work in progress

5. You would elongate a drop shadow to make a _____ shadow.
   a. long
   b. sort
   c. cast
   d. skew

VIP PROFILE

Rob Day, Artist and Author

Rob Day, author of the book *Designer Photoshop*, first started working with Adobe Photoshop in 1989. Rob was trained as a fine art silk screen printer and print-maker.

In 1989, he moved to Newberryport, MA and was working with designer Lance Hidy who was on retainer with Adobe Systems, Inc. In 1989 when Adobe placed Photoshop 1.0 into Beta test, Rob got a first opportunity to work with it—and jumped right in.

Rob began doing a number of assignments in creative education—working on books that were to be placed in school libraries and were written with the intention of encouraging children to read. The books covered sports and famous writers, as well as other topics of interest to young readers. In 1990, the publisher took the risk of letting Rob and Lance do some of the design in Photoshop.

Designer Photoshop was published in 1993 by Random House. It was only the second book available for Photoshop at the time. The book is slender, but it shows Rob's design philosophy and contains very clear, concise instructions. It is beautifully designed. There is an updated version available for Photoshop 3.0.

Rob is currently working as a designer and illustrator with Virginia Evans. He is still doing a lot of design work for book publishing, but the company is also branching out. He has a Web page at `www.evansday.com`, where you can view his portfolio and see some of his very unique designs.

The announcement for his Web page sums up much of Rob's philosophy. "When we wrote, designed, illustrated, and produced *Designer Photoshop,* we used the regular stuff—Quark, Illustrator, Photoshop. We also used some not-so-regular items—Kraft paper, rocks, emu's edges—because in skillful hands great design can happen with a few laser beams and a bag of M&Ms."

Rob is a *complete* artist. He can draw, paint, scan paintings, and use whatever medium is needed to design a job. Photoshop is another tool in his toolbox of techniques—all of which are used to support the art.

Rob's advice to you as a new user of Photoshop: "Take any opportunity you can to produce output from Photoshop. The best way to learn is to be able to see the printed results in as risk-free an atmosphere as possible. Do *pro bono* work and use that as a vehicle for experimentation and learning."

CHAPTER SUMMARY

This chapter is a very important one in that it brings together all of the skills that you have painstakingly mastered in this course so far. There are as many ways to build photomontages as there are artists, but this chapter has given you techniques that you can use as you begin to develop your own style and your own working patterns.

You have learned how to build a road map for your montage, how to extract images from their background, and how to use the various Image commands such as Free Transform, Scale, Skew, Distort, Rotate, Flip, and Perspective. You have also learned how to calculate new image sizes for composite image sections using the Info palette. Finally, you have learned how to use Layer Masks, Apply modes, and Clipping Groups to make your montages flexible and easy to change.

USING SPOT COLOR

O n the Adobe Forum on CompuServe, two questions are asked more frequently than any other. One is: "How can I place transparent output into QuarkXPress?" The other question is, "How can I get Photoshop to use Pantone colors?" These questions are frequently asked because they are the production issues that artists grapple with every day—and because the way to perform both these functions is not obvious, nor is it especially elegant. Using spot colors and making them print is torturous; however, once you understand why Photoshop has trouble with this, it is not impossible to work around.

In this chapter, you will learn how to prepare spot color output from Photoshop, trap it, and place it into a page layout program. At the end of this chapter, you should be able to

555

● Define spot color.

● Describe why the process of using spot color is so difficult in Photoshop.

● Create Layers that are designed in a spot color and transfer them to channels.

● Create grayscale channels at the values needed for spot color work.

● Use the Apply Image command.

● Explain the function of PlateMaker.

LESSON 1

SPOT VERSUS PROCESS COLOR

Just what is this *spot color* that is so problematical? To understand, you have to have some knowledge of how images are printed. Full-color printing is a four-step process. An image is separated into tints of four colors—cyan, magenta, yellow, and black (this is what happens when you convert an image to CMYK mode—you are actually getting it ready for a conventional printing process). Four printing plates are made, and then ink is applied to the paper for each plate—cyan ink, magenta ink, yellow ink, and black ink. This results in the images that you see in magazines and newspapers.

Cyan, magenta, yellow, and black inks are known as *process* colors because, in theory, you can re-create any color using these four inks. It's a nice theory! It is also inaccurate since there is a much smaller number of colors that can be created using these inks than there are possible colors. A lot of colors *cannot* be made from the four process colors. Therefore, there is another set of inks that can be used in order to arrive at the color you want. These are the *spot colors*. These inks require one printing plate per ink, but the color can be picked from a much wider range.

Think of spot versus process color as the difference between purchasing three tubes of acrylic paint (a red, a blue, and a yellow—the *primary* colors) and getting a tube of hot day-glo pink. Although you can mix many colors from the three primary colors, you cannot mix day-glo pink, no matter how hard you try. You probably could not mix Payne's Gray or Alarazin Crimson from the primaries, either.

There are two reasons, then, to use spot or pre-mixed colors in your image. One reason is when a client must have some of a specific color (such as metallic gold, that cannot be mixed from the basic color set) and the other is to cut the cost of printing a job by using fewer than four colors of ink. Spot color is frequently used for brochures and sales marketing pieces that have to look good but which need to be printed for less money.

Spot color inks are sold by many companies, but the most commonly used system of spot color comes from Pantone. Pantone inks are available in thousands of colors, and Pantone has many reference libraries of these colors so that you can choose the color you want from an actual sample. They also license electronic versions of the color libraries to Adobe and to the other graphics software developers. This permits you to select from an online representation of the color.

Why Is Spot Color a Problem?

There are several reasons why it is so difficult to produce spot color separations from Photoshop. The basic problem is that there is no way to define your spot color and have Photoshop "remember" that it needs to go on its own plate. Although you can select a color from the Pantone inks (by choosing Custom in the Color Picker), once you place pixels of that color into your image, the pixels are written to the RGB (Red, Green, and Blue) or CMYK (Cyan, Magenta, Yellow, and Black) channels (depending upon your color mode) just as if they were "ordinary" colors. The channels then become the printing plates when you either ask Photoshop to do a color separation or you place the image into a page layout program such as QuarkXPress.

The second problem area concerns *trapping* (making sure there is no white space that shows if two plates misalign in the printing process). If you are using Photoshop to create a continuous tone image such as a photograph, there is no need to trap. Indeed, if you were unwise enough to do so, your output is likely to resemble mud. However, spot colors, by their nature, are used to color in large discrete areas on an image. Wherever these colors meet, it is very likely that trapping will be needed. Photoshop can trap, and trap very well, but it can only trap images that are in the CMYK channels of a CMYK mode document. Unfortunately, if the images remain on the CMYK plates, they cannot then be output as spot colors.

Why not just use Adobe Illustrator, Macromedia Freehand, or CorelDRAW! to produce spot color images? The illustration programs have no trouble with spot color. That is certainly the easier approach to dealing with spot color. However, if you wish to apply *painterly* effects to your image, you may not be able to do that as easily in an illustration program. The best reason to use Photoshop to prepare spot color (in fact, the only reason to cope with the trauma) is because there are Photoshop features that you *need*.

1. What are the four process colors?
   a. Cyan, white, magenta, and yellow
   b. White, black, blue, and red
   c. Magenta, black, yellow, and cyan
   d. Blue, red, magenta, and cyan

2. In theory what are process colors?
   a. The only colors an image will be printed in.
   b. The three colors when combined can re-create any color.
   c. The four colors when combined can re-create any color.
   d. The five colors when combined can re-create any color.

3. What are spot colors?
   a. A set of inks where you do not mix colors to arrive at the desired color.
   b. Blue is the only spot color.
   c. A set of inks where you do mix colors to arrive at the desired color.
   d. Yellow is the only spot color.

4. Which is best for handling spot color?
   a. Photoshop
   b. Adobe Illustrator
   c. Macromedia Freehand
   d. CorelDRAW!

5. Why would you opt to use Photoshop with spot color?
   a. You can't; it is impossible to do so.
   b. Because they are most compatible.
   c. Because there are features of Photoshop needed to complete a project that can't be done with other programs.
   d. Because Photoshop is the only program capable of using spot color.

USING LAYERS FOR SPOT COLOR

In order to get Photoshop to produce spot color *plates,* there are several things that you need to figure out how to do. You need to find a way to create the spot color image so that Photoshop does not place the image data in the CMYK channels, and you need to create traps for that image. In addition, you need to be able to place this image into a page layout program once Photoshop has finished with it and have the page layout program correctly produce the needed plates.

There are two ways to get color data into a single location so that it can be easily separated—put each spot color into its own Layer, or put each spot color into its own Alpha channel. In order to *print* the image (to create the plates that will print), each spot color must have its own channel, but it is usually easier to start out by working in Layers. This is the approach that you will learn first.

HANDS ON

CREATING SPOT COLOR LAYERS

1. Open the image Lionvase.Psd. This is a detail of a Foo lion that has been extracted from one of Ed Scott's China series of images. Figure 12-1 shows the original image. You are going to change this image into a 3-spots-plus-black image.

2. Duplicate the image (Image → Duplicate → OK). Make a new Layer (click on the New Layer icon at the bottom of the Layers palette).

3. Select the Paintbrush tool (B) and a hard brush (the third brush on the top row of the Brushes palette is a good choice). Trace around the lion with the brush and trace over the major details in the image. You are going to create a woodcut-look on the image, and these black lines will be the emphasis lines, so most of the "personality" that this lion will have comes from the drawing that you do now. You may vary the width of the stroke, and if you have a pressure-sensitive tablet, you can set that up to vary the stroke width depending upon pressure (the tablet controls are in the Brush Options dialog). Figure 12-2 shows the outlines.

Figure 12-1
Foo lion

Figure 12-2
Foo lion outlined

4. These outlines have several purposes. One, the technical, is that it is much easier to trap to black than to trap the other colors against each other. Another purpose is to enable you to easily select the areas to which to apply the Pantone colors. Oh—and of course—there is a design reason as well!

 CMYK Conversion to Black Channel

When you convert an RGB (or grayscale) image that only has gray values in it to CMYK mode, the image usually is split between all four channels. How it is split depends upon the Separation Setup preferences that you are using for the generation of the Black plate. If you want all the grayscale values to end up in the Black plate—and none of them in the Cyan, Magenta, or Yellow plates—then select Black Generation: Maximum. Since this is not the usual setting, make note of your settings before you change them, and change them back again as soon as you have finished the conversion to CMYK mode.

5. The next step is taken for design—there is no reason to blur and level the outlines other than to produce a specific effect.

6. Duplicate the Outline Layer (Layers Palette menu → Duplicate → New) into a new document. Flatten the image (Layers palette menu → Flatten image). This step lets you use the Levels command accurately after the outlines are

blurred. If you don't flatten the image, the Levels command Histogram will show only solid black in the Layer. Change the image mode to CMYK (Image → Mode → CMYK). You could work in RGB, but the image eventually needs to go to CMYK, so it might as well be now!

7. Apply a generous Gaussian Blur to the outlines (Filter → Blur → Gaussian, 4.0). This over-softens the outline, but the next step will both "crisp" them up again and make it look as if the outlines were drawn with a somewhat leaky pen. This is the same stylistic impulse that is popular in many "eroded" new typefaces.

8. Open the Levels dialog (Mac: ⌘+Ⓛ, Windows: CTRL+Ⓛ). Drag the Black Input slider to the right until the image starts to firm up (about where the spike in the Histogram is located). Drag the White Input slider to the left until the image is both firm but smooth. Do not change the Gamma point. This is similar to the way you created a choke mask to preserve image detail. This technique is based on a tip written by Kai Krause of MetaTools when he described a method of smoothing bitmaps and fax input. Figure 12-3 shows the Levels settings used in the example. Figure 12-4 shows the outlines that result from this process.

9. It is time to start applying color to the image. You will use three Pantone colors and black. Each color goes into a different Layer. *As you work, you must keep careful track of which Layer you are supposed to be working on.* Click on the Foreground Color square in the Toolbox. In the Color Picker, press the Custom button. This will let you select a Pantone color. Type in the number 371. Figure 12-5 shows the Pantone color selector. Click OK.

10. Make a new Layer (click on the New Layer icon at the bottom of the Layers palette). Name this Layer Pantone 371CV.

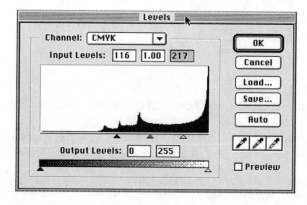

Figure 12-3
Foo lion levels

Figure 12-4
Result of using
levels on blurred
outline

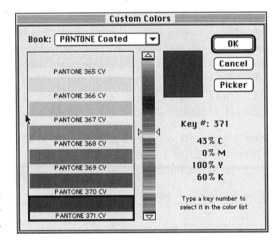

Figure 12-5
Pantone color
selector

11. Click on the Background Layer in the Layers palette to make it the current (active) Layer. Double-click on the Magic Wand tool (W). Set the Tolerance to 200, Anti-Alias on, and Sample Merged off. Click on the lion's belly. Using the dotted areas in Figure 12-6 as a guide, press SHIFT and click on the rest of the dotted areas to add them to the selection.

12. Click on the Pantone 371CV Layer in the Layers palette to make it the current (active) Layer.

Dotted fill shows area to be selected—fill with solid color

Figure 12-6
First areas to be
selected and filled

13. Fill with 70% of the foreground color ((SHIFT)+(DELETE), Use: Foreground Color, Opacity: 70%, Mode: Normal). Deselect (Mac: ⌘+(D), Windows: (CTRL)+(D)).

14. Click on the Background Layer in the Layers palette to make it the current (active) Layer. With the Magic Wand, click in the bottom paw on the left (the one that has no toenails in it). Switch to the Pantone 371CV Layer, and fill ((SHIFT)+(DELETE)) with 90% of the foreground color. Deselect.

15. Switch to the Background Layer and use the Magic Wand to select the lion's mouth, lips, and toenails. Switch to the Pantone 371CV Layer and fill with 20% of the foreground color. *Warning: Be careful not to select too light a tint. You need to determine the smallest screen value that your printer can output.* Deselect.

16. It is now time to fill in the Yellow Layer. Click on the foreground color swatch in the Toolbox. Select Custom... and type in 130 as the Pantone number.

17. Make a new Layer (click on the New Layer icon at the bottom of the Layers palette). Name this Layer Pantone 130CV.

18. Click on the Background Layer in the Layers palette to make it the current (active) Layer. Using the Magic Wand and (SHIFT) to add to selections, select the lion's mane, tail, area over the eye, tassel loop and tassel top, and the two line-shapes on his body and leg. These are the areas in yellow on the original lion image.

19. Click on the Pantone 130CV Layer in the Layers palette to make it the current (active) Layer. Fill with the foreground color ((SHIFT)+(DELETE)) at 70%. Deselect.

20. It is now time to fill in the Brown Layer. Click on the foreground color swatch in the Toolbox. Select Custom... and type in 478 as the Pantone number.

21. Make a new Layer (click on the New Layer icon at the bottom of the Layers palette). Name this Layer Pantone 478CV.

22. Click on the Background Layer in the Layers palette to make it the current (active) Layer. Using the Magic Wand and (SHIFT) to add to selections, select the belt, the bottom of the tassel, and the area between the lion's body and his tail. These are the areas in brown on the original lion image.

23. Click on the Pantone 478CV Layer in the Layers palette to make it the current (active) Layer. Fill with the foreground color ((SHIFT)+(DELETE)) at 100%. Deselect.

The previous steps give you four spot colors to use and are adequate to demonstrate the technique. You can skip to the next section to see how to make channels of these Layers, or you can work on and create a more interesting design.

To save yourself trips to the Toolbox, remember to switch back and forth between the Magic Wand and the Gradient tools by pressing (W) and (G).

The lion is very flat. You can use Gradients and brushwork to restore some of his original contours.

1. Click on the Pantone 130CV Layer to make it active. Since color is already in the Layer, you do not have to select from the Background Layer; you can select from this Layer.

2. Double-click on the Gradient tool. Set the Apply mode to Normal, the Opacity to 100, the Gradient to Foreground to Transparent, the Type to Linear, and check the Mask and the Dither boxes.

3. Change your foreground color to Pantone 130CV.

4. Click on each portion of the lion's mane individually. For each section of the mane, drag the Gradient line from the place that you want to be darkest to the place that should be the lightest. Drag on the angle that you want the Gradient to occur. You can control the amount of light and dark in the Gradient by where you begin and end the drag lines. If you want more dark in the Gradient, click lower in the area to be filled. The area above your first click will get the 100% value. To cut off the Gradient

before it becomes transparent, drag the Gradient line outside of the selected area. To make the transparent area larger, stop the Gradient line before it reaches the edge of the selection. Everything from the end of the drag line to the edge of the selection will not be changed.

5. Repeat Step 4 for the Lion's tail and body lines. For the tassel, select both yellow sections at one time. However, only drag the Gradient line inside of the bottom selected piece. This will make the top of the tassel 100% yellow. Select his top paw and make a very small Gradient toward the bottom of the paw.

6. Make Pantone 371 your foreground color, and activate the associated Layer. Select the lion's mouth and add a Gradient that starts at the base of his mouth and gets transparent as it reaches the part of the mouth closest to his nose. Deselect.

7. By this point, your soft black outlines are starting to look a little ragged. Not to worry. In order to see a more accurate idea of your image, you need to duplicate the Background Layer and raise the duplicate to the top of the Layer stack. Drag the icon for the Background Layer to the New Layer icon on the Layers palette. This will copy the Background Layer into a new Layer. Name this Layer Black Outlines. Drag the new Layer to the top of the Layers palette. Change the Apply mode for the Layer to Multiply.

8. Click on the Pantone 371 Layer. Use the Paintbrush or the Airbrush tool at varying opacities to add tone to the lion's body. Use the original image for clues as to what needs to be made darker and what needs to stay light. Since there is no active selection, just take care to "paint within the lines." *Warning: Do not check the Preserve Transparency box or you will not be able to darken or lighten any tones.* The darkest areas are along the creases in the lion's leg, the front of his stomach, the tops of the toenails, and along the base of his jawbone. You can create the highlights on the top of his nose and around his ear and jaw by using the Eraser with a soft brush and lowered Opacity. If you are not sure how to proceed, look at the layered finished version of this image on the CD-ROM. Figure 12-7 shows the lion with some tone added to him.

 You can work with a very low Opacity and build color densities by working over an area multiple times. This leaves a soft buildup of color rather than an abrupt change. Each time you paint over the same area after you have released the mouse button, you leave another Layer of color. If you have areas of abrupt transitions, you can soften them with the Blur tool.

Figure 12-7
Lion with tonal
values added

9. Now, to give the lion a woodcut look…Drag a copy of the original lion (unedited) onto the spot color document. Make it the top Layer. Apply a High Pass filter with Radius of 1.6. Change the Layer Apply mode to Multiply. Apply the Threshold command (Image → Adjust → Threshold). In the dialog, drag the slider to a point where you like the amount of black. The example used a Threshold of 126. Click OK.

10. To smooth the top Layer and make it resemble the softness of the outlines, apply a Gaussian Blur of 1.0 (you would use more on a larger image). Open the Levels dialog and move the Black and White input sliders toward the middle until you like the size and softness of the result (just as you did for the original lines). Figure 12-8 shows the Levels used in the example image.

11. *Late breaking news!* The client has just decided that he does not want a 4-color spot job. It will be as expensive to print as full-color. He wants to drop out the brown Pantone color and use 100% of the green color instead. This is not a problem. Change your foreground color to Pantone 371. Click on the Preserve Transparency button and fill the area (Mac: OPTION+DELETE, Windows: ALT+DELETE). It's that easy! Figure 12-9 shows the lion completely colored and ready to separate.

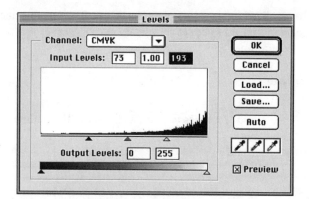

Figure 12-8
Lion detail Levels

Figure 12-9
Lion done

1. Identify the two (2) methods to get color data into a single location so it can be separated.
   a. Put each spot color into its own Layer.
   b. Put each spot color into its own file.
   c. Put each spot color into its own Beta channel.
   d. Put each spot color into its own Alpha channel.

2. To set all grayscale values of an image to a Black plate, what would the Black generation need to be set at?
   a. Minimum
   b. Maximum
   c. High
   d. Low

3. What are two (2) things you can use to select the outline of an object?
   a. Gradients
   b. Magic Wand
   c. Brushwork
   d. Lasso

4. Which tool is the best for adding tone to an image?
   a. Lasso
   b. Paintbrush
   c. Airbrush
   d. Gradients

5. Creating highlights on various places of an image is very similar to
   a. Using a highlighter.
   b. Using a marker.
   c. Using color pencils.
   d. Using an eraser with a soft brush.

PREPARING SPOT COLOR OUTPUT

Now that you have prepared each Layer, you need to get each Layer into its own Alpha channel so that you can trap and separate the image. You will use the Apply Image command to place the contents of each Layer into its own Alpha channel. The only real "trick" to this is to use the *transparency* of the Layer rather than the *color* of the Layer when creating the channel, so that you will end up with gray values in each channel that are the same as the percentage of each spot color that you want to use.

Making the Channels

Making channels from the Layers is mostly straightforward. You need only add a new channel and use the Apply Image command to move the values in the Layer into the correct channel. The only trick to this is that you cannot simply apply the CMYK channel of the Layer to the new channel, you need to apply the *Transparency values* of the Layer instead and then invert the result. In the example image, however, you first need to consolidate the Layers so that there is only one Layer per color. Follow along.

LAYERS INTO CHANNELS

1. Duplicate your working image (Image → Duplicate → OK).

2. Drag the Background Layer into the Layers palette trash can. (You *do* have another copy of this in the Black Outline Layer, don't you?)

3. Remove the Eye icon from all the Layers except the Black Outlines Layer and the Threshold Layer. Merge the Layers (Layers palette menu → Merge Layers).

4. Place the Eye icon on the Pantone 317CV and Pantone 478 Layers *only* (Pantone 478 was the Layer that you converted to Pantone 317). Merge the Layers (Layers palette menu → Merge Layers). You should now have only three Layers in the image.

Now, you need to actually build the channels.

1. Click on the New Channel icon in the center of the Channels palette to create a new channel. This will be Channel #5. Name it Black Outlines. Click on the Color swatch in the Channel Options dialog and select black (CMYK 0, 0, 0, 100). Set the Opacity to 100%.

2. Open the Apply Image dialog. Do not change the Source that appears. Select the Black Outlines Layer as the Layer and CMYK as the channel. Change the Mode to Normal and the opacity to 100%. You do not need a mask. Click OK. (This channel does not use the Layer transparency, because the Black Outlines Layer has no transparency; it is completely opaque).

3. Click on the New Channel icon in the center of the Channels palette to create a new channel. This will be Channel #6. Click on the Color swatch in the Channel Options dialog and select Custom... and Pantone 371. Set the Opacity to 100%. The channel will be named Pantone 371CV automatically once you have selected that as the preview color.

4. Open the Apply Image dialog. Do not change the Source. Select the Pantone 371CV Layer as the Layer. This time, select Transparency as the Channel. Click the Invert check box to flip the values. Figure 12-10 shows this dialog with the correct settings.

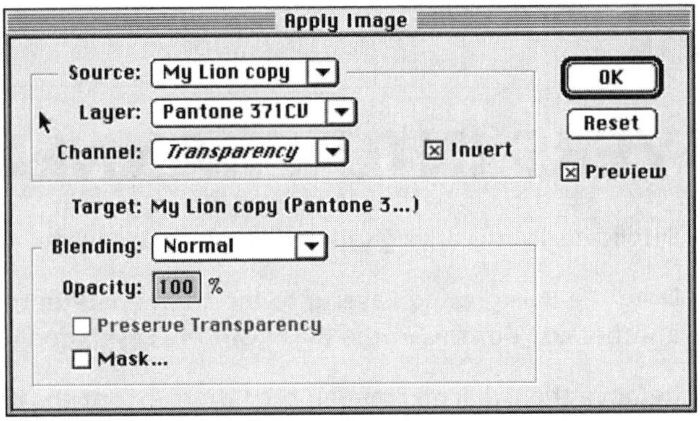

Figure 12-10
Apply Image dialog
for Pantone 371CV
channel

5. Click on the New Channel icon in the center of the Channels palette to create a new channel. This will be Channel #7. Click on the Color swatch in the Channel Options dialog and select Custom... and Pantone 130. Set the Opacity to 100%. The channel will be named Pantone 130CV automatically once you have selected that as the preview color.

6. Open the Apply Image dialog. Do not change the Source. Select the Pantone 130CV Layer as the Layer. Select *Transparency* as the Channel. Click the Invert check box to flip the values.

7. Once you have all the channels you need, switch to the CMYK composite channel (Mac: ⌘+[~], Windows: CTRL+[~]) and select the entire image (Mac: ⌘+[A], Windows: CTRL+[A]) and delete it. You no longer need the actual image (*now* do you know why you copied the image to build these channels?). Even though your CMYK image is solid white, if you click on the Eye icons next to your three Alpha channels, you will see a color preview that is somewhat accurate. The black lines may look a little foggy where the green is covering them, but that is okay. Black will overprint the green anyway.

Why was it necessary to select the Layer transparency rather than the Layer values? When you print the image, you want to be able to see values of the Pantone color ranging from 20% (the lightest screen you applied) to 100%. However, if you simply translate the Pantone color into grayscale values, a 100% dose of Pantone 371 (the darker color) comes to only 73% black in grayscale. The 20% value of the much lighter Pantone 130 is only 5% black. *You need the black values in the channel to be the same as the percentages applied using the Fill dialog.*

Most of the lion's body was filled at 70% of the Pantone 371. That is because a 70% tint is needed. The black values in the Pantone 371 *channel* must also equal 70% when you are through. The only way to make this happen is to apply the Opacity (transparency) values rather than the color values in the Layer.

You need to invert the transparency values because of the way in which Photoshop *sees* transparency values and because of the way the CMYK channels work. In all the channel work you have done so far, white is selected and black is not. It works that way inside an RGB channel as well. Where the channel contains white, the color for that channel is at its highest. Where there is black in the channel, none of the color is present. When all three channels contain 100% of the possible color, you *see* white because red, green, and blue light merges to form white. In CMYK, the opposite is true.

CYMK channels show black where there is 100% of the value. This is because printing inks combine CMY to form *black*. (They don't really, of course, or you would not need that fourth ink, which is black.) The areas of black to gray on a CMYK channel will actually print when the printing plate is placed on the press. When you select the Apply Image command, you come up against the way in which Photoshop reads the transparency and the way you need a channel to appear in order to print from it.

Think of the Apply Image command as a slide projector. It can take any image and *project* it against any desired wall or surface. The active image when you select the command is the *wall*. It is the surface on which the slide will appear. The *slide* is the Source document—a specific image, Layer, and channel that will be reflected to its new home. You can change the Opacity or Apply mode of the slide and you can also mask it as it is being projected.

This brings you (finally) to what is happening when you *project* an image that contains transparency. Areas totally transparent contain nothing that can be seen (or selected). Therefore, those areas will come onto the *wall* as unselected—that is, black. The selected areas (and 100% opacity is the *most* selected) will come in as white (for 100%) or as shades of gray. So, in order to switch these values to get printing plates, you need to invert them. *Whew!*

Trapping

For the most part, this book has tried to ignore (or at least de-emphasize) pre-press issues. You cannot learn both Photoshop and pre-press (the process of preparing images for output) at the same time. The mandate of this book is to teach you how to use Photoshop—and only touch on the issue of how to make these images print. Unfortunately, part of preparing spot color output involves making sure that the plates will print correctly.

When solid colors touch each other, there is always the chance that something will go wrong on press and the touching areas will miss by a hair. This leads to noticeable white spaces in the output—and angry clients. To help prevent this "show-though," most images that are not photographic (continuous tone), require *trapping*. Trapping is the process that adds a bit of color around areas of the image that overlap so that one of the overlapping areas gets a little larger than it should. That way, if the colors misalign, there is still color, rather than whitespace, in that area of the image. The Bibliography in the back of this book gives you some good sources from which to learn more about trapping.

Trapping to black (as you do in this image) is the easiest form of trapping. By making black the *overprint* color (it prints on top of all the other colors), it hides a wide range of potential problem areas. Not only that, but black ink can always use a boost from the colors underneath, so it does not matter if there is color under the black lines. It only makes the black look better (within reason, that is).

In order to trap this image, then, you need to spread the two color plates so that the grays extend under the area to be printed with the black outlines. Sometimes this can be done mechanically in Photoshop using either the technique for making Choke Masks or the Minimum filter in the Filter → Other... submenu. You might also have been able to do this as the image was created by using a higher Tolerance setting on the Magic Wand (though 200 is about as high as it is practical to use). You can also do the trapping manually (with the Paintbrush) so that you can control where and how it is done.

In order to trap this image, you need to work in the Channels palette. Set the Apply mode in the Brush Options to Darken. This makes sure that you do not alter your values. Pick up the gray values near the black lines. If you work with all three Eye icons on, you can see the results as you paint. You can also see where the black lines are! Turn the Black Outlines channel Eye icon on and off frequently to check your work. Figure 12-11(a) shows the Pantone 371 channel before it has been trapped. Figure 12-11(b) shows the channel after the trapping has been painted in. The idea is to place a coating (at least) of Pantone 371 beneath all the black lines and areas that come near this color. When you have finished with the Pantone 371 channel, do the same thing to the Pantone 130 channel.

Figure 12-11
a) Pantone 371 channel, not trapped
b) Pantone 371 channel, trapped

a   b

Using Photoshop's Built-In Trapping Command

This tip is a contribution from David Xanakis, of XRX, Inc. David conducts a series of Photoshop workshops throughout the United States and acts as a consultant to many companies—including the magazines, *Knitter's* and *Weaver's*, published by XRX.

David has found that many companies feel Photoshop's own Trap command (in the Image → Trap menu) causes too much alteration in color at the *trap* line and that a softer trap would be less noticeable. Here's how to get it. You can follow along:

Trapping using the Photoshop Trap command is only possible in the CMYK channels. Therefore, the image (which could be spot color just *occupying* the CMY channels) is in the CMYK channels. The image CMYKflr.Psd on the CD-ROM accompanying this book is from the ArtPattern collection by Art Media, Inc. The colors are too harsh because they are 100% C, M, and Y. The original image (also included on the disk) shows much better use of color. The image is also jagged—once again, to keep the colors all solid in their respective channels. Also, the trap that you will use (2 pixels) is much too large, but it will show you clearly what is happening.

1. Open the image CMYKflr.Psd. Duplicate the image (Image → Duplicate → OK) twice.

2. In the first copy, apply the Trap command (Image → Trap) with a 2-pixel trap.

3. Using the Move tool ([V]), drag a copy of the original on top of the trapped copy.

4. Set the Apply mode to Difference.

5. Flatten the image (Layer → Flatten) and invert (Mac: [⌘]+[I], Windows: [CTRL]+[I]).

6. Drag this image *(which now contains just the trap)* on top of the 2nd copy. Figure 12-12 shows this step.

7. Set the Apply mode to Multiply (the white drops out—leaving just the trap pixels).

8. Adjust the Opacity of the Layer until the trap no longer is so apparent. Figure 12-13 shows an enlargement of the finished trap.

Figure 12-12
Isolated trap

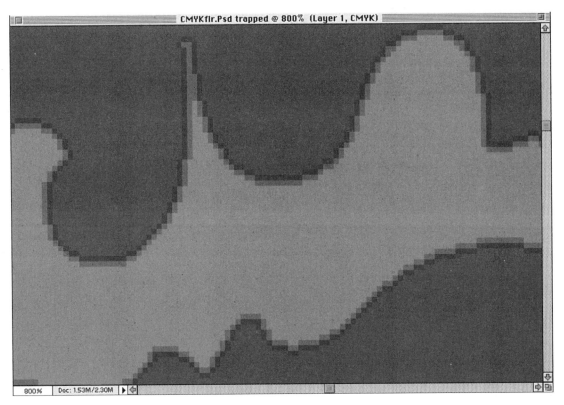

Figure 12-13
Enlarged version of finished trapped image

Going to Press

Once you have the individual Alpha channels trapped, you still need to get the image to print. Here are the possibilities:

1. **The Photoshop image is all that is being printed...If this is the case, then duplicate each channel into its own grayscale image and send it to the imagesetter. Tell the printer which plate gets which color.**

2. **You need to place the image into QuarkXPress or PageMaker.**

If you need to place the image into a page layout program, you have several possible routes. The best one depends upon your budget and the status of the other images that will go along with it in the page layout program. You have two basic strategies to follow:

1. **Keep the Pantone color names associated with the channels.**

2. **Use the CMYK channels to "fake" it.**

If you opt to keep the Pantone colors associated with the image, you can save the image as a TIFF or EPS file. Here's the trade-off. If you save as an EPS file, you can actually send the Pantone color name to QuarkXPress by changing the Mode to Duotone and creating a Monotone image using the Pantone color (Chapter 6, "Color and File Formats," describes the Duotone mode). However, if you *stack* your images in QuarkXPress or PageMaker so that they will print in register, one image will knock out the other—even where there is no color in the EPS file. You cannot get EPS files to overprint.

You could place each image in the same position on a different page, but then you would have to separate all the other text and image elements that you are creating or compositing in the page layout program so that they, too, appear in the correct position, but on the color-specific page. *Yuk!*

You can save your Photoshop file as a TIFF image and place it in QuarkXPress or PageMaker. This technique lets you make a *sandwich* of the images so that they will, hopefully, align. The disadvantage here is that you cannot send the color name when you place the image, and you must add the color in the page layout program. At least you can get the TIFF images to overprint, however. Another disadvantage is that colorized TIFF file images print very slowly on the imagesetter.

Your best solution, if your budget can tolerate it, is to use a Photoshop plug-in called PlateMaker. This is a very elegant piece of software from a company called *a lowly apprentice productions*.PlateMaker lets you export just the channels that you want, and write them to a *DCS2* file. A DCS2 file is a pre-separated file format (similar to the DCS file that you learned about in Chapter 6, but instead of five individual files, it has one combined file) that can use Alpha channels and can be placed into QuarkXPress. There is no need to specify overprinting as all the plates are sent in a single file. All the plates in it will automatically overprint. You can even attach a Clipping Path to the image if

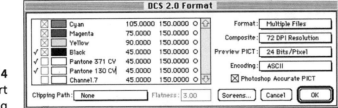

Figure 12-14
PlateMaker export
dialog

you wish. PlateMaker also lets you embed a composite preview of your image (from your CMYK channels—so don't delete them if you use this filter). This lets you see a proof of the image from a composite printer (such as a dye-sublimation printer). PlateMaker is by far the least painful way to do spot color from Photoshop. Figure 12-14 shows the PlateMaker dialog.

You can also trick QuarkXPress into overprinting your plates in an EPS file by using a CMYK image to *hold* the Alpha channels. You can place the Pantone 130 into the Cyan channel and the Pantone 371 into the Magenta channel (use the Apply Image command to do this). So long as you are consistent about the switch of channels (doing the same thing in Illustrator, for example or in text elements in QuarkXPress), you can then separate the image as usual and tell the printer what colors to substitute for the Cyan and Magenta plates (there would be no yellow). This technique works well, but causes you to view a truly weird preview of the image. You can change that preview, however, by changing the Printing Inks setup in the Printing Inks Preferences (as you learned in Chapter 6). Try that now, using another version of the Foo lion.

CHANGING PRINTING INKS

1. Open the image Foo2.Psd. *Surprise!* Didn't you always want a pink-and-blue lion?

2. Select Pantone 371 as your foreground color. Copy down the Lab values for the color. Do not close the dialog.

3. Select Pantone 130 as the color. Copy down its Lab values. Cancel out of the Color Picker.

4. Open the Printing Inks Preferences (File → Color Settings → Printing Inks Setup).

5. In the Ink Colors menu, select Custom. You will see the dialog shown in Figure 12-15. You can click on one of the progressive color Swatches to change the value that is displayed.

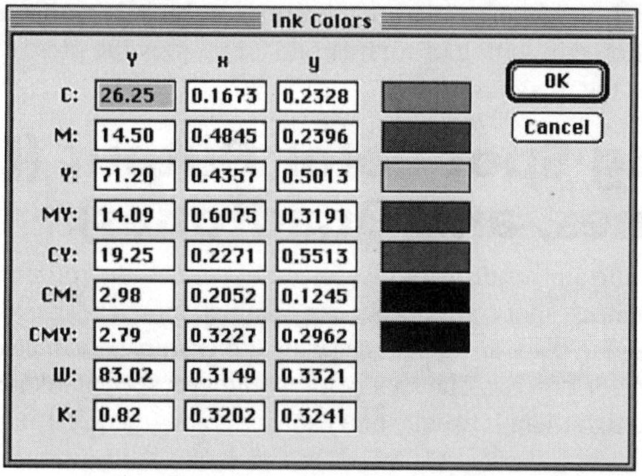

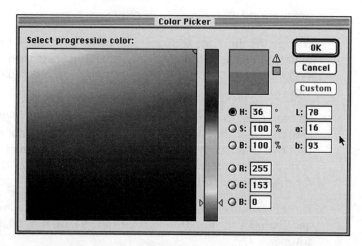

Figure 12-15
Ink Colors dialog

6. Click on the Cyan swatch (the top one). The Cyan channel holds the image that is to be printed in Pantone 130. Therefore, it would be lovely if you could get Photoshop to think that cyan looks like a deep yellow. In the Progressive Color dialog, enter the Lab values for Pantone 130 that you copied in Step 3. Figure 12-16 shows this dialog.

7. Click on the Magenta swatch. Change its values to the Lab values of Pantone 371 (43, –19, 36). There is no need to change any other patches as black is the same and none of the colors overlap.

8. You can also save this setting so that you can recall it when you wish. Click on the Save button and give it a name.

9. When you click OK, your colors should look the way you expect the lion to look.

Figure 12-16
Progressive Color
Picker

One advantage of preparing your images this way is that you can use Photoshop's built-in dot-gain setting to compensate for the way the press causes some values to get darker as the image is printed.

Faking Spot Color Output (Duotones, Tritones, and Quadtones)

After taking all this time to tell you about spot color, you need to know that in some circumstances, spot color output can be much more expensive than using 4-color inks. If you need to place an ad in a magazine, for example, the magazine is likely to be printed in 4-color process. The spot color would be a special ink and you would pay dearly for it (though there is usually one Pantone color—generally a red—available for a lesser fee.

Eric Reinfeld, New York-based artist and trainer, has developed a very useful method of creating a Duotone, Tritone, or Quadtone using standard CMYK inks that does not require using Photoshop's Duotone mode to create. He has used this technique very successfully with clients such as *Time* and *Business Week,* and would like to share it with you.

*H*ANDS *ON*

ERIC REINFELD'S CMYK DUOTONE METHOD

1. Open the image Kids.Psd (Eric's niece and nephew, of whom he is quite proud).

2. Duplicate the image (Image → Duplicate → OK).

3. Change the duplicate to Grayscale (Image → Mode → Grayscale) and then to CMYK (Image → Mode → Grayscale). Duplicate the image again (Image → Duplicate → OK). This is your working copy. It defaults to the name Kids.Psd Copy 2.

4. You can elect to mimic a duotone by selecting the CMYK equivalent of a Pantone color that uses only one color channel, a tritone if the CMYK value uses two channels, or a quadtone if the color uses the C, M, and Y channels in its definition. *In all cases, this technique will not work if the CMYK value for the color contains any black.*

5. For this example, select the CMYK equivalent of Pantone 339C (C91Y60) and change your foreground color to C: 91, M: 0, Y: 60, K: 0. This will be a tritone.

6. Create a new Layer (click on the New Layer icon at the bottom of the Layers palette).

7. Fill the Layer with the foreground color (Mac: OPTION+DELETE, Windows: ALT+DELETE).

8. Change the Apply mode to Screen. If you check the channels in the image, you will notice that there is no data in the Magenta or Black channels. Figure 12-17(a) shows the Layers palette at this point, and Figure 12-17(b) shows the Channels palette.

9. Flatten the image (Layers → Flatten).

10. Click on the Black channel to select it. Make sure that only the Black channel is highlighted.

11. Open the Apply Image dialog (Image → Apply Image). Apply the Kids.Psd Copy image, Black channel. Figure 12-18 shows the Apply Image dialog.

12. Click on the CMYK composite channel to select it. Your *fake* tritone is done.

Figure 12-17
a) Layers palette with base color applied
b) Channels palette showing color in Cyan and Yellow channels only

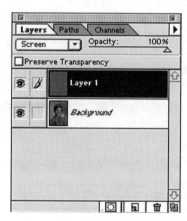

a

b

```
┌─────────────────────── Apply Image ───────────────────────┐
│  ┌───────────────────────────────────┐  ┌──────────┐      │
│  │  Source: [ Kids.Psd Copy    ▼ ]   │  │    OK    │      │
│  │  Layer: [ Background ▼ ]           │  ├──────────┤      │
│  │  Channel: [ Black    ▼ ]  ☐ Invert│  │  Cancel  │      │
│  │                                   │  ├──────────┤      │
│  │  Target: Kids.Psd Copy 2 (Black)  │  │ ☒ Preview│      │
│  │  Blending: [ Normal    ▼ ]        │  └──────────┘      │
│  │  Opacity: [100] %                 │                    │
│  │  ☐ Preserve Transparency          │                    │
│  │  ☐ Mask...                         │                    │
│  └───────────────────────────────────┘                    │
└────────────────────────────────────────────────────────────┘
```

Figure 12-18
Apply Image dialog
correctly filled in

1. What is the correct method to move Layers into channels?
   a. Apply the CMYK channel of the Layer to the channel.
   b. Apply the Transparency values of the Layer.
   c. Apply the Transparency values of the Layer and then invert it.
   d. None of the above.

2. What is trapping?
   a. Catching images in final form to be printed.
   b. Separating plates for printing.
   c. Adding extra color around areas of an image to prevent show through.
   d. All of the above.

3. What is a DCS2 file?
   a. A file that allows images to be sandwiched together to obtain an aligned photo.
   b. A pre-separated file format with two individual files.
   c. A pre-separated file format with five individual files.
   d. A pre-separated file format with one combined file.

4. What is PlateMaker?
   a. A Photoshop plug-in.
   b. Software that allows just the desired channels to be exported.
   c. A DCS2 file.
   d. The hardest way to do spot color from Photoshop.

5. How do you mimic a duotone when faking spot color output?
   a. By selecting the CMYX equivalent of a Pantone color that uses only one color channel.
   b. By selecting the CMYX equivalent of a tritone of the CMYK values that uses two channels.

c. By selecting the CMYK equivalent of a quadtone if the color uses the C, M, and Y channels.

d. All of the above.

VIP PROFILE

Greg Vander Houwen, Interact

Greg Vander Houwen is a principal in the computer graphics firm Interact. He has a background in video, computers, photography, and apple farming. As one of Adobe's "Digital Masters," his images have been shown internationally and are featured on the Photoshop 3.0 CD-ROM. Greg writes articles, does training, and lectures on image retouching and digital illustration. He is an artist by nature, an illustrator by trade.

In the early years, he did some internships in Los Angeles and some assistant work for a number of video companies. He then went back to Washington State and got a job in a computer store. He worked his way up until he was making buying decisions about the hardware and software, and began to purchase graphics software for the company. Since he wanted to purchase the graphics "stuff," he needed to be able to keep sales up to justify the habit.

He purchased one of the first high-quality scanners, obtained access to great new hardware, software betas, and so on, as they were being introduced. A vice president at RasterOps gave him a 24-bit color card using a program called Laserpaint color 2, and he also got a pirated alpha (this is pre-beta software) copy of the program that later became Photoshop.

This not-yet-ready-for-prime-time Photoshop was an absolutely amazing program! It had scratch disk capabilities, and, for the first time, Greg was actually able to scan a 32MB file without crashing.

You need to understand that the late 1980s was a time of tremendous growth and excitement in the computer graphics industry. Up until the advent of Photoshop (originally called BarneyScan), there was not much on the Macintosh platform (or the PC platform, either) that could work with full-color (24-bit) images. There was Time Arts Lumina on the PC—a *lite* version released in conjunction with a special Hercules board that *only* cost $5,000. The remaining 24-bit color software on the PC was even more expensive. On the Mac, Studio/24 from Electronic Arts and PixelPaint were early contenders. Color Studio—released originally by Letraset but written by Mark Zimmer and Steve Hedges of Fractal Design—was released at the same time as Photoshop.

Using an early version of Photoshop, Greg then made his first fine art image, which he submitted to *Verbum* (a magazine then only two or three issues old). This image was one of the highest-resolution photographic images around.

Greg's goal was to print an image to film so that you couldn't see pixels. He sent this image to an LFR film printer. The excitement was really intense. This "computer stuff" was going to work! Those were the glory days, in Greg's mind. It is still fun, but not quite in the same way. Then, the work was about possibilities and each day brought a new discovery.

Greg's working habits with Photoshop vary depending upon whether he is creating commercial art or fine art. If he is working on a commercial art project, the project needs to be tightly controlled as its aim is to communicate a message. He sends a set of sketches to the art director for approval. He then scans the sketch so that he can build the actual image over it. He will frequently scan the sketch into an Alpha channel with the Eye turned on so he can see the sketch (much as you did in Chapter 11, "Photo-Montage").

When Greg creates a fine art piece, he grabs the resources that fit the direction he wants to go—photographs of objects, the actual object, whatever else he feels is relevant. He tends to scatter them around in a huge circle and may walk around them for a full evening until they begin to fall into place. He often works more from intuition than from a tangible image. This is a totally different process than commercial art.

According to Greg, in commercial art, you need to "sing the client's song"; fine art sings your own song and therefore it is more subtle and there is not as much worry as to what comes out. The best pieces occur when the art itself takes over.

"Commercial art teaches you how to work quickly and efficiently and to say something strong with a clear voice, but fine art doesn't have any fences around it and takes much longer. However, that doesn't matter, it is not a money-making endeavor, anyway. Fine art is not about money."

Greg's advice to new users is that you not let a lack of knowledge intimidate you or stop you from trying things. Greg has had the most fun when no one told him that he didn't know what he was doing . It is self-defeating to compare yourself with others. As you work with the program, you will find your own path.

Greg says, "Pursue the act of discovery and the joy of making—you should never feel as if you have mastered the program. Photoshop is like a brush—you can never 'master' it because it is the person who makes the images happen—not the program itself."

Greg's resume is impressive; some excerpts follow.

Exhibitions

- The Computer Pictures Art show—MacWorld, San Francisco, 1995

- The Photoshop Conference Digital Art Gallery—San Francisco Sheraton Palace, 1994

- Digital Masters—Ansel Adams Center for Photography Sponsored by Adobe Systems, Daystar, and Specular International during MacWorld, 1994

- Works on Paper—Sponsored by Iris Graphics during SIGGRAPH, 1993

- Digital Perspectives in Art and Architecture—Contract Design Center, San Francisco, 1993—Sponsored by Cannon, Adobe Systems, and Eastman Kodak

- 6th National Computer Art Invitational Exhibition—Eastern Washington University's Gallery of Art, 1993

- The Imagina Exposition Digital Art Gallery—Monte Carlo, 1993

- Add Noise, Contract Design Center—San Francisco—Sponsored by View by View and Eastman Kodak, 1992

Awards

- 3rd place, fine art—Computer Pictures Annual Art and Design Contest, 1994

- 1st place, technical achievement—Computer Pictures 1st Annual Art and Design Contest, 1993

CD-ROMs

- The Adobe Photoshop 3.0 CD

- The MacWorld Photoshop Bible 3.0 CD

- The Adobe Photoshop 2.5 and 2.5.1 Deluxe Edition CDs

- The Adobe Audition 1.0 CD

Lectures

- The Photoshop Conference, New York, 1994–1996

- PhotoMedia Expo '95, Seattle Center, 1995

- The Photoshop Conference, San Francisco, 1994–1996

- Photoshop 3.0, Seattle and Portland, 1994

- Adobe Photoshop Tips and Tricks, Portland, 1994

- Adobe Photoshop Tips and Tricks, Seattle, 1994

- PhotoMedia Expo '94, Seattle Center, 1994

- The Halftone and Scanning Seminar, Seattle, 1994

- Society of Photo Educators Conference, Tacoma, 1993

CHAPTER SUMMARY

In this chapter, you learned how to use Photoshop's Alpha channels to build spot color plates. You have seen how to use Layers to build channels, learned how to trap manually, and how to set the Printing Inks preferences to simulate the Pantone colors.

CHAPTER 13

BEYOND PHOTOSHOP

Many years ago John Donne wrote a poem that states "No man is an island…". The same sentiment can be expressed of Photoshop. No program exists by itself. It needs to interact with other programs—if only to accept input or prepare output. Photoshop is a brilliant cooperative partner in the quest to create quality output. It not only functions as a full-capacity file translator; it can interact with a wide variety of different types of graphics applications.

In this chapter, you will learn how to move an image between vector programs and Photoshop. You will also learn about some 3D and video applications that coexist nicely with Photoshop, and you will learn the basics of preparing graphics for the World Wide Web. Since you may not have any of the other applications discussed here, however, most of the Hands On material that you will learn concerns the Web.

At the end of this chapter, you should be able to

● Rasterize an image in Adobe Illustrator format

● Describe several 3D programs available

● Rotoscope a filmstrip image

● Explain some of the issues involved in designing Web graphics

● Create a beveled button suitable for a Web project

WORKING WITH VECTOR PROGRAMS

One of the very common questions that is asked in the Adobe Forum is, "Why can't I open an EPS file saved in CorelDRAW! or Freehand?" The answer is that Photoshop's claim to understand EPS files is a bit imprecise. It really only understands the version of PostScript that is written by Adobe Illustrator. If an EPS file was not written by Photoshop itself or written in Adobe Illustrator format, it will not be capable of being opened—at least not in versions of Photoshop earlier than 4.0. Version 4.0 is the first version to contain a generic EPS rasterizer. It can even read files saved as EPS from QuarkXPress and PageMaker. However, it can still have some problems correctly reproducing images that use dedicated features of Freehand or CorelDRAW!. As long as your files are simple and straightforward, you should have no problem.

Using Illustrator Files

When you open a vector file in Photoshop, the program will generally try to *rasterize* it. This means that Photoshop will read the outline paths in the Illustrator file and draw them on the screen so that the paths have been turned into pixels. This is the same process that an imagesetter performs when it outputs PostScript. Photoshop needs to rasterize the image because it is not capable of dealing with vector data.

Actually, the previous statement is somewhat misleading. There is one type of vector data that Photoshop does know how to handle—*paths*. A path is a vector construct within Photoshop. Photoshop can draw one, add and delete points on it, and save and recall it. It can also change the path into a selection or make a selection into a path. These paths, however, do not have any artistic effects applied to them. You cannot color a path (you can stroke it, but the color is in the *document*, not on the path). You cannot fill a path (again, it is the area in the image that gets filled, not the actual path).

So, Photoshop can only deal with paths as outlines that do not print. If your Illustrator image is more than that—if you have added color or patterns to the paths—then you want to rasterize your image so that you can see it. What happens if all you have in the Illustrator document is a blank outline path? You can choose to bring it into Photoshop as a path so long as you work through the clipboard.

You can copy and paste *pure* paths between Illustrator and Photoshop. When you copy a path in Illustrator to the clipboard and select the Paste command from within Photoshop, you are given the choice of rasterizing the image or importing it as paths. If you wish to use the imported area as a path, this is the only way to do it (at least on Windows). On the Macintosh, you can drag a path from Illustrator 6 directly into Photoshop. Figure 13-1 shows the dialog that appears when you paste an Illustrator path.

Why would you want to exchange paths with Illustrator anyway? Photoshop's path management is a bit primitive. You can't rotate or flip a path in Photoshop at all. Therefore, one of the easiest ways to rotate a path is to move it to Illustrator, rotate it there, and bring it back. Also, when you make a path from a selection, it frequently needs major clean-up to remove extra points. There is a plug-in in Illustrator from BeInfinite that enables you to automatically clean up the path and remove redundant points.

Even if you do not own Adobe Illustrator, you can practice rasterizing Illustrator files in Photoshop.

HANDS ON

OPENING ILLUSTRATOR FILES

1. Open the image Drunkard's Path.

2. A dialog box, shown in Figure 13-2, appears. This dialog lets you set the size of the imported image, its resolution, and choose whether or not you wish to anti-alias the image as you rasterize it.

3. Set the resolution to 300 dpi and the size to 600 pixels wide. Set anti-alias off and click OK.

Figure 13-1
Paste dialog from bringing paths into Photoshop

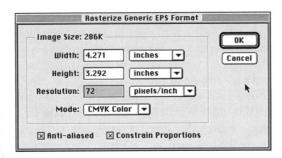

Figure 13-2
Rasterize image
dialog

4. Repeat Steps 1–3. This time, anti-alias the imported image. This lets you see the difference that anti-aliasing makes.

In general, you should anti-alias artwork from Illustrator. The only time that you might not wish to is if you import text or lines that need to remain crisp at a high enough resolution to keep them from looking jagged.

Opening Freehand or CorelDRAW! Files

As you know, Photoshop can only rasterize Illustrator files. Therefore, it has no idea at all as to how to parse (open and interpret) files saved in Freehand native or EPS format or in CorelDRAW! CDR or EPS format. However, both programs are able to save images in Adobe Illustrator format—and this is the format that you need to select.

Some words of caution, however. Every now and then, things get "lost in translation" when you save images this way. If you know you are going to need to move an image into Photoshop, keep it simple. Try not to use advanced program features such as gradients and patterns that are so different between programs.

Handling Text
Photoshop has traditionally had a mixed track record importing text from Adobe Illustrator files—even those saved with Illustrator. When possible, save text as outlines rather than as text. This keeps the kerning and tracking information that is otherwise sometimes lost in transit.

If you find that there is a problem with the images that you have saved in Illustrator format, try saving them as Illustrator 3 or Illustrator 88, and see if that works better. As a last effort, break up compound shapes and save things in pieces. You can put the pieces back together in Photoshop. When you save in Illustrator format from Freehand or CorelDRAW!, be very cautious about trying to use features that Illustrator does not support in the same way (3D, gradients, and patterns are especially problematical).

Importing Photoshop Images into Illustrator, Freehand, or CorelDRAW!

You can also move your Photoshop images into Illustrator, Freehand, or CorelDRAW!. Save your image as a TIFF file. Then use the Place command in the other programs. If you are using Illustrator 6, you can also drag your image directly from Photoshop into Illustrator.

1. In Photoshop why is it not possible to open an EPS file saved in CorelDRAW!?
   a. Photoshop does not understand an EPS file completely.
   b. There is no such thing as an EPS file.
   c. CorelDRAW! is higher quality.
   d. Photoshop 4.0 will open the CorelDRAW! EPS file.

2. What will Photoshop do to a vector file when it is opened from the File menu?
   a. Read it.
   b. Delete it.
   c. Rasterize it.
   d. Eat it.

3. When would you not want to anti-alias artwork from Illustrator?
   a. When you import text that needs to remain crisp
   b. When you import lines that need to remain crisp
   c. When you import text and lines that need to remain crisp
   d. All of the above

4. What is the best way to save text when importing it from Adobe Illustrator?
   a. As text
   b. As color
   c. As a Layer
   d. As outlines

5. When moving a Photoshop image into CorelDRAW!, the image should be saved as
   a. .CDR.
   b. .PCX.
   c. .EPS.
   d. .TIFF.

LESSON 2

PHOTOSHOP AND 3D

Photoshop works very well in conjunction with 3D programs. You can use Photoshop in two ways with these programs: You can create textures and bump maps in Photoshop to apply using a 3D program, or you can render a 3D scene and place it into Photoshop for further work. There are also a variety of Photoshop plug-ins that enable you to work in 3D.

Making Texture and Bump Maps

3D programs achieve their results by simulating the way objects look in the real world. This means that when 3D images are *rendered* (translated into a two-dimensional picture that contains depth cues), the rendering program tries to calculate the way light falls on the object and how the surface texture of an object looks. In the real world, most objects are not perfectly flat on the surface—they have grain or nicks or bumps. They may be hairy or fuzzy. The surface may reflect light or absorb it. 3D programs *know* what a surface should look like because the artist who has created the model has given it a shade or texture or *bump map*.

Bump map is the term given to a grayscale image that tells the rendering program where the highlights and the shadows of an object are located. In the grayscale image, the white areas (typically) show the object highlights and the dark areas show the object shadows. Any grayscale image that you create in Photoshop can be used as a bump map to give an object surface texture.

You do not even need a 3D program to view the effect of a bump map. Photoshop's Lighting filter does a 3D rendering of a bump map when it uses a texture channel.

HANDS ON

BUMP MAPS

The image that you will use in this exercise is a deliberately primitive image of a house, drawn in flat colors over the real image. Figure 13-3 shows the flat house.

1. Open the image House.Psd.

2. Double-click on the Magic Wand and set the tolerance to 3. Set Anti-alias to on. Set Sample Merge to off.

3. Click inside the tall bright green bush at the left of the image.

Figure 13-3
Original house
image

4. Float the selection (Mac: ⌘+Ⓙ, Windows: ⒸⓉⓇⓁ+Ⓙ) to make a new Layer.

5. Apply the Lighting filter to the new Layer (Filter → Render → Lighting). Use the settings in Figure 13-4. Make sure to select the Bush texture as your texture channel.

6. Continue to select bushes on the Background Layer and float them to a new Layer before applying the Lighting filter to them.

7. Select the blue front of the house and apply the Siding texture to it.

8. Select the red brick and apply the Brick texture to it. Figure 13-5 shows the finished house.

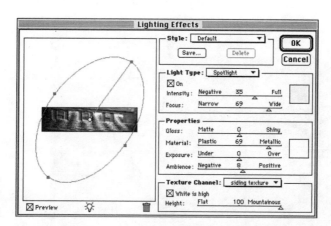

Figure 13-4
Lighting filter
settings

Figure 13-5
Finished bump-
mapped house

This house is not nearly as sophisticated as the bump mapping and surface mapping that can be done within a dedicated 3D program, but it gives you an idea of the possibilities. If you do not like the Lighting filter (sometimes it is difficult to control the lighting to show the texture but not white out or over-darken the other parts of the image), there is another program that does this bump mapping onto an image quite well. It is also by Adobe and is called Adobe TextureMaker. It enables you to apply surface effects and texture to any image. You can use all of the Adobe filters and stack them; you can also create your own textures within the program. When you have created your texture, you can light it using an image that you designate as a bump map. Figure 13-6 shows the interface for TextureMaker. You can also try the exercise again using saved copies of the texture channels as the texture maps within the Texturizer filter (Filter → Texture → Texturizer).

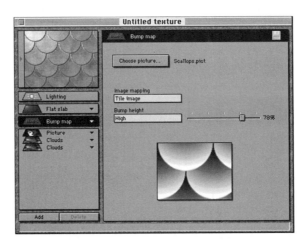

Figure 13-6
Adobe
TextureMaker
interface

Another program, which contains a plug-in for Mac Photoshop, is Alien Skin Textureshop by Virtus. This program creates both texture maps (color regions) and bump maps. Each pattern it creates has both components. The nice thing is that you apply just a bump map to a blank image and then "hijack" the bump map and use it either as a basis for the Lighting filter, a 3D program, or a bump map in Adobe TextureMaker. Figure 13-7(a) shows the interface for Textureshop and Figure 13-7(b) shows the process of creating a bump map. This is a lovely plug-in but it is rather buggy—canceling an operation, for example, crashes the computer. Use it with care. It is annoying, but it really does a nice job.

Figure 13-7
a) Alien Skin Textureshop by Virtus
b) Textureshop creating a bump map

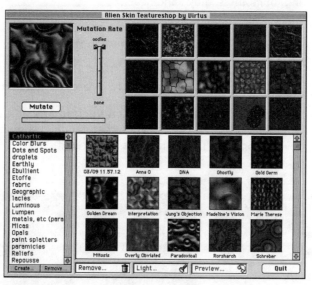

a

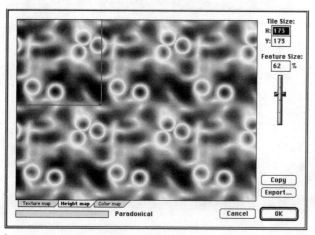

b

A program that creates 3D textures and is worth every penny of its fairly reasonable cost is Specular TextureScape. This is a stand-alone program that uses vector shapes (imported from Illustrator or created in the Shape Editor within the program) to create intricate patterns and textures to which 3D effects can be added. You can bevel the edges of the objects and you can specify shapes to be convex or concave. The patterning ability is quite impressive (it can do unevenly spaced patterns and diagonal repeats). Figure 13-8 shows the TextureScape interface.

The program has some features that make it a wonderful companion for Photoshop:

1. It can render these vector shapes as 3D images with control over the lighting, bumpiness, gloss, and bevel.

2. It lets you create patterns and textures with multiple Layers—and each Layer may use the same or different motifs.

3. It lets you specify the number of times a motif is repeated within the repeat unit—which can be used to create overlapping shapes.

4. It can randomly place the motif on the grid so that it creates patterns that are similar to *sateen* repeats (a sateen repeat is a seamless pattern that uses several copies of the motif as its repeat unit).

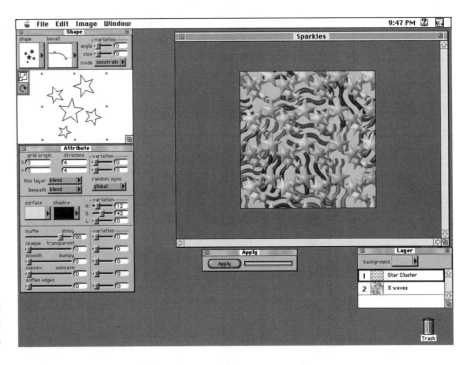

Figure 13-8
TextureScape
interface

5. It can *morph* patterns to create animations (not completely useful for Photoshop but useful in other situations). (You've seen morphs, even if you didn't know the word. Think of the commercial where the car turns into a tiger. That's a morph—where one thing changes into another).

6. Since the pattern is kept as vector data, it can be rendered at any resolution.

7. It can create an Alpha channel for export to Photoshop. This enables you to composite the pattern.

CyberMesh

Regarding the subject of bump maps—using grayscale images to indicate surface height—another Photoshop plug-in should be mentioned. CyberMesh is a plug-in written by John Knoll, one of the brothers who created Photoshop. John has been associated with Industrial Light and Magic for many years (ILM is George Lucas' special effects company that did the SF/X for *Star Wars, Casper, Jurassic Park,* and many other movies). As part of that association, John has seen the need for many programs to help bridge between 2D and 3D design. He wrote CyberMesh to enable you to use a grayscale image created in Photoshop as the basis for a model that could be exported to almost any dedicated 3D program. Figure 13-9 shows what this filter looks like.

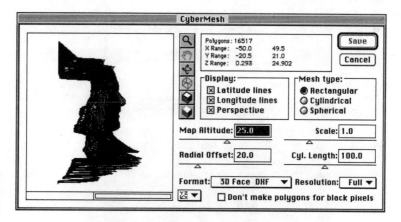

Figure 13-9
CyberMesh by John
Knoll

3D Surface Wrapping Plug-Ins

There are two other Photoshop plug-ins that enable you to work within a limited 3D space inside Photoshop. They are Series II filter from Andromeda Software and HoloDozo, from MMM Software of Germany.

The Series II filter from Andromeda is available for both the Mac and PC. It lets you wrap an image around 3D primitives such as spheres, boxes, cylinders, and planes. You can control the size, placement, and elevation of the 3D object and rotate it to the angle you wish. You can also control how your image is mapped onto the object.

The filter does an excellent job of texture mapping. It has a very dense interface and is fairly complicated to use. It is definitely one filter for which you must read the manual a number of times. However, it is a real time-saver when it does what you want. Figure 13-10(a) shows the Series II filter interface and Figure 13-10(b) shows an image created with the filter.

Figure 13-10
a) Andromeda Series II filter interface
b) Image created with Andromeda Series II filter

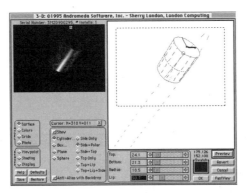

a

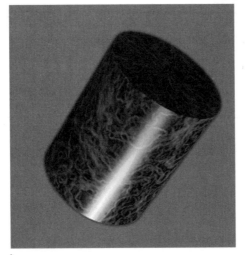

b

HoloDozo is the easiest of the 3D plug-ins to use. It is a series of 28 filters that, in programs such as Adobe Premiere and Macromedia Director, can be applied over time. Each of the 28 filters creates a different 3D primitive. The shapes range from the standard sphere and cube to a flying saucer, 3D bagel, torus, and snail. It also includes shapes that look like the 3D star puzzles based on the Rubik's Cube. This program lets you map an image onto the shape and keep the transparency of the Layer at the same time (while the Series II filter from Andromeda always creates a background). Figure 13-11(a) shows the HoloDozo interface and Figure 13-11(b) shows an image created with the filter.

Figure 13-11
a) HoloDozo interface
b) Image created with HoloDozo

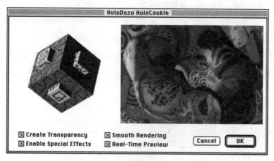

a

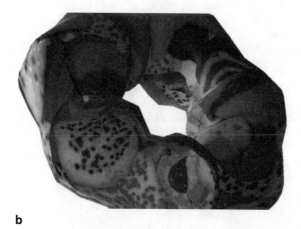

b

G-Buffer Images

Another exciting thing that you can do with some 3D programs is to create scenes that contain distance data. This is referred to as *G-Buffer* data. Ray Dream Designer is a 3D program from Fractal Design that can create an Alpha channel that contains G-Buffer data when it renders a scene to a 2D file. You can take this G-Buffer data and use the channel in Photoshop to apply such special effects as haze and fog that affect the parts of the image in the "back" much more than the closer areas—just as *real* fog would.

Bryce 2.0 by MetaTools

If you don't want to render fog in Photoshop, you can use Bryce, by MetaTools. This is a terrain-modeler that is an amazing time-eater. You can become so engrossed in this program that hours (or days) can slip by unnoticed. Figure 13-12(a) shows part of the Bryce interface and Figure 13-12(b) shows an image created in the program without drawing a single model.

Figure 13-12
a) Bryce interface
b) Image created
with Bryce

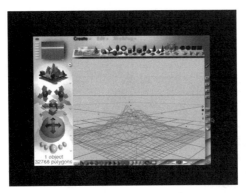

a

b

Bryce is a very deep program. It is easy to use at a basic level—all you need do to create your first scene is to pick a sky and a landscape. However, as you dig into deeper levels, there is always more to explore. You can use a Photoshop file inside of Bryce to set the shape or the height of the landscape, and you can create your own private island based on Marilyn Monroe or the Mona Lisa. Gary Clark, a fine artist who works primarily in Fractal Design Painter, uses Bryce extensively to help generate some of the atmospheric backgrounds for which he is so famous.

Fractal Design Detailer

Fractal Design Detailer is a new program that enables you to paint on 3D objects. You can use a wide variety of brushes and effects, and you can import and export Photoshop files in Layers. Figure 13-13(a) shows part of the Detailer interface and Figure 13-13(b) shows an image created in the program.

Figure 13-13
a) Fractal Design Detailer interface
b) Image created with Fractal Design Detailer

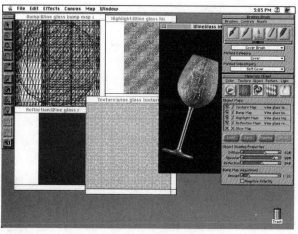

a

b

1. What is a bump map?
    a. A grayscale image that tells the rendering 3D program where the highlights and shadows are
    b. A file extension for 3D figures
    c. A texture channel
    d. A colored image that tells the rendering 3D program where the highlights and shadows are

2. Other programs capable of bump mapping are
    a. Adobe TextureMaker.
    b. Alien Skin Textureshop by Virtus.
    c. Specular TextureScape.
    d. All of the above.

3. What is a morph?
    a. A house turning into a cat in a TV commercial
    b. An alien in a film
    c. When one shape changes into another
    d. A type of algae

4. What is CyberMesh?
    a. A Photoshop video game
    b. A special effects company
    c. A technique used only in film
    d. A plug-in that takes a grayscale image in Photoshop and uses it for a model that can be exported to almost any 3D program

5. When creating scenes that contain distance data in 3D images, what is the data referred to as?
    a. B-Buffer
    b. Fractal Design
    c. G-Buffer
    d. An Alpha channel

LESSON 3

PHOTOSHOP AND VIDEO

Photoshop also works well with video editing and compositing programs. It can be used to create still images to place as titles into Adobe Premiere, or to create images to move and maneuver in Adobe AfterEffects. You can use Photoshop to paint onto video images (the process is called *rotoscoping*) or to create simple animations. You can also use it for *matte painting* (this process involves adding painted content to a video image to make it look as if there were more people or more scenery that was actually shot in the video).

Working with AfterEffects

Adobe AfterEffects is one of the most appealing programs to arrive in a long time—perhaps since Photoshop itself. It is like Photoshop on ice skates. AfterEffects is a video compositing program. This means that you can take any number of still images and video clips and layer them to produce a new QuickTime movie which can be viewed onscreen or exported to videotape or a CD-ROM.

AfterEffects gives you the ability to use Photoshop's Apply modes in the Layers along with opacity and motion. There are additional plug-ins to AfterEffects that add amazing special effects such as rain, wind, fire, and fireworks. AfterEffects can open and place a layered Photoshop file. It can also write a Photoshop file if you just want to use it to apply one of its super effects to a single Photoshop image.

Just to give you an idea of how it can use a still image, picture this. Take an image of the globe viewed from space. You can use this single flat image and create a QuickTime movie that shows the globe entering the image window from one side of the screen as a very tiny ball and rotating as it grows larger and more opaque until it exits the other side as a very large object. You can do all of this with one single image—imagine what you can create stacking many images together! Figure 13-14(a) shows the AfterEffects interface and Figure 13-14(b) shows a "filmstrip" image created in the program (selected frames only).

Figure 13-14
a) Adobe After-Effects interface
b) Filmstrip created with Adobe AfterEffects

a

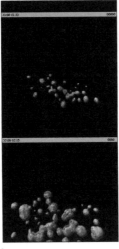

b

Importing Filmstrips

Adobe Premiere is capable of exporting a QuickTime movie in a file format called *film-strip*. This is a PICT file that contains each image frame. You can open this filmstrip file in Photoshop to paint on it or apply special effects. You can then reopen the saved image in Premiere and render it back out as a QuickTime movie. This is the easiest way to get video footage into Photoshop for both rotoscoping and matte painting.

Rotoscoping and Matte Painting

Animations—movies, cartoons, and so on—create the illusion of movement by flashing many *frames* per second (a frame is an individual image that is part of the entire image series) in front of the viewer. If the frame contains a person, for example, the person seems to move because each frame has him (or her) in a slightly different position.

Traditional animation, before the computer, was done by copying the unchanged areas of the frame before and making the needed motion changes to arms, feet, and so forth. This was often done on tracing paper so the artist could see the frame before and know what to change in the sequence. Some programs can do this by showing the frames before as if they were on tracing paper. This ability, called *onion-skinning*, is available in Fractal Design Painter and Macromedia Director, but not in Photoshop.

However, if you open a filmstrip file, you can *rotoscope* (paint onto video frames) by making changes to every (or selected) image(s) in the sequence. You could change the color of a jacket from green to red over a series of frames, or add lightning bolts, if you wish. You could also apply filters to the images—though it's easier to do so within the video-editing program. If you find this process tedious, Strata Corp. has a program called MediaPaint that is specifically designed for rotoscoping. Figure 13-15 shows the MediaPaint interface.

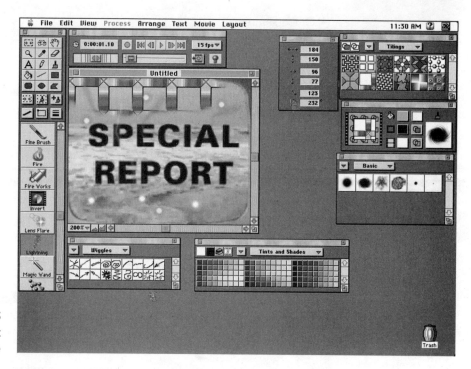

Figure 13-15
Strata MediaPaint
interface

1. What is rotoscoping?
   a. Creating simple animations
   b. Using Photoshop to paint onto video images
   c. Same as matte painting
   d. All of the above

2. What is Adobe's AfterEffects designed to do?
   a. Send Photoshop on ice skates
   b. Composite still images and video to create a QuickTime movie
   c. Paint on 3D objects
   d. Create landscapes

3. What is Adobe Premiere capable of?
   a. Exporting QuickTime movies
   b. Painting on 3D objects
   c. Sending Photoshop on skates
   d. All of the above

4. Onion-skinning is available in
   a. Photoshop.
   b. Fractal Design Painter.
   c. Macromedia Director.
   d. Adobe Premier.

5. What program is specifically designed for rotoscoping?
   a. Photoshop
   b. Media Paint
   c. Fractal Design Painter
   d. Macromedia Director

IMAGING PROGRAMS

Photoshop also gets along well with a variety of other paint programs that can add features or convenience to Photoshop. A brief description of them follows.

Fractal Design Painter

Fractal Design Painter is an intriguing program that should be in the "toolbox" of any Photoshop user who creates images as well as scans them. It features Natural Media—tools that work in the digital world as you expect them to in the *real* world. You can paint with chalk, pencils, marking pens, charcoal, oil, watercolors, and much more. The brushes react to surface texture. The program contains many special effects such as lighting, glass distortion, marbling, weaving, and mosaics. It can read and write layered Photoshop images although the method that it uses for *floaters* (its movable selections) is quite different from Photoshop's Layers. Figure 13-16 shows the Fractal Paint interface.

Specular Collage

Before there were Layers in Photoshop, there was Specular Collage. Collage was designed as an image layout program—sort of a QuarkXPress for picture composition. Photoshop has the major disadvantage that it can be slow and very memory-hungry when you are trying to put a number of images together in one composition. Collage is designed to avoid that problem by enabling you to work with 72-dpi *proxies* of your real image. A proxy is a low resolution preview of the image. You can move these proxies around in multiple Layers, rotate and flip them, add shadows, crop and mask them as you wish. You can also apply some Layer effects such as Multiply and Screen modes.

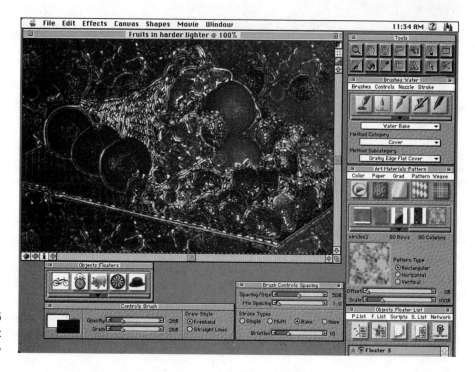

Figure 13-16
Fractal Paint
interface

When you have the image designed so all of the pixels are in place, you then render the image. This process goes back to the original image for its data—so if you rotated a proxy eight times until you got it the way you wanted it, there will be no image degradation. Collage can also write layered Photoshop files, so you can bring images into Collage to arrange them and then do further editing in Photoshop.

Live Picture and OverDrive

At the same time that Collage and Fractal Design Painter were discovering the idea of multiple floating selections or Layers, a program originated in France that took a totally different approach to the issue of image compositing. Live Picture is a high-end, high-speed, image-manipulation program that enables the user to composite huge files (larger than 1GB) seemingly in real-time with only 24MB of RAM.

It performs this feat by changing the image into its own format (called IVUE). This format is a sort-of vector program for images—it keeps the image data in a very compact format as a series of instructions that can be quickly updated. It enables you to view the screen at any resolution, but as you zoom into the screen, Live Picture shows you that magnification at a 72-dpi screen resolution. This means that Live Picture does not carry the overhead that Photoshop does when it tries to move all of the image. Therefore, it can be much faster. Every time you make a change to the image, Live Picture goes back to the original image to *refresh* its screen view. Nothing degrades when it is moved or rotated. The program's Layers are similar to Photoshop's (or Photoshop's are similar to it since Live Picture was first with this feature). However, you never touch the original image files. They stay on Image Layers and are manipulated on Effect Layers that can be changed at any point.

The program features the same kind of "infinite flexibility" that Photoshop has. However, it is so much faster that it makes it possible to edit super-large images. Many artists work with both programs. Live Picture is billed as a companion for Photoshop rather than a replacement.

The program has just acquired a "baby brother" aimed specifically at Photoshop users. This low-cost program, OverDrive, gives you the speed of Live Picture for simple compositing without the expense or the color separation ability of the full version. It comes with a plug-in from Total Integration that enables you to exchange files with Photoshop. Figure 13-17 shows the Live Picture interface.

Macromedia XRes

Macromedia XRes is another program that is aimed at Photoshop users. Although it may some day be a rival, Macromedia is positioning itself as a companion to Photoshop. It has many of the analog tools of Fractal Design Painter (chalk, charcoal, and so on) and it can also composite large images much faster than Photoshop in less RAM.

It works by rendering part of an image when you zoom into it. It stores all of the filters and changes that you make to an image in an "undo" list and does not actually make any of the changes until you tell it to fully render the image. The total editing time

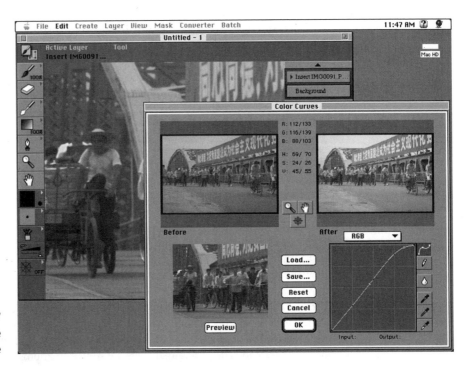

Figure 13-17
Live Picture
interface

may not be any less with XRes, but you can tell the computer to render an image overnight and not have to sit there as each action occurs (Photoshop users often complain of being clock watchers as they wait for each filter or action to get done). XRes is another program for you to explore as your knowledge of Photoshop increases.

1. What is Natural Media?
   a. Painting with chalk
   b. Tools that work in the digital world as expected in the real world
   c. Painting with paints that react to surface texture
   d. All of the above

2. What is Fractal Design Painter?
   a. A partial design painting program
   b. A program with Natural Media
   c. A Photoshop Layer
   d. None of the above

3. Identify one major advantage of Collage over Photoshop.
   a. It uses less space.
   b. It's easier.
   c. It's newer.
   d. It works with proxies of your real image.

4. In what format does Live Picture work?
   a. EPS
   b. TIFF
   c. CMYX
   d. IVUE

5. What is one advantage of Macromedia XRes over Photoshop?
   a. It uses less RAM.
   b. It makes all changes to an image faster.
   c. It will render changes to an image all at once and even overnight.
   d. It will render changes to an image all at once and never takes longer than five minutes.

PHOTOSHOP AND THE WEB

In Chapter 6, "Color and File Formats," you learned about Indexed Color mode and how to create a GIF89a image with transparency. This knowledge is important if you are going to create any images to be placed on the World Wide Web (an online facility that requires a modem to access).

The World Wide Web (the Web) is the portion of the Internet that uses a graphical interface. Unlike the earlier Internet services, which only let you exchange files and text, the Web lets you view images and follow hypertext links (hot links that take you from one location to another by clicking on them). This ability to view graphics comes at a cost.

The cost is the time that it takes to download the images. If you have a slow modem, you could spend more time waiting for images to download than in viewing them or in surfing the Net. Images placed on the Web, therefore, need to be small in size. Because so many people are still using relatively slow modems, you need to figure that 1KB takes about 1 second to download. Therefore, a 60KB file could take a minute. That's marginally okay. No one wants to sit and wait for a 1MB file at that speed, though! One way to make the images smaller in size is to change them to 256 colors or less and save them as GIF files. Another way to make them smaller is to save the images as JPEG files.

JPEG files can contain 16 million colors and can sometimes be smaller in physical size. All too often, however, they are slower to download than GIF images, and progressive JPEG support has been slow to appear (although Photoshop 4.0 lets you write a Progressive JPEG file). *Progressive JPEG* or *Progressive GIF* is a method of downloading a file so that the image begins to appear very fast but at a very low resolution. After the first pass—which looks like jagged blocks—the image begins to come more into focus. With each successive pass, it gets clearer until the entire image has been downloaded to your computer. It really doesn't finish any faster, but seeing it "resolve" helps you decide if you want to wait for it. If you see quickly that it is not an image that you need to view, you can go on to something else.

In order to see the material that is posted on the Web, you need a Web browser. This is a program that dials the telephone number of your Internet provider (the people whom you need to pay to be able to access the Web) and lets you move from Web site to Web site. Each Web site has its own address (called a *URL,* or Universal Resource Locator). When you click on an image or text that contains a URL, you can move directly to the new location. Figure 13-18 shows a Web page "mocked up" for a fictional company. It features a background pattern (which you created in Chapter 4, "Filters") with a transparent GIF file on top of the pattern. There is some text, and one button—similar to the one that you will create shortly. You will have the opportunity to create a similar page in the Lab section in Appendix C.

Figure 13-18
ABC Block's Web
page

Typical Web pages contain a mix of text and graphics that are both entertaining and help you navigate through the content of the site so you can see whatever interests you. Many artists are developing personal Web sites as a means for self-advertisement and a way to show their portfolios easily to a wide audience.

Therefore, the graphics that you need to create for the Web are generally of several varieties:

⚫ Buttons and interface items to help you move through a Web site

⚫ Decorative images to make the site interesting

⚫ Patterned backgrounds

⚫ Images posted as the Web content itself

Creating Buttons and Interface Items

Buttons are the portion of a Web site or interactive presentation that enable you to navigate through the material. They can say things like *Next* or *Previous*, or they can contain icons that symbolize various actions. Although they are practical elements, they can also be quite decorative, and they help to set the tone of the Web site or presentation.

Many buttons contain 3D effects. Here is an easy way to create a 3D button in Photoshop. For this first practice, however, you will create one much larger than you may ever really want.

HANDS ON

CREATING BUTTONS

1. Create a new document (Mac: ⌘+N, Windows: CTRL+N) 300 pixels square.

2. Select any color except black or white as your foreground color.

3. Double-click on the Rectangular Marquee tool. In the Marquee Option palette that appears, make the shape Rectangular and the style Fixed Size. Enter the values for Width=150 pixels, Height=150 pixels, and make sure that the Feather Radius box is set to 0.

4. Drag the Marquee into the center of the image (it does not need to be exact) and fill the selection (Mac: OPTION+DELETE, Windows: ALT+DELETE) with the foreground color.

5. Save the selection to a channel (click on the elliptical Marquee icon in the bottom of the Channels palette.) *Do not deselect.*

6. Make a new Layer (click on the New Layer icon at the bottom of the Layers palette).

7. Press D to set the colors back to the default of black and white.

8. Change the selection (now in the blank Layer) to select only the border (Select → Modify → Border) and set the border amount to 20 pixels.

9. Fill the area (Mac: OPTION+DELETE, Windows: ALT+DELETE) with black.

10. Load Channel 4 (Mac: OPTION+⌘+4, Windows: ALT+CTRL+4)—the selection that you previously saved. Reverse the selection (Select → Inverse).

11. Delete.

12. If the Black bevel looks too dark, decrease the opacity of the Bevel Layer.

When you are satisfied with your button, you can flatten it and convert it to indexed color. In Step 1, if you had created your image as a transparent Layer, you could simply merge both Layers and then take the new button to drag into any other image.

Animations and Animated GIF files

You can create wild animations using Adobe Photoshop—even though Photoshop itself is incapable of animation. Since traditional animation consisted of changing one frame at a time, you can do this manually. The animated GIFs that are now popular on the Web lend themselves to this technique. However, you could also create this manual animation and import it into Macromedia Director (where it could also be a wonderful transition effect) or into the Animation Editor of QuarkImmedia (an Xtension for QuarkXPress that enables you to make QuarkXPress pages move). You could also place it, one frame at a time, into Premiere—or into Adobe AfterEffects, and create a QuickTime movie.

Let's take a gradient-filled circle and turn it into an animated GIF. You will need to retrieve a GIF animation program from the Web—follow the links in the `Animated.Htm` page if you open it from the CD-ROM into your Web browser.

HANDS ON

ANIMATED GIFS

1. Create a new image 80×80 pixels.

2. Double-click on the Marquee tool. In the Marquee Option palette that appears, make the shape Elliptical and the style Fixed Size. Enter the values Width=78 pixels, Height=78 pixels, and make sure that the Feather Radius box is set to 0 and Anti-alias is off.

3. Drag the Marquee into the center of the image.

4. Save the selection to a channel (click on the elliptical Marquee icon in the bottom left of the Channels palette).

5. In the RGB channel, select the Gradient tool (G). Choose the Copper Gradient, Linear, Mask, Dither. Drag the Gradient from the upper-left corner to the lower-right corner of the image.

6. Save this as Frame01 in Photoshop format.

7. Duplicate Frame01 five times (Image → Duplicate → OK).

8. Take one of the duplicates and apply the Twirl filter at the setting of 200 (Filter, Distort, Twirl, 200).

9. Save the image as Frame02.

10. Select another duplicate and load Channel 4 (Mac: OPTION+⌘+4, Windows: ALT+CTRL+4).

11. Reopen the filter dialog (Mac: ⌘+OPTION+F, Windows: ALT+CTRL+F). This time select 400 as the Twirl amount. Save the image as Frame03.

12. Repeat Steps 9, 10, and 11 at settings of 600, 800, and 999 and saving the images as Frame04, Frame05, and Frame06, respectively.

13. The next sequence goes back the other way. Duplicate Frame05 and save it as Frame07.

    Frame04 → Frame08

    Frame03 → Frame09

    Frame02 → Frame10

    Frame01 → Frame11

14. Duplicate Frame01 five more times.

15. Select, Twirl, and Save:

    Frame12 at ×200

    Frame13 at ×400

    Frame14 at ×600

    Frame15 at ×800

    Frame16 at ×999

16. Now it's back to the beginning again.

    Frame15 → Frame17

    Frame14 → Frame18

    Frame13 → Frame19

    Frame12 → Frame20

17. Open GifBuilder or GifConverter or whichever GIF animator you have, and place the frames one at a time. Save as a combined GIF file when you are done. Open the `Twirlme.htm` page in a Web browser such as Netscape that supports animated GIF files and watch it twirl!

Web Design Considerations

One of the challenges of designing for the Web is that you need to design for the lowest common denominator. Not everyone who visits a Web site will have a PowerMac or a Pentium machine. Nor will everyone have the ability to see 16 million colors. Therefore, you need to be very careful in the color palette that you use. While you should be *safe* if you consistently convert images to a *System* palette—an *approved* list of 256 colors—this palette is not the same on the Mac and the PC.

The Mac uses a System palette of 256 colors with white in location 1 and black in location 256. There is no real equivalent Windows palette—the PC needs a specific 20 colors in the first 10 and last 10 locations in the 256-color Lookup Table. It does not care which colors appear in between. Photoshop 4.0 gives you a choice of Mac, Windows, or Web palettes. The Web palette consists of 216-colors that exist both in the Mac and Windows Systems palettes. If you design with this palette (or convert to it), your images will display as you designed them on computers that are capable of showing only 256 colors. If you use a different palette and a person can only view 256 colors, the colors you used will be dithered (colors created to simulate the original by scattering pixels of different colors in an area).

Lynda Weinman has written the *standard* book on Web graphics design. It is called *Designing Web Graphics*. Visit her at her Web site—`http//www.lynda.com`.

1. Identify one of the ways that graphics can be made smaller for the World Wide Web.
   a. Cut out information and include only the significant portion of an image.
   b. Change images to 256 colors and save them as GIF files.
   c. Change images to 256 colors and save them as TIFF files.
   d. Save images as JPEG files.

2. What is a URL?
   a. An animal found in Alaska
   b. A Web address specific to Photoshop graphics only
   c. A graphic address
   d. A Web site's individual address

3. What is a dithered color?
   a. Colors that have been erased due to incompatibility of the color formats on the Web
   b. A Transparent Layer placed over an image
   c. Colors created to simulate the original by scattering pixels and different colors in an area
   d. A system palette of 256 colors

4. How is animation possible with the use of Photoshop?
   a. There is a specific utility in Photoshop that allows this to be done.
   b. By manually changing one frame at time.
   c. It is not possible in any way.
   d. Simply save it as a GIF file.

5. Who is Lynda Weinman?
   a. A professor of graphic design
   b. The author's sister
   c. A designer of Photoshop
   d. Author of *Designing Web Graphics*, a book about graphics on the Web

VIP PROFILE

Deke McCelland, Author of *MacWorld Photoshop Bible*

Deke McCelland is one of the most prolific authors around. He wrote the *MacWorld Photoshop Bible* as well as a number of other books on various graphics programs. Deke is also a contributing editor with *MacWorld* magazine.

Deke worked for a service bureau in Boulder, CO. It was one of the first three in the United States. The service bureau was started in 1985, and Deke became art director in 1986.

He started doing desktop publishing with MacPaint and integrated it with a comic strip in 1984 while still in college. After graduation, he got a job with a local newspaper. He was placed in charge of Mac development. The newspaper printed ads and had been sending them out of the company; they now wanted to bring this process in-house. As a 30,000 copy circulation free newspaper, they wanted to do their display ads by putting them into the computer. Deke didn't have much to work with—he was able to use Times or Helvetica as his fonts and a beta copy of PageMaker.

When he left the newspaper to work for the service bureau, he became the art director almost by default. No one had much experience then. They had no idea of marketing or pricing, and the owner was still in college. They had expected to have customers who were experienced in selecting typefaces and knew what to get from a typesetter, but this was not the clientele that the service bureau attracted. Instead, they attracted folks with no experience at all, and discovered that there was no common language. They hung pictures and samples on the walls to give their customers ideas, and tried a variety of ways to let folks know what they were going to be getting as output. They decided to put out a visual dictionary so people would have some idea. This was a 72-page book on typefaces and leading. They contacted Harcourt Brace Janonivich who agreed to publish it. Eventually, they turned in 300 pages with a paragraph of text per page—and got back 200 marked-up pages. It was a very wobbly first effort.

Deke next wrote a book on Freehand and a book on Adobe Illustrator for Dow Jones Irwin—all Step by Step books. He wrote a book on PageMaker, and then a book called *Painting on the Mac* which won the Ben Franklin award for the best computer book in 1989. He then expanded to writing for larger publishers and doing many more books. The total is now around 40 books—not counting upgrades and reprints.

Deke wanted to do a book on Photoshop for a long time before he had the opportunity to do so. Finally, IDG called out of the blue and asked him to write a book on Photoshop. The task seemed monumental. There was only one other Photoshop book on the market at that time—the David Biedney/Bert Monroy *Official Guide to Photoshop*. IDG wanted a big book—at least 700 pages that could cover everything. Could he write a Photoshop Bible? Once he really got into it, he began to realize how monumental a task it actually was—especially when all of the vendors that he contacted said "good luck." Many times he thought it *was* too much. And then, by the time it was released, everyone was excitedly awaiting the release of the *Photoshop Wow* book from Peachpit Press.

Deke hoped that his book would do half as well. He took to prowling around the online forums to see if anyone mentioned it. When he discovered that an acquisitions editor from a competing publisher trashed the book, he was really soured by the online experience, and after, he avoided the bulletin boards for a long time. However, when he went to MacWorld Expo in Boston two weeks later, 500 copies of the book were sold in a 3-day period—which was a record. Quantum books was the only bookseller at that time, and they had to keep sending for more books. The *MacWorld Photoshop Bible* beat the *Photoshop Wow* book to press by a full month. Then, one day someone left a message asking him to stop by the Adobe forum on CompuServe—which is where he met Robert Phillips, the Windows Section Leader for Photoshop and Illustrator. Robert became the co-author of the *MacWorld Photoshop Bible for Windows*.

Deke does enjoy Photoshop, but his first love was for the program Image Studio. He liked Color Studio as well, but Photoshop was easier to use. He liked Photoshop well enough that it soon became the only image editor he used. In an early product review he wrote the program was reason enough to own a Mac.

Deke's advice to you: Work through your projects incrementally. Don't expect to learn everything at once—or quickly. There is always more to learn. He used Photoshop for a full year before he began to create a mask—and then went hog wild using them. If you feel comfortable using Photoshop, then you are probably at the point where you need to stretch a bit. Photoshop is the kind of program in which you can create exciting stuff in the first few hours but know less than one-tenth of what the program can do. If you keep at it, Photoshop can keep your interest for years. Nothing holds together better for day-to-day work. And—oh yes—one other piece of advice—go out and buy his book!

CHAPTER SUMMARY

In this chapter, you learned about many of the companion programs that can work easily with Photoshop to add 3D imaging, animation, and video support. You also learned about preparing images for the Web.

CHAPTER 14

CONFIGURING AND OPTIMIZING PHOTOSHOP

Photoshop is a *plug-and-play* application—well, almost! In most situations, you can use it as soon as you've installed the program, but knowing how to keep Photoshop happy and well-fed will definitely lead to better working conditions. Much of your success with Photoshop will come from knowing how to use the program efficiently. Efficient use of the program means setting up Preferences and taking advantage of the shortcuts that the program provides. Photoshop has a variety of Preferences, and knowing which of them to choose also results in a better working relationship with the program. Photoshop also has the ability to do a limited amount of scripting (called Actions), and being able to use this tool

617

will also increase your efficiency with the product. When you have finished this chapter, you should be able to

● Set up your scratch disks.

● Figure the amount of RAM your system needs.

● Conserve clipboard memory space.

● Select the best interpolation method for a specific job.

● Set your General Preferences.

● Troubleshoot common setup problems.

● Edit large files using Quick Edit.

● Create and use Actions.

● Batch process a folder of files.

PHOTOSHOP PREFERENCES

Photoshop permits a large degree of flexibility in setting up your working environment. There are two main Preference menus with 12 different submenus. Figure 14-1 shows the Preferences submenu. The Color Settings menu contains the prepress preferences that you will learn in Chapter 15, "Photoshop Output." These settings (Monitor Setup, Printing Inks Setup, Separation Setup, and Separation Tables) work together to help you produce dependable color separations that can be printed.

The Preferences menu items help you to configure your system to best suit your working style or your mood. They are:

1. General

2. Display & Cursors

3. Transparency & Gamut

4. Units & Rulers

5. Guides & Grid

6. Plug-Ins & Scratch Disks

7. Image Cache (Memory & Image Cache in Windows)

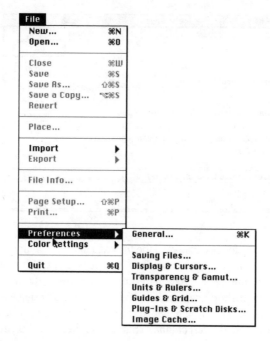

Figure 14-1
The list of
Preferences that
you can change

Choosing a Preference

It is important that you understand the Preferences. They can make a difference between working quickly and efficiently, or wasting time and energy fighting against the program. While you will generally want to set up your preferences only once, some items are flexible and can be changed as your needs change. Let's look at each of the Preferences menu items.

General Preferences

The General Preferences is the most important of the "setup" preferences. It has the most options, and it is the only one of the Preferences Menu items to have a keyboard shortcut (Mac: ⌘+K; Windows: CTRL+K). Figure 14-2 shows the General Preferences screen. From this screen, you can set all of the other Preferences by scrolling Next or Previous or by using a keyboard shortcut.

The first selectable item is the *Color Picker* that you want to use. You can choose either the Photoshop Color Picker, or Windows or Macintosh Picker (depending upon your platform). Normally, you want to select the Photoshop Color Picker. However, if you have a Colortron or other hardware colorimeter (a colorimeter is a device that helps you match colors) that adds functionality to the Color Picker, you might want to use your system's Color Picker instead. Pantone sells a set of colors for Web use that is accessible only via the system Color Picker. This is a setting; therefore, you may wish to change frequently.

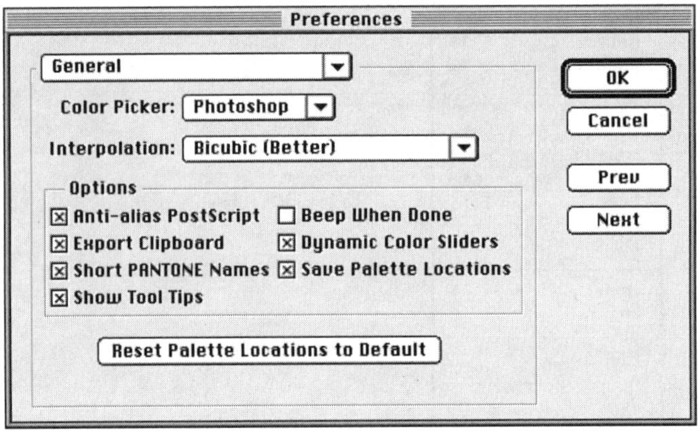

Figure 14-2
General
Preferences screen

The second preference concerns the *Interpolation Method*. In order to select the method that you want, you need to know what the option does. When you resample an image (by changing the number of pixels in the image), or by using the Transform or Free Transform commands, Photoshop has to either *invent* new pixels or determine which ones to toss away. The process of creating new pixels so they look as if they belong on an image when you resize it is called *interpolation*. This is a mathematical term which means to produce a middle value—sort of the way the electric company estimates your bill based on your previous electricity usage pattern.

Photoshop has three interpolation methods. The simplest method to understand is the Nearest Neighbor method. This also produces the most distortion in an image. In Nearest Neighbor interpolation, the computer enlarges the image by repeating the pixel in question. For example, if you had an image with 50 pixels in each direction and wanted to double the size, each pixel in the original would be repeated four times (twice across and twice down) to give the final pixel count of 100×100 pixels. Figure 14-3 shows a picture of a fingernail enlarged by 200% using the Nearest Neighbor interpolation. Even though this is enlarged to show detail, notice how blocky it is. It looks just like the screen preview when you zoom in on an image at greater than 1:1 ratio. Nearest Neighbor creates jaggies. This can be very useful if you want to enlarge your image without creating intermediate colors anywhere, but in general—for fine reproduction quality—you definitely want to avoid this setting. The Lab in Appendix C will allow you to experiment with some examples when you would actually want to use this method.

The preferred method of interpolation is Bicubic. This is the default setting in the Preferences, and you should be careful to change your setting *back* to this when you use a different setting for a special effect. It is too easy to forget that you changed the setting—until you notice pixellation in your image and begin to wonder why. Figure 14-4 shows the same image as Figure 14-3, enlarged using the Bicubic interpolation method. Notice how the color blocks are much smaller even though the image is the same size. Figure 14-5 shows a *difference check* of the two interpolation methods. The two enlargements were composited in Difference mode (just as you check your Lab exercises in Appendix C), and then the image was flattened and the Auto Levels command applied to maximize the difference in values. The black areas are areas where the same value appears in both files. Notice the almost checkerboard pattern of differences. This is typical of the way the Nearest Neighbor interpolation method does its enlargements.

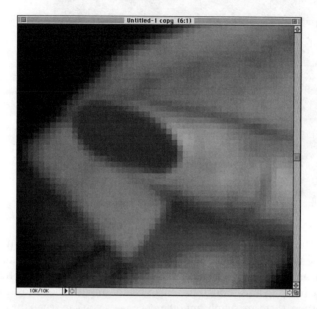

Figure 14-3
Image using
Nearest Neighbor
interpolation

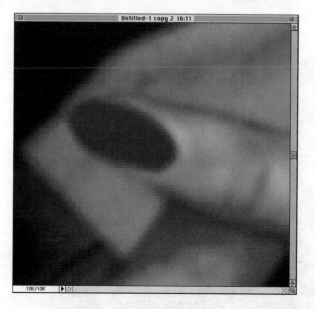

Figure 14-4
Image using Bicubic
interpolation

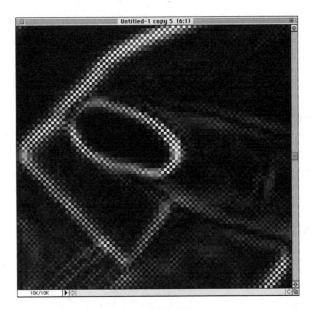

Figure 14-5
Difference Check
between Nearest
Neighbor and
Bicubic
interpolation

The third method of interpolation is Bilinear. This method is much faster than Bicubic (and slower than Nearest Neighbor). It produces a medium-quality enlargement. The Bilinear interpolation method rarely, if ever, needs to be used. There is simply no advantage to using it. Although the enlargement might look almost the same as the Bicubic method, there are significant differences—as you can see in the difference check in Figure 14-6.

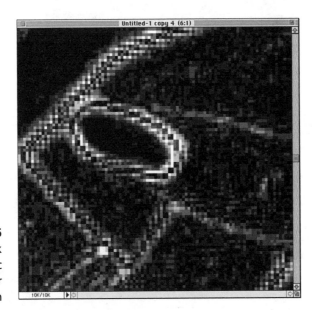

Figure 14-6
Difference Check
between Bicubic
and Bilinear
interpolation

Photoshop 4.0 allows you to change the interpolation method *on-the-fly* as you resample an image. Because of this, you should leave the setting at Bicubic in the Preferences setting. The Preference setting will then be used by the Transform and Free Transform commands. The only times it might need to be changed are if you wish to scale or rotate an image in such a way that it either deliberately leaves jaggies or *blocky* pixel areas, or if you want to scale an image up or down at print time so that it is jagged or blocky (to make a craft chart—for Counted Cross Stitch—from a tiny image, for example).

The next section of the General Preferences allows you to select a variety of options. The *Anti-alias PostScript* preference lets you bring in text or objects from Adobe Illustrator and render them into your image with soft edges. If you turn off the preference, then you may see jaggies when the image is transferred into Photoshop. You have a number of places to override this setting if you wish. When you open or place an EPS image, you can select whether or not to anti-alias the image. You can also change the setting when you create text. The only place that you are not asked to confirm a choice is when you drag an item from Illustrator directly from an open Illustrator file into Photoshop.

If jaggies are *bad,* why might you want to create them? If you are keeping your file at a very high resolution—especially if you are going to create a bitmapped file as output, then it may be undesirable to anti-alias the PostScript since it would degrade the sharpness of the final output. The choice is yours. Generally, you should leave this option on and only set it off in special instances. The Preference setting does not affect either the Line tool or the Text tool. You can anti-alias them—or not—as desired, regardless of this Preference setting.

Another option allows you to *Export Clipboard*—or not—when you leave Photoshop. Even with the option off, you can *import* images via the clipboard—the preference only affects whether the clipboard is *exported.* Unless you specifically need to transfer an image from Photoshop to another program via the clipboard, leave this option off. If you have a large image on the clipboard, switching into the operating system level takes too long. While you are at it, don't use the clipboard any more than absolutely necessary! Learn to know and love the Apply Image command instead.

Short PANTONE Names are only applicable if you are (a) saving a duotone or spot color plates (using PlateMaker) and (b) placing the resulting image into an older version of QuarkXPress where the now-standard Pantone names are not recognized. Otherwise, you do not need this option.

Show Tool Tips refers to the small lines of text that tell you the meaning of icons. This is a totally free choice. The Tool Tips are a bit slow, but they don't show up unless the cursor is stopped over an icon for a while, so they won't really slow down your work. They are convenient—but you won't cause a problem if you turn them off, either.

The *Beep When Done* preference is self-explanatory. A beep will sound when a task that uses a progress bar finishes. If you like to hear chirps or dings or whistles (or whatever sound you have programmed as an alert), by all means select this option. If you'd rather listen to the sound of silence, leave it off.

The *Dynamic Color Sliders* option should be left on unless you are working on a very old, very slow machine. This option gives you a preview of the colors that you can create from any setting in the Color Picker palette. As you move the sliders, the colors update to show what your next move could be. It is a very nice feature and a major help when mixing colors by sliding the controls.

The *Save Palette Locations* option tells Photoshop to remember how you had your desktop arranged when you exit the program and to reopen with the same setup. If you like to work with a Photoshop desktop that is non-default, then this is a valuable setting to select. Unless you are compulsive about having all palettes set to the default, there is no reason *not* to choose this option.

The *Reset Palette Locations to Default* button is valuable for getting your system back on target if you get frustrated with the palette "mess" you create. You can also use it if a window goes under a menu bar and becomes unmovable. If you click the button, it will move all of your palettes back to their factory setting.

Saving Files Preferences

The Saving Files Preference shows you the Mac dialog in Figure 14-7(a) and the Windows version in Figure 14-7(b). The Windows version does not have the options for saving multiple types of image previews, and it does not need the option about file extensions (the PC always saves them). Let's look at each option in turn.

Figure 14-7
a) Saving
Preferences dialog
(Mac)
b) Saving
Preferences dialog
(Windows)

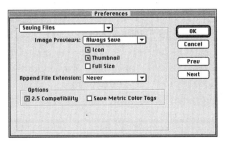

a

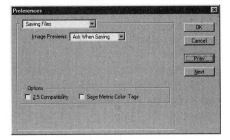

b

Three types of *Image Previews* can be saved on the Mac. These Image Previews can be custom icons you see on the desktop—a miniature of your image, the smaller preview that you see when you are in the File Open dialog (if QuickTime is loaded), and/or a full-size preview of the image that can be placed into a page layout program. Image Previews are a nice feature, but they can be time-consuming and a hard-disk hog when you work with large files. If you want to save only one type of preview, save the Thumbnail (which is the only type of preview on Windows) so that you can see a small representation of the file before you open it. You are best off not saving a full-size preview at all. The image icon is pretty to look at in the Finder and is also very useful; however, it has a very nasty habit of getting mixed up. For some reason—typically after a new piece of software has been installed, or very often on a removable storage device like a Syquest, Zip, or MO unit—the preview icons may become scrambled and link themselves to the wrong documents. This allows you to open the image of your dog, but the icon has a house or an apple on it! For this reason, many Photoshop users have given up on the preview icons. You can always unscramble them by rebuilding the desktop (hold down (OPTION) and ⌘ after your Extensions have loaded and before the disk icons are displayed). You should periodically rebuild the Mac desktop anyway, but it is a real annoyance to have to do it to unscramble mixed-up icons.

If you usually save files that are under 10MB in size, you can set the Image Preview Preference to Always Save with the types of previews you prefer. If your file size sometimes exceeds 10MB (a color file destined for a film recorder, for example, typically weighs in at 150MB), then save yourself a lot of aggravation—set the preference to Ask Before Saving. It can be painful to watch the little wristwatch spin around for five minutes or more while a large file is saved with a preview.

The Mac has an *Append File Extension* feature. You can select from Always, Never, or Ask When Saving. If you exchange files with the PC, a file extension can be valuable to have. If you typically open files from a list or if you save preview icons, it is also handy. However, if you normally click on a document to open it and you never save icon previews, the *standard* icon already tells you the file type. Your choice—you can even open a file without an extension. On Windows, your extension is automatically appended to the file name.

The *2.5 Format Compatibility* option should be left off unless you need to use your files in a program that cannot read the 3.0 format. The only format that can save layered and transparent images is the Photoshop 3.0 standard. However, if you save your files with 2.5 compatibility turned on, an older version of Photoshop can read the layered information as flattened. Good? Yes, if you need to. However, it comes at a heavy price. In order to allow Photoshop 2.5 (or another program) to read this file, it has to be saved with another—flattened—version of the image embedded in it. This can easily add up to as much as another 50% of the file size in hard drive space used. In general, the price is too high. Leave this off unless you really need it.

The *Save Metric Color Tags* preference refers to a feature in QuarkXPress. If you use the EFIcolor engine within Photoshop to convert from RGB to CMYK or to calibrate your output and then place your image into QuarkXPress, then you want this setting checked. It will use the currently selected EFI separation table.

Display & Cursors

The Display & Cursors Preference sets up the display characteristics of your system. The *CMYK Composites* option allows you to choose between Faster and Smoother. The Faster option converts the CMYK values in an image to RGB viewing values using a lookup table. While this method is fast, it is not accurate. It can show much more banding in gradations than is actually in your file. The Smoother option takes longer, but provides a more accurate representation of the actual values. Typically, you can work in the Faster mode and change to Smoother to get a final idea of your image.

Leave the *Color Channels in Color* option *off*—or at least, turn it off once you understand how the color channel is actually just a grayscale representation of your image. Many of the selection techniques you are learning require you to search for the *best* channel to isolate an object. You cannot evaluate that in anything other than grayscale. If you keep the color on when you look at the specific channel, it will only get in the way of your ability to *see* the image in the channel. However, if you are having trouble understanding how a color can be a grayscale image, by all means, leave the option on until it makes sense to you. There is a critical difference between previewing RGB and CMYK channels in grayscale when you look at the image. In an RGB channel, the *white* areas of the channel carry the actual color—any red pixels in the image are white in the Red channel of an RGB image (you can see this by changing the Preference setting to look at the Red channel of an RGB image in color and then in grayscale). In a CMYK image, the reverse is true. It is the *black* areas of a channel that show the color. Look at Figures 14-8 and 14-9. Figure 14-8 shows the Channels palette of an RGB image. It contains a red square on a white background. The Red channel contains solid white—in other words, the Red channel is 100% Red. The Green and Blue channels only contain solid white in the background areas—areas of 100% Green and 100% Blue. The square in both of those channels is black, which indicates that no percentage of Green or Blue is actually in the file in the center part of the image. The fact that all three channels contain 100% color in the background areas means that the background is white (in RGB color, when you mix Red, Green, and Blue in 100% quantities, you get white, just like light). In the CMYK image (see Figure 14-9), however, the channels resemble the printing plates that would actually put ink on paper. The black areas carry the detail; white indicates a total absence of color. If you select the option to view the color channels in color, you will never see white in an RGB image channel (its values would range from black to solid Red, Green, or Blue), and in a CMYK image channel, you will only see black in the Black channel (your color in the other channels will range from white to solid Cyan, Magenta, or Yellow).

Unless you are working with a very limited color card, you do not want to select either the *Use System Palette* option or the *Use Diffusion Dither* option. Use the Diffusion Dither option only if you are working in 256-color mode and need to see a better indication of your colors. If you need to create Indexed Color and look at it as it would look on the lowest common denominator screen, you probably want to let the image do a pattern dither—which is the way it is usually displayed on low-end monitors with 256 colors in the color card. (A common reason to need to do this is to preview images that are to be displayed on the World Wide Web.)

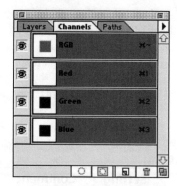

Figure 14-8
RGB channels in
grayscale

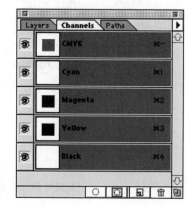

Figure 14-9
CMYK channels in
grayscale

If you have a color card that permits it, however, you *do* want to select the Video LUT animation. This gives you some other desirable features—especially in the Levels dialog. With Video LUT on and the Levels preview turned off, you can see an instant *before and after* of your image just by clicking on the dialog window title bar. You can also see the areas of your image to be clipped by setting specific white and black points on the sliders if you have Video LUT on and preview off (and press OPTION on the Mac and ALT on Windows as you drag the mouse).

You can also have some say in how you want to view the *Painting Cursors* and *Other Cursors* in Photoshop. When you use one of the painting tools (such as something that has an associated brush size—the Airbrush, Eraser, Pencil, Paintbrush, Rubber Stamp, Smudge tool, Tone tools, or Focus tools)—you can work in Standard mode, Precise mode, or Brush Size mode. In Standard mode, all you see is the small icon that indicates which tool is active. It does not vary in size to show you where you are painting. The Precise mode shows you a crosshair cursor. It is excellent for placing the *hot spot* of a tool (the point from which the effect begins) exactly where it needs to go. However, it is frequently less than useful when trying to work with a large size brush. The Brush Size mode is the preferred way to work. While this is totally your choice, most artists feel more comfortable when they can see the size of their brush. It is a definite aid in making the brush go where you want it to! Besides, if you want to see the cursor in Precise mode, all you need to do is press CAPSLOCK down. This works without changing your preference.

The *Other Tools* option should be left in Standard mode—rather than Precise mode—for the same reason; you can always make the cursor appear as a crosshair by pressing CAPSLOCK.

Table 14-1 shows a summary—for fast reference—of the recommended settings discussed so far.

Table 14-1 Recommended settings for General, Saving Files, and Display & Cursors Preferences

Preference Item	Setting	Comment
Interpolation Method	Bicubic	Unless there is a special reason
Anti-alias PostScript	Yes	For normal work flow
Export Clipboard	No	Turn on when needed
Short PANTONE Names	No	Only for old page layout program
Beep When Done	No	Unless you like noise
Dynamic Color Sliders	Yes	
Restore Palette & Dialog positions	Yes	
Image Preview	Ask	
2.5 Compatibility	No	Unless absolutely needed
Save Metric Color Tags	No	Unless using EFI color
CMYK Composites	Faster	Until you are done
Color Color Channels in Color	No	
Use System Palette	No	
Use Diffusion Dither	No	
Video LUT Animation	Yes	
Painting Cursors	Brush Size	
Other Cursors	Standard	

Transparency & Gamut Warning

Photoshop allows you to decide how you want it to display images to indicate transparent areas. The dialog, shown in Figure 14-10 is self-explanatory. You can select the size and color of the grid that is displayed. Unless you have a very good reason, leave the *Transparency Settings* preference alone. The default is the most unobtrusive but still noticeable combination. If you really hate seeing the transparency indicator, you could set both foreground and background colors of the grid to white, but you should

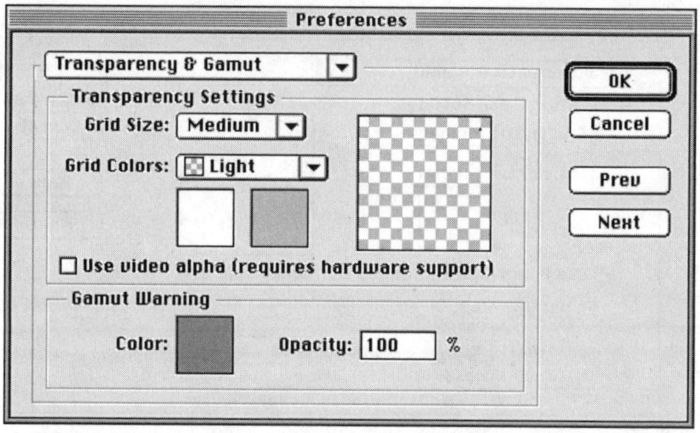

Figure 14-10
Transparency
Preference dialog

make sure that you can see transparency. If you cannot, then you cannot be sure it is behaving as you expect.

The *Gamut Warning* is a feature that allows you to work in RGB color space but test the conversion to CMYK without doing it. While the CMYK Preview (a menu item under the View menu) can show you how your image will look before conversion, the Gamut Warning shows you which colors are out of range in your image. This allows you to use the Tone tool in desaturate mode to help bring the image into gamut (or allows you to see just how bad of a hit your image will take when you convert it). You can turn Gamut Warning on or off on an individual image by selecting the Gamut Warning item on the Mode menu. The Preferences option allows you to select the *color* and *opacity* to be used to show out-of-gamut colors. There is no *right* choice for this option. Pick a color that does not appear in your image. This allows you the best chance of evaluating the out-of-gamut colors in your picture. Figure 14-11 shows you this dialog.

Units & Rulers

The Units & Rulers preference lets you select the unit of measure for Rulers, whether to use PostScript or Traditional points, and the width and gutter sizes for columns. All of this is your free choice. The *Rulers Unit* preference cascades downward, however, so that even if you do not use the Rulers feature (Mac: ⌘+R; Windows: CTRL+R), the unit of measure that you specify is used when you create new files. Setting the Units to pixels may be the most uncomplicated decision that you can make. All of the other settings depend upon the Resolution setting for the image. Measurements made in pixels do not change.

The *Column Size* is totally your call. The *Point/Pica Size* (Traditional versus PostScript pixel measurement) is also your free choice, but in the absence of a reason to change it, select the PostScript size of 72 points/inch. This keeps the measurement easy in that there are also 72 pixels to the inch on most monitors. Figure 14-12 shows the Units & Rulers dialog. It is the same on both platforms.

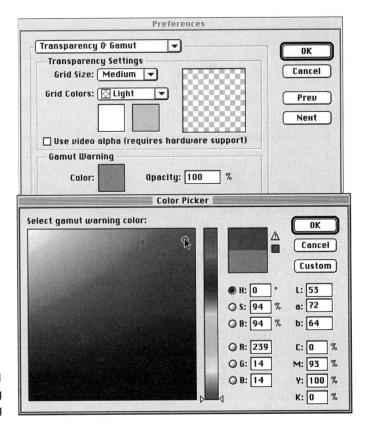

Figure 14-11
Gamut Warning
Preference dialog

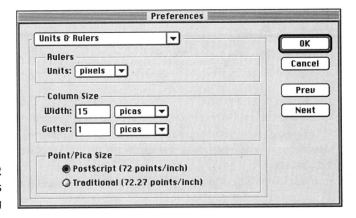

Figure 14-12
Units & Rulers
Preference dialog

Guides & Grid

Guides & Grids are new to Photoshop 4.0, so this is a totally new preference category. This long-requested feature lets you drag snap-to-able guidelines from a ruler to use in compositing or laying out an image. The Grid constrains the paint tools to certain locations or allow you to drag images precisely. For Guides, you have a choice of *Color* and *Style*. The choices are personal. Make sure to select a guide color not in your image (so you can see them). You can select Lines or Dashed Lines for the guidelines—pick whichever style is more visible in your image.

You may also select *Grid Color* and *Style,* and the same recommendations hold true. You have the option of Dots for grids as well as the two line styles. Photoshop defaults to a Gridline Every 1 pixel with four Subdivisions. This is a standard that you will probably change for every job. You might find that working with a grid keyed to 10 lines per *inch*, for example, will work better for you. There is a drop-down menu that allows you to select the unit on the grid. It's too bad it's not possible to select different measurements for horizontal and vertical grid layouts, but this version is limited to square grids only. Figure 14-13 shows the Guides & Grid Preference dialog.

Plug-Ins & Scratch Disk

The Plug-ins preference allows you to specify the folder/directory to use for storing your Photoshop plug-ins. When Photoshop is first installed, the *official* plug-ins folder is called **Plug-ins** and is located inside the Photoshop folder if you are using a Macintosh. If you are using Windows, the directory is called **Plugins** and is a subdirectory of the Photoshop directory.

You do not have to use the specified directory/folder, however. You may want to have several different *sets* of plug-ins that you load at different times. You may want to use a directory/folder that is accessible by more programs and stored outside the Photoshop main directory/folder. As long as you identify the location of the plug-ins to the program, you can store them anywhere you wish on the computer. On the Macintosh, you may also use a folder that actually contains only Macintosh System Aliases to the specific plug-in modules.

Figure 14-13
Guides & Grid
Preference dialog

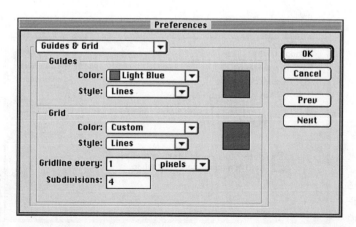

Photoshop allows you to select up to two hard drives as scratch disks. Photoshop uses scratch disks to store pieces of the image that do not fit in RAM as you are editing the file. It also may use the scratch disk to store the Undo buffer (the area of your last action that may need to be reversed).

You cannot specify the folders/directories where Photoshop will store its temp files. You may only locate the disk. Photoshop will use any space on the drive that is empty and release it when it is done. The best thing you can do to maximize your use of the scratch disk is to set aside an entire disk (or disk partition) for Photoshop to use. Keep it empty and keep it optimized with Norton or Central Point Utilities (either platform).

Microsoft Windows maintains its own scratch disk (or Swap disk) for Windows. This is a permanent location on a disk. It is not the same thing as the Photoshop Scratch Disk, however, and should not be confused with it. Increasing the size of the Windows Swap file will not help Photoshop at all. Figure 14-14 shows the dialog to set the preference for locating the **Plug-ins** folder/directory. Figure 14-15 shows the Mac dialog that allows you to specify the Image Cache settings. Figure 14-16 shows the slightly different dialog under Windows. The differences between the two platforms concern the ways in which the two systems handle memory partitions between running applications.

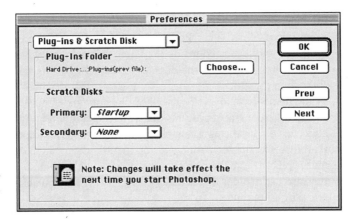

Figure 14-14
Plug-ins preference
dialog

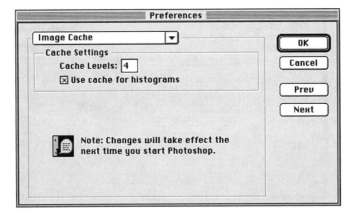

Figure 14-15
Mac Scratch Disk
dialog

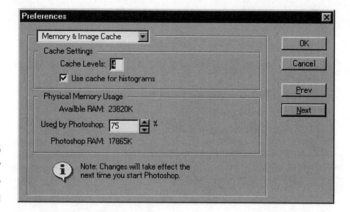

Figure 14-16
Windows Memory
& Image Cache
dialog

Image Cache (Mac) or Memory & Image Cache (Windows)

The *Image Cache* setting is new to Photoshop 4.0. A *cache* is a storage place where something is stashed away for fast retrieval or because it is valuable. An Image Cache is a storage scheme for your document that allows Photoshop to redraw the screen faster with high-resolution images when it is resizing, scaling, compositing, layering, or creating color corrections. The setting defaults to 4—which is the middle of its range. It is faster but less accurate at 8, and slower but more accurate at 1. The decision is yours to make, though there is no good reason to change the settings if you are happy with performance. You can also elect to use the cache for Histograms—which are also slightly less accurate at higher settings. The Image Cache settings are the only options of this Mac preferences screen.

The Windows Memory & Image Cache preference allows you to determine how much of the available RAM is to be used by Photoshop in Windows. By default, Photoshop gets 75%. The Macintosh cannot set RAM allocation in that manner, and so it does not contain an option to set the size of the RAM partition in the Preferences dialog. On the Mac, you need to double-click on the Photoshop application icon at the Finder level in order to increase the amount of RAM for the program. You then change the Preferred amount to whatever you wish it to be. *Never* give Photoshop on the Mac all of your available RAM. That is a recipe for disaster. The Macintosh Operating System needs at least 3–5MB free at all times. A safe bet if you have over 24MB of RAM is to always leave 10MB free for the operating system.

1. Which one of the following Preference Menu options has a keyboard shortcut?
   a. General
   b. Display and Cursor
   c. Units and Rulers
   d. Grids and Guides

2. Identify the three Interpolation methods Photoshop has.
   a. Bicubic
   b. Nearest Neighbor
   c. Trilinear
   d. Bilinear

3. Export the Clipboard option is responsible for which of the following?
   a. Exporting the clipboard and image
   b. Exporting an image
   c. Setting a color scheme
   d. None of the above

4. Identify the three types of image previews that can be saved on a Mac.
   a. A custom icon
   b. There is only one means possible, the custom icon
   c. The small preview you see when in the File Open Dialog
   d. A full size preview of the image

5. What does the Transparency setting do?
   a. Nothing, it doesn't exist
   b. Allows you to choose how you would like to display images to indicate transparent areas
   c. Allows you to work in RGB color space but test the conversion to CMYK without actually doing it
   d. Allows you to choose if the Transparency feature is turned on or off

MEMORY USAGE

Photoshop eats RAM for breakfast. It is powered by RAM; it needs as much of it as you can afford. Adding more RAM is the one major thing that you can do to make Photoshop run faster and more efficiently. Adding RAM is better than adding a Disk Array, a Graphics Accelerator card, a RAM disk, or even a faster motherboard (within reason—it is better to get a Pentium or a Pentium Pro than to put more RAM into a 386 machine, but you then need more RAM for the Pentium anyway). Photoshop has four (or five on Windows) indicators for you to watch to monitor the program's performance and RAM consumption.

File Size and Memory Status Indicators

You can choose between displaying the Image Size, the Scratch disk usage, the Efficiency indicator, or Timing (on Windows, the Cache Overhead) settings. On the Macintosh, there is a drop-down triangle next to the numeric read-out at the bottom of the image window. On Windows, just to the right of the image size figures at the lower left corner of the main Photoshop window, is a right facing arrow. Figure 14-17(a) shows the location of the indicators on the Mac screen, and Figure 17(b) shows them on a Windows screen. Click it for a pop-up menu which allows you to select the desired indicator. The pop-down menu item (on either platform) allows you to choose the numeric display for all the open images.

The *File Size* indicator shows the printing image size as it would be sent, flattened, to a printer. This number is not exactly the same value you would get if you saved the file, as there are other disk overhead considerations involved. The second number indicates the storage space needed to save the image in the same number of layers and channels it has as it is being edited. This number is usually larger than the actual amount of disk

Figure 14-17
a) Mac Memory and File Size indicator drop down
b) Windows Memory and File Size indicator drop down

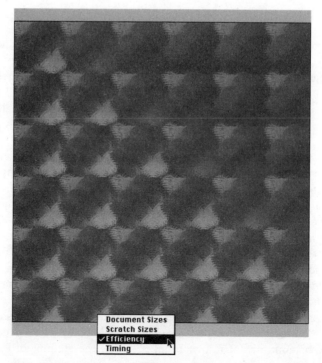

a

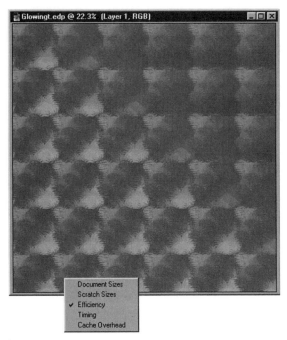

b

space used, as Photoshop can normally compress the image more when it writes the file. However, a large discrepancy shows that you will gain a lot of storage space if you flatten the image. As an example, the image used in the screen capture for Figure 14-17(a) and 14-17(b) occupies 24.1MB of hard disk space. The image contains two layers and a Layer mask. The File Size indicator shows that 11.4MB is the printing size and 26.4MB is the actual size of the image. It did compress by about 2MB on disk.

The *Efficiency* indicator gives you an idea of how well Photoshop is working. When it falls below 100%, this indicates that Photoshop has to make use of the scratch disks. Photoshop always writes to the scratch disk anyway, but this is only a problem (or at least a slowdown) as the Efficiency indicator drops. If you do not have enough RAM to edit the image, you have to accept the slowdown. As you can see from the Efficiency indicator numbers on Figures 14-17(a) and 14-17(b), the Mac efficiency is at 98% and the Windows at 67%. The reason for this to occur on the same file is that the Macintosh is a 9500/120 with 160MB of RAM (110MB devoted to Photoshop) and the Windows machine is a 586 DOS Compatibility card in the Macintosh running Windows 95 with only 32MB total memory and 75% of that total allocated to Photoshop. Naturally, the Windows version will show much more of a slowdown as it is not nearly as high-powered of a machine as the Macintosh in use.

You can also check the usage of the *Scratch disk* by selecting that option in the numeric readout area. The first number shows the amount of RAM used by all open images—the second number shows the available RAM (less the amount needed by the

Photoshop application itself). When the first number grows larger than the second number, your scratch disk is being used to hold the overflow.

The *Timing* indicator shows the amount of time used by the last operation. It took, for example, 15.2 seconds to run a 5-pixel Gaussian Blur against the top layer of the document we have been discussing.

Estimating Needed Memory

Photoshop works fastest when it can keep the entire image that is being edited in RAM. In order to do this, Photoshop needs to have 3–5 times the file size in real RAM (plus about 10MB more). In order to edit the image at all, Photoshop needs at least the file size in a combination of RAM and scratch disk and, to perform many basic tasks, 3–5 times the file size in combination.

Sometimes, you do need to be able to hold all of your image in RAM. Some filters work only in available memory, and if there is not enough RAM, the filter cannot be applied. A work-around for some filters is to filter each channel separately, but even that trick will not work if a filter cannot process grayscale data. Another problem, if you are working under Windows 3.1, is that there is a non-negotiable 16MB RAM that you cannot use and it is not possible to add more.

Your best performance will be achieved when you have 3–5 times your normal file size in RAM. If you create 2-page spreads in Photoshop, then your *average* file size in CMYK mode will be about 66MB. To keep a file this size in RAM, you would need between 200–300MB of RAM—a whopping, super-expensive amount. If that is not feasible (as it is not for most of us), then the next best thing is to have a very fast hard drive with lots of empty space on it to use as the scratch disk.

You may choose up to two scratch disks for Photoshop, and they should be kept clear of any other files and optimized frequently using utilities such as Norton Disk Doctor (on either platform) to keep the disk in perfect shape. One technique that works well with either Windows or the Mac is to create a partition on your hard drive that is only used for the Photoshop scratch disk.

Memory Conservation Strategies

There are a number of ways to make the best use of the RAM that you are able to afford.

● *Never use the Cut and Paste commands.* It is obviously unrealistic to say "never use," but you should use these commands as infrequently as possible. They use valuable memory buffer space. If you do use the Copy command, when you are done with the copy, flush the memory buffer for the clipboard (Edit → Purge → Clipboard). You can use the Apply Image command when you are copying within an image or from an image of the exact pixel count. You can use drag-and-drop between images of different sizes (or press SHIFT as you drag an image of the same pixel count to have it register in place).

Purge the Undo buffer after large actions (Edit → Purge → Undo) or if you are using large patterns that you wish to release (Edit → Purge → Pattern).

● *Use drag-and-drop to move selections between images.* When you drag an object into another image, you do not use the clipboard memory space, so there is nothing that needs to be removed from it.

Duplicate areas in an image by making a "keyboard" copy of the area.

If you need to copy an area of a design within an image, press the OPTION (Mac) or ALT (Windows) and then drag the selection to a new location. This creates a copy of the selected area but does not use the clipboard for it.

● *Float an area to move it.* If you need to move part of an image to another layer and want to "cut" it from the original layer, use the modifier key version of the Float command (Mac: ⌘+OPTION+J; Windows: ALT+CTRL+J) to lift it away from the background. Then move the floating selection in the Layers palette until it is in the correct position in the palette list. If you need to merge the floated Layer with another, move it over the "target" Layer and Merge Down (Mac: ⌘+E; Windows: CTRL+E).

● *Use the Apply Image command.* Apply Image will duplicate your image in a variety of Apply modes and opacities anywhere within your current image or in any open image that has the same pixel count. It does not use the clipboard, and, therefore, is very sparing of RAM.

● *Use the Quick Edit feature.*

Quick Edit

Quick Edit is an Acquire module that comes with Photoshop. It allows you to edit any portion of an image without loading the entire image. You divide your image into a user-selectable number of blocks (you may specify 5 blocks across and 4 down, for example), and load a single block into memory for editing. When you have made the changes, you can export the changes back to your original file and only the edited area in the image is changed. The only catch is that the file must already be in TIFF format for you to be able to use the Quick Edit plug-in. Figure 14-18 shows the Quick Edit Acquire dialog.

You cannot use this technique on a layered file—that must be kept in Photoshop format. You can create layers during the editing process, but they must be flattened before you export your changes, and any channels that you create should be removed as well. Total Integration, a third-party developer for Mac/Photoshop, has a package called FASTedit Deluxe. It not only performs the same functions as Quick Edit, but also enables you to edit files in other formats—most notably, files that are in Photoshop 3.0 format that contain layers. Figure 14-19 shows the FASTedit Deluxe Acquire dialog.

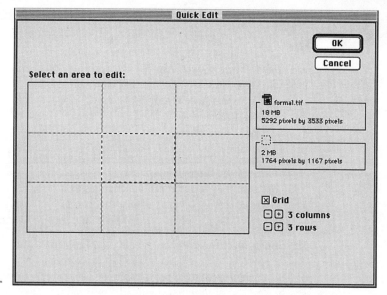

Figure 14-18
Quick Edit Acquire
dialog .

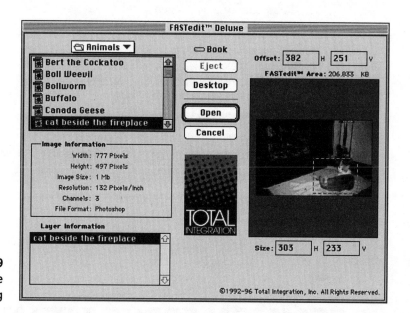

Figure 14-19
FASTedit Deluxe
Acquire dialog

It is a bit more difficult to work on a divided file because you need to be very careful that your "seams" do not show in the final image. If you alter the color of the background, for instance, you must do so in a way that can be precisely applied to all of the sections of your image. The best way to do this is to save the Curves or Levels change that you make. Then, you can recall this setting for every piece of the original file.

1. Which is the best way to improve Photoshop's speed and efficiency?
   a. Add a Disk array
   b. Add a Graphics Accelerator card
   c. Add more RAM
   d. Add a RAM disk

2. The File Size indicator displays what type of information?
   a. The size of the file when you save it
   b. The size of the file as you make changes to it
   c. The size of the file when it is sent to a printer
   d. The size of the file when it is flattened and sent to a printer

3. The timing indicator displays what type of information?
   a. The amount of time used by the last operation
   b. The amount of time to print an image
   c. The amount of time to download a graphic from the Web
   d. The amount of time to open a file

4. If you cannot hold your image entirely in RAM, what is the next best way to achieve the necessary efficiency?
   a. Buy more RAM, which is very expensive
   b. Have a hard drive with a bunch of empty space
   c. Buy a new computer
   d. Forget it and toss in the towel

5. Quick Edit is great for which of the following?
   a. Editing portions of an image without loading an entire image
   b. Maneuvering around if there is not enough RAM available to keep an image in
   c. Editing Layered files
   d. Editing PCX files only

COMMON ERROR SITUATIONS

There are a number of areas where Photoshop has been known to cause problems. Photoshop is generally a very stable program, but since each person has a different system setup and a different mix of possibly incompatible programs, there is sometimes a bit of trouble getting Photoshop to run happily in a given environment. The trouble spots are very platform-specific (the problems on the Macintosh are not the same ones that will plague the Windows user). For this reason, the following section is divided into Macintosh and Windows considerations. The Windows section is contributed by Robert Phillips, the Windows Photoshop Section Leader on the CompuServe Adobe forum, and co-author (with Deke McCelland) of the *Photoshop 3.0 Bible, Windows Edition*.

Macintosh Problem Spots

There are several main problem-solving techniques that can be used on the Macintosh to keep Photoshop happy. When you receive an error message from Photoshop, here, in the order of difficulty and pain-in-the-neck factors, is a list of ways to troubleshoot the problem.

General Strategy

● *Toss the Prefs file.* The Preferences file that Photoshop writes to your System folder is the weakest portion of the program. It is the most prone to corruption—though this seems to be the case with Macintosh Preferences files in general. At a point that you have all of your palettes arranged as you want them, and all of your Preferences set up to suit, you ought to make a duplicate of the Prefs file and tuck it away inside a folder for safekeeping. That way, you do not need to start all over again if you need to remove the Preferences file.

"If you need to remove" should really be *"When you need to remove,"* because you will. The Prefs file tends to give up at least several times a year, and occasionally it self-destructs on its own—showing you a complete default setup when you launch Photoshop. In either case, you should remove the Prefs file at the first sign of trouble and either replace it with your good copy or remove it entirely and let Photoshop create a new one when the program next launches.

● *Start without extensions.* If removing the Prefs file does not help, restart the computer but hold down SHIFT as you reboot. This will disable all extensions. A common reason that Photoshop produces an error message is that something in the Extensions folder is conflicting with a Photoshop function. Photoshop does not need any extensions in order to load— though it might need them in order to use your scanner, and it certainly needs them to access a CD-ROM drive. However, you ought to be able to do enough without any extensions loaded to determine if your specific error is still happening. If it goes away when no extensions are loaded, then you will have the wonderful experience of trying to discover which extension does not like Photoshop (sarcasm intended).

This is probably not the most delightful way to spend a day, but there are a few ways to make the search easier. If you installed something new just before getting errors in Photoshop, disable the new Extension or Control Panel (use the Apple Extensions Manager, a third-party Extensions Manager, or drag the possible offender out of the System folder and onto the desktop). Try again. If that does not help, remove half of your extensions (for example, drag the Control Panels folder to the desktop and reboot). If the error goes away, then the offender was one of the Control Panels. Replace half of the Control Panels and reboot. If the error comes back, then the offending INIT is in that group. Keep removing or restoring extensions and Control Panels by half until you find the one that is causing the problem.

Conflict Catcher, by Cassidy & Greene, is an Extensions Manager that can perform this test for you automatically. It is a highly recommended program.

Some extensions are known to be "bad neighbors." They will work for many people, but cause so many problems for other folks, that they are known to the Adobe tech support people as the "Usual Suspects." This group of suspicious programs is discussed a bit later in this section.

● *Remove the Plug-ins folder or pull all third-party filters from the folder.* Photoshop 4.0 has developed the charming trick of not liking some of the older third-party plug-ins.The program won't crash—it can just behave unexpectedly. For example, perhaps the Offset filter won't offset properly. Removing the older filters seems to fix the problem. At least it gives you a fairly easy way to check for a problem.

● If removing the Prefs file and booting without Extensions does not help, you may need to reinstall Photoshop.

Reinstalling Photoshop is a mid-level pain-in-the-neck. *You need to remove the Prefs file before you begin the reinstall.* You might also want to drag the entire Photoshop folder to the trash (but do not empty the trash). However, if you have third-party plug-ins installed in your Photoshop Plug-ins folder, rescue them before you trash the original installation.

Reinstall the program from the CD-ROM. Replace your third-party filters and Acquire modules (your scanner driver, add-on filters such as Kai's Power Tools, etc.). If you think that a plug-in could be damaged, reinstall it from the original disks as well.

This whole process is made easier if you either do not keep third-party plug-ins in your Plug-ins folder (keep an alias instead), or you keep each plug-in in its own folder so you can easily see which ones need to be moved if you reinstall the program.

- *Reinstall the Apple System.* This is a major pain. If you are constantly getting major system crashes, you may have a corrupt System folder. Unfortunately, when a Macintosh crashes, it has been known to take down not only the application that is running, but the System file as well. Then, even though you find and fix the problem that caused the error, your system is still flaky.

  To perform a clean install of the operating system, drag the Finder and the System file out of the System folder. Reboot with the Apple Tools disk (if your system is on a disk) or with the System CD-ROM. Follow the instructions in the Apple manual for your system as to how to perform a *clean install*.

- If all else fails, reinitialize your hard drive and restore your data from latest backup.

  You *do* have a latest backup, don't you? It is critical that you do. Re-initializing the disk is the most major of all of the suggested steps. It should only be taken after everything else has been tried and the system still seems corrupt and easily crashable. If you are having trouble with the disk media itself, then this drastic step can be the solution.

Photoshop is the canary in the coal mine. If you are not familiar with this expression, miners would often carry a canary into the mines with them. The canary was much more susceptible to the presence of dangerous gases and would sicken and die long before the miners were aware of any problem. Photoshop performs this function for the Macintosh. All too often, what looks like a bug in Photoshop is the symptom of a sick system that has not yet started to affect other programs. A flaky RAM chip will cause Photoshop to crash long before it bothers any other application. A bad SCSI cable or improperly terminated SCSI device will cause Photoshop errors but might work just fine with any other program. However, the problem is really there—it is not Photoshop's fault. The rest of this section will deal with some of the specific errors and their causes, as well as listing some of the "Usual Suspects."

Common Problems

Here is a list of the most common problems that are reported to the Macintosh section of the CompuServe Adobe forum.

- *Cannot initialize disk.* This error message appears when you attempt to load Photoshop. It does not allow the program to load. There are several causes of this. One is a corrupt Prefs file. The other is a corrupt font in the System folder. If trashing the Prefs file does not help, remove the Fonts folder from the System folder. Just drag it onto the desktop or the hard drive. When you reboot, the System will create a new Fonts folder. Launch Photoshop. It should start right up. If it does, return your fonts to the

Fonts folder half at a time until you find the culprit. If it does not work, go on to try the problem-solving steps previously given.

On one occasion, the error message has appeared after a system crash that left the Prefs file both corrupt and open. Since the System thought the file was open, it could not be replaced. When the file was trashed and the trash emptied, a new file could not be created. It took a fix-up with Norton Disk Tools, restoring the Prefs file from a backup tape, and then trashing the restored copy to get the system up and running again. *Do not empty the trash until you are able to reopen Photoshop.*

Another cause of this message—especially on the 603 chip machines—has been the presence or absence of the Macintosh Easy Open extension. If the steps given so far do not work for you, try removing the Easy Open extension. If it is not loaded, enable it. This is becoming a semi-nightmare extension.

- *Lost cursors.* If your cursor disappears when you move it over an image and you cannot see what you are doing, remove the Direct Cursors folder from your Plug-ins Extensions folder. Direct Cursors is the Photoshop extension that allows you to see the actual size brush strokes when you paint. On some systems, it will not work properly and causes the cursor to disappear entirely. With the extension removed, you will not be able to see brushes larger than 16 pixels, but you will be able to see your cursor. This is a problem between Photoshop and the Apple operating system, and as fast as the Adobe engineers "fix" the problem, a new Apple update "breaks" it again *(sigh).*

- *Magnifier keyboard shortcut won't work.* If you press the usual ⌘+SHIFT combination to access the Magnifier and nothing happens, you may have shifted yourself into another language keyboard. This is a glitch in the Mac Operating System. The key combination allows you to scroll through the keycaps and keyboard set-ups for a variety of languages. Remove the WorldScript extension and the extra keyboard definitions, and the problem will go away.

- *Toolbox cannot be moved.* Sometimes, you may discover that the Toolbox looks as if the top is cut off and the Move bar on the Toolbox is "stuck" under the Apple Menu bar—where you cannot get it. This tends to happen if you have hidden the Toolbox and the palettes by use of TAB and then quit Photoshop with the tools still hidden.

  The fix is easy. Press ⌘+K to open the General Preferences. Click on the Restore Palette Locations to Default button. The default tool positions will be back, and you can grab the Toolbox again. Trashing the Prefs file would also work, but this is faster.

● *Crash on Quit.* There are two common causes for this. You may have Norton FileSaver or another Trash Back program installed. Photoshop is not happy with this. Remove the FileSaver extension from your `System` folder. Perhaps someday there will be a version of FileSaver that will co-exist with Photoshop.

The other cause is an original copy of *Kai's Power Tools Version 3.0.* The first release of Version 3.0 had a bug in it, so that if you used the TextureExplorer module and mutated a texture, Photoshop would crash upon quitting. The fix for this is to contact MetaTools for the upgrade to a version that works.

● *Unacceptable scan lines.* This is caused by a noisy SCSI cable that is loose, too long, too short, not the *right* brand, or was otherwise left out during a full moon. SCSI Voodoo is another Mac problem that is not a lot of fun. However, if you are getting odd scan lines, the problem is in the cables somewhere in your SCSI chain—not in Photoshop's ability to process the scan.

● *Type 11 errors.* This problem is limited to the PowerMacs. There are many reasons why Type 11 errors appear and none of them are the result of Photoshop bugs (though they may, sometimes, be the result of buggy third-party filters). There is a file included on the CD-ROM for this book that is called Error.Txt. It was written for the Photoshop Forum on CompuServe to help members solve their Type 11 problems. I was also "bitten" with the Type 11 problem after purchasing a PowerMac. The problem was eventually (after a truly horrid month of working in 15-minute increments between crashes) traced to a flaky DIMM chip. When the DIMM chip was replaced, the Type 11 errors almost totally disappeared. Actually, I was bitten twice. After upgrading from 80MB to 160MB RAM, the same thing happened again. Same solution—and RAM bought from a "name" company rather than the "non-name" brand immediately fixed the problem.

● *System performs slowly.* There are several reasons why Photoshop may seem sluggish. Turn off Virtual Memory—even on PowerMacs. While a small Virtual Memory size may be moderately okay on a PowerMac, it fights with Photoshop's built-in memory management and slows down performance. Also, make sure that your Cache is set to no more than 96KB. It is even better to set it to 32KB. If the program is still slow, you can turn off the previews in the Channels and Layers palettes. That will also significantly speed up your system.

The Usual Suspects

The following is a list of extensions, Control Panels, or plug-ins that do not "play nice-ly" with each other. Check them first when someone misbehaves.

- *Asynch I/O.* This Photoshop plug-in is problematical. If you have tried Steps 1 and 2 of the General Strategy and have ruled out battling INITs, try removing this plug-in. It may make the difference. If it does not—put it back!

- Now Utilities has many programs that are sometimes responsible for Photoshop glitches. WYSIWYG Menus can cause a problem, as can SuperBoomerang. Now Utilities is a wonderful collection of programs and is useful. It works perfectly for the majority of users. However, if you have trouble and you also use Now Utilities, it is one of the first "suspects" on the list.

- *Super Boomerang and Directory Assistance.* SuperBoomerang has already been mentioned. Its partner in function—Directory Assistance—is truly bad news. This program, useful though it may be, is so much a suspect that Norton no longer includes it in the latest version of the Norton Utilities. System 7.5+ has a built-in feature that mimics this and "remembers" the last folder used by an application. It, too, is somewhat problematical but seems much more stable than Directory Assistance.

- *RAM Doubler.* This program by Connectix is a favorite of many Photoshop users, and is another program that should be disabled at the first sign of trouble. Once again, it works flawlessly for the majority of Photoshop users. Make sure that you do not assign a partition to Photoshop that is larger than your available physical RAM. In other words, although RAM Doubler can allow you to use many programs at one time, do not give Photoshop any more than 16MB of RAM if you only have 16MB RAM on your machine. Doing so is one of the major causes of trouble between the programs. All disk compression programs are equally suspect. You are much better off surviving a disk crash if you do not stuff, double, triple, or other-wise squeeze the storage on your system.

- *Suitcase and Master Juggler.* These programs usually work—especially the latest versions. However, they have been known to cause problems in their earlier incarnations and should be among the first Control Panels disabled to test for an extension conflict. In addition, Version 1.9.1 of Master Juggler is incompatible with the PhotoLab filters from Cytopia Software. You can-not run PhotoLab with MasterJuggler installed, as it will crash if you try to do much of anything.

● *ATM and ATR.* Adobe Type Manager and Adobe Type Reunion are essential programs. However, they, too, have been known to kick up a fuss with each other, with Photoshop, and with many other extensions. Disable them early to rule out a problem. If you find one, contact the companies involved or get online as soon as you can. These utilities are too important to be allowed to do battle with Photoshop.

● *QuickKeys.* This is an essential utility for many people. When it works, it is a time-saving miracle. It often gets in the way, however, and needs to be considered a likely suspect in any problems. The new program, OneClick, is similar in many ways to QuickKeys. It, too, has been known to cause a fight on certain systems. Use it, but check it early if a problem appears.

Windows Problem Spots

This material is divided into two sections—Installing and Running, since the problems, and fixes, are unique to those categories. Note that advice will differ depending on whether you're using Windows 3.1/Windows for Workgroups 3.11, Windows 95, or Windows NT. Where the advice is specific to a flavor of Windows, it is indicated. Regardless of your version of Windows, you should be using the very latest version of Photoshop, which is 4.0 at press time. Finally, Photoshop 3.0 in any incarnation does not run under OS/2.

Installing

Here are some pointers for installing on the Windows platform.

● You must be using a video driver of at least 256 colors. If you aren't, the installation will most likely fail, or the application will refuse to start.

● If you're using Windows 3.1/Windows for Workgroups 3.11, the installer will place a Win32 subsystem on your c: partition. You do not have any choice about this—on those versions of Windows, that subsystem is required to run Photoshop. On all versions of Windows, the installer will add color management files. If there is insufficient space on your c: drive to install these files, the installation will fail. For safety's sake, have at least 20MB free—you won't need that much for the files, but you may for starting Photoshop—see the next section.

● Seriously consider doing the Custom Installation and deselecting the Deluxe Tutorial if you're installing from CD-ROM. Otherwise, the installer will place certain QuickTime files on your c: partition. Versions of QuickTime, on the Windows side, do not get along well with each other. You may find, as a result, that you can use the Deluxe Tutorial, but not play some game, or vice versa. You can get out of such a mess but it's, well, a mess. Besides, since you've had the good sense to purchase this book, you shouldn't really need that Deluxe Tutorial.

● Be sure to view the Read Me file on the installation floppies or CD-ROM. There are known installation issues of your using a LaserMaster printer; Adobe's file gives you the workaround which works.

Running: A Baker's Dozen of Tips

1. Per the previous item 1, you must be using at least a 256-color video driver. If not, Photoshop will not start; the error message will tell you this (not all error messages are so helpful).

2. There are a variety of causes for an *insufficient memory* message. First, make sure that you have the recommended minimum of 10MB of physical RAM. Second, if you're on Windows 3.1/Windows for Workgroups 3.11, make sure your permanent swap file (accessed via Control Panel → 386 Enhanced) is equal in size to the amount of your physical RAM. Third, you should make sure you've got at least 10MB of free contiguous space on your c: partition. Here's why: When Photoshop starts, it measures its available scratch disk space—that is, the area it uses for its private virtual memory swapping. It defaults to c:—hence this warning. If you do get an insufficient memory message in these circumstances, do the following: Run chkdsk or scandisk to repair any errors. Run a disk defragmenter to defragment and compress/optimize the free space, since Photoshop only looks for contiguous free space. If none of this works, increase the amount of free space on c: and repeat the previous steps. Once you get into Photoshop, you can use File → Preferences → Plug-ins & Scratch Disk to set the scratch disk to a partition of your choice.

3. Out-of-memory errors when using Photoshop, especially with third-party filters, may often be eliminated by File → Preferences → Plug-ins & Scratch Disk and reducing the percentage there to 75% or less.

4. On Windows 3.1/Windows for Workgroups 3.11, if you get various Win32s error messages, go into \windows\system\win32s and delete the contents of that last directory. Then reinstall Photoshop—your deletion will force a reinstall of the Win32 subsystem. You may have to fully remove it, but the process is too detailed for this book—ask online in the Adobe Forum on CompuServe or AOL, or at the Adobe Web site: http://www.adobe.com.

5. A variety of Photoshop instabilities may be cured by doing the PC equivalent of "trashing the Mac preferences file." In your Photoshop directory there will be a Preferences subdirectory. In it, delete photos30.psp—be sure to do this when Photoshop is not running.

6. Getting error messages when you try to bring in artwork in Adobe Illustrator (AI) format? The jury is still out on this one, but there's some evidence that a corrupt TrueType font may cause this. Go into Control Panel → Fonts and try to view each font in turn. If you find one that Windows balks at, you've found the culprit. Remove it and try the AI test again in Photoshop. If you've still got the problem, and you have many TrueType fonts installed, drastically reduce the number and test again.

7. Getting error messages with the Lighting filter, especially when you try to change the light color via the color picker? Welcome to the club—this is a known problem with no solution as yet.

8. Scanner or digitizing tablet problems? The causes are a function of the hardware you're using × the variety of Windows × the drivers. Not everyone has problems with these two categories of hardware, but many do. There's no one universal fix, alas. Your best bet is to ask online—many of the hardware vendors have an electronic presence, either on CompuServe or the World Wide Web, or both.

9. Problems using third-party filter plug-ins? If they were originally developed on the Macintosh side, the first release can sometimes be buggy—contact the vendor about an update (usually sure to follow). You can also try to be sure that in File → Preferences → Plug-ins & Scratch Disk your percentage is set to 75% (set it even lower if you're having problems with the various Kai's Power Tools "Explorer" modules).

10. Here's a general way to avoid a host of problems. Keep your video drivers up-to-date, but keep the earlier versions around. Usually latest is greatest—but not always. Sometimes an updated driver helps elsewhere, but breaks something in Photoshop. Also, before you start thinking of changing drivers, see if you can re-create the problem using a different resolution and number of colors. Note that many video drivers are at their least stable in 16-bit (*High Color*) mode—this isn't the nature of the beast, it's the prioritizing of the programmers.

11. Stay up-to-date. Adobe often releases new modules for Photoshop, which are available free for the downloading on CompuServe, America Online, Microsoft Network, and its World Wide Web site (www.adobe.com).

12. Get online. Often problems turn up first on Adobe online areas. You may well find other users with precisely your same problem. If not, you'll find sysops (except on the World Wide Web) who will help you do diagnostics and, if necessary, take the problem to Adobe technicians for you.

13. When you run into any error, shut down Photoshop, restart Windows, and restart Photoshop. It may be just a transient glitch—there have been any number of problems that appeared once, and once only.

1. With a Mac, Photoshop is great as a warning tool because
   a. It will prevent crashes.
   b. What appears to be a faulty Photoshop program may in fact be a faulty system.
   c. It has numerous bells and dings that warn when a system crash is about to occur.
   d. None of the above.

2. The message "Cannot Initialize Disk" is an indicator of which of the following?
   a. Corrupt Prefs file
   b. Corrupt font in the system folder
   c. The absence or presence of the Easy Open Extension
   d. All of the above

3. What would be the reason that the ⌘+SHIFT combination (on a Mac) to access the Magnifier would not work?
   a. This shortcut style was not loaded onto your hard drive so it is not enabled.
   b. The keyboard is breaking down.
   c. Another language keyboard has been switched on.
   d. The system is about to crash.

4. When starting on a Windows platform, the video driver must be at least how many colors?
   a. 16
   b. 32
   c. 200
   d. 256

5. How much physical RAM must there be to run Photoshop in Windows?
   a. 10
   b. 20
   c. 30
   d. 40

ACTIONS

The Actions palette is a new feature in Photoshop 4.0, giving users the ability to script certain activities in Photoshop. Almost all Menu commands can be scripted (linked together to perform a series of commands with one click of the mouse). No Painting tools or Toolbox commands can be scripted. This ability gives you a glass that is either half-empty or half-full based on your own expectations.

Actions can be used to process an image in certain defined ways. If you scan a group of photos from the same roll of film and realize that you need to apply a specific color correction, sharpen each scan by the same amount, and convert each image to CMYK before saving it, then the Actions palette can make your life much easier. You can record the commands once and then apply this command to all of the images in a single folder at one time. This is called Batch processing (it comes from a concept in traditional data processing where a group—*batch*—of transactions were all processed at one time, usually at the end of a day). The Batch facility is something for what Photoshop users have been begging for years.

On the flip side, Fractal Design Painter allows you to record paint strokes on an image and play these back on an image that is of higher resolution. The brushstrokes are recorded in relative space so you can paint on a tiny document quickly and then ask Painter to re-do the image at a much larger size suitable for printing while you go out and have lunch. Actions in Photoshop won't do that. They don't even come close. Nor do they allow you to record keystrokes typed into dialog boxes. They will record an entire set of options for a command, but you cannot backspace three times at the end of a file name and type in a new extension.

Now that you have a vague idea of what Actions can and cannot do, we'll look at the Actions palette and see how you can "roll your own" shortcuts to aid in productivity.

Meet the Actions Palette

Figure 14-20(a) shows the Actions palette in Button mode—this is the way it looks when Photoshop 4.0 is first installed. Button mode allows you to treat the Actions much the way the Command palette was used in Photoshop 4.0—that is, press the button, perform the entire action. Figure 14-20(b) shows the Actions palette in Command mode, the way it needs to look for you to be able to record Actions or to edit, duplicate, or delete them. On the side is the drop-down menu giving you a wide choice of additional options.

Now you can play one of the pre-built Actions.

Figure 14-20
a) Actions palette in Button mode
b) Actions palette in Normal mode

a

b

PLAYING AN ACTION

1. Open the image Vista1.Psd.

2. Open the drop-down menu in the Actions palette and make sure that it is in Button mode (there should be check mark next to Button if it is). If the palette is not in Button mode, select the Button mode option, and it will change to that mode.

3. Click on the Action "RGB to Indexed Color." The Action executes the command to change the image to Indexed color.

4. Undo (Mac: ⌘+Z; Windows: CTRL+Z). Since this Action executes only one command, it can be undone.

 If it had executed a sequence of commands, then the Undo command would only have removed the last command performed.

5. Figure 14-21(a) shows the full command that you just executed. The Action used the Image → Mode → Indexed Color command and has the options to use an Adaptive palette, 256 colors, Dithered built into it. Every time that you click on the button for that Action, the same sequence will occur. You can also execute the Action in Normal or Command mode. To see the same view of the Action as is in the figure, click on the right-facing arrow just to the left of the Action name. It will turn around and point down (just as it does in the Finder when you want to see the contents of a folder or directory).

6. Take the Actions palette out of Button mode (select the option on the Actions palette menu again).

7. You can execute an Action when the palette is not in Button mode by clicking on the Play button in the icon row at the bottom of the palette (it is the right-facing triangle—the third icon in the palette). Try it. Undo (Mac: ⌘+Z; Windows: CTRL+Z).

8. You can also execute an Action by double-clicking on it with the modifier key (Mac: ⌘; Windows: CTRL) pressed. Try it. Undo (Mac: ⌘+Z; Windows: CTRL+Z).

9. Perhaps you want to convert the image to Indexed Color but you do not want to use the same options that are recorded. You can set a *break point*. A break point is a place where the Action will stop to allow you to specify new options in a dialog box. You can only inset a break point in a command that has a dialog box (at least, that is the only place that will respond to a break point).

10. Add a break point to the RGB to Indexed Color Action by clicking in the empty box to the right of the check mark column next to the Action name. The box will show a line with three tiny dots under it. Figure 14-21(b) shows this version of the Action.

11. Play the Action again (double-click on the Action name with the modifier key—Mac: ⌘; Windows: CTRL—pressed). This time, instead of just converting to Indexed color, you are asked to select the specific conversion method.

12. Undo (Mac: ⌘+Z; Windows: CTRL+Z).

The ability to set break points is a really useful feature. It lets you record a sequence of events, but does not lock you into using the same settings every time you play the Action. You can record the action for your normal workflow, and simply add a break point after it has been recorded if you decide you need to enter new choices.

Managing Actions Sets

You can save and load your Actions, so that you do not need to keep every Action that you create open at all times.

You need to save your Actions because the Actions that are active in the Actions palette are stored in the Preferences file. As you learned earlier in this chapter, that is a dangerous place to store anything that you do not wish to lose. Make sure you remember to save your Actions every time you create a new one that you want to keep.

Figure 14-21
a) Action expanded to show steps
b) Expanded Action with break point inserted

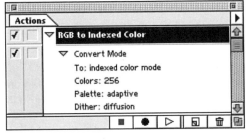

a

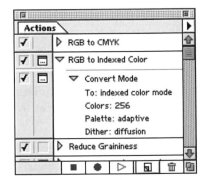

b

Actions can be saved and loaded via the Save and Load commands located on the Actions palette menu. When you *Save* a set of Actions, you save every Action in the palette. You can bring in new Action sets in several ways, however. You can *Reload* them—this appends to or replaces your current Actions with the default Action set. You can *Load* Actions, which simply appends the Actions in the file to your current set, or you can *Replace* your current set with the new one.

Saving Individual Actions

You might find it advantageous to save every Action set individually so that you can bring it—and only it—in when you need it (or you can easily create like-functioned sets with it). To do this, save your current set first. Then, drag every Action but the one that you wish to save to the Actions palette trash can. Now, save the single Action in the palette under its own unique name. You can create a special folder inside the Goodies folder just for it. Name the folder Actions. Then you will know where to look to find all of your Actions and you will be able to group them as you wish.

Creating Your First Action

You can create two basic types of Actions: menu command shortcuts and command sequences. For your first try at creating an Action, you'll recreate the Actions that give instant access to some of the commands that are used most often in this book (these are a few of the ones that were created for you to load, if you wished, in Chapter 1, "Introduction to Photoshop"). Now you can create them yourself.

CREATING MENU SHORTCUTS

1. Save your current Actions set so that you can easily retrieve it (Actions palette menu → Save Actions).

2. Clear your Action palette to remove all of the Actions (Actions palette menu → Clear Actions).

3. Click on the New Action icon at the bottom of the Actions palette. Figure 14-22 shows the dialog that appears.

4. Type Save a Copy in the Name field. The name you use can be anything— it just needs to remind you of what the Action is supposed to do.

5. If you wish to assign a function key to the Action, pull down the list and select one.

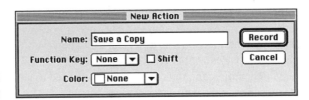

Figure 14-22
New Action dialog

6. If you wish, you can change the color of the Action when it is in Button mode by selecting one of the colors on the list. You can reopen this dialog box after the Action is done by double-clicking on the Action name.

7. Click Record to begin.

8. Now that you have set up the Action, you need to tell it what to do. Since you called this "Save a Copy," that is the action you want to perform. You could select the Save a Copy command—with a file open—and record the dialog, but that would either save a file with the word "copy" added to the end of its current name, or give every file processed that same name, if you type in an actual name. A better solution here is to use the Insert Menu Item command to tell the Action simply to present you with the normal dialog associated with saving a copy of a file.

9. Therefore, select the Insert Menu Item command on the Actions palette menu. Figure 14-23 shows the next dialog that appears. Use the mouse to move the cursor to the File menu, open the File menu, and select the Save a File command as shown. The command will appear in the Action dialog.

10. Click OK. Figure 14-24 shows the Actions palette after the command has been inserted. Click on the Stop Recording icon (the first icon on the left at the bottom of the Action palette). Notice that you can expand the Save command one level more. If you click on the right-facing triangle, it will turn and show you the additional notation "with copy." Click on the main triangle to collapse the Action into one line.

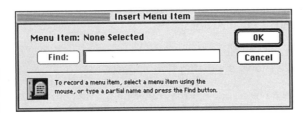

Figure 14-23
Insert Menu Item
dialog

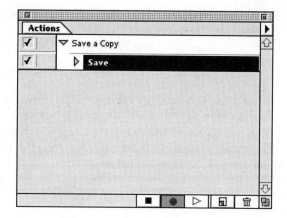

Figure 14-24
Action recorded

11. Reopen the Vista1.Psd image (if you have already closed it).

12. Double-click on the *Save a Copy* Action while pressing the modifier key (Mac: ⌘; Windows: CTRL). Save a copy of this image as "Trial Run."

13. Try setting up Menu item shortcuts for the Image → Duplicate, Filter → Blur, → Gaussian Blur, Edit → Define Pattern, and Filter → Other → Offset commands.

You can record many other activities with Actions. While the Actions palette will not record keystrokes such as arrow key moves, or setting Preserve Transparency, Default Colors, or QuickMask, you can record most commands that are menu-selectable. This lets you string the commands into activities that you can launch with one Action. Now you'll automate the "standard" drop shadow command. The one that comes with Photoshop puts a drop shadow behind an entire image. You just want to put a drop shadow behind a single object.

AUTOMATING A DROP SHADOW

1. Open the image Vane.Psd. This image was created from patterns from the Art Pattern collection from ArtMedia, Inc. using an edge effect from Auto F/X Photo/Graphic Edges, and an EPS image from the Ultimate Symbol collection. It has two Layers.

2. Since the Actions palette cannot record your color choices, pick a foreground color *first*. Choose one of the deeper tones in the Background Layer. Click on the Layer 1 *name* in the Layers palette to make it active.

3. Click on the New Action icon and name the Action DropShad. Click Record.

4. This time, you want to execute the commands rather than insert them. As you choose an item directly from the menus, the Actions palette will record the steps you take. Select the Duplicate Layer command from the Layers menu. Let the command duplicate the Layer into the same image. It will copy Layer 1 on top of the original Layer 1.

5. Then select the Layer → Arrange → Move Backward command. This moves the copy Layer *under* the original.

6. Next, Edit → Fill the Layer with the foreground color with Preserve Transparency on. (Remember, you cannot record a click on the Preserve Transparency button, so you need to do it this way. The advantage is that you do not need to set Preserve Transparency *off* either.)

7. Select the Filter → Other → Offset command and move the Shadow Layer 10 pixels to the right and 12 pixels down (you will be able to change that afterwards). The Undefined Areas do not matter much; however, you may get more reliable results by making it to Set to Transparent.

8. Apply a Filter → Blur → Gaussian Blur of 9 pixels.

9. Click Stop Recording.

10. Toss the Shadow Layer into the Layers palette trashcan and play the Action from the beginning. It should leave a shadow that is oddly colored. You need to set it manually to Multiply mode. The Actions palette does not recognize the Layer Options menu item either. However, if you want to make sure that you remember to change the Shadow Layer Apply mode, continue with the following steps.

11. Click on the Record button again and select Insert Menu item from the Actions palette menu.

12. Choose the Layer → Layer Options command.

13. Click the Stop Recording button.

14. Trash the Shadow Layer again and play the Action from the beginning. When the Action plays, you can select Multiply as the Apply mode and change the Layer Opacity as well.

Figure 14-25 shows the weathervane with the drop shadow added by the Action. Any time you need to make a shadow for an object on a Layer, you can run this script again. In addition, if you wish to change the Offset amount, all you need to do is to set a break point in the Offset command. This will open the filter dialog so you can interactively specify the offset amounts.

Using the Batch Command

In Chapter 13, "Beyond Photoshop," you created an animated GIF file. There were 20 small files that needed to be placed into GifBuilder or whichever other GIF animation program you used. You might have had more control over the final colors if the image were already in Indexed Color space and the files saved as transparent GIF files. Using Actions, it is easy to create a Batch process that will convert your files. Here's how. (There is a new set of the animated GIF files on the CD-ROM in case you deleted the ones that you already created.)

Before you see the actual commands, though, you need to know a little bit more about how Batch Actions work and you need to think about what you want the Batch process to do. Figure 14-26 shows the Batch dialog. The dialog has three main areas: Source, Action, and Destination.

You can select the folder of items that you wish to process (or you can select an Import module to attach to the Batch so you can acquire images from a scanner or other device in Batch). If you decide to process a folder, you can select the source—that is, pick the specific folder to use for this batch. When you click on the Choose button, you get a standard Mac or Windows File Open dialog and a button bar (as shown in Figure 14-27) that lets you select a folder.

Figure 14-25
Drop shadow added to weathervane image

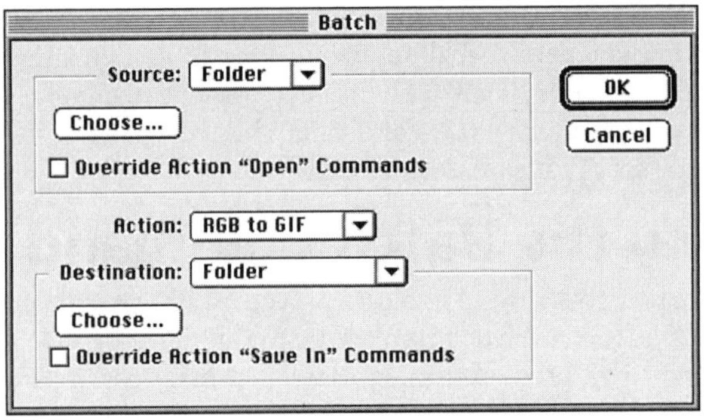

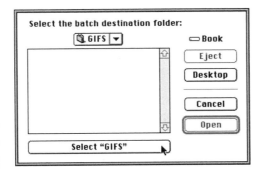

Figure 14-26
Batch Actions
dialog

Figure 14-27
Choose Folder
dialog

In order to save the individual animation frame files as GIF89a, you need to use the Export → GIF89a command. This is the piece that makes the script in Batch mode actually more complex than it appears on the surface. You want to write a script that does the following:

1. Opens the image

2. Converts it to 256 colors using an Adaptive palette and Dither

3. Saves the file as GIF89a

This seems like a simple, three-command script:

1. File → Open → (enter file name)

2. Image → Mode → Indexed Color, Adaptive, 256, Dither

3. File → Export → GIF89a, Interlaced, Get Transparency from Channel #2

There are several problems with this Action. The first, and easiest, is that if you explicitly give the Action the name of the file to open, *it will always and only open that file!* (Not the right idea at all....) Since you can select the folder to process, it is not necessary to have an Open command. The Batch process automatically opens every file in the folder. So, you can remove the first command. This leaves you with these commands:

1. Image → Mode → Indexed Color, Adaptive, 256, Dither

2. File → Export → GIF89a, Interlaced, Get Transparency from Channel #2

There are no problems with the Indexed Color command. While you do not need to change to Indexed Color before using the GIF89a Export module, doing so allows you to specify a precise transparency color for the image (which, in the animated GIF example, gets its transparency from the Alpha channel in Channel 2—the outside of the circle itself). If you feed an RGB image with an Alpha channel to the GIF89a Export module, even though the dialog says it is using the Alpha channel for transparency, it writes the transparency color into the image—and it removes the Alpha channel as well. So, you are more certain of your result if you convert first and then export.

There is a problem with running the Export command in Batch mode, however. When you *Export* (versus *Save*) a file, you are making a *copy* of the file instead of saving the file itself. Therefore, instead of saving the changed image, the Action written above leaves the Indexed Color-converted image open in Photoshop and writes a GIF89a version to *whatever location was specified in the Export module*.

The first problem is that you cannot over-write the location that is specified in the Export command unless you sit there and do it for every image in the batch as it is run (by setting a break point). Bad move. That is not why you wanted to batch process in the first place—you really wanted to be able to walk away and let it run. So, you need to specify the exact location (folder/directory) where you want the exported GIFs placed. You can always re-record that one step when you reuse the Action.

Next, what do you do with the open image? The Batch command gives you three options:

1. None—leave the file open.

2. Save and Close—saves the file and then closes it. This overwrites the original image (almost always a bad idea).

3. Folder—you can select a new location for the file to be saved so that it does not overwrite the original. You can choose a new folder for this from the Batch dialog.

At first glance, the Folder option seems reasonable, but you have already written a copy of the file as a GIF89a. Do you want a second copy that has just been changed to Indexed Color but is still in Photoshop format? Probably not.

You could select Save and Close, even though you really just want to close the open file. However, that would *replace* the RGB versions of the image with Indexed Color versions. But the RGB images could be useful for re-purposing. There is little reason to want to obliterate them. Okay—so this idea is out!

You are left with a choice of None. But do you really want to leave 20 images open to which you need to say "Don't Save" 20 times when trying to Quit Photoshop? I don't think so! You are not quite out of options, however. You could insert a Revert command after the Export, and the let the Batch "Save and Close." This would resave the original image. *Hmmm*...No harm done, but this is clunky and wasteful of time and effort. A much better solution is to insert the File → Close command. When you record this, you will be asked if you want to save the file before closing (since the file was changed by making it Indexed Color). Answer No to this, and the *No* gets recorded as well. Then you can select the None option to leave open the images—since they have been explicitly *closed*, this will cause no problem, and leave a clean environment with no open files at the end. The final Action, therefore, looks like this:

1. Image → Mode → Indexed Color, Adaptive, 256, Dither

2. File → Export → GIF89a, Interlaced, Transparency from Channel #2, default name accepted (original name + .GIF extension), explicit folder set

3. File → Close, Don't Save

Now you'll create this Action and then test it.

CREATING A BATCH ACTION

1. Create a folder or directory for the frames to be placed when they are converted to GIF files.

2. Open the file Frame01.

3. Click the New Action icon in the Actions palette. Name the Action RGB to GIF89a.

4. Click Record.

5. Select Image → Mode → Indexed Color, Adaptive, 256, Dither.

6. Select File → Export → GIF89a, Interlaced, Transparency from Channel #2. Navigate to the correct folder. Press Enter or Return to accept the default name offered.

7. Select File → Close. When asked if you wish to save the file, click No.

8. Click the Stop Recording button at the bottom of the Actions palette. Figure 14-28 shows the expanded Action in the Actions palette.

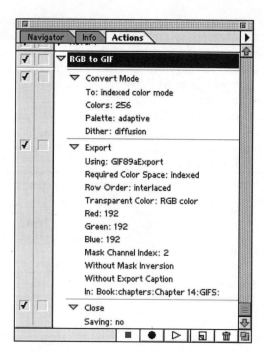

Figure 14-28
Expanded RGB to
GIF Action

9. Go into the target folder (the one where the GIF89a was saved) and delete the file. You want this to be a *clean* process—with no dialogs asking if it is OK to overwrite an already-saved image.

10. Select Batch... from the Actions palette menu.

11. For Source, select Folder and click on Choose. Select the folder that contains the original animation frames.

12. For Action, make certain that RGB to GIF is selected.

13. For Destination, select None.

14. Click OK.

15. When the batch has finished, open one of the original images and make sure that it is still in RGB mode. Then open one of the exported files (named with the extension .GIF in the designated folder) and check that it *is* in Indexed Color and that it has a gray background.

A Word About Debugging

Although Scripting is not usually difficult programming, it *is* programming. There is a saying in the computer industry, "Computers do what you *tell* them to do—not what you *want* them to do." A computer is a maddeningly precise machine. It cannot understand "well, what I really *meant* was…" Because of this, even with simple scripts, things do not always work the way you anticipate. The directions for creating the Batch script are now both precise and correct. While it would be nice to let you think that the author is infallible, how do you think I *knew* that the other methods would not work? Of course, the easy ways were tried first and found wanting. It took a number of tries to make that Batch process work correctly.

The moral? Do not experiment on your only copy of a crucial file. Try out both the recording and the batching for a test run. Check the output and make sure it is what you wanted. It may take you a number of tries to make a complex sequence of steps work the way you really want it to.

1. Which of the following can be scripted?
   a. Menus commands
   b. Painting tools
   c. Toolbox commands
   d. All of the above

2. After running an Action, the Undo command accomplishes which of the following?
   a. Removes the last five commands in a sequence
   b. Removes the last command completed
   c. Removes the last command in a sequence of five commands
   d. Removes the last command in the sequence of three commands

3. When working with the Actions palette, what is the Break Point?
   a. The point at which the Action will stop, allowing the user to enter specifications of new options in a dialog box
   b. The point that allows you to record a sequence of events without locking you into the same settings every time you play the Action
   c. The point that allows you to record a sequence of events but locks you into the same settings every time you play the Action
   d. All of the above

4. How do you save and load an Action?
   a. Via the Save and Load command on the Actions palette
   b. Via the Save and Load command in the File menu
   c. Via the Save and Load command in the Actions menu
   d. Via the Save and Load command on the File palette

5. What are the three options a Batch command will give you when you have an open image?
   a. None
   b. Save and Close
   c. Delete
   d. Folder

VIP PROFILE

Glenn Mitsui, Graphic Designer

Glenn Mitsui is one of the best-known computer illustrators. His work has regularly appeared in *MacWorld* magazine to illustrate their feature articles. He has taught at the Thunder Lizard Photoshop Conferences, and appeared in panels and discussions.

Glenn almost got his associate degree from a Seattle-based community college. It was a two-year course in graphic design—never quite finished—but it gave him a very good base on which to begin. His first job was for Boeing Aircraft as a technical illustrator.

Glenn says of his stint at Boeing that his job consisted of a lot of line drawings of bolts and wings—and that the most exciting part of it was when he had to vary the line widths! However, he did learn about perspective—and discipline—and first started to work with a computer. Boeing used a mainframe-based program called Genigraphics. He worked the graveyard shift and said, "I didn't use my head—but I used everything else." He left Boeing to start his own business. This led to the founding of StudioMD about seven years ago, along with partners Randy Lim and Jesse Doquilo.

Glenn first started using the Mac in 1988. His studio created the first templates for Aldus Persuasion (Aldus was located just up the street from the studio).

He quickly learned to love and use Aldus Freehand. When Photoshop appeared on the scene, it was a challenge to learn the program and to get a head start. Glenn says that one of the most difficult things about being a computer illustrator is that you constantly need to keep up with your software. Just as you master one version, another one appears. And yet, you can only really give your creativity free rein after you have learned the technicalities of the program. You must understand your software before you can be free to concentrate on creative development.

Glenn attributes his success to being in the right place at the right time (though he is being unnecessarily modest—talent certainly helped a lot, too). StudioMD became known as a niche firm doing work for Aldus, Microsoft (also in Seattle), and Apple. The company gained a reputation doing logos and illustrations.

MacWorld magazine gave Glenn a very good break by putting him in their regular rotation list of illustrators—the first non–San Francisco illustrator to become a regular contributor. Working for *MacWorld* brought more business as people saw his artwork in the magazine. Art directors would call *MacWorld* to find the artist and be given Glenn's number.

Glenn wanted to branch out, however. He did not wish to limit himself to working on computer magazines—he wanted to illustrate for mainstream magazines as well. He wanted to do work for *Atlantic Monthly, Time,* and *NewsWeek,* so he bought copies of the magazines that he liked and found the art directors listed in the magazine mastheads. He sent out portfolios and began to get more work. In addition to the editorial work, now he began to bring in higher paid work—which allowed him to keep experimenting and growing.

In the beginning days of StudioMD, he and his two partners each took home $300.00 per month. The first time that Glenn earned $1,000.00 for a month, he thought he had reached nirvana! Now, he has learned how to bid a job, estimate the time needed, and protect his work.

When asked about his first reaction to Photoshop, Glenn said that he found illustration packages to be much easier, faster, and smaller. When he first saw Photoshop, he was working on a MacIIcx. He did a poster for the Washington Department of Ecology in Freehand, and was very pleased with himself. He sent it to the imaging house and went out to celebrate—then he got a phone call. The file sat all weekend long in the RIP (raster image processor) and it did not image. The solution was to purchase Photoshop and create the image as a raster image from the start.

The solution to that problem caused a host of others. His MacIIcx was not up to the job, needed more RAM, more hard drive space, and more speed. He bought a Radius Rocket accelerator but, even so, his first job nearly killed him. It was a job for Aldus and turned out to be an 80MB file. The service bureau had never tried to image anything that large. Everything was brand new and was a problem. Every job broke new ground. One became an expert by walking one step in front of the next person. It was a time for very fast growth.

Glenn's advice to you as you get started is to learn aggressively. Challenge yourself. If you don't have a specific job to do, give yourself a deadline and get one done. Don't fear rejection or folks telling you "no." Eventually, if you keep submitting your work to art directors, someone will like your work—you will find the correct match. Have confidence in yourself and do not take rejection personally. He also feels strongly that if you grasp the technology, you have a big advantage as you can then spend more time on being creative.

Glenn Mitsui can be reached at `Glenn@studiomd.com`.

CHAPTER SUMMARY

This chapter covers a lot of information about how to use Photoshop most efficiently and how to set up your Preferences to that end. It discusses specific problem areas and solutions for both Mac and Windows. It also introduces you to the topic of Photoshop automation via Actions. You learned how to record an Action, manage Action sets, and run an Action in Batch mode.

Key areas to remember about the Preferences are:

1. Use Bicubic Interpolation.

2. Set the channels to display in grayscale.

3. Use the Brush Size display for painting tools.

4. Do not export the clipboard or save your images with 2.5 compatibility.

5. Leave lots of free disk space, preferably an entire drive partition for Photoshop's scratch disk.

6. Optimize the scratch disk space frequently.

CHAPTER 15

PHOTOSHOP OUTPUT

This chapter discusses (finally) some of the issues involved in getting your Photoshop images out of the computer and onto paper. It is easy to create images that do not look at all like they did on your screen. In fact, because the screen is an illuminated surface, it is nearly impossible to make your output match your screen.

This chapter looks at some of the issues involved in getting your images to print and in making 4-color separations. At the end of this lesson, you should be able to

- Calibrate your monitor.
- Correctly set up your monitor preferences to match the monitor calibration.
- Specify the printing inks that you will use.
- Specify the separation setup.
- Convert images from RGB to CMYK.

- Manage dot gain—create images that include dot gain calculations.

- Create an image with Clipping Path.

- Create a bitmap image that will be transparent in the white areas when placed in a page layout program.

Several "systems" are embedded inside of Photoshop that need to work together if you are going to produce the good, consistent separations that are needed in order to print. The subject of this chapter is Photoshop's prepress "engine." This chapter draws heavily on the expertise of Steve Pollock, a New Jersey–based photographer who is an expert in the color management area.

STEP 1: THE CALIBRATION PROCESS

Calibration is the name given to the process of bringing your monitor, scanner, and printer into synch with known "target" input and output. Photoshop provides a built-in method of calibrating monitors in both the Mac and Windows versions of the program. The Mac uses a control panel called Gamma Control Panel (GCP), and Windows has an option within Photoshop called Calibrate.

Gamma Control Panel

This area of Photoshop is the one most functionally different between the Mac and PC platforms. In the former case, the Gamma Control Panel is a system-level utility and, as such, affects the appearance of the screen in both the Finder as well as any and all applications. On the other hand, due to the nonstandardization of PC video cards, similar tools are found within Photoshop itself under File → Preferences → Monitor Setup → Calibrate. The difference here is that settings affect the display only within the Photoshop environment. Figure 15-1 shows the Mac's Gamma Control Panel, and Figure 15-2 shows the PC's Calibrate.

Before making any attempt to actually calibrate the monitor, let's discuss a couple of simple considerations. You'll want to do everything possible to standardize the viewing environment, especially if you are going to be making color-critical decisions on professional work. It is virtually impossible to maintain the necessary level of control if your workspace is flooded with sunlight in the morning and not in the afternoon. Unlike reflective artwork, which simply appears brighter under higher illumination, your monitor begins to lack the same visual snap and contrast that it once had in more subdued lighting conditions.

Figure 15-1
The Mac's Gamma
Control Panel

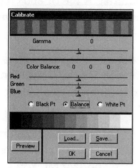

Figure 15-2
The PC's Calibrate

The human eye is a wonderfully adaptive thing, however; it's constantly making subjective comparisons among adjacent surfaces and colors. If the area is decorated with bright, lively colors, this, too, can be expected to have a subtle (or not so subtle) effect on your judgment. Neutral surroundings are the most desirable, and the same can be said of the desktop of the computer screen. If, for whatever reason, you're not at liberty to eliminate a high level of extraneous ambient light, you can probably stop a fair portion of it with a simple three-sided hood over the monitor, even if it's only constructed from black foam core.

Next, you'll want to make sure that the monitor has been turned on for at least a half hour so that the components have had a chance to reach thermal equilibrium. The monitor's brightness and contrast controls should be set and taped in position if there's any possibility of unintentional adjustment in the future. The way to do this is as follows:

LEARNING TO CALIBRATE A MONITOR

1. Create a new grayscale document in Photoshop that's nearly the width of your screen. The height is immaterial. A file of 800×100 pixels is a good start, but you might want to adjust up or down depending on the actual screen resolution of your system.

2. Press ⒟ to make sure that the default black-and-white colors are selected. Press ⒢ to select the Gradation tool. Set the Gradation options to Normal, 100% Opacity, Foreground to Background, and Linear, and uncheck the Mask and Dither check boxes.

3. Begin with the cursor as close to the left as possible and click-and-drag all the way to the right. If you hold down SHIFT along the way, you'll be certain that the effect will be perfectly horizontal. You should wind up with a gradation running from pure black to white.

4. Use the Image → Adjust → Posterize command and enter **40** in the dialog box. This will create a grayscale stepwedge (a document with stripes of gray values—a solid-black gradient) with roughly 6 levels or 2.5% from one patch to the next. Set the Info Palette to display either or both RGB and grayscale values—it's just a matter of taste.

5. Now, turn up the contrast control on the monitor to its maximum. Yes, all the way up! While watching the darkest few steps in your grayscale, adjust the monitor's brightness control until you can just barely detect the slightest difference between the first and second patches. The digital values for these patches should be 0, 0, 0 and 6, 6, 6 as RGB or 100% and 98% in grayscale.

6. Not all monitors are capable of discriminating between these values, especially in high levels of ambient light. Should that become a problem even after turning the brightness to its highest setting, you probably will have difficulty making subjective judgments with very deep shadow detail, but not all is lost. If, at the other end of the stepwedge, you can see separation between the brightest two patches (255, 255, 255 and 248, 248, 248 or 0% and 3%), you're done. Your monitor is now set to use the maximum dynamic range that it's capable of delivering.

7. On the other hand, if a couple or a few of the brightest patches have blended together, you'll want to slowly lower the monitor's contrast control until the difference between the brightest patches reappears. If you've found it necessary to do that, go back to the shadow end, adjust brightness again, and then give a final check to the highlights.

8. Tape over these settings so they won't be changed.

9. Save the grayscale stepwedge in Photoshop's Calibration folder for future referral, but leave it open onscreen as well, for the next steps.

Now you can go into your respective Mac or PC versions of Photoshop's Gamma Control Panel or Calibrate. Here, as its name suggests, you will be actively adjusting other important elements of the display, notably gamma and whitepoint (the "temperature" for the highest highlight value). Gamma can be defined, in an oversimplification, as the contrast of the monitor. Essentially, it's the power to which the monitor's input is raised (in other words, input^x) to allow it to display tonality in a way that's consistent with the monitor's design and the way we see. The match-the-boxes aspect of the Gamma Control Panel is moderately misconceived, due both to its small size (especially on high-resolution monitors) and the fact that it relies on a checkerboard of 1×1 squares of black and white. Many monitors are not capable of accurately reproducing single-pixel alternating blocks in this fashion, which can ultimately lead to improper calibration. As a double-check, obtain a copy of `MONCAL.GIF` (a color calibration target available in the CompuServe Desktop Publishing Forum or from other online sources) prior to going into the calibration. The background of this image is created by a 1×3 checkerboard.

Your actual choice of settings for gamma and whitepoint depends largely on the ultimate use for your Photoshop imagery. In the United States, the de facto standard for prepress work is a gamma of 1.8 and a whitepoint of 5000K. If you are planning output to video or a film recorder, you will probably want to use a gamma of 2.2.

In the GCP (Calibrate) itself, adjust the gamma slider until the row of boxes near its top of the control panel appear to visually match. On the Mac, there is a choice of gamma settings via the radio buttons at the top. The PC version defaults to a setting of 1.8. If you have `MONCAL.GIF` open as well, its sheer size will allow you to more accurately match the appropriate solid box indicating gamma to the 1×3 checkerboard background. It is most advisable that `MONCAL` be viewed at 1:1 resolution. If there is a discrepancy between the two, the design of `MONCAL` makes it a more reliable target.

The choice of whitepoint is somewhat of a bugaboo. Most graphic arts viewing stations are equipped with 5,000K of illumination; hence that can become a noble goal for your display if it happens to be your area of endeavor. However, most monitors have a native whitepoint that is a considerably higher (bluer) value. While 6,500K is typical for many modern displays, a good number of older monitors were built to a 9,300K standard. Native whitepoint is defined as all three of the monitor's RGB electron guns running at full tilt. To see this effect on the Mac, you must hold down the Option key while selecting Options in the Monitor Control Panel and select Uncorrected Gamma, although it's of little more than a curiosity with no real value. The trade-off in setting a 5,000K whitepoint is that some portion of the potential output of the blue (and probably some of the red or green) phosphor guns must be wasted to establish a warmer white. The net result is not only a more accurate display, but one that is often considerably less bright than one that isn't corrected. The proper adjustment of whitepoint, though, should allow you to view original artwork as well as output (under the appropriate 5,000K illumination, of course) next to your monitor with excellent correlation between them.

So how do you set the whitepoint? The best way is through the use of a hardware monitor calibrator. The eyeball method requires a bit of work. What you need is a reference color to attempt to match onscreen. If you are typically going to be attempting to predict the appearance of composite proofs (such as MatchPrints or Chromalins), you could make a case for using its white base or a sample of the paper that will be used in the print run as the basis for white. However, it does not make sense to go to all this trouble if you're going to illuminate it with your desk lamp! While many people manage to stumble along trying to compare color work under the prevailing illumination at the moment, this will create untold gnashing of teeth in the long run. If your work is important, invest in a small graphic arts viewing booth to use next to your monitor. There are even models available that allow the user to control the brightness of illumination to match that of the monitor. As a crude substitute, prepress workers have used an appropriate halftone film to solve the problem. If you plan to work with photographic output, use either a transparency or a print as a reference for whitepoint.

Select the White Point button. Ordinarily, you will wind up reducing the blue slider significantly to bring white in line with the properly illuminated reference sample. It may well be necessary to reduce green or red as well, but there are no circumstances under which you would want to reduce all three from the maximum value at the right—that would simply darken your monitor. Put another way, at least one of the three sliders should remain to the right. If it's not in a place where you can see it, display the 40-step grayscale that you created earlier (if you are on the Mac; this cannot be done on a PC). The white value should look just like the white sample that's being used for reference. Now, select the Balance button in GCP and make whatever changes you feel are necessary to eliminate any cast of color in the midtones of your grayscale. Select the Black Point button and do the same for the shadow range. Unfortunately, the tweaks that you made along the way have probably had an impact on your original gamma setting—no one said this was going to be easy! Readjust gamma, double-check whitepoint, balance, and blackpoint, and save your settings. Your monitor may not behave in exactly the same way next week or next year, but it's a lot easier starting next time from the present point than from scratch.

Gamma Control Panel Versus Monitor Setup

There has been considerable confusion about what functions the GCP (Calibrate) serve versus the settings in the Monitor Setup dialog box, which is shown in Figure 15-3.

As mentioned earlier, the GCP takes active control of the display system in an effort to set it to a known state. By comparison, in Monitor Setup, you are communicating with Photoshop's internal color management system by telling it what gamma, whitepoint, and phosphors you are seeing on the screen. This information is used in Photoshop's calculations in many different ways, especially during mode changes, but it does not calibrate your monitor. That's the function of GCP (Calibrate).

As an aside, you have an alternative means to calibrate for your monitor. While the eye is quite good at judging certain relationships, it is difficult to achieve the consistency obtainable with a good hardware monitor calibrator. Likewise, the possibility of visually matching the settings on a room full of monitors is indeed slim. There are a growing number of calibrators available today from such vendors as X-Rite, Light Source, and Daystar. Whatever gamma and whitepoint you have chosen to use, be certain to enter those same values into the Monitor Setup dialog. It may be self-evident, but do not try to use more than one method of monitor calibration at a time. If you are using an alternative method of calibration, do not load the GCP on the Mac or be sure that the various settings are zeroed in Calibrate on the PC.

1. What is calibration?
   a. A standard unit for measurement
   b. The process of bringing the scanner and printer into synch
   c. The process of bringing the monitor, scanner, and printer into synch
   d. Setting your printer to the correct paper texture

2. In the process of calibrating your monitor and adjusting the brightness control, what should the digital values be for the first and second patches in grayscale?
   a. 0,0,0 and 6,6,6
   b. 100% and 98%
   c. 1,1,1 and 5,5,5
   d. 50% and 100%

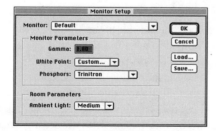

Figure 15-3
Monitor Setup

3. When setting the gamma in prepress for the output of a film recorder, what should the gamma value be set at?
   a. 1.8
   b. 2.2
   c. 3.1
   d. 3.8

4. Which of the following best defines whitepoint?
   a. The blue value of the monitor
   b. The four RGB electron guns of a monitor running at their best
   c. The value of the White channel in printing
   d. The three RGB electron guns of a monitor running at their best

5. Gamma Control Panel setup is different than the Monitor Setup dialog box. What is the Monitor Setup dialog box used for?
   a. Takes active control of the display system and places it in a known state
   b. To calibrate your monitor
   c. To communicate with Photoshop's internal color management system
   d. The font display you see on your monitor

STEP 2: SETTING THE COLOR SETTINGS PREFERENCES

There are several preferences that work together to allow Photoshop to perform color space changes and to display colors onscreen so that they might, possibly, match your output. These are Photoshop's color settings. They interlock and work with each other in some subtle and not-so-subtle ways. However, you need to think of them as a package, even though you set them individually.

Monitor Setup

As mentioned previously, the various fields in the Monitor Setup dialog box are the means through which you tell Photoshop what it is that you're actually seeing onscreen. Look through the list of monitors in the drop-down box and, if you see your model listed, select it. You'll find that doing so automatically enters data into the gamma, whitepoint, and phosphors boxes. Generally, these values reflect the native responses of the monitor and not necessarily those that you'd prefer to use. Be certain to change, if necessary, the gamma and whitepoint figures to agree with the settings made in GCP (Calibrate).

Phosphors are an unchangeable part of the design of your display. Fortunately, they are reasonably stable over the life of a monitor, since many people lack the hardware calibration equipment that would be capable of compensating were the phosphors to drift from their target setting. The easy solution is to select the phosphors in the drop-down box that most closely resemble your particular monitor. The purist will, probably by contacting the manufacturer, obtain the actual x-y chromaticity values and enter them in the Custom box. There are actually few different sets of monitor phosphors in common use, and slight inaccuracies here pale by comparison to poor ambient conditions or improper illumination of your originals or output.

The choice of the Ambient Light setting has a subtle effect on the definition of color that you're trying to describe to Photoshop. In fact, it applies a small gamma change to the program's internal calculations when you, for instance, create a mode change from RGB to CMYK. Look at it as one way to apply a minor tweak in attempting to match your scanner, monitor, and output, but it's not worth considerable obsession. The High selection, in fact, does nothing in this process and is probably the best choice when using alternative forms of calibration. Save the results of your selections again to the Calibration folder by clicking the Save button in the Monitor Setup dialog.

Printing Inks Setup

The combination of Monitors Setup, Printing Inks Setup, and Separation Setup forms an enormously complicated web of interaction in the way that Photoshop manages color. Fortunately, it's not necessary to completely understand what's going on under the hood since the real tough stuff is being handled for you automatically behind the scenes. What is of crucial importance, though, is that you use the opportunity of communicating these various color definitions in the best possible way.

In Printing Inks, you are telling Photoshop about the properties of the actual colorants that will be applied to (normally) paper on output. Figure 15-4 shows this dialog. As an extreme example, it would make no sense to specify SWOP inks (one of the ink choices in the drop-down menu—it stands for Standard Web Output) when, in fact, your newspaper actually uses rubine red in place of magenta. Look through the list of printing inks in the drop-down box. If there is a match with the process that you will eventually use, select it. Normally, for offset printing in the United States, one of the three SWOP choices is the most appropriate.

All of the selections made in Printing Inks affect both the RGB to CMYK conversion during a mode change, as well as the display of CMYK files (which must be explicitly converted to RGB) onscreen. They have no effect on the display of an RGB, Indexed, Grayscale, or Bitmap files.

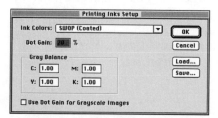

Figure 15-4
Printing Inks Setup
dialog

Since you're trying to describe the appearance of printer's inks to Photoshop, this is a fairly critical stage. What happens if the output process isn't listed in the available choices? Again, not all is lost. However, things will get a little more interesting. You can take a look at this situation further in System Calibration. For now, just notice that the selection of a particular printing ink set has caused a number to be entered in the Dot Gain box, and call it a day. You should also leave Separation Setup alone for now. Meanwhile, let's get a brief understanding of the various color spaces and problems with which you'll be called upon to deal.

1. What are Photoshop's color settings designed to do?
    a. Allow color space changes and display color onscreen so they might match the output
    b. Set the color to printer depending upon the type of output
    c. Set the color to texture of the output
    d. None of the above

2. Which of the following in the Monitor Setup dialog is unchangeable?
    a. Phosphors
    b. Monitor fields
    c. Ambient light
    d. All of the above

3. The Printing Inks dialog indicates which of the following to Photoshop?
    a. Properties of the colorants that will be applied to paper on output
    b. Which SWOP ink to use
    c. Properties of the colorants versus the monitor
    d. Which Standard Web Output ink to use

4. Printing Inks does not affect which of the following?
    a. RGB to CMYK conversion
    b. Display of CMYX files on screen
    c. Grayscale files
    d. Bitmap files

5. What happens if the necessary output process is not listed as an available choice?
    a. Stop, you cannot go any further.
    b. Do not know, it will be tackled in a later lesson.
    c. You can create a custom ink set.
    d. All of the above.

STEP 3: SOME COLOR BASICS

Life would be far simpler if every device in the digital imaging chain related to and reproduced color in a similar manner. The sad fact is that the more scanners, monitors, and printers are grouped together, the more obvious it becomes that, not only do they not all speak the same language, but inevitably, they all create at least a subtly different visual result. There are a couple of immutable reasons behind this, both worth at least momentary consideration.

Color Gamut

Each piece of digital imaging equipment uses a specific means to create what we ultimately perceive as color. That may range from glowing phosphors on a monitor to spots of CMYK ink in a halftone screen on paper. It should not come as too great a surprise to hear that some colors cannot, despite any and all calibration methods, be reproduced in certain media. Just as it is currently impossible to create an onscreen appearance to match 100% process cyan ink on paper, there is no such thing as a vivid saturated blue that can be created using any combination of CMYK process inks. Every device has a particular color gamut that it is capable of reproducing. This is a limitation of the technology in question, the colorants in use, or both.

A major problem arises if you specify a color with one device that has no counterpart in the gamut of another. An example of this would be selecting a brilliant blue RGB value of 0, 0, 255 in the hopes that it can be matched in 4-color lithography.

The practical solution to this problem is to use a technique that restructures the gamut of one device to that of another. This is what Photoshop attempts to do in the course of an RGB to CMYK mode conversion. In the process, it takes into consideration all of the parameters that are present in the Monitor, Printing Inks, and Separation Setup dialogs.

The best approach, referred to as gamut mapping, would be to gently reshape one color space to fit inside the limitations of another. Unfortunately, Photoshop uses a technique that most closely resembles gamut clipping, where colors outside the target space are simply pushed to the closest possible boundary or nearest equivalent. The net result is that, especially with imagery containing information in heavily saturated areas (particularly red and blue), the program has a tendency to create blobs of color lacking in detail. This is simply a limitation of the Photoshop separation engine and is at least part of the reason for the availability of alternative third-party solutions. Nevertheless, with proper attention, many to most images can be separated quite successfully.

You can see the gamut clipping in operation for yourself. Try this:

A COLOR GAMUT

1. Click on the Foreground color selector in the Toolbox.

2. Set the RGB values for the foreground color to RGB 0, 0, 255 (true blue). Notice that a triangle with an exclamation point appears next to the color. This means that the foreground color being selected cannot be printed using process (4-color or CMYK) inks. In other words, the color is out-of-gamut. Figure 15-5 shows the Color Picker dialog with the Gamut Warning flag.

3. Click on the small color square under the triangle. The color selector cursor will move to a much less saturated blue of a darker value. If you drag the cursor through the values on the screen, you will notice that, in order to keep the Gamut Warning flag from showing, you need to select colors that are mostly in the bottom-left triangle (as if you drew a line from the upper-left corner of the color selection area to the lower-right corner).

4. Set the new color to RGB 0, 0, 255 and click OK.

5. Repeat the instructions for Steps 1 to 4 of the Monitor Calibration exercise above, using blue as your foreground color and white as your background color to create a 40-step blue-to-white stepwedge. Create it in RGB mode.

6. Duplicate the image (Image → Duplicate → OK).

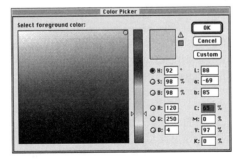

Figure 15-5
Color Picker dialog
with Gamut
Warning flag

7. Convert the image to CMYK (Image → Mode → CMYK). Your results will vary somewhat based on whatever settings are already in the Separation Setup settings. However, that is not critical right now. Regardless of the specific settings, you should see a dramatic change in color from the original RGB image to the CMYK image. Worse—and here the gamut clipping becomes very apparent—where the RGB stepwedge indicated a smooth gradation of color, the CMYK stepwedge shows clumps and gaps. The color moves from magenta-y to purple-y and back again, and it is anything but smooth. In addition, some of the colors look identical (even though they are not, quite, if you use the Info Palette on them). Do not close these files just yet.

If the change is this dramatic, is there any way to see what will happen to your image before you convert it? Of course (or the question would not have been asked!). Photoshop provides two ways for you to measure the "hit" that your image will take when it is moved from RGB color space into CMYK. You can work with CMYK Preview (View → CMYK Preview or Mac: ⌘+Y, Windows: CTRL+Y) or Gamut Warning on (View → Gamut Warning or Mac: SHIFT+⌘+SHIFT+Y, Windows: SHIFT+CTRL+SHIFT+Y). The CMYK Preview does exactly what it says—it uses your current color settings to display the RGB image as if it were in CMYK color space.

The Gamut Warning, on the other hand, specifically locates the colors that are out of gamut. You can set the color that you wish the warning to use by changing the Preference in the Transparency and Gamut Preference dialog. It does not matter which color you choose, but it should be a color that is not in your image or not common in your image. With Gamut Warning on, all colors that are out-of-gamut are shown in the warning color that you selected. Try it. Click on the RGB blue stepwedge and turn on the Gamut Warning. Almost the entire image turns gray (or whatever your warning color is). You may want to turn that off and turn CMYK Preview on. Notice that with CMYK Preview on, the RGB image looks just like the CMYK one.

Device-Independent Color

Another major problem that has existed since the dawn of digital imaging is the method chosen to specify color. Rather than basing the solution on the appearance of color, the graphics industry has been firmly rooted in the formula used instead. A walk through the television department in an electronics store should put to rest any notion that a given signal might produce a similar picture on the rows of sets. Specifying color by formula is akin to walking into a paint store and asking for a gallon of paint tinted with 3 drops of burnt umber and 27 drops of cadmium yellow. Depending on, at the least, the pigments themselves, the type of tinting base, and the size of the drops, one would never be quite certain what the ultimate effect might be. Likewise, a trip to two or three other stores might produce rather different results. In practice, we bring a sample of wallpaper, fabric, or carpeting to match and have little interest in what goes into the can to achieve the desired color.

Working in this fashion has been largely a matter of convenience and, in lieu of better technology, has made reasonable sense in a tightly integrated, proprietary prepress system. Shops that specialize in color separation typically use a small number of similar or identical scanners, use identical monitors provided by their system's vendor, and maintain tight control on the imagesetting and proofing process. By comparison, many of us in the real world must contend with scanned imagery from diverse sources (for example, desktop scanners, Photo CD, prepress, or unknown pedigree) and a wide variety of monitors and viewing conditions in the hopes that we can create predictable color with a huge variety of dissimilar media (such as dye sublimation, inkjet, composite proofs, or even photographic film). This situation is exponentially more complicated than the previous scenario, and begins to explain why color has not been a simple matter to master for many people. This is not to say that it's impossible, only that it's rather unlikely to happen by accident.

Since we have a huge sampling of device-dependent colors, it would be lovely if there were some way to try to specify color in a vacuum, so that red would be red regardless of whether that red was on the screen or in the dye sub printer. This is the goal (though not necessarily the reality) of device-independent color management systems.

1. Define Color Gamut.
   a. A range of colors a particular monitor displays
   b. A range of colors a printer will process
   c. A range of colors a particular device is capable of reproducing
   d. The range of colors Photoshop is capable of working with

2. What is gamut clipping?
   a. Reshaping one color space of one device to fit inside the limitations of another device
   b. Designing a template for colors in Photoshop
   c. A utility that enables CMYK process inks to create a vivid saturated blue
   d. None of the above

3. What onscreen feature signifies when a color is out-of-gamut?
   a. A percentage sign within a circle
   b. An explanation point within a circle
   c. A explanation point within a triangle
   d. A question mark within a triangle

4. Define when a color is out-of-gamut.
   a. When the foreground color being selected cannot be printed using process inks
   b. When the background color being selected cannot be printed using process inks

    c. When the RGB values for the foreground color are RGB 0,0,255
    d. When the RGB values for the foreground color are 1,1,300

5. How can you see the Color Gamut changes before converting the image?
    a. CMYK preview
    b. Gamut Warning
    c. CTRL + Y
    d. CTRL + SHIFT + Y

STEP 4: COLOR MANAGEMENT SYSTEMS

The relatively immature world of color management is a deep subject and one that could easily be addressed in a book of its own. The intention here is simply to provide a brief overview that may offer some assistance in selecting tools appropriate to a particular work flow or set of conditions. Even though some of the features described are not included in the standard Photoshop installation, the program does manage color in a way that's consistent with many of these basic principles.

A Bit of History

All color management systems are based, at least in part, on research performed in the 1930s by the French *Commission Internationale de l'Eclairage* (CIE). The perception of color was based not only on an object's characteristics, but also on the viewing illumination and its surroundings as well. The definition of a standard observer was based on measurements of individuals with normal color perception. This can be thought of as an imaginary scanner that can perceive color in the same manner as the human eye. The CIE defined three imaginary primaries called X, Y, and Z and chromaticity coordinates called x and y that can be combined at various levels to produce all visible colors. CIEXYZ and permutations derived from this original work (CIELUV, CIELAB, as well as some proprietary specifications) form the basis for all modern attempts at color management.

    Most often, the actual device-independent color space is not something that the end user addresses directly. Rather, it's managed in a transparent fashion behind an interface that will, hopefully, be intuitive to us mere mortals. You can think of this color space as a universal translator between any pair of devices that will be likely to be speaking a different language. The operative element here is that RGB and CMYK values predict nothing about the actual appearance of a particular formula unless they are accompanied by a comprehensive description of the color space itself. Unfortunately, this description is notably lacking in almost all popular file formats and applications. Photoshop's Lab color mode is one notable exception.

Just as a given RGB image is likely to appear differently on two different monitors, a CMYK file will print differently given any change in ink, paper, or press conditions. The same file that prints beautifully in a premium annual report will become an unmitigated mess when placed in a newspaper ad. In other words, CMYK is not just CMYK. It is a color space that is very tightly purposed for its intended output. What this means, though (and this is the important part), is that the converse is also true—if the same file is responsible for a different visual appearance on different devices, then we must create different files to send to each device to approximate the same appearance. Figure 15-6 shows the general structure of a color management system.

The System Part of Color Management

Until just recently, with the advent of ColorSync 2 on the Mac platform, all of the various color management solutions were both proprietary and incompatible with each other. The major players have been Kodak, Agfa, Candela, Linotype-Hell, and, at one time, EFI. The formation of the International Color Consortium has prompted a universal standard for much of what was previously a Tower of Babel. Once the various vendors have all produced ICC-compatible profiles to replace their original proprietary versions, most of the system-level color management solutions will be in place on the Mac. What remains, unfortunately, is for the key desktop imaging and page makeup applications to implement a complete interface to this new capability. At the moment, there is a series of free ColorSync 2 plug-ins for the Mac to provide functionality within Photoshop, but one can hardly say that it's totally integrated into the program.

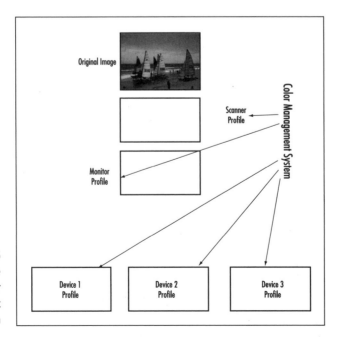

Figure 15-6
General structure of a color management system

Developments on the PC platform are not quite so far along. Microsoft has chosen Kodak to provide system-level color management for Windows 95, but as yet no applications have been designed to use it. However, both Kodak's and Agfa's systems are well in place in the form of plug-in support in both Photoshop and Quark. The myriad of video cards available has continued to stand in the way of any widespread attempts at hardware monitor calibration.

The main components of a color management system are

⚫ Profile-building tools

⚫ The device profiles themselves

⚫ The color management engine

A profile carefully describes a particular device's relationship to the human perception of color (the device-independent color space). For instance, if you present enough samples of known color to a scanner, you can begin to form a matrix of conversions that can account for the peculiarities of that particular model. This process eventually determines that "every time we show you color X, you give us something that's a little too yellow and a shade too dark; color Y appears to be the right hue, but it's not quite saturated enough," and so on.

Determining this relationship is referred to as characterization. Although it might seem like a fine line, this is different from calibration, which is, essentially, returning a device to a desired state of linearity. With enough information (a typical scanner characterization involves in excess of 200 samples, whereas one for a printer might involve 500 to more than 2,000), the color management software can construct a mathematical transformation that brings the actual output of the scanner in line with the known colorimetric values of the colors originally presented to it. For monitors and printers, the process is reversed, that is, digital values are fed to them and the colorimetric values of the resulting output are analyzed to create a similar transformation that accounts for the characteristics of the particular device.

ColorSync 2 is the only system-level engine that's been designed for the Mac. Kodak, Agfa, and others have provided support for their individual efforts through a series of plug-ins in Photoshop and Quark. This is a kind way of saying that color management is not yet a reality in, for instance, Freehand or Illustrator—at least until they are rewritten to use ColorSync's system-level capabilities. This might lead you to wonder of what use all this is at the moment. Actually, complete, functional color management systems that fully support Photoshop are available from at least four different vendors.

If you need to predict the limited gamut result of 4-color printing on a dye sub or inkjet printer, this would be a good place to look. If you frequently need to output a given image to a variety of different output devices, these systems can aid tremendously in achieving the closest uniformity. If you have an ongoing need to determine accurate CMYK tint specifications for a variety of tangible color samples (such as for printed pieces, plastics, leather, or textiles), color management can be of tremendous help. Perhaps most importantly, if you must have an accurate, onscreen Soft Proof prior to committing to the output of film and proofs, this technology is probably the easiest and, in the long run, least expensive way to get there. These are only some of the advantages offered by color management; however, it's a safe conclusion that this thinking makes more sense as the number of imaging devices in your arsenal proliferates.

This is not to say that similar results can't be achieved by way of Photoshop's inherent functionality, only that color management will, more than likely, make it happen more quickly and, in some cases, better than you would be able to accomplish on your own. This discussion can only begin to scratch the surface of what is obviously a complex topic. Hopefully, it will provoke further thinking and research in the quest for accurate, predictable color. Because the methods that Photoshop uses to manage color are closely related, this background information should help you better understand the interactions among its various preference settings. If your initial efforts to control color are less than completely successful, rest assured that you are following in the footsteps of a long, illustrious procession of desktop publishers who have had to wrestle with the situation before you.

1. Identify the imaginary primaries the CIE defined.
   a. X,Y, and Z
   b. A,B, and C
   c. 1,2, and 3
   d. A and B

2. Which plug-in helps the Mac along in color management?
   a. EFI
   b. Lino-Hell
   c. ColorSync 2
   d. Agfa

3. What is a profile when referring to color management?
   a. The designer of the color scheme
   b. A device's relationship to human perception of color
   c. A Kodak utility for PCs
   d. Agfa's utility for PCs

4. Characterization is which process?
   a. The same as calibration
   b. Naming color files
   c. Setting colors between two monitors to be exact
   d. Determining the profile relationship

5. Which of the following summarizes color management's purpose(s)?
   a. Predicting limited gamut results of 4-color printing on an inkjet printer
   b. Outputting an image to a variety of output devices

c. Determining accurate CMYK tint specifications for leather

d. All of the above

STEP 5: SYSTEM CALIBRATION

With that behind us, it's time to use some of our new-found knowledge in an effort to establish a sense of working harmony with our tools.

How Photoshop's Internal Color Management Works

The underlying concepts that have already been covered are quite applicable to the way that Photoshop manipulates color. The interface to the system is by way of the Monitor Setup, Printing Inks Setup, and Separation Setup dialogs. In the case of the Monitor Setup, you're defining, for the program's benefit, what you're seeing on the screen as you base subjective judgments on the visual result. The RGB values in the image files don't define a color in the absolute sense until you've further specified what these values mean. That is, they are being displayed on a SuperMac monitor with a gamma of 1.8, a whitepoint of 5,000K, and Trinitron phosphors.

In reality, you've now been provided with enough information to allow for a reasonably accurate translation between RGB and Lab, which, as you already know, is a device-independent color space. Lab color space is used internally as the basis for all subsequent RGB to CMYK (and CMYK to RGB) conversions. Only then, does Photoshop's understanding of the RGB values and the visual interpretation of them jive. If you tell Photoshop that your monitor is set to a gamma of 1.8, but it's actually set to 2.2 or 1.4, any further conversions it makes based on this improper setting will be flawed.

In the Printing Inks and Separation Setup dialogs, you are, in a somewhat crude fashion, defining the characteristics of your output device. A full-featured color management system can account for a relatively warm or cool paper stock by tweaking the color balance such that neutral colors remain so. Likewise, the definition of your printer's color space in Photoshop is through the specification of a total of nine colors, whereas a color management system will consider hundreds or thousands. While Photoshop doesn't allow this level of control, there is quite a bit lurking beneath the surface. We'll take a look at this and the Separation Setup in greater depth shortly.

Making Things Match

Reproducing Color (Chapter 5 in the *Photoshop User Guide*) is actually a rather concise look at the problem and solution. Due to its brevity, it may create more questions, though, than answers. We'll use the same basic procedure here, but will provide a more in-depth look at some of the functions and choices along the way. The manual suggests these steps in the process:

1. **Calibrate your monitor.**

2. **Enter the Monitor Setup information.**

3. **Enter the Printing Inks Setup information.**

4. **Print a color proof.**

5. **Calibrate the screen image to the proof.**

By now, you've already accomplished the first three steps of calibrating the monitor, entering Monitor Setup information, and entering Printing Inks Setup information. You'll pick up, then, from Step 4: Print a color proof.

Notice that the bulk of this calibration concern is related to trying to match the results of the CMYK output to its appearance on the RGB monitors. The difficulty involved in doing so, while certainly not completely insurmountable, is perhaps the main reason that many people working with color have a hard time gaining control of the process. If your output is to an RGB device (a film recorder), you have a far simpler work flow to consider. CMYK output is complicated by the fact that many combinations of the four inks can be responsible for an identical visual result (different combinations of CMY inks with different amounts of black).

We've already discussed the problems associated with the various color gamuts of a monitor and printed output. If you take a little deeper look into how Photoshop deals with creating and displaying CMYK files, you'll see that it's actually two problems in one. You need not only to be able to separate RGB images into CMYK, but to come up with a way of accurately viewing them as well (CMYK to RGB). These two halves of this concern are represented internally by color lookup tables (CLUTs), one to handle conversion in each direction. These separation tables can be saved and reloaded through the File → Color Settings → Separation Tables menu. This is also the vehicle through which you can import separation tables from other applications, but that, unfortunately, is beyond the scope of this chapter.

Once you save a separation table, you have locked up, in compact form, all of the prevailing settings in effect at the moment in the Printing Inks Setup and Separation Setup dialogs (but not Monitor Setup). If nothing else, this becomes a simple method to ensure that those elements are set to the specifications of a particular form of output. If you need to handle color imagery that is output to a variety of printing technologies and suppliers, this represents a good way of keeping the various parameters organized.

You'll want to proceed with this process by outputting a preseparated CMYK file, in other words, one that has not been made as a result of an RGB to CMYK conversion in Photoshop. The basic Photoshop installation provides the venerable *Olé No Moiré* as one solution (in the Separation Sources folder of your Photoshop installation). If you have access to other CMYK images, most likely from a prepress source, you may want to include them as well. The only caveat is that you'll want to specify any tint or color values directly in CMYK mode. You will probably find that the more different types of images you include in your testing, the more feedback you have to judge down the road. If possible, try to include both high-key and low-key images, one that has particular concentration on neutral subjects and another that features brightly colored saturated values. Of course, if you are interested in a specific type of imagery (for example, if you find yourself dealing with considerable amounts of food, jewelry, or textiles), be sure to include at least a representative sample.

With the hard-copy output at hand, illuminate it alongside the monitor in a way that's consistent with the whitepoint setting that you've made in Monitor Setup. Be careful that this light does not spill onto the monitor itself. If you cannot justify the expense of a small graphic arts viewing booth, appropriate 5,000K fluorescent tubes (GE Chroma 50) are available through most professional photographic and graphic arts suppliers. You will not need tubes of considerable brightness to balance the output of your monitor, so you may want to begin with a bulb in the 20-watt range. Open the file(s) that are responsible for the output and first study the relationship between the overall density of the proof and the image(s) onscreen.

Dot Gain

Again, the term dot gain is responsible for considerable confusion. Let's take a moment to understand Photoshop's assumptions, as well as how they might fit in with a typical print run. The program treats dot gain as a simple power function that is centered at the 50% midtone point—much like a gamma correction. This view may be a bit simplistic, but it is, nevertheless, how dot gain is treated in Photoshop. When we refer to a 20% dot gain, we are saying that a 50% digital value in a file will ultimately be represented by a 70% dot on paper, that is, it's nothing more than an additive relationship.

Another basic assumption is that the files are being output to a linearized imagesetter, in other words, one that is capable of providing a 13%, 52%, or 93% dot on demand without further correction. Your service bureau should be able to provide actual density values read from the screened film of your output as a check on this. If your film varies from the specifications in your files by more than a percent or two over the entire range of tonality, you should attempt to find out why (or even consider a different service bureau).

So where is this dot gain likely to originate? The easy answer is anywhere after the output of film until ink dries on paper. This can include halftone dots spreading slightly as ink is applied to paper, the platemaking process itself, and even within the press as dots are transferred between rollers and blankets in the course of offset printing. Where additional confusion occurs is in the communication of various types of dot gain. What we have been referring to so far can be considered total dot gain. When you have a composite proof (MatchPrints, Chromalin) made from separated films, the proofing process attempts to predict the dot gain (the amount by which some of the dots in the darker values will expand—thus making your image darker than you wished it to be) inherent in the actual printing process. These proofing systems are capable of being tuned to the characteristics of a particular press, paper, and ink combination, but in many to most cases, they represent little more than a reasonable guess about the results that you'll actually achieve at printing time. Typically, proofing systems build in an assumption of a 15 to 25% dot gain.

Additionally, you may talk with your printers or service bureaus and find them referring to a very low value (2-5%) of dot gain. Undoubtedly, what they are speaking of is a different phenomenon that describes the dot gain between the composite (or contract) proof and the final printed piece. This number has little value in what's being considered here; although, if this does prove to be the case, you may want to aim for a slightly lighter overall density at the proofing stage in anticipation of darkening on press.

While proof and digital images are being properly displayed, open the Printing Inks Setup dialog and notice that increasing the value in the dot gain field will eventually darken the onscreen appearance of all CMYK images (after selecting OK and closing the dialog box). The reverse is true as well. You want to use this variable as a means of tweaking the overall density of the onscreen images to most closely match their appearance in the proof. This parameter will have no effect on the appearance of RGB images, but it will come into play the next time that an RGB to CMYK conversion is done.

Let's look at the difference that selecting a Dot Gain setting can make. The following Hands On shows you the effect of the Dot Gain setting on the conversion from RGB to CMYK when used on a file that is already in CMYK color space. You will use a setting of 40% dot gain—hopefully much higher than you will ever see in the real world, but it will certainly make a point.

*H*ANDS ON

DOT GAIN

1. Open the image BoatFest.Psd.

2. Duplicate the image (Image → Duplicate → OK).

3. Convert the duplicate image to CMYK mode (Image → Mode → CMYK).

4. Open the Printing Inks dialog (File → Color Settings → Printing Inks) and change the Dot Gain setting to 40%. Click OK. Yuk! That would be one burned out, dark image if that is what really happened on press. Figure 15-7(a) shows this result.

5. Duplicate the original image again.

6. Convert this new copy to CMYK mode. Hmm... Big difference! It looks just fine. Figure 15-7(b) shows this version.

Figure 15-7
a) 40% dot gain applied after CMYK conversion
b) 40% dot gain applied before CMYK conversion

a

b

What happened here? When you changed the Dot Gain setting after the image was converted to CMYK mode, all Photoshop could do was shrug and say "Oh well...send this image to press and that's what you are going to get—and won't you be sorry!" However, if you convert the image to CMYK with a 40% Dot Gain setting in place, Photoshop compensates for the dot gain so that you get the values that you actually want, and the image will not darken either onscreen or on press.

The Use Dot Gain for Grayscale Images check box determines whether Photoshop will attempt to predict the effect of dot gain in both grayscale and duotone files. It will also have its way during the display of individual grayscale color or mask channels. Unlike with color images, since there is often no specific conversion to either of these modes, there is no place to build in the effect, like there is during an RGB to CMYK mode change. As you might guess, turning this feature on will cause Photoshop to try to simulate onscreen what will occur when actual output is made. It only changes the onscreen display and has no effect on the digital values in the files. The actual use of the feature is somewhat a can of worms, since one might expect any dot gain value to cause a darkening of the image on the monitor, but this isn't necessarily the case with every setting. Some people consider this feature a loose cannon due to its unpredictable nature, and elect to avoid it at all cost. You are probably best advised not to use it either.

Gray Balance

The set of four values in the Gray Balance section of Printing Inks represents gamma curves that can be applied to the individual color plates of the images, both during the separation process and while displaying CMYK images. If you get output from your now-calibrated system that does not match the screen, you can change the Gray Balance settings to make your computer screen look like the printed image. Use these settings with caution; a little bit goes a long way.

Unfortunately, there is no interactive interface to using this tool. What must be done is to open the Levels dialog box and make appropriate gamma adjustments to the individual CMYK channels, by using either the middle (gamma) slider directly beneath the histogram or by entering numeric values in the middle of the three Input Levels fields (remember, you did this in Chapter 7 to color-correct your images and remove color cast). Write down the values for each channel (do not attempt to make any adjustments to the composite CMYK channel) and CANCEL out of the dialog box. Do not select OK, which will apply these changes to the image data onscreen. Instead, go back into Printing Inks and enter the same number(s) next to the appropriate C, M, Y, or K fields. If, for some reason, your initial CMYK values in Printing Inks are not each set to 1.00 (the default), you should multiply the original and new values to obtain a final one. Again, once you OK the settings and leave the dialog box, all CMYK files onscreen should be redrawn to reflect these changes. Likewise, any RGB images that are subsequently separated will be done with your adjustments taken into consideration.

Custom Ink Colors

If your work is being printed via conventional 4-color offset printing, the chances are good that you can get acceptable results by selecting the appropriate set of predefined ink colors in the Printing Inks dialog. However, you will notice a rather short list of desktop printers that are directly supported. There are two basic approaches to this problem—one a by-the-seat-of-the-pants approach and the other far more scientific but potentially expensive. If you select Custom from the list of ink colors, you'll be presented with a formidable chart listing CIE xyY values next to the various inks and their over-printing permutations. Figure 15-8 shows this dialog (though you have already worked to change these patches in Chapter 12, "Using Spot Color," but now you know why the changes occur). If you are in a position to know these values for your printer, they can be entered here. Practically, the only way to determine this information is by way of a spectrophotometer or colorimeter used to measure patches on an actual printed sample. You may have success in obtaining this information from the manufacturer of your printer.

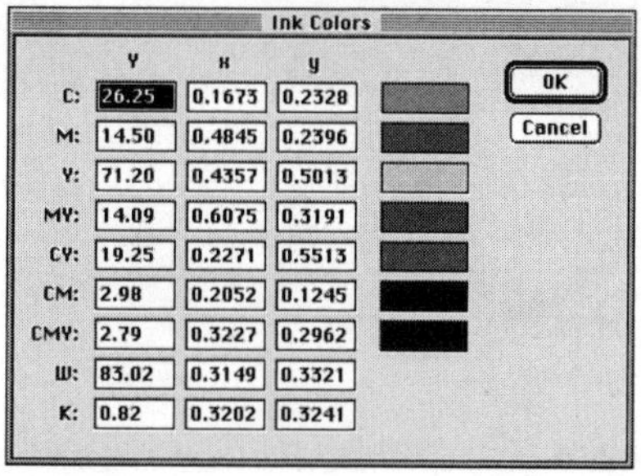

Figure 15-8
Custom Printing
Inks dialog box

The more typical scenario is that we don't know these values; however, you might get better results than you would otherwise by attempting to match your printed output to the screen by eye. With properly illuminated output of the seven possible combinations of ink listed in the dialog, click on each color, one at a time, and try to find the most appropriate color in the Picker to simulate its appearance onscreen. If you're going to all this trouble, it's probably worth saving a copy of these settings with an appropriate name when you're done. After accepting and closing the Printing Inks dialog, again, all CMYK images are redrawn in an effort to simulate the new definition of inks. With any luck, the onscreen appearance will result in a closer match to the printed sample than you had previously, but the further acid test will be the separation of RGB images and subsequent output. You will probably want to take another look at gray balance and dot gain for further adjustment. This process isn't for everyone, but with care, you should be able to improve on the agreement between what you see on your monitor and what comes out of a supported printer.

Separation Setup

In this particular area of Photoshop, caution is the operative concern. In a nutshell, you're telling the program both the maximum amount of ink to apply to the press sheets and exactly how the black plate is created from the values in the RGB files. Improper choices in either or both areas can spell disaster on press.

Determining optimum settings for a given set of press conditions is something that may well require a number of attempts. If you are consistently working with a single printer (and a commensurate budget) to try to nail down the situation, it could be in your best interest to reach for the brass ring. On the other hand, if you are more typically supplying separations for a variety of publications over which you have no control, it's probably best to aim for a least-common-denominator approach.

Figure 15-9 shows the Separation Setup dialog. Taking the contents of the dialog from the top, you must make a choice of UCR (Undercolor Removal, sometimes referred to as skeleton black) or GCR (Gray Component Replacement) by way of the two radio buttons. In either case, Photoshop will remove a certain percentage of cyan, magenta, and yellow density (that would otherwise combine to create gray—this is referred to as the achromatic component) and replace it with a suitable amount of black.

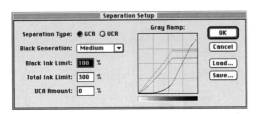

Figure 15-9
Separation Setup
dialog

Why go to all this trouble and not simply translate the RGB values to CMY? The main reason is that, due to the nonideal characteristics of printing inks, a 100% application of CMY does not create the rich black that you'd hope for. Instead, you wind up with a rather muddy dark brown. Once you find that you must rely on black ink to increase the visual density, another concern is that you cannot, in offset printing, lay down 100% of the four process inks—at least not without creating a mess on press.

In practice, we find that, depending on the selection of paper, press, and inks, the maximum value falls into the range of from below 250% to 350% of the possible 400%. The reasons for this are primarily related to ink drying and trapping (this use of the word trapping is unrelated to press registration and chokes and spreads). Let it suffice to say that, if you exceed the limitations of the process, the works will be gummed up. The simple fact that you can build up more apparent density with a given percentage of black relative to the other three colors allows you to get away with less ink. (As an aside, black ink is less expensive.)

You can get a sense of the differences between UCR and GCR separations by studying the shape of the black curve displayed in the Separation Setup dialog box. Notice that with UCR, Black Generation is confined to only the shadow areas or those heavier than approximately 75%. In GCR, black is being introduced, with the Light Black Generation curve, at approximately 40% in the tonal range. With a UCR setting, you have similar choices of Black Ink Limit and Total Ink Limit, period. GCR additionally provides a selection of Low, Medium, Heavy, None, Maximum, and Custom Black Generation. It also allows for the Black Ink Limit and Total Ink Limit available in UCR, but adds the option of UCA (Undercolor Addition). A small level of UCA can help regain density in neutral shadows that would have otherwise existed with the GCR separation by itself. In other words, you've first removed CMY ink from these areas and replaced it with black; the black alone may not provide you with an area with enough visual density, so you're adding back a little of the CMY to enrich the effect and give some life to the shadow or neutral areas.

In reality, unless you are prepared to run a press proof to gauge the effects on the actual printing process, this isn't a particularly wonderful place for experimentation. Many of the potential pitfalls will not be discernible at the stage of a composite proof. It is, however, an excellent point at which to discuss the situation with your printer. While there are preferences within the industry toward one form of separation or the other, it would seem that these are not always entirely justifiable.

Light Black Generation is probably a good place to start for sheetfed printing, although lesser processes (newspaper reproduction) may benefit from the choice of Medium. Good communication with your printer and service bureau will help with any necessary alterations to Total Ink Limit or Black Ink Limit.

Another Viewpoint: Prepress Settings

The following dialog is extracted from a series of messages posted on the Compu-Serve Adobe Forum by Dan Margulis (author of *Professional Photoshop* and *MakeReady*) and Bruce Fraser (co-author of *Real World Photoshop*). It is repeated here with permission from both authors. The conversation was in response to someone's question about his printer not knowing the "correct" settings and asking which settings to use. The conversation shows that the topic is really a complex one, and that conflicting answers are both possible and likely. Both men are experts in this area of Photoshop.

In reality, it will take a lot of testing (and, probably, disasters) for you to find the settings that work with the paper, inks, and press that you are using. Your printer is not likely to know the Photoshop settings that yield the best result on his equipment unless you work with a Photoshop-based service bureau that offers that knowledge as a value-added service. The two pieces of information that the printer should know, however, are the minimum and maximum dot (the shadow and the highlight) that his press can hold.

Dan writes:

"In terms of your setups...the big-ticket item is the handling of the black. Photoshop's defaults are not very good. Two ways to avoid muddy-looking shadows: (1) set maximum black to 85%, 90% at most. In principle this shouldn't matter; in real life it matters a lot on press for a number of reasons that I could get into if you like. (2) Black dot gain is heavier than in the other inks.... In Printing Inks Setup, lower the value for black from 1.0 to .92 or thereabouts. (3) Unless you feel you have a specific reason to do otherwise, use Light GCR.

"The dot gain percentage varies with the work you are doing. Photoshop's default is 20%. I recommend substituting the following: 30% for newspaper work, 25% for magazine or similar Web work, 22% for sheetfed and high-quality Web work, 20% for high-quality sheetfed work. Deduct 3% if you are imaging to positive rather than negative film.

"Dot gain appears heavier in the darker inks. Thus, the order of dot gain, heaviest to lightest, is KMCY. Magenta and cyan are sometimes roughly equal, but black is always highest and yellow always lowest. To compensate, change gray balance settings to: C=1, M=1, Y=1.04, K=.92 (lower number = more dot gain anticipated). If you have a lot of experience with the same printer, you may find you want to reduce the M value as well. If you prepare files for more than one kind of work, you should be storing more than one kind of printing inks setups.

continued on next page

continued from previous page

"The two important numbers we need to guess—and it is, indeed, a guess—are (1) what the dot gain will be; (2) how heavy a black the job can accommodate without losing dot integrity.

"The two realities to keep in mind are (1) what these 2 numbers will actually be on a given job are subject to huge variation, depending on the ink, the particular unit of the press, the paper, the pressman, the weather, the condition of the blankets and how tightly they are packed, bearer pressure, who washed the press last and how long ago, and so on, and (2) that on press, it is much easier to cope with a job that starts out too light than it is with one that starts out too dark."

Bruce writes:

"All experts have their own favorite starting points. All are correct in some situations, if only in the same way that a stopped clock is right twice a day. In *Real World Photoshop*, we say upfront that any set of numbers is only a general guideline.

"The difference between Dan's values and mine would probably be wiped out by the differences in the way we treated the RGB images. The one exception would be the dot gain—I think 22% would be a bit high for a good sheetfed press on good coated stock unless you were printing a pretty high line screen, 200 lpi [lines per inch] or greater. With the sheetfed shop I use most (a pretty high-quality shop with a new Heidelberg Speedmaster), I use 20% at 200 lpi, 18% at 175 lpi, and 14% at 150 lpi....

"If they say they can get good results with 280% total ink, go for it, and back off the black a bit—95% is probably fine. Basically, I have no reason to distrust your printer's numbers.

"The higher ink limits I suggest rarely appear on the film because I usually set-limit my highlight and shadow points with the Eyedropper tool on the RGB file so that the heaviest shadow comes out around 78c67m67y93k.

"I generally advocate not messing with the gray balance controls unless you find a good reason to. The SWOP ink setups already have differential dot gains built in—when you set all inks to 1, the cyan and black have a heavier gain than the magenta, which is in turn a hair heavier than the yellow. Dan has sufficient experience to have determined that he gets better results when he tweaks them—I'd advise you to try everything else first unless you're having an obvious problem holding neutral balance.

"UCA is an image-dependent thing, really. If you need the shadows to be significantly non-neutral, UCA will counteract the tendency of GCR to make them flat and overly neutral. It also affects contrast a bit.

"...I could write a book full of clarifications and qualifications about all the reasons to depart from them in a given set of circumstances. I think Dan's about to publish a book like that, which I anticipate eagerly." (Note: Dan's book, *MakeReady*, was published in October 1996.)

1. What is Lab?
   a. A device-independent color space
   b. A device-dependent color space
   c. A course in college
   d. None of the above

2. What does the term *dot gain* indicate?
   a. The gain of pixels when calibrating a monitor
   b. The expected darkening of an image after printing measured at a 50% midtone point
   c. The expected darkening of an image after printing measured at a 45% midtone point
   d. The expected darkening of an image after printing measured at a 55% midtone point

3. Where is dot gain likely to originate?
   a. When halftone dots spread slightly as ink is applied to paper
   b. The plate-maker process
   c. When dots are transferred between rollers and blankets in the course of offset printing
   d. All of the above

4. What does the Separation dialog tell Photoshop?
   a. The maximum amount of ink to apply to press sheets
   b. How the black plate is created from the values in the RGB files
   c. Both a and b
   d. Neither a nor b

5. In the Separation Setup dialog box, what does UCR indicate?
   a. Under Cover Reply
   b. Undercolor Removal
   c. Skeleton Black
   d. Undercare Removal

LESSON 6

STEP 6: THE PRINTING PROCESS

Here is a brief summary of the steps needed to produce a printed piece:

1. The image is designed (scanned, color-corrected, manipulated).

2. The image is converted into CYMK color from the original RGB, so that its gamut matches that of the printing press.

3. The image is then sent to an imagesetter, a machine that takes the PostScript instructions from the image and produces one film for each color plate (channel). The film contains the halftone for each plate (a screened pattern that changes the color information for that channel from grayscale to black and white—somewhat similar to doing a bitmap conversion within Photoshop).

4. The films are then taken to a printer who uses them to burn metal plates that will be attached to the rollers on a printing press.

5. The plates are developed in such a way that the areas that have image data will accept ink and repel water, and the areas that do not contain image data will repel the ink and accept water.

6. The roller revolves and, as it does, it picks up both the ink color and water on each pass.

7. The roller transfers the image to the blanket—a rubber surface on another roller in the printing press. It is the blanket that transfers the image to the paper—hence the term offset printing.

8. For full-color printing, each sheet of paper must travel through 4 sets of rollers—one for each of cyan, magenta, yellow, and black ink. If a spot color or varnish is to be used, it requires another pass. Four-color presses are common, so most jobs do not need to be physically fed through a press 4 times. Six- and eight-color presses are also becoming more common as the printing industry copes with the customer's desire for more vibrant color printing.

9. There is also the issue of Pantone Hexchrome and Hi-color printing specifi-cations (ink systems using 6 or 7 inks to produce an expanded gamut of saturated colors) and stochastic screening (a screening method similar to diffusion dither conversion to bitmap). However, this is a beginning book on Photoshop—not an advanced text on digital prepress, so these issues are beyond the scope of this volume.

Creating Color Separations

You create color separations (also known as color seps) in Photoshop by changing an RGB image into CMYK. It is at this point that all of your selections in the Preferences dialogs come together to produce an image that will either print well or not. When you save your image as a CMYK file, you are saving a 4-color separation to be used direct-ly or, more commonly, to be placed into a page layout program like QuarkXPress or Adobe PageMaker and then output to film as separations.

You can also save your file as a DCS-EPS file. This option, under the EPS File Save dialog, creates a preseparated file to be placed into your page layout program.

As difficult as it is for many beginning users to understand, when you have changed an image from RGB to CMYK, you have created your color seps. The channels in a CMYK image are your color plates.

Transparent Output

One of the most popular questions in the Adobe forum is, "How do I get transparent output in QuarkXPress from files in Photoshop that have transparency in them?" The answer, unfortunately, is that you don't. This is a system and PostScript issue rather than a Quark or Photoshop issue.

People frequently need to place the subject of an image on top of either another image or on top of a QuarkXPress or PageMaker object. They want the background of the image to be clear, not white, and not the color of the original background. The way to achieve this is either to use Clipping Paths or to change your image to Bitmap and save it in a format that sees white pixels as transparent.

Clipping Paths

You create a clipping path from the Paths palette. After you have drawn a path around the subject or part of your image that you wish to isolate, select the Clipping Path... option on the Paths palette menu. The resulting dialog box allows you to select, from the list of paths in the image, the one that you wish to use as the clipping path. You can also set the Device Flatness at this point. The Device Flatness controls the length of the straight-line segments that the Raster Image Processor (RIP) uses to trace the edges of the curves. A higher flatness setting makes the RIP work less hard, but can cause straight lines where you want to see curves. A setting of 2 is fine for most basic shapes. A Flatness setting that is too low for a complex image can cause the RIP to choke up and not produce any output at all. Ask your printer or service bureau for the best setting if you have any questions or concerns about your image.

You must then save your image as an EPS file in order to use the clipping path (PageMaker permits clipping paths in TIFF files, but is the only page layout program that does). If you have a clipping path set in the Paths Palette, this choice will be the default when you save your image.

When you place your image into a QuarkXPress layout, you need to select None as the color of the picture box background. The clipping path will then remove the background of your image so that you can see around it. (Note: On Windows, there has been some difficulty in seeing the preview of a clipping path. Often the path will not look as if it is clipping out the background, but it will print just fine).

Let's try this whole process using the Pigeon image for which you prepared paths in Chapter 9, "Advanced Selection Techniques".

CLIPPING PATHS

1. Open the image Pigeon.Psd. Duplicate the image (Image → Duplicate → OK).

2. In the Paths palette (Window → Show Paths), select the Bird path by just clicking on it. The pigeon will be surrounded by the path.

3. In the drop-down menu in the Paths palette, select the Clipping Path option. Figure 15-10 shows this menu.

4. The dialog shown in Figure 15-11 appears. Select Bird path from the Paths drop-down menu. You do not need to set a flatness at this point (though a setting of 2 is usually a safe choice for an uncomplicated path). Click OK. Figure 15-12 shows the Paths palette after the Clipping Path has been selected. Notice that the path name is in outline text.

5. Change the image mode to CMYK (Image → Mode → CMYK).

Figure 15-10
Paths palette menu
with Clipping Path
option

Figure 15-11
Setting the clipping
path

Figure 15-12
Paths palette menu
showing clipping
path

6. Save the file as Pigeon.EPS in Photoshop EPS format. What? There is no such option; it is grayed out. Cancel the command and select the Save A Copy command instead. There are alpha channels in this image that cannot be saved in Photoshop EPS format. If you wish to keep your original image, select the Save A Copy command and click on the box labeled Don't include Alpha channels (and Don't Include Layers, if your image is layered). Then you can save your file in EPS format.

7. You are presented with another dialog box that asks for specific settings. Use the values shown in Figure 15-13. Do not use EPS-JPEG, though if you are working in Windows, you should select the TIFF 8 bits/pixel option.

8. If you have QuarkXPress or PageMaker, open that application and place the Pigeon.EPS image into an open document. Change the background to None. You should not be able to place the image on top of another image (such as a native Quark gradient) and should see only as much of the pigeon image as was included in the path (in other words, just the pigeon).

EPS File with Transparent Whites

You can also save an EPS file that is in bitmap format (only black or white pixels) and choose the option Transparent Whites. With this option, any white pixel is transparent and you can see behind it. The only problem with this approach is that you cannot apply any trapping settings to an EPS file (if you do not know what trapping is, then do not worry about this statement). Generally, you want black to overprint, but black in an EPS file will knock out the image beneath it.

TIFF Options

White pixels in a bitmap file saved in TIFF format are automatically transparent and the black ink automatically overprints. That makes this a very good format for transparent output.

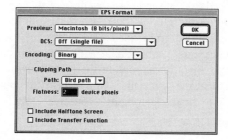

Figure 15-13
Save a copy as EPS

Creating Shadows

One of the most common reasons to need a clipping path is to create a shadow behind text that picks up the colors in several images. This is a complex subject. With permission from *Computer Artist* magazine, the CD-ROM contains an article written by the author for the July 1996 issue that discusses the problem in detail. Take the time to read it now.

Best File Formats for Prepress

TIFF and EPS are the file formats of choice for prepress. Review the material in Chapter 6, "Color and File Formats," if you do not remember the reasons for using one versus the other.

Going to Film

Another somewhat less common output format is photographic film. This approach is used when you want to print an image as a photograph or display it on a slide projector. The "printing press" in this instance is the film recorder.

Preparing an image for a film recorder is substantially different than preparing it for a printing press. For one thing, the image needs to remain in RGB color space rather than be converted to CMYK. This gives you an expanded color gamut, but the gamma point of a film recorder is different. It is 2.2 instead of 1.8. If you do not correct for this difference in gamma (either in the Gamma Control Panel or by lightening your image), the image will be much darker than you expect it to be.

The other area in which film recorder output causes a major difference is that of image resolution. The rule of thumb for typical prepress is screen ruling × 1.5 or 2, but a film recorder has no need to screen (halftone) output. It is a continuous-tone device. It also produces film that can only be an inch wide and yet must contain a large number of pixels.

Therefore, forget the image resolution setting for a film recorder. It is meaningless. You can set it to anything at all. The only thing that matters is the number of pixels in your image. Film recorders "write" to film at 2K, 4K, and 8K sizes (a "K" is 1024 pixels). Therefore, you need to create an image that has exactly that number of pixels across its largest side. The film aspect ratio is 3:2. Therefore, if your file conforms to the aspect ratio, a 4K file should contain 4096 pixels × 2730 pixels.

You also need to be careful about sharpening images that are going to a film recorder. You cannot use nearly as much unsharp masking on an image that is to be printed on a continuous-tone device like a film recorder as you can on an image to be halftoned. If you can see the sharpening halos onscreen, you have oversharpened the image.

1. How are color separations created in Photoshop?
   a. By changing an RGB image into CMYK
   b. By changing an RGB image into CMY
   c. They aren't.
   d. None of the above

2. When placing the subject of a Photoshop image on top of a QuarkXPress object, how do you obtain the desired clear background?
   a. Paths palette.
   b. Clipping paths.
   c. Change the Photoshop image to Bitmap.
   d. It can't be done.

3. Where is a clipping path created from?
   a. Toolbox
   b. Lasso tool
   c. File menu
   d. Paths palette

4. What are the two best file formats for prepress?
   a. EPS
   b. PCX
   c. TIFF
   d. Bitmap

5. Which path is useful for creating shadows?
   a. Clipping
   b. Preferences
   c. File
   d. None of the above

VIP PROFILE

Steven Pollock, Digital Artist and Photographer

Steven Pollock is a New Jersey-based power user of Photoshop. He was trained as a commercial photographer and had his own studio for 20 years. He specialized as a "visual problem solver"; when people wanted weird effects that they didn't know how to create, they came to him.

His goal was to get as much to happen at a photo shoot as possible—when it couldn't, he became the prepress intermediary between the art director and the Scitex technician (between the "blue-sky" artistry and technical reality).

In the mid- to late 1980s, the Quantel Paintbox and other high-powered and expensive graphics systems were used to get computer power into creative environments. It was the first time that the "creatives" themselves were able to "play" and make effects happen.

In the late 1980s, Steve was ready to try this Brave New World himself. He hired a consultant, who found a number of possible systems for him—and only one of them was under $100,000. The Macintosh did not even make the list. Most of the workstations were in the seven-figure range—way too high for a single photographer working alone and wondering if he would have any clients for this new service.

The package that Steve purchased was a DOS-based turn-key system called Networked Picture Systems. Its target audience was the small print shop that had not been able to cost-justify a computer in its work flow. Typically, these printers only had scanners whose output went directly to film—a film plotter attached to the scanner itself. Steve was one of only three creatives (as opposed to small businesses) to purchase the system.

He used it to retouch images and apply digital effects. It was limited in the video cards, monitors, and peripherals that it could use. It could only edit a large image by means of a Quick-Edit-like feature that allowed you to work on images 512×482 pixels in width at a time. If you wanted to draw a diagonal airbrushed line on an image, it was fairly close to impossible—by the time you draw each "tile" separately, the line was jagged and not even aimed in the right direction. It was, to quote Steve, "quite an experience."

When Photoshop appeared in 1990, Steve viewed it as a toy. It was not useful to him until it got CMYK abilities. He stuck with the NPS and the PC. His first Mac was a Mac II, purchased for opening client files. He beta-tested Photoshop 2.5 for Windows.

How does Steve feel about Photoshop? It does not have many competitors—Micrografix Picture Publisher and Macromedia Xres, for example, all do much the same thing. In some cases, the Photoshop feature set may be spartan, but the implementation is excellent, and the program is so rock-stable that the idea of changing to another program is almost unthinkable.

Steve also has some advice for you as a new user of Photoshop. "Use whatever happens to be representative of your work flow and pick some files. Get your feet wet with a 1, 2, or 3 Mb image—don't try to manipulate 40 Mb as a learning exercise. When you feel comfortable with the process, then pull hardware, software, and work flow together. Remember to utilize the margins of 4-color jobs as "scratch areas" to test a variety of Separation and Printing Inks Setups to find the ones that work best for you."

CHAPTER SUMMARY

This chapter just scratches the surface of what you need to know about prepress (the name given to the preparation steps for printing). One of the best sources of Photoshop prepress knowledge is Bruce Fraser and David Blatner's book *Real World Photoshop*. Dan

Margulis's two books, *Professional Photoshop* and *MakeReady*, also belong on your bookshelf. Another good source for prepress knowledge is Agfa's Pre-Press series. Originally a six-book series, it is now available as an interactive CD-ROM. Two more sources worth noting are International Paper's *Pocket Pal* and Frank Romano's *Pocket Guide to Electronic Pre-press*.

You have learned quite a lot about monitor calibration, setting Monitor, Printing Inks, and Separation Setup preferences, and creating images with clipping paths. You have also come to the end of this course. There is always much more to learn, and you have made an excellent beginning. Now is a good time to flip back through the other lessons and review anything that is still unclear. It is also a good time to try to design some portfolio pieces for yourself. As a perfect final project, design a business card for yourself in four colors. Have it printed. Look in the back of the computer magazines for low-cost, 4-color, short-run printers. This is an excellent first step into the real world. Good luck to you!

APPENDIX A
THIRD-PARTY FILTERS AND COMPANION PRODUCTS

The companies listed here produce plug-ins for Photoshop or products that work well in concert with Photoshop. The phone numbers of the companies are included so you can easily contact them.

Company	Product	Phone
a lowly apprentice productions	PlateMaker	619-743-7502
Adobe	After Effects	415-961-4400
	Dimensions	
	Gallery Effects	
	Illustrator	
	Photoshop	
	TextureMaker	
	Type faces	
Alien Skin	Eye Candy filters	919-832-4124
Andromeda Software	Series I	805-379-4109
	Series II (3D)	
	Series III (Screens)	
	Series IV (Techtures)	
	Velociraptor	
AufoFX Corporation	Photo/Graphic Edges	603-875-4400
Binuscan, Inc.	Binuscan	212-681-0600
BoxTop Software	PhotoGif 2.0	601-323-6436
	ProJpeg 2.0	
Chroma	Chromatica	415-375-1100

continued on next page

continued from previous page

Company	Product	Phone
Cytopia	PhotoLab	415-364-4594
DataStream	WildRiverSSK	606-259-1541
Daystar	multiprocessing	770-967-2077
Digital Dominion/Nova Design, Inc.	Cinematte	804-282-6528
Digital Frontiers	HVS Color	847-869-2053
Equilibrium	DeBabelizer	415-332-4343
Extensis	Intellihance PhotoTools	503-274-2020
Fractal Design	Detailer Expression Painter AddDepth Ray Dream Designer	408-430-4100
Image Express	ScanPrep Pro	404-564-9924
Live Picture	Live Picture OverDrive	
MetaTools	Kai's Power Tools KPT Bryce KPT Convolver	805-566-6200
MultiMedia Marketing GmbH	SISSNIKK HoloDozo	415-241-8806
Olympus Image Systems	CD-ROM writers	800-347-4027
Seattle Support Group	Photo CD collections	800-995-9777
Second Glance Software	Chromassage LaserSeps PaintThinner/PhotoSpot ScanTastic	714-855-2331
Specular	Collage Infini-D TextureScape	413-253-3100
Strata	StrataType StrataVision 3d StudioPro	801-628-5218
Total Integration	Epilogue Fast/Edit Deluxe	708-776-2377

Company	Product	Phone
Valis	Flo MetaFlo MovieFlo	415-435-5404
Virtus	Alien Skin Textureshop	919-467-9700
Vivid Details	Stock photography TestStrip	805-646-0217
Xaos Tools	Paint Alchemy Terrazzo	415-558-9831

APPENDIX B
BIBLIOGRAPHY

Books are not written in a vacuum. I did not just wake up one morning with a head full of Photoshop knowledge and decide to write a book.

PHOTOSHOP BOOKS

The following books on Photoshop form the basis of my library. These are the books used for background; the original Biedny/Monroy book and *Design Essentials* have "osmosed" into my consciousness over the years. You can never have too many Photoshop books. Each book on this list has something very important, and unique, to say. Every one of them—even the outdated Biedny/Monroy books if you can find copies—should be on your shelves if you are serious about Photoshop.

Biedny, D. and Monroy, B.; *Official Adobe Photoshop Handbook;* Bantam Books, 1991.

Biedny, D.; Monroy, B.; and Spirut, M.; *Adobe Photoshop Handbook 2.5 Edition;* Random House, 1993.

Cohen, L.; Brown, R.; Jeans, L.; and Wendling, T.; *Design Essentials;* Adobe Press, 1992.

Day, Rob; *Designer Photoshop;* Random House, 1995.

Dayton, L. and Davis, J.; *The Photoshop Wow Book;* Peachpit Press, 1995.

Fink, Peter; *Photoshop 3.0: Knock Their Socks Off!;* Mis:Press, 1995.

Fraser, Bruce and Blatner, David; *Real World Photoshop;* Peachpit Press, 1995.

Haynes, Barry and Crumpler, Wendy; *Photoshop Artistry—A Master Class;* Sybex, 1995.

Margulis, Dan; *Makeready;* Mis:Press, 1996.

Margulis, Dan; *Professional Photoshop;* Wiley, 1995.

McClelland, Deke; *MacWorld Photoshop 3.0 Bible;* IDG Books, 1995.

McClelland, Deke and Phillips, Robert; *MacWorld Photoshop 3.0 Bible, Windows Edition;* IDG Books, 1996.

MAGAZINES

These are excellent resources and ideal sources to use in your quest for excellence.

Computer Artist magazine; Pennwell Publishing, 10 Tara Blvd. 5th Floor, Nashua, NH 03062, 918-831-9405 (subscriptions).

McWade, John; *Before & After—How to design cool stuff;* 1830 Sierra Gardens Drive, Suite 30, Roseville, CA 95661, 916-784-3880.

Step-by-Step Electronic Design; Dynamic Graphics, 800-255-8800.

Swanson, Craig; *Photoshop Techniques*—a weekly magazine; Swanson Technical Support, P.O. Box 30049, Seattle, WA 98103.

APPENDIX C
LABS

CHAPTER 1

Using the Paint tools in a precise manner

Exercise Type: Experiment

Purpose: To compare the brushstrokes made by the Paint tools and see how the Eraser affects them. The second purpose is to teach you to use the Info palette to read precise locations on the canvas, and to show you to compare your work to the final file on the CD-ROM for those times when your work should match the example *exactly*.

This exercise is not a lot of fun unless you are a precision loony. However, it *is* good practice. To make it a bit less taxing, a blank image with Guides located in the critical places was created for you. The exercise asks you to paint straight lines from top to bottom across the image, then use the Eraser horizontally to see how it interacts with the painted lines. The Guides fall at each intersection where you should start and stop. In addition, if you select the Option marked Snap to Guides from the View menu, your cursor will easily find the general vicinity.

Starter File: `Guides.Psd`

Environment: Make sure you have selected Brush Size as your Painting Tools cursor in the General Preferences dialog. Set your colors to the default. Make the Info palette visible. Turn Show Guides on in the View menu (if the menu says Hide Guides, it is already on). Turn on Snap to Guides in the View menu. Select it from the menu, and a check mark appears.

Do:

1. Open the image Guides.Psd.

2. Press D to set the colors back to the black and white default.

3. Select the Pencil tool at 100% Opacity, Normal mode. Do not set a Fade amount for any of the tools used in this exercise. Using the brush labeled 35, move it to location 55, 55 on the image. Click.

4. Move your cursor to location 55, 363. Press the SHIFT+C. This leaves a straight line.

5. Select the Brush tool at 100% Opacity, Normal mode, Wet Edges *off*. Using the brush labeled 35, move it to location 136, 55 on the image. Click. Move your cursor to location 136, 363. Press SHIFT+click.

6. Select the Brush tool at 100% Opacity, Normal mode, Wet Edges *on*. Using the brush labeled 35, move it to location 221, 55 on the image. Click. Move your cursor to location 221, 363. Press SHIFT+click.

7. Select the Airbrush tool at 50% Pressure, Normal mode. Using the brush labeled 35, move it to location 317, 55 on the image. Click. Move your cursor to location 317, 363. Press SHIFT+click.

8. Select the Airbrush tool at 10% Pressure, Normal mode. Using the brush labeled 35, move it to location 376, 55 on the image. Click. Move your cursor to location 376, 363. Press SHIFT+click. (Remember, you can change the Pressure or Opacity by typing the number on the keyboard—10% is the number 1.)

9. Select the Eraser tool with the Block method. Move it to location 12, 81 on the image. Click. Move your cursor to location 390, 81. Press SHIFT+click.

10. Select the Eraser tool with the Paintbrush method, 100% Opacity, Normal mode, Wet Edges *off*. Move it to location 12, 137 on the image. Click. Move your cursor to location 390, 137. Press SHIFT+click.

11. Select the Eraser tool with the Paintbrush method, 100% Opacity, Normal mode, Wet Edges *on*. Move it to location 12, 208 on the image. Click. Move your cursor to location 390, 208. Press SHIFT+click.

12. Select the Eraser tool with the Airbrush method, 50% Pressure, Normal mode. Move it to location 12, 284 on the image. Click. Move your cursor to location 390, 284. Press SHIFT+click.

13. Select the Eraser tool with the Airbrush method, 10% Pressure, Normal mode. Move it to location 12, 350 on the image. Click. Move your cursor to location 390, 350. Press SHIFT+click.

Solution File: EX01-1A.Psd

Result: Your file and the Result file should match *exactly* (or be very close).

Here is how you check an exact match. Whenever you are told an exercise should be an exact match, the following technique is the one you should use for checking your work.

1. Select the Move tool ([V]).

2. Click on EX01-1A.Psd. Press [SHIFT] and drag the image on top of *your* solution (this creates a new layer). Change the Layer Apply mode to Difference (it's in the same location on the Layers palette as on the various Tool Options dialogs). The image should turn black. This proves the images are identical.

3. You can drag Layer 1 to the Trash Can at the lower right of the Layers palette if you want to save your own work. If not, simply close the image without saving.

Discussion: Notice that the Pencil tool leaves definite markings in which you can see the brush spacing quite clearly. If you were to zoom into this edge, you would see that there are only black pixels; nothing is shaded to white. The Paintbrush has a much softer edge; the Airbrush is even softer and more diffuse. The Wet Edges setting on the Paintbrush affect even black paint. The black paint is much lighter in the center of the stroke, so you can clearly see the brush buildup between your first click and the rest of the stroke.

EXERCISE 1B

Using the Paint tools in a playful manner

Exercise Type: Exploration

Purpose: To try different combinations of Opacities and Fadeout rates.

Starter File: None

Environment: Nothing special.

Do: Select any Foreground and Background colors you like, create a new document (File → New → Name: Practice, Width: 400 pixels, Height: 400 pixels, Resolution: 72,

Mode: RGB Color, Contents: White). You may change colors as you wish throughout this exercise.

Use the Paint tools freely on the image and change the Fadeout rates and methods. Change the Opacity settings as well, and see how the tools react.

Solution File: None.

Result: You will have a fairly good idea of what to expect when you change either the Opacity or Fadeout rates.

Discussion: Notice that when you change the Fadeout method to Fadeout to Background, if your Background color is not white, it looks as if you are creating a color ramp to change from one color to another. When you Fadeout to transparent, it looks as if the brush is drying.

EXERCISE 1C

Pencil tool: Using Auto Erase

Exercise Type: Experiment

Purpose: To determine exactly how the Pencil knows something should be erased when the Auto Erase flag is turned on.

Starter File: None

Environment: Turn Auto Erase *on* in the Pencil Options dialog. You may select any Foreground and Background colors you want.

Do:

1. Create a new document (File → New → Name: Practice, Width: 400 pixels, Height: 400 pixels, Resolution: 72, Mode: RGB Color, Contents: White).

2. Draw several lines with the Pencil. Vary the brush size on them from very small to the biggest you have.

3. Repeat Step 2 using the Paintbrush, and again using the Airbrush.

4. Switch to the Pencil again and go over some of your lines with it. Change the size of the brush as you do this. See if there's a pattern in which the brush starts to paint with the Foreground color or erase to the background. See if you can determine when this happens. Make sure you click on only *part* of your original lines at times.

Solution File: EX01-1C.Psd

Result: The solution file will not resemble your results at all, since both are random scribblings. The solution file is only provided in case you did not understand the exercise.

Discussion: You should have discovered that Auto Erase has no idea if a line is created by the Pencil tool or not. It erases rather than leaves new paint if the cursor is clicked on an area with more than 50% of the current brush size filled with the current Foreground color.

EXERCISE 1D

Airbrush practice

Exercise Type: Practice

Purpose: To gain an understanding of the technique for using the Airbrush tool to apply graduated tones.

Starter File: None

Environment: Make sure you select Brush Size as your Painting Tools cursor in the General Preferences dialog.

Do: Create a new image 200 pixels×400 pixels. Select the 65-pixel brush. Chose a shade of green for your Foreground color, and set the Airbrush Pressure to 10%. Quickly move your brush back and forth across the width of the image, starting at the top. As you work your way down to the bottom, overlap rows of brushstrokes so the color gradually darkens. Cover the entire image in one pass (do not let go of the mouse button until you finish). Try to get as even a coverage as possible. Undo your work if you need to start over. If you cannot control the brush at 10% Pressure, try the exercise at 1% Pressure and keep trying until you can do it at 10%. When you are happy with your results, set the Fadeout rate to 300 and select a sky blue as a Background color. Work on getting a smooth transition of Foreground to Background color with the airbrush.

Solution Files: EX01-1D1.Psd and EX01-1D2.Psd

Result: You should gradually begin to feel like you can control the pressure and speed with which you move the brush across the image.

Discussion: Notice that the faster you move the brush, the less time the color has to build up. If you gradually change the amount of overlap between the brush's horizontal passes without changing the speed at which you move the brush, the paint darkens in a very gradual and pleasing manner.

Using the Fixed Size Marquee

Exercise Type: Technique

Purpose: To see how the Fixed Size Marquee is used in a practical manner. Also, to get a first look at Photoshop's ability to create patterns.

In this exercise, you will copy 1/4 of a pattern and repeat it (rotated) in each corner of the image—as if you were laying a tile floor.

Starter File: SmPat.Psd

Environment: Colors should be at the black and white default.

Do:

1. Open the image SmPat.Psd.

2. Determine the number of pixels in the image in each direction. On the Mac, press OPTION while clicking on the size box in the lower-left corner of the Image Window. You need to pull on the grow box in the lower-right corner to let the size box appear. On Windows, you can determine the size by pressing ALT as you click on the size box along the bottom bar of the application Window. (This image is 30 pixels × 30 pixels).

3. Duplicate the image (Image → Duplicate → OK).

4. Double the size of the image using the Canvas Size Command (Image → Canvas Size → 60×60, click on the upper-left box in the dialog to anchor the position of the current image).

5. Press M to get the Marquee. Set the Fixed Size of the Rectangular Marquee to 30 pixels × 30 pixels.

6. Drag the Fixed Size Marquee into the upper-left corner of the image until it cannot move any farther. *Do not release the mouse button from when you first click until the Marquee is in the upper-left corner.* Copy the selection to the Clipboard (Mac: ⌘+C, Windows: CTRL+C). Deselect (Mac: ⌘+D, Windows: CTRL+D).

7. Drag the Marquee into the upper-right corner of the image. Paste (Mac: ⌘+V, Windows: CTRL+V). The image you copied pastes into the place in

which the Marquee was located, the Marquee disappears, and the copy becomes a new Layer. Flip the image horizontally (Layer → Transform → Flip → Horizontal). Drag the Marquee back over the upper-right corner. Copy it to the clipboard (Mac: ⌘+C, Windows: CTRL+C). Deselect (Mac: ⌘+D, Windows: CTRL+D).

8. Drag the Fixed Size Marquee into the lower-right corner of the image. Paste in the selection from the clipboard (Mac: ⌘+V, Windows: CTRL+V). Flip the image Vertically (Layer → Transform → Flip → Vertical). Drag it back over the lower-right corner. Copy it to the clipboard (Mac: ⌘+C, Windows: CTRL+C). Deselect (Mac: ⌘+D, Windows: CTRL+D).

9. Drag the Fixed Size Marquee into the lower left-hand corner of the image. Paste in the selection from the Clipboard (Mac: ⌘+V, Windows: CTRL+V). Flip Horizontal (Layer → Transform → Flip → Horizontal).

10. Select the entire image (Mac: ⌘+A, Windows: CTRL+A).

11. Define this as a pattern (Edit → Define Pattern).

12. Create a new document (File → New → Name: Practice, Width: 400 pixels, Height: 400 pixels, Resolution: 72, Mode: RGB Color, Contents: White). Fill the image with the pattern (SHIFT+DELETE → Pattern, 100% Opacity, Normal).

Solution File: EX01-2A.Psd

Result: Your result should match the solution file exactly. Check your results the way you learned in Exercise 1A.

Discussion: The Fixed Size Marquee makes it easy to control exactly where the Marquee is placed, since it cannot be dragged outside the image boundaries. This method creates a seamless pattern much like floor tiles. If you enjoyed this, there is another file SmPat2.Psd in the C01LabSt folder you can try.

*EXERCISE 2*B

Creating op art with Auto Erase

Exercise Type: Just for Fun

Purpose: Just for fun, to see how an interesting image is created.

Starter File: None

Environment: Make sure you have selected Brush Size as your Painting Tools cursor in the General Preferences dialog.

Do:

1. Create a new document (File → New → Name: Practice, Width: 640 pixels, Height: 480 pixels, Resolution: 72, Mode: RGB Color, Contents: White).

2. Select the Pencil and click on the 17-pixel brush (fourth brush from the left in Row 2). In the Options dialog, make sure Auto Erase is checked.

3. Double-click on the brush to edit it and change the spacing to 125%.

4. Select a hot pink for the Foreground color.

5. Click once in the image to leave a brush mark and press (SHIFT). Drag the brush to the right and hold down (SHIFT) to make a straight line of little circles.

6. Release (SHIFT). Click to start Row 2 so it fits in between the circles just below Row 1 and almost touches Row 1. Press (SHIFT) to make the line horizontal.

7. Line up the cursor back on Row 1 so it falls in between the first and second circles. Click. If the circle is in the Foreground color, click again for the Background color. Press (SHIFT) and drag it across Row 1. You will eat circles out of the original row.

8. Do the same thing on Row 2. The final effect looks like zipper teeth.

9. Use the Zoom tool to enlarge the image so you can see the individual pixels. Using the rectangular Marquee, select just one pattern unit repeat, for example, from the beginning of one zipper tooth to the pixel before the next one. The selection should be just as high as both rows and not one pixel more. Define your selection as a pattern (Edit → Define Pattern). Deselect.

10. Fill the entire image with the pattern ((SHIFT)+(DELETE), fill with pattern).

11. Now use the Distort → Polar Coordinates filter in the Rectangular to Polar mode to filter the image

Solution File: EX01-2B.Psd

Result: Watch the screen whirl! Your image should look very similar to the solution file. It is unlikely to match pixel by pixel, though.

Discussion: There are some interesting effects you can make with Auto Erase turned on. You could do them without it, but this setting makes it easier.

Creating a custom brush

Exercise Type: Practice

Purpose: To create and use custom brushes. To discover the difference gray values make in a brush.

Starter File: FORBRUSH.Psd

Environment: Make sure you have selected Brush Size as your Painting Tools cursor in the General Preferences dialog. Set your colors to the default. Make the Info palette visible.

Do:

1. Open the file FORBRUSH.Psd.

2. Drag a Rectangular Marquee around the small squiggle.

3. In the Brushes palette, select Define Brush. The new brush appears on your palette.

4. Drag a Rectangular Marquee around the larger, smooth doodle. Define it as a brush.

5. Create a new document (File → New → Name: Practice, Width: 400 pixels, Height: 400 pixels, Resolution: 72, Mode: RGB Color, Contents: White).

6. Paint, using the new brushes in a variety of tools, colors and opacities. Make sure you try the Wet Edges Options on the Paintbrush.

7. Find a clean corner of your image (or drag the Marquee around an area, then press (DELETE)). Set your Foreground color to RGB 1268, 128, 128 (a neutral gray—the easiest way to do this is to drag the cursor up and down the left edge of the Color Picker until the numeric RGB readout shows the desired values).

8. Use the Marquee to enclose a small area of the canvas (Fixed Size 32×32 pixels). Fill with the Foreground color. Define this area as a brush.

9. Change the Marquee to an Elliptical shape (Hint: Press (M) again). Leave the Fixed Size active. Click on another area of the canvas and fill the selection. Define this as a brush.

10. Choose a different Foreground color. Use both new brushes to paint over other areas of your image that have paint on them.

Solution File: EX01-3A.Psd

Result: You should see brush effects similar to the ones in the solution file. Notice that the square custom brush retains its sharp edges when used, but the round brush looks like a transparent version of the normal brushes.

Discussion: The tool you use makes a difference in how the brush appears. The gray custom brush you defined does not paint in a lighter shade of your Foreground color—rather, it paints with 50% transparency when you have the Opacity setting turned to 100%. This is the first time you are seeing a shade of gray used to determine Opacity. This is a consistent Photoshop feature, and understanding the action of this brush will help you in later discussions of channels and selections.

Using the Gradient tool

Exercise Type: Practice

Purpose: To use the Gradient tool to create a simple sunset.

Starter File: None

Environment: No special requirements.

Do:

1. Create a new document (File → New → Name: Sunset, Width: 400 pixels, Height: 400 pixels, Resolution: 72, Mode: RGB Color, Contents: White).

2. Double-click on the Marquee tool. In the Marquee Option palette that appears, set the Shape as Rectangular and the Style as Fixed Size. Enter the values Width: 400 pixels, Height: 300 pixels and make sure the Feather Radius box is set to 0. Select the top portion of the image with the Marquee.

3. Set your Foreground color to purple (R: 74, G: 15, B: 142) and your Background color to orange (R: 245, G: 124, B: 9). Double-click on the Gradient tool. Set the Apply mode to Normal, the Opacity to 100%, the Gradient to Foreground to Background, the Type to Linear, and check the Dither and Mask boxes. Drag the Gradient from the top of the selection to the bottom and press (SHIFT) to constrain the Gradient to the vertical.

4. Change the size of the Fixed Size Marquee to 400 pixels × 100 pixels and select the bottom portion of the image.

5. Change your colors to a foreground of deep sand (R: 47, G: 31, B: 13) and a background of medium sand (R: 195, G: 132, B: 42). Drag the Gradient in this selection as you did for the sky Gradient. There's your instant sunset!

6. This exercise was designed by Roberts Howard, one of the most talented illustrators around.

Solution File: EX01-04.Psd

Result: You will see two Gradients colored in a way resembling a sky against an empty dirt plain. Your result should match the solution file exactly, but if it is off a little, don't worry. There is really no need to do a formal check, as long as a visual check of the file looks about the same.

Discussion: This was a very easy exercise. It simply shows that Gradients can create smooth runs of color and simple techniques can mimic reality quite well. Compare the color and richness of the Gradient to the results you achieved with the airbrush. Could you have done this as easily or convincingly with the airbrush?

Challenge

Can you re-create the results of this exercise by creating one Gradient in the Gradient Editor? Try it. Then load the Gradient file **Sunset.Grd**. Look at the way the Gradient was created and how the nearly solid break between colors was achieved. Apply the Gradient to your image from top to bottom with SHIFT pressed.

The math behind the Apply modes

Exercise Type: Experiment

Purpose: To determine exactly what happens when you select various Apply modes.

Starter Files: PIXELS.Psd, PIXELS2.Psd, PIXELS3.Psd

Environment: Make sure you have selected Brush Size as your Painting Tools cursor in the General Preferences dialog. Make the Info palette visible. The second set of readouts in the palette must be RGB. The top set should be Actual Color.

Do:

1. Open the file PIXELS.Psd. Double-click on the Hand tool to enlarge it to 16:1 view. There are a number of pixels in the image. All are value 155 gray.

2. Select the Pencil with the 1-pixel brush. Move it over the first pixel in the second row and read the RGB value in the Info palette (since all three numbers are the same for grayscale, reading any one of them is fine).

3. Set your Foreground color to RGB 55, 55, 55 (another gray).

4. Set the Apply mode to Normal and the Opacity to 100%, and click on the first pixel in the first row. What is the resulting value of the pixel?

5. Set the Apply mode for the Pencil to Dissolve and change the Opacity to 50%. Click on the second pixel in Row 1. It may or may not change color. Why? Drag the cursor a few pixels in either direction around the pixel. Sometimes the color appears; sometimes it does not.

6. Use a calculator to solve this math problem: $155 \times 65 \div 255$. If the answer is .5 or greater, round up to the next whole number.

7. Set the Apply mode for the Pencil to Multiply and change the Opacity to 100%. Click on the first pixel in Row 2. Read the color in the Info palette. Is this what you calculated?

8. Screen mode takes the starting pixel and subtracts it from 255. It then takes the new color and subtracts that from 255. It multiplies both results and subtracts the answer from 255. The equation for this example is $255 - (((255-155) \times (255-65)) \div 255)$. What is the answer? Does it match what happens when you change the Pencil's apply mode to Screen and click on the second pixel in Row 2?

9. The next three pixels in Row 2 should be replaced with the Foreground color in Overlay, Soft Light, and Hard Light mode. Check their values. What are they? How do the values relate to one another?

10. Calculate the values for Darken (the darker of the two), Lighten (the lighter or the two), and Difference mode (the absolute value of (the existing pixel minus the Foreground color)). Replace the pixels in Row 3 with the Foreground color in Darken, Lighten, and Difference Mode. Did you match the calculated values?

11. Leave Row 4 alone. This is a grayscale image, so the remaining Apply modes are not valid.

12. For extra practice, try to calculate what happens using the color image PIXELS2.Psd. You should be able to calculate the results for all modes except Overlay, Soft Light, and Hard Light. The original pixel is RGB 255, 41,

243 (a magenta), and the replacement pixel is RGB 93, 255, 227 (a cyan). You need to set your Foreground color to RGB 93, 255, 227. The calculations work on each channel separately, which is why the color change is so dramatic when you change the Apply mode.

Solution Files: EX01-5A1.Psd and EX01-5A2.Psd

Result: Here are the values for the grayscale image:

- *Original value:* 155, replacement 65
- *Normal mode:* 65—straight replace
- *Dissolve mode:* 65—straight replace, but only percent of pixels in Opacity slider
- *Multiply mode:* 40—formula: rounded integer of (155×65÷255))
- *Screen mode:* 180—formula: rounded integer of (255÷(((255÷155)×(255−65))÷255))
- *Overlay mode:* 106 (value is darker than original pixel, but not as dark as replacement)
- *Soft Light mode:* 125 (value stays much closer to original pixel)
- *Hard Light mode:* 79 (value stays much closer to replacement pixel)
- *Darken mode:* 65 (darker pixel is selected)
- *Lighten mode:* 155 (lighter pixel is selected)
- *Difference mode:* 90—formula: absolute value of (155−65)

Discussion: The Apply modes of Multiply, Screen, Darken, Lighten, and Difference are reciprocal. It does not matter which is the original value and which the replacement value—the result is the same. This *does* matter, however, in Overlay, Hard Light, and Soft Light modes. It gets even trickier in color. This exercise is good preparation for understanding the Apply modes in the Layers palette and in the Channel Calculations. Although you eventually won't need to know the math—only the expected results—it is very helpful to understand what is happening and why. If you wish to explore this further, try the exercise again using white and black as your original and replacement pixels in both orders. Try white and black with different values too, and see how the modes react to them. Also try choosing the *same* color for your Foreground and existing colors. Which Apply modes change and which remain the same?

Using the Paintbrush in various Apply modes

Exercise Type: Exploration

Purpose: To see how the Paintbrush responds to changes in Apply modes when painted over an existing image.

Starter File: BOATFEST.Psd

Environment: Make sure you have selected Brush Size as your Painting Tools cursor in the General Preferences dialog. Set your Foreground color to RGB 0, 191, 10. This color is used throughout the exercise.

Do:

1. Open the image BOATFEST.Psd.

2. Select the Paintbrush. Set the Apply mode to Dissolve with 50% Opacity. Paint over the base of the single boat on the right. Use whichever brush size feels most comfortable to you. Remember that you can use the keyboard to zoom in closer to the image, and you can change brush sizes using the bracketkeys (⊡ and ⊡).

3. Set the Apply mode to Multiply and the Opacity back to 100% (where it remains for the rest of this exercise). Paint the right portion of the sail on the single sailboat to the right.

4. Set the Apply mode to Screen. Paint the left portion of the sail.

5. Set the Apply mode to Overlay. Paint over the large white sail (and the numbers) on the boat to the front and left of the image.

6. Set the Apply mode to Soft Light. Paint the other half of the brightly colored sail.

7. Set the Apply mode to Hard Light. Paint the right half of the sail directly behind (and to the left) of the one painted in Step 6.

8. Set the Apply mode to Darken. Paint the other half of the sail.

9. Set the Apply mode to Lighten. Paint the orange sail behind the white sail at the center of the image.

10. Set the Apply mode to Difference. Paint the right half of the white sail in the center of the image (include the numbers).

11. Set the Apply mode to Hue. Paint the very dark back sail at the center of the image.

12. Set the Apply mode to Saturation. Paint the remaining half of the white sail in the center of the image.

13. Set the Apply mode to Color. Paint the base portion of the boat in the center of the image.

14. Set the Apply mode to Luminosity. Paint the sky.

Solution File: EX01-5B.Psd

Result: You should see results similar to the solution image. They won't match pixel for pixel, but they should be close. If you do want to use the Difference method of checking your result, now you know why it works as it does!

Discussion: Notice that the Multiply, Overlay, and Soft Light modes do an excellent job of preserving the image detail as they paint. Screen seems to obscure more of the detail (a function of the specific colors being screened together). Hue shows up on the lighter portions of the sail, but makes no apparent change to its darker areas. Saturation mode shows all the different ranges of pixels in the original sail—even though it looked mostly white. Difference mode made a dramatic change in color.

EXERCISE 6A

Using the Toning tools

Exercise Type: Exploration

Purpose: To see how the various controls affect the Dodge, Burn, and Sponge tools.

Starter File: BUBBLES.Psd

Environment: Make sure you select Brush Size as your Painting Tools cursor in the General Preferences dialog.

Do: Open the image BUBBLES.Psd. Set the Fixed Size of the Rectangular Marquee to 100×100 pixels. Drag the Marquee to the upper-left corner of the image. For each of the following activities, select the Marquee (Ⓜ) first, then drag to the next unused space in the image, and press Ⓞ to get the Toning tool back. Use the 45-pixel brush.

1. Dodge tool, 100% Exposure, Highlights

2. Dodge tool, 100% Exposure, Midtones

3. Dodge tool, 100% Exposure, Shadows

4. Dodge tool, 11% Exposure, Midtones

5. Burn tool, 100% Exposure, Highlights

6. Burn tool, 100% Exposure, Midtones

7. Burn tool, 100% Exposure, Shadows

8. Burn tool, 11% Exposure, Midtones

9. Sponge Tool, 100% Pressure, Desaturate

10. Sponge Tool, 11% Pressure, Desaturate

11. Sponge Tool, 100% Pressure, Saturate

12. Sponge Tool, 11% Pressure, Saturate

There are four remaining spots. Try out any other combinations you want.

Solution File: EX01-6A.Psd

Result: Your results should match the solution file closely.

Discussion: Notice how the tools react differently to the specific tonal ranges. The Dodge tool is most extreme when it is asked to act on the shadow areas, while it produces the most change in the highlights. All the tools are much easier to control at a lower exposure or pressure. Try using the Dodge and Burn tools in the same image again with very small brushes. Even at a lower exposure, the tools seem to have a more pronounced effect. These tools are designed to help retouch photographs, allowing the artist to darken and lighten specific areas of the image. Make sure you use a small brush (the first one in Row 2) to dodge a highlight around one of the bubbles and burn a deeper shadow on another one.

Using the Smudge tool

Exercise Type: Just for Fun/Exploration

Purpose: To see how the Smudge tool is used to produce a special effect.

Starter File: TOMARBLE.Psd

Environment: Make sure you have selected Brush Size as your Painting Tools cursor in the General Preferences dialog.

Do:

1. Open the image TOMARBLE.Psd.

2. Select the Smudge tool in Normal mode at 75% Pressure. In the Brushes palette, select the second brush in Row 2.

3. Open the Paths palette (T). Click on the Grow box at the top left until you see all five Paths in the image.

4. Click on the Path marked Pass 1 to select it. Click on the Stroke Path icon at the bottom of the Paths palette (the second one from the left). The Smudge tool is used to stroke that Path in the brush size you selected.

5. Click on Pass 2, then click on the Stroke Path icon.

6. Click on Pass 3, then click on the Stroke Path icon.

7. Click on Pass 4, then click on the Stroke Path icon.

8. Click on the Fine Line path, then click on the Stroke Path icon.

9. Click on the Layers palette to view the image without any Paths.

Solution File: EX01-6B.Psd

Result: Your result should match the solution image exactly.

Discussion: The Smudge tool is used to create a marbled image from an original. To see how the Smudge tool reacts to the Apply mode settings, you can try the exercise as many times as you wish using a different Apply mode each time.

Exploring various ways to fill a selection with an image

Exercise Type: Experiment/Exploration

Purpose: To see how many ways Photoshop has of using a portion of a saved image.

Starter Files: CALIPATT.Psd and OPAL.Psd

The image in **CALIPATT.Psd** is a pattern created from a photo by Ed Scott, a photographer living in California.

Environment: Make sure you select Brush Size as your Painting Tools cursor in the General Preferences dialog. The Layers palette must be open.

Do:

1. Open both starter files.

2. Select the Move tool (V), press SHIFT, and drag the OPAL image on top of the CALIPATT image. Flatten the image (Layers palette → Layers palette menu → Flatten image).

3. Double-click on the Marquee tool. In the Marquee Option palette that appears, set the Shape as Rectangular and the Style as Fixed Size. Enter the values Width: 100 pixels, Height: 100 pixels·and make sure the Feather Radius box is set to 0. Drag the Marquee to the upper-left corner of the image.

4. Select the Eraser tool with a 45-pixel Paintbrush and 100% Opacity. Click on the Erase to Saved Option. Erase the area in the Marquee.

5. Select the Rubber Stamp tool and set the Option to From Saved. Use Normal mode and 100% Opacity. Select the 45-pixel brush. Paint inside the selection.

6. Press M and move the Marquee to the lower-left corner. Select the Rubber Stamp again.

7. Change the Rubber Stamp Option to Clone (Aligned). Press OPTION (Mac) or ALT (Windows). The cursor changes. With the key pressed, click on the pixel as close to the upper-right corner as possible. Release the key. Move the cursor to the upper-right corner of the new selection area. Paint.

8. Press M and move the Marquee to the lower-right corner.

9. Press SHIFT+DELETE and change the Used item to Saved. Set the mode to Normal and the Opacity to 100%.

10. Change the tools, opacities, and Apply modes to find various ways to combine the saved image with other areas of the file. You can use the Marquee or not, and you can change the shape if you wish.

Solution File: EX01-7A.Psd

Result: The four corners of the image should look like the solution, unless you drew over them a second time.

Discussion: Photoshop frequently offers many ways to do the same thing. The Eraser: Erase to Saved, Rubber Stamp From Saved, and Fill Command using Saved do exactly the same things. The method you use depends on how you feel at the moment, or on which tool gives you the most control. Fill command can only fill a selection, while the other two methods can be used with custom brushes or any type of fancy brush-strokes. However, the Eraser has no Apply modes.

Using the Impressionist Option in the Rubber Stamp tool

Exercise Type: Exploration

Purpose: To see how the Impressionist Option works.

Starter Files: OPAL2.Psd and OPAL.Psd

Environment: Make sure you select Brush Size as your Painting Tools cursor in the General Preferences dialog. The Layers palette must be open.

Do:

1. Open both starter files.

2. Select the Move tool (V). Press SHIFT and drag the OPAL image on top of the OPAL2 image. Flatten the image (Layers palette → Layers palette menu → Flatten image).

3. Select the Rubber Stamp tool with the Impressionist Option. Use 100% Opacity and Normal mode.

4. Use a very large brush and brush in the new image. Gradually decrease the brush sizes, and watch the different effects you get.

5. Repeat Step 2 to get a fresh copy of the OPAL image. This time, change Opacities and Apply modes as you brush.

Solution File: None

Result: You will only see scribbles and colors, though your first pass with the large brush creates a very soft, pleasing effect.

Discussion: The Impressionist Option pulls color from the saved image, based on the size of the brush being used. It can create a variety of effects when used in different apply modes.

Scratchboard technique using Clear mode

Exercise Type: Just for Fun

Purpose: Conventional scratchboard designs are made by removing a layer or coating over an image to reveal a painted area beneath. You can get the same effect using the Line tool or the Stroke command in Clear painting mode while you are in a layer.

Starter File: Scratch.Psd

Environment: Nothing special.

Do:

1. Open the starter file. It consists of two Layers. You need to work only on Layer 1 (the top Layer).

2. Select the Line tool (N). Press ENTER or RETURN to bring up the Line Tool Options dialog, and change the Apply mode to Clear. Select a Line Width of 4—though you can change this as you wish.

3. Create a design or image with the Line tool. You may also use the Lasso if you wish to select an area, then apply the Stroke command to it (Edit → Stroke).

Solution File: EX01-08.Psd

Result: Your image will not resemble the solution at all, but the idea is the same. You are removing areas of paint from the top Layer to reveal the design on the Layer beneath.

Discussion: There is no trick to this, but it opens up a number of design possibilities. If you wish to paint with randomly colored lines, it is a lot easier to remove color to reveal a design than to create the design on top of something else.

CHAPTER 2

Using Quick Mask

Exercise Type: Exploration

Purpose: To show how various tools work in Quick Mask mode.

Starter Files: Stars.AI and Grapetex.Psd

Environment: Nothing special.

Do:

1. Open the two starter files. When you open the image Stars.AI and are asked for the size, select 75 as the width. Leave Constrain Proportions and Anti-Alias Edges checked.

2. In the Stars image, select the entire image (Mac: ⌘+Ⓐ, Windows: CTRL+Ⓐ). Define it as a pattern (Edit → Define Pattern).

3. Click on the Grapetex image. Press Ⓠ to enter Quick Mask mode. If your colors do not change to the black and white default, press Ⓓ to change them.

4. Press SHIFT+DELETE to bring up the Fill dialog. For the Contents use Pattern, and leave the Opacity at 100%. The mode is Normal. Click OK.

5. Because of the default colors, the stars pattern appears in red, which means that it is protected. The part of the image *that is not the stars* is what will be changed.

6. Duplicate the image (Image → Duplicate → OK).

7. The Quick Mask follows the image. Press Ⓠ to turn it into a selection.

8. Hide the marching ants (Mac: ⌘+Ⓗ, Windows: CTRL+Ⓗ).

9. Select the Adjust Hue/Saturation command (Mac: ⌘+Ⓤ, Windows: CTRL+Ⓤ). This is a dialog that you have seen before. Change the Hue to −59, the Saturation to 54, and the Lightness to 31. This creates an optical effect similar to the famous Faces-and-Vase example which causes the viewer to notice both foreground and background interchangeably. Deselect (Mac: ⌘+Ⓓ, Windows: CTRL+Ⓓ). You can check your work in EX02−01A.Psd.

10. Click on the original Grapetex image again and duplicate (Image →
Duplicate → OK).

11. This time, apply the Add Noise filter (Filter → Noise → Add Noise, Gaussian,
150). This has the effect of splattering tiny paint droplets on your image. It
adds the noise to the unmasked areas and removes some of the mask on
the protected areas.

12. Press Q to make a selection from the mask. Press DELETE to remove all
selected areas. Deselect.

Solution Files: EX02-1A.Psd and EX02-1B.Psd

Result: EX02-01A.Psd has the solution to the first example using Hue/Saturation
controls, and EX02-021B.Psd has the solution to the filter exercise.

Discussion: The shape of the Quick Mask has a pronounced effect on the final result.
You can use all of the tools in Photoshop on a Quick Mask, and the tools only affect
the mask. Quick Masks that are active are copied along with an image when the image
is duplicated. If the image is saved with an active Quick Mask, the mask is saved to
Channel 4 permanently. The action that you take once the Quick Mask is changed back
into a selection is also critical to the final look of the image. From two masks that were
very similar, two extremely different images were generated based on the actions performed upon the selection.

EXERCISE 2A

Selecting against a solid
background

Exercise Type: Challenge

Purpose: Can you move the images in the picture to the bottom of the file without
leaving edge pixels behind?

Starter File: Dots.Psd

Environment: Nothing special.

Do: Open the Dots.Psd image. Using any selection methods you have learned, select
the dots and the flower. When you have selected them, drag them away from their original location to an empty place in the image. Check to make sure they have left no parts
of themselves behind.

Solution File: None

Result: You should see no traces of the original images in their original locations.

Discussion: There are several solutions to this. A "right-but-not-what-I-wanted" solution is to use the Rectangular Marquee to select the entire area where the images are located and drag them to the bottom of the file.

The correct solution is for you to realize that by setting the Tolerance to 0 and clicking on a white pixel, you can select the entire file that is *not* part of the image area. If you then Inverse the selection, you have no edge pixels left unselected.

A companion approach to the Inverse technique is to use the Lasso tool to select white space around the dots and flower and to use the Shrinking Marquee method of selecting (Tolerance set to 0, click on a white pixel inside the selection Marquee select Subtract-From-Selection and press the modifier key—Mac: ⌘, Windows: CTRL). This solution is equally acceptable.

EXERCISE 2B

Selecting with Tolerances

Exercise Type: Experiment

Purpose: To see where the Tolerance setting needs to be set in order to select all of the edge pixels without selecting the entire background.

Starter File: Dots.Psd

Environment: Make the Info palette visible.

Do:

1. Open the Dots.Psd image again. Duplicate the image (Image → Duplicate → OK).

2. Set your Magic Wand Tolerance to 50 with Anti-alias *on*.

3. Click on a purple splotch. Use the Magic Wand, Grow, and/or Similar to pick up all of the non-white pixels. For this exercise, do *not* use the Inverse or Shrinking selection methods.

4. When you have a selection that looks complete but does not contain the background as well, hide the selection Marquee. Check around the outside of the selection edges with the Info palette. The outer edges should be white (RGB 255, 255, 255). If they are not, then you have left edge pixels unselected.

5. If you cannot get the edge pixels with the current Tolerance setting, try various settings and do the best you can.

When you think you have a "clean" image (one that only contains the flower, check your work using the Difference method from Chapter 1. There is one needed modification, however. After you have dragged the images into the same file ((SHIFT) selected) and set the Apply mode to Difference, Flatten the image (Layers palette menu → Flatten). Then apply the Auto Levels command (Image → Adjust → Auto Levels). This will graphically show you if the images are the same. *Do not spend more than 15 minutes playing with the exercise.*

Solution File: EX02-2B.Psd

Result: You should have close to an exact match.

Discussion: This is very possibly a "trick" assignment. The best way to get the edge pixels is the solution file to the previous exercise. It is almost impossible to make the Magic Wand tool sensitive enough to pick up all of the edges pixels and none of the background. With the Magic Wand Tolerance set to 10, it took one Similar command and 26 Grow commands to get the dots selected before selecting the entire background.

A good result can be obtained by setting the Tolerance to 155 and selecting each dot individually. Depending upon the exact pixels on which you click, you may be able to get a totally clean match or leave some small dot edge pixels.

EXERCISE 2C

More fun with edge pixels

Exercise Type: Experiment

Purpose: To see whether it is better to expand or contract a selection in order to move it seamlessly onto a different background.

Starter Files: Dots.Psd and Fleurtex.Psd

Environment: Make the Info palette visible.

Do: Select just the flower in the **Dots.Psd** image. You may use the Magic Wand or any other selection method you want. Save the selection to a channel so you can easily recover it. When you have the entire object selected, use the Move tool ((V)) to move it onto the **Fleurtex.Psd** image. If you are not happy with the way the image looks, undo the drag operation and fix your selection until you do like the way the flower blends into the background. You may want to Expand or Contract the selection, and you may wish to Feather it. To see exactly what you are doing, work at 16:1 magnification (you may double-click the Hand tool, or use the Magnifying Glass around the flower to get to that level). When you drag onto the Fleurtex image, also work at 16:1 magnification. *Remember to press* SHIFT *before you drag-and-drop if you want the image to fit exactly.*

Solution File: EX02-2C.Psd

Result: Your result should be similar to the solution file. It is not acceptable if you have left obvious white pixels around the selection. You should have decided on a small (1- to 2-pixel) feather.

Discussion: The problem in Exercise 2B really *was* a trick question. As you have seen, it is almost impossible to pick up every edge pixel on a soft-edged selection unless you select the background and then inverse. However, you usually will not want to recover every pixel—especially if your reason for selecting an object is to blend it into another image (which is a common need).

Objects with soft edges pick up a blend of colors at the edge—part object color and part background color. When you move this type of object onto a differently colored background, you get a very messy situation. The old edge color is called *spill* and it is often hard to remove this spill. One thing that helps is the Contract command. To get the result image, contract the selection by 3 pixels and feather it by 1 pixel. It blends softly.

You can create blends that are more crisp but yet have no spill when you work on larger images. The reason for giving you such a small image was to allow you to work at 16:1 magnification where you can see every pixel all at once. You would not have been able to do so with a larger image. Seeing the pixels should give you a better feel for what is happening.

EXERCISE 3

Selection challenge

Exercise Type: Practice

Purpose: To practice adding, subtracting from, or intersecting a selection.

Starter File: Happy.Psd

Environment: Nothing special.

Do:

1. Open the image Happy.Psd. Duplicate the image (Image → Duplicate → OK). Also open the solution file—EX02-03.Psd.

2. The solution file contains a simple "happy face." The face components are contained in the channels in the Channels palette. What channels do you need to load in order to duplicate the solution?

3. Start by loading the channels for eyes—both at once. Fill them with black.

4. Next, load the channel for the mouth. Fill with red.

5. Now, can you figure out how to fill the face with yellow without covering up the features you have already placed?

Solution File: EX02-03.Psd

Result: Your result should be very close to the solution file.

Discussion: To create the eyes, load Channel 5 by pressing ⌘ (Mac) or CTRL (Windows) and clicking on it in the Channels palette. Then load Channel 6 by pressing ⌘+SHIFT (Mac) or CTRL+SHIFT (Windows) and clicking on the channel name. Fill the area (Mac: OPTION+DELETE, Windows: ALT+DELETE).

Deselect and then load Channel 7 for the mouth (change your Foreground color).

The face is tricky. The "A+" solution is to load the channels for the eyes and mouth at the same time and then inverse the selection (leaving the features unselected). Next, load Channel 4 by pressing ⌘+OPTION+SHIFT (Mac) or CTRL+ALT+SHIFT (Windows) and clicking on Channel 4 to *intersect* the selection.

The "B+" answer would be to load the face and then subtract each of the features from the selection.

Cookie cutter selections

Exercise Type: Just for Fun

Purpose: To use a selection in one image to "pick up" a design area from a second image in order to create a third image.

Starter Files: Afribird.Psd and AfriFibr.Psd

Environment: The Layers palette must be visible.

Do:

1. Open both starting images and the solution image (EX02-04.Psd).

2. Select the bird figure in the Afribird image. The Magic Wand works well.

3. Using the Magic Wand tool (or the Marquee or the Lasso tool), drag the selection Marquee into the AfriFibr image.

4. Drag the selection Marquee to wherever you like the pattern under it.

5. Create a new document (Mac: ⌘+Ⓝ, Windows: ⒞⒯⒭⒧+Ⓝ). Select Window and choose AfriFibr.Psd as the model.

6. Return to the AfriFibr image. Using the Move tool (or press ⌘ or ⒞⒯⒭⒧), drag the selection into the new image to match the position in the solution file.

7. In order to create a copy of this selection, you need to get the Marquee back. Press ⌘ and click on the name Layer 1 in the Layers palette. This reloads the selection Marquee. Select the Move tool, press the modifier key (Mac: ⒪⒫⒯⒤⒪⒩, Windows: ⒜⒧⒯) and drag a copy of the bird to another location in the image.

8. Drag a third copy of the bird to the location of the black outlined bird in the solution file. Set the Opacity back to 1% on the Layers palette slider and Stroke the selection (Edit → Stroke) with a 4-pixel black center stroke.

9. Click on the AfriFibr image. The selection should still be active. You can change the location of the selection if you wish by moving the Marquee without moving the image (remember how to do that?). Create a Border selection of 4 pixels and, with the Move tool, drag it into the new image.

10. Drag it into the position indicated by the solution file.

Solution File: EX02-04.Psd

Result: Your image should resemble the solution image very closely.

Discussion: It is very easy to use a shape in one image to pick up a pattern or texture area in another image. You can combine methods to create a new composite image. You can stroke a selection created this way, drop it and pick up another area, or create a border area to pick up a texture. The variations are endless.

Using the Stroke and Border commands

Exercise Type: Experiment

Purpose: To learn exactly what happens when you stroke a selection or select the border area. Also, to learn the differences and similarities in Stroke and Border commands.

Starter File: None

Environment: Nothing special.

Do:

1. Create a new document (File → New → Name: Practice, Width: 400 pixels, Height: 400 pixels, Resolution: 72, Mode: RGB Color, Contents: White).

2. Double-click on the Marquee tool. In the Marquee Options palette that appears, set Shape to Rectangular and the Style to Fixed Size. Enter the values Width: 100 pixels, Height: 100 pixels and make sure that the Feather Radius box is set to 0.

3. Press D to set the colors back to the black and white default.

4. Drag a Marquee into the upper-left corner of the image (you need to leave room to get three rectangles across and three down).

5. Stroke the selection (Edit → Stroke, 4 pixels, center). Notice you get a solid black line around the edge.

6. Drag a Marquee into the center of the top "row" of the image. Select the Border command (Select → Modify → Border, 4 pixels).

7. Fill the area (Mac: OPTION+DELETE, Windows: ALT+DELETE). Instead of a solid line, you have a soft edge.

8. Drag a Marquee into the right corner of the top "row" of the image. Select the Border command (Select → Modify → Border, 4 pixels).

9. Stroke the selection (Edit → Stroke → 4 pixels, center, Opacity: 100%, Mode: Normal). This produces a double line with a soft gray center.

10. Drag a Marquee into the center left of the image (start a second row). Feather the selection (Select → Feather, 4 pixels). Stroke the selection (Edit

→ Stroke → 4 pixels, Center, Opacity: 100%, Mode: Normal). This leaves a lighter edge.

11. Drag a Marquee into the center of the image. Feather the selection (Select → Feather, 4 pixels). Select the Border command (Select → Modify → Border, 4 pixels). Fill the area (Mac: OPTION+DELETE, Windows: ALT+DELETE). This leaves a lighter edge. Instead of the sharp miter line that you saw in the filled border above it, this set of actions gives you a slightly softer inner edge that breaks up and lets you almost notice blocks of pixels.

12. Drag a Marquee into the center right of the image. Feather the selection (Select → Feather, 4 pixels). Select the Border command (Select → Modify → Border, 4 pixels). Stroke the selection (Edit → Stroke → 4 pixels, Center, Opacity: 100%, Mode: Normal). This gives you a soft round-cornered double ring with pixellated edges.

13. Drag a Marquee into the bottom center of the image. Select the Border command (Select → Modify → Border, 4 pixels). Feather the selection (Select → Feather, 4 pixels). Fill the area (Mac: OPTION+DELETE, Windows: ALT+DELETE). This gives you a very soft edge—even softer than the plain feathered stroke in the center left of the image.

14. Drag a Marquee into the center right of the image. Select the Border command (Select → Modify → Border, 4 pixels). Feather the selection (Select → Feather, 4 pixels). Select the Border command (Select → Modify → Border, 4 pixels). You are not able to stroke the selection as the command is grayed out.

15. Undo the Feather command (Mac: ⌘+Z, Windows: ALT+Z). Feather the selection (Select → Feather, 4 pixels). Stroke the selection (Edit → Stroke → 4 pixels, Center, Opacity: 100%, Mode: Normal). This gives you a very soft round-cornered double ring with tiny white spaces in the corners.

Solution File: EX02-5A.Psd

Result: Your results should resemble the solution file.

Discussion: The original stroked square (top left) is quite solid. It is the only final rectangle that is. This is because the Stroke command does not add feathering or softening. As you can see from the square that is below it, the Stroke command will take advantage of a feather that is already there. The Border command always creates a softened selection. The only hard edge at all on a border is at the line of the original selection (the center of the border). That will only show up if the border is not feathered. You can also see that it makes a difference if you stroke a border selection or fill it. It also makes a difference if you feather the selection before you create the border or after you create the border.

When you tried to stroke a border selection that had been feathered at the same radius as the border, you were not allowed to proceed. This is because you no longer had anything to stroke. The selection was completely soft. You could fill it, but you could not apply the stroke. You had to lessen the amount of the feather in order to be able to use the Stroke command.

EXERCISE 5B

More on strokes and borders

Exercise Type: Experiment/Just for Fun

Purpose: To see if the size of the border, stroke, or feather changes the behavior. To evaluate the potential of the various combinations for creating 3D buttons.

Starter File: None

Environment: Make sure the Channels palette is visible.

Do: Repeat Exercise 5A. Make two modifications to the exercise:

● Change the amount of the Stroke, Border, and Feather to 10 pixels (you will need to drop back to an 8-pixel feather for the last one).

● After you place the Marquee in your image, press SHIFT and drag the marching ants icon at the bottom left of the Channels palette *up to* Channel 4. This *adds* the current selection to Channel 4.

When you have completed this example, duplicate the image. In the duplicate, load Channel 4 and reverse the selection (Select → Inverse). Press DELETE to fill the background with white. Look at your sample 3D buttons. Which techniques do you like best?

Solution File: EX02-5B.Psd

Result: The filled, un-feathered border selection is the closest to a "real" 3D button. Some of the other gray shapes have potential if they are created with a round-cornered rectangle.

Discussion: The results mirror the results you got in Exercise 5A. The same proportions hold true. You might find different results if you change the pixel values for the Border, Stroke, and Fill so they are no longer identical. If you have the time, try that.

In addition, you have also learned how to quickly create 3D buttons. If you want to capture a round-cornered rectangle shape, use the Smooth command with a Radius of 1 to 3 before you save the selection Marquee to the channel. Be very careful to position the non-smoothed rectangle directly over your channel in order to create the shape. This is easier if you click on the Eye icon next to the channel. This will show the unselected areas in red, making it easy to see where your channel selection is located.

EXERCISE 6A

Exploring Tolerance

Exercise Type: Exploration

Purpose: To determine the formula that Photoshop uses to determine if a color is within "range" of another.

Starter File: `Turquois.Psd`

Environment: Make the Info palette visible. The Color Method needs to be set to Actual Color or RGB for the first readout. Use the Palette Options to change it if that is not your setting.

Do: Open the starter image. Set the Tolerance on the Magic Wand tool to 30. The center two "boxes" in each object are the same color and are the "starting" color of RGB 40, 210, 170. You need to find out which colored squares are within range and which are out of range and decide why that is occurring.

There is a relationship between the color values in each object. You need to determine what that is. You can read the values of each of the color squares simply by placing your cursor over the square and reading the numbers on the Info palette.

What Tolerance setting is needed to bring all of the colors in range?

Solution File: None

Result: Photoshop looks at the deviation from the "original" of each pixel next to the original in each channel. If one channel changes by 30 and the Tolerance is set to 30, it is in range. If two or three channels change by 30 in one direction, they are still in range. If one channel goes up by 30 and the other goes down by 30, the color is out of range. If one goes up by 15 and another down by 15, the color is in range.

Discussion: The first group object changes only channel. The second object changes two channels at a time but in the same direction. The third object moves two channels in opposite directions. The fourth object changes all three channels in one and two directions by both 15 and 30 (and one square changes by 15 and 16 in opposite directions). A Tolerance of 60 is needed to bring everything in range. Finally, with a Tolerance of 30, click on the fourth object in the center and then try both the Similar and Grow commands. Repeat this using the center of the first object. Why are the results different? (Answer: because the starting "population" of pixels was different.)

Grow and Similar commands

Exercise Type: Experiment

Purpose: To learn the differences and similarities between the Similar and Grow commands.

Starter File: Testgrad.Psd

Environment: Nothing special.

Do:

1. Open the starter file and set the Tolerance on the Magic Wand to 30.

2. Click on the band of pure cyan inside of one of the red rectangles. You will see a rectangular selection that is within range.

3. Grow the selection (Select → Grow). How many times can you grow the selection before it stops expanding?

4. Select similar (Select → Similar). What happens? Is there any change if you repeat the command?

5. Deselect (Mac: ⌘+D, Windows: CTRL+D). Click on approximately the same pixel again. This time, select Similar as your first action. How many times can you use that command before the selection stops getting bigger?

6. Click on a section of color outside of the rectangles and repeat Steps 2 through 5.

7. Can you find the lowest Tolerance value that will ultimately let you grow the selection to include the entire image?

Solution File: None

Result: Grow looks only at contiguous pixels. Similar reads the entire image and looks for pixels. By either method, you can only grow the selection about 9 to 13 times with a Tolerance setting of 30. Somewhere between 100 and 125 you will find the correct Tolerance setting that allows you to eventually select the entire image.

Discussion: The first pixel on which you click sets the stage for all subsequent activity. The Tolerance setting puts boundaries on that activity. Even within gradients there are "jumps" of color beyond which the Tolerance setting cannot leap (unless you increase it).

Replacing a sky

Exercise Type: Practice

Purpose: To use the skills that you have learned so far on a real image of moderate difficulty.

Starter Files: Wupatki.Psd and Sky.Psd

Environment: Make sure you have selected Brush Size as your Painting Tools cursor in the General Preferences dialog. Make sure you have easy access to both the Layers and the Channels palettes.

Do: In this exercise, you need to replace the sky with a new one. In order to do that, you will need to select either the sky or the rest of the image. The replacement will be trickier than it needs to be because you have not yet learned about layers or about the Apply Image command. The method that is used for the actual replacement works and builds on what you have already learned—but you will find better methods of doing this shortly.

1. Open the starter files.

2. Using any tool you feel is appropriate, build a selection that isolates the sky from the rest of the image (part of this exercise is in discovering which tool is best for the task).

3. Make sure that you feather your selection very slightly or at least anti-alias it.

4. Save the selection to a channel. If the channel has a black sky, invert the entire channel (Image → Map → Invert). *You must have no selection active at the time that you use the Invert command.*

5. Click on the Sky image and select the entire image (Mac: ⌘+Ⓐ, Windows: CTRL+Ⓐ). Copy it to the clipboard (Mac: ⌘+Ⓒ, Windows: CTRL+Ⓒ).

6. Click on the Wupatki image.

7. Load Channel 4 (Mac: OPTION+④, Windows: ALT+CTRL+④).

8. Select the Paste Into command from the Edit menu. The new sky replaces the old one.

Solution File: EX02-7A.Psd

Result: Your result should be very close to the solution image. Also check your mask against that in Channel 4 of the solution image.

Discussion: Hopefully, you decided to use the Magic Wand tool for this problem. The easiest solution requires only a few steps: set the Tolerance on the Magic Wand to about 50. Click once in the sky area. This selects almost all of the sky and none of the mesa. Use the Lasso tool to add to the selection by circling the few missed areas of sky. Save the selection to a channel. Deselect.

If you look at the Layers palette, you will see that the Paste Into command looks like it pasted in the entire sky—over your image and left the shape of the channel in another thing that shares the space in the Layers palette with it. It did. The "thing" is a Layer Mask, and it keeps you from seeing that the entire sky was pasted. You will learn more about this in Chapter 3,"Layers and Channels."

EXERCISE 7B

Advanced simple selections

Exercise Type: Practice

Purpose: To add additional practice to your selection skills with a more challenging problem. This one is still in the "simple" category because it is basically a black and white selection that only needs minor anti-aliasing.

Starter File: Family.Psd

Environment: Make sure you have selected Brush Size as your Painting Tools cursor in the General Preferences dialog. Set your colors to the default.

Do: Your mission is to remove the background from the four figures in this image. There is a minimum of fly-away hair in this picture—which means that you can just make a hard-edged selection around the figures. You do not need to worry about wisps of hair (which you will learn to select in Chapter 9, "Advanced Selection Techniques"). Do not select the shadow detail around the figures. It is much too dark to be realistic against a white background, and can be re-created later (though not in this exercise).

Use any selection tools you prefer, but you will get your best results right now by painting in at least part of the selection in Quick Mask mode. Save your selection to a channel when you are done. Save the file to your hard drive as you will use it—and the channel again—in later chapters. After you have saved the image, delete the background of the image to white (you need to save the background with the image for right now).

Solution File: EX02-7B.Psd

Result: Your result should closely match the solution file.

Discussion: Painting in the entire background with a brush in Quick Mask mode works, but is very tedious. A better approach is to use the Marquee tool to select as many rectangular areas of the background as possible and switch to Quick Mask mode. You can then use the Lasso to fill additional large areas. You need to paint in the detail—using white or black as needed to make the selection on the Quick Mask. Remember you can paint straight lines by clicking and then pressing (SHIFT) at your next click. Hopefully, you also discovered you needed to use a hard-edged Paintbrush in order to keep the edges of the selection from getting too soft. It is also to be hoped that you did not use the Pencil to paint the selection—that leaves a jagged edge that is not attractive.

CHAPTER 3

EXERCISE 1A

Layers and transparency

Exercise Type: Experiment

Purpose: To show the difference between using a solid color and a transparent color.

Starter File: None

Environment: Open the Info palette (Window → Palettes → Show Info) and the Layers palette. In the Info palette, set the First readout to RGB and the Second to Opacity.

Do:

1. Create a new document (File → New → Name: Practice, Width: 400 pixels, Height: 400 pixels, Resolution: 72, Mode: RGB Color, Contents: White).

2. Press D to set the colors back to the black and white default.

3. Make a new layer (click on the New Layer icon at the bottom of the Layers palette).

4. Press M once or twice to select the Rectangular Marquee and then press (RETURN). In the Marquee Options dialog, select the Fixed Size Marquee and set it to 100 pixels wide and high.

5. In the next two exercises, you will create nine squares inside of the image—3 rows of 3—so plan accordingly. Drag the Marquee near the upper-left corner of the image.

6. Fill the area (Mac: OPTION+DELETE, Windows: ALT+DELETE). Deselect (Mac: ⌘+D, Windows: CTRL+D).

7. Drag the Marquee to the center of the top "row" in the image. Fill the selection by pressing SHIFT+DELETE. In the resulting dialog box, use the Foreground color in Normal mode at 50% opacity. Deselect (Mac: ⌘+D, Windows: CTRL+D).

8. Drag the Marquee near the upper-right corner of the image (top row). Press SHIFT+DELETE and fill the selection with 50% Gray (from the drop-down menu) at 100% Opacity. Deselect (Mac: ⌘+D, Windows: CTRL+D).

9. Measure the three color Swatches by dragging the cursor over them and reading the answer in the Info palette. *What value do you get for each swatch?*

10. Turn off the Eye icon for the Background layer. What immediate change do you see to your color? *How have the color values changed?*

11. Change your foreground color to RGB 255, 0, 0 (true red).

12. Click on the Background layer to select it in the Layers palette. Click on the Eye icon column to make the background visible. Fill the Layer (Mac: OPTION+DELETE, Windows: ALT+DELETE). *What changes do you see in the values of the color squares?* Undo (Mac: ⌘+Z, Windows: CTRL+Z). Leave this image open for the next exercise.

Solution File: EX03-01A.Psd

Result: When the Background Layer is visible, the two gray squares look the same (the 50% black square reads RGB 127, 127, 127, and the 50% gray square reads RGB 128, 128, 128).

When the Background Layer is turned off, the checkerboard pattern shows through only on the 50% black square. The Info palette shows RGB 0, 0, 0 for the black and 50% black squares, and RGB 128, 128, 128 for the 50% gray square. However, the Opacity indicator reads 50% for the center square but 100% for the left and right squares.

When red is added as the background color, the black and 50% gray values are unchanged (with the Background Layer on), but the 50% black square reads RGB 127, 0, 0—which is half-red.

Discussion: There is a substantial difference between painting on a layer in 50% black or using the actual gray value. The difference is that 50% black is a *transparent* color—a black pixel with an opacity value of 50%—and the 50% gray pixel is totally opaque. The transparent pixels react to anything placed under them, whereas the opaque pixels do not.

This knowledge must be applied to selection edges in particular. When you "lift" a selection into a layer, you want to make sure that there is transparency along the edges of the selection, or you get unpleasing effects when you replace the background.

Loading Transparency

Exercise Type: Experiment

Purpose: To show the difference between selecting and duplicating pixels on a Layer and Loading the Layer Transparency.

Starter File: EX03-01A.Psd (or the open file from the last exercise)

Environment: Open the Info palette (Window → Palettes → Show Info) and the Layers palette.

Do:

1. Open the starter file if for some reason you do not have the file open from the last exercise.

2. Select the Marquee tool (M), and change the Style back to Normal in the Marquee Options dialog.

3. Select the entire image (Mac: ⌘+A, Windows: CTRL+A).

4. Select the Move tool (V). Press the modifier key (Mac: OPTION, Windows: ALT) and drag the rectangles toward the center of the image. Press SHIFT (in addition to the modifier key) after you start to drag to constrain the movement vertically. What colors are the squares as you drag them? What happens to the selection Marquee after you have dragged the squares? *Deselect.*

5. Select the nontransparent layer pixels (Mac: ⌘+click, Windows: CTRL+click on the Layer name in the Layers palette).

6. Select the Marquee tool (M). Remove the lower group of squares from the selection by pressing the modifier key (Mac: OPTION, Windows: ALT) and dragging the Marquee around the lower group of squares. Only the top three squares should be selected.

7. Select the Move tool again (V) or press ⌘ (Mac) or CTRL (Windows) and then press the modifier key (Mac: OPTION, Windows: ALT) and drag the rectangles toward the bottom of the image. Press SHIFT (in addition to the modifier keys) after you start to drag to constrain the movement vertically. What happens to the colors as you drag? What happens to the colors of the squares after they are dragged to the new location?

8. Measure the colors of each square with and without the Background Layer visible.

9. Turn on the Background Layer. Make the top layer active.

10. Using the Rectangular Marquee, drag a selection Marquee around the top row of squares. Fill the area (Mac: [OPTION]+[DELETE], Windows: [ALT]+[DELETE]) with red. What happens? Deselect (Mac: [⌘]+[D], Windows: [CTRL]+[D]).

11. Press the modifier key (Mac: [⌘], Windows: [CTRL]) and click on the layer to select the non-transparent pixels on the layer. Using the Rectangular Marquee, press the modifier key (Mac: [OPTION], Windows: [ALT]) and surround the top and bottom rows to remove them from the selection. Now, you have three individually selected squares in the center of the image. Fill the area (Mac: [OPTION]+[DELETE], Windows: [ALT]+[DELETE]) with red. Deselect (Mac: [⌘]+[D], Windows: [CTRL]+[D]).

12. Press the modifier key (Mac: [⌘], Windows: [CTRL]) and click on the layer to select the non-transparent pixels on the layer. Using the Rectangular Marquee, press the modifier key (Mac: [OPTION], Windows: [ALT]) and surround the top and center rows to remove them from the selection. Now, you have three individually selected squares in the bottom of the image. Fill the area ([SHIFT]+[DELETE], 100%, Normal, Foreground color, *Preserve Transparency On*) with red. Deselect (Mac: [⌘]+[D], Windows: [CTRL]+[D]).

13. Turn off the Background Layer and measure each of the Squares with the Info palette.

Solution File: EX03–01B.Psd

Result: When the squares were copied using the Select All method, the middle square changed to black as it was dragged, but the colors were unchanged when moved to the new location. The marching ants shrank down around the squares as they were moved.

Using the Load Transparency method, exactly the same thing happened. If, by chance, you were familiar with Photoshop 3.0, this is a *significant* difference. Loading the Layer transparency selects *100% of every pixel in the layer that is not totally transparent.*

On the first fill, with a plain selection, you covered all of the pixels with 100% red. The center section, loaded with the Transparency settings, fills the black and gray squares with 100% red. The center square which was 50% opaque becomes 75% opaque. This is because it filled 50% of the area with red and added it to the values already there. When you fill with Transparency on, the 100% black and 50% gray squares fill completely and the 50% black square becomes 50% red—the transparency amount is unchanged.

Discussion: When you need to move an object on a layer, ideally, you should move the entire layer using the Move tool. If you need to move just a portion of it, you can either select all and nudge the image 1 pixel using an arrow key or you can load the image transparency (by clicking on the Layer preview with ⌘ or (CTRL) pressed). You can then subtract out the portion that is to remain in its original location.

If there is data in the "margins" of the image that you cannot see, and you either load the transparency or Select all and move the visible data, you will "break" the connection to the data on the pasteboard—though it will still be left there.

EXERCISE 2

Selecting fringed areas and saving to a Layer

Exercise Type: Experiment

Purpose: What happens when you create feathered selections in the Background Layer and try to make a transparent layer out of them? This exercise lets you see what happens. This is in preparation for Chapter 9, "Advanced Selection Techniques."

Starter File: Feathers.Psd

Environment: Layers palette must be open.

Do:

1. Duplicate the starter image (Image → Duplicate → OK) two times.

2. Your task now is to re-create the selection to put it into a layer. In one of the copies, select the Magic Wand tool (W). Set the Tolerance to 0 with Anti-Alias *off* and click on a white background pixel. Reverse the selection (Select → Inverse).

3. Float the selection, cutting it from the background (Mac: ⌘+(OPTION)+(J), Windows: (ALT)+(CTRL)+(J)) to make a new layer. That doesn't look too bad.

4. Make red your Foreground color (RGB 255, 0, 0).

5. Select the Background Layer and fill it with red (Mac: (OPTION)+(DELETE), Windows: (ALT)+(DELETE)). What do you see now?

6. Turn off the Background Layer. Is there any transparency in the shapes that are in the top layer?

7. Try the same exercise with the second copy but this time, set Anti-Alias *on*.

Solution File: EX03-2B.Psd

Result: You see an awful mess. The white fringe pixels (areas where the circle feathered) are glaring and ugly when lifted to another layer and the background changed. These pixels are fully opaque. They have no transparency and cannot blend with a changed background color. With Anti-Alias on, the second image looks better for the center circle since it added some transparency around the edges, but it is almost as bad on the heavily feathered circle.

Discussion: This is another example of the problem of edge or fringe pixels. Images that have any anti-aliasing in them need to become partially transparent at the edges in order to blend in with new surroundings. Chapter 9 will show you how to re-create that edge transparency.

Preserve Transparency

Exercise Type: Exploration

Purpose: To show how Preserve Transparency and Load Transparency combine and interact.

Starter File: Circle.Psd

Environment: Nothing special.

Do:

1. Open the starter file. It contains a single blue feathered circle on a layer.

2. Duplicate the image (Image → Duplicate → OK).

3. Select magenta as your Foreground color (RGB 255, 0, 240).

4. Fill the area (Mac: OPTION+DELETE, Windows: ALT+DELETE). *Whoops!* The entire layer filled with magenta. Undo (Mac: ⌘+Z, Windows: CTRL+Z).

5. Check the Preserve Transparency box in the Layers palette. Fill the area (Mac: OPTION+DELETE, Windows: ALT+DELETE). What happens?

6. Click on the original image. Duplicate the image (Image → Duplicate → OK). Make sure that Preserve Transparency is *off*. Select the nontransparent layer pixels (Mac: ⌘+click, Windows: CTRL+click on the Layer name in the Layers palette). Fill the area (Mac: OPTION+DELETE, Windows: ALT+DELETE). What happens?

7. Click on the original image. Duplicate the image (Image → Duplicate → OK). Turn Preserve Transparency *on*. Select the nontransparent layer pixels (Mac: ⌘+click, Windows: CTRL+click on the Layer name in the Layers palette). Fill the area (Mac: OPTION+DELETE, Windows: ALT+DELETE). What happens?

Solution Files: EX03-03A.Psd, EX03-03B.Psd, and EX03-03C.Psd

Result: The image with Preserve Transparency *on* and no selection simply exchanges one color for the other. There is no blue in the image after it is filled.

When Preserve Transparency is *off* and the transparency is loaded, the blue is only partially replaced at the time the image is filled with magenta, but there is more magenta then blue.

When both Preserve Transparency and Load Transparency are turned on, much more blue is left in the filled circle.

Discussion: Preserve Transparency keeps the level of transparency in the pixel the same regardless of what color is used as a fill color.

When a selection that is made by transparency is filled with a color, the new color overlays a portion of the original one. This adds to the Opacity of the pixel. If an area that is 50% transparent is 50% selected and filled, then it gains another 25% Opacity (50% of 50% is 25%. Added to 50% it becomes 75% opaque).

However, when both Preserve Transparency and Load Transparency are used, the area has to keep the same Opacity regardless, and cannot change as much.

Filling with neutral color

Exercise Type: Just for Fun

Purpose: To show how the combination of Apply mode and filter can change an image.

Starter File: Marina.Psd

Environment: The Layers palette must be visible (Window → Palettes → Show Layers).

Do:

1. Open the starter file. Notice it has two hidden layers. Leave them hidden for now.

2. Create a new layer by clicking on the New Layer icon at the lower-left of the Layers palette. In the dialog box, set the Apply mode to Overlay and click in the box that says Fill with Overlay-neutral color (50% gray). Click OK.

3. Add a Lens Flare to the image (Filter → Render → Lends Flare, 128% Brightness, 105mm prime). Drag the center of the flare to the center of the upper-right quarter of the image. Click OK. The image gets a little bit brighter and picks up a set of circles in the lower-left section.

4. Click off the Eye icon to hide the layer, and turn on Layer 1. This is mostly the same Lens Flare as you created, but it is using Hard Light mode. Change the Apply mode to cycle through the various Options, and see how that affects the image. Return the layer to Hard Light mode. Hide the layer.

5. Turn on Layer 3—OPTION+click (Mac) or ALT+click (Windows)—on the Eye icon by the Layer name. This turns the other layers off at the same time. This image looks almost identical to the original image. It is—but not quite. It has been slightly sharpened and some of the pixels are different. How different? Turn on the Background layer by clicking on its Eye icon. As you do so, notice that Layer 2 is set to Difference mode. This view of the image shows you the difference between them (and creates a somewhat mysterious, attractive image as well). You can get another attractive image by duplicating the image (Image → Duplicate, Merged Layers only → OK).

6. In the new image, select the Auto Levels command (Image → Adjust → Auto Levels). This process of using Difference Apply mode on two closely related images is called *Difference Painting.*

7. To see what effect lighting the scene will have, return to the original image and turn on Layer 1. It makes a big difference.

Solution Files: EX03-04A.Psd, EX03-04B.Psd, and EX03-04C.Psd

Result: EX03-04A.Psd shows the unlit Difference Apply mode.
EX03-04B.Psd shows the Difference Apply with Auto Levels applied.
EX03-04C.Psd shows the lit Difference Apply mode.

Discussion: By choosing to apply a Lens Flare to an empty layer (one filled with a neutral color), you can keep your original image untouched. The neutral color allows you to "see through" the layer, almost as if the filter were applied to a totally blank layer.

This exercise also shows that some of the effects of the Difference Apply mode—when used with two very similar images—can be spectacular. This is a very easy special effect. Two similar images typically produce a very dark "Difference" image—as you would expect since two identical images produce a totally black image. Auto Levels can lighten and dramatically change the result when used on the flattened image.

Exercise 5

Embossing using Layers

Exercise Type: Just for Fun

Purpose: In the apply Image section of the lesson, you used an image called `Lifeboss.Psd`. This image looks like an embossed version of the text in the `Life.Psd` image. It is. In this exercise, you learn how to create this embossed effect using Layers.

Starter File: `Life.Psd`

Environment: Nothing special.

Do:

1. Open the starter file. This time, notice both layers are visible. Duplicate the image (Image → Duplicate, Merged Layers only → OK). If you forgot to merge the layers in the duplicate, flatten the image now.

2. Drag the icon for the Background Layer to the New Layer icon at the lower-left of the Layers palette. This will copy the Background Layer into a new layer.

3. Invert the top layer (Mac: ⌘+Ⅰ, Windows: CTRL+Ⅰ).

4. Set the opacity to 50%. What happened to the image? Why is it a totally neutral gray?

5. Select the Move tool (Ⓜ). Using the arrow keys, press ⬆ twice and ⬅ twice. Now the image looks embossed.

6. To see how the image would look with a softer edge, open the Gaussian Blur filter dialog (Filter → Blur → Gaussian Blur). Start with a value of 2 and slowly move the slider in stages up to 9 pixels. Click on Cancel to exit without doing anything.

7. Make the bottom layer active and try the Gaussian Blur dialog again. Do not really apply the filter.

8. Apply a Gaussian Blur filter of 3 to both layers (one at a time).

Solution Files: `EX03-05A.Psd` and `EX03-05B.Psd`

Result: Your image should be identical to the one in the solution file.

Discussion: The embossing technique works nicely and gives you different control over the results than you have with the Emboss filter. This trick owes its origin to a tip posted by Kai Krause, one of the first masters of Photoshop, on America Online.

This works because any pixel that is inverted and mixes 50-50 with the original will cancel out to neutral gray. Mathematically, picture the following: Pick a number from 1 to 100. Subtract it from 100. Add this remainder to the original number and divide by 2. No matter what number you started with, you have to end up with 50.

When you move the layers out of alignment with one another, you reveal the black or white edges of the original. This produces the embossed look. If the image has hard edges, the embossing will look hard. If both images are blurred using the Gaussian Blur filter, then the embossing is much softer.

If you enjoy this use of layers and channels for special effects, *Photoshop 3.0 Special Effects How-To* covers these topics in minute detail.

Drop shadows using Channel Operations

Exercise Type: Practice

Purpose: This exercise shows how to create a drop shadow for an object that is against a background in a flat image. This technique, like most of those dealing with Channel Operations, is the brainchild of the remarkable Kai Krause. You can download all of Kai's tips from a variety of online locations—the MetaTools forums on CompuServe and AOL, the Photoshop forum on CompuServe, and the MetaTools World Wide Web page (`http//www.metatools.com`). This gives you more practice using the Calculations and Apply Image commands.

Starter File: `Candycup.Psd`

Environment: The Channels palette must be open (Window → Palettes → Show Channels)

Do:

1. Open the starter file. The file already contains a Channel 4 with the proper selection in it. If it did not, then your first step would be to create a selection in the shape of the object that you wish to shadow.

2. Drag Channel 4 to the New Channel icon in the bottom of the Channels palette (it is the icon that looks like a square with its corner bent). This duplicates the channel.

3. Apply a Gaussian Blur of 7 to the channel (Filter → Blur → Gaussian Blur, Radius: 7).

4. Offset the channel by 5 pixels to the right and 7 pixels down (Filter → Other → Offset, 5 pixels right, 7 pixels down). Click OK.

5. Open the Calculations dialog (Image → Calculations). Source 1 is Channel 4. Source 2 is Channel 4 Copy. The Blending mode is Subtract. Send the result to a new channel (Channel 6).

6. Duplicate Channel 6 by dragging it onto the New Channel icon. It will be named Channel 6 Copy. Invert the channel (Mac: ⌘+⎌, Windows: CTRL+⎌. This is your Shadow Multiplier.

7. Return to the RGB channel of the image (Mac: ⌘+0, Windows: CTRL+0).

8. Open the Apply Image dialog. Use Channel 6 Copy in Multiply mode at 100%. Your drop shadow appears.

Solution File: EX03-06.Psd

Result: Your result should be channel-for-channel identical to the solution file.

Discussion: Most of the steps should be self-explanatory at this point. The blurring and offsetting of the drop shadow channel is similar to the actions you performed when you made the drop shadow using layers.

The only tricky part is creating the channel to multiply with the image. The way to make this produce the right image is to use the Calculations Command and subtract the blurred shadow from the original channel. This is similar to the work you did interactively in Chapter 2 with adding images to a single selection channel. In this case, you are removing the original selection from the final shadow selection. You need to "cut" the original channel out of the shadow channel so that the object in your original RGB image is not altered.

The Subtraction command produces an image that is the reverse of the one you want, however. You need to have a mostly white image to multiply with only the drop shadow in black. Therefore, inverting the result of the Calculations command gives you a channel that can easily be multiplied with the original RGB channel using Apply Image. The Calculations command cannot be used as it only works in grayscale.

 **7**

More practice with Layers, Apply modes, and calculations

Exercise Type: Exploration/Practice

Purpose: This exercise shows you another way to create shadow multipliers—one that can be used in layers to add dimension to a totally solid background image.

Starter File: `Multiply.Psd`

Environment: Layers and Channels palettes should be visible.

Do:

1. Open the starter file. It is a grayscale image with two channels.

2. Open the Calculations dialog. Source 1 is the Black channel and Source 2 is Channel 2. Subtract is the Blending mode at 100%. Put the result into a new channel. This gives a very complex image.

3. Set your Foreground color to neutral 50% gray (RGB: 128, 128, 128).

4. Drag Channel 3 to the New Channel icon in the bottom of the Channels palette (it is the icon that looks like a square with its corner bent). This duplicates the channel.

5. You want to change all the pixels that are darker than 50% black to solid black. This will give you a highlight multiplier. Open the Levels dialog (Mac: ⌘+L, Windows: CTRL+L). At the right side of the dialog towards the bottom are three eyedroppers. Click on the left eyedropper (it has a black tube). Now, click on the 50% foreground swatch in the toolbar. All of your darker shades turn black. Click OK to exit the Levels dialog.

6. Double-click on the name Channel 3 Copy in the Channels palette. In the dialog, change the name to Highlight.

7. Drag Channel 3 (the "complex" channel) to the New Channel icon in the center bottom of the Channels palette (it is the icon that looks like a square with its corner bent). This duplicates the channel (again).

8. This time, you want to turn all of the lighter shades white. Open the Levels dialog (Mac: ⌘+L, Windows: CTRL+L). Click on the right eyedropper (it has a white tube). Now, click on the 50% foreground swatch in the toolbar. All of your lighter shades turn white. Click OK to exit the Levels dialog.

9. Double-click on the name Channel 3 Copy in the Channels palette. In the dialog, change the name to Shadow.

10. Create a new document (Mac: ⌘+N, Windows: CTRL+N). Pull down the Window menu to select a file the same size as Multiply.Psd. Change the Mode to RGB.

11. Change your Foreground color to red (RGB 255, 0, 0). Fill the area (Mac: OPTION+DELETE, Windows: ALT+DELETE).

12. Make a new layer (OPTION+ or ALT+click on the New Layer icon at the bottom of the Layers palette). In the dialog box, choose Multiply Layer and fill with neutral color. Use the Add Noise filter (Filter → Noise → Add Noise, Gaussian, 52, do not check Monochromatic). Set the Layer Opacity to 68%.

13. Make a new layer (click on the New Layer icon at the bottom of the Layers palette). This time, it is OK to create a totally transparent layer.

14. Open the Apply Image dialog. Select Multiply as the Source and Shadow as the Channel. Blending mode is Normal, 100%. Click OK.

15. Set the Layer Apply mode to Multiply and the Opacity to 65%.

16. Make a new layer (click on the New Layer icon at the bottom of the Layers palette).

17. Open the Apply Image dialog. Select Multiply as the Source and Highlight as the Channel. Blending mode is Normal, 100%. Click OK.

18. Set the Layer Apply mode to Screen and the Opacity to 69%. Your image now has dimension and depth but it is totally artificial—created through the skillful use of Layers, Channels, and Apply modes.

Solution File: EX03-07A.Psd and EX03-07B.Psd

Result: Your results should be nearly identical to the two solution files.

Discussion: The technique of using one grayscale image for highlights and another one for shadows gives you a high degree of flexibility in controlling the final image. Contrast the exercise above to simply multiplying Channel 3 of the Multiply image with the red background. It looks good at about 76% Opacity, but the look is totally different from the one you produced in the exercise above. It is much softer—which in some cases is just what you want. However, you should have a variety of techniques at your disposal.

Gradient compositing

Exercise Type: Exploration/Practice

Purpose: To show how Gradients can be used in a Layer Mask.

Starter File: Japan.Psd

Environment: The Layers palette must be visible.

Do:

1. Open the Japan.Psd file. Notice that there are two Layers in this image already—just for your convenience.

2. Press D to set the colors back to the black and white default.

3. Double-click on the Gradient tool. Set the Apply mode to Normal, the Opacity to 100%, the Gradient to Foreground to Background, the Type to Linear, and check the Dither box and the Mask box.

4. Create a Layer Mask (click on the Add Layer Mask icon—the left icon at the bottom of the Layers palette).

5. Drag the Gradient tool from the upper-right corner of the image to the lower-left corner. You are working in the Layer Mask, so the Gradient only changes that which is visible—not the actual image data.

6. Try other Gradients: Drag from the bottom of the image in a straight line to the top. Try dragging in many other directions. Each Gradient overwrites the previous one, so you do not need to undo or "wipe clean" the Layer Mask.

7. Try dragging the Gradient end points only short distances rather than from one end of the image to the other. This keeps more areas of solid black or white.

8. Try some radial Gradients.

Solution Files: EX03-08A.Psd, EX03-08B.Psd, and EX03-08C.Psd

Result: Some of your results should resemble the ones in the three solution files. EX03-08A.Psd has a linear Gradient dragged from the upper-right to lower-left corner. EX03-08B.Psd has a linear Gradient dragged from the bottom of the image to the top. EX03-08C.Psd has a radial Gradient dragged from over the center of the location of the teacher's face in the bottom layer out about two inches.

Discussion: A Gradient-controlled Layer Mask is very simple and effective as a means of seamlessly compositing two images together. The variations are endless. If you have the Kai's Power Tools filters, you can create very wild Gradients to use as Layer Masks.

CHAPTER 4

Applying a one-step filter

Exercise Type: Practice

Purpose: The Find Edges filter is a one-step filter, but it can give you unique results.

Starter File: Costume.Psd

Environment: Nothing special.

Do:

1. Open the starter file.
2. Apply the Find Edges filter (Filter → Stylize → Find Edges).
3. Invert the image (Mac: ⌘+Ⓘ, Windows: CTRL+Ⓘ).

Solution File: EX04-01.Psd

Result: Open the solution file and check your results. The images should be identical.

Discussion: One-step filters have no controls. You cannot specify anything about their performance except to select the filter itself. Using a one-step filter is like putting a nickel in a gumball machine that only has red gumballs. Every time you put in a nickel, you get a red gumball. There is no variation. The Find Edges filter will look different if it is applied to two different images because the image itself is different. However, if you applied the Find Edges filter to 1,000 copies of the same file, all of the results would be identical.

Applying a parameter filter

Exercise Type: Practice/Exploration

Purpose: This technique creates a woodcut look on an image. It is a fun technique to use on many different types of images.

Starter File: `Costume.Psd`

Environment: Nothing special.

Do:

1. Open the starter file. Duplicate it (Image → Duplicate).

2. Drag the icon for the Background layer to the New Layer icon (the center icon at the bottom of the Layers palette).

3. Apply the Dust&Scratches filter to the Background Layer (check to make sure that it is the selected layer). Use a Radius of 16 and a Threshold of 1.

4. Make the top layer the active layer (click on it in the Layers palette).

5. Change the Layer Apply Mode to Multiply.

6. Apply the High Pass filter with a setting of 1.6.

7. Open the Threshold command dialog (Image → Adjust → Threshold). Drag the slider to the left until you leave just a bit of black outlines on the image (on the example, this was Level 127).

Solution File: `EX04-02.Psd`

Result: Open the solution file and check your results. The images should be nearly identical.

Discussion: This exercise shows how you can combine filters and layers to create a stylized image. The Dust&Scratches filter smoothed the values in the image so the image detail was lost. Try the Dust&Scratches filter at less drastic settings to see how it can be used to remove imperfections in the image. In addition, applying the High Pass filter to the next layer at such a low amount lessened the contrast of the image everywhere except at the edges of color, so applying the Threshold command immediately afterward allowed more edge detail to be found.

Filtering selections using the Fade Filter command

Exercise Type: Practice/Exploration

Purpose: To experiment with using the Fade Filter command after applying a filter.

Starter File: CrabText.Psd

Environment: Nothing special.

Do:

1. Open the starter file and duplicate it (Image → Duplicate).

2. Apply the Diffuse filter (Filter → Stylize → Diffuse, Normal) to the image 15 times (Remember—press ⌘+F or CTRL+F to reapply the same filter). Apply the Diffuse filter (Lighter) to the file three times (Mac: OPTION+⌘+F, Windows: ALT+CTRL+F). Then apply the Diffuse filter to the image two times in Darker mode.

4. Load Channel 4 (Mac: OPTION+⌘+4; Windows: ALT+CTRL+4).

5. Apply the Crystallize filter to the image (Filter → Pixellate → Crystallize, 14).

6. Fade the filter (Mac: SHIFT+⌘+F, Windows: SHIFT+CTRL+F). Change the Apply mode on the Fade to Multiply and the Opacity to 80%.

7. Load the Blue channel (Mac: OPTION+⌘+3, Windows: ALT+CTRL+3).

8. Apply the Sumi-e filter (Filter → Brush Strokes →Sumi-e) at whatever settings you like. Fade the filter to 30%.

9. Load the Green channel (Mac: OPTION+⌘+2, Windows: ALT+CTRL+2).

10. Apply the Pointillist filter (Filter → Pixelate → Pointillist) at whatever settings you like. Fade the filter to 77% and change the filter Apply mode to Hard Light.

11. Load the Red channel (Mac: OPTION+⌘+1, Windows: ALT+CTRL+1).

12. Select a purple from the image as your Foreground color.

13. Apply the Clouds Filter (Filter → Render → Clouds) twice. On the second application, Fade the filter to 66% and change the Filter Apply mode to Hard Light.

14. Load Channel 4 (Mac: OPTION + ⌘ + 4 ; Windows: ALT + CTRL + 4) again.

15. Apply the Emboss filter (Filter → Stylize → Emboss) at whatever settings you prefer.

16. Fade the filter to Multiply mode at 80%.

Solution File: EX04-03A.Psd

Result: Open the solution file and check your results. You should obtain results similar though not identical to the solution.

Discussion: This exercise shows how you can filter using the Fade Filter command to change the result that you obtain.

EXERCISE 3B

Filtering in Layers

Exercise Type: Practice/Exploration

Purpose: To experiment with filtering in layers.

Starter File: CrabText.Psd

Environment: Nothing special.

Do: Open the starter file in Photoshop, duplicate it (Image → Duplicate). Repeat Exercise 3A until you reach Step 3. After you load Channel 4, float the selection (Mac: ⌘ + J , Windows: CTRL + J). Apply the filter to the resulting layer. Continue to follow the instructions in Exercise 3A, but click on the Background Layer to make it active before you load each subsequent selection, and float the selection before you filter it. Do not merge the layers. When you are done, experiment with changing opacities, apply modes and stacking orders for the layers.

Solution File: EX04-03B.Psd

Result: Open the solution file and check your results. You should obtain results similar though not identical to the solution.

Discussion: This exercise shows how you can filter within layers. By filtering within a layer, you keep your options open to change and rearrange your final output.

Making a filter effect your own

Exercise Type: Practice/Exploration

Purpose: To practice creating custom effects.

Starter File: Rudolph.Psd

Environment: Nothing special.

Do:

1. Open the starter file and duplicate it (Image → Duplicate → OK).

2. Drag the icon for the Background Layer to the New Layer icon (the center icon at the bottom of the Layers palette)

3. Apply the Colored Pencil filter to the image (Filter → Artistic → Colored Pencil). Make sure that your Background color is white and the Paper Brightness is at the maximum of 50%. Change the other settings however you wish.

4. Duplicate either the original or an already filtered layer and continue to apply filters or effects. Change the Apply modes and opacities to blend the effect back into the other layers. You can apply a filter to a selection made from one channel (the Red channel works well here). Play until you like what you have done. Make the filters your own.

Solution File: EX04-04.Psd

Result: Open the solution file. Your results should be completely different. The layer names and the apply modes/opacities should let you see what was done.

Discussion: When you use a distinctive filter, you do not have to accept the results of that filter. An image that leaves the viewer wondering, "How was that done?" is usually much more effective than one in which the viewer says, "Oh, I can see the Mosaic filter and the Crystallize filter and…." You see how you can take filter output and customize it.

More filter play

Exercise Type: Practice/Exploration/Just for Fun

Purpose: To practice creating custom effects.

Starter Files: Flowers.Psd (two images from the *KPT Power Photos IV* collection) and Edge197.Psd from *Auto F/X Photo/Edges Volume III*.

Environment: Nothing special.

Do:

1. Open the starter files and duplicate the Flowers.Psd image (Image → Duplicate → OK).

2. Select the Background Layer as your active layer.

3. Apply the Mosaic filter (Filter → Pixelate → Mosaic, 8) at 8 pixels per square.

4. Apply the Find Edges filter (Filter → Stylize → Find Edges).

5. Fade the filter (Mac: SHIFT + ⌘ + F, Windows: SHIFT + CTRL + F). Change the Opacity to 90% and the Filter Apply mode to Difference.

6. Click on the top-layer name in the Layers palette to make it active.

7. Apply the Mosaic filter (Filter → Pixelate → Mosaic, 6) at 6 pixels per square.

8. Apply the Find Edges filter (Filter → Stylize → Find Edges).

9. Invert the image (Mac: ⌘ + I, Windows: CTRL + I).

10. Select a deep red from the image as your Foreground color.

11. Drag the icon for Layer 1 (the tulip) to the New Layer icon (the center icon at the bottom of the Layers palette). Drag it below Layer 1 in the Layer stack (Mac: SHIFT + ⌘ + [, Windows: SHIFT + CTRL + [).

12. Fill the Shadow Layer with Preserve Transparency (Mac: SHIFT + OPTION + DELETE, Windows: SHIFT + ALT + DELETE). Change the Apply Mode to Multiply (this will allow the shadow color to softly darken the image). Change the Opacity to about 86%.

13. Drag the shadow—press ⌘ (Mac) or CTRL (Windows) for the Move tool—to the right and up a bit.

14. Open the Gaussian Blur filter. A radius of 10.0 pixels will work here. Click OK.

15. Now, to get rid of the boring straight edges in the image, you will apply an edge effect from the *Photo/Graphic Edges* collection by Auto F/X. To do that, you need to increase the canvas size, but you need to "float" the Background Layer first. Double-click on the Background Layer name in the Layers palette to change it to Layer 0.

16. Make a new Background Layer—press OPTION (Mac) or ALT (Windows) and click on the New Layer icon at the bottom of the Layers palette. In the dialog, select Background as the new Layer type.

17. Press D to set the colors back to the black and white default.

18. Increase the Canvas Size (Image → Canvas Size) by 150 pixels in both width and height (929×817). Anchor in the middle. Notice the bottom of the tulip is no longer at the same edge as your image. That is fine—the tulip's bottom was previously hidden by the image's size.

19. Click on Layer 0 to make it active.

20. Load the Inset channel from the Edge197.Psd document (Select → Load Selection, Document: Edge197.Psd, Channel: Inset 1, Invert). Make sure you check Invert so the selection is around the edges of the image. Press DELETE.

21. Make a new layer (click on the New Layer icon at the bottom of the Layers palette). Drag it beneath Layer 0.

22. Pick a light-but-vibrant yellow-green from the image (look on the underside of the bent leaf) as your Foreground color.

23. Load the Outset channel from the Edge197.Psd document (Select → Load Selection, Document: Edge197.Psd, Channel: Outset 1). Do *not* check Invert this time. Fill the area (Mac: OPTION+DELETE, Windows: ALT+DELETE).

24. Drag the icon for the Outset layer to the New Layer icon (the center icon at the bottom of the Layers palette), and create a drop shadow for the frame using this layer. Select black as your Foreground color, use an 18 pixel Gaussian Blur, and make the transparency 50% on the shadow.

Solution File: EX04-05.Psd

Result: Open the solution file. You should obtain results that are very close.

Discussion: The Find Edges filter creates a very colorful, square grid when used on a Mosaic filtered image. This exercise showed you some ways to control that and also introduced you to the joys of edges that are not flat and even. Often an artistic presentation is greatly enhanced by an edge treatment, and they are very easy to apply.

CHAPTER 5

Contrast and levels adjustment on paper textures

Exercise Type: Exploration

Purpose: To show how changing the relationship between light and dark values in a paper texture changes the nature of the texture produced.

Starter File: `Rafting.Psd`

Environment: Nothing special.

Do:

1. Open the starter file. There is an image in the RGB channel and four textures in additional Alpha channels. Duplicate the image (Image → Duplicate → OK). *Do not close the original.*

2. Use the Fixed Size Rectangular Marquee (set it to 247×240 pixels). Drag the Marquee into the image and change the values of the pixels in the selection. Some possible ways are to

   ● Use the Auto Levels command (Image → Adjust → Auto Levels).

   ● Invert the selection (Mac: ⌘+Ⓘ, Windows: CTRL+Ⓘ).

   ● Use the Levels command (Mac: ⌘+Ⓛ, Windows: CTRL+Ⓛ) to move the white point, the black point, the Gamma point, and/or the black-and-white output levels.

   ● Try the Curves command (Mac: ⌘+Ⓜ, Windows: CTRL+Ⓜ) and either draw arbitrary curves with the Pencil or change any of the tonal ranges by moving points on the curve up or down.

3. When you are done manipulating the textures, load the changed texture channel by dragging it onto the Load Channel icon at the lower left of the Channels palette.

4. Click on the RGB channel to make it active and press DELETE. Deselect (Mac: ⌘+Ⓓ, Windows: CTRL+Ⓓ).

Solution File: EX05-01.Psd

Result: The solution file shows one set of possible outcomes. Look at the Channels palette in it. The last channel has a key as to how the texture was changed from the original (the one on the upper left).

Discussion: There are an infinite number of possibilities for changing a single paper texture. When you add to that all of the possible paper textures, it is a staggering number of combinations.

There are two ways to apply the paper texture to the already-created image (such as the photograph by Ed Scott, which is included in the starter file). The method used in the solution was to load the texture channel and delete. This removes color from the image based on how much white or light values were in the texture. Areas where the texture was lightest show the most removal of color. Why? White or light areas are the most selected; dark or black areas are the least selected, and therefore, the least changed.

The other way to add the texture is to copy the original image to the clipboard. Then, load the texture channel and use the Paste Into command (Edit → Paste Into). To do this, there should be no image in the RGB channel at the start. This produces the opposite type of texture from the first method. The areas of the texture channel that are darkest end up with the lightest amount of the pasted image. Since they are the "least selected" areas, they receive the least amount of the new image.

You can strengthen the amount of the texture effect by repeating either of the two methods. If you Paste Into a second time, you will strengthen and deepen the colors in the image.

EXERCISE 2

Weaving a texture

Exercise Type: Just for Fun

Purpose: To show how to create a woven pattern that can be used for a paper texture. The first part of the directions (that show how to create a woven pattern) are taken from the book *Photoshop 3.0 Special Effects How-To*.

Starter File: Rural.Psd (to use late in the process)

Environment: You need to change the Interpolation method to Nearest Neighbor. Remember to set it back to Bicubic when you are done.

Do:

Create the Warp (Vertical Threads)

1. Create a new document (File → New → Name: *Tartan,* Width: 22 pixels, Height: 1 pixel, Resolution: 72, Mode: RGB Color, Contents: White).

2. Enlarge the view of the image as far as it will enlarge ([OPTION]+[⌘]+Spacebar+[+]), or drag the Navigator palette slider all the way to the right).

3. Make sure the Color palette is available as a fast way to select colors (Window → Show Color). Press [D] to get the black and white default, and then move the Red slider as far right as possible. This will pick a pure red as Color 1.

4. Select the Pencil tool ([Y]). Choose the smallest (1-pixel) brush (press [[until the brush size goes no smaller or use the Brush palette to select). Press [RETURN] to look at the Pencil Options. Make sure Apply mode is set to Normal and Opacity is 100%. Fade should be set *off.*

5. Click six times from the left edge of the image to fill the first six pixels with red.

6. Press [D] for default colors, and color the next four pixels black.

7. Move the Green slider in the Color palette as far to the right as it will go. Leave the next two pixels in your image white, and fill the next six pixels with green (six clicks of the Pencil).

8. Press [D] for default colors again, and make the next two pixels black.

9. Finally, choose a gold as your last color (R: 145, G: 133, B: 0). Make the remaining two pixels gold.

10. This is the complete pattern for the warp. You could select it as a pattern at this point and use it to fill another image. However, there is an easy and non-obvious way to get a stripe you may not have seen, so let's do it that way first. Change the Interpolation method (File → Preferences → General Preferences → Interpolation → Nearest Neighbor).

11. Increase the size of your document (Image → Image Size). Uncheck Constrain Proportions and then set the height to 22 pixels. You are making an even plaid, and the warp repeat is 22 threads (or pixels). Click OK. Your top stripe has almost magically repeated itself along the length of the image.

Create the Weft (Horizontal Threads)

12. Double-click on the icon for the Background Layer and change the layer name to Warp.

13. Drag the icon for the Warp Layer to the New Layer icon at the lower left of the Layers palette. This will copy the Warp Layer into a new layer. Double-click on the Warp Copy Layer and change its name to Weft.

14. Rotate the Weft Layer 90 degrees clockwise (Layer → Transform → Rotate 90 degrees CW).

Create the Pattern

15. Create a new document (File → New → Name: *Weave1*, Width: 2 pixels, Height: 2 pixels, Resolution: 72%, Mode: Bitmap, Contents: White). Magnify the image as far as it will go (double-click on the Hand tool).

16. The patterns are very small, so you need to be able to see each pixel as you work on it. Set your colors to black and white ($\boxed{\text{D}}$). Select the Pencil tool ($\boxed{\text{Y}}$) with a 1-pixel wide brush.

17. Draw a dot in the upper-left corner of the document. Draw another dot in the lower-right corner.

18. Select the entire image (Mac: $\boxed{\text{⌘}}$+$\boxed{\text{A}}$, Windows: $\boxed{\text{CTRL}}$+$\boxed{\text{A}}$). Define this as a pattern (Edit → Define Pattern).

Make the Weave

19. Click on Tartan to select it. Create a Layer Mask (click on the Add Layer Mask icon—the leftmost icon at the bottom of the Layers palette).

20. The Layer Mask is active and selected. Fill it with the weave pattern ($\boxed{\text{SHIFT}}$+$\boxed{\text{DELETE}}$ → Pattern, 100% Opacity, Normal). The result: instant Tartan plaid.

21. Click on the Weft icon so that it, rather than the Layer Mask, is now active.

Now that you have a woven pattern tile, here's how to use it as a texture:

22. Select the entire woven image (Mac: $\boxed{\text{⌘}}$+$\boxed{\text{A}}$, Windows: $\boxed{\text{CTRL}}$+$\boxed{\text{A}}$). Define this as a pattern (Edit →Define Pattern).

23. Open the starter file (Rural.Psd).

24. Click on the New Channel icon in the Channels palette to create a new channel. This will be Channel 4.

25. Fill the new channel with the pattern ($\boxed{\text{SHIFT}}$+$\boxed{\text{DELETE}}$ → Pattern, 100% Opacity, Normal).

26. Emboss the pattern (Filter → Stylize → Emboss, Angle: 45, Height: 2, Amount: 60%).

27. Apply a Gaussian Blur of 1.5 (Filter → Blur → Gaussian Blur, 1.5) to the embossed pattern.

28. Return to the RGB channel (Mac: ⌘+~, Windows: CTRL+~). Select the entire image (Mac: ⌘+A, Windows: CTRL+A). Cut the image to the clipboard (Mac: ⌘+X, Windows: CTRL+X).

29. Load Channel 4 (Mac: OPTION+⌘+4, Windows: ALT+CTRL+4).

30. Paste the cut image into the main image (Edit → Paste Into).

31. Repeat Steps 8 and 9 to give the image another "dose" of texture.

Solution Files: EX05-2a.Psd and EX05-2b.Psd

Result: Your results should be very similar to the example images. EX05-2a.Psd has the woven pattern, and EX05-2b.Psd contains the Rural image with the paper texture applied.

Discussion: You can vary the weave by the pattern you use in the Layer Mask. You can also vary the look of the final applied texture by varying the amount of the Gaussian Blur or of the Embossing filter. You can also try this using the woven pattern without any embossing or blurring. Of course, the warp and weft values and arrangement also have a major effect on the pattern.

One way to explore this effect is to repeat the entire exercise. This time, instead of planning your warp and weft colors, use the Add Noise filter at a high setting on the 22×1-pixel file. Do everything else the same. This actually makes a more satisfactory woven texture because the value changes with every pixel.

Creating seamless textures

Exercise Type: Practice

Purpose: To show how you can make a texture that is seamless using the Rubber Stamp tool.

Starter File: Marble.Psd

Environment: Rubber Stamp Tool Options: Normal Apply mode, 100% Opacity, Clone Aligned

Do:

1. Open the starter file.

2. Offset the image (Filter → Other → Offset, 87 pixels right, 94 pixels down, Wraparound). This measurement is one-half of the image width and height.

3. You see a sharp line in the center of the image that shows where the edges meet. At this point, the pattern would have an obvious seam. Select the Rubber Stamp tool (⑤).

4. Click with the modifier key pressed (Mac: OPTION, Windows: ALT) to select a starting point somewhat away from the seam. Paint over the seam with the Rubber Stamp. Keep moving the starting point for the tool by pressing the modifier key and clicking somewhere else. Do not change the pixels at the edges of the image.

5. When you think you have removed the seam, offset the image again (Mac: ⌘+F, Windows: CTRL+F to re-apply the last filter). If the image still looks seamless, you should be okay.

6. Define this as a pattern (Edit →Define Pattern).

7. Create a new document (File → New →, Width: 600 pixels, Height: 600 pixels, Resolution: 72%, Mode: RGB Color, Contents: White). Fill with pattern (SHIFT+DELETE → Pattern, 100% Opacity, Normal).

Solution File: EX05-03.Psd

Result: You should see no seams in your pattern.

Discussion: This exercise is very straightforward. The only skill needed in this is the use of the Rubber Stamp tool. As you select the areas to clone over the seam, try to make them blend with the areas nearby. Also, if you wish to create a texture where no part of the image pulls the eye, clone areas of the texture that are less obvious. If you clone spots or dark or light portions, you will create a pattern that shows the repeat almost as much as if you had left in the seams.

Using Lighting textures

Exercise Type: Exploration

Purpose: To show how you can combine the textures that come with Photoshop and the Lighting Filter to create paper textures.

Starter File: Monkey.Psd

Environment: Nothing special.

Do:

1. Open the starter file. Duplicate the image (Image → Duplicate → OK).

2. Drag the Monkey Light lighting style from the book's CD-ROM to the Lighting Styles folder/directory of your copy of Photoshop.

3. Click on the New Channel icon in the Channels palette to create a new channel. This will be Channel 4.

4. Apply the Texture Fill filter (Filter → Render → Texture fill). Select the Thick Hair texture that is located in the Textures for Lighting Filters folder that comes with Photoshop (or use the ThickH.Psd file in the Labstart folder on the book's CD-ROM).

5. Apply the Lighting filter (Filter → Render → Lighting). Choose the Monkey Light setting. Select Channel 4 as the texture channel and click *white is high*. The surface texture amount should be 50%. You can accept these settings or experiment as you wish. Click OK when you are satisfied.

6. Look at the image for a few moments and then Undo (Mac: ⌘+Z, Windows: CTRL+Z).

7. Drag the icon for the Background Layer to the New Layer icon in the Layers palette. This will copy the Background Layer into a new layer.

8. Reapply the Lighting filter (Mac: ⌘+OPTION+F, Windows: ALT+CTRL+F). This reopens the dialog so you can set the texture back to Channel 4 again. This time, you are filtering the layer. Now, you can play with the Layer Opacity and Apply modes until you get an effect you like.

Solution File: EX05-04.Psd

Result: Your image should look similar to the example.

Discussion: The starting image was so out of focus, it is almost merciful to add texture to the poor thing. It is always a good idea to apply the Lighting filter to a layer that is a copy of the original. This expands your options—including keeping open the option of tossing the entire channel if you really hate the effect!

Try the exercise a number of times using different lighting styles and different textures. Get a feel for how these fit together. Also try the exercise by creating a new Overlay Layer filled with neutral color over your original (rather than making a layer from a copy of the original).

Another thing to try is to take the Overlay Layer with the texture in it and use the Apply Image command to copy it to a channel. Now, use that channel as a paper texture as you did in Exercises 1 and 2.

EXERCISE 5

Colorizing an image

Exercise Type: Exploration

Purpose: To compare several methods of colorizing.

Starter File: `Iceflowr.Psd`

Environment: Nothing special.

Do:

1. Open the starter file. Duplicate the image (Image → Duplicate → OK). Leave the original open.

2. Select the Paintbrush tool (B). Change Apply mode to Multiply.

3. Drag a Rectangular Marquee around the picture of the flower. Desaturate (Image → Adjust → Desaturate). Hide the marching ants (Mac: ⌘+H, Windows: CTRL+H).

4. Use whichever brushes and brush sizes feel best to you to paint over the image. Pick up the colors from the color palette at the side of the image (remember, you can get the Eyedropper tool while you are using the Paintbrush by pressing the modifier key (Mac: OPTION, Windows: ALT).

5. When you are finished, activate the original image and duplicate it (Image → Duplicate → OK).

6. Repeat Steps 2–4 using Color mode in Paintbrush.

7. Finally, just to compare, use the directions from the "trick" method in Lesson 2 of this chapter to copy the image into a layer and add a Layer Mask. Manipulate the Layer Mask so the flower portion of the image is colorized against a grayscale background.

Solution Files: `EX05-5a.Psd`, `EX05-5b.Psd`, and `EX05-5c.Psd`

Result: Your results should be similar to the ones in the solution files. `EX05-5a.Psd` contains the image done in Multiply mode, `EX05-5b.Psd` has the image in Color mode, and `EX05-5c.Psd` has the two-layer image.

Discussion: There is no right or wrong as to whether Color mode or Multiply mode looks best. The result depends on the starting image and your artistic sensibility to the way in which the image needs to be colorized.

Using the Airbrush

Exercise Type: Practice

Purpose: To give you a more complex image to airbrush.

Starter Files: `Tulip.Psd` and `Template.Psd`

Environment: Nothing special.

Do:

1. Open the two starter files. The Template image has all of the needed paths and the palette for you to use. Look at the paths carefully. Perhaps, first open the solution file—which is still layered. If you are adventurous, do not use the enclosed template. Create your own. Make your own paths.

2. Create a new layer for each image element (each petal, the stem, and the stamen). Airbrush from the part of the flower that is farthest away to the closest.

3. To get the random dots, set the airbrush to Dissolve mode. Then use either the Gaussian Blur filter or the Blur tool to soften the specks of color. Paint the fine lines with a small brush and blur them when finished, as well.

Solution File: `EX05-06.Psd`

Result: Your result should look at least as good as the solution file.

Discussion: This exercise uses the same process that you learned in the chapter. It is simply a more complicated image. Even a complex image, however, becomes manageable when you have a method of working. Knowing how to organize your airbrushing project (and how to use a very light touch on the airbrush) makes all the difference.

Soft embossing

Exercise Type: Technique

Purpose: To show how you can create a soft, embossed look.

Starter File: Swirl.Psd

Environment: Nothing special.

Do:

1. Open the starter file. This contains the basic texture in the RGB Background Layer, and the word Swirl in a channel (the text is set in ITC Highlander Bold). Make sure you are in the RGB channel.

2. Make a new Layer (click on the New Layer icon at the bottom of the Layers palette).

3. Load Channel 4 (Mac: OPTION+⌘+4, Windows: ALT+CTRL+4).

4. Press D to set the colors back to the black and white default. Fill the area (Mac: OPTION+DELETE, Windows: ALT+DELETE).

5. Double-click on the Layer name to open the Layer Options dialog. Name this Layer Shadow.

6. Apply a 3.0 pixel Gaussian Blur (Filter → Blur → Gaussian Blur, 3.0).

7. Drag the icon for the Shadow Layer to the New Layer icon at the lower left of the Layers palette. This will copy the Shadow Layer into a new Layer. Click on the Preserve Transparency button.

8. Exchange Foreground and Background colors (X). Fill the area with white (Mac: OPTION+DELETE, Windows: ALT+DELETE). Turn the Preserve Transparency button *off*.

9. Double-click on the Layer name to open the Layer Options dialog. Name this layer Highlight.

10. Press the modifier key (Mac: ⌘, Windows: CTRL) and click on the Layer name to select the non-transparent pixels on the Highlight Layer.

11. Click on the Background Layer in the Layers palette to make it the current Layer.

12. Float the selection (Mac: ⌘+Ⓙ, Windows: ⒸⓉⓇⓁ+Ⓙ). This creates a new Layer. Name the layer Top Layer, and drag it to the top of the Layer stack.

13. Click on the Shadow channel to select it.

14. Offset the image (Filter → Other → Offset, 5 pixels right, 5 pixels down, Wraparound).

15. Click on the Highlight Layer to select it.

16. Offset the image (Filter → Other → Offset, –5 pixels right, –5 pixels down, Wraparound). The image is now softly embossed.

Solution File: EX05-07.Psd

Result: Your result should be the same as the solution file.

Discussion: The image embossing can be made softer or harder by changing the amount of the Gaussian Blur.

There is an almost inexhaustible number of ways to do embossing (in addition to the Emboss filter). The Alien Skin Black Box filters have a very good Outer Bevel filter that can create a sharper version of this effect very easily and also add the highlights as if the bevel were created in a 3D program. Extensis PhotoTools can do bevels and embossing, and Wild River SSK has an amazing range of effects. **EX05-07.Psd** shows the exercise done with some of the PhotoTools, Alien Skin, and Wild River filters. Just look at one layer at a time!

Photoshop 3.0 Special Effects How-To also has a number of different ways to achieve embossed effects.

CHAPTER 6

 EXERCISE 1

Exploring color modes

Exercise Type: Exploration

Purpose: To see how changing the color mode/color space of an image affects the editing you can do on it, the channels or layers you can add, and the way in which the color is displayed. The starter file is an impressionistic rendering by the author of a photograph. It contains deliberately saturated colors so that you can see how they react to changes in the image mode.

Starter File: Snowbird.Psd

Environment: Make sure your Printing Inks Setup uses the SWOP (Coated) profile.

Do:

1. Open the starter file. Make six duplicates of the image.

2. Change the duplicates so that you have one of each of the following image modes:
   CMYK
   Lab
   Indexed Color
   Duotone
   Grayscale
   Bitmap

2. For each of the files (including the original RGB) *try* to do the following:

3. Make a note of the size indicator in the image window information area.

4. Apply a filter (look at all the filters in the menu that are not grayed out).

5. Create a new Layer.

6. Use the Gradient and Blur tools on part of the image.

7. Use the Brush and Pencil tools on the image.

8. Select a color from the default System Palette Swatches.

9. Use the Curves command on the image.

10. Create a selection and save it to a channel.

11. Pull down the Image menu and see which commands can be used.

Solution File: None

Result: See discussion below.

Discussion: The RGB mode allows the most manipulation of an image. Some filters are not active in Grayscale or CMYK mode, and many filters will not work in Lab mode. No filters work on a Bitmap or Indexed Color image. You can add channels to files in every mode but bitmap, but you cannot add layers to an image that is in Bitmap or Indexed Color mode. Neither Lens Flare nor Lighting Effects will work on an image that is a duotone.

Borrowing a color table

Exercise Type: Just for Fun

Purpose: To see how you can change an image by using the color table from another image.

Starter Files: `Parkview.Psd`, `Cabbage.Psd`, `Cabbage2.Psd`

Environment: Nothing special.

Do:

1. Open the starter files.

2. Click on the `Cabbage.Psd` image and change it to Indexed Color (Image → Mode → Indexed Color → Adaptive, OK).

3. Save the Color Table (Image → Mode → Color Table → Save, `Cabbage.LUT`).

4. Click on the `Parkview.Psd` image. Duplicate the image (Image → Duplicate → OK).

5. Change it to Indexed Color (Image → Mode → Indexed Color → Previous). It now uses the colors of the Cabbage image.

6 Repeat Step 4. Change to Indexed Color mode again, but this time, use an Adaptive palette (i.e., the colors in the Parkview image).

7. Swap the color table (Image → Mode → Color Table → Load → `Cabbage.LUT`). A much different color set emerges. (This is `EX06-02B.Psd`).

8. Change the image back to RGB and apply a 2.0 Gaussian Blur filter.

9. Click on the `Cabbage2.Psd` image. Change it to Indexed Color using an Adaptive palette and save the Color Table in `Cabbage2.LUT`.

10. Repeat Steps 4–8 substituting the `Cabbage2.LUT` for the `Cabbage.LUT`.

11. Repeat Step 4. Using the Move tool, drag the blurred image with the Cabbage2 Color Table on top of this duplicate. Change the Apply mode to Luminosity and the Opacity to 75%. (This is the `EX06-02C.Psd` image).

12. Experiment with different Apply modes and opacities. You can also double-click on the Background Layer to make it into Layer 0 and then drag it on top of the other layer. Try the various modes and opacities again.

Solution File: EX06-02A.Psd, EX06-02B.Psd, and EX06-02C.Psd

Result: Your results should match.

Discussion: When you convert an image to Indexed Color mode using a Previous or a Custom palette, the program tries to find the closest match it can between the original colors in the image and the colors in the palette. If there are any greens in the palette, for example, the greens in your image will be mapped to those. That is why there was not much change the first time you converted the Parkview.Psd image to the Cabbbage.LUT.

The second time you performed the sequence—using Cabbbage2.LUT—there was a bit more change because the Color Table itself had many fewer types of colors in it. Cabbbage2.LUT contains mostly pinks and purples.

Your biggest changes occurred when you converted the image first to Indexed Color using the Adaptive method, which saved 256 of the original image colors and then switched Color Tables to either Cabbbage.LUT or Cabbbage2.LUT. This happened because once the image was in Indexed Color mode, a Color Table switch is linear. Old color 1 becomes new color 1 and so on. If red were color 1 in the Adaptive palette and you switched it for a palette that used Yellow as color 1, all of your reds from that "bucket" would become yellow.

You can get very moody images from the Palette Switch method. If you change the Indexed Color image back to RGB mode and apply a small Gaussian Blur, you improve the color range. You can then combine the image with the original in many different ways.

EXERCISE 3

Duotones using the CMYK channels

Exercise Type: Practice

Purpose: To try another example of changing a duotone image into a CMYK image and creating a Printing Ink Setup to preview it correctly.

Starter File: AmandaGS.Psd

Environment: Make sure your Printing Inks Setup uses the SWOP (Coated) profile to start and put it back when you are done.

Do:

1. Open the starter file. Duplicate the image (Image → Duplicate → OK).

2. Change the image to a duotone using the preset Blue 286 Bl 2.

3. Follow the procedure given in the chapter to change the duotone to Multichannel mode and from there to a CMYK image with black in the Cyan channel and Pantone 286 CV in the Magenta channel.

4. Create a Printing Ink Setup to preview the image in the correct colors.

Solution File: EX06-03.Psd

Result: Your result should match.

Discussion: When you open the Solution file, you need to also load the P286BL.INK file into the Printing Inks Setup, or you will not see the colors properly.

Exploring file sizes

Exercise Type: Exploration

Purpose: To see what you can save and how much room is occupied by saving images in various formats. The Starter image contains a layer with a Layer Mask and an extra channel.

Starter File: NewYear.Psd

Environment: Turn off Photoshop 2.5 compatibility in the General Preferences dialog.

Do:

1. Open the starter file.

2. Use the Save a Copy command on the File menu to save a copy of the image in Photoshop 3.0, Photoshop 2.0, EPS (Binary with 8-bit TIFF or PICT preview), TIFF (Uncompressed), PICT (uncompressed), PCX, JPEG (High), and Targa (32-bit) format. Take note of which formats allow you to save channels and which allow you to save layers. Notice you cannot save a CompuServe GIF file from this menu.

3. Look at all of the images you have saved. Get the actual file sizes of the images on disk.

Solution File: None

Result: Here are the file sizes from the author's system:

NewYear.Psd	2.9MB
NewYear2.Psd	1.5MB (Photoshop 2.0 format)
NewYear.PCX	1.2MB
NewYear.PCT	1.5MB
NewYear.TGA	1.5MB
NewYear.TIF	1.5MB
NewYear.EPS	1.9MB
NewYear.JPG	174K

Discussion: Your mileage will vary—files on your disks are likely to have different sizes than those listed here. However, the relative size should be the same. The Photoshop 3.0 file is the largest because it contains the channels and layers and Layer Mask. The JPEG image is the smallest since it tosses away image data. The PCX file is smaller than the PICT, TARGA, TIFF, or Photoshop 2.0 files since it cannot be stored with the extra channel that the other formats can hold. EPS cannot hold the extra channel either, but it is larger than any format except for the Layered Photoshop 3.0 image.

EXERCISE 5

Creating JPEG images

Exercise Type: Experiment

Purpose: To examine the damage caused by creating JPEG images at different quality settings.

Starter File: IceStorm.Psd

Environment: Nothing special.

Do:

1. Open the starter file. Make four copies of the image.

2. Save the duplicates as JPEG files so you have one of each of the following quality settings:
   Maximum
   High
   Medium
   Low

3. Open all the images and compare the damage both in the screen 1:1 representation and in a zoomed-in approach.

4. Also note the file sizes on the hard drive.

Solution File: None

Result: See discussion below.

Discussion: It is no surprise the images get less pleasing as you do more compression. The file sizes, as expected, get smaller. You can use the Difference command on various combinations of the images (as you learned to do in Chapter 1 to compare your results to the book's) to see exactly how different one compression level is from the other.

EXERCISE 6

Creating a GIF89a image

Exercise Type: Practice

Purpose: To make sure you understand how to create a GIF89a image. The Starter image is from *Kai's Power Photo II Collection, Volume VII, HotRods*.

Starter File: Hotrod.Psd

Environment: Nothing special.

Do:

1. Open the starter file. Make five duplicates of the image.

2. Convert three of the images to Indexed Color mode using the Adaptive palette.

3. Select one of the converted images and Export it as GIF89a. Select the Interlace Option and click on as many Background colors as needed to get rid of everything but the car. Save the image. (This is EX06-06A.GIF.)

4. Select another converted image. Export it to GIF89a but do not drop out the red shaded area behind the car.

5. Select the final converted image. Instead of selecting specific dropout colors, use the channel to produce the transparency. Export as GIF89a. (This is EX06-06B.GIF.)

6. Select one of the unconverted images. Double-click on the image to change the Background to Layer 0. Load the Alpha channel 4 (Mac: OPTION+⌘+4, Windows: ALT+CTRL+4), reverse the selection (Select → Inverse), and delete the selected area. Export as GIF89a.

7. Finally, load Channel 4 (Mac: OPTION+⌘+4, Windows: ALT+CTRL+4) in the last duplicate image. Reverse the selection (Select → Inverse). Fill the area (Mac: OPTION+DELETE, Windows: ALT+DELETE) with black. Now convert the image to Indexed Color mode and Export using Channel 4 to GIF89a format.

8. Reopen all five images and examine them. Decide which one you like best.

Solution File: EX06-06A.GIF and EX06-06B.GIF

Result: Your images should match.

Discussion: It's not surprising if you are unhappy with all five images. The Hotrod image used had too much black where the wheels are located to make a really successful "dropout." However, the **EX06-06A.GIF** is by far the *least* successful as it also dropped out half of the car. The channel looked smooth enough, but it became very choppy after it was converted to Indexed Color mode. However, using the mask for the dropout area was better than not using it. Chapter 13, "Beyond Photoshop," discusses the challenge of getting images ready for the Web in somewhat more detail.

CHAPTER 7

EXERCISE 1A

Learning about "good" color

Exercise Type: Exploration

Purpose: If you are going to be able to correct color that is not what it is supposed to be, you need to know what *good* colors look like. What is a "proper" value for magenta? For skin tones? This exercise lets you explore those values using a standard IT8 Target. This is a table of pre-built values of "known" quantity that is used to help calibrate your scanner, monitor, or printer. You can also explore the *Olé No Moiré* that comes as a separation source with Photoshop.

Starter Files: IT8.TIF and *Ole No Moire* (in the Goodies folder, Calibration/Separation Sources)

Environment: The Info palette needs to be set to RGB and CMYK color.

Do:

1. Open the two starter files.

2 Using the Info palette, read the values of the solid areas. Contrast the RGB and CMYK numbers. The IT8 target is a scanned photograph, so the values are less precise in the solid colors. Compare the Magenta ranges (column 14 on the IT8) with the "pure" magenta patch on the *Olé No Moiré* image.

3. Compare the values for cyan, magenta, and black as well.

4. Then look at the skin tones. For Caucasian skin tones, what seems to be the "normal" CMY balance?

Solution File: None

Result: If it helps you, you can make a chart of the RGB and CMYK comparisons.

Discussion: The IT8 target shows colors in columns 13–19 that are much less "pure" than *Olé No Moiré*. However, these are also normal photographic ranges for these colors. The flesh tones both on the small samples and on the model (and in *Olé No Moiré*) seem to indicate the CMYK values should be approximately even in the magenta and yellow and a bit more than half of the amount in cyan.

Correcting flesh tones

Exercise Type: Practice

Purpose: To use the knowledge gained from the previous exercise about flesh tone balance to correct an image.

Starter File: `Carolyn.Psd`

Environment: Nothing special.

Do:

1. Open the starter file. Duplicate the image (Image → Duplicate → OK).

2. Use the Curves command along with the Info palette to adjust the skintones (actually, the entire image) so that the balance of Magenta=Yellow=.5 Cyan is approximately maintained in the Yellow and Cyan channels with curves of at least 3–5 points.

Solution Files: EX07-1b.ACV and EX07-1b.Psd

Result: Your result should be fairly close to the solution files.

Discussion: This exercise did flesh tone correction "by the numbers." You did not look at whether the original was more pleasing to the eye, agreed more with the original photograph, or matched the person's actual skin tone better. You also ignored the fact that more magenta was introduced into the whites of Carolyn's eyes and into some of her hair. In this exercise, you only worried about the flesh tones. If you were correcting the entire image, you might have needed to make fewer corrections to ensure the neutrality of the eyes and hair.

EXERCISE 2A

Creating a 4-point lockdown curve

Exercise Type: Exploration

Purpose: To create curves as Locked points that can be used as starter curves.

Starter File: None

Environment: Nothing special.

Do:

1. Open an image—any image—or create a new file. You need an open file for this, but you are not going to change the file at all.

2. Open the Curves dialog (Mac: ⌘+M, Windows: CTRL+M).

3. Make sure the curve is set up so it is in Levels mode, and it has four divisions (if you are seeing 10 divisions, click on the grid with OPTION (Mac) or ALT (Windows) pressed).

4. In the Master channel, click on each of the three grid intersections to leave a point. Make sure the input and output points are the same. They should be at 64, 128, and 191 (as well as the original points at 0 and 255).

5. Make the same changes to the Red, Green, and Blue channels.

6. Save this curve as 4point.Acv.

Solution File: EX07-2A.ACV

Result: Your curve should be identical to the example.

Discussion: The only skill needed here is to make sure the input and output points are identical.

EXERCISE 2B

Creating a Transfer curve

Exercise Type: Practice

Purpose: It can be tedious to create a 10-point lockdown curve. It is also subject to hand-wobbling which can change the values you need. A more precise method of creating this lockdown curve is to take advantage of the fact that the Page Setup dialog can create a curve with values entered numerically that can be opened by the Curves command.

Starter File: None

Environment: Nothing special.

Do:

1. Open an image—any image—or create a new file. You need an open file for this, but you are not going to change the file at all.

2. Open the Page Setup dialog (ideally for the Laserwriter). There should be a Transfer Option. The Transfer Option shows 13 points—from 0–100 with 5% and 95% points as well.

3. Ignore the 5% and 95% boxes. Enter the matching number into each of the other boxes (10 into the 10% box, 20 into the 20% box, and so forth).

4. Save the Curve as Xfer.ACV.

Solution File: EX07-2b.ACV

Result: Your curve should be the same.

Discussion: The transfer curve will take care of the lockdown points for the Master channel, but will not create the individual channels for you.

EXERCISE 2C

Creating a 10-point lockdown curve

Exercise Type: Practice

Purpose: To create a locked curve with 10 points for future use.

Starter File: None

Environment: Nothing special.

Do:

1. Open an image—any image—or create a new file. You need an open file for this, but you are not going to change the file at all.

2. Open the Curves dialog (Mac: ⌘+M, Windows: CTRL+M).

3. Make sure the curve is set up so that it is in Levels mode, and it has 10 divisions (if you are seeing four divisions, click on the grid with OPTION or ALT pressed).

4. In the Master channel, load the Xfer.ACV curve. All of the points are locked.

5. In the Red channel, click on each of the nine grid intersections to leave a point. Make sure the input and output points are the same. They should be at 22, 56, 76, 102, 128, 153, 179, 203, 229 (as well as the original points at 0 and 255).

6. Make the same changes to the Green and Blue channels.

7. Save this curve as 10point.Acv.

Solution File: EX07-2C.Acv

Result: Your curve should be the same.

Discussion: This curve can be used as a starter curve for your own color corrections.

Using selections in Adjustment Layers

Exercise Type: Exploration/Practice

Purpose: To let you experiment with multiple layers and selections in an Adjustment Layer. For this, you will use the corrected BlueRoom image that was used earlier in the chapter.

Starter File: BlueRm2.Psd

Environment: Nothing special.

Do:

1. Open the starter file.

2. First, put a bit more saturation into the image as a whole. Create an Adjustment Layer (Mac: ⌘+click, Windows: CTRL+click on the New Layer icon at the bottom of the Layers palette).

3. Make it a Hue/Saturation Adjustment Layer, and set the Saturation slider on the Master to +29. Click OK.

4. Since this looks as if it is making the shadows too blue again, select the Paintbrush and paint with black over the bottom area of the table to remove this area from the color correction (you can paint over the legs as well). Remember, this is just like a Layer Mask in that it can be painted upon in black, white, and gray.

5. Change the Apply mode to Multiply, and drag the Opacity to 52%.

6. Load Channel 4 (Mac: OPTION+⌘+4, Windows: ALT+CTRL+4). This selects the oranges in the cornucopia on the table. They are very anemic-looking, so make them brighter.

7. First, you need to remove the oranges from the first correction or else they will get over-corrected. Make sure the first Adjustment Layer is the active layer. Fill the selection (Mac: OPTION+DELETE, Windows: ALT+DELETE) with black. *Do not deselect.*

8. Create an Adjustment Layer (Mac: ⌘+click, Windows: CTRL+click on the New Layer icon at the bottom of the Layers palette). This is also a Hue/Saturation Adjustment.

9. This time, click on the Colorize button and pick a shade of orange in the Hue slider. The values Hue: 25, Saturation: 100, and Lightness: –12 work well. Click OK.

10. Change the Apply mode to Multiply and the Opacity on this new layer to 66%.

11. Click on the first Adjustment Layer and load Channel 5 (Mac: OPTION+⌘+5, Windows: ALT+CTRL+5). To remove this area from the first correction, fill the selection with black (Mac: OPTION+DELETE, Windows: ALT+DELETE). *Do not deselect.* You are going to restore the pink to the pink icing.

12. Create an Adjustment Layer (Mac: ⌘+click, Windows: CTRL+click on the New Layer icon at the bottom of the Layers palette). This one, too, is a Hue/Saturation Layer.

13. Click on the Colorize box and move the Hue to –41. Set the Saturation to 80%, and the Lightness to –3.

14. Click OK. You can leave this layer in Normal mode at 100% Opacity.

Solution File: EX07-03.Psd

Result: Your result should be identical.

Discussion: The values selected for this image are not etched in stone. Feel free to experiment and see if you can create an effect that you prefer.

Using Adjustment Layers for special effects

Exercise Type: Just for Fun

Purpose: To show you can create some wild adjustments in this Dining Room by Gaugain.

Starter File: BlueRoom.Psd

Environment: Nothing special.

Do:

1. Open the starter file. Duplicate the image (Image → Duplicate → OK).

2. Create an Adjustment Layer (Mac: ⌘+click, Windows: CTRL+click on the New Layer icon at the bottom of the Layers palette).

3. Select Invert as the Adjustment Layer type, and set the Apply mode to Screen.

4. This certainly changes the character of the room! But it is too light. Add a Levels Adjustment Layer. Set the levels as you think they should be and click OK.

Solution File: EX07-04.Psd

Result: See how close your result is to the solution file.

Discussion: How could you have done this without an Adjustment Layer? (Hint: Start by duplicating the Background Layer as a new layer in the same image. Invert and set to Screen mode. However, you cannot apply the levels to the joint layers—you need to flatten the layers, at which time you lose the ability to change them.)

CHAPTER 8

Calculating scanning parameters

Exercise Type: Practice

Purpose: To practice the calculations needed to scan images that differ in size from the originals.

Starter File: None

Environment: Nothing special.

Do: For each of the following situations, calculate the correct scanning parameter:

Physical Size	Print Resolution	Output Size	Calculate
4×6 inches	300 dpi	2.75 inches wide	Percent
10×8 inches	133 dpi	6 inches wide	Scan resolution
5×7 inches	266 dpi	8 inches wide	Pixels

Solution File: None

Result: 68.75% enlargement
159 dpi (approximate)
2128×1163 (approximate) pixels

Discussion: The second calculation was a "trick." You need to realize that a screen of 133 will usually require a dpi of 266 (though it could be a bit less). Assuming a 266 dpi, however, means that you need 6×266 pixels in the image. You then divide this number by 10 (the number of current physical inches) to get the new resolution.

EXERCISE 2

Cleaning scans

Exercise Type: Practice

Purpose: To let you practice touching up a scanned image.

Starter File: Snowflak.Psd

Environment: Nothing special.

Do:

1. Open the starter file.

2. Make the snowflake all black against a white background so it would be easy to autotrace.

3. Smooth out the jagged edges.

Solution File: EX08-02.Psd

Result: Your result should be similar to the example image.

Discussion: This was a difficult image to clean if you actually wanted to make all of the edges sharp. The easy way was to select the background, inverse the selection, and then fill the snowflake with black. This still left wobbly edges, however. You should then have blurred it just slightly (about a 1.5 point Gaussian Blur) and evened out the scan using Levels. If you really need sharp edges for autotracing, the image still needs more work.

CHAPTER 9

Using the Path tool

Exercise Type: Practice

Purpose: To practice creating paths.

Starter Files: `Pigeon.Psd`, `Relief.Psd`, and `Lionhead.Psd`

Environment: Nothing special.

Do:

1. Open the starter files. For each file, create a path around the main element in the file.

2. When you have created the path, adjust it as needed to make it conform to the shape.

3. Test your path by changing it into a selection and then floating the selection. Make the selection into a new layer to see how accurate the path is.

Solution Files: `EX09-1A.Psd`, `EX09-1B.Psd`, and `EX09-1C.Psd`

Result: The paths you create should be very similar to the paths that are in each of the solution files. You need to open the Paths palette to be able to see the paths.

Discussion: The Pigeon is a fairly easy image for which to create paths. The Lionhead is a bit more tricky, and the Relief image is actually a relief to finish—it is surprisingly tricky.

On the three images use the keyboard shortcuts to set the correct position of the points while you are drawing them—as best you can. Changing the smooth points into corner or sharp points as you create makes it easier to see what the next move should be.

You may have trouble with the points along the bottom edge of the lion as you really need to bend the direction points on the right edge rather than create a corner point with no direction lines. If it gives you trouble, enlarge the canvas size. On the Relief image, you will definitely need to increase the canvas size in order to form the point at the top of the medallion.

The other places on the Relief that are a problem are the S-curves at the top, bottom, and sides of the medallion. You need to place an additional point in each of them about halfway into the S.

Using the Color Range command

Exercise Type: Exploration/Practice/Just for Fun

Purpose: To practice with the Color Range command and to show another technique you can use once you have a selection.

Starter File: Mums.Psd

Environment: Nothing special.

Do:

1. Open the starter file.

2. Use the Color Range command to select the background of the mums. Try to get as little of the mums as possible while getting as much of the background as you can. Use the Fuzziness slider as much as you need to. When you are satisfied, click OK.

3. Feather the selection by 1 pixel to get a bit more softness to the edge.

4. Create a new layer (there is still an active selection).

5. Choose a medium gray as your Foreground color. Apply the Clouds filter to the new layer (Filter → Render → Clouds).

6. Create a Layer Mask (Layers menu → Add Layer Mask). Press D to set the colors back to the black and white default. Select the Gradient tool (G). Make a linear Gradient by clicking about one-third down from the top edge and dragging the Gradient line to the bottom of the image. This leaves the top third of the image out of the clouds, and brings in more clouds toward the bottom of the image.

7. Double-click on the layer in the Layers palette to open the Options dialog. Set the This Layer black slider to 0/171 (you need to press the modifier key—Mac: OPTION, Windows: ALT—in order to get the black point slider to split in half so you can move each half). Set the Underlying white slider to 27/136. This cuts out the clouds based on the colors in both layers.

To give the image a nice soft glow, you can apply a Gaussian Blur filter though a self-mask (a density mask). There are a few steps that you need to do to make this work:

1. Make a new layer (click on the New Layer icon at the bottom of the Layers palette). Press the modifier key (Mac: OPTION; Windows: ALT) and select the Merge Layers command from the Layer palette menu. This makes a fully

opaque copy of all the layers and places it in the new layer. If it is not at the top of the layer stack, drag it there. This is so you can experiment but easily change your mind if you need to. It also gives you a channel to use for the blur.

2. In the Channels palette, drag the icon for the Green channel to the New Channel icon in the bottom center of the Channels palette to duplicate the channel. Select the Auto Levels command (Image → Adjust → Auto Levels). This forces the end values in the channel to white and black (fast, but not as good for color correction as using Levels—it is fine for this, though).

3. Select the RGB channel (Mac: ⌘+⓪; Windows: CTRL+⓪). Load Channel 4 (Mac: OPTION+⌘+④; Windows: ALT+CTRL+④).

4. Inverse the selection. You want to blur the shadows rather than the highlights of this image.

5. Apply a Gaussian Blur of about 2.9 (you can try other values to see how they differ in the image).

Solution File: EX09-2.Psd

Result: Your image should be very similar to the example.

Discussion: There is a bit of fiddling needed to make the Color Range give you what you want. If you cannot pick up the background colors just by dragging through them with the Eyedropper+, you might find it easier to set the preview to either White or Black matte (white in this image). You can then specifically click on the spots in the background that have white "preview-paint" on them.

Simple compositing

Exercise Type: Exploration

Purpose: To see how the choice of feather or defringing affects a finished composite image.

Starter Files: Pigeon.Psd and Grass.Psd

Environment: Nothing special.

Do:

1. Open the two starter files. Use the Pigeon file you created in Exercise 1 so you have a path already created, or open the EX09-01A.Psd file to use that path.

2. Change the path into a selection. Make the selection anti-aliased but with no feather. Float the selection (Mac: ⌘+Ⓙ, Windows: CTRL+Ⓙ).

3. Select the Move tool (Ⓥ) and drag the layer into the grass image. Notice how the edges crisply blend with the new image.

4. Click on the Pigeon image again. Drag Layer 1 into the trashcan in the Layers palette.

5. Load the Pigeon path again.

6. Feather the selection by 4 pixels. Float the selection (Mac: ⌘+Ⓙ, Windows: CTRL+Ⓙ). Defringe by 3 pixels.

7. Drag the layer into the Grass image. Turn off the icon of the layer beneath so you can see this effect.

8. Repeat Steps 4 and 5.

9. Contract the selection by 3 pixels (Select → Modify → Contract).

10. Feather by 3 pixels. Float the selection (Mac: ⌘+Ⓙ, Windows: CTRL+Ⓙ), and drag it into the Grass image. Turn off the lower layers (except for the grass) so you can see how it looks.

11. Continue to try other combinations of feather, defringe, and contract to see which way gives you the most satisfactory results.

Solution File: EX09-03.Psd

Result: Your solutions should be close to the solution file.

Discussion: The methods used here provide similar but subtly different results. Which one works best sometimes depends on the image itself. The method of contracting the image selection before feathering it does the best job of removing color spill.

EXERCISE 4A

Building a detail-saving mask

Exercise Type: Practice

Purpose: Another mask-making example.

Starter Files: `Ram.Psd` and `Rampat.Psd`

Environment: Nothing special.

Do:

1. Open the two starter files.

2. Use the methods you learned in this chapter to create an Image Mask and an Edge Mask and build up the two layers as you did in the Hands On parts of Chapter 9. Extract the ram and the surrounding rocks for this example.

3. Make the solid Background Layer behind the ram the deep gold of the rocks. Drag the Ram image on top of the solid layer and drop the Opacity of the layer where you like it.

4. Create a Drop Shadow using the deep gold in the rocks as the shadow color. Set the shadow where you think it looks best and change the Apply mode to Multiply.

Solution File: `EX09-4A.Psd`

Result: Your results should be somewhat similar and the detail on the ram's coat should be apparent.

Discussion: This example is basically the same as the one in Chapter 9. It should give you no real difficulty. The one place that can be a bit tricky is on the ram's horn— you need to remove color spill without removing the dark areas of the horn.

EXERCISE 4B

Detail-preserving masks, Part II

Exercise Type: Practice

Purpose: To give you more practice masking self-masks.

Starter File: `Yappie.Psd`

Environment: Nothing special.

Do:

1. Open the starter file. Get Yappie dog into her own layer(s) with as much of her fur present and uncontaminated as possible.

2. Create whatever you wish as the background for this. It probably does need a shadow.

Solution File: EX09-4B.Psd

Result: Your solution should be close to the example.

Discussion: Yappie's fur is more of a challenge than the ram's. In order to get a good mask, you might want to make a duplicate of the image and use the Unsharp Mask command to almost over-sharpen the fur. This can help to build the best edges. You might also want to build this mask up from several sources and try several color modes to find the best candidate channels.

CHAPTER 10

More grayscale practice

Exercise Type: Practice

Purpose: To practice retouching scratches and damaged photos.

Starter File: Popgram.Psd

Environment: Nothing special.

Do: Open the starter file. Do the best job you can on retouching the image.

Solution File: EX10-1A.Psd

Result: You should be able to get fairly close to the solution file.

Discussion: In order to set the tone for this image, you need to use Screen instead of Multiply.

EXERCISE 1B

More grayscale practice

Exercise Type: Practice

Purpose: To practice retouching scratches and damaged photos.

Starter File: Brothers.Psd

Environment: Nothing special.

Do: Open the starter file. Do the best job you can on retouching the image.

Solution File: EX10-1B.Psd

Result: You should be able to get fairly close to the solution file.

Discussion: This should be starting to get easier.

EXERCISE 1C

More grayscale practice

Exercise Type: Practice

Purpose: To practice retouching scratches and damaged photos.

Starter File: Boygirl.Psd

Environment: Nothing special.

Do: Open the starter file. Do the best job you can on retouching the image.

Solution File: EX10-1C.Psd

Result: You should be able to get fairly close to the solution file.

Discussion: The difficult thing on this image is trying to restore the damaged greenery at the top of the image.

EXERCISE 2A

Sepia-tones from Indexed Color

Exercise Type: Practice

Purpose: To try out the Indexed Color method of applying a sepia-tone.

Starter File: Dancer.Psd

Environment: Nothing special.

Do:

1. Open the starter file.

2. Duplicate the image and change it first to RGB mode and then to Indexed Color mode using the Custom Color Table Sepia.ACT on the CD-ROM.

3. Change the image back to RGB mode.

4. Apply a Gaussian Blur of 4 pixels.

5. Duplicate the original image again. Drag the color image on top of it and set the Apply mode to Color. The image will no longer be blurred, and the main image will use the colors from the top layer.

6. Flatten the image.

Solution File: EX10-2A.Psd

Result: Your image should be nearly identical to the example image.

Discussion: This is a very easy method of creating a sepia-tone—especially if you are given the Color Table to use.

EXERCISE 2B

Sepia-tones from solid color

Exercise Type: Practice

Purpose: To try out the desaturate method of applying a sepia-tone.

Starter File: Dancer.Psd

Environment: Nothing special.

Do:

1. Open the starter image.

2. Change the mode to RGB (Mode → RGB).

3. Make a new layer (click on the New Layer icon at the bottom of the Layers palette).

4. Set your Foreground color to RGB 51,19, 9. Fill this layer (SHIFT+DELETE) with solid color.

5. Set the Apply mode to Color.

6. In the Channels palette, click on the New Channel icon to create a new channel.

7. Use the Apply Image command to place a copy of the Background Layer into this channel.

8. Use the Levels command to make the channel darker. The values of 27, 0.73, 248 for Black, Gamma, and White slider should be sufficient.

9. Load Channel 4 (Mac: OPTION+⌘+4; Windows: ALT+CTRL+4). Hide the marching ants (Mac: ⌘+H; Windows: CTRL+H).

10. Desaturate the image through this mask (Image → Adjust → Desaturate).

11. If you want to change the actual sepia color, use the Hue/Saturation command to push the image toward a new color.

Solution File: EX10-2B.Psd

Result: Your image should be nearly identical to the example image.

Discussion: This method works very well once you find a good sepia color as the base. It gives results that are nearly the quality of the CSI GradTone filter.

EXERCISE 3

Colorizing an image

Exercise Type: Practice

Purpose: To practice adding color to flesh tones. The two photos here are another parent-child combination. While the two children in this example do not look like one another, they are father and son.

Starter Files: `Norm.Psd` and `Dan.Psd`

Environment: Nothing special.

Do:

1. Open the two starter files. `Dan.Psd` is the color file to use as a reference.

2. Make a duplicate of the `Norm.Psd` image.

3. Sample flesh tone colors from Dan's image and apply them to Norm in Color mode using the Paintbrush. Color Norm's face and hair to match Dan's coloring. Not that you can tell from the closed eyes, but both children's eyes are blue.

Solution File: `EX10-03.Psd`

Result: Your image should look similar to the example.

Discussion: If you wish, you can colorize the entire image and Norm's clothes. The main object, however, is to give you practice in colorizing the flesh tones in the face.

EXERCISE 4

Creating a new image from an old one

Exercise Type: Practice

Purpose: To practice removing a person from an image and re-creating needed detail.

Starter File: `Bernie.Psd`

Environment: Nothing special.

Do: Can you remove the young boy from this image and put him in a new image? Fix up the damaged pieces of his head and redraw the piece of his arm that was never in the image. Continue the rug texture. Put him on top of a graduated background (a Gradient that goes from light to medium-dark).

Solution File: EX10-04.Psd

Result: Your results should be similar to those in the example.

Discussion: This exercise is not all that difficult. Hopefully you realized that you could continue the arm by using a copy of the other one.

EXERCISE 5

Batch dust and scratch removal

Exercise Type: Practice

Purpose: To practice the technique of float and move in Darken mode. The image being used is a fragment taken from an old image. It only contains the area for which the technique is valid.

Starter File: Jacket.Psd

Environment: Nothing special.

Do: Open the starter file. Select the image and float it. Move the selection in Darken or Lighten mode (whichever you feel is appropriate) until you have covered up most of the damaged spots. Take care that you do not move it so much that you create a motion blur.

Solution File: EX10-05.Psd

Result: Your image should be very similar to the example.

Discussion: You should have moved the image in Darken mode just a few pixels. When using this technique, you really do need to take care not to create an unintended motion blur.

EXERCISE 6

General dirt removal

Exercise Type: Practice

Purpose: This example is a mixture of several techniques for you to practice. You can work with the Paintbrush in Darken or Lighten mode to get rid of some of the grime on the image. You can also patch up the shoes and other areas of damage.

Starter File: Apron.Psd

Environment: Nothing special.

Do:

1. Open the starter file.

2. Lighten the image—correct the tones.

3. Try to bring out the lines on the apron using the technique for finding hidden detail taught in the chapter.

4. Clean up the apron a bit using the same technique shown for getting rid of paper texture.

5. Repair the remaining holes and make the background beneath the feet complete.

Solution File: EX10-06a.Psd, EX10-06b.Psd

Result: Your results should be similar to those in the example.

Discussion: The apron is nasty to clean up. You should have chosen a medium-light color and worked at about 30% Opacity. In order to adjust the tones, you could have either used the Levels command or screened the image several times. As a last resort, in **EX10-06b.Psd**, the apron was reworked by creating a Gradient in the Gradient Editor.

Rubber Stamp continuation

Exercise Type: Practice

Purpose: It's not worth the effort to continue the background of the Thanksgiving image so that it would actually fit the 8×10 aspect ratio. In this example, you are given a piece of the wallpaper and asked to use the Rubber Stamp tool to make enough wallpaper to repaper the back wall. The challenge is to continue the pattern.

Starter Files: Wallpapr.Psd and Backwall.Psd

Environment: Nothing special.

Do: Use the techniques you learned about continuing patterns with the Rubber Stamp tool to make more wallpaper. Apply it to the **Backwall.Psd** image.

Solution File: EX10-07.Psd

Result: Your results should be similar to those in the example.

Discussion: The real trick here is you cannot work in totally straight lines as the wall itself has a perspective that must be followed.

Object removal

Exercise Type: Practice

Purpose: To remove image detail.

Starter File: Shirley.Psd

Environment: Nothing special.

Do: Open the starter file and make a duplicate of the image. Remove the barbershop pole, the door frame, and the dark flag-like thing from the right and left sides of the image. Try to keep the detail of the houses.

Solution File: EX10-07.Psd

Result: Your results should be similar to those in the example.

Discussion: You should be able to duplicate pieces of existing houses to compensate for the image areas you were asked to remove.

EXERCISE 9

Compositing

Exercise Type: Practice

Purpose: This exercise gives you practice in putting images together.

Starter Files: Elf.Psd, Cyclist.Psd, and Cyclist2.Psd

Environment: Nothing special.

Do: Your task in this exercise is to extract the elf and the very young motorcycle baby from the first two starter images and put them together on grassy background borrowed from the Cyclist2.Psd image. You need to resize the images to match each other. Look at the final image before you begin.

Solution File: EX10-09.Psd

Result: Your results should be similar to those in the example.

Discussion: If this one was easy, then you have become a pro! Do not worry if you had a difficult time of it. This was not an easy example, but it is typical of the things that you will be asked to do if you work at photo-retouching.

CHAPTER 11

EXERCISE 1A

Image resolution and image size

Exercise Type: Exploration

Purpose: To show the benefits of using pixels as your unit of measure.

Starter Files: `ZooGator.Psd` and `Pigeon.Psd`

Environment: Nothing special.

Do: In the first part of this exercise, you will place the pigeon on top of the alligator's back.

1. Open the two starter files.

2. Open the Info palette and use the Palette Options (in the small triangle pop-down menu) to set the Units to inches.

3. Drag a Rectangular Marquee around the area on the alligator's back where you want the pigeon to fit.

4. Read the inch measurement from the Info palette for the size of the selection.

5. Duplicate the Pigeon image and crop it so it includes only the pigeon. Use the Image Size command to change the Pigeon image to the size you measured on the Info palette (approximately 1/2 inch). Enter the height measurement in the Print Size area of the Image Size dialog.

6. Load the Choke Mask and drag the selection into the Alligator image. Did you get your expected results? Delete the Pigeon layer.

7. Change the Units on the Info palette to pixels and repeat the exercise (setting the number of pixels when you resize the image to the height that you read from the Info palette). You need to enter the pixels in the Pixel Dimensions area of the dialog. Save this image as `Comp1.Psd` to use in the next lab exercise.

Solution File: None

Result: The first method created a pigeon that was much larger than needed; using pixels as Units created a pigeon of the right size.

Discussion: The two starting images are of different resolutions. The Pigeon image is set to 300 ppi whereas the alligator is set to 132 ppi. Therefore, if you selected 1/2 inch as the size for the pigeon, you created a pigeon that was about 150 pixels. When you dragged the pigeon into the Alligator image, those pixels occupied over one inch of space rather than the 1/2 inch you wanted.

When you did all of the calculations in pixels, you got the expected results. Since pixels are an absolute rather than a relative measurement, the image resolution is not important. It is easier, therefore, to work with pixels as your unit of measure under most circumstances.

Making a composite work

Exercise Type: Practice

Purpose: To make the pigeon you placed in the last exercise look as if it belongs in the image.

Starter File: Comp1.Psd (output of Exercise 1A)

Environment: Nothing special.

Do: Look at the pigeon that you placed in the Comp1.Psd image. Does it look natural? What's wrong with the image? What do you need to do to make it look like it was part of the original photograph?

Identify the problems and fix them.

Solution File: EX11-01.Psd

Result: Your solution should be similar to the example.

Discussion: There are several problems with the image:

● The color of the pigeon does not match the tone of the Alligator image.

● The pigeon needs a shadow.

● The pigeon is too sharply focused for the image.

Here are the steps you should have taken to correct the problems:

● Added a solid color layer using Color mode and a pink cast from the image over the pigeon and reduced the opacity a bit so that some of the original color shows through (or used an Adjustment Layer to do this).

● Made a Shadow Layer under the pigeon using black as the shadow color and used the Distort command to turn the drop shadow into a cast shadow.

● Added a Layer Mask to the pigeon to better feather the edges into the base image, and then blurred the pigeon using a very small Gaussian Blur.

Using a Gradient in a Layer Mask

Exercise Type: Practice

Purpose: To show how a Gradient in a Layer Mask can be used to softly hide the joining of two images.

Starter Files: `CreoleQ.Psd` and `Ocean.Psd`

Environment: Nothing special.

Do:

1. Open the two starter files.

2. Drag the Creole Queen into the ocean where it looks reasonable to place her.

3. Create a Layer Mask (click on the Add Layer Mask icon—the leftmost icon at the bottom of the Layers palette).

4. Drag a very short Gradient over the area at the bottom of the boat (while you are working in the Layer Mask). The black end of the Gradient should start a little above the keel and the white end should begin where you want the water line to appear (too long of a Gradient and you will sink the ship).

5. Add some mist over the ship by selecting a blue from the atmosphere. With white as your Background color, apply the Clouds filter to a totally empty, transparent layer. Clip the layer over the ship, and turn down the Opacity.

Solution File: `EX11-02.Psd`

Result: Your results should be similar to the example.

Discussion: The small Gradient in the Layer Mask covers the bottom of the ship and makes it look as if the boat has been placed in the ocean. If you want to add more realism, you could clone some of the waves to make it look as if the ship is traveling fast.

The Clouds Layer provides an instantly misty environment for the ship. Without it, the ship is much too sharply focused for the ocean photograph.

Using a Gradient in a Layer Mask, Part II

Exercise Type: Exploration

Purpose: To show how Layer Mask gradients can seamlessly blend two images.

Starter Files: XmasTree.Psd and Candy.Psd

Environment: Nothing special.

Do:

1. Open the two starter files.

2. Drag the Candy image on top of the XmasTree image.

3. Create a Layer Mask (click on the Add Layer Mask icon—the leftmost icon at the bottom of the Layers palette).

4. Using black and white as your colors, drag a Gradient in the Layer Mask. Experiment with various angles and length of gradient-drags to see what effects you prefer.

Solution File: EX11-03.Psd

Result: Your result should show a seamless blend of the two images but may not look at all like the example.

Discussion: This is a very easy exercise. There is no right or wrong way for the Gradient to be placed. Any angle will work—it just depends on what you like. Hopefully, you have tried enough options to begin to be able to predict your results.

Using clipping groups for text

Exercise Type: Practice

Purpose: To show how you can place an image inside of text.

Starter Files: Text.Psd, Leaves.Psd, and Jack0_L.Psd

Environment: Nothing special.

Do:

1. Open the starter files.

2. Drag the Text Layer into the Jack O'Lantern image.

3. Drag the Leaves Layer on top of the Text Layer in the Jack O'Lantern image.

4. Clip the leaves to the shape of the text. If you want specific areas of the leaves to show through, you can copy and paste the sections within the Leaves image (if the clip-to Layer were smaller, you could also move the Leaves image around to choose what shows through).

5. Add a glow to the text: create a drop shadow for the Text Layer using white as the shadow color, and do not offset the shadow. Use a large Gaussian Blur on the white text, and it will become a glow.

Solution File: EX11-04.Psd

Result: Your result should be similar to the example.

Discussion: You can clip one layer to another by selecting the Group with Previous Layer option in the Layer Options dialog, or you can use the *grouping* cursor by pressing the modifier key (Mac: [OPTION]; Windows: [ALT]) and clicking on the line that divides the two layers in the Layers palette.

   The glow is produced by duplicating the Text Layer (it may replace the Clipping Group Layer, but that is okay so long as one of the layers is not part of the clipping group). Turn on Preserve Transparency and fill the text with white. Turn off Preserve Transparency and apply a large Gaussian Blur. Do not move the white glow—if it remains in its original position, you get the glowing effect.

Making multiple rotations

Exercise Type: Exploration/Just for Fun

Purpose: To show how you can create a snowflake, string art, or a kaleidoscopic effect. This exercise (repeated in three variations) shows how you can rotate a squiggle using the Actions palette. This makes five copies and rotates each one 60 degrees more than the previous copy. You can also do it manually (without a script), but the script makes it easier—and helps prepare you for learning more about scripting in Chapter 14, "Configuring and Optimizing Photoshop."

Starter Files: Squiggle.Psd, Multi-R.Act (Action file)

Environment: Nothing special.

Do:

1. Open the image Squiggle.Psd and duplicate it (Image → Duplicate → OK).

2. Load the action file Multi-R.Act into your Actions palette (Action palette menu → Load Actions...).

3. Click on the Multi-Rotate action in the Actions palette to select it and then press the Play button (the forward-pointing triangle). The solution file for this is EX11-05a.Psd.

4. Click on the original image to make it active (the one with only one layer).

5. Press the modifier key (Mac: ⌘; WINDOWS: CTRL) and click on the layer to select the non-transparent pixels on the layer.

6. Copy it to the clipboard (Mac: ⌘+C; Windows: CTRL+C) and paste it into a new file (Mac: ⌘+N; Windows: CTRL+N). Click OK, and paste in the copy (Mac: ⌘+V; Windows: CTRL+V).

7. Use the Canvas Size command to double the height of the image, and place the Anchor in the top-center square.

8. Using the Line tool, draw a very thin line across the bottom of the image.

9. Play the Multi-Rotate Action again.

10. Use the Canvas Size command to increase the canvas size to 400×400 pixels with the anchor in the center. The solution file for this is EX11-05b.Psd.

11. Repeat Steps 4–6. This time, double both the height and width of the image (using the values that appear in the Canvas Size dialog). Anchor the image to the upper-left corner.

12. Using the Line tool, draw a very thin line across the lower right of the image.

13. Play the Multi-Rotate Action again.

14. Increase the canvas size to 660×600 pixels with the Anchor in the center. The solution file for this is EX11-05c.Psd.

Solution Files: EX11-05a.Psd, EX11-05b.Psd, EX11-05c.Psd

Result: Your result should be similar to the example.

Discussion: The Rotate command always rotates around the center point of the object being rotated. In the first pass, you had a small area of non-transparent pixels on a larger layer. You produced a small snowflake because the image overlapped itself. When you rotated the image in the second pass, you doubled the canvas size and placed some non-transparent pixels at the bottom of the image. This created a new center for the rotation—a center that was the mid-way between the left and right edges of the canvas and at the base of the original squiggle. The third pass placed the center of rotation at the lower-right corner of the original image by doubling both the height and width of the canvas and placing non-transparent pixels diagonally opposite to the area that was already filled.

By increasing the canvas size in the second and third passes, you could see the entire image and "prove" that Photoshop keeps all of the data on a layer—even if it cannot be seen.

Question: How would you get the squiggle to rotate around the bottom point of the green "hook" on the squiggle (hint—you have to determine a new center of rotation that is twice as high and wide as the distance to the "top" of the shape, enlarge the canvas to that size, anchor the top-left corner, and place some pixels in the bottom of the transparent area).

EXERCISE 6

Using Free Transform

Exercise Type: Exploration/Practice

Purpose: To give you extra time to explore both the Free Transform and the Numeric Transform commands. The Ram image you used in Chapter 9 has been prepared so the ram is on the center layer with the rock in the front and a mountain-type background in the bottom layer.

Starter File: Ram.Psd

Environment: Nothing special.

Do:

1. Open the starter file and duplicate it (Image → Duplicate → OK).

2. Explore using the Free Transform and the Numeric Transform commands—skewing, rotating, distorting, applying perspective. Just play with the commands. What happens when you use the Numeric Transform command to position the layer 100 pixels × 100 pixels?

Solution File: None

Result: You should have a good idea as to how to control both commands.

Discussion: The Positioning command in the Numeric Transform command uses relative numbers. If the image started at screen location 25, 38 and you moved it 100 pixels in each direction, the new coordinates would be 125, 138.

It is extremely convenient to be able to control the scaling of an object numerically. This feature is new to Photoshop 4.0.

EXERCISE 7

Creative project

Exercise Type: Exploration

Purpose: To apply a design technique to your own work.

Starter File: Anything you wish.

Environment: Nothing special.

Do: This is an optional exercise to stimulate your creativity. It is based on a technique for designing surface stitchery that was first introduced by Wilke Smith, one of the most talented fiber artists working today. This exercise is part technique and part *mind game*.

1. Make a list of all of the *opposing* sets of words that you can think up that deal with the senses. Examples are: thick–thin, soft–hard, hot–cold, nubby–smooth, salty–peppery, etc.

2. Think of a concept you wish to illustrate. It can be anything from "spring" to "peace"—as ordinary or as esoteric as you wish.

3. Using your list of opposites, circle the word in each pair that applies to your concept (is *peace* hot or cold, nubby or smooth?).

4. Now that you have a list of attributes, tear paper into shapes that remind you of (some of) the words you have circled. The paper can be ordinary construction paper or can be pages whose colors you like from magazines.

5. Scan these shapes—one to an image, and remove the backgrounds on the shapes.

6. Use these shapes as clipping shapes to build a composite or photo-montage that seems appropriate to your concept. Add images that represent your concept or create textures that have the *feel* of your circled words. Let your

creativity take flight. You can also composite using various Apply modes and Layer Masks as needed.

Solution File: None

Result: Hopefully, some fun and challenge.

Discussion: There is no right or wrong. There is just creativity and experience.

CHAPTER 12

Creating spot color image in Layers

Exercise Type: Exploration/Practice

Purpose: To show how you can use grayscale data from a color image to create a spot color image. You will create a two-spot-plus-black image from this using Pantone 151 for the flowers and Pantone 364 for the foliage. The black will be added by the same High Pass of 1.6 and Threshold that you used in the chapter.

Starter File: Flower.Psd

Environment: Nothing special.

Do:

1. Open the starter file. This image is an RGB image of a field of flowers. A mask has already been created for you in Channel 4 to pull the flowers away from the foliage.

2. Create a new document (Mac: ⌘+N; Windows: CTRL+N). Use the Window menu to set the size of the new image to match the Flower image.

3. Click on the New Channel icon in the Channels palette to create a new channel. This will be Channel 4. Double-click on the channel name to open the Channel Options dialog. Click on the Color swatch in the dialog box and select Pantone 151. This channel will hold the flowers.

4. Use the Apply Image command and select the Flower.Psd image for the Source, Background for the Layer, and RGB for the Channel, Normal for the Apply mode, and 100% for the Opacity.

5. Drag the icon for the Pantone 151 CV channel to the New Channel icon in the Channels palette. This will duplicate the channel. Double-click on the channel name to open the Channel Options dialog and select Pantone 364 as the preview color. Use the Load Selection dialog on the Select menu to load Channel 4 from the `Flower.Psd` image. Fill the selected area with white. This will remove the flowers from the image.

6. Click on the Pantone 151 CV channel to make it the active channel. The flowers are still selected. Reverse the selection (Select → Inverse). Fill the selection with white. Deselect (Mac: ⌘+D, Windows: CTRL+D).

7. Change the image mode to CMYK.

8. Duplicate the original Flower image, apply a High Pass filter of 1.6 and then a Threshold of about 124.

9. Click on the spot-color-in-process image. In the Channels palette, select the Black channel and make sure it is the only selected channel. Use the Apply Image command to place the threshold image into the Black channel. You need to select the Red, Green, or Blue channel in the `Flower.Psd` copy image as you do not have access to the RGB channel. Since the image is all black and white, however, all three RGB channels contain the same data.

10. Turn on the Eye icons for all of the channels and preview your image.

11. Since the green looks a bit anemic, make the Pantone 364 your active channel and open the Levels dialog. Load the `Flower.Map` curve and apply it to the channel. This S-curve darkens the darks and somewhat lightens the lights. It adds more variety of tone.

12. Now that you have the channels built, apply the Pantone 151 channel to the Cyan channel and the Pantone 364 channel to the Magenta channel.

13. Build your preview in the Printing Inks Setup the way you did in the chapter. Here is a "no-brainer" work-around from author and designer Rob Day to set the color swatch for the Printing Inks. Make Pantone 151 your Foreground color. When you go into the Progressive Image Color Picker in the Printing Inks Setup, click on the Foreground color to set the color swatch. No need to copy down formulas for the color. Close the dialog and make Pantone 364 your current color. Open the Printing Inks again (selecting Custom) and set the color for the Magenta plate.

14. To get an idea of the overprint color, create a small, new, grayscale file and fill it with a black to white Gradient. Change the mode to Duotone and select Pantone 151 and Pantone 364 as your colors. Make both curves the same. Click on the Overprint... button and then on the color swatch that appears for 1+2. Copy down the Lab values for the color. Add that color as the Cyan + Magenta color.

15. Select the Trap command from the Edit menu. A 1-pixel trap is too much for this tiny image, but it is the smallest amount you can do. Trap the image using Photoshop's built-in trapping facility. (You can also use the tip from David Xanakis to soften the trap.)

Solution Files: EX12-01.Psd and EX12-01A.Psd

Result: Your image should look like **EX12-01.Psd** if you do not have your Printing Inks set up to the Pantone colors and **EX12-01A.Psd** if you do. The latter file is in RGB mode as the only way of preserving color.

Discussion: The Trap command can be used in this example because the colors actually touch one another. They are not being trapped to black as they were in the exercise in the chapter.

This exercise should open up to you a variety of ways to use the gray tones in color images as a way of getting spot color output.

Building a CMYK preview using regular printing inks

Exercise Type: Exploration/Practice

Purpose: To show how you can re-create a CMYK image from the spot color Alpha channels. This technique is contributed by Michael Doyle, a Nova Scotia artist who has used this for many years in order to get color comps for his clients.

Starter File: FChannel.Psd (the mid-point of the last exercise)

Environment: Nothing special.

Do:

1. Open the starter file.

2. Select Pantone 151 as your Foreground color. In the Color Picker, copy down the CMYK formula for the color.

3. Select Pantone 364 as your Foreground color. In the Color Picker, copy down the CMYK formula for the color.

4. Select the Cyan channel of the image in the Channels palette. Use the Apply Image command to apply the percentage of cyan that is in Pantone

364 to the channel (there is no cyan in Pantone 72, but there is 72% cyan in Pantone 364). Make the Pantone 364 channel your Source channel and use 72% as the Opacity. The Apply mode is Multiply (since the channel is white, this is the same as using Normal but works as well when you need to apply multiple Alpha channels into the same color channel).

5. The Magenta channel receives 43% of the Pantone 151 channel.

6. The Yellow channel gets 87% of the Pantone 151 channel and 100% of the Pantone 354 channel. This time, you really need to use Multiply as the Apply mode for the second channel.

7. The Black channel gets 43% of the Pantone 364 channel in addition to the data already in the Black channel.

Solution File: EX12-02.Psd

Result: Your image should look like EX12-02.Psd.

Discussion: Michael Doyle usually creates his spot color images directly inside Alpha channels rather than layers. Then, when he wants to see what the image looks like, he builds the CMYK preview as you just did. He usually sets up two QuarkXPress files—using the same image names. One has the "phony" spot color in CMYK mode so he can show his clients a composite proof, and the other has the version that will generate the actual printing plates.

EXERCISE 3

Designing a spot color image

Exercise Type: Just for Fun

Purpose: To explore your creativity with image pieces suitable for spot color.

Starter Files: Candy1.Psd through Candy6.Psd

Environment: Nothing special.

Do: Open the starter files and use whatever you want out of them. Arrange them as you wish and color them with Pantone colors as you wish. When you like the design, prepare the image for spot color output using one of the methods you have learned.

Solution File: EX12-03.Psd

Result: Your image should look nothing at all like EX12-03.Psd.

Discussion: EX12-03.Psd shows one approach to design with the components you were given. The file is in RGB mode, however, and is not set up for spot color. It was designed to use a limited number of colors so as to be suitable for spot color output.

CHAPTER 13

Creating a transparent GIF from a 3D image

Exercise Type: Exploration/Practice

Purpose: To show how you can take an image created in a 3D program and modify it in Photoshop to repurpose it for the Web. The ABC Blocks image was created by Eric Reinfeld.

Starter Files: ABC.Psd, Shadow.AI

Environment: Nothing special.

Do:

1. Open the ABC.Psd image. Duplicate the image (Image → Duplicate → OK).

2. Load Channel 4 (Mac: OPTION+⌘+4; Windows: ALT+CTRL+4). This is an Alpha channel that was created when the 3D model was rendered in ElectricImage (a high-end 3D package). The Alpha channel lets you composite the blocks without getting the background as well.

3. Float the selection (Mac: ⌘+J; Windows: CTRL+J).

4. Drag the Background Layer into the Layers palette trash can.

5. Increase the Canvas Size to 900 pixels wide (Image → Canvas Size, 900 pixels wide, Anchor: Middle Right).

6. Place the image Shadow.AI (File → Place). Double-click inside the box to accept the defaults, and drag the shadow outline—using the Move tool—so that the lower-left edge of the shadow lines up with the bottom leftmost edge of the blocks. The Shadow was created from a path made from the original Alpha channel. This path was placed into Adobe Illustrator and the

BeInfinite Pure Transformation filter was used to rotate the shadow in 3D space to make it into a path for a cast—rather than a drop—shadow. If you have Illustrator, it would be easier to copy the path in Illustrator and then paste it or drag it onto Photoshop as a path—not as a rasterized object.

7. Click inside of the shadow shape with the Magic Wand (Tolerance of 15, Anti-alias *On*). *Save the selection to a channel.*

8. Drag the layer containing the `Shadow.AI` Layer to the Layers palette Trashcan, and create a new layer (click on the New Layer icon at the bottom of the Layers palette). The shadow shape should still be selected.

9. Press ⒟ to set the colors back to the black and white default. Fill the selection (Mac: OPTION+DELETE; Windows: ALT+DELETE). Deselect (Mac: ⌘+⒟; Windows: CTRL+⒟).

10. Apply the Gaussian Blur filter (Filter → Blur → Gaussian, 8). Change the Layer Opacity to 50%.

11. Now, you need to make the master Alpha channel for transparency. You need to combine the original Alpha channel and the Shadow Alpha channel. Here is the easiest way (though there are other ways to do this). Load Channel 4 (Mac: ⌘+click; Windows: CTRL+click on Channel 4 in the Channels palette). Then press SHIFT and Mac: ⌘+click; Windows: CTRL+click on Channel 5 in the Channels palette. This adds the shadow to the original selection. Save the selection (click on the Save Selection icon in the Channels palette).

12. The image is too large for the Web page. You need to reduce it to 1/4 of its size (Image → Image Size, change the percent to 25% in either the pixels or the Print Size box and make sure that Constrain Proportions and Resample Image are checked).

13. Since you want to make a transparent GIF from this image, you also need to do something about the shadow. If the background of the Web page is very different in color than your image, the shadow will look awful. The best solution is to have the shadow look as if it were created over the background itself. In Exercise 3 for Chapter 13, you will create a Web page using the Boucle texture that you made in Chapter 4, "Filters," as the background pattern. In this exercise, you will use it *under* your shadow as in the following steps.

14. Open the file `Texture.Psd` (an RGB version of the GIF image). Drag it into the Blocks image and position it so that it is under the blurred shadow (both under it in the Layers palette and under it physically in the image itself).

15. Select the nontransparent layer pixels (Mac: ⌘+click; Windows: CTRL+click on the Layer name in the Layers palette). Reverse the selection (Select → Inverse). Delete.

16. Flatten the image (Layers palette menu → Flatten image).

17. Change the Mode to Indexed Color (Image → Mode → Indexed Color, Adaptive, 256 colors, No Dither).

18. Export the image as Blocky.Gif as a GIF89a. Interlace the image and select #4 as the Transparency channel in the Transparency From drop down. Save. You will use this again.

Solution File: EX13-01.Psd

Result: Your image should look like the example.

Discussion: There were two main "tricks" in this exercise. One was grabbing an image from a 3D program to re-purpose for the Web by manipulating it in Photoshop. The other was the use of an underlay of the actual background to make the soft shadow look reasonable when its background is removed. You will see in Exercise 3 if this was successful. A 256-color adaptive palette is used simply because this is a demo and the Web palette—either dithered or non—did not do this image justice. If this were really for a Web page, you would need to evaluate the pros and cons of this choice more carefully and evaluate the probable systems of your intended audience.

EXERCISE 2

Creating a textured button

Exercise Type: Exploration/Practice

Purpose: To show how you can create a button that "matches" the background on a Web page.

Starter File: Texture.Gif

Environment: Nothing special.

Do:

1. Open the Texture.Psd image.

2. Create a new document in RGB mode, 100 pixels wide by 50 pixels high.

3. Make a new layer (click on the New Layer icon at the bottom of the Layers palette).

4. Double-click on the Marquee tool. In the Marquee Option palette that appears, make the shape Rectangular and the style Fixed Size. Enter the values Width=50 pixels, Height=30 pixels, and make sure that the Feather Radius box is set to 0.

5. Drag the Marquee into the image. It should be near the center, but you do not need to measure exactly.

6. Save the selection to a channel (click on the shaded Marquee icon in the bottom left of the Channels palette).

7. Select the border area (Select → Modify → Border, 7). Fill the area with black (Mac: OPTION+DELETE; Windows: ALT+DELETE).

8. Select the Text Tool (T), and click in the center of the button. Type the word **Next** in a bold font, probably at 14 point (the font used will make a difference). Make sure the word fits on the button.

9. Load Channel 4 (Mac: OPTION+⌘+4; Windows: ALT+CTRL+4). Crop the image (Image → Crop). This is the easiest way to get the button to be the correct size and get everything where it should be.

10. Drag and drop the Texture.Psd image into the button, and drag it so it is under the text and the Button layer.

11. Adjust the Opacity of the button and the texture until you are satisfied.

12. Export the image as Buttons.Gif as a GIF89a. You can convert the image to Indexed Color in one step this way. Make sure the channel is selected as the Transparency (it will select everything).

Solution File: EX13-02.Psd

Result: Your image should look like the example.

Discussion: This button is now custom made to sit on the background of the Web page.

Mocking up a Web page in PageMill 1.0 Demo

Exercise Type: Exploration/Practice

Purpose: To show how you can create a Web page.

Starter File: Blocks.HTM, Texture.Gif, Blocky.Gif, Button.Gif

Environment: Install the Demo version of *PageMill 1.0* that is included on your Photoshop 4.0 CD-ROM.

Do:

1. Start PageMill.

2. Open the file Blocks.HTM. It will appear inside a new page.

3. In the upper-right corner of the window, there is a block that contains a Globe. That is the Browse/Preview mode. If you click on it, it will toggle to Edit mode (which looks like a sheet of paper with a quill pen).

4. Open the Blocky.Gif image. You can do this by dragging it out of Photoshop, by dragging the icon from the Finder or Desktop into PageMill, or by opening it in PageMill. To open it from PageMill, click on the 7th icon from the left (it looks like a little person).

5. As long as you are in Edit mode, you can drag the image around where you would like it to go. However, it won't always stay where you put it. Image placement in a Web page depends on what else is in the page. Just like you cannot type into the middle of a totally empty line in a word processor, you cannot place an image in the center of a totally empty page. Drag the Blocky.Gif image so that it is at the top left of your image. If needed, press [RETURN] a few times to make sure that the text is below it.

6. Insert the cursor to the left of the Blocky image and press the spacebar 11 times. The image moves from the left margin. You are actually creating blank text to space it out.

7. Select the text **American Block Company** and click on the second icon at the top of the window. This makes the text sit in the center of each line.

8. Select the text that discusses the company. From the Format menu, Indent Left and Indent Right. On the same menu, select the Heading submenu and choose Large. On the Style Menu, select Strong.

9. Finally, open the Buttons.Gif file and place it below everything else. You can leave a few lines between it and the text above because the original HTML file has several codes for blank lines under the text.

10. With the button selected, click on the center align textbox (the second icon at the top of the window) to move the button to the center of the line.

Solution File: EX13-03.Psd

Result: Your image should look like the example (which is a screen shot since the demo will not save anything).

Discussion: PageMill 1.0 is not the latest version. PageMill 2.0 has many more features. However, this gives you a taste of drag-and-drop editing and Web page creation without the need to master HTML. Notice that if you change the size of the window, everything except the top image adjusts. You can make the top image sit in the center by selecting the Center alignment for it, too. However, the shadow throws the center of the image "off-center" so it might not look right if you did that. Your call! Remember, the user can make this any size he/she wants. That is part of the major challenge of Web design.

CHAPTER 14

EXERCISE 1A

Interpolation Methods—reducing

Exercise Type: Exploration

Purpose: To compare Bicubic and Nearest Neighbor interpolations when reducing images.

Starter File: `Angel.Psd`

Environment: Nothing special.

Do:

1. Open the starter file, `Angel.Psd`.

2. Duplicate the image (Image → Duplicate → OK).

3. Set your Interpolation Method to Bicubic (Mac: ⌘+K; Windows: CTRL+K) to open the General Prefs dialog).

4. Reduce the image size to 50% (Image → Image Size, 50%).

5. Duplicate the original image again.

6. Set your Interpolation Method to Nearest Neighbor (Mac: ⌘+K; Windows: CTRL+K) to open the General Prefs dialog).

7. Reduce the image size to 50% (Image → Image Size, 50%).

8. Compare the images both visually and by magnifying them.

Solution Files: `EX14-1A1.Psd` and `EX14-1A2.Psd`

Result: The file that was reduced using Bicubic Interpolation is much smoother than the one that was reduced with Nearest Neighbor, which is pixelated and jaggy.

Discussion: This is a "trick" image to reduce. The original image has a lot of noise (single pixels of spotty areas) in it. Because of this, there is really not a *right* interpolation method for this image. The reduction done with Bicubic is smooth but the one done with Nearest Neighbor has more punch and more life to it. It retains the character of the original a bit more successfully. The trick is that usually it is always *right* to use Bicubic Interpolation rather than Nearest Neighbor; but in this case, it is an artistic decision where there is merit in both methods.

EXERCISE 1B

Interpolation methods— enlarging images

Exercise Type: Exploration/Just for Fun

Purpose: To show a circumstance where you might want to use Nearest Neighbor interpolation to produce a special effect. In general, one should never enlarge an image. When you resample an image upwards, you create data that did not exist. At a certain level, you destroy the image beyond repair—and you expose the underlying pixels that should never be apparent.

Watch out for that word *never.* There can definitely be times when you want to see the pixels. If you do, then using Nearest Neighbor interpolation makes sense. This exercise blends both interpolation methods into a unified image.

Starter File: Kamakura.Psd

Environment: Nothing special.

Do:

1. Open the starter file and duplicate it (Image → Duplicate, Name: NN → OK).

2. Set the Interpolation Method to Nearest Neighbor.

3. Increase the size of the file 600% (Image → Image Size → 600%).

4. Click on the original file and duplicate it again (Image → Duplicate, Name: BiC → OK).

5. Set the Interpolation Method to Bicubic.

6. Increase the size of the file 600% (Image → Image Size → 600%).

7. Compare the images—the NN image has blocks of pixels 6×6, the BiC image looks like it was stretched too thin and is very soft and noisy.

8. Drag the NN image on top of the BiC image.

9. Apply the Find Edges filter (Filter → Stylize → Find Edges) to the NN layer.

10. Invert the image (Mac: ⌘+Ⓘ; Windows: CTRL+Ⓘ).

11. Double-click on the Layer icon or Layer name in the Layers palette to open the Layer Options dialog.

12. Press the modifier key (Mac: OPTION; Windows: ALT) and move the lefthand This Layer slider until the split numeric readout shows 0/11. Set the Apply mode to Multiply and click OK.

Solution File: EX14-01B.Psd

Result: Your result should be identical to the solution file.

Discussion: This exercise shows you how to create an image with a deliberate grid in it. This grid will always occur if you enlarge an image using the Nearest Neighbor interpolation method and then the Find Edges filter. Inverting the image simply makes the colors more powerful.

In this, you were told to combine the result with a copy of the original that was up-sampled using the preferred Bicubic interpolation method. In reality, you can see that up-sampling an image 600% is not a very good idea for raw image quality. This example, however, covers that deficiency with the applied layer.

If you need to enlarge an image and want to either cause color blocks to appear or keep a hard edge, you need to set your interpolation method to Nearest Neighbor. You get the best results when you enlarge by a whole number (use the percent units in the Image Size dialog to enlarge).

This technique of using Nearest Neighbor is excellent for making grids for counted cross stitch or for any gridded craft project.

Here is a bonus exercise: You might want to create a graph for Peyote beading some day (or if you don't ever want to weave beads, the gridding technique may still prove useful). Peyote beading uses a half-dropped grid—almost like brickwork. Here's how to do it.

1. Create your basic pattern tile (the file Peyote.Psd has a 50-pixel image that you can use).

2. Set the Interpolation Method to Nearest Neighbor and enlarge the image 1000%. Each grid square is now 10 pixels by 10 pixels.

3. Create a new layer. Magnify the image so you can see individual pixels. Draw a half box around one of the squares on the layer below (use the 1-pixel Pencil with black and draw half of a square that is 10 pixels high by 10 pixels wide).

4. Select the half-square using a Fixed Size Rectangular Marquee that is 10 pixels by 10 pixels. Turn off the Eye icon on the bottom layer so all you can see is the start of your grid.

5. Define this as a pattern (Edit →Define Pattern). Fill the area (Mac: OPTION+DELETE; Windows: ALT+DELETE) and select Pattern, Normal. Turn the Eye icon back on for the Bottom Layer. It now looks as if the pattern were drawn on graph paper.

6. Duplicate the image as Merged Layers only (Image → Duplicate, Merged Layers only → OK).

7. Click on the New Channel icon in the center of the Channels palette to create a new channel.

8. Set the size of the Fixed Size Rectangular Marquee to 10 pixels wide (the width of one grid square) by 500 pixels high (the height of the image). Press D to set the colors back to the black and white default. Drag the Marquee to the left edge of the channel. Press DELETE to fill the selection with white.

9. Change the width of the Fixed Size Rectangular Marquee to 20 pixels (twice the size of the grid square). Drag the Marquee to the left edge of the channel. Define this as a pattern (Edit → Define Pattern).

10. Fill the channel (Mac: OPTION+DELETE; Windows: ALT+DELETE) with the pattern. Invert the channel (Mac: ⌘+I; Windows: CTRL+I) so the left edge of the channel is black.

11. Click on the RGB channel again (Mac: ⌘+0; Windows: CTRL+0). Load the pattern channel (Mac: ⌘+OPTION+4; Windows: ALT+CTRL+4).

12. Offset the image 0 pixels right and 5 pixels down (Filter → Other → Offset, 0 pixels right, 5 pixels down, wraparound). This moves every other grid column down by half of the grid size.

Note

EX14–1C1.Psd has the resized image with the grid, and EX14–1C2.Psd shows the result. Enjoy!

EXERCISE 2

Using Quick Edit

Exercise Type: Practice

Purpose: To show how to use Quick Edit.

Starter File: WaterBuf.Tif (Quick Edit will only open TIFF files). This is another of Ed Scott's China photographs.

Environment: Nothing special.

Do:

1. Open the starter file and save it as a TIFF file to your hard drive.

2. Open a portion of the saved file—pull down the File menu and select Acquire. Choose Quick Edit. Click on Grid and select 3 rows and 3 columns.

3. Select the upper-left corner of the image and click OK.

4. Open the Levels dialog (Mac: ⌘+Ⓛ; Windows: CTRL+Ⓛ). Set the White input numeric readout to 208 (instead of 255) and the Gamma to 1.10 (instead of 1.0). Click OK.

5. Apply the Unsharp Mask filter (Filter → Sharpen → Unsharp mask, Amount: 184%, Radius: 1.4, Threshold: 12).

6. Save the image (File → Export → Quick Edit).

7. Repeat steps 1–5 eight more times—until you have processed each of the grid areas in the Quick Edit screen.

8. Finally, open the image using the File → Open command to see the entire file. There should be no indication that the file was ever processed in pieces.

Solution File: EX14-02.Psd

Result: Your result should be identical to the solution file.

Discussion: This is a very simple practice using Quick Edit. It can be very useful if you need to correct a large image and are tight on RAM.

Using a Complex Action

Exercise Type: Just for Fun

Purpose: This has a dual purpose. One is to show you an Action that is much more complex than the ones created in the chapter and to let you play with it. The second purpose is for you to study the way it was created by working with it and reading the entire sequence.

Starter File: None.

Environment: Nothing special.

Do: This Action allows you to rotate whatever is on Layer 1 in increments of 60 degrees. In order to understand the effect, you need to know how Photoshop rotates a layer. A layer or selection always rotates from its center point, but the center point is calculated as the center of the *non-transparent* pixels on the layer. This means if you draw a straight line on a layer and rotate it, it will rotate around its center—since the line is the only thing on the layer. Try this exercise a number of times. What it does is fairly simple:

● It duplicates Layer 1 five times (so you end up with six layers).

● It rotates the top layer by 60 degrees and positions itself to the next layer down in the stack.

● It continues to add 60 degrees to each rotation. This is hard-wired into the Action. If the Action were to rotate a layer 60 degrees and then copy it and rotate the copy 60 degrees, and so on, you would get mud by the final rotation. Therefore, it has to be explicitly set up that the first layer rotates 60 degrees, the second 120 degrees, etc.

The one condition the Action makes is that there be only one additional layer and that it be named Layer 1. If there is no Layer 1, the Action will get confused and not work.

1. Create a new document (Mac: ⌘+N; Windows: CTRL+N) 400×400 pixels.

2. Make a new layer (click on the New Layer icon at the bottom of the Layers palette). It must be named Layer 1 (which it will be automatically).

3. Select the Paintbrush tool and draw a squiggly line in the general direction of upper-left corner to lower-right corner.

4. Load the Action "mrotate" from the CD-ROM into your Actions palette (Actions palette menu → Load Action). This will append the Action to your current Actions set.

5. Select mrotate in the Actions palette and click Play. You should see a rough approximation of a snowflake shape.

6. These shapes can be embellished quite a bit, now that you know what the Action does.

7. Try the exercise again in a new image. This time, embellish the line with additional colors, and shapes that continue off of the main one.

To make the image rotate around the center of the image itself:

1. Create another 400×400 pixel file.

2. Using any round brush and any color, place a dot in the Background Layer of the image.

3. Click on the background white pixels with the Magic Wand tool and reverse the selection (Select → Inverse). Copy it to the clipboard (Mac: ⌘+C; Windows: CTRL+C). Deselect (Mac: ⌘+D; Windows: CTRL+D).

4. Paste in the selection from the clipboard (Mac: ⌘+V; Windows: CTRL+V). It will land in the exact center of Layer 1 (a pasted selection always lands in the center of the image if there is no selection active in the target image).

5. Now that you know the exact center, you can draw an embellished line in one direction only—as fanciful as you wish.

6. Place a tiny dot in each corner of the image. This makes Photoshop think the entire layer contains pixels, and will cause Photoshop to rotate the layer around the layer's center point (which is, by design, also an endpoint of the line that you drew).

7. Play the mrotate Action. This time, you will really get a snowflake form.

Solution File: EX14-03.Psd

Result: Your result will be quite different from the solution file, but perhaps the solution will give you some ideas.

Discussion: Once you understand what this Action does, you can have fun with it. Try wild scribbles all over Layer 1. If you create a line that does not go through the center of the layer, you leave very interesting shapes and "kaleido-forms" as well.

CHAPTER 15

Reality check

Exercise Type: The Lab exercises for this chapter are different from those in the other lessons. Following are suggestions for you to try based on the lecture.

1. Calibrate your monitor.

2. Send the *Olé No Moiré* image from the Photoshop/Goodies/Calibration/ Separation Sources folder to a CMYK printer.

3. Create and save a Printing Inks setup that enables your monitor to match the output.

4. Print an image with a Clipping Path in it from QuarkXPress or PageMaker.

5. Print an image with transparent whites from QuarkXPress or PageMaker as an EPS or a TIFF.

6. Try designing and printing a business card or a cover for a CD-ROM or tape.

APPENDIX D
QUIZ ANSWERS

CHAPTER 1

Quiz 1
1. a,b,c,d
2. c
3. b
4. a,c,d
5. a,b

Quiz 2
1. a,c,d
2. d
3. b
4. a,b,c,d
5. b

Quiz 3
1. d
2. c
3. b,d
4. b
5. a,b,c

Quiz 4
1. d
2. a,c
3. b
4. d
5. a,b,c

Quiz 5
1. b,d
2. c
3. b,c,d
4. c
5. b

CHAPTER 2

Quiz 1
1. c
2. a,b,c,d
3. b,c,d
4. a
5. d

Quiz 2
1. a,c,d
2. a,c
3. c
4. d
5. c

Quiz 3
1. d
2. a
3. c
4. b,c
5. a,b,d

Quiz 4
1. b
2. a,c
3. a,b
4. b
5. a,c

Quiz 5
1. b
2. c
3. a,c,d
4. b
5. a,d

Quiz 6
1. b,d
2. c
3. a,c
4. a,b
5. b,c

Quiz 7
1. a,c
2. b
3. a
4. b,c,d
5. b,d

CHAPTER 3

Quiz 1
1. a,b,d
2. b,c,d
3. b,d
4. a,b,c
5. b

Quiz 2
1. b
2. a,c,d
3. d
4. a,b
5. b

Quiz 3
1. b,d
2. a,b,c,d
3. d
4. a,c,
5. c,d

833

Quiz 4
1. b
2. b
3. a,b,c
4. a,b
5. a

Quiz 5
1. b
2. a,b,c
3. d
4. a,b
5. b

CHAPTER 4

Quiz 1
1. b,c,d
2. a,b,d
3. a
4. b
5. a,b,c

Quiz 2
1. d
2. a,c
3. a,b,c,d
4. a,d
5. c

Quiz 3
1. c
2. b
3. b,c,d
4. a,d,b
5. b,c

Quiz 4
1. c,d
2. c
3. d
4. a,b
5. a,c,d

Quiz 5
1. a
2. a,b
3. d
4. b,c
5. c

Quiz 6
1. b
2. d
3. a,b,c
4. a,c,d
5. c

CHAPTER 5

Quiz 1
1. b
2. d
3. a,d
4. b
5. b,c,d

Quiz 2
1. b
2. a,c,d
3. a,c,d
4. b
5. a,b,d

Quiz 3
1. a,d
2. b,c
3. b,a
4. c
5. b

CHAPTER 6

Quiz 1
1. d
2. b
3. a,c,d
4. c
5. a,b

Quiz 2
1. b
2. a,b,c
3. a,b,c,d
4. a,c,d
5. b

Quiz 3
1. b,c
2. a,d
3. a,c
4. b
5. a,b,d

CHAPTER 7

Quiz 1
1. b
2. a
3. a,b,d
4. a,b,c
5. b,c

Quiz 2
1. b
2. c
3. a,c
4. b,c
5. c,d

Quiz 3
1. b,c
2. b
3. b,d
4. b,c
5. b

Quiz 4
1. a,d
2. b
3. b
4. b
5. a,b,c,d

Quiz 5
1. a,c
2. a,b,c
3. b,d
4. b,c
5. c

CHAPTER 8
Quiz 1
1. a,b,d
2. a,b,d
3. b
4. d
5. c

Quiz 2
1. a,b,c,d
2. b
3. c
4. a,b
5. b

Quiz 3
1. a,b,c
2. d
3. b
4. a,c
5. c

Quiz 4
1. a,c
2. b
3. a,b,c,d
4. b
5. d

Quiz 5
1. b,c,d
2. c
3. a,b,c
4. c
5. b

CHAPTER 9
Quiz 1
1. b
2. d
3. c
4. a
5. d

Quiz 2
1. a
2. d
3. b
4. d
5. a

Quiz 3
1. d
2. c
3. c
4. a
5. b

CHAPTER 10
Quiz 1
1. c
2. a
3. d
4. b
5. c

Quiz 2
1. b
2. b
3. a
4. a
5. d

Quiz 3
1. d
2. a
3. c
4. b
5. d

Quiz 4
1. c
2. a,c
3. d
4. b
5. c

Quiz 5
1. d
2. a
3. c
4. b
5. d

Quiz 6
1. b,c,d
2. a,b
3. c
4. c
5. b

Quiz 7
1. d
2. b,c
3. a
4. c
5. b

CHAPTER 11
Quiz 1
1. a
2. b
3. c
4. d
5. b

Quiz 2
1. b
2. c
3. a
4. b
5. c

CHAPTER 12

Quiz 1

1. c
2. c
3. a
4. b,c,d
5. c

Quiz 2

1. a,d
2. b
3. a,c
4. b or c
5. d

Quiz 3

1. c
2. c
3. d
4. a,b
5. d

CHAPTER 13

Quiz 1

1. d
2. c
3. d
4. d
5. d

Quiz 2

1. a
2. d
3. a,c
4. d
5. c

Quiz 3

1. b
2. b
3. a
4. b,c
5. b

Quiz 4

1. d
2. b
3. a
4. d
5. c

Quiz 5

1. b and d
2. d
3. c
4. b
5. d

CHAPTER 14

Quiz 1

1. a
2. a,b, and d
3. d
4. a,c, and d
5. b

Quiz 2

1. c
2. d
3. a
4. b
5. a and b

Quiz 3

1. b
2. d
3. c
4. d
5. a

Quiz 4

1. a
2. b,c, and d
3. a,b
4. a
5. a,b, and d

CHAPTER 15

Quiz 1

1. c
2. b
3. b
4. d
5. c

Quiz 2

1. a
2. a
3. a
4. c and d
5. c

Quiz 3

1. c
2. a
3. c
4. a
5. a,b,c,d

Quiz 4

1. a
2. c
3. b
4. d
5. d

Quiz 5

1. a
2. b
3. d
4. c
5. b,c

Quiz 6

1. a
2. b,c
3. d
4. a,c
5. a

APPENDIX E

INTERNET EXPLORER 3.0: A FIELD GUIDE

A new day dawned. The sun reached its fingers over the digital outback. The mighty Navigators (*Netscapus navigatorus*)—a species that reproduced like rabbits and ran nearly as fast—covered the landscape. Yonder, on a cliff that seemed to be beyond the horizon, a trembling new creature looked out over the Internet jungle. This strange new creature, calling itself the Explorer (*Microsoftus interneticus explorus*), sniffed around, considering whether it should enter the fragile ecosystem. Netscape gators gnashed their teeth, but the Explorer was not daunted. Explorer was a formidable beast. It became a part of the jungle and thrived. And even though it began as a mere pup, it evolved, and it evolved and it evolved.

Now the jungle is rife with two intelligent species.

What follows is a guide to domesticating Internet Explorer. You will learn how to care for your Explorer and even how to teach it tricks. Before long, you shall find truth behind the old axiom that the Explorer is man's (and woman's) best friend.

INTRODUCING EXPLORER TO YOUR ECOSYSTEM

Whether you're running a Macintosh, Windows NT or Windows 95, installing Explorer is easy. Explorer's own installation program makes setup a breeze, and you need only to select the appropriate file on the CD-ROM to launch this installer. Make sure the CD-ROM included with this book is in the CD-ROM drive; then, depending upon your system, follow the directions below for either a Macintosh, Windows 95 or Windows NT.

Macintosh Installation Instructions

1. Insert the CD-ROM into your CD drive.

2. You will see a CD icon when the CD is mounted by your Macintosh. Double-click on the CD icon.

3. You will see four folders: 3RDPARTY, ARCHIVES, CHAPTERS, and EXPLORER. Double-click on the EXPLORER folder.

4. Launch Internet Explorer's installer by double-clicking on IE Installer. A dialog box similar to the one shown in Figure E-1 appears. Follow the onscreen prompts to finish the installation.

Windows 95 Installation

1. Click the Start button in the lower-left corner of your screen.

2. Click on the Run... option in the Start menu. A dialog box similar to the one shown in Figure E-2 appears.

3. Using the Run dialog box, type in a pathname and specify the location of the Explorer installation program. IE301M95.EXE is in the CD's \Explorer directory, so if your CD-ROM drive is designated as D:, you'd type

   `d:\explorer\ie301m95.exe`

   If your CD-ROM drive has a different designation letter, type in the appropriate drive designation letter in place of d:.

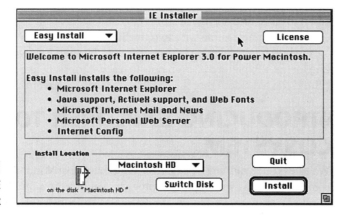

Figure E-1
The Macintosh IE
Installer box

Figure E-2
The Windows 95
Run dialog box

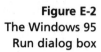

4. After typing the proper pathname, click the OK button to start the Explorer's installation program. Depending upon your system, it may take a moment to load.

5. Once the installation program loads, follow the onscreen prompts to set up Explorer on your computer.

Windows NT 4 Installation

1. Click the Start button in the lower-left corner of your screen.

2. Click on the Run... option in the Start menu. A dialog box similar to the one shown in Figure E-3 appears.

3. Using the Run dialog box, type in a pathname and specify the location of the Explorer installation program. MSIE30M.EXE is in the CD's \Explorer directory, so if your CD-ROM drive is designated as D:, you'd type

```
d:\explorer\ie301mnt.exe
```

If your CD-ROM drive has a different designation letter, type in the appropriate drive designation letter in place of d:.

4. After typing the proper pathname, click the OK button to start the Explorer's installation program. Depending on your system, it may take a moment to load.

5. Once the installation program loads, follow the onscreen prompts to set up Explorer on your computer.

Figure E-3
The Windows NT
Run dialog box

Once you've run the installation, you'll need to restart your system. You can then click on the Internet icon on your desktop. If you've already selected an Internet provider with Windows dial-up networking, you'll be connected. If not, you'll be walked through the dial-in process. You'll need to enter the phone number of your Internet provider, your modem type, and other related information. Ultimately, you'll be taken to Microsoft's home page, where you can register your Explorer and find out about its latest features.

The Explorer is a constantly evolving animal. For the latest updates, plug-ins, and versions, be sure to regularly check out Microsoft's neck of the woods at `http://www.microsoft.com/ie/`.

Explorer Components

Explorer is more than a plain-Jane Web browser. As you work through the installation, you'll be able to choose a variety of components. You can select the following add-ons:

- *Internet Mail*—This is a comprehensive e-mail package. Using simple icons, you can write and read your mail offline and then log on quickly to send and receive your latest batch of correspondence. See Figure E-4.

- *Internet News*—This is a window that lets you browse through thousands of newsgroups, read through the threads, and post your own messages. The News system is very easy to use. You can easily keep track of your favorite topics and automatically be updated with the latest news.

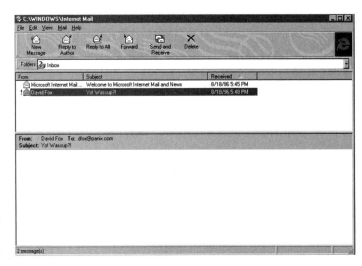

Figure E-4
The Internet Mail
main window

● *ActiveMovie*—This feature of Explorer lets you watch all sorts of video clips—MPEG, AVI, and QuickTime formats. It even supports a special streaming version of video that downloads movies as you watch them, letting you view video with little delay. The ActiveMovie system also lets you listen to all popular formats of audio files—AU, WAV, MIDI, MPEG, and AIFF. This makes it easy to add background sound to Web pages.

● *VRML Support*—This feature is a separate module that lets you download and coast through Virtual Reality Modeling Language worlds. This allows you to explore true 3D landscapes and objects.

● *NetMeeting*—This is a full-featured package that lets you hold entire meetings over the Internet. You can chat with one person or with dozens. If you have a microphone, you can use the Internet phone feature to hold voice conversations with other people. You can share applications. For example, you and a client can edit the same word processing document together. A whiteboard feature lets you draw on a "digital blackboard" that can be updated live across the Internet.

● *HTML Layout Control*—This tool lets Web page publishers create spiffy versions of HTML pages, the way professional designers would lay out a magazine page or a newspaper. Designers can choose exactly where to place elements within a Web page. You can make objects transparent and layer objects over each other, which helps make a Web page eye-catching yet uncluttered.

THE NATURE OF THE BEAST

Internet Explorer features very up-to-date HTML. It supports HTML 3.2, including the following:

● *Frames*—These break up the Web page window into several areas. For example, you can keep an unchanging row of navigation controls along the top of the page while constantly updating the bottom. You can use *borderless frames*, which split up the page without making it seem split. A special type of frame known as the *floating frame* lets you view one Web page within another.

● *Cascading Style Sheets*—This allows all your Web sites to have the same general look and feel.

● *Tables*—You can create or view all sorts of fancy tables, with or without graphics, borders, and columns.

● *Embedded Objects*—Internet Explorer can handle Java applets, ActiveX controls, and even Netscape plug-ins. These objects are discussed later, in the Symbiotic Partners section of this appendix.

● *Fonts*—Explorer supports many fonts, allowing Web pages to have a variety of exciting designs.

From the get-go, Internet Explorer has included a few special bells and whistles. For example, it's easy to create and view marquees across Web pages. This lets you scroll a long, attention-drawing message, similar to a tickertape, that puts a great deal of information in a very small space.

TRAINING THE EXPLORER

By its very nature, the Explorer is a friendly beast. You can access the full range of the Explorer's talents by pushing its buttons. These buttons, which appear in the toolbar at the top of the screen as depicted in Figure E-5, are as follows:

● *Back*—Use this to return to the Web page you've just come from. This will help you retrace your steps as you take Explorer through the Internet maze.

● *Forward*—Use this after you've used the Back button, to jump forward again to the page from which you began.

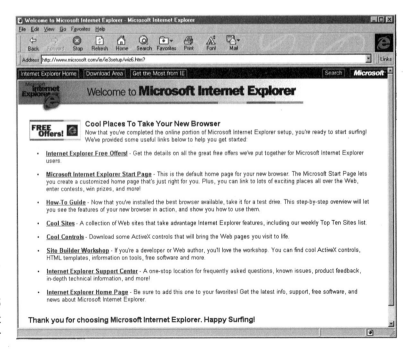

Figure E-5
A cosmetic look at Explorer

- *Stop*—If a Web page is taking too long to load, press this button. Any text and graphics will immediately stop downloading.

- *Refresh*—If your Web page is missing some graphics, or if you've previously stopped its loading using the Stop button, you can reload it using Refresh.

- *Home*—This takes you to your pre-set home page. By default, this is Microsoft's main Web page, but you can set your home to any you'd like. See the Taming the Beast section.

- *Search*—This takes you to a special page that allows you to search for a Web page, using a number of cool search engines. See the Hunting Skills section.

- *Favorites*—This button lets you access a list of your favorite Web sites. See the Favorite Haunts section.

- *Print*—This allows you to print out the current Web page, allowing you to keep a perfect hard copy of it.

- *Font*—Find yourself squinting at a Web page? Just click here to zoom in. The font size will grow several degrees. Too big now? Click a few more times and the size will shrink once again.

- *Mail*—This will launch the Internet Mail program, which allows you to send and receive e-mail and to access newsgroups.

PLAYING FETCH

Your Explorer is a devoted friend. It can scamper anywhere within the Internet, bringing back exactly what you desire.

If you know where you want to go, just type the URL into Explorer's Address box at the top of the screen. If you like, you can omit the `http://` prefix. The Web page will be loaded up. You can also search for a page or load up a previously saved page.

You can now click on any *hyperlink*—an underlined or colored word or picture— to zoom to that associated Web page or Internet resource. Some hyperlinked graphics may not be obvious. Explorer will tell you when you are positioned over a valid hyperlink, because the cursor will change into a pointing finger. Continue following these links as long as you like. It's not uncommon to start researching knitting needles and end up reading about porcupines.

If you're an aspiring Web page writer, you might want to take a peek at the HTML source code to see how that page was created. Just select View|Source.

HUNTING SKILLS

If you want to find Web pages dealing with a specific category, the Explorer makes it easy to find them. Click the Search button. The Search screen will appear, as in Figure E-6. You can search for more than Web pages. With Explorer, it's easy to find

- Phone numbers, ZIP codes, and addresses

- Information on a number of topics—health, home, education, consumer affairs, finance, weather, sports, travel, and so on

- References—maps, a dictionary, a thesaurus, quotations, and an encyclopedia

- Online books, newspapers, and magazines

You can also quickly hunt for any idea, word, or category. Simply type GO in the Address box at the top of the screen, followed by the word or phrase you want to search for.

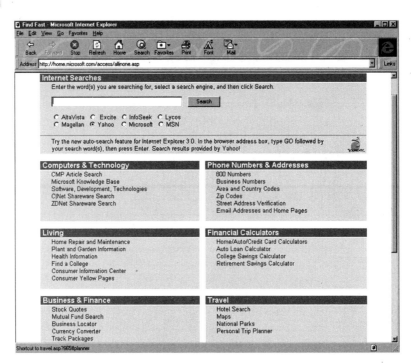

Figure E-6
The Search screen

FAVORITE HAUNTS

It's easy to keep track of the Web pages you visit most. When you want to save a page for future reference, simply click the Favorites button or choose the Favorites menu item. Select the Add To Favorites option. The current Web page will now be added to the list of favorites, which appears each time you click on the Favorites button or menu.

After a while, your list of favorites will get long and cluttered. It's simple to keep track of huge lists of favorites—just put them into separate folders. Organize your favorites, as shown in Figure E-7, by selecting Favorites|Organize Favorites.

To create a new folder, click on the New Folder icon (the folder with the little glint on it) at the top of the window. Now drag and drop your Web page bookmarks into the appropriate folders. You can also move, rename, or delete a folder by selecting it and using the corresponding buttons at the bottom of the screen.

You can even include or attach a favorite Web document within an e-mail message, the way you would attach any other file.

On Windows systems, the Favorites list is actually a folder within your Windows directory. This reflects a Microsoft trend—treating the entire World Wide Web as just another folder to explore on your desktop. Eventually, you'll be able to drag and drop documents across the Internet as easily as you would within your own hard drive.

MEMORY

Internet Explorer keeps track of every Web page you visit. This is kept in a vast History list. You can view the entire History list, in chronological order, by clicking the View History button. Just click on any page you'd like to revisit.

Figure E-7
Organizing the
Favorites list

The History list is cleared every 20 days—you can set this value within the Navigation properties sheets.

TAMING THE BEAST

Now that you and your Explorer are getting acquainted, why not tame it so that it acts and looks exactly like you want? Select View|Options and pick a tab at the top of the window to customize the following properties:

- *General*—The general properties sheet is illustrated in Figure E-8. Since multimedia content (such as sounds, movies, and graphics) takes longer to load in Web pages, you can choose not to load certain media types. You can also easily customize the color of the text and hyperlinks. Finally, you can decide how little or how much information appears in your toolbar.

You can change the size and position of your toolbar simply by clicking on its borders and dragging it to a desired location.

- *Connection*—You can adjust your connections settings, as shown in Figure E-9, by clicking on this tab. This lets you choose your Internet provider. If you're connecting to the Internet through a network firewall, you can also set your proxy server information here.

- *Navigation*—You can customize which page you'd like to use as your starting home page. Just enter its URL in the Address box here.

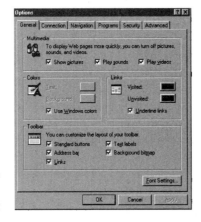

Figure E-8
The General
properties sheet

Figure E-9
The Connection
property sheet

● *Programs*—This allows you to set which programs you'd like to use for
e-mail and for Usenet news. By default, you can use Microsoft's Internet
Mail and Internet News, which are included with Explorer. You can also
tell Explorer how to handle various types of files by selecting the File
Types button. It allows you to designate which program or plug-in should
be launched whenever Explorer comes across various unfamiliar file
formats.

● *Security*—You are able to customize how securely documents will be handled by Explorer. If you want to keep your computer extremely safe, you
may tell Explorer not to download possible security risks such as ActiveX
controls, Java applets, or other plug-ins. Another nice feature is a
Content Advisor. Click on Settings; the Content Advisor window will
appear as in Figure E-10. You may now decide which Web pages to skip
based on Adult Language, Nudity, Sex, or Violence. Many questionable
Web pages are written with certain tags so that the pages can be weed-
ed out by people who don't want to see them. This is a great option to
use if your kids surf the Internet, or if your sensibilities are offended. To
turn ratings on, click on the Enable Ratings button. You can also lock this
window with a password.

● *Advanced*—This properties sheet lets you customize when Internet
Explorer will issue warnings. This is useful if you deal with sensitive information and want to know which Web pages are secure and which are
not. You can also set a number of other advanced Java and Security
options here.

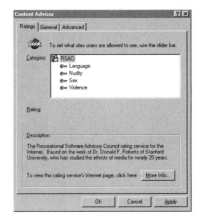

SYMBIOTIC PARTNERS

Explorer includes many of the latest Web technologies. These make your Web pages sing, dance, and even act as entire applications. The line between what a computer can do in general and what a computer can do over the Internet is thinning.

ACTIVEX

Microsoft's proprietary ActiveX technology lets you drop controls into your Web pages. Controls are software components such as specialized buttons, input forms, graphics viewers, sound players, and so forth.

When you load a page with an ActiveX control, Explorer will check if you already have that control on your system. If not, you'll be asked whether you'd like to download it. You'll be told whether the control has been authenticated by Microsoft. If the control is secure, it'll automatically be downloaded and installed for you. The resulting Web page may look more like a software program than a Web page. Don't be surprised to find all new types of buttons, such as the up and down arrow controls in Figure E-11.

SCRIPTS

Internet Explorer allows Web page writers to add different types of scripts right into the source code of the Web page itself. This means you can get instantaneous feedback and control of the Web browser, ActiveX controls, Java applets, and other plug-ins. This makes interactivity fast and easy. Internet Explorer supports the Visual Basic, Scripting Edition and JavaScript languages.

JAVA

Finally, Explorer fully supports the popular Java language. Java is a programming language that lets you write full applications that run directly within your Web browser. Java is great for writing games, graphics demonstrations, databases, spreadsheets, and much more.

Figure E-11
Loading a page
with an ActiveX
control

TOTAL MASTERY

Now that you are fully in control of Explorer, you can learn, work, and have fun using it with the greatest of ease. Wandering through the Internet faster than ever, you are ready to investigate new paths of adventure with your trusty, obedient Explorer guiding you every step of the way.

INDEX

Symbols

A

Books have a substantial influence on the destruction of the forests of the Earth. For example, it takes 17 trees to produce one ton of paper. A first printing of 30,000 copies of a typical 480-page book consumes 108,000 pounds of paper, which will require 918 trees!

Waite Group Press™ is against the clear-cutting of forests and supports reforestation of the Pacific Northwest of the United States and Canada, where most of this paper comes from. As a publisher with several hundred thousand books sold each year, we feel an obligation to give back to the planet. We will therefore support organizations that seek to preserve the forests of planet Earth.

About Moore College of Art and Design

Technological Leadership Starts with Educational Leadership

Moore College of Art and Design approaches its 150th anniversary with a keen appreciation of its unique place in American higher education. It was the first and now the only accredited college of art for women in the nation. Moore was the pioneer for teaching industrial art in the United States and even antedated the great South Kensington School of London, England.

The Institution was founded by Sarah Worthington Peter, a philanthropist and humanitarian with an interest in art who was concerned with the need for women to be trained in order to be self-supporting. Sarah Peter recognized that Philadelphia led the United States in the manufacturing of textiles, wallpapers, floor coverings, and upholstery, as well as lithography, illustration, and wood engravings for books. She also knew that because of lack of available local talent, these manufacturers imported designs for these products from Europe at considerable expense.

Sarah Peter was a woman ahead of her time—she coupled the need for practical yet profitable career options for women, with the demand to increase the expertise and talent of the local design manufacturing industries. Thus began Moore's continuing tradition of educating women in the visual arts and its partnership in the greater Philadelphia business community. It is a college dedicated to tradition, yet alive with the diversity, the innovation, and the intellectual ferment that are the hallmarks of an enduring institution.

Moore College Today

Moore College of Art and Design is a small, independent, four-year women's college with an enrollment (in 1996) of 379 students from 22 states and eight foreign countries. The College is located on beautiful Logan Circle in center city Philadelphia. Four world-renowned museums, including the Philadelphia Museum of Art and the Rodin Museum, are within walking distance.

Meeting the Needs of a Competitive Marketplace

Open to men and women, Moore has addressed the demands of those who need to learn the basics or increase their knowledge of emerging technologies through its Division of Continuing Studies. The Desktop Publishing and Computer Graphics (DP/CG) certificate program, one of the College's most popular options, is available to graphics professionals and others who seek to retain or upgrade their positions. This three-semester course of study was created to prepare graphic designers to use current computer technology to its maximum effectiveness. The College's state-of-the-art computer labs house 48 PowerMacintoshes and 12 Windows-based PCs. The latest software, including Quark, Illustrator, Photoshop, and Director, allows students to integrate digital imagery and multimedia sources, such as video, audio, film, and printing processes.

Message from the
Publisher

WELCOME TO OUR NERVOUS SYSTEM

Some people say that the World Wide Web is a graphical extension of the information superhighway, just a network of humans and machines sending each other long lists of the equivalent of digital junk mail.

I think it is much more than that. To me, the Web is nothing less than the nervous system of the entire planet—not just a collection of computer brains connected together, but more like a billion silicon neurons entangled and recirculating electro-chemical signals of information and data, each contributing to the birth of another CPU and another Web site.

Think of each person's hard disk connected at once to every other hard disk on earth, driven by human navigators searching like Columbus for the New World. Seen this way the Web is more of a super entity, a growing, living thing, controlled by the universal human will to expand, to be more. Yet, unlike a purposeful business plan with rigid rules, the Web expands in a nonlinear, unpredictable, creative way that echoes natural evolution.

We created our Web site not just to extend the reach of our computer book products but to be part of this synaptic neural network, to experience, like a nerve in the body, the flow of ideas and then to pass those ideas up the food chain of the mind. Your mind. Even more, we wanted to pump some of our own creative juices into this rich wine of technology.

TASTE OUR DIGITAL WINE

And so we ask you to taste our wine by visiting the body of our business. Begin by understanding the metaphor we have created for our Web site—a universal learning center, situated in outer space in the form of a space station. A place where you can journey to study any topic from the convenience of your own screen. Right now we are focusing on computer topics, but the stars are the limit on the Web.

If you are interested in discussing this Web site or finding out more about the Waite Group, please send me email with your comments, and I will be happy to respond. Being a programmer myself, I love to talk about technology and find out what our readers are looking for.

Sincerely,

Mitchell Waite

Mitchell Waite, C.E.O. and Publisher

200 Tamal Plaza
Corte Madera, CA 94925
415-924-2575
415-924-2576 fax

Website:
http://www.waite.com/waite

CREATING THE HIGHEST QUALITY COMPUTER BOOKS IN THE INDUSTRY

Waite Group Press

Come Visit
WAITE.COM
Waite Group Press
World Wide Web Site

Now find all the latest information on Waite Group books at our new Web site, **http://www.waite.com/waite**. You'll find an online catalog where you can examine and order any title, review upcoming books, and send email to our authors and editors. Our FTP site has all you need to update your book: the latest program listings, errata sheets, most recent versions of Fractint, POV Ray, Polyray, DMorph, and all the programs featured in our books. So download, talk to us, ask questions, on **http://www.waite.com/waite**.

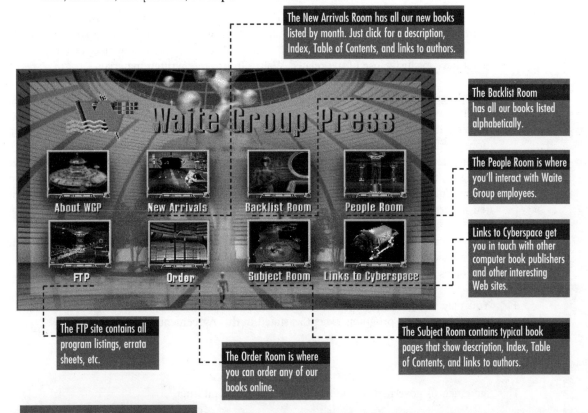

The New Arrivals Room has all our new books listed by month. Just click for a description, Index, Table of Contents, and links to authors.

The Backlist Room has all our books listed alphabetically.

The People Room is where you'll interact with Waite Group employees.

Links to Cyberspace get you in touch with other computer book publishers and other interesting Web sites.

About WGP

New Arrivals

Backlist Room

People Room

FTP

Order

Subject Room

Links to Cyberspace

The FTP site contains all program listings, errata sheets, etc.

The Order Room is where you can order any of our books online.

The Subject Room contains typical book pages that show description, Index, Table of Contents, and links to authors.

World Wide Web:

COME SURF OUR TURF—THE WAITE GROUP WEB

http://www.waite.com/waite
Gopher: gopher.waite.com
FTP: ftp.waite.com

This is a legal agreement between you, the end user and purchaser, and The Waite Group®, Inc., and the authors of the programs contained in the disk. By opening the sealed disk package, you are agreeing to be bound by the terms of this Agreement. If you do not agree with the terms of this Agreement, promptly return the unopened disk package and the accompanying items (including the related book and other written material) to the place you obtained them for a refund.

SOFTWARE LICENSE

1. The Waite Group, Inc. grants you the right to use one copy of the enclosed software programs (the programs) on a single computer system (whether a single CPU, part of a licensed network, or a terminal connected to a single CPU). Each concurrent user of the program must have exclusive use of the related Waite Group, Inc. written materials.

2. The program, including the copyrights in each program, is owned by the respective author and the copyright in the entire work is owned by The Waite Group, Inc. and they are therefore protected under the copyright laws of the United States and other nations, under international treaties. You may make only one copy of the disk containing the programs exclusively for backup or archival purposes, or you may transfer the programs to one hard disk drive, using the original for backup or archival purposes. You may make no other copies of the programs, and you may make no copies of all or any part of the related Waite Group, Inc. written materials.

3. You may not rent or lease the programs, but you may transfer ownership of the programs and related written materials (including any and all updates and earlier versions) if you keep no copies of either, and if you make sure the transferee agrees to the terms of this license.

4. You may not decompile, reverse engineer, disassemble, copy, create a derivative work, or otherwise use the programs except as stated in this Agreement.

GOVERNING LAW

This Agreement is governed by the laws of the State of California.

LIMITED WARRANTY

The following warranties shall be effective for 90 days from the date of purchase: (i) The Waite Group, Inc. warrants the enclosed disk to be free of defects in materials and workmanship under normal use; and (ii) The Waite Group, Inc. warrants that the programs, unless modified by the purchaser, will substantially perform the functions described in the documentation provided by The Waite Group, Inc. when operated on the designated hardware and operating system. The Waite Group, Inc. does not warrant that the programs will meet purchaser's requirements or that operation of a program will be uninterrupted or error-free. The program warranty does not cover any program that has been altered or changed in any way by anyone other than The Waite Group, Inc. The Waite Group, Inc. is not responsible for problems caused by changes in the operating characteristics of computer hardware or computer operating systems that are made after the release of the programs, nor for problems in the interaction of the programs with each other or other software.

THESE WARRANTIES ARE EXCLUSIVE AND IN LIEU OF ALL OTHER WARRANTIES OF MERCHANTABILITY OR FITNESS FOR A PARTICULAR PURPOSE OR OF ANY OTHER WARRANTY, WHETHER EXPRESSED OR IMPLIED.

EXCLUSIVE REMEDY

The Waite Group, Inc. will replace any defective disk without charge if the defective disk is returned to The Waite Group, Inc. within 90 days from date of purchase.

This is Purchaser's sole and exclusive remedy for any breach of warranty or claim for contract, tort, or damages.

LIMITATION OF LIABILITY

THE WAITE GROUP, INC. AND THE AUTHORS OF THE PROGRAMS SHALL NOT IN ANY CASE BE LIABLE FOR SPECIAL, INCIDENTAL, CONSEQUENTIAL, INDIRECT, OR OTHER SIMILAR DAMAGES ARISING FROM ANY BREACH OF THESE WARRANTIES EVEN IF THE WAITE GROUP, INC. OR ITS AGENT HAS BEEN ADVISED OF THE POSSIBILITY OF SUCH DAMAGES.

THE LIABILITY FOR DAMAGES OF THE WAITE GROUP, INC. AND THE AUTHORS OF THE PROGRAMS UNDER THIS AGREEMENT SHALL IN NO EVENT EXCEED THE PURCHASE PRICE PAID.

COMPLETE AGREEMENT

This Agreement constitutes the complete agreement between The Waite Group, Inc. and the authors of the programs, and you, the purchaser.

Some states do not allow the exclusion or limitation of implied warranties or liability for incidental or consequential damages, so the above exclusions or limitations may not apply to you. This limited warranty gives you specific legal rights; you may have others, which vary from state to state.

MACMILLAN COMPUTER PUBLISHING USA

A VIACOM COMPANY

Technical ----┐
└---- Support:

If you need assistance with the information in this book or with a CD/Disk
accompanying the book, please access the Knowledge Base on our Web
site at **http://www.superlibrary.com/general/support**. Our most
Frequently Asked Questions are answered there. If you do not find the
answer to your questions on our Web site, you may contact Macmillan
Technical Support **(317) 581-3833** or e-mail us at **support@mcp.com**.

SATISFACTION REPORT CARD

Please fill out this card if you wish to know of future updates to
Photoshop 4 Interactive Course, or to receive our catalog.

First Name: _____   **Last Name:** _____

Street Address: _____

City: _____   **State:** _____   **Zip:** _____

E-Mail Address _____

Daytime Telephone: (   ) _____

Date product was acquired: Month _____ **Day** _____ **Year** _____   **Your Occupation:** _____

Overall, how would you rate *Photoshop 4 Interactive Course?*
- ☐ Excellent   ☐ Very Good   ☐ Good
- ☐ Fair   ☐ Below Average   ☐ Poor

What did you like MOST about this book? _____
_____
_____

What did you like LEAST about this book? _____
_____
_____

Please describe any problems you may have encountered with installing or using the disk: _____
_____

How did you use this book (problem-solver, tutorial, reference...)?
_____

What is your level of computer expertise?
- ☐ New   ☐ Dabbler   ☐ Hacker
- ☐ Power User   ☐ Programmer   ☐ Experienced Professional

What computer languages are you familiar with? _____
_____

Please describe your computer hardware:
Computer _____   Hard disk _____
5.25" disk drives _____   3.5" disk drives _____
Video card _____   Monitor _____
Printer _____   Peripherals _____
Sound Board _____   CD ROM _____

Where did you buy this book?
- ☐ Bookstore (name): _____
- ☐ Discount store (name): _____
- ☐ Computer store (name): _____
- ☐ Catalog (name): _____
- ☐ Direct from WGP   ☐ Other _____

What price did you pay for this book? _____

What influenced your purchase of this book?
- ☐ Recommendation   ☐ Advertisement
- ☐ Magazine review   ☐ Store display
- ☐ Mailing   ☐ Book's format
- ☐ Reputation of Waite Group Press   ☐ Other

How many computer books do you buy each year? _____

How many other Waite Group books do you own? _____

What is your favorite Waite Group book? _____
_____

Is there any program or subject you would like to see Waite Group Press cover in a similar approach? _____
_____

Additional comments? _____
_____
_____

Please send to: **Waite Group Press**
200 Tamal Plaza
Corte Madera, CA 94925

☐ **Check here for a free Waite Group catalog**

STOP!